*Meriwether Lewis*

# THE HISTORY
# OF THE
# LEWIS AND CLARK
# EXPEDITION

BY
## MERIWETHER LEWIS
AND
## WILLIAM CLARK

EDITED BY
### Elliott Coues

*IN THREE VOLUMES*
*Volume I*

DOVER PUBLICATIONS, INC.
NEW YORK

Published in Canada by General Publishing Company,
Ltd., 30 Lesmill Road, Don Mills, Toronto, Ontario.
Published in the United Kingdom by Constable and
Company, Ltd.

This Dover edition is an unabridged republication of
the four-volume edition published by Francis P. Harper
in 1893. The fourth volume of the Harper edition
consisted of illustrations and the Index; in this Dover
edition five illustrations and the Index are appended to
Volume III, and the remaining illustrations are arranged
on large plates inserted at the end of Volumes I and II.

*International Standard Book Number: 0-486-21268-8*
*Library of Congress Catalog Card Number: 64-15500*

Manufactured in the United States of America
Dover Publications, Inc.
180 Varick Street
New York, N.Y. 10014

# Dedication.

---

*To the People of the Great West:*

*Jefferson gave you the country. Lewis and Clark showed you the way. The rest is your own course of empire. Honor the statesman who foresaw your West. Honor the brave men who first saw your West. May the memory of their glorious achievement be your precious heritage! Accept from my heart this undying record of the beginning of all your greatness.*

*E. C.*

# HISTORY OF THE EXPEDITION

UNDER THE COMMAND OF

# LEWIS AND CLARK,

To the Sources of the Missouri River, thence across the Rocky Mountains and
down the Columbia River to the Pacific Ocean, performed during
the Years 1804-5-6, by Order of the

GOVERNMENT OF THE UNITED STATES.

## A NEW EDITION,

FAITHFULLY REPRINTED FROM THE ONLY AUTHORIZED EDITION OF 1814, WITH COPIOUS
CRITICAL COMMENTARY, PREPARED UPON EXAMINATION OF UNPUBLISHED
OFFICIAL ARCHIVES AND MANY OTHER SOURCES OF INFORMATION,
INCLUDING A DILIGENT STUDY OF THE

## ORIGINAL MANUSCRIPT JOURNALS

AND

# FIELD NOTEBOOKS OF THE EXPLORERS,

TOGETHER WITH

A New Biographical and Bibliographical Introduction, New Maps
and other Illustrations, and a Complete Index,

BY

## ELLIOTT COUES,

*Late Captain and Assistant Surgeon, United States Army,*
*Late Secretary and Naturalist, United States Geological Survey,*
*Member of the National Academy of Sciences, etc.*

IN FOUR VOLUMES.
VOL. I.

NEW YORK.
FRANCIS P. HARPER.
1893.

---

*Title page of the Harper edition of 1893 (see page vi).*

# PREFACE TO THE NEW EDITION.

**L**EWIS AND CLARK'S Expedition from the Mississippi river to the Pacific ocean was the first governmental exploration of the "Great West." The History of this undertaking is the personal narrative and official report of the first white men who crossed the continent between the British and Spanish possessions. When these pioneers passed the Rocky mountains, none but Indians had ascended the Missouri river to the Yellowstone, and none had navigated the Columbia to the head of tide-water. The route was from Illinois through regions since mapped as Missouri, Kansas, Iowa, Nebraska, South Dakota, North Dakota, Montana, Idaho, Washington, and Oregon. The main water-ways on the Atlantic side of the mountains were the Missouri and Yellowstone ; on the Pacific side, Lewis' river, the Kooskooskee, and the Columbia. The Continental Divide was surmounted in three different places, many miles apart. The actual travel by land and water, including various side-trips, amounted to about one-third the circumference of the globe. This cost but one life, and was done without another serious casualty, though often with great hardship, sometimes much suffering, and occasional imminent peril. The discipline of the party was perfect. The comparatively youthful and inexperienced captains developed the qualities of ideal leaders, dauntless, resourceful, indefatigable, vigilant, absolute in command, solicitous for the welfare of their men, and imposing no privation unshared by themselves. The duration of the journey was from May, 1804, to September, 1806; and from April, 1805, to August, 1806, all communication with the world was suspended. The story of this adventure stands easily first and alone. This is our national epic of exploration, conceived by Thomas Jefferson, wrought out by Lewis and Clark, and given to the world by Nicholas Biddle.

Perhaps no traveler's tale has ever been told with greater fidelity and minuteness, or has more nearly achieved absolute accuracy. Our heroes proved also model journalists. The imagination of Defoe, which evolved a fiction with startling verisimilitude, has been matched by those acute powers of actual observation which gave us what we may call the "Robinson Crusoe" of fact.

It is singular that this History, which has held its own for nearly a century as a standard work of reference, has never before been republished in full, nor ever until now been subjected to searching and systematic criticism. The more closely it is scrutinized, in the light of our present knowledge, the more luminous it appears. The severest tests which contemporaneous criticism can apply serve mainly to develop its strength and worth. The printed narrative would carry easily twice as much commentary as is now put upon it; for it continually challenges and solicits the editorial pen, even without reference to those manuscript records which have proved a very mine of new wealth.

The present edition is accurately described upon its title-page. The editorial notes are so copious and so various that there is little left to be said by way of preface. In undertaking the work, I expected to do little more than supervise a reprint of the original text. The acquisition of the manuscripts was not foreseen; nor had I any idea of the embarrassing richness of resources about to become mine. The publisher, with not less sagacity than liberality, altered his previous plans accordingly, and left the whole matter in my hands. The question whether a new History of the Expedition should be written was promptly answered in the negative. The present edition gives the Biddle text with scrupulous fidelity, even to indicating the original pagination—a convenience which every scholar will appreciate as highly as he does the unbroken numbering of pages of the present volumes. But I have not found it necessary to make a fetich of that text. I have punctiliously preserved the orthography of proper names [1] in all their variance and eccentricity; and wherever I have amplified any statement in the text, or diverted the sense of a passage by a hair's breadth, square brackets indicate the fact. Yet I have not hesitated to touch the text here and there in a mere matter of grammar or punctuation. For the rest, I have prepared new titles and synopses of the chapters, and new headlines of the pages; one new chapter is interpolated, by digesting the Clatsop diary for that purpose. Excepting in these several respects, the present edition is literally true to the original. Nothing whatever is omitted.

The copy for this edition was actually in the printer's hands, in December, 1892, when I first found myself in possession of over 3,000 pages of Lewis' and of Clark's manuscript. Consequently, what would otherwise have been simple supervision was turned into the very arduous and exacting editorial function which is represented by my notes. With scarcely an exception these were penned while a lively corps of compositors was setting type, from January to June, 1893. As this work upon press-proofs included all the research which the notes represent, the demand upon my mental alertness and staying powers proved more severe than I should care to meet again. It was a daily draft upon a fund of omniscience which I am satisfied I never possessed. These circumstances are not cited to forestall criticism, or condone any offense of which I may be convicted. I hope that every error which I have not detected in the orginal text, and every one which I have committed, whether in ignorance or by inadvertence, may be exposed and corrected—to the end that " Lewis and Clark," whose develop-

---

[1] Excepting Captain Clark's, which was wrongly " Clarke " throughout, and is now correctly respelled ; and except in one or two other cases, notably of Kansas for " Kanzas," in which the modern spelling of a familiar name is inadvertently given.

ment ought to be brought abreast of that of the Great West, may approximate to that perfection which is said to belong to the gods.

My commentary relates mainly to geography, ethnology, and natural history; but it is too extensive and diversified to be concisely described, and if it cannot speak for itself, there is nothing to be said about it. I wish that the literal extracts from the codices were more copious than they are; but all books, even such as this one, have necessary limits. The rest of the new matter in these volumes consists of a Supplement to Jefferson's Memoir of Lewis, Memoirs of Clark and of Gass, respectively, a bibliography, a much-needed index, this preface, and various illustrations. The modern map was selected as being on about the same scale as Captain Clark's original, thus facilitating comparison of his with our geography. But as it was not drawn for this work, I am responsible for nothing that appears upon it excepting the red marks I have made to indicate the route. These will be found as accurate as the map permits them to be; but the result is to be taken simply as a diagram.[*]

Many friends, both known and unknown to me personally, have shown their interest in this work, and contributed to such excellence as the new matter it contains may be found to possess. My most sincere as well as most formal acknowledgments are due to the American Philosophical Society of Philadelphia, which did not hesitate to trust the precious manuscripts to my keeping, and whose Secretary, Mr. Henry Phillips, Jr., showed me every personal attention. Mr. Alfred J. Hill of St. Paul, Minn., helped me more than any other individual, with constant suggestion and criticism, and by the loan of several manuscript charts he had prepared for his own use with special reference to Lewis and Clark, as well as by calling my attention to various things which I might or should have otherwise overlooked. My citations of certain authorities, notably Perrin du Lac, are upon Mr. Hill's representations. Access to and use of the archives of the State and War Departments, by permission of the respect-

[*]In this Dover Edition, the map referred to is reproduced on a large plate inserted at the end of this volume. The illustration is reproduced in black and

ive secretaries, was facilitated, in the former, by Mr. Andrew H. Allen, Chief of the Bureau of Rolls and Library, and Mr. Walter Manton, of the same Bureau, as well as by Mr. W. W. Rockhill, Chief Clerk; and in the latter, by Mr. Samuel Hodgkins, Chief of the Record Division, and Mr. David Fitz Gerald, Librarian, as well as by Mr. John Tweedale, Chief Clerk, and Gen. Lewis A. Grant, Assistant Secretary of War. Mr. A. R. Spofford of the Library of Congress; Major J. W. Powell, Director of the U. S. Geological Survey and of the U. S. Bureau of Ethnology; Mr. Henry Gannett, of the same Survey; Prof. G. Brown Goode, Director of the U. S. National Museum, Prof. T. C. Mendenhall, Superintendent of the U. S. Coast and Geodetic Survey; Mr. R. A. Brock, Secretary of the Virginia Historical Society; Hon. Charles Aldrich of the State Historical Department of Iowa; and Mr. M. S. Hill, Secretary of the Tacoma Academy of Sciences, each rendered valued official and personal favors. Judge Craig Biddle of Philadelphia; Mr. Horace Howard Furness of the same city; Judge James T. Mitchell of the Supreme Court of Pennsylvania; Mr. Jefferson K. Clark of St. Louis; Mr. Wm. Hancock Clark of Detroit, Mich.; Col. Meriwether Lewis Clark of Louisville, Ky.; Mr. F. L. Billon of St. Louis, Mo.; and Mr. R. S. Voorhis of Hannibal, Mo., supplied various data, biographical and historical. In natural history, my thanks are due to Prof. Theodore Gill of the Smithsonian Institution; Mr. B. W. Evermann; Prof. E. D. Cope of the University of Pennsylvania; Mr. L. O. Howard of the Agricultural Department; and especially Mr. F. H. Knowlton, who made most of the botanical identifications. I have also to thank for various favors the Hon. the Commissioners of the General Land Office and of the Indian Bureau, respectively; the Directors of the Black Eagle Falls Dam; the Mayor of Benton, Mont.; Professor Alfred Newton of Cambridge, Eng.; Mr. W. P. Garrison of the New York Nation; Judge James Wickersham of Tacoma, Wash.; Prof. J. A. Allen of the American Museum of Natural History, N. Y.; Mr. James E. Babb of Lewiston,

white and Dr. Coues' tracing of the route appears as a heavy solid and broken line.

Idaho; Mr. Peter Koch of Bozeman, Mont.; Governor Buchanan of Tennessee; Mr. James D. Park of Franklin, Tenn.; Mr. J. G. Jacob of Wellsburg, W. Va.; Col. E. Polk Johnson of Frankfort, Ky.; Judge R. T. Durrett of Louisville, Ky.; Judge John M. Lea of Nashville, Tenn.; Dr. W. C. N. Randolph of Charlottesville, Va.; Mr. F. Firmstone of Easton, Pa.; Rev. Dr. Edward D. Neill of St. Paul, Minn.; Gen. John Gibbon, U. S. Army; Mrs. Mary B. Anderson of Washington, D. C., who prepared the index under my direction; and Mr. Robert M. Trulan, of the Mershon Printing Company, whose faithful and skillful attentions were animated by an intelligent interest in the subject-matter, and who very ably seconded my efforts to produce an accurate impression. Most of my correspondents are also named in the course of my notes, where each such recognition seemed not less a pleasure than a duty.

ELLIOTT COUES.

SMITHSONIAN INSTITUTION, WASHINGTON, D. C.,
*June 30th*, 1893.

# CONTENTS

OF

# THE FIRST VOLUME.

*HISTORY OF THE EXPEDITION.*

CHAPTER I.

CHAPTER II.

CHAPTER III.

CHAPTER IV.

# LIST OF MAPS AND OTHER PLATES.

## VOLUME I.

## VOLUME II.

## VOLUME III.

*(The following five maps are reproduced in facsimile
from the Philadelphia Edition of 1814.)*

# PREFACE TO THE ORIGINAL EDITION.

In presenting these volumes to the public, the editor owes equally to himself and to others to state the circumstances which have preceded the publication, and to explain his own share in compiling them.

It was the original design of Captain Lewis to have been himself the editor of his own travels, and he was on his way toward Philadelphia for that purpose when his sudden death frustrated these intentions. After a considerable and unavoidable delay, the papers connected with the Expedition were deposited with another gentleman [Nicholas Biddle], who, in order to render the lapse of time as little injurious as possible, proceeded immediately to collect and investigate all the materials within his reach.

Of the incidents of each day during the Expedition, a minute journal was kept by Captain Lewis or Captain Clark, and sometimes by both, which was afterward revised and enlarged at the different periods of leisure which occurred on the route. These were carefully perused in conjunction with Captain Clark himself, who was able, from his own recollection of the journey, as well as from a constant residence in Louisiana since his return, to supply a great mass of explanations, and much additional information with regard to part of the route which has been more recently explored. Besides these, recourse was had to the manuscript journals (*p. iv*) kept by two of the sergeants [John Ordway and Patrick Gass], one of which [Gass'], the least minute and valuable, has already been published. That nothing might be wanting to the accuracy of these details, a very intelligent and active member of the party, Mr. George Shannon, was sent to contribute whatever his memory might add to this accumulated fund of information.

From these copious materials the narrative was sketched nearly in its present form, when other pursuits diverted the attention of the writer and compelled him to transfer his manuscript, in its unfinished state, with all the documents connected with it, to the present editor, to prepare them for the press and superintend the publication. That he may not seem to arrogate anything from the exertions of others, he should therefore state that, although the whole work was thus submitted to his entire discretion, he found but little to change, and that his labor has been principally confined to revising the manuscript, comparing it with the original papers, and inserting such additional matter as appears to have been intentionally deferred by the writer till the period of a more mature revisal. These circumstances, which would otherwise be indifferent to the public, are mentioned merely to account for imperfections, which are in some degree inseparable from any book of travels not written by the traveler. In a work of pure description indeed, like the present, where the incidents themselves are the sole objects of attraction, the part of an editor is necessarily subordinate, nor can his humble pretensions aspire beyond the merit of rigid adherence to facts as they are stated to him. This has been very diligently attempted, and for this, in its full extent, the editor deems himself responsible.

The present volumes, it will be perceived, comprise only the narrative of the journey. Those parts of the work which relate to the various objects of natural history observed or collected during the journey, as well as the alphabets of the (*p. v*) Indian languages, are in the hands of Professor [Benjamin S.] Barton, and will, it is understood, shortly appear. [See note ¹⁷, p. 400.]

To give still further interest to the work the editor addressed a letter to Mr. [Thomas] Jefferson, requesting some authentic memoirs of Captain Lewis. For the very curious and valuable information contained in his answer, the public, as well as the editor himself, owe great obligations to the politeness and knowledge of that distinguished gentleman.

PAUL ALLEN.

PHILADELPHIA, *January* 1st, 1814.

# MEMOIR OF MERIWETHER LEWIS.

---

*[Letter from Ex-President Thomas Jefferson.]*

MONTICELLO, *August* 18*th*, 1813.

SIR: In compliance with the request conveyed in your letter of May 25th,[1] I have endeavored to obtain, from the relations and friends of the late Governor Lewis, information of
such incidents of his life as might be not unacceptable to
those who may read the narrative of his Western discoveries.
The ordinary occurrences of a private life, and those also
while acting in a subordinate sphere in the Army, in a time
of peace, are not deemed sufficiently interesting to occupy
the public attention; but a general account of his parentage,

---

[1] This letter is not on file among the Jefferson Papers in the Bureau of Rolls
and Library of the State Department at Washington, and probably was not preserved. The rest of the record of Mr. Jefferson's connection with the History
of the Expedition is complete in these archives. The original manuscript of the
Memoir of Lewis, in Mr. Jefferson's hand-writing, six folios or twelve pages of
letter-paper, now forms Docs. Nos. 222 and 223 of Vol. 13 of the 1st series of
the Jefferson Papers. Doc. No. 138, Jeff. Papers, 2d. ser., Vol. 3, is a letter
from Mr. Jefferson to Mr. Allen, requesting to be informed when the Memoir
would be required, etc. Doc. No. 139, *ibid.*, letter from the same to the same,
forwards the manuscript of the Memoir therewith, orders 13 copies of the History, etc. Doc. No. 136, *ibid.*, is a letter from Mr. Allen to Mr. Jefferson,
dated Philadelphia, Aug. 18th, 1813, in which is exhibited an achievement in
impudence that deserves to become historical. The person says: '' I am not
apprehensive that the fulness of your Biography [of Lewis] will be an obstacle
to its publication, now that I have prevailed upon the Booksellers to procras-
tinate the volumes. I wish very much to enliven the dulness of the [Biddle]
narrative by something more popular, splendid and attractive. The publick
taste,'' etc., *ad nauseam*. Doc. No. 137, *ibid.*, is a letter from the same to the
same, dated Philadelphia, Dec. 18th, 1813, in which the writer patronizes the name
and fame of Captain Lewis, does not care to have any biography of Captain
Clark, and favors the Ex-President of the United States with sundry reflections
and opinions. In this matter, of course, the real understanding was between

with such smaller incidents as marked his early character, are briefly noted ; and to these are added, as being peculiarly within my own knowledge, whatever related to the public mission of which an account is now to be published. The result of my inquiries and recollections shall now be offered, to be enlarged or abridged as you may think best ; or otherwise to be used with the materials you may have collected from other sources.

Meriwether Lewis, late Governor of Louisiana, was born on the 18th of August, 1774, near the town of Charlottesville, in the County of Albemarle, in Virginia, of one of the distinguished families of that state. John Lewis, one ( *p. viii* ) of his father's uncles, was a member of the king's council before the Revolution. Another of them, Fielding Lewis, married a sister of General Washington. His father, William Lewis, was the youngest of five sons of Colonel Robert Lewis of Albemarle, the fourth of whom, Charles, was one of the early patriots who stepped forward in the commencement of the Revolution, and commanded one of the regiments first raised in Virginia and placed on con-

Mr. Jefferson and Mr. Biddle ; the correspondence shows that Mr. Allen was a mere dummy. The Memoir of Lewis was actually transmitted and submitted by Mr. Jefferson to Mr. Biddle ; witness Doc. No. 52, Jeff. Papers, 2d. ser., Vol. 11, as follows :

Monticello, Aug. 20, 1813.

Sir

In a letter from mr Paul Allen of Philadelphia I was informed that other business had obliged you to turn over to him the publication of Gov<sup>r</sup>. Lewis's journal of his Western expedition ; and he requested me to furnish him with any materials I could for writing a sketch of his life. I now enclose him such as I have been able to procure, to be used with any other information he may have received, or alone, if he has no other, or in any way you & he shall think proper. The part you have been so good as to take in digesting the work entitles you to decide on whatever may be proposed to go out under it's auspices, and on this ground I take the liberty of putting under cover to you, and for your perusal, my letter to mr Allen, which I will request you to seal & hand on to him. I am happy in this occasion of expressing my portion of the thanks all will owe you for the trouble you have taken with this interesting narrative, and the assurance of my sentiments of high esteem and respect.

Th : Jefferson.

Mr. Biddle.

tinental establishment. Happily situated at home, with a wife and young family, and a fortune placing him at ease, he left all to aid in the liberation of his country from foreign usurpations, then first unmasking their ultimate end and aim. His good sense, integrity, bravery, enterprise, and remarkable bodily powers marked him as an officer of great promise ; but he unfortunately died early in the Revolution. Nicholas Lewis, the second of his father's brothers, commanded a regiment of militia in the successful expedition of 1776 against the Cherokee Indians; who, seduced by the agents of the British government to take up the hatchet against us, had committed great havoc on our southern frontier, by murdering and scalping helpless women and children, according to their cruel and cowardly principles of warfare. The chastisement they then received closed the history of their wars, and prepared them for receiving the elements of civilization, which, zealously inculcated by the present government of the United States, have rendered them an industrious, peaceable, and happy people. This member of the family of Lewises, whose bravery was so usefully proved on this occasion, was endeared to all who knew him by his inflexible probity, courteous disposition, benevolent heart, and engaging modesty and manners. He was the umpire of all the private differences of his county—selected always by both parties. He was also the guardian of Meriwether Lewis, of whom we are now to speak, and who had lost his father at an early age.

He [Meriwether] continued some years under the fostering care of a tender mother, of the respectable family of Meriwethers, (*p. ix*) of the same county; and was remarkable, even in infancy, for enterprise, boldness, and discretion.

When only eight years of age he habitually went out, in the dead of night, alone with his dogs, into the forest to hunt the raccoon and opossum, which, seeking their food in the night, can then only be taken. In this exercise, no season or circumstance could obstruct his purpose—plunging through the winter's snows and frozen streams in pursuit of his

object.  At 13 he was put to the Latin school, and continued
[under the tuition of Dr. Everett, Parson Maury, and Parson
Wardell] at that until 18, when he returned to his mother
and entered on the cares of his farm; having, as well as a
younger brother, been left by his father with a competency
for all the correct and comfortable purposes of temperate
life.  His talent for observation, which had led him to an
accurate knowledge of the plants and animals of his own
country, would have distinguished him as a farmer; but at
the age of 20, yielding to the ardor of youth and a passion
for more dazzling pursuits, he engaged as a volunteer in the
body of militia which were called out by General Washington, on occasion of the discontents produced by the excise
taxes in the western parts of the United States; [2] and from
that situation he was removed to the regular service as a
lieutenant in the line.  At 23 [in 1797] he was promoted to
a captaincy; and, always attracting the first attention where
punctuality and fidelity were requisite, he was appointed
paymaster to his regiment.  About this time a circumstance
occurred which, leading to the transaction which is the subject of this book, will justify a recurrence to its original idea.

While I resided in Paris, John Ledyard of Connecticut
arrived there, well known in the United States for energy of
body and mind.  He had accompanied Captain Cook on his
voyage to the Pacific ocean, and distinguished himself on that
voyage by his intrepidity.  Being of a roaming disposition,
he was now panting for some new enterprise.  His immediate object at Paris was to engage a mercantile company in
the fur trade of the western coast of America, in (*p. x*)
which, however, he failed.  I then proposed to him to go by
land to Kamtschatka, cross in some of the Russian vessels to
Nootka Sound, fall down into the latitude of the Missouri,
and penetrate to and through that to the United States.
He eagerly seized the idea, and only asked to be assured of

_____

[2] The " discontents " thus delicately suggested are better known to history as
the " Whisky Insurrection " of 1794.   The malcontents were called " insurgents."
Young Lewis enlisted as a private under one T. Walker.

the permission of the Russian government.    I interested, in obtaining this, M. de Simoulin, Minister Plenipotentiary of the Empress at Paris, but more especially the Baron de Grimm, Minister Plenipotentiary of Saxe-Gotha, her more special agent and correspondent there in matters not immediately diplomatic.    Her permission was obtained, and an assurance of protection while the course of the voyage should be through her territories.    Ledyard set out from Paris, and arrived at St. Petersburgh after the Empress had left that place to pass the winter, I think, at Moscow.    His finances not permitting him to make unnecessary stay at St. Petersburgh, he left it with a passport from one of the ministers; and at 200 miles from Kamtchatka, was obliged to take up his winter-quarters.    He was preparing, in the spring, to resume his journey, when he was arrested by an officer of the Empress, who by this time had changed her mind and forbidden his proceeding.    He was put into a close carriage, and conveyed day and night, without ever stopping, till they reached Poland; where he was set down and left to himself.    The fatigue of this journey broke down his constitution; and when he returned to Paris his bodily strength was much impaired.    His mind, however, remained firm, and he after this undertook the journey to Egypt.    I received a letter from him, full of sanguine hopes, dated at Cairo, the 15th of November, 1788, the day before he was to set out for the head of the Nile; on which day, however, he ended his career and life.    Thus failed the first attempt to explore the western part of our northern continent.

In 1792 I proposed to the American Philosophical Society that we should set on foot a subscription to engage some (*p. xi*) competent person to explore that region in the opposite direction—that is, by ascending the Missouri, crossing the Stony [Rocky] mountains, and descending the nearest river to the Pacific.    Captain Lewis being then stationed at Charlottesville, on the recruiting service, warmly solicited me to obtain for him the execution of that object.    I told him it was proposed that the person engaged should be attended by a single companion only, to avoid exciting alarm among the Indians. This did not deter him ; but Mr. André Michaux, a professed botanist, author of "Flora Boreali-Americana" and of the "Histoire des Chesnes d'Amèrique," offering his services, they were accepted. He received his instruction, and when he had reached Kentucky in the prosecution of his journey, he was overtaken by an order from the Minister of France, then at Philadelphia, to relinquish the Expedition,[3] and to pursue elsewhere the botanical inquiries on which he was employed by that government ; and thus failed the second attempt for exploring that region.

In 1803, the act for establishing trading-houses with the Indian tribes being about to expire, some modifications of it were recommended to Congress by a confidential message[4] of

[3] I believe that Michaux's case is here presented with the reserve of the true diplomatist. It is a matter of common tradition, if not of verifiable history, that the already celebrated French botanist, who had been selected by the President to accompany the Expedition in the capacity of a scientific specialist, was discovered or at any rate suspected to be a spy in the secret service of the French Government ; and that his services were therefore declined by Mr. Jefferson himself, who probably had no trouble in securing his recall by an "order" from the French Minister. But however this may have been, certainly the most serious defect in the organization of the Expedition was the lack of some trained scientist, who should also have been a medical man, and thus united the professional functions of physician, surgeon, and naturalist.

[4] This is an occult document, not easy to find in print. It is not included in The Writings of Thomas Jefferson, nor in ordinary collections of State Papers. It is contained in The Addresses and Messages of the Presidents of the United States, Inaugural, Annual, and Special, from 1789 to 1846, etc., 2d ed., 2 vols., 8vo, New York, Edward Walker, 1846, Appendix, pp. xxv–xxvii, entitled "Jefferson's Confidential Message, recommending a Western Exploring Expedition," Jan. 18th, 1803. It is addressed "Gentlemen of the Senate and House of Representatives." Its astuteness and wariness may be judged by the words with which it concludes : "The interests of commerce place the principal object within the constitutional powers and care of Congress, and that it should incidentally advance the geographical knowledge of our own continent, can but be an additional gratification. The nation claiming the territory, regarding this as a literary pursuit, which it is in the habit of permitting within its own dominions, would not be disposed to view it with jealousy, even if the expiring state of its interests there did not render it a matter of indifference. The appropriation of

January 18th, and an extension of its views to the Indians on the Missouri. In order to prepare the way, the message proposed the sending an exploring party to trace the Missouri to its source, to cross the Highlands, and follow the best water-communication which offered itself from thence to the Pacific ocean. Congress approved the proposition, and voted a sum of money for carrying it into execution. Captain Lewis, who had then been near two years with me as Private Secretary,[5] immediately renewed his solicitations to have the direction of the party. I had now had opportunities of knowing him intimately. Of courage undaunted ; possessing a firmness and perseverance of purpose which nothing but impossibilities could divert from its direction ; careful as a father of those committed to his charge, yet steady in the maintenance of order and discipline ; intimate (*p. xii*) with the Indian character, customs, and principles ;

two thousand five hundred dollars, ' for the purpose of extending the external commerce of the United States,' while understood and considered by the executive as giving the legislative sanction, would cover the undertaking from notice, and prevent the obstructions which interested individuals might otherwise previously prepare in its way." This message, perhaps penned by Private Secretary Lewis from President Jefferson's dictation, was favorably acted upon by Congress, with the result of placing the Expedition in the field. The estimate of $2,500 was Lewis' own, as witness Doc. No. 96a, Jeff. Papers L, 2d ser., Vol. 51, being the following " Recapitulation of an Estimate of the sum necessary to carry into effect the Miss^ie Expedicion," in Lewis' handwriting : " Mathematical Instruments, $217 ; Arms and Accoutrements extraordinary, $81 ; Camp Ecquipage, $255 ; Medicine & packing, $55 ; Means of transportation, $430 ; Indian presents, $696 ; Provisions extraordinary, $224 ; Materials for making up the various articles into portable packs, $55 ; For the pay of hunters, guides, and interpreters, $300 ; In silver coin, to defray the expences of the party from Nashville to the last white settlement on the Missisourie, $100 ; Contingencies, $87 ; Total, $2,500."

[5] State Dept., Bur. of Rolls and Libr., Jeff. Papers L, 2d ser., Vol. 51, Doc. No. 110, is a press-copy of the President's tender of the Private Secretaryship, in highly complimentary terms, dated Washn., Feb. 23d, 1801. Acceptance of same, in Lewis' handwriting, *ibid.*, Doc. No. 95, is in part as follows :

Pittsburgh, March 10th. 1801,

Dear Sir,

Not untill two late on friday last to answer by that days mail, did I recieve your much esteemed favour of the 23rd. Ult. in it you have thought proper so

habituated to the hunting life; guarded, by exact observation of the vegetables and animals of his own country, against losing time in the description of objects already possessed; honest, disinterested, liberal, of sound understanding, and a fidelity to truth so scrupulous that whatever he should report would be as certain as if seen by ourselves—with all these qualifications, as if selected and implanted by nature in one body for this express purpose, I could have no hesitation in confiding the enterprise to him.[6] To fill up the measure desired, he wanted nothing but a greater familiarity with the technical language of the natural sciences, and readiness in the astronomical observations necessary for the geography of his route. To acquire these he repaired immediately to Philadelphia, and placed himself under the tutorage of the distinguished professors of that place, who, with a zeal and emulation enkindled by an ardent devotion to science, communicated to him freely the information requisite for the purposes of the journey. While attending at Lancaster to the fabrication of the arms with which he chose that his men should be provided, he had the benefit of daily communication with Mr. Andrew Ellicot, whose experience in astronomical observation, and practice of it in the woods, enabled him to apprise Captain Lewis of the

far to honour me with your confidence, as to express a wish that I should accept the place of your private Secretary ; I most cordially acquiesce, and with pleasure accept the office ; nor were further motives necessary to induce my complyance, than that you, Sir, should conceive that in the discharge of the duties of that office, I could be servicable to my country, or ucefull to yourself : permit me here, Sir, to do further justice to my feelings, by expressing the lively sensibility with which I received this mark of your confidence and esteem. . . .

Receive I pray you, Sir, the most undisembled assurance, of the attatchment and friendship of

Your most obedient,<br>
& Very Humble Servt,<br>
Meriwether Lewis

Thomas Jefferson.
President of the U. States.

[6] The substance of the eulogy of this sentence forms the inscription on the east face of Lewis' monument, erected by the Legislature of Tennessee in 1848. See p. lx, beyond.

wants and difficulties he would encounter, and of the substitutes and resources offered by a woodland and uninhabited
country.

Deeming it necessary he should have some person with
him of known competence to the direction of the enterprise,
in the event of accident to himself, he proposed William
Clark, brother of General George Rogers Clark, who was
approved, and, with that view, received a commission of
captain. [On this point see Memoir of William Clark,
beyond.]

---

In April, 1803, a draught of his instructions was sent to
Captain Lewis, and on the 20th of June, they were signed
in the following form : [7]

[7] Press-copy of the original of these instructions, in Jefferson's handwriting, now
forms Doc. No. 269 of Vol. 9 of 1st ser. of Jeff. Papers, in Bur. of Rolls and Libr.,
State Dept. The writing is very small ; the impression is much blurred, and
scarcely legible in all places. Signature is " Th : Jefferson, Pr. US. of America"
The doc. occupies 4 folios.—Doc. No. 305, *ibid.*, 2 folios, is letter from T. J. to
M. L., Wash[n]. Nov. 16th, 1803, giving further instructions, with details of then
expected transfer of Louisiana to the U.S.—Doc. No. 8, Vol. 10 of Jeff. Papers,
dated Wash[n]. Jan. 22d, 1804, is letter of T. J. to M. L., chiefly occupied with
instructions and suggestions for intercourse with Indians ; item, identifies a
Mr. Evans as a Welshman " whose original object I believe has been to go in
search of the Welsh Indians said to be up the Missouri ": see note [31], p. 159,
beyond ; item, incloses a transl. of the journ. of an agent of a trading comp'y of
St. Louis up the Mo. R.; item, incloses a letter from the Amer. Philos. Soc. of
Philada., conveying to M. L. diploma of membership in that Society.—Doc. No.
1, *ibid.*, is letter of T. J. to M. L., Wash[n]. Jan. 13th, 1804, inclosing a map of
the Mo. R. to the Mandans, " said to be very accurate," having been done by a
Mr. Evans, by order of the Spanish Govt. This letter concludes as follows : " The
acquisition of the country through which you are to pass has inspired the country generally with a great deal of interest in your enterprise. The inquiries are
perpetual as to your progress. The Feds. [*i. e.*, Federalists] alone still treat it
as a philosophism [*i. e.*, as we should now say, crankery], and would rejoice at
its failure. Their bitterness increases with the diminution of their numbers and
despair of a resurrection. I hope you will take care of yourself, and be the living witness of their malice and folly. Present my salutations to Mr. Clarke.
assure all your party that we have our eyes turned on them with anxiety for their
safety & the success of their enterprize. accept yourself assurances of sincere
esteem and attachment." Various other letters of T. J. to M. L. are also preserved in press-copies in Jeff. Papers L, 2d ser., Vol. 51 ; as, *e. g.*, Doc. No. 111.

(*p. xiii*) " To Meriwether Lewis, Esquire, Captain of the First Regiment of Infantry of the United States of America :

" Your situation as Secretary of the President of the United States has made you acquainted with the objects of my confidential message of January 18th, 1803, to the legislature ; you have seen the act they passed, which, though expressed in general terms, was meant to sanction those objects, and you are appointed to carry them into execution.

" Instruments for ascertaining, by celestial observations, the geography of the country through which you will pass,

Apr. 27th, 1803 ; No. 112, Apr. 30th, 1803 ; No. 113, May 16th, 1803 ; No. 114, July 11th, 1803 ; No. 115, July 15th, 1803 ; No. 116, Apr. 23d, 1803.  These are Jefferson's side of the continued correspondence with Lewis during that year and the beginning of 1804.  The originals of Lewis' side of this correspondence are also on file, bound in the same volume.  These have never been published ; and as they enable us to trace all his movements in preparing for the Expedition, in 1803-4, I will abstract them, as follows : Doc. No. 97, five pages, Lancaster, Pa., Apr. 20th, 1803.  M. L. arrives there Apr. 19th, and puts himself under instructions of Mr. Andrew Ellicot to learn to work astron. insts.; steps taken to engage recruits from posts of Southwest Point, Massac, Kaskaskais (*sic*) and Illinois ; one John Conner engaged as interpreter (engagement later canceled) ; rifles and tomahawks being made at Harper's Ferry, where Lewis was long detained about the building of his boat " Experiment " (see p. 406, beyond).— Doc. No. 98, Philada., Pa., May 14th, 1803; various matters, but chiefly Mr. Ellicot's and Mr. Patterson's views regarding astron. insts.—Doc. No. 99, Philada., May 29th ; preparations so far forward that he expects to leave for Washn. June 29th ; has submitted Jefferson's instructions to Drs. Rush, Barton, and Wistar, who approve them ; is informed by Major McRea,com'd'g at S.W. Point that out of 20 volunteers for the Exped. only 3 possessed the requisite qualifications ; has taken sketches from Vancouver's work for composing a map Mr. Gallatin promised to project and complete ; has been unable to procure " Danvill's," *i. e.*, D'Anville's, map ; and " the maps attached to Vancouver's Voyage cannot be procured seperately from that work, which is both too costly and too weighty for me either to purchase or carry."—Doc. No. 109, Philada., June 27th, 1803 ; wholly personal matters.  Doc. No. 108, dated 12 o'clock Harper's Ferry, July 8th, 1803; leaves in an hour, " taking the rout of Charlestown, Frankfort, Uniontown and Redstone old fort to Pittsburgh."—Doc. No. 100, Pittsburgh, July 22d, 1803, delayed there by non-completion of a boat which had been promised for July 20th, was now promised for Aug. 5th (but in fact was not finished till Aug. 31st).—Doc. No. 101, Pittsburgh, July 26th, 1803.  (☞This is the Lieut. Hook matter : see

have been already provided. Light articles for barter and presents among the Indians, arms for your attendants, say for from ten to twelve men, boats, tents, and other traveling apparatus, with ammunition, medicine, surgical instruments, and provisions, you will have prepared, with such aids as the Secretary of War can yield in his department; and from him also you will receive authority to engage among our troops, by voluntary agreement, the number of attendants above mentioned ; over whom you, as their commanding officer, are invested with all the powers the laws give in such a case.

"As your movements, while within the limits of the

in full in my Memoir of Clark, beyond.)—Doc. No. 102, Wheeling, Sept. 8th, 1803, in part as follows : "It was not until 7 O'Clock on the morning of the 31st. Ultm⁰· that my boat was completed, she was instantly loaded, and at 10 A. M. on the same day I left Pittsburgh, where I had been moste shamefully detained by the unpardonable negligence of my boat-builder . . . according to his usual custom he got drunk, quarreled with his workmen, . . I spent most of my time with the workmen alternately presuading and threatening . . . I shall leave this place tomorrow morning, and lose no time in geting on." . . —Doc. No. 103, dated "On board my boat opposite Marietta," Sept. 13th, 1803 ; just arrived there ; been obliged to use horses or oxen to drag his boat over shoals ; "I find them the most efficient sailors in the present state of the navigation of the river, altho' they may be considered rather clumsy."—Doc. No. 104, Cincinnati, Oct. 3d, 1803 ; chiefly devoted to discovery by Dr. Wm. Goforth of bones of "mammoth" (mastodon), found at Big Bone Lick ; item, interpreter Conner has declined ; William Clark has accepted ; item, so refreshing in its naïveté that I must quote it : "As this Session of Congress has commenced earlyer than usual, and as from a variety of incidental circumstances my progress has been unexpectedly delayed, and feeling as I do in the most anxious manner a wish to keep them in a good humour on the subject of the expedicion in which I am engaged," this ingenuous young diplomat, who evidently had not served a Jefferson in vain, proposes to make a side-trip, perhaps up the Canceze (Kansas) river, and prevail on Captain Clark to make a feint somewhere else, as a sop to a congressional Cerberus thirsting for information about "Jefferson's Purchase."—Doc. No. ——, St. Louis, March 26th, 1804, describes Osage plum and apple, and incloses specimens.—Doc. No. 105, St. Louis, May 18th, 1804 (when the Exped. had started, but Captain L. had not joined it), is a list of articles for'd to Prest. Jefferson by Mr. Peter Chouteau, not in the handwriting of M. L. This closes the correspondence, so far as I have examined it, up to the date last given ; the next documents on file among the Jeff. Papers are the advices from Fort Mandan, Apr. 7th, 1805 : see beyond, p. xxxvi.

United States, will be better directed by occasional communications, adapted to circumstances as they arise, they will not be noticed here. What follows will respect your proceedings after your departure from the United States.

"Your mission has been communicated to the Ministers here from France, Spain, and Great Britain, and through them to their governments; and such assurances given them as to its objects, as we trust will satisfy them. The country of Louisiana having been ceded by Spain to France, the passport you have from the Minister of France, the representative of the present sovereign of the country, will be a protection with all its subjects; and that from the Minister of England will entitle you to the friendly aid of any traders of that allegiance with whom you may happen to meet.

(*p. xiv*) "The object of your mission is to explore the Missouri river, and such principal streams of it, as, by its course and communication with the waters of the Pacific ocean, whether the Columbia, Oregan [*sic*], Colorado, or any other river, may offer the most direct and practicable water-communication across the continent, for the purposes of commerce.

"Beginning at the mouth of the Missouri, you will take observations of latitude and longitude, at all remarkable points on the river, and especially at the mouths of rivers, at rapids, at islands, and other places and objects distinguished by such natural marks and characters, of a durable kind, as that they may with certainty be recognized hereafter. The courses of the river between these points of observation may be supplied by the compass, the log-line, and by time, corrected by the observations themselves. The variations of the needle, too, at different places, should be noticed.

"The interesting points of the portage between the heads of the Missouri, and of the water offering the best communication with the Pacific ocean, should also be fixed by observation; and the course of that water to the ocean, in the same manner as that of the Missouri.

" Your observations are to be taken with great pains and accuracy ; to be entered distinctly and intelligibly for others as well as yourself ; to comprehend all the elements necessary, with the aid of the usual tables, to fix the latitude and longitude of the places at which they were taken ; and are to be rendered to the War Office, for the purpose of having the calculations made concurrently by proper persons within the United States. Several copies of these, as well as of your other notes, should be made at leisure times, and put into the care of the most trustworthy of your attendants to guard, by multiplying them against the accidental losses to which they will be exposed. A further guard would be, that one of these copies be on the cuticular membranes of the paper-birch [*Betula papyrifera*], as less liable to injury from damp than common paper.

(*p. xv*)  " The commerce which may be carried on with the people inhabiting the line you will pursue renders a knowledge of those people important. You will therefore endeavor to make yourself acquainted, as far as a diligent pursuit of your journey shall admit, with the names of the nations and their numbers ;

" The extent and limits of their possessions ;

" Their relations with other tribes or nations ;

" Their language, traditions, and monuments ;

" Their ordinary occupations in agriculture, fishing, hunting, war, arts, and the implements for these ;

" Their food, clothing, and domestic accommodations ;

" The diseases prevalent among them, and the remedies they use ;

" Moral and physical circumstances which distinguish them from the tribes we know ;

" Peculiarities in their laws, customs, and dispositions ;

" And articles of commerce they may need or furnish, and to what extent.

" And, considering the interest which every nation has in

extending and strengthening the authority of reason and justice among the people around them, it will be useful to acquire what knowledge you can of the state of morality, religion, and information among them ; as it may better enable those who may endeavor to civilize and instruct them, to adapt their measures to the existing notions and practices of those on whom they are to operate.

"Other objects worthy of notice will be :

"The soil and face of the country ; its growth and vegetable productions, especially those not of the United States ;

"The animals of the country generally, and especially those not known in the United States ;

"The remains and accounts of any which may be deemed rare or extinct ;

"The mineral productions of every kind, but more particularly metals, limestone, pit-coal, saltpetre ; salines (*p. xvi*) and mineral waters, noting the temperature of the last, and such circumstances as may indicate their character ;

"Volcanic appearances ;

"Climate, as characterized by the thermometer, by the proportion of rainy, cloudy, and clear days ; by lightning, hail, snow, ice ; by the access and recess of frost ; by the winds prevailing at different seasons ; the dates at which particular plants put forth or lose their flower or leaf ; times of appearance of particular birds, reptiles, or insects.

"Although your route will be along the channel of the Missouri, yet you will endeavor to inform yourself, by inquiry, of the character and extent of the country watered by its branches, and especially on its southern side. The North river, or Rio Bravo [Rio Grande del Norte], which runs into the Gulf of Mexico, and the North river, or Rio Colorado, which runs into the Gulf of California, are understood to be the principal streams heading opposite to the waters of the Missouri and running southwardly. Whether the dividing grounds between the Missouri and them are mountains or flat lands, what are their distance from the

Missouri, the character of the intermediate country, and the people inhabiting it, are worthy of particular inquiry. The northern waters of the Missouri are less to be inquired after, because they have been ascertained to a considerable degree, and are still in a course of ascertainment by English traders and travelers; but if you can learn anything certain of the most northern source of the Missisipi [*sic*], and of its position relatively to the Lake of the Woods, it will be interesting to us. Some account too of the path of the Canadian traders from the Missisipi at the mouth of Ouisconsing [Wisconsin river] to where it strikes the Missouri, and of the soil and rivers in its course, is desirable.

" In all your intercourse with the natives, treat them in the most friendly and conciliatory manner which their own conduct will admit; allay all jealousies as to the object of your journey; satisfy them of its innocence; make them (*p. xvii*) acquainted with the position, extent, character, peaceable and commercial dispositions of the United States; of our wish to be neighborly, friendly, and useful to them, and of our dispositions to a commercial intercourse with them; confer with them on the points most convenient as mutual emporiums, and the articles of most desirable interchange for them and us. If a few of their influential chiefs, within practicable distance, wish to visit us, arrange such a visit with them, and furnish them with authority to call on our officers on their entering the United States, to have them conveyed to this place at the public expense. If any of them should wish to have some of their people brought up with us, and taught such arts as may be useful to them, we will receive, instruct, and take care of them. Such a mission, whether of influential chiefs, or of young people, would give some security to your own party. Carry with you some matter of the kine-pox; inform those of them with whom you may be of its efficacy as a preservative from the smallpox, and instruct and encourage them in the use of it. This may be especially done wherever you winter.

" As it is impossible for us to foresee in what manner you

will be received by those people, whether with hospitality
or hostility, so is it impossible to prescribe the exact degree
of perseverance with which you are to pursue your journey.
We value too much the lives of citizens to offer them to
probable destruction.  Your numbers will be sufficient to
secure you against the unauthorized opposition of individuals, or of small parties ; but if a superior force, authorized
or not authorized by a nation, should be arrayed against
your further passage, and inflexibly determined to arrest it,
you must decline its further pursuit and return.  In the
loss of yourselves we should lose also the information you
will have acquired.  By returning safely with that, you may
enable us to renew the essay with better calculated means.
To your own discretion, therefore, must be left the degree
of danger you may risk, and the point at which you should
decline ; ( *p. xviii*) only saying, we wish you to err on the
side of your safety, and to bring back your party safe, even
if it be with less information.

" As far up the Missouri as the white settlements extend,
an intercourse will probably be found to exist between them
and the Spanish posts of St. Louis opposite Cahokia,[8] or
St. Genevieve opposite Kaskaskia.[9]  From still further up
the river the traders may furnish a conveyance for letters.
Beyond that you may perhaps be able to engage Indians to

[8] The Cahokia was a tribe of Indians of the Illinois confederation, who occupied
a village about the mouth of Cahokia creek, St. Clair Co., Ill., and are supposed
to have become extinct about 1800.  The name survived as that of a village on
the E. bank of the Mississippi, four or five miles below St. Louis.

[9] The river of this name runs S. W. in Illinois and falls into the E. side of the
Mississippi at Chester, Randolph Co., Ill.  The old French town of St. Genevieve was on a creek called Gabaree, near the W. bank of the Mississippi, a little
higher up ; it is now the principal town of the county of the same name in Missouri.  The Kaskaskia was named from an Indian tribe, and was also called
Ocoa.  At its mouth was started the town of Portland before 1819, to rival the
old town of Kaskaskia.  There commences the celebrated valley along the Mississippi which became known as the "American bottom," extending along the
E. bank to the Piasa Hills, four miles above the mouth of the Missouri.  This
tract contained the villages of Kaskaskia, Prairie des Roches, Cahokia, Prairie du
Pont, Harrisonville, and Fort Chartres.  The latter, originally built too close to
the river, was undermined in 1808.  It stood about 20 miles above Kaskaskia.

bring letters for the government to Cahokia, or Kaskaskia, on promising that they shall there receive such special compensation as you shall have stipulated with them. Avail yourself of these means to communicate to us, at seasonable intervals, a copy of your journal, notes, and observations of every kind, putting into cipher [10] whatever might do injury if betrayed.

" Should you reach the Pacific ocean, inform yourself of the circumstances which may decide whether the furs of those parts may not be collected as advantageously at the head of the Missouri (convenient as is supposed to the waters of the Colorado and Oregan, or Columbia), as at Nootka Sound, or any other point of that coast; and that trade be consequently conducted through the Missouri and United States more beneficially than by the circumnavigation now practiced.

" On your arrival on that coast, endeavor to learn if there be any port within your reach frequented by the sea vessels of any nation, and to send two of your trusty people back by sea, in such way as shall appear practicable, with a copy of your notes ; and should you be of opinion that the return of your party by the way they went will be imminently dangerous, then ship the whole, and return by sea, by the way either of Cape Horn, or the Cape of Good Hope, as you shall be able. As you will be without money, clothes, or provisions, you must endeavor to use the credit of the United States to obtain them ; for which purpose open letters ( *p. xix*) of credit [11] shall be furnished you, authorizing you to draw on the Executive of the United States, or any of its officers, in any part of the world, in which draughts

[10] The construction of the cipher for communication between President Jefferson and Captain Lewis is displayed on a doc. now bound between Docs. Nos. 97 and 98, in Jeff. Papers L, 2d ser., Vol. 51. The key-word was "artichokes."

[11] Following is this open letter of credit, probably the most remarkable ever held by any individual. It has been printed, but never once correctly. I publish it from the hand-press copy of the original document, in Jefferson's handwriting ; this is a half-sheet, or one folio, written one side, of letter-paper, being Doc. No. 94, Jeff. Papers, 1st ser., Vol. 9, Bureau of Rolls and Library, State

can be disposed of, and to apply with our recommendations to the consuls, agents, merchants, or citizens of any nation with which we have intercourse, assuring them in our name that any aids they may furnish you shall be honorably repaid, and on demand. Our consuls, Thomas Hewes, at Batavia in Java, William Buchanan in the Isles of France and Bourbon, and John Elmslie at the Cape of Good Hope, will be able to supply your necessities by draughts on us.

" Should you find it safe to return by the way you go, after sending two of your party round by sea, or with your whole party, if no conveyance by sea can be found, do so ; making such observations on your return as may serve to supply

Dept. It is accompanied, *ibid.*, by the first rough draft, in Jefferson's hand, full of interlineations and erasures. Captain Lewis received the following final text :

Washington. US. of America. July 4. 1803.

Dear Sir

In the journey which you are about to undertake for the discovery of the course and source of the Missouri, and of the most convenient water communication from thence to the Pacific ocean, your party being small, it is to be expected that you will encounter considerable dangers from the Indian inhabitants. should you escape those dangers, and reach the Pacific ocean, you may find it imprudent to hazard a return the same way, and be forced to seek a passage round by sea, in such vessels as you may find on the Western coast. but you will be without money, without clothes, & other necessaries ; as a sufficient supply cannot be carried with you from hence. your resource in that case can only be the credit of the US. for which purpose I hereby authorise you to draw on the Secretaries of State, of the Treasury, of War & of the Navy of the US. according as you may find your draughts will be most negociable, for the purpose of obtaining money or necessaries for yourself & your men ; and I solemnly pledge the faith of the United States that these draughts shall be paid punctually at the date they are made payable. I also ask of the Consuls, agents, merchants & citizens of any nation with which we have intercourse or amity, to furnish you with those supplies which your necessities may call for, assuring them of honorable and prompt retribution. and our Consuls in foreign parts where you may happen to be, are hereby instructed & required to be aiding and assisting to you in whatever may be necessary for procuring your return back to the United States. And to give more entire satisfaction & confidence to those who may be disposed to aid you, I Thomas Jefferson, President of the United States of America, have written this letter of general credit for you with my own hand, and signed it with my name.                                                    TH : JEFFERSON

To

　　Capt. Meriwether Lewis.

[*i. e.*, supplement or complete], correct, or confirm those made on your outward journey.

" On re-entering the United States and reaching a place of safety, discharge any of your attendants who may desire and deserve it, procuring for them immediate payment of all arrears of pay and clothing which may have [been] incurred since their departure, and assure them that they shall be recommended to the liberality of the legislature for the grant of a soldier's portion of land each, as proposed in my message to Congress, and repair yourself, with your papers, to the seat of government.

" To provide, on the accident of your death, against anarchy, dispersion, and the consequent danger to your party, and total failure of the enterprise, you are hereby authorized, by any instrument signed and written in your own hand, to name the person among them who shall succeed to the command on your decease, and by like instruments to change the nomination, from time to time, as further experience of the characters accompanying you shall point out superior fitness ; and all the powers and authorities given to yourself are, in the event of your death, transferred to and (*p. xx*) vested in the successor so named, with further power to him and his successors, in like manner to name each his successor, who, on the death of his predecessor, shall be invested with all the powers and authorities given to yourself.

" Given under my hand at the City of Washington, this twentieth day of June, 1803.

" THOMAS JEFFERSON,

" *President of the United States of America.*"

While these things were going on here, the country of Louisiana,[12] lately ceded by Spain to France, had been the

---

[12] " Louisiana " is a name whose widely varying geographical and political implications require explanation here.    At the time this History opens " Louisiana " was all that country which had been ceded by Spain to France, and by the latter to the United States ; it was practically then the United States west of the Mississippi.    A map of the period just before the cession would show :

subject of negotiations at Paris between us and this last
power ; and had actually been transferred to us by treaties
executed at Paris, on the 30th of April, 1803. This information, received about the 1st day of July, increased infi-
nitely the interest we felt in the Expedition, and lessened the
apprehensions of interruption from other powers. Everything in this quarter being now prepared, Captain Lewis left
Washington on the 5th day of July, 1803, and proceeded to

United States, east of the Mississippi ; British Possessions, north of 49° and
along the Great Lakes, etc.; Spanish possessions, on the southwest, up to about
38° at point of furthest northward extension ; the rest being " Louisiana."
A straight line from the Straits of Fuca on the Pacific coast to the mouth of the
Mississippi river would run through " Louisiana " from northwest to southeast.
Such was the vast area acquired by the United States through Jefferson's mag-
nificent stroke. It was often called " Jefferson's Purchase."

The treaty ceding this country by France to the United States was executed
at Paris, April 30th, 1803, by Robert R. Livingstone and James Monroe, Ministers Plenipotentiary, on the part of the President of the United States, and Barbe
Marbois, Minister of the Public Treasury, on the part of the First Consul of
France. This treaty was ratified July 31st, 1803. The lower part of Louisiana
was formally transferred by Laussat, Commissioner of France, to General James
Wilkinson and Governor Wm. C. C. Claiborne, at New Orleans, Dec. 20th, 1803
(see Jefferson's Message of Jan. 16th, 1804) ; the upper part was likewise transferred to Captain Amos Stoddard, at St. Louis, Mar. 9th or 10th, 1804. Captain
Lewis, while waiting for the advance of spring to enable him to go up the Missouri, was present at the latter transfer. His name is said to be affixed as that of
one of the witnesses to the official document executed by the Spanish authorities
and Captain Stoddard ; but I have not seen it.

An Act of Congress of March 26th, 1804, divided the thus acquired territory of
Louisiana along the parallel of 33° N. into a southern part, called the " District
of New Orleans," and a northern part, the " District of Louisiana." The latter
District was then temporarily attached to the already existing " Territory of
Indiana," of which William Henry Harrison was at the time Governor, and who
thus became also the first Governor of the new " District of Louisiana." His
governorship of the latter began at St. Louis, Oct. 1st, 1804. An Act of Congress of March 3d, 1805, changed the name " District of Louisiana " to
" Louisiana Territory," to be governed by a Governor and three Judges. This
arrangement took effect July 4th, 1805, when General James Wilkinson entered
upon his gubernatorial functions. These he held for two years, when Governor
Lewis was appointed to the office, Mar. 3d, 1807, and entered upon his functions
in July, 1807, at St. Louis ; he held the position till his death, Oct. 11th, 1809,
and was succeeded by Governor Benjamin Howard, appointed April 17th, 1810.

How " Missouri " grew out of " Louisiana " may also be here noted, as Cap-

Pittsburg, where other articles had been ordered to be provided for him. The men too were to be selected from the military stations on the Ohio. Delays of preparation, difficulties of navigation down the Ohio, and other untoward obstructions retarded his arrival at Cahokia until the season was so far advanced as to render it prudent to suspend his entering the Missouri before the ice could break up in the succeeding spring.

tain (afterward General) Clark became Governor of that Territory.   Originally "Missouri" was the name of certain Indians and their river.   An Act of Congress of June 4th, 1812, taking effect the first Monday of October, 1812, created Missouri as a Territory of the second grade : "The Territory heretofore called 'Louisiana' shall be hereafter called 'Missouri.'"   (This was the former "District of Louisiana," as separated from the "District of New Orleans"—both these having been in the first instance "Louisiana.")   A proclamation of Governor Benjamin Howard, of Oct. 1st, 1812, divided the new Missouri Territory into five counties—St. Charles, St. Louis, St. Genevieve, Cape Girardeau, and New Madrid—the same that had before been the five "districts" of the "District of Louisiana."   The total of representation in the General Assembly of the new Territory of Missouri was 13.   Governor Howard was succeeded by Governor Clark, 1813-1820.   The first delegate to Congress from Missouri was Edward Hempstead, elected Nov., 1812, to serve two years : he had been Attorney-General of the former District of Louisiana, under a commission from Governor Lewis, presented before the proper court May 29th, 1809.   At the date of creation of Missouri Territory, James Madison was President of the United States, and Henry Clay Speaker of the House of Representatives.   Missouri was authorized to adopt a State Constitution by an Act of Congress approved by President Monroe, March 6th, 1820.   The Legislature met for this purpose at St. Louis, Sept. 18th, 1820, and Alexander McNair was inaugurated Governor ; the first Senators elected were David Barton and Thos. H. Benton ; the first Representative was John Scott.   But certain objections to the State Constitution which Missouri had adopted, caused Congress, March 2d, 1821, to require amendments thereto ; which being made by the Legislature which convened at St. Charles, June 4th, 1821, the President's proclamation of Aug. 10th, 1821, admitted Missouri as the twenty-fourth State of the Union.

Thus it appears that Captain Lewis became Governor of "Louisiana Territory" (which had been the "District of Louisiana"), Mar. 3d, 1807–Oct. 11th, 1809, succeeding Governor Wilkinson, and succeeded by Governor Howard.   And General Clark became Governor, not of "Louisiana Territory" but of "Missouri Territory," succeeding Governor Howard (after a short interregnum of an acting Governor), July 1st, 1813, and holding the office till 1820, when, declining the dust of the political arena, he was defeated by the election of Alexander McNair. General Clark was never Governor of Missouri as a State.

From this time his journal, now published, will give the history of his journey to and from the Pacific ocean, until his return to St. Louis on the 23d of September, 1806."³ Never did a similar event excite more joy through the United States. The humblest of its citizens had taken a lively interest in the issue of this journey, and looked forward with impatience for the information it would furnish. Their anxieties too for the safety of the corps had been kept ( *p. xxi* ) in a state of excitement by lugubrious rumors, circulated from time to time on uncertain authorities, and uncontradicted by letters or other direct information, from the time they had left the Mandan towns, on their ascent up the river in April [Apr. 7th ¹⁴] of the preceding year, 1805, until their actual return to St. Louis.

¹³ As stated in my note ⁴⁷, p. 283 of the History, we have the original draft of Lewis' letter of Sept. 23d, 1806, announcing to President Jefferson the return of the Expedition in safety to St. Louis. We also have the original draft of the President's reply, now forming Doc. No. 117, Jeff. Papers L, 2d ser., Vol. 51, dated "Washington Oct. 20 1806." It begins abruptly : "I received, my dear Sir, with unspeakable joy your letter of Sep. 23 announcing the return of yourself, Capt Clarke & your party in good health to St. Louis. the unknown scenes in which you were engaged & the length of time without hearing of you had begun to be felt awfully," etc. The joy was felt nowhere more intensely and sincerely than in the heart of the most exalted citizen of the United States.

¹⁴ Here the allusion to the last direct information Mr. Jefferson had of the Expedition implies the celebrated Mandan letter of Captain Lewis, which was one of the Accompanying Documents of Jefferson's Message to Congress of Feb. 19th, 1806, later taken up in various Apocrypha (see Bibliography, beyond). Besides having its date misprinted April " 17th," instead of 7th, this letter was judiciously pruned down for publication by Mr. Jefferson himself, and consequently has never been printed in full. The original occupies six pages or three folios of letter-paper size, in Lewis' usual fine and even hand. It is now Doc. No. 107 of the Jeff. Papers, 2d ser., Vol. 51, in the archives of the State Dept., and it shows the pencilings of Mr. Jefferson for deletion of certain passages which he thought best not to publish at that time.

Regarding other Mandan matters of this date, if the reader will turn to note ³, p. 250 of the History, he will find mention of the complete invoice of articles which were sent by the barge to President Jefferson. The *original* of this invoice is extant, as Doc. No. 105a, Jeff. Papers L, 2d. ser., Vol. 51. This is in Captain Clark's hand ; it is headed : " Invoice of articles forwarded from Fort Mandan to the President of the United States through Captⁿ· [Amos] Stoddard at St. Louis and Mʳ· H. B. Trist the Collector of the Port of New Orleans."

It was the middle [15] of February, 1807, before Captain Lewis, with his companion, Captain Clark, reached the City of Washington, where Congress was then in session. That body granted to the two chiefs and their followers the dona-

[15] He was certainly in Washington by the 11th, as witness the following letter, addressed to Auguste Chouteau, sen. (b. New Orleans, Sept. 26th, 1750 ; d. St. Louis, Feb. 24th, 1829), who was appointed colonel of militia by Governor Lewis in 1808. I copy it from Billon's Annals, 1888, p. 384—the only place where it occurs in print, to my knowledge.

CITY OF WASHINGTON, Feb. 11, 1807.

SIR.—This will be handed to you by a particular friend and acquaintance of mine, Mr. Fleming [qu. Frederick?] Bates, late Judge of the Michigan Territory and Receiver of Public Moneys at Detroit.

Mr. Bates has been recently appointed the Secretary of the Territory of Louisiana and Recorder of the Board of Commissioners for adjusting the Land Claims in that Territory, and is about to establish himself at St. Louis, in order to take on him the discharge of the duties incumbent to those offices.

The situation of Mr. Bates as a public officer sufficiently shows the estimation in which he is, in my opinion, deservedly held by the Executive of the United States, and consequently renders any further observations in relation to his talents or integrity unnecessary on my part. You will confer an obligation on me by making Mr. Bates acquainted with the respectable inhabitant of St. Louis and its vicinity or by rendering him any service which it may be in your power to give him.

The papers you confided to my care have been laid before the Executive, but as yet I have received no answer on the subject ; nor do I believe that any definite answer will be given, or measures taken in relation to the land claims of Louisiana, until after the passage of a law on that subject which is now under the consideration of Congress.

I shall probably come on to St. Louis in the course of the next fall, for the purpose of residing among you ; in such an event I should wish timely to procure a house by rent or otherwise for my accommodation, and I have fixed my eye on that of Mr. Gratiot, provided we can come on terms which may be mutually agreeable. I would prefer renting or leasing to purchase ; in either case the enclosure of the garden must be rendered secure, and the steps and floor of the piazza repaired by the 1st of October next. I would thank you to request Mr. Gratiot to write me on this subject and to state his terms distinctly, as to price, payment, etc., in order that I may know whether my resources will enable me to meet these or not, or whether it will become necessary that I should make some other provision for my accommodation.

My respectful compliments to your lady, Mad'e P. Chouteau, and to my friends of St. Louis and its vicinity, and believe me your sincere friend and

Obed't servant,

MON'R AUG'T CHOUTEAU.                    MERIWETHER LEWIS.

tion of lands which they had been encouraged to expect in reward of their toil and dangers.[16]    Captain Lewis was soon after [March 3d [17]] appointed Governor of Louisiana, and Captain Clark [March 12th] a General of its militia and Agent of the United States for Indian affairs in that department.

A considerable time intervened before the Governor's arrival at St. Louis.    He found the territory distracted by feuds and contentions among the officers of the government, and the people themselves divided by these into factions and parties.    He determined at once to take no side with either, but to use every endeavor to conciliate and harmonize them.    The even-handed justice he administered to all soon established a respect for his person and authority, and perseverance and time wore down animosities and reunited the citizens again into one family.[18]

[16] On this matter of the grant of lands by Act of Congress, see the note [1], p. cxi, beyond, in the Bibliographical Introduction.

[17] Meanwhile Captain Lewis had resigned from the Army, Mar. 2d, 1807.   See his letter of resignation, in facsimile from a photograph of the original (now on file in the Record Division of the War Dept.), among the plates which illustrate the present work.*   It is extraordinary that the date of Governor Lewis' appointment is left out from every place where it might confidently be expected to appear in print, for it is of official record in the Bureau of Commissions of the State Department, being of almost equal date with his resignation from the Army.   Captain Lewis was nominated as Governor of the Louisiana Territory, by President Jefferson, Feb. 28th, 1807, confirmed by the senate Mar. 2d, and commissioned Mar. 3d.

[18] To this just eulogium of Lewis as governor may be added a few details I have been able to glean, chiefly from Billon's Annals of St. Louis for 1804-21, pub. 1888.   Governor Lewis' appointment is dated Mar. 3d, 1807.   He entered upon his duties in July of that year, at St. Louis, to be performed until his death, Oct. 11th, 1809—a brief period of office in which to do all the good he undoubtedly effected.   One of his important acts was the proclamation establishing "Arkansas," which was formed of a part of the inconveniently large District of New Madrid.   His successor, Benjamin Howard, was appointed April 17th, 1810.

We find that on Nov. 1st, 1807, Silas Bent, Auguste Chouteau, Bernard Pratte, and Louis Labeaume presented their commissions from M. Lewis, the new Governor, and took their seats in the Court of Common Pleas.

Among the Acts of the Legislature of the District of Louisiana, consisting then of Meriwether Lewis, Governor, and two judges, may be noted one of June 18th, 1808, " concerning Towns," and one of June 20th, 1808, " to lay out a road from St. Louis to St. Genevieve, thence to Cape Girardeau, thence to New Madrid."

In August, 1808, Governor Lewis held at St. Louis a Council with the Sacs,

*In this Dover edition, the illustration referred to is reproduced on the large plate at the end of this volume.

Governor Lewis had from early life been subject to hypo-
chondriac affections. It was a constitutional disposition
in all the nearer branches of the family of his name, and
was more immediately inherited by him from his father.
They had not, however, been so strong as to give uneasiness
to his family. While he lived with me in Washington I
observed at times sensible depressions of mind ; but, knowing their constitutional source, I estimated their course by
what I had seen in the family. During his Western Expedi-

Foxes, and Iowas ; a tract of three miles square was ceded to them, and in
the autumn of that year was built Fort Madison, the first fortification established by the United States in that region. At the same time his comrade
General Clark, then Indian Agent for Louisiana, concluded an important treaty
with the Osages, to which nation he was escorted by a troop of cavalry
under Captain M. Wherry. One result of this affair was the establishment of
Fort Osage, for which see notes on p. 30.

The militia of Louisiana Territory was organized in 1808 by Governor Lewis,
who appointed Auguste Chouteau, Sen., to be Colonel of the St. Louis Regiment. In October of this year he had issued general orders to the militia to
parade according to law. One of his latest proclamations was that published
in July, 1809, discharging militia which had been held under his requisition of
Nov. 28th, 1808, to be again enrolled as before with the other militia, with his
thanks for their promptness in volunteering.

Among the Jeff. Papers on file in the Bureau of Rolls and Libr., State Dept.,
of about this date, and relating to Lewis as Governor, may be noted : Doc. No.
220, in Vol. 12 of 1st ser., T. J. to M. L., dated Monticello, Aug. 8th, 1807,
relating to the militia, etc.—Doc. No. 529, *ibid.*, T. J. to M. L., Washn., July
17th, 1808, chiefly concerning the getting of the Mandan chief, Big White, back
home safe. There was great trouble in this matter, on account of the Sioux, and
it assumed a very grave aspect. This letter also recommends to Gov. Lewis " a
Mr. Astor of N. York "—low be it spoken at the present day !—Docs. No. 570 and
No. 573, *ibid.*, T. J. to M. L., Monticello, Aug. 21st and Aug. 24th, 1808, concerning Indian Affairs.—Doc. No. 7K, Misc. Jeff. Papers, 5th ser., Vol. 16, is perhaps
the last letter ever received by Governor Lewis from Mr. Jefferson—if, indeed, it
ever reached him. It is dated Monticello, Aug. 16th, 1809. It opens by recommending the bearer of it, Mr. Bradbury, the subsequently distinguished English
botanist. It includes the following reference to the History of the Expedition :
" I am very often applied to to know when your work will begin to appear ; and
I have so long promised copies to my literary correspondents in France, that I
am almost bankrupt in their eyes. I shall be very happy to receive from yourself information of your expectations on this subject. everybody is impatient
for it."

The first post-office at St. Louis was established early in 1808, with Rufus

tion, the constant exertion which that required of all the faculties (*p. xxii*) of body and mind suspended these distressing affections; but after his establishment at St. Louis in sedentary occupations, they returned to him with redoubled vigor and began seriously to alarm his friends. He was in a paroxysm of one of these when his affairs rendered it necessary for him to go to Washington.[19] He proceeded to the Chickasaw bluffs,[20] where he arrived on the 16th of September, 1809, with a view of continuing his journey

Easton as postmaster. Mails were then usually about six weeks from New York, Philadelphia, and Washington; and the only mail routes west of Indiana and Kentucky were to Cahokia and thence to St. Louis and St. Charles. During this year of Governor Lewis' incumbency the first book ever printed in St. Louis was published in December. It was a volume of 372 pages, being the Laws of the Territory of Louisiana, compiled by Frederick Bates and printed by Joseph Charless. Already had the first newspaper appeared, July 12th, 1808. This was the Missouri Gazette, founded by Mr. Charless; the first issue was a sheet of foolscap 8 x 12 inches. The name was changed Nov. 30th, 1809, to Louisiana Gazette, and this was changed back to the original name July 18th, 1812 ("Congress having changed the name of this Territory, the editor also changed his paper to its first appellation"). Mr. Charless conducted it through twelve volumes to Sept. 13th, 1810, when it had 1,000 subscribers, having started with 170; it was then transferred to another editor. There was no opposition paper till May, 1815, when appeared the Western Journal, which, in 1817, became the Western Emigrant, and, in 1819, the St. Louis Enquirer, with the subsequently famous Thomas H. Benton as editor.

[19] It appears from Billon's sketch (Annals of St. Louis, 1888, p. 378) that before leaving St. Louis on his last journey, Governor Lewis had, on the 19th day of August, 1809, appointed his "three most intimate friends, William Clark, Alexander Stuart, and William C. Carr, his lawful attorneys, with full authority to dispose of all or any part of his property, real and personal, and to pay or receive all debts due by or to him," etc. This power of attorney was executed in the presence of Jeremiah Connor and Samuel Solomon as witnesses. From the fact of his naming three attorneys, clothed with such full powers as are usually exercised by executors only, Mr. Billon remarks that he might have had some foreboding that he would never return to St. Louis, even if he then entertained no idea of self-destruction. In 1810 Edward Hempstead was appointed administrator of his estate by the General Court of Louisiana Territory. He had purchased several pieces of land in the vicinity of the village of St. Louis, among them a 3½ arpent piece, just above the then north end of the village. On a part of this is now the Belcher sugar refinery, and a part of it now forms Lewis street.

[20] On the Mississippi, at present site of the city of Memphis, Shelby Co., Tenn.

thence by water.  Mr. Neely, Agent of the United States with the Chickasaw Indians, arriving there two days after, found him extremely indisposed and betraying at times some symptoms of a derangement of mind.  The rumors of a war with England, and apprehensions that he might lose the papers he was bringing on, among which were the vouchers of his public accounts and the journals and papers of his Western Expedition, induced him here to change his mind and to take his course by land through the Chickasaw country [Tennessee].  Although he appeared somewhat relieved, Mr. Neely kindly determined to accompany and watch over him.  Unfortunately, at their encampment, after having passed the Tennessee [river] one day's journey, they lost two horses, which obliged Mr. Neely to halt for their recovery.  The Governor proceeded under a promise to wait for him at the house of the first white inhabitant on his road.  He stopped at the house of a Mr. Grinder,[21] who not being at home, his wife, alarmed at the symptoms of derangement she discovered, gave him up the house and retired to rest herself in an outhouse, the Governor's and Neely's servants lodging in another.  About three o'clock in the night [of Oct. 11th, 1809] he did the deed which plunged his friends into affliction and deprived his country of one of her most valued citizens, whose valor and intelligence would have been now employed in avenging the wrongs of his country, and in emulating by land the splendid deeds which

[21] In what is now Lewis Co., Tenn., two miles west of the county town of Newburgh.  For circumstances of the journey and the question of suicide or murder, see the Supplement to this Memoir, beyond.  I have a letter dated Ætna, Tenn., July 9th, 1890, addressed to Mr. James D. Park, of Warner, Tenn., by one Joel P. Morrison, of whom I know nothing.  From this letter it appears that the name was not Grinder, but Griner, and that his place was near a creek of the same name.  But several names occur in this letter mistakenly, and the following statement can only pass for what it may be worth : " Lewis stoped at the house of One Robert E. Griner Near the head of what is known as Griners Creek in what is now lewis County Next Morning he was found Dead with Marks of violence on his person, and the report went out that he committed suicide but there has always been suspicion of foul play how this was will never be known."

have honored her arms on the ocean. It lost, too, to the nation the benefit of receiving from his own hand the narrative (*p. xxiii*) now offered them of his sufferings and successes, in endeavoring to extend for them the boundaries of science and to present to their knowledge that vast and fertile country which their sons are destined to fill with arts, with science, with freedom and happiness.

To this melancholy close of the life of one whom posterity will declare not to have lived in vain, I have only to add that all the facts I have stated are either known to myself or communicated by his family or others, for whose truth I have no hesitation to make myself responsible; and I conclude with tendering you the assurances of my respect and consideration.

TH. JEFFERSON.

Mr. PAUL ALLEN, Philadelphia.

# SUPPLEMENT TO JEFFERSON'S MEMOIR
# OF MERIWETHER LEWIS.

## BY DR. COUES.

Ex-President Jefferson's Memoir of Lewis is a noble and fitting tribute, leaving little to be desired as a contemporaneous biography. It has been accepted as authoritative and final, and has furnished the basis of every memoir of Lewis I have seen. As will be observed, however, I have found much historical matter to incorporate with it in the form of notes. What else I have to say concerns not Lewis' life, but the circumstances of his death; and certain subsequent events, which may be brought together in the form of a supplement to Jefferson's Memoir. The affirmation of suicide, though made without qualification, has not passed unchallenged into history; and the mystery of the tragic event will probably never be cleared up. Undoubtedly Jefferson wrote in the light of all the evidence that had reached him in 1813; but it appears that his view of the case was far from being that of persons who lived in the vicinity of the scene at the time. That Governor Lewis did not die by his own hand, but was murdered and robbed, was common report at the time, as vouched for by some persons still living; and the question came up in the Legislature of Tennessee at its session of 1849–50, in connection with the erection of the monument for which the Legislature had provided in 1848.

By far the most circumstantial account we have of the tragedy is that given by Alexander Wilson, the famous ornithologist, in a letter which was written to his friend and the engraver of his birds, Alexander Lawson, and which was published originally in The Portfolio, Vol. VII., No. 1, pp. 34–

47, of date January, 1812, under the caption " Particulars of the Death of Capt. Lewis." This was known and accessible to ex-President Jefferson; in fact, a letter from Paul Allen to him, which I have seen, calls his attention to it. But it is not noted in his Memoir of Lewis, and in the course of time has been practically forgotten, though it is included in the Rev. Alexander B. Grosart's The Poems and Literary Prose of Alexander Wilson (2 vols., 8vo, Paisley, 1876). This important letter is dated " Natchez, Missisippi Ter., May 28th, 1811." It tells the story of Lewis' death as Wilson took it down from the lips of Mrs. Grinder, in her own house. I quote from The Portfolio those portions, pp. 36–38, which are pertinent to my purpose :

" . . . Next morning (Sunday) I rode six miles to a man's of the name of Grinder, where our poor friend Lewis perished. In the same room where he expired, I took down from Mrs. Grinder the particulars of that melancholy event, which affected me extremely. This house or cabin is 72 miles from Nashville, and is the last white man's as you enter the Indian country. Governor Lewis, she said, came there about sun-set, alone, and inquired if he could stay for the night; and, alighting, brought his saddle into the house. He was dressed in a loose gown, white, striped with blue. On being asked if he came alone, he replied that there were two servants behind, who would soon be up. He called for some spirits, and drank a very little. When the servants arrived, one of whom was a negro, he inquired for his powder, saying he was sure he had some powder in a canister. The servant gave no distinct reply, and Lewis, in the mean while, walked backwards and forwards before the door, talking to himself. Sometimes, she said, he would seem as if he were walking up to her; and would suddenly wheel round, and walk back as fast as he could. Supper being ready he sat down, but had eaten only a few mouthfuls when he started up, speaking to himself in a violent manner. At these times, she says, she observed his face to flush as if it had come on him in a fit. He lighted his pipe, and draw-

ing a chair to the door sat down, saying to Mrs. Grinder, in
a kind tone of voice, ' Madam this is a very pleasant evening.' He smoked for some time, but quitted his seat and
traversed the yard as before. He again sat down to his
pipe, seemed again composed, and casting his eyes wishfully
towards the west, observed what a sweet evening it was.
Mrs. Grinder was preparing a bed for him; but he said he
would sleep on the floor, and desired the servant to bring the
bear skins and buffaloe robe, which were immediately spread
out for him; and it being now dusk the woman went off to
the kitchen, and the two men to the barn, which stands about
200 yards off. The kitchen is only a few paces from the
room where Lewis was, and the woman being considerably
alarmed by the behaviour of her guest could not sleep, but
listened to him walking backwards and forwards, she thinks,
for several hours, and talking aloud, as she said, ' like a lawyer.' She then heard the report of a pistol, and something
fall heavily on the floor, and the words ' O Lord!' Immediately afterwards she heard another pistol, and in a few
minutes she heard him at her door calling out ' O madam!
give me some water, and heal my wounds.' The logs being
open, and unplastered, she saw him stagger back and fall
against a stump that stands between the kitchen and room.
He crawled for some distance, raised himself by the side
of a tree, where he sat about a minute. He once more got
to the room; afterwards he came to the kitchen door, but
did not speak; she then heard him scraping the bucket with
a gourd for water; but it appears that this cooling element
was denied the dying man! As soon as day broke and not
before, the terror of the woman having permitted him to
remain for two hours in this most deplorable situation, she
sent two of her children to the barn, her husband not being
at home, to bring the servants; and on going in they found
him lying on the bed; he uncovered his side and shewed
them where the bullet had entered; a piece of the forehead
was blown off, and had exposed the brains, without having
bled much. He begged they would take his rifle and blow

out his brains, and he would give them all the money he had in his trunk.  He often said 'I am no coward; but I am so strong, so hard to die.'  He begg'd the servant not to be afraid of him, for that he would not hurt him.  He expired in about two hours, or just as the sun rose above the trees.  He lies buried close by the common path, with a few loose rails thrown over his grave.  I gave Grinder money to put a post fence round it, to shelter it from the hogs, and from the wolves; and he gave me his written promise he would do it.  I left this place in a very melancholy mood, which was not much allayed by the prospect of the gloomy and savage wilderness which I was just entering alone. . . ." [1]

Such is the horrible story told to Wilson by an eye- and ear-witness.  We must accept the substantial accuracy of Wilson's version, written almost immediately after he heard the narrative of Mrs. Grinder, and by one noted for habitual precision of statement.  There is no more room to doubt Wilson's painstaking correctness than there is reason for doubting his veracity.  But the narrative of Mrs. Grinder is very extraordinary.  A woman who could do as she said she did, after hearing and seeing what she testifies, must be judged "fit for treason, stratagem, and spoils," and not to be believed under oath.  The story is wildly improbable upon its face; it does not hang together; there is every sign that it is a concoction on the part of an accomplice in crime, either before or after the event.  On the theory that Mrs. Grinder was privy to a plot to murder Governor Lewis, and therefore had her own part to play in the tragedy, even if that part were a passive one—or on the theory that, becoming afterward cognizant of the murder, she told a story to shield

---

[1] The " melancholy poet-naturalist," as Wilson has often been styled, was moved to compose an elegy on Lewis, which was published with the letter of which the above is an extract.  The first and also the last of the nineteen verses is :

" Far hence be each accusing thought !
With his my kindred tears shall flow ;
Pale Pity consecrates the spot,
Where poor lost LEWIS now lies low ! "

the actual criminal or criminals—on either of these theories we could understand Mrs. Grinder; otherwise her story is simply incredible. Yet it is upon such evidence as this that the imputation of suicide rests.

Governor Lewis' alleged actions, before he retired to his room " about dusk," seem nothing extraordinary. He certainly appears to have been fretted or worried about something; but there was nothing in his conduct which should have so alarmed Grinder's wife that she could not sleep, but lay listening " she thinks for several hours." The sort of a woman likely to be the wife of a keeper of a " stand " on the Natchez Trace in 1809 is not likely to have had such weak nerves as that. And where was Grinder himself on this fateful night? Then she hears two pistol-shots, a heavy fall, and an appeal for help. This, however, only moves her to peep through the cracks in the logs of the detached kitchen. There she sees her guest staggering, falling, and crawling about in the yard in search of water. Still she does not stir, and it is not till daybreak, about " two hours " after the shots were fired, that the terror of the woman permits her to give the alarm. This she does by sending " two children " to the barn to bring the servants, who meanwhile had heard nothing; and the whole party now, for the first time, musters courage enough to enter Governor Lewis' room. Two hours more pass, during which they are begged and offered money to put him out of his misery; but nothing is done, and the governor expires as the sun tops the trees.

Governor Lewis may have committed the deed which history has laid to his charge, in a fit of suicidal mania; and the woman's incoherent story may not have been intended to deceive, but may have arisen from confused memories of an exciting night. That is conceivable; but my contention is that the testimony, as we have it, does not suffice to prove suicide, and does raise a strong suspicion that Governor Lewis was foully dealt with by some person or persons unknown— presumably Grinder, or him and some accomplices. Until other evidence is forthcoming the victim of untimely fate should be given the full benefit of the doubt, that no stigma may rest on his illustrious name.    History may never be able to disprove the alleged suicide; neither has history thus far proven the allegation.    This death remains a mystery; but mystery should not be paraded as history.

Very recently the question has been reopened, with a view of setting aside the verdict of posterity, by Mr. James D. Park, a lawyer of Franklin, Tenn., who inclines strongly to the theory of murder and robbery, not suicide. Mr. Park's article, over the pseudonym "John Quill," was published in the Nashville (Tenn.) American of Sunday, September 6th, 1891.    It occupies 4¼ columns of the newspaper, and has two illustrations—one a portrait of Lewis, from the miniature profile in the possession of the State Historical Society of Tennessee at Nashville;[2] the other a picture of the monument, from a sketch made by Mr. Park on the spot.    Whatever view be taken of the tragedy, Mr. Park's article is a valuable historical document, bringing news to most persons.    Some of it is biographical, citing the brief notice in Howe's Historical Collections of Virginia,[3] and the more extended sketch of Lewis' life in the Analectic Magazine and Naval Chronicle, VII. April, 1816, pp. 329–333 (with frontisp. portrait)—both of which were in turn based on Jefferson's Memoir; another portion is historical, giving the

[2] On Nov. 16th, 1892, I delivered in Washington, before the American Ornithologists' Union, an off-hand address nominally relating to the birds of Lewis and Clark, but mainly occupied with the question of Lewis' death.    A reporter who was present took me down, with the result of a somewhat sensational, but in the main correct, article of two columns' length in the St. Louis Globe-Democrat of Nov. 19th, 1892.    This has two portraits, of Lewis and of Clark respectively. I allude to this article partly from my bibliographical instincts, but mainly to say that the portrait of Lewis is there given as that of Clark, and vice versa; also, that the former is from a photograph of this same Nashville miniature.

[3] Historical Collections of Virginia : Containing a Collection of the most interesting Facts, Traditions, Biographical Sketches, Anecdotes, etc., relating to its History, Antiquities, etc., to which is added a historical and descriptive sketch of the District of Columbia.    By Henry Howe.    Published by William R. Babcock, Charleston, S. C., 1856, 1 vol. 8vo.    (Biographical notice of Captain Lewis, p. 171.    Biographical notice of Captain Clark, p. 234.    Both inaccurate in some particulars.)

action of the Tennessee Legislature, and the first report of
the committee appointed to erect the monument, including a copy of the several inscriptions.   The most original
matter is the result of Mr. Park's researches on the spot,
which inclined him to the view of murder and not suicide.
The picture of the monument is the first ever printed ;
though roughly executed, as usual with newspaper cuts, it
gives an excellent idea of the object.   I was put in private
correspondence with Mr. Park, through the good offices
of Governor Buchanan of Tennessee, and will adduce the
substance of his new evidence, nearly in his own words.

As adequate to support the theory of suicide has been
held Mr. Jefferson's statement of hereditary hypochondria,
developed to desperation under worry over some trouble
about public money accounts.   Mr. Jefferson touches very
lightly upon the latter feature of the case, but others have
spoken more pointedly.   Thus in Howe's Historical Collections, p. 171, we read : " He was subject to constitutional
hypochondria, and while under the influence of a severe
attack, shot himself on the borders of Tennessee in 1809, at
the age of 35.   This event was ascribed to the protest of
some bills which he drew on the public account."   Again,
we find in Jacob's Life and Times of Patrick Gass, pp. 110,
111, remarks upon the same score, with some particulars to
which ex-President Jefferson does no more than allude.
Says Jacob :

" Lewis was appointed very shortly after his return in
1806, Governor of Louisiana Territory, as some acknowl-
ment of his merit, and compensation for his services.   In
this capacity he acted for some time, but unfortunately a
misunderstanding arose between him and the government
in regard to the settlement of his public accounts.   He was
the very soul of honor and of unimpeachable integrity, and
the implied imputation dwelt too heavily upon his proud
and sensitive spirit.   He started to Washington City for an
explanation, but never reached his destination.   In company with another man [Mr. Neely] he traveled the old

route followed by the boatmen at that day, through the Indian country, and having reached a small cabin occupied by a man named Grinders [Grinder] as a kind of tavern for travellers, just within the Chickasaw nation, near the Tennessee line, and between 25 and 30 [read 60 or 70] miles of Nashville, his man left him to go in search of a horse that had strayed. During his absence after the horse, Lewis shot himself twice with a pistol, and this failing to effect his purpose, he killed himself by cutting his throat with a knife [!]. No one saw him commit the act, but some of the [Grinder] family afterwards reported that they had observed indications that his mind was affected, on the morning of [evening before] his death. His body was buried at the corner of the cabin, and for a long time after, the spot was remembered by the adventurous traders who passed that way [along the Natchez Trace], between New Orleans and the upper country. Thus was ushered into eternity a brave and chivalrous spirit, goaded to desperation by the chafing of wounded honor. . . It is enough for the historian to say that he died with the cloud on his memory ; and while he records his fate with a careful pen, he would ask of the world its most charitable judgment. The charges against him were hushed, communities and States vied to do him honor, and [in 1848] the Legislature of Tennessee, his adopted State, to manifest an appreciation of what was high and noble in his character and services, ordered a monument to be erected to his memory at the State's expense."

Mr. Jacob's paragraph in Gass fairly reflects accredited history, excepting what he says of recourse to the knife.

A similar view of the case is presented in J. B. Killebrew's Resources of Tennessee (Nashville, 1874), p. 791, where Lewis county is described : " In the very centre of the present county, on the line of the old Natchez Trace, while on a journey from the Territory of Louisiana, of which he was Governor, Merriwether [sic] Lewis committed suicide, being at the time a little over 35 years of age. On this very spot he was buried, and the Legislature of Tennessee in

1848 had a suitable monument erected to his memory. . . In the midst of dense woods, several miles from any human habitation, on the crest of a bold broad ridge, with deep gorges running toward the northeast and west, and near the commencement of the flat lands, this monument stands, seldom visited, and almost forgotten by the present generation. Its entire height is about 25 [read 20½] feet, and it is surrounded by an iron fence in a state of great dilapidation, many of the rods having been taken away."

The Analectic Magazine and Naval Chronicle,[4] Vol. VII., No. 40, April, 1816, gives a full-length portrait of Captain Lewis in Indian dress, as a frontispiece; and the same number of this magazine contains, pp. 329–333, a " Notice of Captain M. Lewis." This is simply abridged from the Jefferson Memoir, and is mostly in the words of the latter. Concerning the portrait the editor says:

" The portrait of captain Lewis, given in the present number, is taken from a drawing of that officer belonging to his fellow traveler, governor Clark, who considers it an excellent likeness, and prizes it highly. The gentleman [name not given] who lent it to us remained here but a short time, and was obliged to take it with him; to which circumstance it is owing that our engraving from it is not executed in so good a style as we could have wished. But that engraving is a faithful copy of the original, which is believed to be the only likeness of Captain Lewis now extant. The ornaments

---

[4] Published monthly by Moses Thomas, 8vo, Philada.; printed by J. Maxwell—the same who printed the History of the Expedition for Bradford & Inskeep. In saying that the portrait he published was from the only likeness of Lewis extant in 1816, the editor is mistaken, unless the others we possess were executed after the death of their subject. The portrait in Indian dress is at present in St. Louis, and may be learned of through Mr. J. K. Clark, 3121 Locust St. The one from which the engraving contained in the present work was prepared is the oil painting by Charles Wilson Peale, which has for many years hung in Independence Hall in Philadelphia, with its companion-piece, Captain Clark, also reproduced by my publisher. Besides this, there is left the profile miniature in the possession of the Tennessee Historical Society in Nashville. Of the latter, which is very beautiful, photographs are abundant, and I suppose may be procured at the usual price for pictures of cabinet size.

worn by him when in the costume of an Indian warrior, (as represented in the picture) are preserved in the Philadelphia [Peale's] Museum."

We may now recur to Mr. Park's article above described. Jefferson's account (says Mr. Park in substance) was written in the light of such information as had reached him in 1813, at his home in Virginia. It would be interesting to know the exact sources of his information were this possible now, to judge for ourselves whether they were entirely free from suspicion. Probably such accounts did not convey the idea of murder and robbery. It then required several weeks for the news to travel from the scene to Washington ; and whether the details of the death of Governor Lewis ever reached the national capital in official form cannot now be learned.

During the first years of this century a great military road was cut through the then wilderness of Tennessee and Mississippi, known as the " Natchez Trace." It was made by Lieutenant Edmund Pendleton Gaines, U. S. A., who rose to be a major general during the war of 1812–15. It led southwest from Nashville, Tenn., to Natchez on the Mississippi river, and was the only public road in that region, cut to facilitate the movement of troops and the transportation of supplies to and from the newly acquired " Spanish country." This old road has since been abandoned in many places, but in other parts of its length it is still (1891) used. Even where given up, and passing through open woods or inclosed in fields, its course can still be traced through Tennessee and Mississippi by its well-worn bed, lower than the adjoining land. Governor Lewis struck across country directly eastward from the Chickasaw Bluffs (the present site of Memphis, Tenn.), and probably made the Natchez Trace at or about where this Trace crosses the Tennessee river, in what is now Lauderdale Co., in northern Alabama, about 20 miles below the town of Florence, and traveled it for about a day's march west of Newburgh, Lewis Co., Tenn., the scene of the tragedy. At this point in the journey, observes Mr.

Park, "the conduct of Mr. Neely, the Indian agent, as mentioned in Mr. Jefferson's account, seems to have been very strange. He had at the Chickasaw Bluffs volunteered to accompany Governor Lewis from there through the Indian country to the seat of government, in order to look after and watch over his distinguished guest, whom he had found quite indisposed, and, as alleged, showing signs of a disordered mind. They had servants and horses in their train; yet the recapture of two horses that had strayed from the camp was deemed by Mr. Neely of more importance than the welfare and safety of his friend, whom he permitted to go forward with the servants while he remained a whole day behind to look up the horses. The accounts do not show that he ever found them, or ever caught up with Governor Lewis."

Thus it appears that from the point above noted Governor Lewis kept on, unattended by Mr. Neely, along the Natchez Trace. On this road, at intervals of about a day's journey, say some 30 miles, there were primitive places of entertainment for man and beast, called "stands." Governor Lewis reached one of these, kept by a Mr. Grinder. The site of "Grinder's stand" is still seen, on a spot about sixty miles in an air-line southwest of Nashville, marked by the ruins of a stone chimney, a mound of earth, and the remains of a garden or small clearing in the forest. It is on the crest of a ridge, along which runs the Natchez Trace, not now used at this point. Even at this day the nearest habitation is a mile and a half or two miles distant. North of the site of the old house, and about 150 yards from it, on the east side of the road, is the great explorer's grave, and the monument erected by the State of Tennessee to his memory.

I give the results of Mr. Park's inquiries on the spot, Nov. 21st, 1889, in his own words: "It has always been the firm belief of the people of this region that Governor Lewis was murdered and robbed. The oldest citizens now living remember the rumor current at the time as to the murder, and it seems that no thought of suicide ever obtained footing here. The writer recently had an interview with Mrs.

Christina B. Anthony, who lives some two miles from
the Lewis grave, and has lived all her life of 77 years
in the neighborhood. She says that 'old man Grinder'
kept a 'stand' for travelers on the Natchez Trace. Polly
Spencer, whom she knew well before her death about 40
years ago, was a hired girl at Grinder's when Governor
Lewis was killed. Polly had often told the circumstances
of the murder so far as she personally knew them. She
was washing dishes in the kitchen after supper with some
of the females in the family, when they heard a shot in the
room where Captain Lewis was sleeping. All rushed into
the room and found him dead in his bed. Captain Lewis,
being fatigued from his journey, had retired immediately
after supper. His only companion, she said, was a negro
boy, who was attending the horses in the barn at the time.
Old Grinder, who was of Indian blood, was at once suspected of the murder, ran away, was captured on Cane
creek, brought back, and tried; but the proof not being
positive, he was released. Only 25 cents was found on the
person of Captain Lewis after he was shot. Old Grinder
soon afterward removed to the western part of the State,
and it was reported in his old neighborhood had bought
a number of slaves and a farm, and seemed to have
plenty of money. Before this he had always been quite
poor.

"Mrs. Anthony says the people always believed old
Grinder killed Mr. Lewis and got his money. She had
never heard of the theory of suicide until the writer mentioned it to her. Mrs. Anthony was a young married
woman, boarding with the father of Polly Spencer, when
Polly told her of these circumstances. Mrs. Anthony thus
heard an ear-witness, so to speak, relate the story of the
murder, which is pretty direct evidence. She is a bright,
active, intelligent old lady, and has for many years kept the
little hotel at the hamlet of Newburgh, the county seat of
Lewis County, which is just two miles east of the monument. She refers to her brother, Jason Boshears, 80 years

of age, living near Mount Pleasant, 20 miles distant, and
Mrs. Sallie Barham Sims, 82 years of age, living at Ætna
Furnace, Hickman County, who were born and formerly
lived near by, and who, she thinks, could give more in detail
the circumstances of the murder, as developed on the trial
of old Grinder. It was, however, inconvenient for the
writer to look up these two old persons.

" Others living in Lewis and adjoining counties have been
conversed with, who remember the general belief at the time
that Grinder killed his guest for the purpose of robbery.
He must have observed that Captain Lewis was a person of
distinction and wealth ; that he was almost alone and probably had money with him. It seems incredible that a
young man of 35, the governor of the vast territory of
Louisiana, then on his way from his capital to that of his
nation, where he knew he would be received with all the
distinction and consideration due to his office and reputation, should take his own life. His whole character is a
denial of this theory. He was too brave and conscientious
in the discharge of every duty, public and private ; too conspicuous a person in the eyes of the country, and crowned
with too many laurels, to cowardly sneak out of the world by
the back way, a self-murderer. This idea was doubtless in-
vented to cover up the double crime of robbery and murder,
and seems to have been the only version of his death that
reached Mr. Jefferson and his other friends in Virginia."

This is literally a lawyer's brief, summing such evidence
as could be procured to defend Governor Lewis from the
charge of suicide. It is probably as strong a presentation
of the case as is now possible. It also falls in well with the
Wilson evidence already adduced—which is the more remarkable, in that Wilson took Mrs. Grinder's wild story to
be a statement of fact, and evidently believed that poor
Lewis had killed himself. That the new Park testimony is
conclusive, however, Mr. Park himself would probably not
urge. That the theory of murder was a matter of common
report, acted upon at the time to the extent of the arrest

and trial of Grinder, and that it has ever since been believed by the community, is established by direct testimony. But the evidence, mainly circumstantial, did not suffice to convict Grinder or anyone else of murder. The fragmentary evidence which has come down to us, moreover, does not hang together well. It is even opens up the doubt that we have the true date of death within 24 hours. Jefferson's account makes the hour "about three o'clock in the night," when Polly Spencer is not likely to have been washing dishes in the kitchen with others of the household. This means 3 a. m., of the historical date, October 11th, 1809; but from what Mr. Park has adduced, it would appear that, irrespective of mode of death, Governor Lewis lost his life shortly after the usual hour of an evening meal, on October 10th. Had Polly and all the rest " rushed into the room " on hearing the shot, and " found him dead in his bed," it seems likely that more positive and detailed accounts of the scene would have at once come into existence and been perpetuated. But nothing appears of the whereabouts of the supposititious murderer at this moment ; and an intending murderer would hardly have chosen so early an hour, when all the family were up and about, and he knew he had the whole night in which to execute his design at leisure. It is not unreasonable to translate Mrs. Anthony's report to Mr. Park—made about 80 years after the event, it must be remembered—in somewhat these words : Polly Spencer (had been) washing dishes (the evening before; and some hours afterward, when the family had been abed and asleep) they heard the shot, and rushed into the room, etc. This might easily have been past midnight of October 10th, or about the hour alleged of October 11th. But even were the date fixed to the hour, the question of murder or suicide would not, thereby, be left other than it was before.

Mr. Park seems to me to present a strong case,—perhaps the strongest that will ever be drawn up,—and deserves much credit for thus undertaking to clear so great a name from so grave an imputation. Prior to making his investigations he had never heard of the Wilson testimony above given, and had read only Mr. Jefferson's account of the death. In fact he had nothing but the common belief of the people to go upon. He cites Governor Lewis' established reputation and well-known circumstances; he brings forward an actual arrest and trial for murder; and he establishes the facts that murder was at the time a matter of common allegation and belief, and has been from that day to this the tradition of the community. These are strong points. But the actual testimony adduced at this time is from the memory of one person as to events of about eighty years ago; it is at second-hand, indirect, and circumstantial only; thus being fatally defective. It is also offset by the unqualified statements of Mr. Jefferson, a wary and astute man of the world, accustomed to weigh his words well; one who must have been satisfied in his own mind that he had the facts of a case beyond his personal knowledge; and one who had every imaginable reason—personal, official, or other—to put the matter in the most favorable light. The mystery remains, and it is not probable that the truth will ever be known.

It is a relief to turn from this sad scene, and see what has been done to honor Governor Lewis by the country he loved and served so well. The erection of his monument is an incident in the history of a State.

On the 21st of December, 1843,[5] the legislature of Tennessee passed an act creating the County of Lewis, " In honor of Capt. Merrewether Lewis, who has rendered dis-

[5] Acts passed at the First Session of the Twenty-fifth General Assembly of the State of Tennessee, 1843-44, pub. 1844, 1 vol., 8vo, pp. 41-44 : " An Act to establish the County of Lewis. Sect. 1. Be it enacted by the General Assembly of the State of Tennessee, That a new county be, and the same is hereby established, to be composed of fractions taken from the counties of Maury, Lawrence, Wayne and Hickman, and to be known and designated by the name of Lewis County, in honor of Captain Merrewether [*sic*] Lewis, who has rendered distinguished services to his country, and whose remains lie buried and neglected within its limits," etc., to Sect. 15 inclusive—being the usual provisions for forming and maintaining a county. Passed Dec. 21st, 1843. D. L. Barringer, Speaker of the House of Representatives ; J. M. Anderson, Speaker of the Senate.

tinguished services to his country, and whose remains lie buried and neglected within its limits." The grave is in the exact center of this county, which was surveyed from this point and carved out of the then surrounding counties of Maury, Hickman, Wayne, and Lawrence.

On the 4th of February, 1848,[6] the same legislature appropriated $500 for the erection of a suitable monument, and appointed four distinguished citizens of Tennessee as a committee to carry out this design and report to the next legislature. The gentlemen accepted the commission as a labor of love and duty. The " Report of the Lewis Monumental Committee," made to the legislature of 1849–50, as appears from the Appendix to the Journal of the House of Representatives, pp. 238–240, is as follows :[7]

" To the General Assembly of the State of Tennessee :

" By the ninth section of an act passed at the last session of the General Assembly of this State, entitled an act to

----

[6] Acts of the State of Tennessee passed at the First Session of the Twenty-seventh General Assembly for the years 1847–48, pub. 1848, 1 vol., 8vo, p. 217, Chap. cxxxv. An Act to amend an act, passed the 21st of Dec. 1843, entitled an " act to establish the County of Lewis." Sect. 9 is : " Be it further enacted, That the sum of five hundred dollars be, and the same is hereby appropriated out of any money in the Treasury not otherwise appropriated, or so much thereof as may be necessary to preserve the place of interment, where the remains of the Gen. Meriwether Lewis were deposited, and that Robert A. Smith, of the county of Lewis, Hon. Edmund Dillahunty and Barclay Martin, of Maury county, and Dr. Samuel B. Moore, of Hickman county, be, and are hereby made the agents of the General Assembly to carry into execution the provisions of this act, and report to the next General Assembly." Passed Feb. 4th, 1848. F. Buchanan, Speaker of the House of Representatives ; J. M. Anderson, Speaker of the Senate.

[7] I have cited the foregoing Acts of the Tennessee Legislature from the originals ; but the Journal of the House of Representatives I have not been able to lay hands on. The set of volumes in the Congressional Library happens to lack 1849–50, and this volume is not to be found in the library of the Supreme Court or in that of the State Department. My citation of the report of the committee is therefore at second hand, from Mr. Park's printed article ; but this gentleman informs me that he has taken great pains to correct what is cited above, by comparing a press-proof which I sent him with a copy of the original official report in the State Library at Nashville—" carefully verified, June 10th, 1893." he says.

[amend an act to] establish the County of Lewis, the sum of $500 was appropriated, or so much thereof as might be necessary, to preserve the place of interment where the remains of General MERRIWETHER LEWIS were deposited ; and the undersigned were appointed the agents of the General Assembly to carry into execution the provisions of the act, and report to the present General Assembly.

" Looking upon the object to be accomplished to be one highly honorable to the State, the undersigned entered upon the duties assigned them most cheerfully, and with as little delay as possible. They consulted with the most eminent artists and practical mechanics as to the kind of monument to be erected, and a plan being agreed upon they employed Mr. Lemuel W. Kirby, of Columbia, to execute it for the sum of five hundred dollars.

" The entire monument is twenty and a half feet high. The design is simple, but is intended to express the difficulties, successes, and violent termination of a life which was marked by bold enterprise, by manly courage and devoted patriotism. The base of the monument is of rough unhewn stone, eight feet high, and nine feet square where it rises to the surface of the ground. On this, rests a plinth of cut stone four feet square, and eighteen inches in thickness [height], on which are the inscriptions which are given below. On this plinth stands a broken column eleven feet high, two and a half feet in diameter at the base, and a few inches smaller at the top. The top is broken to denote the violent and untimely end of a bright and glorious career. The base is composed of a species of sandstone found in the neighborhood of the grave. The plinth and shaft, or column, are made of a fine limestone, commonly known as Tennessee marble. Around the monument is erected a handsome wrought-iron rail fence.

" Great care was taken to identify the grave. George Nixon, Esq., an old Surveyor, had become very early acquainted with its locality. He pointed out the place ; but to make assurance doubly sure the grave was reopened and the upper part of the skeleton examined, and such evidences found as to leave no doubt of the place of interment. Witnesses were called and their certificate, with that of the Surveyor, prove the fact beyond dispute.

"The inscription upon the plinth was furnished by Prof. Nathaniel Cross, of the University of Nashville. It is beautiful and appropriate. It is placed on the different sides of the plinth, and is as follows: [8]

[WEST FACE.]

MERRIWETHER LEWIS,
Born near Charlottesville, Virginia, August 18, 1774,
Died October 11, 1809, aged 35 years.

[SOUTH FACE.]

An officer of the Regular Army—Commander of the Expedition to
the Oregon in 1803–1806—Governor of the Territory of
Louisiana—His melancholy death occurred
where this monument now stands,
and under which rest his
mortal remains.

[EAST FACE.]

In the language of Mr. Jefferson : ' His courage was undaunted : His firmness and perseverance yielded to nothing but impossibilities : A
rigid disciplinarian, yet tender as a father of those committed to his charge ; honest, disinterested,
liberal, with a sound understanding
and a scrupulous fidelity
to truth.'

[NORTH FACE.]

Immaturus obi : sed tu felicior annos
Vive meos, Bona Respublica ! Vive tuos.

———

Erected by the Legislature of Tennessee.
A. D. 1848.

[8] In attempting to reproduce these inscriptions as copied by Mr. Park from the stone, certain errors which appear in the printed report are ignored. The worst of these is the wrong date of Oct. "17" instead of 11. Lewis' Christian name is misspelled both on stone and on paper. The Latin word Respublica is also misspelled "Republica" in the report. The alignment here presented is not exactly true to the stone, but gives the same general effect to the eye.

"In the Latin distich, many of your honorable body will no doubt recognize as the affecting epitaph on the tomb of a young wife, in which, by a *prosopopocia* [*sic*— read prosopopœia], after alluding to her immature death, she prays that her happier husband may live out *her* year and his own:

> "*Immatura peri : sed tu felicior annos*
> *Vive meos, conjux optime ! Vive tuos.*

"Under the same figure the deceased is represented, in the Latin distich as altered, after alluding to his early death, as uttering as a patriot a similar prayer, that the republic may fulfill her high destiny, and that her years may equal those of time. As the distich now stands, the figure may be made to apply, either to the whole Union, or to Tennessee that has honored his memory by the erection of a monument.

"The impression has long prevailed that under the influence of disease of body and mind—of hopes based upon long and valuable services—not merely deferred but wholly disappointed—Governor Lewis perished by his own hands. It seems to be more probable that he died by the hands of an assassin. The place at which he was killed is even yet a lonely spot. It was then wild and solitary, and on the borders of the Indian nation. Maj. C. L. Clark,[9] a son of Governor Clark, of Missouri, in a letter to the Rev. Mr. Cressey, of Maury Co., says: ' Have you ever heard of the report, that Governor Lewis did not destroy his own life, but was murdered by his servant, a Frenchman, who stole his money and horses, returned to Natchez, and was never afterwards heard of ? This is an important matter in connection with the erection of a monument to his memory, as it clearly removes from my mind, at least, the only stigma upon the fair name I have the honor to bear.'

"The undersigned would suggest to the General Assembly the propriety of having an acre of ground, or some other

---

[9] Misprint or other mistake for M. L. Clark, *i.e.*, Meriwether Lewis Clark, eldest son of William Clark by his first wife.

reasonable quantity, around the grave, secured against the entry of private persons. This can be done either by reserving the title in the State, or by directing a grant to issue in the name of the governor and his successors in office. The first mode would probably be the best.

"All of which is respectfully submitted.

                               "EDMUND DILLAHUNTY,
                               "BARCLAY MARTIN,
                               "ROBERT A. SMITH,
                               "SAMUEL B. MOORE."

At the time of Mr. Park's visit to the grave, November 21st, 1889, the base of the monument was somewhat moss-grown, the inscriptions on the plinth were scarcely legible, and the iron fence was nearly all gone. It is said that the iron was taken away during the War of the Rebellion to make horseshoes, as the production of iron was then almost entirely suspended in the South. The acre reserved around the monument has since become "God's Acre" indeed, where rest the remains of one of his noblest works, albeit now indistinguishable from humbler dust in a common burying-ground. "Far out in the native forest, on the highlands, with no human dwelling near, it is indeed a lonely spot, where the wild deer and the fox are still pursued by the hunter's hounds. The existence of such a grave and monument is scarcely known outside of the State, and to but few anywhere of the present generation. Tennessee would be loath to give up the honored dust which has slept in her bosom for more than eighty years; but would it not be a graceful, if too long neglected, act, should Congress authorize the erection of an appropriate monument of bronze at the national capital, to the memory of the accomplished soldier and scientist who led the first expedition through the unknown gateways of the mountains to the Pacific, and the mystery of whose untimely end will perhaps never be solved?"

# MEMOIR OF WILLIAM CLARK.

BY DR. COUES.

WE possess a genealogy of that Clark family of which William is the most illustrious member, from about the beginning of the last century to the present day. In the early part of the eighteenth century, John Clark 1st and Miss or Mrs. Burd resided in King and Queen Co., Va. They married, and were William's grandparents. Their children were John 2d, Benjamin, and Elizabeth.

John Clark 2d, b. K. and Q. Co., Va., Oct. 20th, 1724, d. Mulberry Hill, Ky., Aug. —, 1799, aged 75 years ; and Ann Rogers, b. K. and Q. Co., Va., Oct. 20th, 1734, d. at Mulberry Hill, Ky., Dec. 24th, 1798, aged 64 years ; were married in K. and Q. Co., Va., in 1749, lived together 49 years, and were William's parents. They had the following six sons and four daughters :

1. *Jonathan :* b. Albemarle Co., Va., Aug. 1st, 1750 ; d. Mulberry Hill, Ky., in 1816. He married Sarah Hite, by whom he had four sons and two daughters.

2. *George Rogers 1st :* b. Albemarle Co., Va., Nov. 19th, 1752 ; d. Locust Grove, Ky., Feb. 13th, 1818, aged 66 years, and was buried there. He never married. He was the most distinguished member of his family until his fame was shaded by the greater renown to which William attained. George Rogers and William held several positions of the same military or civic title, and hence have been sometimes confused. When " the brother " of William is mentioned in annals, etc., George Rogers is generally meant.

3. *Ann :* b. Caroline Co., Va., July 14th, 1755 ; married Owen Gwathmey, Oct. 25th, 1773 ; had five sons and

five daughters; d. in 1822, aged 66 years, at Locust Grove, Ky.

4. *John 3d :* b. Caroline Co., Va., Sept. 15th, 1757 ; d. Oct. 17th, 1783, aged 26 ; never married ; was "imprisoned by British during war five years on Long Island." (So family bible : but see next paragraph.)

5. *Richard :* b. Caroline Co., Va., July 6th, 1760 ; never married ; lost in Feb. or Mar., 1785, aged 25 years; "supposed to have been killed by Indians at Little Wabash." (So family bible ; some obscurity and confusion of record regarding Richard and John 3d. Another account, furnished to Mr. Jefferson K. Clark by his cousin, Mrs. Caroline O'Fallon Pope, states that Richard, a lieutenant in the Continental army, was captured at Germantown, Pa., and died in a prison-ship at New York, in 1783 ; and that John, a captain in the army, was killed by Indians on the Wabash in 1785.)

6. *Edmund 1st :* b. Caroline Co., Va., Sept. 25th, 1762 ; d. Louisville, Ky., in 1817, aged 55 years ; never married ; was an army officer with rank of captain, left out when the army was reduced.

7. *Lucy :* b. Caroline Co., Va., Sept. 15th, 1765 ; married William Croghan ; had five sons and two daughters; d. at Locust Grove, near Louisville, Ky., Mar. 4th, 1837 or 1838.

8. *Elizabeth :* b. Caroline Co., Va., Feb. 11th, 1768 ; married Colonel Richard Clough Anderson ; had one son and three daughters; died in 1795, aged 27 years.

9. **William :** b. Caroline Co., Va., Aug. 1st, 1770; married (1) Julia Hancock, at Fincastle, Va., Jan. 5th, 1808 ; she died at Fotheringay, Va., June 27th, 1820, leaving four sons and one daughter; he married (2) Harriet Kennerly (b. Fincastle, July 25th, 1788, widow of Dr. John Radford), at St. Louis, Mo., Nov. 28th, 1821 ; she died there Dec. 25th, 1831, leaving two sons and one daughter by Dr. Radford, and one son

living (one having died) by William Clark; he died at St. Louis, Mo., at the residence of his son, Meriwether Lewis 1st, Sept. 1st, 1838, and was buried at Athlone, from the residence of Colonel J. O'Fallon, near St. Louis.

10. *Frances*, commonly called *Fanny:* b. Caroline Co., Va., Jan. 20th, 1773; married (1) in 1790, Dr. James O'Fallon (b. Athlone, Ireland; d. Louisville, Ky., 1793), (2) Charles M. Thruston, (3) Dennis Fitzhugh; had (1) two children, John and Benjamin; (2) four children; (3) one child; died at St. Louis, Mo. Her eldest son, John, acquired the title of colonel in the military service, from which he resigned in July, 1818; he survived till Dec. 17th, 1865, in business in St. Louis.

———

Regarding William's first wife's family, we have the following genealogy:

Robert Hancock (son of Robert Hancock), b. Mar. 22d, 1711; Edward 1st, b. June 30th, 1713; Dinah or Diana, b. Jan. 14th, 1717, married; Patterson, b. ——, had no heirs; William, b. May 30th, 1720; *George 1st*, b. July 22d, 1724, married Mary Jones; Thomas, b. Oct. 15th, 1727, lost at sea; Joshua, b. Feb. 9th, 1729, lost at sea. In the next generation: Edward 2d, son of George Hancock 1st and Mary Jones his wife, b. Mar. 8, 1752, in Montgomery Co., Va.; *George 2d*, b. June 13th, 1754, d. at Fotheringay, Va., July 18th, 1820; Augustus, b. Oct. 14th, 1756, d. in the army; Mary, b. Nov. 4th, 1759, married (1) Mr. Rayford, (2) Samuel Kennerly.

George 2d, above, married at Fincastle, Va., Sept. 18th, 1781, Peggy Strother (dau. of Mary Kennerly Strother, b. Sept. 10th, 1746, married (1) George Strother of Culpepper Co., Va., (2) Patrick Lockhart, who d. at Fincastle, Va., in 1809; d. at Fotheringay, Va., June 2d, 1830), who was b. Sept. 16th, 1763.

The children of George 2d and Peggy Strother his wife, were:

1. *Mary*, b. Friday, Feb. 14th, 1783 ; married J. D. Griffin ;
   d. Apr. 26th, 1826, leaving three sons and one daughter.
2. *Caroline*, b. Saturday, Mar. 26th, 1785 ; married Wm.
   Preston ; d. at Louisville, Ky.   3. *John Strother*, b. Sunday,
   Mar. 25th, 1787 ; d. Aug. 2d, 1795.   4. **Julia,** also called
   **Judith,** b. Monday, Nov. 21st, 1791 ; married **William
   Clark,** Jan. 5th, 1808, at Fincastle, Va.; d. at Fotheringay,
   Va., June 27th, 1820, leaving four sons and one daughter.
   5. *George 3d*, b. Good Friday, Apr. 6th, 1798 ; married (1) E.
   Croghan (dau. of Wm. Croghan and Lucy Clark, of Locust
   Grove), (2) Mary Davidson, of New Orleans, Miss.

---

The children of William Clark and Julia Hancock his first
wife, were :

1. *Meriwether Lewis 1st :* b. St. Louis, Mo., Jan. 10th, 1809 ;
   married (1) Abby Churchill, Louisville, Ky., Jan. 9th,
   1834 ; he died at Frankfort, Ky., Oct. 28th, 1881.   His
   first wife was b. Louisville, Ky., Mar. 9th, 1817 ; d. St.
   Louis, Jan. 14th, 1852.   Their children were: William
   Hancock, b. St. Louis, Mo., Dec. 25th, 1839, now living ;
   Samuel Churchill, b. St. Louis, Mo., Sept. 12th, 1843,
   killed in battle of Elk Horn, at Pea Ridge, Ark., com'd'g
   the Clark battery, 10 a. m., Mar. 8th, 1862, buried at
   Fort Smith, Ark.; Mary Eliza, b. St. Louis, Mo., May
   31st, 1845, d. Spring Grove, Ky., May, 1847 ; Meriwether
   Lewis 2d, b. Louisville, Ky., Jan. 27th, 1846, living ;
   John O'Fallon 2d, b. St. Louis, Mo., July 7th, 1848, d.
   Frankfort, Ky., Feb., 1863, killed by accidental discharge
   of a pistol in hands of a schoolmate at Sayre Institute ;
   George Rogers 2d, b. St. Louis, Mo., Apr. 19th, 1850,
   d. of yellow fever at Greenville, Miss.; Charles Jefferson, b. St. Louis, Mo., Jan. 10th, 1852, living.   Meriwether Lewis 1st married (2) Julia Davidson, at Louisville, Ky., Dec. 30th, 1865 ; she was b. in New Orleans,
   La., July 8th, 1826, and is living ; they had no issue.
2. *William Preston :* b. St. Louis, Mo., Oct. 5th, 1811 ;

never married; d. there, suddenly, of heart disease, May 16th, 1840; buried at Athlone.

3. *Mary Margaret:* b. St. Louis., Mo., Jan. 1st, 1814; d. at Mrs. Preston's, near Middletown, Ky., Oct. 15th, 1821; buried at Mulberry Hill, near Louisville, Ky.

4. *George Rogers Hancock:* b. St. Louis, Mo., May 6th, 1816; married there Ellenor Ann or Eleanor Ann Glasgow, Tuesday, Mar. 30th, 1841. Their children were: Julia, b. St. Louis, 3 a. m., Friday, Mar. 6th, 1842; Sarah, Sadie, or Seddie Leonida, b. there 2 a. m., Oct. 6th, 1843, d. Dec. 18th, 1864; John O'Fallon 1st, b. there 3 p. m., Dec. 17th, 1844; Ellen Glasgow, b. there 3 p. m., Jan. 22d, 1846. He died Sept. 29th, 1858, at the residence of his half-brother, Jefferson K. Clark, at Minoma, St. Louis Co., Mo., in his 43d year, and was buried Oct. 2d, 1858, in Bellefontaine cemetery.

5. *John Julius:* b. St. Louis, July 6th, 1818; d. there Sept. 5th, 1831.

The children of William Clark and his second wife, Mrs. Harriet Kennerly[1] Radford (widow of Dr. John Radford), who were married at St. Louis, Nov. 28th, 1821, were:

1. *Thomas Jefferson* or *Jefferson Kearny*, b. St. Louis, Mo., Feb. 29th, 1824;[2] married Mary Susan Glasgow (dau. of William Glasgow, Sr.) there, May 8th, 1849: both are living there now (1893).

2. *Edmund 2d*, b. St. Louis, Sept. 9th, 1826; d. there, Aug. 12th, 1827.

---

[1] Harriet Kennerly (b. Fincastle, Va., July 25th, 1788, d. St. Louis, Mo., Dec. 25th, 1831) and John Radford were married at Fincastle, Va., Dec. 23d, 1806. He was born there Jan. 25th, 1788. Their children were : William, b. Sept. 9th, 1807; Mary P., b. Mar. 5th, 1812 (who married Gen. S. W. Kearney) ; John D., b. June 6th, 1816 (who married Sophia Menard, of Kaskaskia, Ill.). William Clark's two wives were first cousins, being respectively children of a brother and a sister—the last being a sister of James and George H. Kennerly.

[2] The year 1824, in which Mr. Jefferson K. Clark was born, was memorable in the annals of Missouri, the then youngest State in the Union, and about to participate for the first time in a presidential election. It was the closing year of the administration of our first five Presidents of Revolutionary stock or connection, and was marked by a visit, after an interval of 40 years, from one who had strenuously assisted in the struggle for independence—General Lafayette.

The late Admiral Radford, U. S. N. (formerly owner of the house 1726 N St., Washington, D. C., in which I now reside), was a half-brother of Mr. J. K. Clark, being a son of William Clark's second wife by her first husband.

The foregoing data for five generations are derived in part from records in the family bible of George Rogers Hancock Clark, copied Oct. 1st, 1881, by Frederick L. Billon, of St. Louis, and lately secured from him ; in part from William Hancock Clark, who at my request obligingly prepared and furnished a tabular statement of the lineal issue of William Clark, living and dead at the present date of July, 1893. This genealogical chart, including two more generations, is published on a separate folding sheet with this work.

---

William Clark's parents resided in Albemarle Co., Va., until their two eldest children had been born ; when, in 1754, they removed to the vicinity of Charlottesville, Caroline Co., in the same State, where all their other children first saw the light.[3]   In 1784, or about that year, when William was 14 years old, they moved again to what was then called the Falls of the Ohio, now Louisville, Ky. Their place of residence was known as Mulberry Hill. Louisville at that time consisted merely of a few cabins clustered about a fortification which had been erected by his elder brother, George Rogers Clark.

William received his first title or distinction of any sort while yet a mere lad, being made a member of the Society of the Cincinnati on March 1st, 1787, before he had completed his seventeenth year.   His original certificate of membership is extant ; it bears the signatures of George Washington, President, and General Henry Knox, Secretary.   His first military title was that of Ensign U. S. A., to which grade he was appointed in 1788.   On the 8th of January, 1790, he received the following commission, which is curious enough to be presented in full.   I copy from a careful copy of the original :

---

[3] Dr. W. C. N. Randolph, son of President Jefferson's executor, writes to me from Charlottesville, Va., under date of Jan. 11th, 1893, that the house in which William was born was situated within a mile and a half from that town; and that the exact spot is identifiable, though the building has disappeared.

*Territory of the*
U N I T E D  S T A T E S
*North West of the*
*River Ohio*

{ Seal. }

### By HIS EXCELLENCY
### ARTHUR St CLAIR *Esq ;*

*Governor and Commander in Chief of the Territory of the United States*
*North West of the River Ohio*

To William Clark Esquire Greeting

You being appointed a Captain of Militia in the Town & vicinity of Clarks-ville—By Virtue of the Power vested in me, I do by these presents (reposing Special Trust and Confidence in your Loyalty, Courage and Good Conduct) commission you accordingly—You are therefore carefully and diligently to discharge the Duty of a Captain in leading, ordering and exercising said Militia in Arms, both Inferior Officers and Soldiers ; and to keep them in good Order and Discipline. And they are hereby commanded to obey you as their Captain, and you are yourself to observe and follow such Orders and Instructions as you shall from Time to Time receive from me or your Superior Officers—

Given under my Hand, and the Seal of the Said Territory of the United States, the eighth day of January in the Year of our Lord 1790 and of the Independence of the United States of America, the fourteenth

Aʳ Sᵗ CLAIR

By His Excellency's Command

WINTHROP SARGENT Secretary

Captain Clark was commissioned as a lieutenant of infantry, March 7th, 1791, and assigned to the fourth Sub-Legion, Sept. 4th, 1792. While holding this rank, at the date of March 19th, 1793, he acted as adjutant and quartermaster. We find him on sick-leave in 1795, and July 1st, 1796, he resigned from the army on account of ill-health.[4]

[4] We hear of one William Clark in business connections in St. Louis about this time. It is of public record, May 19th, 1798, Solomon Link to William Clark, for $70 cash, a lot 150 ft. square, with a log house, in the village of Marais des Liards (Owens Station, now Bridgton), bounded by John Hildebrand and Joseph Williams on two sides, on the other two sides streets ; and Isaac Hildebrand to Wm. Clark, for $20, a lot 150 ft. square, bounded by David Hildebrand and Wm. Clark, and by two streets ; also, about the same date, Wm. Clark to Gregoire Sarpy, of St. Louis, mortgage for $128.50 on above, etc. It is likewise of record, July 5th, 1800, concession by Gov. Delassus to William Clark of 800 arpents of land, unlocated, and some other transactions connected with this property, etc. But *this* William Clark was another person of the same name, sometime of Portage des Sioux. The subject of this memoir became in due course a sort of sun-god in the myths of the West, and like another Hercules absorbed various tradition that lacked fixity of time, place, and circumstance. The most remarkable instance that has come to my knowledge is that of one William Clark who, though he became a judge of the Supreme Court of his State, has thus far completely, and perhaps permanently, lost his identity. The sometime association of this Judge Clark with George

The year 1803 saw the beginning of Captain Clark's real career, to which previous events of his life merely led up. His friend, Meriwether Lewis, at this time President Jefferson's private secretary, who as an ensign had at one time served under Captain Clark's orders, desired his association on equal terms in the conduct of the Expedition then about to be set on foot. Captain Clark assented, and the two young officers entered into those relations which linked their names forever.[5] It is commonly said that Captain Clark re-entered the regular army under these circumstances in 1803. It is also said in Jefferson's Memoir of Lewis, *anteà*, that he was commissioned as a captain. These are mistakes. The commission he received was that of second lieutenant, Corps of Artillerists, and not the

Rogers Clark (brother of our William), as trustees of a certain town, tended to promote this confusion. On looking up this case, I find the date to be when William was about 13 years old, and therefore not likely to have been the trustee of anything more than the contents of a boy's pockets. Item, I find among the MS. Clarkiana in my possession that on March 3d, 1801, William Clark, Henry Vanderburg, and John Griffin, judges appointed by Gov. W. H. Harrison, of the newly organized Indiana Territory, held their first term at Vincennes. Here again is no doubt the lost *Judge* William Clark. Item, one of our best biographical cyclopedias has a short notice of this jurist, in which I think some matters pertaining to *General* Clark are involved.

[5] As a matter of curious history, perhaps known to no other person at the moment of my penning this note, I will cite the fact that in July, 1803, it looked as if " Lewis and Clark " was going to be " Lewis and Hook," or " Hooke." Captain Lewis had extended his invitation to Captain Clark, and had received no answer. Mails were infrequent and irregular in those days ; no doubt Captain Clark took time to sleep over the proposition ; but delays seemed dangerous if not fatal, to Captain Lewis' ardent imagination, already at a white heat of most puissant purpose. He had actually sought a substitute, in anticipation of Captain Clark's declination, when he penned the letter, now forming Doc. No. 101. Jeff. Papers L, 2d ser., Vol. 51, of which the following are some extracts :

Pittsburgh July 26th. 1803.

Dear Sir,

I have recieved as yet no answer from Mr. Clark ; in the event of Mr. Clark's declining to accompany me Lieut Hooke of this place has engaged to do so, if permitted ; and I think from his disposition and qualifications that I might safely calculate on being as ably assisted by him in the execution of the objects of my mission, as I could wish, or would be, by any other officer in the Army. Lieut Hooke is about 26 years of age, [etc.] . . . Should I recieve no answer from Mr. Clark previous to my leaving this place, or he decline going with me, I would be much gratifyed with being authorized to take Lieut. Hooke with me, [etc.] . . . If Lieut. Hooke sets out twenty days after me, by taking the rout of Limestone, Louisville and Vincennes, he will reach the mouth of the Missourie as early as I shall.

I am with the most sincere attachment
Your Obt. Servt.
Meriwether Lewis.

The President of the
United States.

captaincy of Engineers he had been led to expect.    The
date of this commission was March 26th, 1804 ; his routine
promotion to a first lieutenantcy came Jan. 31st, 1806.    It
will be recollected that his *title* was already that of captain,
from prior military service ; but during that Expedition,
which was to convert all possible titles into sounding brass,
his actual rank in the army was that of a subaltern.    On
this point, once a matter of some delicacy, now simply a
question of historical accuracy, I am fortunately able to sink
the biographer in the autobiographer.    We will hear what
Captain Clark once had to say on the subject himself.

In the extensive unpublished Clark-Biddle correspondence, mainly relating to the History of the Expedition,
obligingly placed in my hands by Judge Craig Biddle, of
Philadelphia, son of Nicholas Biddle, Esq., I find the following two letters :

Phila. July 8. 1811

Dr Sir,

[A page about engraving, etc., and then ]    There is one and only one
more thing about which I wish you would give me information.    It is the exact
relative situation in point of rank and command between Captain Lewis and
yourself.    I think you mentioned to me that your commission was that of Lieutenant of Engineers [read of Artillerists], which placed you completely on an
equality with Captain Lewis who was a Captain of Infantry or Artillery [the for-
mer], and that in all other respects you were equal in command.    I am desirous
of being correct and I will get you to state to me whether I have understood
you precisely, so as to avoid all errors on that subject.    With my Compts to
Mrs. Clarke [*sic*] I remain yrs sincerely

N[icholas]. B[iddle].

Genl William Clarke [*sic*]
St Louis
Upper Louisiana

———

St Louis 15th. August 1811

Dear Sir,

By the last mail I had the honor of receiving your letter of the
8th. of July, which I do assure you gave me much pleasure ; as well to hear
from you as to learn that you had got thro' the work, and had it ready for the
press as soon as Mr. Conrad pleased.    I hope Mr. C. is getting it in a state of
forwardness,—I feel convinced that your arrangement of the Map is a good one,
I wish it was engraved and out.

You express a desire to know the exact relation which I stood in point of Rank
and Command with Captain Lewis—*equal in every point of view*—(I did not

think myself very well treated as I did not get the appointment which was promised me, as I was not disposed to make any noise about the business have never mentioned the particulars to anyone, and must request you not to mention my disapointment and the cause to anyone.—

In March [Mar. 7th] 1791 I was appointed a Lieut. in Waynes army and was kept on command about 18 months before I joined the main army [Sept. 4th, 1792]. When I joined I was anexed to a Chosen Rifle Company, of which I had the command, and received a Staff appointment, both of which I retained untill after the Treaty at Greenville and at the time of takeing possession of the Western posts, I *resigned* [July 1st, 1796] and returned to a Farm in in Kentucky on which I lived several years in bad health (Capt. Lewis was appointed an Ensign and arranged to the company which I commanded a fiew months before I resigned) During the time I [was] liveing on my Farm in Kent.y. I had frequent occasions to visit the Eastern States & Washington where I became acquainted with the Presidt. Mr. Jefferson.    In [July] 1803 I was applied to by Captain Lewis by Letter, who was then Private Secty to the President, to accompany him on an Expedition to the Pacific, stating the genl. plan and objects, and offered by the apprbn of the President to place me in a situation in every respect equal to himself, in rank pretentions &c &c.    On those conditions I agreed to undertake the expedition made my arrangements and set out, and proceeded on with Capt. Lewis to the mouth of the Missouri where we remained the winter 1803 made every necessary arrangement to set out early in spring 1804 every thing arranged I waited with some anxiety for the commission which I had reason to expect (Capt. of Indioneers [Engineers]) a fiew days before I set out I received a Commission of 2nd Lieutenant of Artillerist [dated Mar. 26th, 1804], my feelings on this occasion was as might be expected.    I wished the expedition suckcess, and from the assurence of Capt. Lewis that in every respect my situation command &c &c. should be equal to his ; viewing the Commission as mearly calculated to autherise punishment to the soldiers if necessary, I proceeded.    No difficuelty took place on our rout relative to this point—On my return to this town, I inclosed the Commission to the Secty of War and wrote to him that the Commission had answered the purpose purpose for which it was intended &c.

I do not wish that anything relative to this Comsn or appointment should be inserted in my Book, or made known, for very perticular reasons, and I do assure you that I have never related as much on the subject to any person before.    Be so good as to place me on equal footing with Capt. Lewis in every point of view without exposeing anything which might have taken place or even mentioning the Commission at all.

I hope you will do me the honor to write to me often and without reserve— Accept the acknowledgements of Mrs. Clark and my self for the friendly sentiments expressed in the latter part of your letter and accept of our wormest wishes for your [health] and hapiness.

I remain your sincere

Mr. Nichs. Biddle                                            Friend
Atty at Law Phila.                                          Wm Clark

No question concerning the relations of the two noble young officers during the Expedition is possible. On the one hand, it is certain that Captain Lewis was absolutely in command of the Expedition, taking official precedence over his lieutenant, Captain Clark, whom he outranked, and who was as fully subject to his lawful orders as any enlisted man of the party. On the other hand, it is not less certain that in their mutual relations the technical point was never raised between the two captains, and that the actual command and conduct of the Expedition devolved upon each in exactly equal degree.

It would appear from the foregoing letter that Captain Clark tendered his resignation in 1806, immediately upon his return to St. Louis. The official date of his resignation is Feb. 27th, 1807, and thus but a few days before that of the next commission which he received, a copy of a copy of which is as follows:

Thomas Jefferson<br>
President of the United States of America

To all who shall see these Presents, Greeting

Know Ye, that reposing special trust and confidence in the patriotism, valour, fidelity and abilities of William Clark, I do by these presents appoint him the said William Clark, Brigadier General of the Militia of the Territory of Louisiana: He is therefore carefully and diligently to discharge the duty of Brigadier General—And he is to observe and follow such orders and directions from time to time as he shall receive from the President of the United States of America for the time being, or other superior officer set over him according to the laws for regulating and disciplining the Militia of said Territory—And I do strictly charge and require all officers and soldiers under his command to be obedient to his orders—This commission to continue in force until the end of the next Session of the Senate of the United States and no longer——

Given under my hand at the City of Washington the Twelfth day of March in the year of our Lord One Thousand Eight Hundred and Seven, and in the thirty-fourth year of the Independence of said States.

By the President of the                                      Thos Jefferson
United States of America

{ Seal }          Hy Dearborn

With this commission General Clark was also made Indian Agent for Louisiana. In those days this title was not synonymous with "thief," and the position was one of honor, not to be sought or used for dishonest purposes. I have examined much official correspondence (on file in the War Department) between General Clark and General Henry Dearborn, then Secretary of War. The official signature of the former is usually "Wm. Clark, I. A. L."—sometimes written in full, as "Indian Agent for Louisiana." Most of these letters bear dates of the first year of his agency, and their contents show that Agent Clark had his hands full at this time. I revert to some of his Indian affairs beyond.

General Clark was reappointed Brigadier General of the Militia of˙ Louisiana, Feb. 27th, 1811, by President James Madison, William Eustis being Secretary of War.

Meanwhile he married Miss Julia Hancock, Jan. 5th, 1808, at Fincastle, Va. In that year also, the Grand Lodge of Ancient York Masons of Pennsylvania, having chartered St. Louis Lodge No. 111, William Clark was entered, passed, and raised therein, as witness his diploma of Sept. 18th, 1809, signed by Frederick Bates. On the 16th of November, 1810, he was appointed Inspector General of the Militia of Missouri, by Governor Benjamin Howard.

It will be convenient to continue with the list of official honors and dignities of which General Clark was the recipient. Governor Lewis had met his untimely fate in 1809. Governor Benjamin Howard, his successor, in 1810 (April 17th) was himself succeeded [6] by General Clark, July 1st, 1813, as Governor of Missouri Territory, by virtue of the following appointment (copied from a copy of the original):

James Madison, President of the United States of America
To all who shall see these presents, Greeting
Know Ye, that reposing special Trust and Confidence in the Integrity, Patriotism and Ability of William Clark, of St. Louis—I do appoint him Governor in and near the Missouri Territory, and do authorize and empower him to

---

[6] After a short interval, during which Frederick Bates acted as Governor. Governor Clark reached St. Louis the last of June or first of July, 1813. The Missouri Gazette of July 3d, 1813, has an item noticing his arrival "on Thursday last." During the first session of the General Assembly, which convened at St. Louis on Monday, July 5th, 1813, both houses united in an address to the new Governor, whose reply, owing to his absence on public business, was not received till July 26th.

execute and fulfil the duties of that office according to Law ; and to Have and
to Hold the said office with all the powers, privileges and emoluments to the
same of right appertaining until the end of the next session of the Senate of
the United States and no longer, unless the President of the United States for
the time being should be pleased sooner to revoke and determine this Commission
 In Testimony whereof, I have caused these letters to be made patent and
the Seal of the United States to be hereunto affixed—Given under my hand
at the City of Washington the first day of July A. D. 1813 ; and of the
Independence of the United States the Thirty Seventh.

James Madison.

{ Seal } By the President :
James Monroe
Sec. of State.

Governor Clark was recommissioned [7] as such, by the same,
June 16th, 1816; as such, by the same, Jan. 21st, 1817 ; and
as such, by James Monroe, President of the United States,
John Quincy Adams being Secretary of State, Jan. 24th,
1820. The latter year determined his gubernatorial functions ; for on the first election of a governor for the State
of Missouri he was defeated by Alexander McNair. Nevertheless, he was soon placed in other important official positions. In May, 1822, President Monroe appointed him
Superintendent of Indian Affairs; [8] in October, 1824, he was
commissioned by the same as Surveyor General of the States
of Illinois and Missouri, and of the Territory of Arkansas;
and on March 4th, 1825, he was recommissioned [9] by President John Quincy Adams, Henry Clay being Secretary of

[7] During his early incumbency of this office, Governor Clark's chief clerk was James
Kennerly, who was married in 1817, and whose first son, born in 1825, was named William
Clark Kennerly. A daughter of the same, born Aug. 2d, 1829, received the name of Harriet
Clark Kennerly. During his next incumbency of the same office, it was his function to pre-
side over the first celebration of Washington's birthday ever held west of the Mississippi,
Feb. 22d, 1817, in the ball-room of Kibby's Washington Hall, which was the seventh brick
building erected in St. Louis, and the first one built for a hotel.

[8] An office which had lately been created by Act of Congress. Superintendent Clark held
this position until his death, in 1838. His successor was Joshua Pilcher, appointed by
President Van Buren.

[9] The long famous post of Jefferson Barracks was established and named about Christmas,
1826. In July of that year Col. Talbot Chambers, with a battalion of the 1st U. S. Infantry,
abandoned the old post of Bellefontaine which had been established by General James Wilkinson in 1807, and went down to the new site, naming their camp Cantonment Adams, after the
President of the United States. In September of the same year they were joined by Col.
Henry Leavenworth, with the 3d U. S. Infantry, whose camp was called Camp Miller, after
the then Governor of Missouri. This was the origin of Jefferson Barracks, where, on the
completion of winter-quarters, the officers gave a ball to the citizens of St. Louis on January 8th,

State.   He laid out the town of Paducah, Ky., in 1828, and in 1830 effected the important treaty of Prairie du Chien.

Meanwhile, the first Mrs. Clark having died, June 27th, 1820, General Clark married Mrs. Harriet Kennerly Radford, Nov. 28th, 1821.   At the latter date he had had five children ; the four sons were growing up ; the only daughter, Mary, had died a few weeks before.   Of the two children of the second marriage, the elder is still living (1893) ; the younger died in infancy.[10]   General Clark himself paid the debt of nature on the 1st of September, 1838, on the first day of the second month of his sixty-ninth year, at the residence of his eldest son.   The Missouri Saturday News of Sept. 8th, 1838, appeared in mourning, and had a feeling and appreciative obituary, by the editor, Chas. Keemle, together with a poem to his memory, by Mr. Field.   His funeral was the most impressive that had ever taken place in St. Louis ; it was a public demonstration of the profound respect and warm affection of the community in which he had resided for more than thirty years, during the whole of which period he had been prominently identified with the administration of public affairs, both civil and military.

It is simply impossible, within the limits of a mere sketch like the present article, to do anything like justice to the full-

1827.  The compliment was returned by the citizens to the military on January 31st, and the local " Jenkins " gave an account of the latter affair in the columns of the Missouri Republican of February 8th, where we read :

"The large Indian Council Room (General Clark's) was selected for the occasion, and was decorated in a style reflecting much credit on those who superintended its arrangement "— with much more on the music, dancing, toilets, and toasts of the occasion—altogether forming, in the language of Jenkins, " a toute ensemble that would have done honor to any city, and was a favorable evidence of the advance of society west of the Mississippi."

[10] It is interesting to turn from dry data like these and those which have preceded, to a father's own words about his children.  General Clark wrote as follows to Mr. Jefferson, in a letter, dated St. Louis, Dec. 15th, 1825, now filed in Jeff. Papers C, 2d ser., Vol. 21 : " . . . I have *five* sons the oldest of them Meriwether Lewis of 17 years of age is a Cadet at West Point ; he is a youth of Capacity & Application, anxious to receive an education which he wishes to complete at some university after he leaves W. Point.  My secon[d] son William [Preston] is 14 years of age, Boald, Sprightly with good Capacity deficient in application.—My 3d Son George Rogers [Hancock] is 11 years old possessing application and a mind equal to any boy of his age—my 4th Son John [Julius] is 8 years old is Sprightly but unfortunately Deformed—my 5th Son Thomas Jefferson is only 2 years old and very promising."  The last-named is the still (1893) living one ; whence it appears that at some time the given name of " Thomas Jefferson " was changed to " Jefferson Kearny."

rounded life of a man of William Clark's remarkable personal character, versatile accomplishments, and brilliant achievements. What has preceded merely points to some of the milestones of his long journey ; to fill in the details would require a volume, and that is a labor which must be left to his future biographer. Should it ever fall to my share, it would be assuredly a labor of love ; for the study of a single episode in his career has filled me with the most vivid admiration for the man himself, aside from his exploits. The few bare facts which I have already presented will be found more numerous and more accurate than those which have hitherto appeared in any single article—so little does the world really know of some of our greatest men ! I am tempted to desist at this point from any further presentation of a subject my treatment of which must necessarily be inadequate, and, therefore, in a case where personal name and fame are concerned, unjust. But since I am in possession of some datum-points of Clark's career which are either entirely unknown or inaccurately known, these may be appropriately placed on record here and now, with the understanding that they shall be taken as materials only, and not as a finished work. I will first present some items touching the man of business; next give some illustrations of what the Indians thought of this friend ; and finish with various particulars pertinent to any history of that exploration which immortalized twin names.

——

Mr. Clark was eminently a man of affairs, who could turn a trade as well as he did various other things. Some of his transactions are of record. On Aug. 18th, 1808, Peter Chouteau and wife transferred to him, for $800, 1,400 arpents of land in St. Louis Co., 2½ leagues N.W. of St. Louis, bounded on the north by a tract belonging to Meriwether Lewis. On Jan. 7th, 1811, he bought of Alexander McNair, for $1500, the north half of block No. 9, 120 French feet, on Main Street, St. Louis, running east to the river, with the old

French house built of posts by Rene Kiersereau, and the three small stone stores of Alexis Marie. He lived here for a time, and had his Indian office in one of these stores, where is now the corner of Main and Pine streets. On Oct. 7th, 1814, he purchased from Jno. G. Comegys, for $1,000, 47 feet front on Main street, back east to the river, in block 10, between Pine and Olive streets. Here he built, in 1816, on the south, 21 feet front, a two-story brick house, when only about half a dozen structures of that material existed in St. Louis. The lower story was used as a store; the upper was first occupied by the Missouri Masonic Lodge No. 12 for a couple of years; from 1823 to 1827 it was occupied by Mr. Frederick L. Billon, the noted annalist of St. Louis (b. Apr. 23d, 1801, and still living, 1893). The north 26 feet front was sold to James Kennerly, for $3,500, July 19th, 1821. On Dec. 13th, 1815, Mr. Clark bought from Antoine Flandrin, for $1,300, the N.E. quarter of block 39, on the S.W. corner of Main and Almond streets, with the house built of posts by N. Beaugenou in 1765. The first marriage ever recorded in St. Louis, that of B.'s daughter, in April, 1766, took place in this house. Mr. Clark occupied it for two or three years, and after him Captain M. Wherry for several more. On April 2d, 1816, Mr. Clark purchased of Col. A. Chouteau, for $4,500, the north half of block 12, on the S.E. corner of Main and Vine streets, with the old stone house built by Louis Chancellier in 1767. This structure was removed; in 1818–19 Mr. Clark erected here his large brick mansion, and afterward his brick row south of it for his Indian council-house and museum of Indian curiosities. But after these and other dealings in real estate, Mr. Clark died in the house which had been the year before bought from George Atchison by Meriwether Lewis Clark.

Almost throughout the History of the Expedition we read of fur-bearing animals, and of the fur-trade. It does not surprise us to learn that Captain Clark became pecuniarily interested in this then remunerative and flourishing industry, in which many thousands of men were engaged and a vast amount of capital was invested. One of the earliest if not the first indications of activity on his part in this direction is of record at the date March 7th, 1809, when were associated, for the purposes of a trading-camp on the Missouri, Benjamin Wilkinson, Pierre Chouteau, Sr., Auguste Chouteau, Jr., Manuel Lisa, Reuben Lewis, William Clark, and Sylvestre Labbadie, all of St. Louis; Pierre Menard, and William Morrison, of Kaskaskia; Andrew Henry, of Louisiana, and Dennis Fitzhugh, of Kentucky. The Louisiana Gazette of Feb. 1st, 1812, prints the following advertisement: " Missouri Fur Company. Capital $50,000; 50 shares at $1,000. Sylvestre Labbadie, Wm. Clark, and Manuel Lisa, the old Company, hold $27,000 in goods, &c., up the Missouri River. Subscriptions desired for the remaining $23,000."

We have every reason to believe that a fair share of profit accrued from most if not all of William Clark's business ventures. The same cannot be said of the only literary enterprise with which his name ever was or ever will be associated.[11] The inside history of Lewis and Clark's

---

[11] A certain connection which may be called literary is represented in his election as a corresponding member of the U. S. Naval Lyceum, June 28th, 1837. In zoölogy, his name attaches to several species of animals, discovered by or dedicated to him. In palæontology, he lent a hand to help Mr. Jefferson secure specimens of important fossils which were named and described by Cuvier. Thus in Jeff. Papers, 1st ser., Vol 12, Doc. No. 340, is a letter from Mr. Jefferson to him, dated Washington, Dec. 19th, 1807, relating to the collection of bones of the mammoth, which Mr. Jefferson wished to procure to send to the Institute of France ; item, *ibid.*, Doc. No. 802, another letter from the same to him, of date Sept. 10th, 1809, relating to bones upon which the genus *Mastodon* was based. In this letter Mr. Jefferson apologizes for the trouble he is putting General Clark to, saying handsomely : " The world has, of right, no further claims on yourself & Govr. Lewis, but such as you may voluntarily render according to your convenience or as they may make it your interest." Let me also mention here a letter from Lafayette to General Clark, dated Paris, Feb. 1st, 1830, a copy of which is before me, and one clause of which I will cite : " The grisley bear you had the goodness to send to me, has been the more admired on this side the Atlantic as it was the first animal of the kind, living or dead, that has ever made its appearance in Europe. I was inclined to make a pet of him, as he was then very gentle. But it was thought wiser to put him under the care of the Board of Professors at the Jardin des Plantes. . . . His large size and ferocious temper have since been developed." In botany, F. Pursh erected the genus *Clarkia*, of the evening primrose family (natural order *Onagraceæ*), which contains annual herbs of Oregon and California, some species of which are cultivated for ornament, as *C. pulchella* and *C. elegans.* They have alternate, mostly entire leaves, with showy flowers in the upper axils, or the upper running into a loose raceme ; flowers regular and symmetrical ; calyx-tube extended beyond the ovary ; petals 4, cuneate or rhombic, sometimes 3-lobed, raised on a slender claw, never yellow ; stamens 8, with slender filaments alternately longer and shorter ; stigmas 4 ; pod 4-sided, linear, tapering upward. *C. pulchella* is about 1 foot high, with narrow lance-linear leaves, and deeply 3-lobed petals, purple or in cultivation rose-colored or white, and producing a partly double blossom.

immortal book is a yawning chasm between cash and glory. Lewis was dead; Clark pushed the work to publication. His total receipts from this business were no dollars and no cents; but the assignees of his insolvent publishers, who had failed while the book was in press, generously gave him the copper-plates, as likewise permission to try it again, if he liked to be literary. These old coppers are serviceable at present writing as paper-weights on my desk; but Captain Clark never ventured to avail himself of the copyright thus made over to him.

---

General and Governor Clark was known far and wide to the Indians as the "Red-head." It is significant of his repute among them that St. Louis was for them simply the Red-head's town—as we should say, "Clarksville." The pith of this whole matter is in the words of a Sac chief who had been called in council by Major Benjamin O'Fallon at St. Louis, April 3d, 1821, on the subject of certain hostilities which were to be suppressed : "American chief! We have opened our ears to your words and those of the Red-head. Brother! We receive you as the son of the Red-head; inasmuch as we love him, we will love you and do not wish to offend you." General Clark possessed in an eminent degree those personal qualities which commanded the respect of Indians as well as of all other persons whose privilege it was to know him; they recognized in him a great chief, whether friend or foe. They saw he preferred to be the former;[12] and they found this to be to their own advantage. They compared his fair and honorable dealings with the lying and cheating which to them were no novel elements in the character of

C. *elegans* is more commonly seen in conservatories; it is fully 2 feet high, with lance-ovate or oblong leaves on long branches and entire lilac-purple petals, broader than long. *Clarkia* is one of a group of genera including *Œnothera*, the evening primroses proper, and belongs to that order which contains the familiar fuchsias.

[12] A letter of General Clark to Mr. Jefferson, dated St. Louis, Dec. 15th, 1825, now filed in Jeff. Papers C, 2d ser., Vol. 21, gives a sign of the amity that inspired his policy with the Indians : "In my present situation of Superintendent of Indian affairs, it would afford me pleasure to be enabled to meliorate the condition of those unfortunate people placed under my charge, knowing as I do their retchedness, and their rapid decline.—It is to be lamented that the deplerable situation of the Indians do not receive more of the humain feelings of the nation."

many whites with whom they were brought in contact; they discovered him to be a man of his word; and they reposed unbounded confidence in all that he said. Probably no officer of the government ever made his personal influence more widely and deeply felt; his superintendency grew to be a sort of lawful autocracy, wielded in the best interests of all concerned, on the strong principle of even-handed justice; his word became Indian law, from the Mississippi to the Pacific. Thousands of Indians had made his personal acquaintance when he traveled among them; and in later years there could have been few who did not regard his signature as "medicine" of the most salutary sort.

We sometimes hear of persons who are credited with great insight into what is called "the Indian character." Granting that Indians have all the defects of their qualities, and that some of these are peculiar to this remarkably picturesque race of men, it does not follow that there is not as much human nature in an Indian as in any other person. No professional secret is violated in saying that to treat an Indian as if he were a human being is to encourage him to return the compliment. General Clark received back from the Indians only what he gave out to them; reciprocity in fair dealing was established; for the rest, they recognized his superiority in mental and material resources; they felt and feared his power. Had he not been at heart their sincere friend and well-wisher—had the moral element been eliminated from the equation—had he only made terms with them with the idea that it is cheaper to feed than to fight Indians—he never could have acquired that ascendency which enabled him to exercise perfect control. During his long administration of Indian affairs, beginning soon after his return from the Expedition, and ending only with his life, he was instrumental in bringing about many important treaties, not only between his government and the Indians, but also between different tribes of the latter. He was master of a situation whose possibilities, both for good and evil, were enormous; in his hands, possible evil turned to

certain good. This man was a large factor in the civilization of that great West which Lewis and Clark discovered.
It may be said of him with special pertinence, *stat magni
nominis umbra*—for the explorer stands in the shadow of
his own great name as such, obscuring that of the soldier,
statesman, diplomat, and patriot. The world is slow to
concede the greatness of any man in more than one thing.

We will now turn to the light another facet in the complex
of this many-sided man, namely, his instrumentality in the
publication of that History of the Expedition which was
rewritten for the press by Nicholas Biddle from the manuscript journals and field notebooks of Lewis and Clark.
Captain Lewis is believed, no doubt rightly, to have been
on his way East to attend to this matter when he met his
fate; whereupon, that duty devolved upon his comrade,
and was almost immediately assumed by him. My information upon this score is not less accurate than extensive, and
will be found almost entirely novel, as it is derived mainly
from the never published Clark-Biddle correspondence, now
in my hands. These letters speak autobiographically for
themselves, and I will therefore select a few for presentation.
The one of earliest date is as follows:

Near Fincastle Virga. 20th. Feby 1810

Dear Sir

I expected to have had the pleasure of hereing from you previous to my setting
out from Philadelphia but as I did not receve a note from you at that time calculated on receeving a letter from you at this place on the Subject of writing my
Western Tour &c. as I have been disappointed in hereing from you on this Subject feel my self much at a loss to adress you—I shall not employ the gentleman
in Richmond to write the Book whom I mentioned haveing in view, from his
offer made previous to my seeing you. I have calculated on your writing for
me, and if you will undertake this work ; cant you come to this place, where I
have my books and memorandoms and stay with me a week or two ; read over
& make yourself thereby acquainted with everything which may not be explained
in the Journals ? if you will come it may enable me to give you a more full view
of those parts which may not be thereby explained and inable you to proceed
without deficuilty. Such parts as may not be full, I can explain, and add such
additional matter as I may recollect—

I brought the Books with me to Copy such parts as are intended for the Botanical work which I shall send to Doctr. Barton, and will deliver the Books to you if you will engage to write the naritive &c. I mentioned to Mr John Conrad of Philadelphia to request you to come on here if possible and spend a short time. I am at present with Col. Hancock my father in Law who is on a retired and plesently situated [place] in view of the Town of Fincastle—should you Come on to this place, I would advise the rout by Hagerstown Winchester & Staunton in the *Stage* which passes this place once a week.—

Please to write me on the subject of this letter, your intentions and accept my Highest respect & esteem

Your Obe Servt

Wm Clark

Mr. Nicholis Biddle
    Phila.

This letter is folded, sealed without envelop, super-scribed "Nicholis Biddle esquire Atty at Law Philadelphia," marked by postmaster, in MS., "Fincastle Fab'y 25th 20" [cents], and indorsed by Mr. Biddle, "From Genl W. Clarke 20 Feby. 1810".

--------

Philada. March 3. 1810

Sir,

I have to acknowledge the receipt of your letter of 20th Feby which reached me yesterday—Before you receive this my brother's note will have apprized you that it will be out of my power to undertake what you had the politeness to offer, and the only object of the present is to renew my regret at being obliged to decline complying with your wishes. My occupations necessarily confine me to Phila. and I have neither health nor leisure to do sufficient justice to the fruits of your enterprize and ingenuity—You cannot be long however without making a more fortunate selection, but if I can be of any assistance to you here in the proposed publication it shall be very cheerfully given.

Being with high respect

Genl Wm Clark.                                 Yr obt s
      FinCastle                                    N. Biddle
           Virginia

Before Mr. Biddle could have heard from General Clark again he changed his mind and wrote as follows:

Philadelphia<br>Saturday March 17, 1810.

Sir,

I had the pleasure of writing to you on the 3d inst. upon the subject of your intended publication—Being unwilling to disappoint you, I was afraid of under-taking a work which I feared I might not be able to execute to my own and your satisfaction.  Having since then seen Mr. Conrad, & Dr Barton, what I learnt from them, joined with a prospect of better health & more time than I had originally expected induced me to consent provided you had not in the mean time, as I thought probable, made a better choice.  Mr Conrad mentioned to me to day that your last letter of the 9th inst. represents you as under no engagements of that sort.  I will therefore very readily agree to do all that is in my power for the advancement of the work ; and I think I can promise with some confidence that it shall be ready as soon as the publisher [Mr. John Conrad] is prepared to print it.  Having made up my mind today, I am desirous that no delay should occur on my part.  As therefore you express a wish that I should see you, I am arranging my business so as to leave this on Wednesday next, & take the route by Hagerstown Winchester &c.  In this way I hope to make you a short visit very soon after the receipt of my letter.  In the mean time I remain with high respect Yrs &c                              N. Biddle

Genl Wm Clark.
    Fincastle
      Virginia

But before General Clark received the above he wrote .

                   Fin Castle Vga March 25th. 1810
Dear Sir

I was extreamly sorry to find by your letter of the 3rd. inst. that your health was bad, and that your Occupation would confine you to Philadelphia, and would not afford your leasure to Comply with my wishes of writing my Journals &c.  The proffered assistance in the later part of your letter, creates much solicitude and my most sincere acknowledgements for the friendly sentiments it contains.

I am much gratified by Mr Mr Conrads letter of the 13th. inst : to learn, the state of your health ; and that you are willing to undertake the writing of my Journal, and to have it ready for publication in 12 months &c.

Mr Conrad also informs me that you will comply with my request to see me at this place before I set out to the westward.  The roads are now fine and I hope your health may have permitted you to have set out before this time.  I must request you to Come on, as soon as possible, as my business call me to Louisiana ; and nothing detains me, but the business I wish with you

            With the highest respect & esteem
                    I am yr ob Sert.
Mr. N. Biddle                                              Wm Clark

Mr. Biddle, having made his visit, returned home, and began to write the book.  Mr. George Shannon, who was one of the members of the Expedition, next appears on the scene :

Louisville, May 22nd. 1810

Dear Sir

This will be handed to you by Mr. George Shannon the young man I spoke to you about, who was with me on the N W expedition ; he has agreed to go to Philadelphia and give such information rilitive to that Tour as may be in his power. This young gentleman possesses a sincere and undisguised heart, he is highly spoken of by all his acquaintance and much respected at the Lexington University where he has been for the last two years. Any advice and friendly attentions which you may show to this young man will be greatfully acknowledged by him, and confur an additional obligation on me.

Mr. S connections are respectable. Since the misfortune of loseing his leg, he has been studeously employed in persute of an edducation to enable him to acquire a profession by which he can make an honorable and respectable liveing —he wishes to study Law, and practice in the Western Country.

May I request of you to give him such advice or assistance as may be agreeable & convenient to you to enable him to prosue those studies while in Phila.

Accept my highest respect & Friendship

Mr. N. Biddle                                              Wm Clark

The History of the Expedition having been thus launched, Mr. Biddle was already navigating the Missouri, en route to the Pacific and back. We have a glimpse of his progress in following extract of an eight-page letter:

Philadelphia July 7. 1810

My Dear Sir,

. . . ever since my return to Philadelphia I have been engaged seven or eight and even more hours a day on our work, . . . the map was immediately forwarded to Mr. Hassler, and Dr Barton received all his papers. On consulting with Mr Conrad he agreed with me in opinion that it was much better to have a large connected map of the whole route & the adjacent country than to form an atlas of detached parts. The map can embrace as many degrees of latitude as you think your Indian information will authorize. . . The portages of the Columbia & Missouri we have already & they will form very interesting charts which may be put into the work opposite to the pages which contain a description of them [which was done]. The only other part which I think it would be well to have on a larger scale than is contained in the general map is the passage across the Rock mountains—that is, the country comprized between the head of Jefferson's river northward to the point where you struck the Kooskooskee and extending eastward to the falls [of the Missouri] As that square is so important a part of your route it should be shown very distinctly. In all other respects your present map, on a scale rather larger, and diminished or increased as to degrees of latitude [$i.\ e.$, taking in less or more country north and south of the route] as you may judge best, will be quite sufficient. [But the map as published was on a scale much reduced from the original.]

On my arrival I found that proposals were circulating here for a second edition of Gass's journal [of which three Philadelphia editions *did* appear—1810, 1811, 1812], which I thought it best to stop by announcing immediately our work & therefore published the Prospectus. I see also by the English journals that some man in England has printed a sort of account of the Expedition, compiled from Gass chiefly, and from the documents which you and Captain Lewis sent to Congress.[13] The work seems to have met with a favorable reception in England, which is a good sign for our own. . .

Today I have sent you and ten men up into a bottom to look for wood to make canoes after the unhappy failure of your iron boat ; so that you see how far I am [on July 7th, 1805—above Great Falls of the Missouri : see p. 407]. . .

I find that Gass's journal in the original manuscript is also deposited in our library [of the Philosophical Society], and at my service. Ordway's, which is much better than Gass's, is really very useful : and as these two as well as your's and Captain Lewis's and my own notes are all to be examined, in order to leave nothing omitted, the labor is by no means light. . . Shannon has not yet arrived. . .

I must now begin my catechism of inquiries with which you remember I importuned you not a little when I had the pleasure of seeing you [*cf.* p. 31]. . .

In the mean time I remain with my best respects to Mrs Clarke, & my very warmest wishes for your fine little son [Meriwether Lewis Clark].

Your's very sincerely<br>Nicholas Biddle

Gen William Clarke
  St Louis
    Upper Louisiana

The next letter in point of date is a long one from Mr. F. R. Hassler, who was getting up the map, dated Schenectady, Aug. 12th, 1810, full of astronomical calculations for longitude, etc. It is addressed to Mr. Biddle. The next on my file is from General Clark :

St. Louis Decr. 20th. 1810

Dear Sir

I herewith Inclose to you a map which I have drawn for my Book, it is much more correct than any which has been before published, it is made on the same scale of the one you have, containing more Country, I wish you to anex as much of it to the book as you think best, you will observe that I have not inclosed it in lines,—The Ohio is not correct, mearly shows the rivers as they mouth—I am sorry that I could not get the calculations from Mr. Hosler [Has-

---

[13] Mr. Biddle means that miserable spurious "Lewis and Clark" published in London in 1809—the main body of it stolen from Jonathan Carver and fathered on Lewis. See my account of the Apocrypha in the Bibliographical Introduction. The prospectus above mentioned must be extant, as it was published ; but it has become so rare that I have never seen it. I should be much obliged to anyone who would favor me with a copy, or inform me where one could be procured.

sler] to correct the map, but, I hope it will doe without, This package is inclosed to the Secty of War to be fowarded.—

I have not collected any information since my last letter to you

I think I mentioned having heard a rumbling noise at the falls of Missouri, which was not accounted for, and you accounted for them by simelating them to Avelanchers of the Alps.

Please to give my compliments to Geo Shannon and accept my sincere friendship I shall write you again soon

Wm Clark

Mr. Biddle

The above-mentioned map is doubtless that one of which the draughtsman's (Mr. Samuel Lewis') copy was finally engraved and published with the work.

St Louis Januy 24th: 1811

Dear Sir

I hope you have received my several letters my new map, and sundery other papers relative to such information as I could collect. Inclosed I send you some rough notes which I made at the Mandans the 1st year of my tour, perhaps you may collect from this something which you may wish to know.—A copy of these notes were sent to Mr. Jefferson from the Mandans—I send this as I have sent several others papes thro' the Secty of War. I should be hapy to here from you on the subject of my book.

Accept the assurance of my highest respect & esteem

Your Friend

Wm Clark.

Mr. Nicholis Biddle
　　　Philadelphia

We may pass over several letters relating to the progress of the work under Mr. Biddle's editorship, but must include the following announcement that he had completed it—for this letter also opens up the long chapter of accidents that befell the fateful History.

Phila July 4. 1812

Dear Sir,

I have been for some time anxiously expecting you in Phila, but observing by the papers that you were at Louisville about the middle of June I write this in expectation that it will find you in Pittsburgh

It is now almost a whole year since on the 8th of July 1811 I wrote to you that I had completed the work agreeably to our engagement, & was ready to put it to the press whenever Mr. Conrad chose. Since that time I have been constantly endeavouring to commence the publication not only from a regard to the interests of both of us, but because while this work remained on my hands it interfered very much with all my other occupations, besides that the work would lose some of its interest by so much delay.   Last winter I was prevented from going to the legislature chiefly by a desire to stay & superintend the printing yet notwithstanding all my exertions the publication has been prevented from time to time till at last Mr Conrad's difficulties have obliged him to surrender everything to his creditors & give up business.   This misfortune is very much to be regretted on his account, & I am sorry that we did not know sooner that he would not be able to publish.   But since things have taken this turn, it is perhaps better that the printing was not begun than that we should be entangled with his assignees, since now we can place it in other hands.   I have already spoken to Mr Bradford, one of the best booksellers here, & if we come to an arrangement he can soon print the work.   I am in hopes that he will take it on the same terms as Mr. Conrad did, but [T. O.] but Mr Conrad has been so embarrassed & occupied that they have not yet been able to understand each other.   In a few days however I expect that some agreement can be made & then we can proceed vigorously & soon get the volumes out. . .

I am truly yrs

N. B.

So this publisher failed and assigned just as the book was ready to go to press—and as we shall see another publisher failed just before it came out.   But those were war times, and nothing was secure.   General Clark replied promptly:

Washington City Augt. 6th. 1813

Dear Sir

On my arrival at this place I recved your letter of the 4th of July, in which you inform me the falue [failure] of Mr. Conrad, and the State of our work. Mr. Conrad has disapointed us both I find ; he has disapointed me in a way I had not the smallest suspicion of.

I think we might have expected from him some intimition of his situation which would [have] prevented a delay of the work—

I hope you have suckceeded in engageing Mr. Bradford to print the work and in makeing such other arrangements as you may have thought best—I expect to go on to Philadelphia in a week or ten days, where I hope to have the pleasure to meet you ; as I shall take Indian Chiefs with me, it will not be in my power to stay in your City as long as I could wish.   I must therefore intrude on your goodness and assistance

Mrs. Clark and my two sons came on with me as far as Hagers Town from thence they proceded to Col. Hancocks to remain untill our deficueltes are adjusted to the N W

Accept of my wormest Solicitations

Yours Truly

Wm Clark

Nicholas Biddle Esq
    Phila.

The course of publication never ran more crookedly than about this time, and was as full of shoals as the Kooskooskee. Here is an interesting letter from a great man—one who, however, was greater in steering boats than books :

Philadelphia September 5th. 1812

Dear Sir

I had the pleasure of receiving your letter of the 24th ulto. two days ago at this place, and am extreemly sorry that you were not in the City dureing the time of my remaining in the place, which has been four days, my only Indivdl. business here was to see you, and make some arrangements respecting the publication of the work (Lewis and Clarks Journal). From the situation of my publick duties, I am compelled to return tomorrow without effecting the objects of my wishes—I have expected you for two days, and have delayed one longer than the Contract made with the man to Carry the Indian Chiefs to Pittsburgh autherised—I am a publick officer and must move with a parcel of people (Indians) who are placed under my Charge.

Cant' I persuade you to become *Interested* in Lewis and Clarks work, I hope you will Concent, and under that hope I take the liberty of offering you the half of every profit arising from it, if you will attend to it, have it Completed as far as it is possible and necessary, prented published &c. including the advances which have and may be necessary &c. If you will agree to this proposition (which I hope you will) please to write to me at Pittsburgh or Louisville, inclose agreements which I can excutee there ; and I will send you orders for such specimens &c. as are in the hands of Mr. Conrad and other gentlemen in this City.

Should you not incline to become interested in this way, be so good as to write to me at pittsburgh, and give me your oppinion on this subject.

I have not seen Mr. Bradford, thinking it probable you would become interested and Could make a much better bargain with him than I could.

Doctr. Bartain [Barton] says he can do his part in a very short time. should you become interested you will in Course employ some other persons if the Doctr. should not please you

Please to write to me as soon as possible and accept the assurance of my highest respect and Esteem

Yr most Ob He Sert

Mr. Nichs. Biddle                                                                                    Wm Clark

It began to look very much as if no publisher could be found willing to undertake Lewis and Clark. For example :

Dear Sir

Johnson & Warner have, at last, positively declined making any sort of offer for Genl Clarkes book, & from their conversation seem to have so incorrect an idea of the value of the work and probable profits arising from the publication of it, that it would in my opinion be useless to make them an offer, there is not the smallest probability of their acceding to a fair and reasonable one.—Mr.

Dobson also appears to have little inclination to embark in the work and declines making proposals for it—I can now, I believe, do nothing more in the business for you or Genl Clarke, unless you will permit me to substitute advice for services. If I may do this, I will say very decidedly, agree to Mr. Bradfords offer. It is I am confident the best bargain you can make for Genl Clarke.— The copyright I presume will be in him (Genl C.) & I suppose he will derive the entire benefit of the sale of the M. S. in England—

Yours sincerely<br>John Conrad

[To N. B.]                                    Philada Nov 12. 1812.

Phila Feby 23. 1813

Dear Sir

. . . The times have thrown some obstacles in the way of our work which have prevented its making as much progress as I could have wished. Soon after you left us I consulted Mr. Bradford, but finding his terms not such as I thought advantageous I made proposals to all the booksellers in town. The stagnation in that branch of business however was so great that no one was willing to embark in it, and after a great deal of fruitless negociation I was obliged to return and on the advice of Mr. Conrad accept Mr. Bradford's proposals. This I was desirous of deferring in hopes of obtaining better terms, but none could be had owing to the nature of the times. I now wait only for the engravers who will soon I hope finish their work and then we can strike off the printing im-immediately & in a little time the work will be published. The agreement with Mr. Bradford you will see when you arrive, but as I am not sure whether you are not already on this side of Washington I will add no more than that I am

Very sincerely

Genl William Clarke                              Yrs
Washington                                       N. B

The spectacle of a Biddle begging all Philadelphia to publish Lewis and Clark! Mr. Conrad's advice proved sound. Mr. Biddle was forced to Mr. Bradford's terms. These were doubtless as liberal as the latter could afford to make them —for the sequel showed that Bradford and Inskeep would fail even before they could publish the book.

The next document I possess is a power of attorney— ominous of much litigation to come :

I William Clark of the Missouri territory do hereby constitute Nicholas Biddle of Philada my lawful Attorney in all things relative to my transactions with Bradford & Inskeep or any other persons concerned in the publication of Lewis & Clark's travels, and do hereby empower him for me to demand, recover & receive all my claims and rights thereto or to the profits thereof—make such arrangements and commence such legal processes, consent to such compromises as he may judge proper & generally to do every thing relative to the said work as fully as I could were I personally present—with power also to make such substitutes as he may think advisable. Hereby ratifying whatever he or his substitutes may lawfully do in the premises. In witness whereof I have set my hand and seal hereto this 29th day of March 1813 at Philadelphia

Witness at signing                  Wm Clark   { Seal. }
    Benjn O'Fallon

Meanwhile the work was put to press by Bradford and Inskeep. The composition and presswork occupied about one year, in the course of which the publishers became insolvent, and made an assignment. I have inspected the original manuscript of the balance-sheet headed " Dr. Lewis and Clarks Travels in acc. currt. with the Estate of Bradford & Inskeep, Cr.," showing every item of debit and credit. The net price of the books was $6.00 the set, with various discounts to the trade of 50 per cent. or less. The cost of manufacture, etc., was $3,496.97. The total sales credited amounted to $5,535.47, showing a profit. This, however, was offset by amt. of unpaid bills, $686.27; and of bad debts and cops. not paid for, $1,198.13—altogether a debit of $5,381.37, against a credit of $5,535.47, reducing net profits to $154.10. Whereupon, one Paul Allen appears on the scene for the first time to the naked eye of history, with a claim for alleged services of $500, or so much thereof as he had not taken out in trade with the publishers; which more than wiped out the nominal credit of $154.10. This dismal story is not quite told yet. The edition was ostensibly of 2,000 copies; but when the above-described balance-sheet was drawn up, there were 392 of them lacking plates, probably not delivered because certain bills were unpaid; there were 35 otherwise defective copies, and 156 copies were missing, " supposed to be destroyed in binder's or printer's hands." Deducting 583 copies, defective or missing, from an ostensible edition of 2,000, it appears that no more than 1,417 perfect copies of Lewis and Clark ever existed.[14]

[14] For an itemization of the above account, see my note in the New York Nation of January 12th, 1893. The original number of 1,417 copies became, in the course of time, so much reduced by ordinary wear and tear, mutilation, and destruction, that the price of a perfect copy has of late years settled somewhere about $50—more or less, according to the respective tempers of buyers and sellers. What it will rise or fall to in 1894 remains to be seen.

Thus, by dint of luck, pluck, and perseverance on the part of the surviving author and his steadfast editor, the History that was to make so much history appeared, in February, 1814. If we take the day on which was made the first sale credited in the above account, as that of actual publication, the exact date was Feb. 20th, 1814. Mr. Biddle soon afterward announced the fact of publication to Governor Clark, as follows:

Phila. March 23, 1814.

My dear Sir,

I have at last the pleasure of informing you that the travels are published, that they have sold very well I understand, and have been well thought of by the readers. Henceforth you may sleep upon your fame, which must last as long as books can endure. Mr. Bradford has I presume sent you a copy of the work. The gentleman who received and prepared it for the press, Mr. Allen, is a very capable person [!], and as I did not put the finishing hand to the volumes I did not think it right to take from him the credit of his own exertion and care by announcing personally the part which I had in the compilation. I am content that my trouble in the business should be recognized only by the pleasure which attended it and also by the satisfaction of making your acquaintance, which I shall always value. I could have wished that your time had permitted you to revise the whole of the work, as no doubt some errors and inadvertencies have from the nature of the volumes and the circumstances attending the publication crept into them. I hope however that you will not find them very numerous or important. . .

Let me hear from you often. Neither you nor I are great letter writers but I will always be happy to learn that you are well and your affairs prosperous, with my comp'ts to Mrs. Clark I am very truly,

N. Biddle.

Gen. Wm. Clark,
    St. Louis.

Mr. Biddle doubtless had reasons satisfactory to himself for surrendering to another the credit justly his own, as well as for his rosy vision of Mr. Paul Allen's ability; but both these are beyond my comprehension. General Clark's private opinion in this matter is equally occult. We do not hear from him on the subject of the History, in correspondence with Mr. Biddle, until Sept. 16th, 1814, when, in the course of a long letter from St. Louis, on military and domestic topics, he simply says:

"I have borrowed a Copy of my Book which has reached this place but have not had time to read it as yet."

The rest of the inside history of the book, as represented in this correspondence, is simply the dreary story of lawyering in settlement of an insolvent estate. Mr. Biddle had full power of attorney from General Clark, as we have seen; he was able and indefatigable in his efforts to protect and benefit his client. The case dragged its slow length along till 1818; and much of the correspondence is between the lawyers on each side. Charles Chauncey, Esq., atty. at law; Thomas Astley, ditto; Mr. G. W. Thomas (with an offer to take the remaining stock of books on certain terms); Mr. Mathew Carey (publisher of the Phila. eds. of Gass); Mr. Paul Allen (whining in accents of injured innocence); and others too numerous to specify, appear on the scene; the arithmetic of the eminent counsel for and against the estate of Bradford and Inskeep fetched out variant sums—in fine, no feature of total failure was lacking, for the devil on two sticks had stalked through the whole business. Far from this scene of legal action after mercantile disaster, in St. Louis, was General Clark, who seems to have been slow to realize that nothing can be made of nothing. In 1816 he is still anxious to know how his book-property stands. One letter brings up yet another aspect to the case:

St. Louis March 31st 1816.

Dear Sir

   . . . As Doctr. Marks the half Brother of Gov Lewis has expressed to me in a letter some concern about his brothers interest in the Books, and asked of me for a power of Atty. to receive of the publisher the Books I must request you to deliver to the order of his mother Mrs. Marks, such Books Papers &c. as you may think Govr Lewis's Heirs should receive at least fully the one half of my part. . .

Your mo. ob.t Hl Sert

[To N. B.]                                        Wm Clark

But the half of nothing is nothing again; and having already mentioned the fact that in the final settlement of the unhappy affair, General Clark's total receipts were some copper-plates and the right to bring out a second edition—

of neither of which did he ever avail himself—I will conclude a history cf the History with the following letter:

St Louis Dec<sup>r</sup>. 28th. 1817

Dear Sir

Your letter of the 21st of October informing me of the State of my business with the asse of Mess<sup>r</sup>. Bradford & Inskeep in relation to the publication
of Lewis & Clarks Journal was only received a few days ago ; The proposition
made by Mr. Astley as recommended by you meets my decided approbation ;
I have written to the mother of the late Gov<sup>r</sup> Lewis [Mrs. Marks] & sent her a
statement of the accounts, and asked her to assent to the arrangement, This
measure is important to me as it enables me to satisfy the old lady who I have
reasons to believe has been persuaded that profit arrising from that work has
been received   I wish something done with the Copy rights but what should be
done I cant say, must leave it to your own judgement and better experience,   I
am realy sorry that you have been at so much trouble in acting for me I console
myself that I may yet have it in my power to do you a service ; M<sup>rs</sup>. Clark joins
me in Compliments, respectfully to Mrs. Biddle & hope you will accept my best
wishes

Your Ob<sup>t</sup> H<sup>le</sup> Servant

Wm Clark

Such were the throes of delivery to the world of an
immortal book.  It only remains for me to close a very
imperfect memoir of one of its authors by setting forth the
disposition made of the precious manuscripts upon which
the original and the present editor both worked.  If the
patient reader will turn to the plate which is bound in
front of this Memoir,*he will find reproduced in facsimile
a letter from General Clark to Mr. Biddle, dated Washington, 27th Jany., 1818, in which the former indicates
his wishes in this matter, concerning those volumes of the
Journals and Field Notebooks of Lewis and Clark which Mr.
Biddle had in his possession, and certain other manuscript
records of the Expedition.  All of these writings were
deposited by Mr. Biddle with the American Philosophical
Society in Philadelphia, with the exception of Ordway's
journal (presumably returned to General Clark), and perhaps
with the further exception of Gass' MS. journal (to which
all clew has been lost).  The Biddle deposit was of fourteen
(14) bound volumes of MS., the same being two (2) small

*In this Dover edition, the illustration referred to is reproduced on the large
plate at the end of this volume.

marble-covered books, one (1) brown book, and eleven (11) red books; together with a number of loose letters and other documents. Meanwhile, in November, 1817, Mr. Jefferson[15] had deposited with the same Society three (3) more bound volumes which had been in his hands, the same being two (2) small marble-covered notebooks, and one (1) red book. A thirteenth red book was also deposited about this time, but by whom is not now known; but it seems probable, from the letter of Mr. Jefferson cited in the note

[15] The three MS. Vols. deposited by Mr. Jefferson have memoranda to such effect on the fly-leaves. The Writings of Thomas Jefferson, by H. A. Washington, 8vo. ed. 1854, Washington, Taylor and Maury, include : Vol. VI., pp. 267-270, Letter to Alex. Humboldt, dated Dec. 6th, 1813, alluding to the L. and C. MSS., hoping the Biddle History will soon be out, etc. Vol. VI., pp. 595-597, Letter to M. Correa de Serra, dated Poplar Forest, Apr. 16th, 1816, giving an account, not quite correct, of the L. and C. MSS., as known to him. Vol. VII., pp. 91-93, Letter to M. Duponceau, dated Monticello, Nov. 7th, 1817, saying : "After his [Lewis'] death, I obtained, through the kind agency of Mr. Correa, from Mrs. Barton, three of those books [*i. e.*, L. and C. MSS.], of which I knew there had been ten or twelve [there were at least 18], having myself read them. These were all she could find." Some further light is thrown on the whereabouts of the L. and C. MSS., in the interval between the publication of the History and the final deposit of the MSS. with the Philosophical Society, by the following letter from Mr. Jefferson to General Clark, now on file in the Bureau of Rolls and Library of the State Department. As it is specially interesting in connection with General Clark's somewhat peremptory requisition upon Mr. Biddle, above mentioned as being reproduced in facsimile, I will give it entire :

Monticello, Sep. 8. 1816
Dear Sir

The travelling journal of Govr. Lewis and yourself having been published some little time ago, I had hoped to hear that something was doing with the astronomical observations, the biographical chart, the Indian vocabularies, and other papers not comprehended in the journal published. With a view to have these given to the public according to the original intention, I got a friend to apply for them to mr Biddle in whose hands I understood them to be, referring him for authority to the instructions inserted in the life of Govr. Lewis prefixed to the journal. He said he could not deliver them even to the War office, without an order from you. it is to sollicit this order that I now trouble you, and it may be given in favor either of the War office or of myself. if the latter, I should deliver the astronomical observations to the Secretary at War, who would employ someone to make the calculations to correct the longitudes of the map, and to have it published thus corrected ; and I should deliver the papers of natural history & the vocabularies to the Philos. Society at Philadelphia, who would have them properly edited, and I should deposit with them also for safekeeping the travelling pocket journals as originals to be recurred to on all interesting questions arising out of the published journal. I should receive them only in trust for the War office to which they belong, and take their orders relating to them. I have received from Dr. Barton's exrs. 4 vols. of the travelling pocket journals, but I think there were 11 or 12. the rest I suppose mr Biddle has. I hope the part I have had in this important voyage will excuse the interest I take in securing to the world all the beneficial results we were entitled to expect from it, and which would so fully justify the expences of the expedition incurred by the United States in that expectation. I salute you with constant friendship and respect.

Th : Jefferson
Genl. Wm. Clarke

below, that this was one of " four " books deposited by Mr.
Jefferson, who certainly received that number (not three)
from the executors of Dr. Barton's estate. I have before me
the original and also a copy, both in Mr. Biddle's hand, of
the letter making his own deposit, dated Philada., April 6th,
1818, and addressed to Hon. Wm. Tilghman, Chairman of
the Historical Committee of the Philosophical Society;
item, a copy of the receipt given by the Society in accepting
the custody of these records.[16] In the terms of this agreement it was expressly provided that William Clark, his heirs
or assigns, were and are always to have access to and use
of these manuscripts for the preparation of any other edition of the History. *Manent verba scripta*—the " written
words " slept the sleep of the just, while the printed words
went round the world, during three-quarters of a century,
till one day they awoke to a new lease of life. The following letter requires no comment beyond my profound
acknowledgment of its significance :

SAINT LOUIS, *Nov. 25th*, 1892.

PRESIDENT AND DIRECTORS OF THE
PHILOSOPHICAL SOCIETY.

GENTLEMEN :—

According to the inventory and receipt given in 1818 by your Society for
the papers and manuscripts of Lewis and Clark, explorers of the Missouri and
Columbia rivers, it was agreed that the heirs of Genl. Clark should at all times
have access to them for any future edition of his travels.

Mr. Elliott Coues is now engaged in writing one, and I request that you will
let him have access and use of the manuscripts for that purpose.

Very respectfully,

[Signed]        JEFFERSON K. CLARK,
(only surviving son of
General William Clark).

---

[16] With regard to this finishing of the deposit of the L. and C. MSS. with the Philosophical
Society, see also Jeff. Papers, 2d ser., Vol. 51, Doc. No. 86, letter of N. Biddle to Wm. Tilghman, Phila., April 10th, 1818, endorsed by Jno. Vaughan. Mr. Vaughan was at the time the
Recording Secretary of the Historical and Literary Class of the American Philosophical
Society. A copy of the receipt he gave Mr. Biddle is before me, of date April 8th, 1818. That
clause of this receipt which expresses the conditions of the custody of the MSS. is in these
terms : " It is understood and agreed on the part of the Historical Committee in receiving
these books and papers, that Governor William Clark his heirs or assigns shall at all times
have the full use of them for any future edition of his travels. By order of the Historical
Committee."

My presentation of this letter, together with a formal request to be placed in possession of the MSS. for a limited period, resulted in an immediate vote by the Society in open meeting, Dec. 16th, 1892, by which the whole of this material passed into my hands.[17]   The present edition will show what use has been made of a golden opportunity to prepare for the twentieth century that History of the Expedition of Lewis and Clark which Mr. Biddle wrought for the nineteenth.

[17] For an article entitled: " Description of the Original Manuscript Journals and Field Note-books of Lewis and Clark, on which was based Biddle's History of the Expedition of 1804-6, and which are now in the possession of the American Philosophical Society in Philadelphia," see : Proc. Amer. Philos. Soc. XXXI,, Jan. 20th, 1893, pp. 17-33.

# MEMOIR OF PATRICK GASS.

## BY DR. COUES.

I COMPILE the following biographical sketch of the famous Irish sergeant mainly from material presented by one who knew him well, Mr. J. G. Jacob, author of The Life and Times of Patrick Gass, cited on p. cxxiii, and editor of the Wellsburg Herald, of Wellsburg, W.Va. In private correspondence Mr. Jacob informs me that the substance of it appeared in the columns of his paper before it was made up in book form.

Gass was born June 12th, 1771, at Falling Springs, Cumberland Co., near what was afterward Chambersburg, Franklin Co., Pa. When Mr. Jacob wrote of him, in 1858, he was a hale, hearty old man, and already long the sole survivor of Lewis and Clark's Expedition. His vigor and vitality were astonishing; the more so, considering the hardships he had long endured, and his many years of the besetting sin of an old soldier. In stature he was low, having in his most erect manhood never exceeded five feet seven ; he was compactly built, broad-chested and strong-limbed, lean and wiry; only very late in life was he bowed and crippled with rheumatism. When nearly 99 years old he retained his mental faculties, and had a good, sound memory for the events of almost a century. He died April 3d, 1870.

In 1775 Gass' father moved over South mountain into Maryland. From 1777 to 1780 the boy lived with his grandfather, and was supposed to go to school ; but he says himself that he never learned to read, write, and cipher till he had come of age. His next recorded move was in 1780, memorable for the severity of its winter and the deplorable state of the American army. In 1782 the family " went west "—that is, across the Alleghenies. In 1784 they reached the forks of Yough, and located near Uniontown, then called Beasontown; but next year was again " up stakes " with them, and they finally settled at Catfish camp, so called from a noted Indian chief of the time, and serving as a sort of halfway place between the Monongahela and the Ohio rivers. Here Patrick seems to have first developed some of his qualities, for he used to explore the vicinity, and has left his impressions of the site, as it was in 1790, of what is now Wellsburg, W. Va. There was at that day but one house, a log cabin, built and occupied for many years by one Alexander Wells; it was still standing in 1858.

We next hear of the Irish lad in 1792, when, having attained his majority, he was stationed as a soldier under Captain Caton at Yellow creek, guarding the frontier against Indians. These had long been troublesome, and were just then elated at having defeated General Arthur St. Clair's army, in November, 1791. General Anthony Wayne was sent against them, and the militia all along the frontier was drafted into service. Patrick had been serving in the place of his father, who had been drafted; he was soon after pressed into the service himself, and stationed at Bennett's fort, on Wheeling creek, near Wheeling; but he does not seem to have been in any actual engagement. Indian hostilities were soon after put down entirely and forever in that region by the defeat of the redskins on the Miami by General Wayne, in August, 1792.

While stationed at Wheeling creek young Gass met the scout, Lewis Wetzel, a tall, slim, dark-visaged man, notorious for his deadly hatred of Indians, and credited by tradition with having killed more of them than perhaps any man of his time. They had murdered some of his relations, and he wreaked upon them a terrible vengeance, which in his case, as in many others, became a monomania. He used to shoot peaceable Indians on sight; and on one occasion, being arrested and jailed in consequence, he was released by a mob—such being public sentiment on this score. Wetzel became a boatman, of the kind facetiously called " half-horse, half-alligator," and died a sot a few years later.

Peace being restored, young Gass became a carpenter, having bound himself in 1794 for two years or more. He built about this time at least one house which was standing in Wellsburg in 1859, and also worked on a house for Mr. James Buchanan, father of the boy who was afterward President of the United States, and whom Gass used to call "little Jimmy." The elder Buchanan was an Irishman who had emigrated to this country at an early day, and in York county had married a Miss Speer, the future mother of a president. The Gass family was connected by marriage with the Speers, and Patrick used to say that "little Jimmy" must have got his qualities from his mother, as his father was more thrifty than statesmanlike.

About this time, in 1794, Patrick met General Washington, when the latter was out with some troops to suppress the Whisky Insurrection of 1794. His biographer remarks that he "was too much of a patriot to resist the government, and he loved good old Monongahela too well to enlist against the Whisky Boys; so he wisely remained neutral."

Gass seems to have stuck to his trade for the most part till May, 1799, when, under the presidency of the elder Adams, a war-cloud appeared on the horizon in the prospect of a rupture with the French. Throwing down his jack-plane, he enlisted in the 19th Regiment under Gen. Alexander Hamilton. He was sent from Carlisle to Harper's Ferry in June, 1800, and was soon afterward discharged from the service at Little York, Pa. But being evidently "cut out for the army," he immediately re-enlisted for five years under Major Cass, the father of General Lewis Cass. His intelligence and other merits caused his promotion as a non-commissioned officer, and he was intrusted with some responsible duties in recruiting, and in arresting deserters. His career was about to begin.

In 1801 Gass went with a company under Captain Bissell up the Tennessee river, and in the autumn of 1802 Bissell's company, with a battery of artillery, was sent to Kaskaskia, in Illinois. There they were when, in the autumn of 1803, a call was made by the government for volunteers to accompany the Expedition of Lewis and Clark. Captain Lewis himself came to Kaskaskia in search of suitable material for his corps; and here was the meeting of two soldiers who were to tempt fate together—Meriwether Lewis, American patrician, in command, and Patrick Gass, Irish plebeian, in the ranks—each in his own sphere on the very edge of fame.

To one of Gass' adventurous and hardy nature, this was a golden opportunity. Of course he instantly volunteered—to tread where white man had never set foot before seemed glory mountain-high. But he did not very easily secure his captain's permission to transfer. He was a good carpenter as well as a good soldier, and was wanted in the garrison. So Captain Bissell objected. Whereupon the resolute Patrick persisted, and having found out Captain Lewis' whereabouts hunted the latter up and put the case plump. The result was his enlistment under Captain Lewis, his own commanding officer's objections notwithstanding.

Here I send Sergeant Gass to the Pacific ocean and back to St. Louis; for I shall use his Journal all through the following pages to check and corroborate the narrative of his commanding officers. Shoulder-straps and chevrons understand each other well, and the latter may be heard to advantage with the former. The following extract [1] of a certificate delivered by Captain Lewis to Sergeant Gass, dated St. Louis, October 10th, 1806, attests the high character and good conduct of this non-commissioned officer during the Expedition:

" As a tribute justly due to the merits of the said Patrick Gass, I with cheerfulness declare, that the ample support, which he gave me, under every difficulty; the manly firmness, which he evinced on every necessary occasion ; and the fortitude with which he bore the fatigues and painful sufferings incident to that long voyage, intitles him to my highest confidence and sincere thanks, while it eminently recom-

---

[1] Quoted from the publisher's (David M'Keehan's) Preface to the original edition of Gass' Journal, dated March 26th, 1807.

mends him to the consideration and respect of his fellow citizens."

At St. Louis, Gass and his companions were of course lionized. Very real lions they were, with a story to tell that is immortal. Gass' biographer remarks upon the sergeant's story, as subsequently published in 1807, that "it gives evidence of close observation and much shrewdness of reasoning. It is strictly and conscientiously accurate, for, contrary to the received aphorism regarding travelers' tales, we have never perused a work so devoid of the imaginative, or where was manifested so little desire to garnish plain prose with poetic tinsel. All is unpretending matter of fact. . . We see the adventurers just as they were; and with rare modesty the author—although we have authority for saying he was one of the most useful, efficient, and intelligent men of the party—is kept strictly in the background, or, if mentioned at all, it is only incidentally in connection with some special party of which he was a member."

Remaining but a short time at St. Louis, Gass went to Vincennes, Ind., and thence to Louisville, Ky., where, with a couple of comrades, he rejoined Lewis and Clark. They had with them a deputation of Indians, headed by a chief called Big White, whom they were taking to Washington. The party paid their respects to President Jefferson, made their report to the proper officials, delivered their specimens and curiosities, and were discharged. Gass received his pay in gold, with the promise of future consideration, and went home to his friends in Wellsburg. Here it was that he arranged with the Irish schoolmaster, David M'Keehan, for the publication of his Journal, which appeared early in 1807, thus seven years before Lewis and Clark's own narrative was published. This prompt piece of work ended his connection with Lewis and Clark, during which he had spanned America from the tide-water of the Potomac to that of the Columbia, and thus formed a link in the chain that bound the Atlantic with the Pacific for the first time in the history of the United States.

Gass never exchanged the pen for the sword, for he was one of those who are marked by nature for heroism in very humble life; but he quickly threw down the pen and shouldered the musket again. In the spring of 1807 we find him a soldier still, and he served at the then frontier post of Kaskaskia for the next four years of his life.

Embers of the Revolutionary War smoldered till 1812, when they burst into the second War of Independence. Formal declaration of war was made June 18th, 1812, under the administration of President Madison. Shortly before this Gass was at Nashville, Tenn., where he was drafted into the regiment raised by General Jackson to fight the Creeks, during some Indian disturbances which had broken out. He had, however, the option of enlistment for five years in the regular army. This he promptly accepted, with a bounty of $100, and marched north under General Gaines. He was at Fort Massac in Illinois, in 1813; and the 1st of July, 1814, found him at Pittsburgh, in a battalion under command of Colonel Nichols, with the Northern Army commanded by General Brown. He took part in the assault on Fort Erie, and was conspicuous for his bravery in the famous battle of Lundy's Lane, where he was attached to the 21st Regiment under the gallant Colonel Miller. Gass is said to have distinctly recollected hearing Miller's memorable answer, when ordered by General Ripley to capture the British battery: "I will try, sir." Sergeant Gass shows up gallantly in a sortie made on the 17th of August, where he was intrusted with the duty of spiking the enemy's guns. His selection for such duty, requiring cool courage, was a high compliment to the sergeant, and shows the estimation in which he was held. He was discharged from the service at Sackett's Harbor, in June, 1815, and returned to Wellsburg once more.

The war closed, and with it Gass' career. He retired to an obscurity whence he never emerged. He was past forty, and had lived his life, though his years were not yet half counted. He had nothing to show for the past, and nothing but memory to live on.   His book was financially a failure, and temporarily forgotten; in fact, it has always been rare, and practically known only to the bibliographer.   So he simply settled down to make a living as best he could, tell his soldier's stories, and reap the wild oats he had sown. Having all the "defects of his qualities," he naturally gave way to drink, and for forty years was a sad drunkard. The marvel is that he lived so long with such habits, and that, too, after he had endured hardship enough to undermine the constitution of most men.   He seemed made of steel that would neither break nor bend.

What romance may have entered into the young soldier's life we can only infer from his character and habits.   But love conquered the old soldier at 58, and he was married in 1831 to Miss Maria Hamilton.   During their married life, which lasted for 15 years, till her death in 1846, Mrs. Gass presented her husband with seven children.   "It was customary," says his biographer, "to joke the old soldier on his rapid increase of family.   Such jokes were always good-naturedly received, and he would characteristically remark that, 'as all his life long he had striven to do his duty, he would not neglect it now, but by industry make amends for his delay.'"   He is represented as being a good husband and father, kind and affectionate in his family.

To the statement that Mr. Gass never emerged from obscurity, one slight exception must be made.   He was naturally interested in pension laws, considering that the pittance he drew from the government was ostensibly his only means of support, and that very late in life, when infirmity overtook him, he was thrown in part on the charity of the county.   In some action taken by old soldiers Mr. Gass came to the fore, and figured at the convention held in Washington, January 8th, 1855.   A call had emanated from the veterans of the war of 1812, who had assembled in Philadelphia, January 9th, 1854, for surviving soldiers to meet in their respective neighborhoods and elect delegates to the Washington convention.   Mr. Gass had the post of honor at Wellsburg, December 25th, 1854, and was one of a committee of three selected to go to Washington. During the convention they were received by President Pierce and his Cabinet. The veterans memorialized Congress, and returned to their homes—with the usual barren result.

Writing in 1858, his biographer does not hesitate to say: "There is probably not now living a single man who has done so much for the public as Mr. Gass, and received so little. Among the many unique features of his character, this is not the least singular. He has never been a beggar, neither has he ever had emolument thrust upon him by the country he so faithfully served; hence he is both poor and humble. He is still living, December, 1858, a hale, hearty Virginia Democrat of the old school."

I might have been excused if at this point I had concluded my sketch with the remark that no doubt Mr. Gass soon died. But I wished if possible to complete the record of this wonderful life. I sent to Wellsburg a letter of inquiry, which the postmaster was requested to deliver to "any friend, relative, or descendant of the late Patrick Gass." This was answered in a few days, and my respondent proved to be Mr. Jacob himself. From him I learned that Mr. Gass did not answer his last roll-call till the 3d of April, 1870, when he was in his 99th year. A short time before his death he professed the Campbellite faith, and was baptized in the Ohio river in the presence of a large concourse. His remains were interred in the cemetery at Wellsburg.

Thus ended a life in some respects unparalleled. Gass was one of the most extraordinary men America ever produced. Men have turned their centenary—but how many have done so after such sieges of war, whisky, and women as Gass withstood for nearly a hundred years? It may help us to appreciate the duration of his life, if we remember that he attained nearly the average period of human existence in the eighteenth century, and then rounded out to the full the traditional three-score and ten years in the nineteenth.

# BIBLIOGRAPHICAL INTRODUCTION.

BY DR. COUES.

PUBLICATION of the results of this memorable undertaking was attended by the untoward circumstances that neither Lewis nor Clark became the ostensible author, and that, pending the preparation of their MSS. for the press at other hands, two separate sources of incomplete information respecting their Expedition became available. These were eagerly seized by certain dishonest publishers, who appreciated the lively and general interest which the intrepid explorers had awakened. The result was the appearance of several spurious books which purported to be, in one way or another, the " Narrative," " Travels," or " Journey," of " Lewis and Clark," though the claim of none of them to be so considered rested upon any proper foundation. The bibliography of the subject, if not more extensive than would be expected, was in a confused state, until the appearance of my monograph in 1876; and quotation of " Lewis and Clark " has too often been made with reference to the bogus books. I have been led to examine this matter with care, and with the result here presented, which should place the subject in a white light. I have examined almost every edition, whether authentic or apocryphal, and am able to give the titles of others not seen. Probably the best account of these books, aside from my special bibliography of 1876, is contained in Sabin's Bibliography of Americana, and the next in Field's Essay towards an Indian Bibliography, New York, 8vo, 1873. The latter author includes none of the foreign versions, and omits several others I have seen.

All of the numerous editions and versions of " Lewis and

Clark" which I have seen or heard of may be traced to one or another of three sources, namely :

I. The *Jefferson* Message and Accompanying Documents. (1806.)

II. The *Gass* Journal. (1807.)

III. The *Biddle* History of the Expedition. (1814.)

Of these, the last-named alone is the complete, authentic, and authorized account, prepared by Nicholas Biddle from the original MSS. of Lewis and Clark. The Gass Journal is a perfectly authentic narrative of the journey, by a non-commissioned officer attached to the party, but is *not* a "Lewis and Clark." From President Jefferson's official communication, which is, of course, exactly what it purports to be, sprung a number of books to which the names of Lewis and Clark are more or less prominently attached ; all of which are, nevertheless, spurious in as far as they claim to be narratives of the Expedition. These three classes of books will be successively considered.

### I.—THE JEFFERSON PRODROME AND THE APOCRYPHA.

On the 19th of February, 1806, the Expedition being then at Fort Clatsop, in Oregon, President Jefferson addressed to Congress a communication, entitled as follows :

[1806.] *Message | from    the | President    of    the    United States | communicating | Discoveries | made in exploring | the Missouri, Red River and Washita, | by | Captains Lewis and Clark, Doctor Sibley, | and Mr. Dunbar ; | with | a Statistical Account | of the | Countries adjacent. | — | February* 19, 1806. | *Read, and ordered to lie on the table. | — | City of Washington : | A. & G. Way, printers. | . . . |* 1806.

*8vo. pp.* 1–171, 3 *l.* (*State Papers.*)

It is necessary to examine this State Paper closely, in order to see how the Apocrypha depend upon it. The Message itself is a curt official letter. (This is also to be found, unaccompanied by the documents, in various places, as *e. g.*, in The Addresses and Messages of the Presidents of the United States, etc., 2d ed., 2 vols., 8vo, New York, Edward Walker, I. pp. 185, 186 ; in The Writings of Thomas Jefferson, ed. by H. A. Washington, 1854, Washington, Taylor and Maury, VIII. pp. 59, 60 ; also, in various eds. of the Apocrypha, serving as a dishonest advertisement of the same.) Next comes : (1) A semi-official letter to the President from Captain Lewis, misdated Fort Mandan, April 17th, (*i. e.*, 7th) 1805, giving a progress-report of the Expedition at that date, &c. (2) "A Statistical View of the Indian Nations inhabiting the Territory of Louisiana and the Countries Adjacent to its Northern and Western Boundaries," by Captain Lewis, is the second of the accompanying documents ; this is an elaborate set of statistics of various tribes, with miscellaneous particulars. It is these last particulars—abridged, mutilated, and patched together—that constitute the " Statistical View" printed in the various Apocrypha. (3) The third paper is Dr. Sibley's " Historical Sketches of the Several Indian Tribes in Louisiana, south of the Arkansas River, and between the Mississippi and the River Grand." These Sketches are transferred bodily, with some abridgment and mutilation, to the Apocrypha. (4) Dr. Sibley's Indian Sketches are followed by an account of Red River, in the form of a letter to General Henry Dearborn, Secretary of War. This does not seem to have found favor with the compilers of the Apocrypha, for it is generally omitted, and an anonymous article entitled " Origin of the American Indian Population," stolen bodily from Jonathan Carver, is inserted instead. But Sibley's Red River is duly and truly given in Phillips' English ed. of 1807. (5) The fifth article consists of " Observations made in a Voyage commencing at St. Catharine's Landing, on the East Bank of the Mississippi, proceeding downwards to the Mouth of Red River, and from thence ascending that River, the Black River, and the Washita River . . . from the Journals of William C. Dunbar, Esq., and Dr. Hunter." With omission of some meteorological tables appended to the original, this document, like Dr. Sibley's Sketches, is introduced into the Apocrypha with little change. But it is obvious that none of these documents concerns Lewis and Clark, excepting (1) and (2) ; and that only (1) of these concerns the actual History of the Expedition.

The President's Message, with the Accompanying Documents, was reprinted in New York as a pamphlet, which I have not seen ; but the title of which, nearly identical with that of the original, except as relates to the imprint, is kindly furnished to me by Mr. F. B. Perkins, late of the Boston Public Library, as follows:

[1806.] *Message | from the | President of the United States, | communicating | Discoveries | made in exploring the | Missouri, Red River and Washita, | by | Captains Lewis and Clarke, Doctor Sibley | and Mr. Dunbar ; | with | a Statistical Account | of the | Countries adjacent. | — | Read in Congress, February* 19, 1806. | — |

*New-York :* | *Printed by Hopkins and Seymour,* | *and sold
by G. F. Hopkins, No.* 118, *Pearl-street.* | — | 1806.
*One vol., 8vo, pp.* 178+1 *folded l. not paged.*

Sabin gives another New York imprint of this, as G. F.
Hopkins, 1806, pp. 178 and folder; also, an edition described
as of Natchez, printed by Andrew Marshal, 8vo, pp. 174,
reprinted in part in the Political Cabinet, an appendix to the
Monthly Anthology, Boston, 1807, later collected under
title of American State Papers, Boston, 1808, pp. 39–92 ; of
these I know nothing further. In London, the President's
Message, with the Accompanying Documents, was republished in a faithful reprint under a modified title, as follows :

[1807.] *Travels* | *in the* | *Interior Parts of America ;* | *com-
municating* | *Discoveries* | *made in Exploring* | *the Mis-
souri, Red River and Washita,* | *by* | *Captains Lewis and
Clark,* | *Doctor Sibley,* | *and* | *Mr. Dunbar ;* | *with* | *a
Statistical Account* | *of the* | *Countries adjacent.* | — | *As
laid before the Senate,* | *by the* | *President of the United
States.* | *In February,* 1806, | *and never before published
in Great Britain.* | — | *London :* | *Printed for Richard
Phillips,* 6, *Bridge Street,* | *Blackfriars,* | *By J. G. Barnard,*
57, *Snow-hill.* | — | 1807.

*8vo., pp.* 1–24, *then a folding table, then pp.* 17–116.
*Forming a part, separately paged, of Vol. VI. of Phillips'
Collection of Modern and Contemporary Voyages, &c.*

The contents of this tract are as follows : Title, backed blank, pp. 1, 2 ;
Jefferson's Message, pp. 3, 4 ; Extract of a Letter from Captain Lewis to President Jefferson, being the Fort Mandan letter of Apr. " 17th," *i. e.*, 7th, pp. 4–7;
A Statistical View of the Indian Nations, etc., by Captain Lewis, pp. 7–24,
table, and pp. 17–39 ; Historical Sketches of the several Indian Tribes, etc., by
Doctor Sibley, pp. 40–74 (including an account of the Red River, etc., in a
letter to Gen. Henry Dearborn, from Dr. Sibley) ; Observations made on a
voyage commencing at St. Catharine's Landing, etc., by William Dunbar, Esq.,
and Dr. Hunter, pp. 74–113 ; Meteorological Observations, by the same, pp.
114–116. Thus, as will be seen by comparing the synopsis given of the original
(1806) Message, etc., this tract is genuine, in the sense that it is exactly what it
purports to be. But the Lewis and Clark matter only occupies pp. 4–24, table,

and pp. 17-39, the rest of the volume being Sibley's, Dunbar's, and Hunter's matter, relating to other affairs, and to a different expedition ; though throughout, the words "Lewis and Clarke" appear as signature-marks on the first leaf of every sheet (back lower margin of pages 9, 17, 25, etc.), and p. 116 has as colophon "End of Lewis and Clarke's Travels." This is not, however, intentionally wrong, being merely a sort of printer's mark to keep together the various documents of the Jefferson Message in Phillips' Collection of Voyages, Vol. VI.

From this official *Prodrome*,[1] the earliest available source of much-desired information, books quickly sprung, which, however modified in title or in contents with successive editions, are essentially the same. These are mostly anonymous as to author, compiler, or editor; and though containing matter of intrinsic merit and interest for the time, they are all, as just stated, spurious in as far as they pretend to be " Lewis and Clark," and therefore properly to be styled the *Apocrypha*. These books consist chiefly of accounts of the Indians, in part compiled from the three sources indicated in the title of the President's Message ; but most of the Indian matter is simply a mutilated and garbled version of Jonathan Carver, padded with an account of the Knisteneaux and Chippeways, from Alexander Mackenzie. The curious essay entitled " Origin of the American Population," and credited to an anonymous " ingenious

---

[1] Among collateral publications bearing on the subject may be noticed the following State Paper—in some evidence against the proverbial ingratitude of republics :

[1807.] *Documents | accompanying | a Bill making compensation | to | Messieurs Lewis and Clarke, | and | their companions | presented | the 23d January,* 1807. | — | *Washington City : | A. & G. Way. | . . . |* 1807. *8vo. pp.* 1-8, 1 *leaf folded.*

This is a rare tract, hard to find. Mr. A. R. Spofford showed me the only copy I have seen, in the Library of Congress. The contents are : (1) Letter of Hon. Willis Alston, jun., dated Committee Room, January 12th, 1807, to the Secretary of War, requesting certain information of Lewis and Clark's Expedition. (2) Letter of Gen. H. Dearborn, in reply, dated War Department, Jan. 14th, 1807, transmitting to the Committee a copy of Captain Lewis' muster-roll of his party, together with a copy of his letter to the Secretary of War relative to the same. (This muster-roll and letter of Captain Lewis are those that I cite, from the original MSS., on p. 167 and pp. 254-259 of the present work). Gen. Dearborn's proposition for grants of land to be made to all the members of the Expedition is in these terms : " I take the liberty of proposing, for the consideration of the committee, a grant to each non-commissioned officer and private, of 300 acres of land ; to lieutenant Clarke, of 1,000 ; and to captain Lewis, of 1,500, with the addition of double pay to each while engaged in the enterprize." The Secretary of War adds, that Captain Lewis objected to receiving any more land than should be granted also to Captain Clark. The folding sheet which forms part of this tract is Captain Lewis' muster-roll, printed very closely after the autograph MS. The Bill which these several documents accompanied passed and became an Act of Congress.

traveller," is stolen bodily and copied word for word from Jonathan Carver's " Travels," etc., of which the third edition appeared in 1781 ; being Chap. I. of that part of his book subtitled " Of the Origin, Manners, Customs, Religions, and Languages of the Indians," occupying pp. 115-139 of the Phila. ed. of 1796—as anyone may see by making the comparison.  Here the plagiarism is barefaced ; but elsewhere it is disguised, and some little patience is required to discover the full proportions of the scheme to make Carver's old work pass for Lewis and Clark's.  It is really a notable literary forgery, in constructing which the operator even went so far as to cut out of Carver's narration names which would serve to identify tribes of which Carver treated, in order that what was said of them might be misapplied to other tribes met with by Lewis and Clark.  This miserable trick, by which Carver was robbed and ethnology travestied, has misled every bibliographer.  I myself was at a loss to account for much of the matter of the Apocrypha, when, in 1876, I prepared my original bibliography.  Some of the Apocrypha are illustrated ; others are not.  The titles and captions are well contrived to make them appear as the work of our authors.  The Apocrypha were not wholly superseded by the appearance of the authentic History in 1814, but continued to be published at least until 1840, though they are now scarce and seldom if ever quoted.

Two editions of the Apocrypha appeared the same year in England and America.  They are very similar, but not identical.  I do not know which has actual priority, but suppose that the English was taken from the American. The title of the English 8vo, 1809, is as follows :

[1809.]  *The | Travels | of | Capts. Lewis & Clarke, | from | St. Louis, by way of the Missouri and Columbia rivers, | to the | Pacific Ocean ; | performed in the years 1804, 1805, & 1806, | by order of the | Government of the United States. | Containing | delineations of the manners, customs, | religion, &c. | Of the Indians, | compiled from | Various Authentic*

*Sources, and Original Documents, | and | A Summary of the Statistical View of | the Indian Nations, | from the official communication of | — | Meriwether Lewis. | — | Illustrated with a Map of the Country, inhabited by the | Western Tribes of Indians. | — | London : | Printed for Longman, Hurst, Rees, and Orme. | Paternoster Row. | 1809. |*

*One vol., 8vo, map (frontisp.), pp. i–x, 1–309. (No illustrations except the map. No copyright. Title-p. backed " Printed by C. Stower, Paternoster-Row, London," and the same reset on p. 309.)*

The composition of this motley volume is as follows : After frontispiece (map) and title-page comes : (1) " Message from the President, to the Senate and House of Representatives of the United States," pp. iii, iv. (2) " Introduction," anonymous, pp. v–ix. (3) " Travels to the Pacific Ocean," pp. 1–117, purporting to be by Captain Lewis. Not a word of this audacious forgery is by or from Captain Lewis. Some of it is garbled from Gass ; two authentic and genuine letters of Captain Clark, to his brother George Rogers Clark and to Governor W. H. Harrison, respectively, are interpolated, ending on p. 24 ; then comes, pp. 25–117, the great theft from Jonathan Carver, ingeniously mutilated and garbled, in order that it might be palmed off as Lewis and Clark matter. Next we have (4), pp. 117–156, an account of the Knisteneaux and Chepewyan Indians, summarized from Alexander Mackenzie (1789), and duly credited to him. Then comes (5), pp. 157–183, a " Statistical View of the Indians," based upon Captain Lewis' paper of like title in the Jefferson Message, but abridged, mutilated, and patched together ; (6) then follows, pp. 184–210, " Historical Sketches of the Several Indian Tribes in Louisiana, South of the Rakansas [Arkansas] River, and between the Mississippi and River Grand [Rio Grande] " which is by Dr. Sibley, though not so stated, being the third paper accompanying the Jefferson Message, with some mutilation ; (7) then continues, pp. 211–237, an anonymous essay, *i. e.,* Jonathan Carver's, on the " Origin of the American Indian Population"; (8) then concludes, pp. 238–309, the fifth of the papers accompanying the Jefferson Message, namely : " Observations made on a voyage, commencing at St. Catharine's Landing, on the East Bank of the Mississippi, proceeding downward to the mouth of Red River," etc., extracted from the Journals of William C. Dunbar, Esq., and Dr. Hunter. Such is the dishonest patchwork which was paraded under a title devised to make it appear to be the Travels of Lewis and Clark, and to be by Captain Lewis himself. As remarked of this book by Rees, editor of the London editions (4to, 1814, and 3 vols. 8vo, 1815) of the authentic History : " As far as relates to Lewis and Clarke's Travels, this work is not, however, what it pretends to be, for it contains no further account of them than was contained in the above message [*i. e.,* President Jefferson's], and some private letters of Captain Clarke, addressed to his friends before and after his return. But, in other respects, it is of considerable value, the other documents inserted in it being curious and contained in no other English publication."

The corresponding American edition, in 12mo, 1809, of which I have several copies before me, is as follows:

[1809.] *The | Travels | of | Capts. Lewis & Clarke, | by order of the | Government of the United States, | performed in the years 1804, 1805, & 1806, | being upwards of three thousand miles, from | St. Louis, by way of the Missouri, and | Columbia Rivers, to the | Pacifick Ocean : | Containing an Account of the Indian Tribes, who inhabit | the Western part of the Continent unexplored, | and unknown before. | With copious delineations of the manners, cus- | toms, religion, &c., of the Indians. | Compiled | From various authentic sources, and Documents. | To which is subjoined, | A Summary of the Statistical View of the Indian | Nations, from the Official Communication of | — | Meriwether Lewis. | — | Embellished with a Map of the Country inhabited by | the Western Tribes of Indians, and five Engravings | of Indian Chiefs. | — | Philadelphia : Published by Hubbard Lester. | . . . . | 1809. | Price— 1 dollar 62½ cts. |*

*One vol., 12mo, pp. i–xii, 13–300, pll. 5, map, and tail-piece (scroll and pen). (Copyright dated April 17, 1809.)*

The composition of this wretched meretricious compilation is very much the same as that of the foregoing, of which I suppose it to be really the parent, as it seems to have been published as early as April. The typography of the title-page is ingeniously so arranged as to make it appear, at first sight, that Meriwether Lewis is the author of the book. The title-page is followed by Lester's copyright. Then comes the "recommendation" from President Jefferson, artfully twisted into a recommendation of the book itself. A mutilated version of Jefferson's Message succeeds. Then comes the compiler's introduction, consisting of some meditations on the value of geographical knowledge, and a statement, from some person unknown, of the commerce of the Missouri. The running heads of the pages to p. 153 read, " New Travels among the Indians." This part of the book is meant to pass for Lewis and Clark's Narrative ; the anonymous compiler audaciously opens with the now familiar " On the 14th of May, 1804, we embarked from St. Louis," etc.; but most of this matter is stolen from Jonathan Carver, as already sufficiently indicated. The other pieces are from Mackenzie, Lewis (his "Statistical View"), Sibley, Dunbar, Hunter, and Carver again, as noted above. The volume closes with some anecdotes, one of which is the story of "Master Neddy," copied from William Buchan's "Domestic Medicine," and not having the most remote connection with anything that precedes. Yet this is one of the twin apocryphal books which, with their several offspring, doubtless many thousand worthy American citizens and loyal British subjects have read for "Lewis and Clark"—and, indeed, they are very readable books, as might be judged from the names of the various authors whom the compiler pressed into his service.

We have next to notice two Baltimore editions of the Apocrypha, published by Fisher. None of the former editors of Lewis and Clark alludes to these books, nor are they represented in Field's bibliography. I have before me two editions, of 1812 and 1813 respectively; their titles are as follows:

[1812.] *An | Interesting Account | of the | Voyages and Travels | of | Captains Lewis and Clark, | in the years 1804, 1805, and 1806. | Giving a faithful description of the river Missouri and | its source—of the various tribes of Indians through | which they passed— | manners and customs—soil—climate | —commerce — gold and silver mines—animal and vege- | table productions interspersed with very enter- | taining anecdotes, and a variety of other useful and | pleasing information remarkably calculated to de- | light and instruct the readers—to which is added a | complete dictionary of the Indian tongue. | By William Fisher, Esq. | — | Baltimore. | Printed by Anthony Miltenberger, For the purchasers. | 1812.*
*One vol., 12mo, 2 portraits, pp. v–xv, 16–326.*

For note on this, see next edition, 1813. Sabin gives under Fisher, W., something that seems to be like this; but with imprint Philadelphia, James Sharan, 1812, pp. 300, with two woodcut portraits; but I have never seen this Philadelphia issue of the Fisher fraud.

[1813.] *An | Interesting Account | of the | Voyages and Travels | of | Captains Lewis and Clarke, | in the years 1804–5, & 6. | Giving a faithful description of the river Missouri and | its source—of the various tribes of Indians through | which they passed—manners and customs—soil | —cli-*

*mate—commerce—gold and silver | mines—animal and
vegetable | productions. | Interspersed | With very enter-
taining anecdotes, and a variety of | other useful and
pleasing information, re- | markably calculated to delight
and | instruct the readers. | To which is added | A com-
plete Dictionary of the Indian tongue | — | by William
Fisher, Esq. | — | Baltimore : | printed and published by
P. Mauro, | No 10, North Howard St. | 1813.
One vol., 12mo, portraits ? pp. iii–xii, 13–262, with 3
full-page woodcuts. (No copyright.)*

William Fisher, Esq., must have been a bold man, and he may not have been
a bad man too. Whereas the compiler, editor, thief, or whatever he may have
been, of the London and Philadelphia editions of 1809, retired behind an anonym,
William Fisher not only stole his production bodily, and gave it another name,
but also formally announced himself as the author of the same ; for the edition
of 1812 is a literal reprint, as nearly as may be, of that of 1809, published by
Lester in Philadelphia. The edition of 1813 is nearly another reprint ; the title
reads substantially the same, though the typography of the title-page is entirely
different. In this edition " Master Neddy " is dropped.

In the interval between 1813 and 1840 there may have
been, and probably were, other editions of the Apocrypha ;
but the following, published by Ells at Dayton, O., 1840, is
the only one I have seen or heard of :

[1840.] *The | Journal | of | Lewis and Clarke, | to the Mouth
of the Columbia River | beyond the Rocky Mountains. | In
the years 1804–5, & 6. | Giving a faithful description of the
River Missouri | and its source—of the various tribes of
Indians | through which they passed—manners and cus- |
toms—soil—climate—commerce—gold and | silver mines—
animal and vegetable | productions, &c. | New Edition,
with Notes. | Revised, corrected, and illustrated with
numerous | wood cuts. | To which is added | a complete
dictionary of the Indian tongue. | — | Dayton, O. | Pub-
lished and sold by B. F. Ells. | John Wilson, printer.
| . . . . | 1840.
One vol., 16mo, pp. i–xii, 13–240, portraits of Lewis and
Clark, and 14 other full-page woodcuts.*

The advertisement of the proprietor of this edition says : "The great demand for the Journal of Lewis & Clarke, has induced the republication of the work, with the additions of extensive and interesting notes, and numerous illustrations on wood. We have divided the work into Chapters, with appropriate captions, corrected much that was erroneous in the Topography, and especially in the Nomenclature and Orthography of the Proper Names, and the Philological errors (of which there were many,) have been corrected, where it could be done, without too materially infringing the text." But this volume, aside from changes in the general make-up, addition of table of contents, insertion of wood-cuts, and the minor points noted in the advertisement just quoted, is the same as its Philadelphia and London prototypes of 1809, and the Baltimore steals of 1812 and 1813, notwithstanding the notable modification of title, by which it attempts to lay still stronger claim to be the authentic " Narrative," and by which perhaps it acquired an undeserved copyright. The standing heads of the pages, throughout the volume, are the words "Journal of Lewis and Clarke." The addition of " a complete dictionary of the Indian tongue," as per the title, is a false claim (as it was in Fisher's case), as this " dictionary " is simply the glossary (Alexander Mackenzie's) of Knisteneau words and phrases which was contained in the editions of 1809. The notes added would probably be called " extensive and interesting " only by the publisher. The volume closes with an appendix, containing some irrelevant anecdotes, not entirely the same as those of the 1809–1812–1813 editions ; " Master Neddy " being replaced by a story about a " Great African Serpent, killed by Regulus, the Roman General." The illustrations are most of them additional to any I have seen elsewhere.

## II.—THE GASS JOURNAL.

This publication is perfectly authentic, in the sense that it is exactly what it purports to be—a narrative of the Expedition, by a known person who accompanied Lewis and Clark ; though it is not, nor does it pretend to be, the journal of his leaders. Patrick Gass was an intelligent and observant person of very limited education, who kept a diary of his own, in which events of the journey and their impressions upon the writer were recorded from day to day. His general good character and the faithful and efficient service he rendered are formally certified by Captain Lewis. The Gass Journal is a plain, straightforward, and connected account. It serves as a valuable check upon the narrative of Lewis and Clark itself, in the minutiæ of dates, names, places, etc., and on this account may not inaptly be termed the *Concordance*. Gass had kept notes during the entire Expedition, but they were not in shape for publication; and as his limited education prevented him from arranging them for the press, he secured the literary services of an Irish schoolmaster, David M'Keehan. The result was the Pittsburgh book of 1807, cited below. M'Keehan presented his materials in the raw, stating in his preface that "neither he or Mr. Gass had attempted to give adequate representations of the scenes portrayed." Gass received as his share of the work the copyright and 100 copies of the book; M'Keehan had the balance of the edition, which he sold at some profit.

Gass' Journal was superseded by the publication of the Biddle History; I know of no edition later than 1812, though Sabin cites one of 1815. I have handled five editions of this Concordance, namely: Pittsburgh, 12mo, 1807; London, 8vo, 1808; Philadelphia, 12mo, 1810, 1811, and 1812; and French version, 8vo, 1810. Excepting the French, they only differ from each other in details of typography, and are nothing more than reprints, though some of them are illustrated, others not. All the American editions are in fact identical books. I have minutely compared, for instance, the Philadelphia edition of 1811, with the Pittsburgh princeps of 1807, and find them not only page for page the same (i–viii, 9–262), but paragraph for paragraph, word for word, and almost point for point. I never saw books more exactly alike, when the type had been reset; they only differ in the text in their respective errors of the press; but the Philadelphia book has six pictures that were not in the original, and a modified title page. The original edition is as follows:

[1807.] *A Journal | of the | Voyages and Travels | of a Corps of Discovery, | under the command of Capt. Lewis and Capt. | Clarke of the Army of the United States, | from | the mouth of the River Missouri through the | interior parts of North America | to the Pacific Ocean, | during the years* 1804, 1805, & 1806. | *Containing | An authentic relation of the most interesting transactions, during the expedition,—A description of the country,—* |

*And an account of its inhabitants, soil, climate, curiosities |
and vegetable and animal productions. | — | By Patrick
Gass, | one of the persons employed in the expedition. | — |
With geographical and explanatary notes | by the pub-
lisher. | — | [Copy-right secured according to law.] |
Pittsburgh, | printed by Zadok Cramer, | for David
M'Keehan, Publisher and | proprietor . . . . . 1807. |*
     *One vol., 12mo, pp. i–viii, 9–262. (No illustrations.)*

In my bibliography of 1876 I said : " There appears to
have been another Pittsburgh edition, in 8vo, probably of
1808 ; the one from which a London edition was reprinted."
This is a mistake of mine, arising from my misunderstanding
of the title as given by Field.   There never was a Pittsburgh
octavo, or any Pittsburgh edition after the princeps.   This
was followed by a London 8vo, 1808, and also by three successive Philadelphia 12mos, of 1810, 1811, 1812.

[1808.]   *A | Journal | of the | Voyages and Travels | of |
a corps of discovery, | under the command of Captain Lewis
and | Captain Clarke, of the Army of | the United
States ; | from the mouth of the | River Missouri, |
through the | Interior Parts of North America, | to the
Pacific Ocean ; | during the years 1804, 1805, & 1806. |
Containing | An Authentic Relation of the most interest-
ing Transactions during | the Expedition : | A Description
of the Country : And an | Account of its Inhabitants, Soil,
Climate, Curiosities, | and Vegetable and Animal Produc-
tions. | — | By Patrick Gass, | One of the Persons employed
in the Expedition. | — | Pittsburgh : | printed for David
M'Keehan. | London : | Reprinted for J. Budd, Bookseller
to | His Royal Highness the Prince of | Wales, Pall-Mall. |
1808.*
     *One vol., 8vo, pp. i–iv, 1–381, no map or any other illust.*

A faithful and complete reprint of the original of 1807 ; textually identical
(barring points of diversity incident to resetting the type) ; large plain print,
much better than that of any American edition.   Imprint " Brettell & Co.,
Marshall-Street, Golden-Square," verso of title and on p. 381.   There is a new

" Advertisement by the English Publisher," pp. iii, iv, dated London, April 18th, 1808. The publisher also furnishes new chapter-heads, by dates of the Journal comprehended in each chapter, and summary of contents of each. (These date-heads are used by Lallemant in his French edition.) There is no new editorial text. This edition is the best one in the English language—for those who do not care for princeps editions.

[1810.] *Voyage | des Capitaines | Lewis et Clarke, | Depuis l'embouchure du Missouri, jusqu'à l'entrée | de la Colombia dans l'Océan Pacifique; | fait dans les années 1804, 1805 et 1806, | par ordre du Gouvernement des États-Unis : | contenant | Le Journal authentique des Événements les plus remar- | quables du Voyage, ainsi que la Description des | Habitants, du Sol, du Climat, et des Productions | animales et végétales des pays Situés à l'ouest de | l'Amérique Sep- tentrionale. | Rédigé en Anglais par Patrice Gass, Employé dans | l'Expédition ; | Et traduit en Français par A.J.N. Lallemant, | l'un des Secrétaires de la Marine. | Avec des Notes, deux Lettres du Capitaine Clarke, | et une Carte gravée par J. B. Tardieu. | — | A Paris, | Chez Arthus- Bertrand, Libraire, rue Hautefeuille, n°. 23. | — | 1810. One vol., 8vo, pp. i–xxiij, 1–443, and map.*

This is a faithful and complete French translation of Gass' Journal, doubtless made from the English ed. of 1808 : but whether Lallemant had this text or the original of 1807 before him is immaterial, as the two are substantially the same. The original editor's (M'Keehan's) notes are translated, and the French editor adds a few of his own. The vol. opens with a half-title, verso advts., pp. i, ii ; title, verso blank, pp. iii, iv ; Message du Président des États-Unis, etc., pp. v–vij (not in the original) ; p. viij, blank ; pp. ix–xviij, abridged translation of the original editor's preface ; pp. 1–415, the Journal, entire ; pp. 416–432, two Letters of Clark, genuine and authentic, translated in French (being the same that are given in the spurious London ed. of 1809 and in other Apocrypha) ; pp. 433–443, table of contents, by chapter-heads, not in the orig. ed. Vol. ends " de l'imprimerie de Me Ve Jeunehomme, rue Hautefeuille, N°. 20." The map measures 7¾ x 9½ inches ; it is legended | Carte | Pour servir au Voyage | des Capes. Lewis et Clarke, | à l' Océan Pacifique. | Gravé par J. B. Tardieu. | It is copied from the familiar old London Longmans map of 1809, with French names lettered instead of English.

I had never seen this book when my former Bibliography was prepared, in 1876, and could only give an abridged title at second hand. I was right in then supposing it to be a version of the Gass Journal.

The next edition (the second American) appeared in Philadelphia in 1810, as follows:

[1810.]  *A | Journal | of the | Voyages and Travels | of a Corps of Discovery, | under the command of Capt. Lewis and Capt. | Clarke of the Army of the United States, | from | the mouth of the River Missouri through the | interior parts of North America, | to the Pacific Ocean, | During the Years 1804, 1805 and 1806. | Containing | an authentic relation of the most interesting transac- | tions during the expedition,—A description of | the country,—And an account of its inhabi- | tants, soil, climate, curiosities, and ve- | getable and animal productions. | — | By Patrick Gass, | one of the persons employed in the expedition. | — | With | geographical and explanatory notes. | — | [Copy-Right secured according to Law.] | — | Philadelphia : | Printed for Mathew Carey, | No. 122, Market-street. | — |* 1810.

*One vol., 12mo, pp. i–viii, 9–262, with 6 full page illustrations on separate inserts backed blank.*

The title of this edition is substantially the same as that of the foregoing, though the arrangement of the title-page is quite different, as shown by the bars in the preceding paragraphs. The pagination is identical ; in fact, the edition, as far as the text is concerned, is a literal copy and exact reprint of the Pittsburgh 12mo of 1807 ; though the typography of pp. 9 and 11 is different. To this edition, however, are added six full-page illustrations, in which the figures of men, trees, and animals are notable rather for the mathematical regularity of their lines than for any approach to "curves of beauty."

This Philadelphia edition of 1810 was reissued the following year, 1811, though I can find no allusion to it in any bibliographies examined. Fortunately I have a copy before me—one of the best-thumbed books I ever handled. Though it is mutilated, the upper half of the title-page and the whole last leaf of the book being torn out, enough of the title remains for identification. It is as follows:

[1811]. . . . . . . . . | — | *By Patrick Gass, | One of the persons employed in the expedition | — | With Geo-*

*graphical and Explanatory Notes.* | — | *Third Edition—
with six Engravings.* | — | [*Copy-right secured according
to Law.*] | — | *Printed for Mathew Carey,* | *No.* 122
*Market street,* | *Philadelphia.* | — | 1811.
*One vol.* 12*mo, pp. i–viii,* 9–262, *with* 6 *full page illustrations on separate inserts backed blank.*

This is exactly the same as the Phila. ed. of 1810, but title-page is reset in
a little different typography. The title-page is backed with copyright, certified
by D. Caldwell, Clerk of the District of Pennsylvania, pp. i, ii ; Preface by the
publisher of the first edition (M'Keehan, Pittsburgh, 1807), dated March 26th,
1807, pp. iii–viii ; half title ( | *Journal of the* | *Voyages and Travels* | *of* | *a
Corps of Discovery* | ), p. 9, backed blank ; Journal, pp. 11–262.

This edition is said to have been re-issued at Philadelphia
in 12mo, 1812. I have seen no copy bearing this date.
The title, as quoted by Field, is substantially identical ; the
illustrations are continued. This is spoken of as the
" fourth " (*i. e.*, the fourth American) edition ; but as the
London 8vo reprint, 1808, of the Pittsburgh 12mo, 1807,
is to be counted as one, and the French version as another,
then the Philadelphia 12mo of 1812 is the sixth. Sabin
gives a Phila. re-issue of 1815, and alludes to a possible
Dutch translation; of neither of these do I know anything
further.

Very copious extracts, together amounting to an epitome
of the Journal of Gass, have lately (1892) been published
by Colonel John Doniphan, in a series of eight articles,
running through as many numbers, weekly, of the Daily
News of St. Joseph, Mo. These articles average nearly two
columns apiece. They are of the following dates : I, May
7th ; II, May 14th ; III, May 21st ; IV, May 28th ; V, June
4th ; VI, June 11th ; VII, June 18th ; VIII, June 25th, 1892.
These articles collectively are a fuller and clearer reflection
of the Journal than is contained in Jacob's Life and Times
of Patrick Gass, 1859. The latter is our only biography of
the famous sergeant, and incidentally a booklet of much
curious information. Following is the full title :

[1859]. *The | Life and Times | of | Patrick Gass, | now sole survivor | of the overland expedition to the Pacific, | under Lewis and Clark, in* 1804-5-6; | *also, | a soldier in the war with Great Britain, from* | 1812 *to* 1815, *and a participant in the | Battle of Lundy's Lane. | Together with | Gass' Journal of the Expedition condensed; | —and— | sketches of some events occurring during the | last century in the upper Ohio country, | biographies, reminiscences, etc. | — | By J. G. Jacob. | — | Jacob & Smith, Publishers and Printers, Wellsburg, Va. |* 1859.

*One vol.,* 12*mo, pp. i-viii,* 9-280, *cuts, including frontisp. portrait and autograph of Gass.*

The Life of Gass extends to p. 193, of which only Chap. II, pp. 32-142, entitled " Overland Journey to the Pacific," relates to the Expedition of Lewis and Clark. It is greatly condensed, or rather a mere digest of the original, but fully deserves mention in this connection. The biographical sketch of Gass' life which I give is mainly prepared from this book.

### III.—THE AUTHENTIC HISTORY OF THE EXPEDITION.

[1814.] *History | of | the Expedition | under the command of | Captains Lewis and Clark, | to | the sources of the Missouri, | thence | across the Rocky Mountains | and down the | River Columbia to the Pacific Ocean. | Performed during the years* 1804-5-6. | *By order of the | Government of the United States. | Prepared for the press | by Paul Allen, Esquire. | In two Volumes. | Vol. I* [*II* ]. | *Philadelphia : | Published by Bradford and Inskeep ; and | Abm. H. Inskeep, Newyork. | J. Maxwell, Printer. |* 1814.

*Two vols.,* 8*vo. Vol. I., pp. i-xxviii,* 1-470, *with* 1 *large folding and* 2 *small maps. Vol. II., pp. i-ix,* 1-522, *and* 3 *small maps.*

The *editio princeps.* What is in these two volumes is the original, genuine, and only authoritative History of the Expedition which has come down to us. The Jefferson Message and Accompanying Documents are original, genuine, and authentic, but not the History of the Expedition at all, though repeatedly dressed up to appear as such, in the various Apocrypha. The Gass Journal is an original, genuine, and authentic account of the Expedition, but is not Lewis and Clark's narrative. The author of this book is Nicholas Biddle, whose work was faced, prefaced, and defaced by one Paul Allen.

*Vol. I.* Title leaf, on which Clark's name is spelled correctly, backed with original copyright of Bradford and Inskeep, 1814, certified by David Caldwell, Clerk of the District of Pennsylvania, pp. i, ii ; original preface, signed Paul Allen, pp. iii–v (p. vi blank) ; Life of Captain Lewis, by Th. Jefferson, pp. vii–xxiii (p. xxiv blank). Contents, pp. xxv–xxviii, recapitulating the synopses of chaps. i–xvii, which this vol. contains ; main text of the Narrative, pp. 1–470.

*Vol. II.* Title leaf as before ; contents, pp. iii–ix (p. x blank) ; main text of the Narrative, pp. 1–433 (p. 434 blank). Appendix begins p. 435, and consists of the following pieces : (1) " Observations and reflections on the present and future state of Upper Louisiana, in relation to the Government of the Indian nations inhabiting that country, and the trade and intercourse with the same. By Captain Lewis," pp. 435–461. Then comes, without break in the text, and without sign of its being a new heading, (2) " A summary statement of the rivers, creeks, and most remarkable places," . . . etc., by Captains Lewis and Clark, pp. 462–470, being an itinerary, in tabular form, with notes ; then comes (3) an " Estimate of the Western Indians," pp. 471–476 ; then starts in on the middle of p. 476 (4) certain " Thermometrical Observations," etc., which run to the middle of p. 495, and are followed by " Remarks and Reflections," making a new heading, and running to p. 522 inclusive, the end of the volume. This is a confusing thing, from the way it is set in type ; it really makes four appendices, as will be found fully explained in the present new edition.

The work thus described makes two octavo volumes of ordinary size, 36 lines to the page, type-bed 6½ x 3⅝ inches, l. p. type, very thick and heavy, almost like a full-face font, not pleasant to the eye, though the lines look as if leaded ; the paper very thin, though rough, bringing an average of about 500 pages into a moderately thick volume ; the binding was very strong, so that copies remain to-day in excellent state. The running head of all the left-hand pages is the words " Lewis and Clarke's Expedition," and of the right-hand pages " Up the Missouri "—which latter is misleading before the close of Vol. I, when the Expedition had long left the Missouri and was across the Rocky mountains. After p. 433 of Vol. II the running head is simply " Appendix " on both odd and even pages. The type-setting is bad—very bad ; misprints abound, to the number of several thousand ; in fine, the individual who is announced as having prepared the work for the press, and is supposed to have read the proofs, capped the climax of all possible typographical terrorization. The punctuation is exasperating, in more particulars than one ; besides the thousands of superfluous commas with which the text is peppered, as was the fashion in the close pointing of the period, there runs through the book a peculiarly vicious use of colons, quite aside from their proper office. There is hardly a case of such colons that were not better replaced by a full stop and beginning of a new sentence, or even of a new paragraph. The Dublin edition reproduces the text *punctuatim*, as a rule ; in the London editions the pointing is somewhat improved.

In the capitulation of the text the editor has shown good judgment. As nearly as seemed consistent with making chapters of approximately equal lengths, the divisions accord in the main with marked stages in the journey, as will be seen by the titles I have put to the several chapters in this new edition.   The original has a summary heading of each chapter, and all these are reproduced in the table of contents.

The illustrations consist of one large folding map and five copper-plates, page size.   The map is gone from many if not most copies of the book now extant. For the reason given in my memoir of Clark, *anteà*, p. xci, this important feature of the book was not inserted in all the copies of the original edition. Besides this folder, there should be in a perfect copy, two other plates, page size, in Vol. I and three in Vol. II.   Two in Vol. I are : (1) Plan of the Ancient "fortification" on the Missouri river at Bon Homme island ; (2) Plan of the Portage at the Great Falls of the Missouri.   (That view of the Great Falls which is in the Dublin 1817 ed., I have yet to see in a copy of 1814.)   The three plates in Vol. II are : (1) The Great Falls of the Columbia ; (2) The Great Shoot or Rapids of the Columbia ; (3) The Mouth of the Columbia.   Some copies are without any illustrations at all.

The work was not indexed—a serious defect, for which the ostensible editor should be taken to task, as this omission has made consultation of the wonderful book difficult and tedious, when one has wanted to look up a point, only to be found by searching the pages ; for the analyses of the chapters are far from being minute enough to condone the offense of which someone was guilty. There ought to be a law against indexless books, with heavy penalty.

An extended review and analysis of the work, with copious extracts, and signed "B," will be found in the Analectic Magazine, Philada. 1815, V. n. s. pp. 125–149, 210–234.   Some of the other contemporaneous reviews of which I once made memoranda, are : One by Robert Southey, in Lond. Quart. Rev. XII. Jan., 1815, pp. 317–368, thus very extensive ; one by Gordon, in Edinb. Rev. XXIV. Feb., 1815, beginning p. 412 ; also, Southern Quart. Rev. VIII. p. 191 ; Methodist Quart. Rev. II. p. 556 ; Monthly Rev., July, Aug., Sept., 1815.   But these are mere samples ; to discover and adduce all the places where "Lewis and Clark" appears in literature would require more than any man's lifetime, and result in a voluminous "bibliography of bibliography."

During the same year (1814), the Biddle History was republished in London, under the editorship of Dr. Thomas Rees, in one Vol. 4to, with the following title :

[1814.]   *Travels | to the | Source of the Missouri River | and across the | American Continent | to the | Pacific Ocean. | Performed | by order of the Government of the United States, | in the Years 1804, 1805, and 1806. | — | By Captains Lewis and Clarke. | — | Published from the Official Report, | and | illustrated by a map of the route, | and other maps. | — | London : | Printed for Longman,*

*Hurst, Rees, Orme, and Brown, Paternoster-Row.* | — |
1814.

*One vol., 4to, pp. i–xxiv,* 1–663, 1 *folding and* 2 (*or* 5 ?)
*full-page maps.*

"The present edition is printed nearly verbatim from the original ; the
sheets of which were forwarded to this country by the American proprietors :
the only liberty that has been taken with the language, has been merely the
correction of a few inadvertent grammatical or typographical errors.   The
American copy contained an Appendix drawn up by Captain Lewis on the State
of the Indian Nations ; . . . but as the subject is altogether of a local nature,
and the observations possess little interest for the British reader, it has been
omitted." Besides the whole Appendix, which occupies 89 pages of the original, Jefferson's Life of Lewis and the American editor's preface are also
omitted ; the place of the latter being occupied by a new preface of the English
editor.   This preface consists chiefly of a sketch of other explorations in the
West, especially Pike's (which Rees had edited in 1811) ; it also includes President Jefferson's Message of Feb. 19th, 1806, and an extract of the Mandan letter,
of Apr. "17th", *i. e.,* 7th, 1805, from Captain Lewis to the President, with
bibliographical references to the Jefferson pamphlet of 1806, to the English
edition (1809) of the Apocrypha, and to Gass' Journal ; which latter is spoken of
in more complimentary terms than those used by the American editor.   Excepting these points and those mentioned above in quotation marks, this English 4to
edition is identical with the original American one.

It was succeeded the next year by a 3-vol. 8vo reprint, as
follows :

[1815.]   *Travels* | *to the source of* | *the Missouri River* | *and
across the* | *American Continent* | *to* | *the Pacific Ocean.* |
*Performed by order of* | *the Government of the United
States,* | *in the years* 1804, 1805, *and* 1806. | — | *By Cap-
tains Lewis and Clarke.* | — | *Published from the Official
Report,* | *and illustrated by a map of the route,* | *and other
maps.* | — | *A new edition, in three volumes.* | *Vol. I.*
[*II. III.*] | — | *London :* | *Printed for Longman, Hurst,
Rees, Orme, and Brown,* | *Paternoster-Row.* | 1815.

*Three vols., 8vo.   Vol. I, pp. i–xxvi,* 1 *l. not paged,* 1–411,
3 *maps.   Vol. II, pp. i–xii,* 1–434, 3 *maps.   Vol. III, pp.
i–xii,* 1–394.

Except in form, and in some minor details of typography incident to resetting
of the type, this is identical with the 4to edition of 1814.   Being convenient in

form and otherwise unexceptionable, it is a favorite, perhaps oftener met with, even in this country, than the original of 1814.   It was re-issued under date of 1817, apparently from the same plates ; though I observe, on the last two pages of Vol. I, a slight decrepancy in the set of the type.   If re-issued subsequent to 1817, as may easily have been the case, the fact has not come to my notice.   These two English 3-vol. 8vo editions of 1815 and 1817 may be quoted without distinction, as the pagination is the same.

Meanwhile, in the year 1815, the work (?) was translated into German and published in that language.   The abridged title of something in German, not seen by me, is thus given by Kayser ; I regret that I am unable to complete the title :

[1815.]   "(*Lewis und Clarke.*)  *Tagebuch e. Entdeckungsreise durch Nord. Amerika in d. Jahren* 1804–6, *Aus d. Engl. v. Weyland.   Mit.* 1 *Karte.*"
< *Neue Bibliothek der wichtigsten Beschreibungen, u. s. w.* (*Weimar, gr.* 8vo.) *Bd. I,* 1815.

To judge from the title and date of publication, this may be a version of the authentic narrative.   But it may be something else—a mere review, for example, or a Gass.   I have never seen it, and do not know.

The next edition of the authentic narrative is a Dutch version, by Van Kampen, published in three 8vo vols., at Dordrecht, 1816–18.   It is entitled as follows :

[1816–18.]   *Reize | naar | de Bronnen van den Missouri, | en door het vaste land van America | naar de Zuidzee. | Gedaan op last van de Regering der Vereenigde Staten van America, | in de jaren* 1804, 1805 *en* 1806. | *Door de Kapiteins | Lewis en Clarke. | Met eene Kaart. | — | Uit het Engelsch vertaald door | N. G. Van Kampen. | — | Eerste [tweede, derde en Laatste] Deel | * | Te Dordrecht, | Bij A. Blussé & Zoon. |* 1816 [1817, 1818].
   *Three vols., 8vo.   Vol. I,* 1816, *pp. i–xxxii,* 1–398, *map. Vol. II,* 1817, *pp. i–viii,* 1–390. *Vol. III,* 1818, *pp. i–xii,* 1–335.

This is a fair and complete version, doubtless made from the English 3-volume edition of 1815 (Rees' preface being reproduced and the original preface and memoir of Lewis omitted). The Dutch translator prefixes a preface of his own (Voorberigt van den Vertaler, pp. iii–xviii of Vol. I) and furnishes a number of new footnotes. But the appendices of the original edition are omitted, and in their stead are given as appendices Jefferson's Message of February 19th, 1806, and Lewis' Mandan letter to the President, these two occupying pp. 327–335. The book ends with Aanteekeningen on p. 335. There are no illustrations. The map is legended | Kaart | der Reizen van Lewis en Clarke | door het Westelijk Gedeelte van | Noord Amerika | van den Mississippi tot de Zuid Zee, | op last van de Uitvoerende Magt der | Vereenigde Staten, | en 1804, 5 en 6. | In lower margin is " C. van Baarsel en Zoon, sculps." and " Te Dordrecht, bij A. Blussé & Zoon." This map was redrawn and re-engraved, and the execution is better than that of the original. The size is about the same—a trifle higher and a trifle shorter. The lettering is mostly in Dutch, but with most of the Indian and some of the English and French names unchanged. It is faithfully done, though I observe several slips of the draughtsman or engraver—which would yield a little crop of synonyms of rivers, etc., as " Missourri," "Mil" for Milk R., Meir " Eusue " and " Riddle" for Lakes Eustis and Biddle, "Quamash Vlakte " in one place and " Quamash Flats " in another, etc., etc.

While this Dutch translation was in progress, there appeared an Irish 2-vol. edition at Dublin, in 1817, as follows:

[1817.] *History | of | the Expedition | under the command of Captains Lewis and Clarke, | to | the sources of the Missouri, | thence | across the Rocky Mountains | and down the | River Columbia to the Pacific Ocean. | Performed during the years* 1804–5–6. *| By order of the | Government of the United States. | Prepared for the press | by Paul Allen, Esq. | With the Life of Captain Lewis, | by T. Jefferson, | President of the United States of America. | In two Volumes. | Vol. I [II]. | Philadelphia : published by Bradford and Inskeep ; and Abm. H. | Inskeep, Newyork. | Dublin : | printed by J. Christie,* 170, *James's-street. |* 1817. |

*Two vols.,* 8vo. *Vol. I, map as frontisp., title-leaf backed with Caldwell's Pennsylvania copyright, 4 unpaged leaves of Contents, preface pp. iii–vi, Life of Capt. Lewis pp. iv–xxviii, Narrative pp.* 1–588, *with* 3 *pll. opp. pp.* 78, 326, 327. *Vol. II, title-leaf as before, contents pp. i–xii, 2 unpaged leaves of List of subscribers and directions for placing plates, pp.* 3–643, *with* 3 *pll. opp. pp.* 40, 67, 90.

Of all the reissues this one is the best, being nearest the original, of which it is a faithful and literal reprint, and would be an exact copy but for the slight changes about to be noticed.   The form is the same, with the same divisions of chapters in the two volumes ; the copy makes a little taller and slightly deeper book, with more margin, and a larger, clearer type, wider spaced between the lines, so that there are only 32 lines to the page as against 36 of the princeps edition ; but the type-bed is within one em of the same width.   Whereas the Rees' London eds. of 1814 and 1815 substituted a new preface in place of the original one, and omitted the Life of Lewis, this Dublin ed. retains both of these, and pointedly notes the fact, even adding to the title of the book, " With the Life of Captain Lewis, by T. Jefferson," etc.   The unpaged leaves giving " contents " are identical with those of the original ; in Vol. II a couple of unpaged leaves gives subscription list of the new ed., and directions for placing the plates.   The main text is word for word, barring some typographical discrepancies incident to resetting the type ; nothing is added, taken away, or transposed in the narrative itself, the greater number of pages resulting from the larger and more open type, of 32 instead of 36 lines to the page.   In the appendix some slight modifications are introduced ; a leaf backed blank says " Appendix" (being pp. 545, 546), another leaf backed blank (pp. 547, 548) gives half-title ( | Observations and reflections | on the | present and future state | of | Upper | Louisiana, | in relation to the government of the Indian | nations inhabiting that country and the | trade and intercourse with the same. | By Captain Lewis. | ), headed again, on p. 549, " Observations on the State of Upper Louisiana," running to p. 583, which is backed blank.   Then comes a leaf backed blank (pp. 585, 586) with the half-title | Estimate | of | the Western Indians., pp. 587–596, in substance the same as the original, but in better form, the awkward tabular shape being replaced by an unbroken text ; then the meteorological tables of the original are *omitted*, but the " Reflections and Remarks " which follow these tables in the original as a running commentary are reproduced entire, half-titled | Reflections and Remarks | on a leaf backed blank (pp. 597, 598) and running to p. 630 ; finally comes the Summary Statement, pp. 631–643, identical with the original, but thus transposed, so that, instead of preceding the Estimate of the Western Indians, it becomes the last of the appendicial pieces and ends the volume.

The map which accompanies this edition is unfortunately so much reduced in size as to be very obscure—in fact, the " track " of the Expedition is scarcely visible in some places and does not show at all in others.   On the other hand, the other plates are reproduced in facsimile from their respective originals, and actually superior ; the impressions, at least in the copy I have examined, being much clearer.   This edition—at any rate the copy I handled—had *six* plates, besides the map.   The extra one is a view (scenery) of the Great Falls of the Missouri.   This I know nothing about, never saw elsewhere, and do not pretend to account for.   Lewis says somewhere that he took a sketch of these Falls ; but if any such picture was ever engraved for the orig. ed. of 1814, the fact has escaped my very diligent inquiry into the composition of that work.

Excepting the very defective map, this Dublin ed. of 1817 is a better made book than the princeps itself, superior in every particular of its mechanical execution ; besides which, it is literally true to the original, and thus by far the best reprint.

During the period from 1817 to 1842, there were no editions or imprints of Lewis and Clark that I know of. At the later date, the Messrs. Harper & Brothers, having procured a copyright, made the first issue of a new and modified edition, prepared for them by the Rev. Dr. M'Vickar. There have been a great many (see beyond) successive re-issues of this handy little abridgment, all of which, however, appear to have been printed from the same plates. They are in fact the same edition, though in some of the copies I have seen the maps are omitted. The following title is quoted from the issue of 1868 :

[1842-91.] *History* | *of* | *the Expedition* | *under the command of* | *Captains Lewis and Clarke,* | *to* | *the sources of the Missouri, thence across the Rocky* | *Mountains, and down the River Columbia to the* | *Pacific ocean : performed during the* | *years* 1804, 1805, 1806, | *by order of the Government of the United States.* | *Prepared for the press* | *by Paul Allen, Esq.* | *Revised, and abridged by the omission of unimportant de-* | *tails, with an introduction and notes,* | *by Archibald M'Vickar.* | *In two volumes.* | *Vol. I.* [*II.*] *New York :* | *Harper & Brothers, Publishers,* | *Franklin Square.* | 1868.

*Two vols.,* 18*mo, some of the issues forming part of Harpers' series, "The Family Library."* | *Vol. I, pp. i–vi, (title and advt.) i\*–v\*, (contents), vii–li,* 53–371, 1 *folding and* 3 *other maps. Vol. II, pp. i–x,* 11–395, 3 *maps.*

By the obliging attentions of the publishers themselves, I have been put in possession of the following memoranda of the dates of the successive issues, most of which consisted of 250 copies : September, 1842 ; January, 1843 ; May, 1843 ; January, 1844 ; July, 1845 ; April, 1847 ; May, 1850 ; August, 1851 ; June, 1855 ; April, 1858 ; November, 1860 ; February, 1868 ; March, 1871 (Vol. II) ; April, 1872 (Vol. I) ; February, 1874 (Vol. II) ; December, 1875 (Vol. I) ; February, 1881 ; March, 1882 ; July, 1883 ; April, 1886 ; February, 1886 ; June, 1891—in all 20 issues of the whole work, under 22 different dates.

The advertisement of this edition, dated March, 1842, fully explains its character, in the following extract : " The work [*i. e.*, the Biddle edition] being now nearly out of print, it seemed to the publishers a suitable time to put forth an edition of the Journal of Lewis and Clarke pruned of unimportant details, with a sketch of the progress of maritime discovery on the Pacific coast, a summary account of earlier attempts to penetrate this vast wilderness, and such extracts and illustrations from the narratives of later travelers, led by objects of trade, the love of science, or religious zeal, as the limits of the undertaking would allow. [The editor's (M'Vickar's) introduction, pp. vii.–li. of Vol. I, consists of this matter.]   The matter of the original journal is indicated by inverted commas, and where portions of it, embracing minute and uninteresting particulars, have been omitted, the leading facts have been briefly stated by the editor in his own words, so that the connection of the narrative is preserved unbroken, and nothing of importance is lost to the reader. . .  The seventh chapter of the second volume [of the American edition of 1814], giving an account of the quadrupeds, birds, and plants found on the Columbia and its tributaries, has, to avoid unnecessary interruption of the course of the narrative, been transferred to the appendix."

This, then, is an editorial abridgment, or digest, of the original ; faithfully and, on the whole, judiciously executed.   The natural history chapter, besides being relegated to an appendix, is transposed as to its botanical and zoölogical portions, the botany coming first in the original, the zoölogy in the present edition ; it is, furthermore, like the rest of the work, abridged at the editor's discretion, the omissions being indicated by asterisks.   In this appendix the Estimate of the Western Indians is given, headed however, " Enumeration of Indian Nations and their Places of General Residence," and is not printed in the awkward form of the original.   The original Summary Statement follows, printed in different form from the original.   The Thermometrical Tables, and their accompanying Remarks and Reflections, are omitted.

There is a slight change in contents of the two Vols., the last chapter (xvii.) of Vol. I of the original being carried over to make chap. i. of Vol. II of this edition ; and by the relegation of chap. vii. of Vol. II of the original to the appendix of the present edition, the numeration of the chapters is altered, though they come out the same number in Vol. II, namely, xix.

The " contents " call for one folding map and 6 other plates, 3 in each Vol. I accordingly so collate the book, though I have seen copies without the folder, and others with this but no other illustrations.   These are all reduced to suit the small size of the book, and the map, particularly, is too small to trace satisfactorily the route.

Besides the important and interesting editorial introduction, as above noticed, Dr. M'Vickar supplies various footnotes, but attempts no systematic criticism of Lewis and Clark's geography, ethnology, or natural history.

Sabin says that the M'Vickar ed. was reprinted in London, 1842, 2 vols., 12mo, with modified title, to suit the English demand that grew out of the " Oregon fever " in 1842.   For title, see Sabin's No. 40,834, on p. 313 of Vol. X. of his Bibl. Amer.

*Résumé of the several publications noticed in the foregoing
pages.*

I. Jefferson's Message and Accompanying Documents,
8vo, Washington, A. & G. Way, 1806.—The same, 8vo, New
York, Hopkins & Seymour, 1806.—The same, 8vo, London, R. Phillips, 1807.—(The three preceding genuine.)—
The same, mutilated, abridged, and " Carverized " with irrelevant matter, 8vo, London, 1809.—The same, do., do., do.,
12mo, Philadelphia, H. Lester, 1809.—The same, with slight
modification, 12mo, Baltimore, W. Fisher, 1812 and 1813.—
The same, with slight further alteration, 16mo, Dayton, B. F.
Ells, 1840.—8 editions (all spurious except the first three).

II. Gass' Journal, 12mo, Pittsburgh, D. M'Keehan, 1807.
The same, 8vo, London, J. Budd, 1808. The same, 12mo,
Philadelphia, M. Carey, 1810, 1811, and " 1812 " (latter not
seen by me).—The same, 8vo, Paris, A. Bertrand, 1810
(French translation).—6 editions (all genuine).

III. The Biddle History of the Expedition, 2 vols.,
8vo, Philadelphia, Bradford & Inskeep, 1814.—The same,
1 vol., 4to, London, T. Rees, 1814.—The same, 3 vols., 8vo,
London, T. Rees, 1815 and 1817.—The same (?) " 8vo,
Weimar, 1815 " (German something, not seen by me).—The
same, 3 vols., 8vo, Dordrecht, A. Blussé & Zoon, 1816–18
(Dutch translation).—The same, 2 vols., 8vo, Dublin, J.
Christie, 1817 (the best of all).—The same, much abridged,
with notes, 2 vols., 18mo, New York, Harper & Bro., 1842–
91.—27 editions.

In all,[2] 40 or 41 different imprints of the three series of
books, about 20 of which may be considered as actually
different editions, prior to the appearance of the 4 vol. ed.
of the History, New York, Francis P. Harper, 1893.

---

[2] Exclusive of certain issues, unknown to me, but indicated in Sabin's Bibl. Amer., as duly
noted in the foregoing pages.

The basis of the foregoing Bibliographical Introduction is my article entitled : An Account
of the various Publications relating to the Travels of Lewis and Clarke [*sic*], with a Commentary on the Zoölogical Results of their Expedition, in Bull. U. S. Geol. and Geogr. Surv. Terr.,
2d ser., No. 6, Feb. 8th, 1876, pp. 417-444, and separate, 8vo, Washington, 1876—the same
having been recast and improved for the present occasion.

# LEWIS AND CLARK'S EXPEDITION.

## CHAPTER I.

### UP THE MISSOURI TO THE PLATTE.

ON the acquisition of Louisiana, in the year 1803 [April 30th], the attention of the Government of the United States was earnestly directed toward exploring and improving the new territory. Accordingly, in the summer of the same year, an expedition was planned by the President [Jefferson] for the purpose of discovering the courses and sources of the Missouri, and the most convenient water communication thence to the Pacific ocean. His private secretary, Captain Meriwether Lewis, and Captain William Clark, both officers of the Army of the United States, were associated in the command of this enterprise. After receiving the requisite instructions, Captain Lewis left the seat of government [July 5th, 1803], and being joined by Captain Clark at Louisville, in Kentucky, proceeded to St. Louis,[1] where they arrived in the month of December. Their original intention was to pass the winter at La Charrette (*p. 2*), the highest settlement on the Missouri. But the Spanish commandant of the province, not having received an official account of its transfer to the United States, was obliged by the general policy of his government to prevent strangers from passing through the Spanish territory. They therefore camped at the mouth of Wood [Du Bois] river, on the eastern side of the Mississippi, out of his jurisdiction, where they passed the winter in disciplining the men, and making the necessary preparations for setting out early in the spring, before which the cession was officially announced.

The party consisted of [the two officers] ; nine young men from Kentucky ; 14 soldiers of the United States Army, who had volunteered their services ; two French watermen [Cruzatte, Labiche] ; an interpreter and hunter [Drewyer] ; and a black servant [York] belonging to Captain Clark. All these, except the last, were enlisted to serve as privates during the expedition, and three sergeants [Floyd, Ordway, Pryor, were] appointed from among them by the captains. In addition

[1] Before it was named St. Louis, this place had been called Pain Court. It was founded by Pierre La Clede and his associates in 1764, or not until 84 years after the establishment of Fort Crèvecœur on the Illinois river, and was long inhabited almost exclusively by the French. In Lewis and Clark's time it was a mere village. The inhabitants undertook to incorporate as a town July 23d, 1808, under an act of the Territorial Legislature of June 18th, 1808. But an election of trustees made on the former date proved illegal, and the mistake was not rectified till November 9th, 1809, when the Court of Common Pleas was petitioned for incorporation. The Court approved, and the first valid election of trustees was ordered for December 4th, 1809. Probably the best pen-picture of St. Louis during the next few years is in Irving's Astoria. Up to 1816 St. Louis was confined to its original three streets. The first official survey of the town was made in June, 1818, by Joseph C. Brown, Deputy United States Surveyor. In October, 1817, "Illinois Town" was laid out, opposite St. Louis.

[2] For ratification of the treaty, and actual transfer of Louisiana to the United States, in which latter transaction Captain Lewis had a hand, see my notes near the end of Jefferson's memoir of Captain Lewis, *anteà*.

to these were engaged a corporal and six soldiers, and nine
watermen, to accompany the expedition as far as the Mandan nation, in order to assist in carrying the stores, or in re-
pelling an attack, which was most to be apprehended between
Wood river and that tribe.[3]  The necessary stores were
subdivided into seven bales, and one box containing a small
portion of each article in case of accident.  They consisted
of a great variety of clothing, working utensils, locks, flints,
powder, ball, and articles of the greatest use.  To these
were added 14 bales and one box of Indian presents, distributed in the same manner, and composed of richly laced
coats and other articles of dress, medals, flags, knives, and
tomahawks for the chiefs, with ornaments of different kinds,
particularly beads, looking-glasses, handkerchiefs, paints,
and generally such articles as were deemed best calculated

[3] This enumeration of forty-five persons agrees with the number stated in the
Journal of Gass, who counts forty-three, besides the two captains.   The original
text is ambiguous ; for '' an interpreter and hunter '' might be one person or two
persons, and in the latter case, the same or not the same as the '' two French
watermen.''  But the two French watermen were Cruzatte and Labiche ; and
the interpreter and the hunter was one George Drewyer ; thus making the total
45, with no discrepancy from Gass.   It will be observed that 16 of the men were
only engaged to go as far as the Mandans.   Who they were is unknown now,
excepting Corporal Warfington.   The muster of the party given in Chapter vii,
when the Expedition left the Mandans, April 7th, 1805, includes all the names
which have come down to us together with that of Charles Floyd, then already
deceased.   Gass says (p. 12) : '' The corps consisted of forty-three men ( [besides]
including Captain Lewis and Captain Clarke, who were to command the expedition), part of the regular troops of the United States, and part engaged for
this particular enterprise.   The expedition was embarked on board a batteau
and two periogues.''   Billon's Annals of St. Louis (1888, p. 376) makes a correct
count of the party, though with a wrong composition.   '' Capt. Lewis's party
consisted originally of 28 persons, viz.: 9 young men from Kentucky, 14 U. S.
soldiers, 2 Canadian boatmen, Capts. Lewis and Clark, and a negro servant of
Capt. Clark.   When leaving here in the spring, Captain Lewis added to his
party 1 Indian interpreter [who was also the] 1 hunter, and 15 [i. e., 16] boat
hands, the party then numbering 45 in all.''   See further on this subject in Chapter vii, where I discuss the official list of twenty-nine persons recognized by the
government as belonging to Captain Lewis' party—this being the number of
names on the original manuscript muster-roll which I have examined in the
archives of the War Department at Washington.

for the taste of the Indians. The party was to embark on board of three boats : the first was a keel-boat 55 feet long, drawing three feet of water, carrying one large square-sail and 22 oars. A deck of ten feet in the bow and stern formed a fore- (*p. 3*) castle and cabin, while the middle was covered by lockers, which might be raised so as to form a breastwork in case of attack. This was accompanied by two perioques[4] or open boats, one of six and the other of seven oars. Two horses were at the same time to be led along the banks of the river for the purpose of bringing home game, or hunting in case of scarcity.

Of the proceedings of this expedition, the following is a succinct and circumstantial narrative.[5]

All the preparations being completed, we left our camp on Monday, May 14th, 1804.[6] This spot is at the mouth of Wood [Du Bois] river, a small stream which empties into the Mississippi [on the east side], opposite the entrance of the Missouri. It is situated in latitude 38° 55′ 19.6″ north, and longitude from Greenwich 89° 57′ 45″ west. On both sides of the Mississippi the land for two or three miles is

---

[4] *Sic*—misprint for "periogue," the usual form of the word in Lewis and Clark, and also in Gass. The letter of Captain Lewis to President Jefferson, dated Fort Mandan, April 7th, 1805 (published with Jefferson's Message of February 16th, 1806), prints "peroque." Sometimes the word occurs as "perogue"; never once *pirogue*, the accepted spelling, to which M'Vicker alters in his edition of 1842. I leave it as I find it—"periogue." Similar boats would now be named Mackinaws. They have been much used on the Missouri. I traveled in one nearly a thousand miles down the river, from the head of navigation to Bismarck, and found it safe and commodious. It was shaped like a flat-iron, with pointed bow but square stern, flat-bottomed, roomy yet with little draft, manned with four oars, and steered with a long pivoted sweep. It carried a crew of twelve men, besides myself and three companions, with a month's provisions, and could be fitted with a mast and sail (made of a tent-fly) to help along when the wind was abaft ; yet it was not too heavy to be shoved off a sand-bar when we ran aground, if we all jumped overboard—an incident that no day passed without.

[5] The foregoing is an original editorial introduction ; the narrative of Lewis and Clark begins at this point.

[6] Captain Clark in command ; Captain Lewis was detained a few days (till May 21st.)—Gass, p. 11.

rich and level, but gradually swells into a high pleasant country, with less timber on the western than on the eastern side, but all susceptible of cultivation. The point which separates the two rivers on the north extends for 15 or 20 miles, the greater part of which is an open level plain, in : which the people of the neighborhood cultivate what little grain they raise. Not being able to set sail before 4 p. m., we did not make more than four miles, and camped on the first island, opposite a small creek called Cold-water.[7]

*May* 15*th.* The rain, which had continued yesterday and last night, ceased this morning. We then proceeded, and after passing two small islands about ten miles further, stopped for the night at Piper's landing, opposite another island. The water is here very rapid, and the banks are falling in. We found that our boat was too heavily laden in the stern, in consequence of which she ran on logs three times to-day. It became necessary to throw the greatest weight on the bow of the boat, a precaution very necessary in ascending (*p. 4*) both the Missouri and Mississippi rivers, in the beds of which lie great quantities of concealed timber.

The next morning [May 16th] we set sail at five o'clock. At the distance of a few miles, we passed a remarkable large coal hill on the north side, called by the French La Charbonnière,[8] and arrived at the town of St. Charles [at 2 p. m.]. Here we remained a few days.

[7] "Camped on the north bank six miles up the river."—Gass, p. 12. This creek is just above Bellefontaine, where a military post was established by General James Wilkinson in 1803. The original site of the fort was in the bed of the river in 1819. The works in existence at the latter date were begun in 1810. See Long's Exped. Rocky Mts.. I., 1823, p. 61 of the London ed. The spot interests the naturalist as that of the discovery of *Fringilla grammaca*, by Say, in 1819.

[8] Without any accent in the original text ; also, often spelled with one *n* in books of that date and subsequently. It means a coal-pit or colliery. The name was given by the French watermen and the early settlers, from the beds of coal near the water at the base of a cliff of soft sandstone. The sulphurous smell of the place has been supposed to be due to the decomposition of pyrites. Another place, further up the river, receives the same name.

St. Charles[9] is a small town on the north bank of the Missouri, about 21 miles from its confluence with the Mississippi. It is situated in a narrow plain, sufficiently high to protect it from the annual rising of the river in June, and at the foot of a range of small hills, which have occasioned its being called Petite Côte,[10] a name by which it is more known to the French than by that of St. Charles. One principal street, about a mile in length and running parallel with the river, divides the town, which is composed of nearly 100 small wooden houses, besides a chapel. The inhabitants, about 450 in number, are chiefly descendants from the French of Canada. In their manners they unite all the careless gayety and amiable hospitality of the best times of France. Yet, like most of their countrymen in America, they are but ill qualified for the rude life of the frontier—not that they are without talent, for they possess much natural genius and vivacity; not that they are destitute of enterprise, for their hunting excursions are long, laborious, and hazardous; but their exertions are all desultory; their industry is without system and without perseverance. The surrounding country, therefore, though rich, is not generally well cultivated; the inhabitants chiefly subsist by hunting and trade with the Indians, and confine their culture to gardening, in which they excel.

*May 21st.* Being joined by Captain Lewis who had been detained by business at St. Louis, we set sail on Monday, May 21st, in the afternoon [4 p. m.], but were

[9] Now at the same site and by same name, in St. Charles Co., Mo. The town declined somewhat after Lewis and Clark's visit, but had begun to revive when Major Long's party passed it on the "Western Engineer," June 26th, 1819. Pop. lately 5,000.

[10] Not accented in the original text. This French name for a range of hills or the like acclivity, formerly very common in the West, is usually superseded now by its synonym in this sense, *coteau;* as, Coteau de Missouri. The latter is often spoken as an English word in the West; as, a prairie coteau. The most notable instance of the retention of the word is probably its application to the very long, but low, dividing ridge which separates the Missouri watershed from that of Mouse river, a tributary of the Assiniboin.

prevented by wind and rain from going more than about three miles, when we camp- (*p. 5*) ed on the upper point of an island, nearly opposite a creek which falls in on the south side.

*May 22d.* We made about 18 miles, passing several small farms on the bank of the river, a number of islands, and a large creek on the south side, called Bon Homme, or Good Man's river.[11] A small number of emigrants from the United States have settled on the banks of this creek, which are very fertile. We also passed some high lands, and camped on the north side, near a small creek. Here we met with a camp of Kickapoo[12] Indians, who had left us at St. Charles with a promise of procuring us some provisions by the time we overtook them. They made us a present of four deer, and we gave them in return two quarts of whisky. This tribe reside on the heads of the Kaskaskia and Illinois rivers, on the other side of the Mississippi, but occasionally hunt on the Missouri.

*May 23d.* Two miles from our camp of last night we reached a river emptying itself on the north side, called [Femme Osage or] Osage Woman river.[13] It is about 30 yards wide, and has a settlement of 30 or 40 families from

[11] Of varying form, Bon Homme or Bonhomme; Lewis and Clarke use the latter (misprinted Bonhommer in the Dublin ed., 1817). Gass spells it "Bonum," p. 13. There is still a place of this name in St. Louis Co., Mo., not to be confounded with one of the same name in S. Dakota. See Sept. 1st, beyond.

[12] The Kickapoos come of the great Algonquian family or linguistic stock, and were among the principal tribes, of which about 36 are now recognized. The name, according to different authorities, is either (1) a corruption of the Fox word gîkápu, signifying "smooth, without rapids or obstruction," as a river; or (2) a Pottawattomi word, meaning "one who stands firmly," from kakábu, to stand; or (3) a derisive term, meaning "otter's ghost." Of all the Algonkins, in a broad sense, there are now left about 95,600, of whom 35,600 are in the United States and 60,000 in Canada. Of these the Kickapoos are a mere handful—according to the latest returns, 325 at the Sac and Fox agency, Indian Terr., and 237 at the Pottawattomi agency, Kas. Besides these, there are supposed to be some 200 Kickapoos in Mexico.

[13] In Gass noted simply as "the Osage River," with editorial foot-note surmising "perhaps Little Osage." The mistake was in not noting "*Femme* Osage." On Lewis' map of 1806 (pub. 1887) the name stands "Ossage Womans Cr."

the United States.    About a mile and a half beyond this is
a large cave on the south side, at the foot of cliffs nearly 300
feet high, overhanging the water, which becomes very swift
at this place.    The cave is 120 feet wide, 40 feet deep,
and 20 high; it is known by the name of the Tavern[14]
among the traders, who have written their names on the
rock and painted some images which command the homage
of the Indians and French.    About a mile further we passed
a small creek called Tavern creek, and camped on the south
side of the river, having gone nine miles.

*May 24th.*    Early this morning we ascended a very difficult rapid, called the Devil's Race-ground, where the current
sets for half a mile against some projecting rocks on the
south side.    We were less fortunate in attempting a second
rapid of equal difficulty.    Passing near the southern shore,
the (*p. 6*) bank fell in so fast as to oblige us to cross the river
instantly, between the northern side and a sand-bar which
is constantly moving and banking with the violence of the
current.    The boat struck on it, and would have upset
immediately if the men had not jumped into the water and
held her till the sand washed from under her.    We camped
on the south side, having ascended ten miles.

*May 25th.*    Passed on the south side the mouth of Wood[15]
river, on the north two small creeks and several islands,
and stopped for the night at the entrance of a creek on the
north side, called by the French La Charrette,[16] ten miles
from our last camp, and a little above a small village of the
same name.    It consists of seven small houses, and as many
poor families, who have fixed themselves here for the con-

---

[14] Gass calls it Tavern cove, p. 13.    See Brackenridge's Journal, 1814, p. 203.

[15] Not to be confounded with another of the same name : see May 14th.

[16] Gass calls this St. Johns, p. 13.    This village was founded by the original
French colonists.    It was about this time a residence of the famous Daniel
Boone (b. Bucks Co., Pa., Feb. 11th, 1735), type of American backwoodsman,
who was met here by the overland party of "Astorians," in January, 1811, a very
old man, but still erect in form, strong in limb, and unflinching in spirit.    This
Nestor died in La Charrette, Sept. 26th, 1820, full of sylvan honor and renown.
His latter years were spent with his son-in-law Flanders Callaway. (Compare

venience of trade. They form the last establishment of whites on the Missouri. It rained last night, yet we found this morning that the river had fallen several inches.

*May 26th.*—The wind being favorable, we made 18 miles to-day. We passed in the morning several islands, the largest of which is Buffalo island, separated from the southern side by a small channel which receives the waters of Buffalo creek. On the same side is Shepherd's creek, a little beyond which we camped on the northern side.

*May 27th.*—We sailed along a large island called Otter island, on the northern side. This is nearly ten miles in length, narrow but high in its situation, and one of the most fertile in the whole river. Between it and the northern shore, three small creeks, one of which has the same name [Otter[17]] with the island, empty. On the southern shore is a creek 20 yards wide, called Ash creek. In the course of the day we met two canoes loaded with furs, which had been two months on their route from the Mahar [Omaha] nation, residing more than 700 miles up the river, one large raft from the Pawnees on the Platte river, and three others from the Grand Osage river. At (*p. 7*) the distance of 15 miles we camped on a willow-island, at the entrance of Gasconade river.[18] This river falls into the Missouri from the south, 100 miles from the Mississippi. Its length is about 150 miles,

Irving's Astoria, ed. 1861, p. 146, and Appleton's Amer. Cyclop. II., p. 83.) The Missouri Gazette of Jan. 17th, 1814, notes an Act of Congress for the relief of Colonel Daniel Boone, confirming to him 1000 arpents of land, claimed by him under a grant of Jan. 28th, 1798, and the Recorder of Land Titles for the Territory of Missouri is directed to issue to him a certificate for the same. Approved by James Madison, President U. S.

[17] Or in those days the corresponding French name *Loutre*, which our text translates into English. Thus we read in Long's Expedition of Loutre island, creek, and prairie, the latter described as 23 miles long (p. 68 of the London ed). A Mr. Talbot of Kentucky settled at Loutre or Otter creek, in 1810. When Major Long's Expedition passed in 1819 several forts had been built for protection against the Indians, chiefly Sacs and Kickapoos. Near here was the scene of the massacre of Captain Callaway and his men.

[18] The first considerable river that falls into the Missouri entirely within the State of the same name. Its mouth is in Gasconade Co., Mo., half a mile above

in a course generally northeast, through a hilly country. On its banks are a number of saltpetre caves, and it is believed some mines of lead are in the vicinity. Its width at the mouth is 157 yards, and its depth 19 feet.

*May 28th.*—Here we halted for the purpose of hunting, drying our provisions, and making the necessary celestial observations.

*May 29th.*—We set sail at four o'clock [p. m.] [19] and at four miles distant camped on the south side, above a small creek, called Deer creek.

*May 30th.*—We set out early, and at two miles distant reached a large cave, on the north, called Montbrun's ["Mombran's" in Gass] tavern, after a French trader of that name, just above a creek called after the same person. Beyond this is a large island. At the distance of four miles, Rush creek comes in from the south; at 11, Big Muddy river on the north, about 50 yards wide; three miles further is Little Muddy river on the same side [in Callaway Co., Mo.], opposite to which we camped, at the mouth of Grindstone creek [Osage Co.]. The rain which began last night continued through the day, accompanied with high wind and some hail. The river has been rising fast for two days, and the country around appears full of water. Along the sides of the river we observe much timber, the cottonwood, sycamore, hickory, white walnut, some grapevines, and rushes. The high west wind and rain compelled us to remain all the next day, May 31st. In the afternoon a boat came down from the Grand Osage river, bringing a letter from a person sent to the Osage nation on the Arkansaw river, which mentioned that the

a marked mass of rocks which were ornamented with Indian pictographs. It rises in hilly country near some of the sources of the Youngar or Yungar branch of the Grand Osage, and has a clear, rapid current, navigable for a few miles only. The name was often spelled "Gaskenade," as in Gass, p. 14.

[19] The late start is accounted for by Gass, who says : "*Tuesday 29th.*— Seven men were sent out to hunt, six of whom returned. We waited here till 5 o'clock p. m. for the man who had not come in, and then proceeded," etc., p. 14.

letter announcing the cession of Louisiana had been committed to the flames; that the Indians would not believe
that the Americans were owners of that country, and dis-
regarded St. Louis and its supplies.    The party was occupied in hunting, in the course of which they caught in (*p. 8*)
the woods several very large rats [*Neotoma floridana:* see
note under date of July 7th, beyond].

*Friday, June 1st,* 1804.—We set sail early this morning,
and at six miles distant passed Bear creek, a stream about
25 yards wide; but the wind being ahead and the current
rapid, we were unable to make more than 13 miles, to the
mouth of the Osage river.    Here we camped and remained
the following day, for the purpose of making celestial observations.[20]

The Osage empties itself into the Missouri at 133 miles
distant from the mouth of the latter.    Its general course
is west and west-southwest through a rich and level country.[21]    At the junction the Missouri is about 875 yards
wide, and the Osage 397.[22]    The low point of junction
is in latitude 38° 31' 16" north, and at a short distance
from it is a high commanding position, whence we enjoyed
a delightful prospect of the country.

The Osage river gives or owes its name to a nation in-

[20] Gass notes here that the periogue which had been left at the mouth of the
Gasconade for the missing hunter came up with the man who had been lost.

[21] The Osage rises in Kansas, south of the Kansas river, in a range of hills
which were known as the Ozark mountains.    It enters Missouri, and empties
into the Missouri below Jefferson City, separating Cole from Osage Co.    The
course is eastwardly—the direction stated by the authors being *from* the Missouri.
The largest tributary was called the Youngar or Yungar, falling in about 140
miles from the mouth of the Osage.    In Long's Expedition, which passed here
in July, 1819, there are noted, between the Gasconade and the Osage, "Bear
creek, the Au Vase, and other tributaries," but the only locality marked on
Long's map is the village of Côte sans Dessein, opposite the lower mouth of the
Osage, and then containing about 30 families, mostly French.    This place was
established about 1808, and so named from a neighboring hill.    Here was an
attack and massacre during the late war by Sacs, Foxes, and Iowas; the hero
of which affair was there when Long's Expedition passed.    See Brackenridge's
Journal, 1814, p. 209.

[22] Gass makes it 197, and gives the Missouri as 875, as in our text.

habiting its banks at a considerable distance from this place. Their present name, however, seems to have originated from the French traders, for both among themselves and their neighbors they are called the Wasbashas.[23] They number between 1,200 and 1,300 warriors, and consist of three tribes: the Great Osages, of about 500 warriors, living in a village on the south bank of the river; the Little Osages, of nearly half that number, residing at the distance of six miles from them; and the Arkansaw band,[24] a colony of Osages, of 600 warriors, who left them some years ago, under the command of a chief called Big-foot, and settled on the Vermilion river, a branch of the Arkansaw. In person the Osages are among the largest and best-formed Indians, and are said to possess fine military capacities; but residing as they do in villages, and having made considerable advance in agriculture, they seem less addicted to war than their northern neighbors, to whom the use of rifles gives a great superiority.

Among the peculiarities of this people, there is nothing more re- (*p. 9*) markable than the tradition relative to their origin. According to universal belief, the founder of the

[23] Wabasha, whence our familiar word Wabash, is corrupted from *Wazhazha*, the Dakotan name of the Osage Indians. Other forms of the word are *Wajaja* and *Wawsashe*. The Osages call themselves *Wacace*, pronounced nearly "Wazhazhe." Osage is twice misspelled "Ossage" on Lewis' map of 1806.

[24] This "Arkansaw band" of Osages must not be confounded with the Arkansaw or Arkensa Indians of early times, now known as the Quapaw (Kwapa) tribe of the great Siouan family. In 1805, according to Dr. Sibley, the latter lived along the Arkansaw river, in three villages on the south side, about twelve miles above the post or station. He believed that at that date they did not exceed 100 men in number, and were diminishing. They were at war with the Osages, their own relations, but friendly with all other Indians, and with the whites. They were considered the proprietors of the country on the Arkansaw up to the forks, or to the country claimed by the Osages, and cultivated corn.

The native name of the Arkansaw band signifies "Dwellers in a Highland Grove." This band spoke the Osage language.

The two Osage nations and the Arkansaw band constituted a principal tribe of the great Siouan family. They numbered, in 1891, 1,509 at the Osage agency, Indian Terr.; besides which there were 65 at school in Lawrence, Kas., and six at Carlisle, Pa.

nation was a snail passing a quiet existence along the banks of the Osage, till a high flood swept him down to the Missouri, and left him exposed on the shore.  The heat of the sun at length ripened him into a man ; but with the change of his nature he had not forgotten his native seat on the Osage, toward which he immediately bent his way.  He was, however, soon overtaken by hunger and fatigue, when happily the Great Spirit appeared, and giving him a bow and arrow, showed him how to kill and cook deer, and cover himself with the skin.  He then proceeded to his original residence, but as he approached the river, he was met by a beaver, who inquired haughtily who he was, and by what authority he came to disturb his possession.  The Osage answered that the river was his own, for he had once lived on its borders.  As they stood disputing, the daughter of the beaver came, and having by her entreaties reconciled her father to this young stranger, it was proposed that the Osage should marry the young beaver, and share with her family the enjoyment of the river.  The Osage readily consented, and from this happy union there soon came the village and the nation of the Wabasha, or Osages, who have ever since preserved a pious reverence for their ancestors, abstaining from the chase of the beaver, because in killing that animal they killed a brother of the Osage.  Of late years, however, since the trade with the whites has rendered beaver-skins more valuable, the sanctity of these maternal relatives has visibly reduced, and the poor animals have nearly lost all their privileges of kindred.

*June* 3*d.*  On the afternoon we proceeded, and at three miles distant reached a creek, called Cupboard[25] creek, from a rock of that appearance near its entrance.  Two miles

---

[25] Not marked on Clark's map, 1814 ; not on Nicollet's map, 1843, nor Gen. Land Office map, 1876, nor on U. S. Geol. Surv. map, nor on Mo. R. Commission map ; an insignificant stream ; by the text three-fifths of the way from the Osage to the Moreau, by the Mo. R. Comm. distances 140 miles from mouth of the Missouri, and now called Rising creek.

further we camped at Moreau[26] creek, a stream 20 yards wide, on the southern side.

*June 4th.* This morning we passed, at an early hour, Cedar island on the north, so called (*p. 10*) from the abundance of the tree of that name. Near this is a small creek, which we named Nightingale[27] creek, from a bird of that species which sang for us during the night. Beyond Cedar island are some others of smaller extent, and at seven miles' distance is a creek 15 or 20 yards wide, entering from the north, known by the name of Cedar creek.[28] At 7½ miles further, we passed on the south side another creek, which we called Mast[29] creek, from the circumstance of our mast being broken by running under a concealed tree. A little above is another creek on the left, one mile beyond which we camped on the southern shore under high projecting cliffs. The French had reported that lead ore was to be found in this place, but on examining the hills we could discern no appearance of that mineral.[30] Along the river on the south, is a

[26] Present name of that river which empties into the Missouri in Cole Co., a little below the capital of the state, Jefferson City (formerly Missouriopolis, as on Long's map, 1823). It is laid down, unlettered, by D'Anville, 1752; it is R. à Morou of Perrin du Lac, 1805; Marrow Cr. of Lewis, 1806 (laid down, unlettered, by Clark, 1814) ; of Gass, 1807 ; of Brackenridge, 1816 ; Murrow in Lewis and Clark's text later on. The name is French, certainly personal (Moreau's Cr. of Long, 1823), but of uncertain sense in its application to the river, as it might mean either " nose bag " or " black-horse."

[27] No species of nightingale (*Daulias luscinia*), in any proper sense of the word, is found in North America. The so-called " Virginia nightingale " is the cardinal red-bird (*Cardinalis virginianus*).

[28] Cedar island and creek (or river) are present names on ordinary maps ; at mouth of the stream is Cedar City, Calloway Co., opposite Jefferson City. Several other places called " Cedar " will occur in our text.

[29] Marked, unlettered, on Lewis' map, 1806 ; not on Clark's, 1814, nor on any other maps examined. The name occurs in Long's text, 1823, but has long since lapsed, and the creek is probably not identifiable with certainty. It may be sought on the south side of the river, about 150 miles up, by Mo. R. Commission distances.

[30] This place is elsewhere called Lead-mine hill, as also by Brackenridge, 1814, who locates it nine miles above Cedar creek.

low land covered with rushes and high nettles, and near the mouths of the creeks supplied with oak, ash, and walnut timber. On the north the land is rich and well situated. We made 17½ miles this day. The river is falling slowly.

*June 5th.* We continued our route this morning early. A small creek called Lead creek, on the south ; another, on the north, known to the French by the name of Little Good Woman creek ; and again Big Rock creek, on the south, were the only streams we passed this morning.[31] At eleven o'clock we met a raft made of two canoes joined together, in which two French traders were descending, from 80 leagues up the Kansas river, where they had wintered and caught great quantities of beaver, but had lost much of their game by fires from the prairies. They told us that the Kansas nation is now hunting buffalo in the plains, having passed the last winter on this river. Two miles further we reached on the south Little Manitou[32] creek, which takes its name from a strange figure resembling the bust of a man with the horns of a stag painted on a projecting rock, which may represent some spirit or deity.

[31] No sign of the first and third of these creeks on Lewis', or Clark's, or any ordinary map ; may be sought near a prominent point now called Sugar-loaf rock, about 160 miles up the river. The second creek, usually by its French name Bonne Femme, is laid down on any good map, emptying into the Missouri between Burlington and Claysville, Boone Co.

[32] To be distinguished from another (Big) Manitou creek, beyond. The present stream empties at the junction of Cole and Moniteau (*sic*) counties on the south, and is down on any good map by its modern corrupt name. It is the R. au Diable of D'Anville, 1752 ; the Petit Manitou of Perrin du Lac, 1805 (whence *Little* Manitou of our text) ; Maniteau creek of Nicollet, 1843; Manitoo of Brackenridge, 1814, p. 210, but his "Hamilton" creek, p. 265. The "painted rocks" of the text naturally acquired the name of Manitou rocks (as Long, 1823, who says that in 1819 there were along here a number of hamlets, called Nashville, Smithton, Rectorville, etc., of one to half a dozen houses). These rocks, like the stream, must not be confounded with others of the same name, higher up the river. The word is Algonkin, meaning spirit, whether god or devil. It has suffered the usual permutations in spelling, and is now usually Manito or Manitou in English literature, but Moniteau in Missouri geography.

Near this is a sand-bar extending several miles, which (*p. 11*) renders navigation difficult, and a small creek called Sand creek[33] on the south, where we stopped for dinner, and gathered wild cresses and tongue-grass from the sand-bar. The rapidity of the current, added to our having broken our mast, prevented our going more than 12½ miles. The scouts and hunters, whom we always kept out, reported that they had seen fresh tracks of Indians.

*June 6th.* This morning we left our camp, which was on the south side, opposite a large island in the middle of the river, and at five miles reached a creek on the north side, about 20 yards wide, called Split Rock[34] creek, from a fissure in the point of a neighboring rock. Three miles beyond this, on the south, is Saline[35] [or Salt] river; it is about 30 yards wide, and has its name from the number of salt-licks and springs, which render its water brackish. The river is very rapid and the banks falling in. After leaving Saline river, we passed one large island and several

[33] Sand creek is not easily identified. It should be about 168 miles up the river, nearly opposite a considerable island which appears on the Commission map. The wild cresses and the tongue-grass are the same (for I find that Clark writes "creases *or* tung-grass") and are a species of *Lepidium*, tongue-grass being another name of pepper-grass, which latter is applied to all the numerous species of these cruciferous plants, but especially to *L. sativum*. Two of the species which occur along the Missouri are *L. ruderale* and *L. virginianum.*

[34] So lettered on Lewis' map ; on Clark's, laid down, but unlettered; to be found on most maps, next below (Big) Manitou river, usually by its earlier French name, Roche percée or Rocher percé, but variously misspelled or unaccented (as for example Roche à Pierce and a Piercè of Long's text, 1823). This stream runs south through Boone Co., west of the county seat Columbia, and empties just above Providence. Nearly opposite its mouth is the forked rivulet called Splice creek by Long, 1823, but not noticed in our text.

[35] Now Little Saline, running chiefly in Cooper Co., but emptying in Moniteau Co., according to G. L. O. map of 1876. Name Saine creek in Gass, ed. 1811, by misprint. Salt R. lettered on Lewis' and on Clark's maps, and on Pike's, 1810. Little Saline of Long's text, 1823, but not laid down on his map. Mr. A. J. Hill's MS. river-chart remarks that it is apparently the R. à la Bargue of Renaudière, 1723. It is not to be confounded with another Salt or Saline river, a little higher up, on the north side of the Missouri. The large island noted in the text is plainly shown on the Mo. R. Commission map.

smaller ones, having made 14 miles.    The water rose a foot last night.

*June 7th.*    We passed at 4½ miles, Big Manitou[36] creek, near which is a limestone rock inlaid with flint of various colors, and embellished, or at least covered, with uncouth paintings of animals and inscriptions.    We landed to examine it, but found the place occupied by a nest of rattlesnakes, of which we killed three.    We also examined some licks and springs of salt water, two or three miles up this river.    We then proceeded by some small willow-islands, and camped at the mouth of [Big] Good Woman[37] river on the north.    It is about 35 yards wide, and said to be navigable for boats several leagues.    The hunters, who had hitherto given us only deer, brought in this evening three bears [*Ursus americanus*], and had seen some indications of buffalo.    We had come 14 miles.

*June 8th.*    We saw several small willow-islands, and a creek[38] on the south, near which are a number of deer-licks ; at nine miles' distance we came to Mine river.[39]    This river,

[36] Which Gass naturally calls the river of the Big Devil, p. 16 ; lettered simply Manitou R. on Lewis' map, but G. Manitou R. on Clark's ;  R. grand Manithou of Perrin du Lac, 1805 ; Manitoo of Brackenridge, 1814 ; Big Manito of Long, 1823 ;  Grand Maniteau of Nicollet, 1843 ;  now commonly Moniteau creek, in Howard Co., emptying at town of Rocheport, at or near junction of Boone Co.    The rock noted in the text has the same name as the river.    The text does not notice a rivulet, just above the river, and on the same side, which Long (1823) called Little Saline river, and which is on the Commission map as Salt creek.    Long also names a Big Manito island near here ; and a large island appears on the map just cited, 190 miles up the river.    This is the I. de Manithou of Perrin du Lac.

[37] In Howard Co., emptying below the town of Franklin ; the R. Bonne Femme of Perrin du Lac, 1805, and still better known by its French name than by the English equivalent.    No qualifying term appears in L. and C.'s text or map to distinguish this river from another of same name lower down the river (see above) : but Gass inserts " Big."    Note that *this* is the river marked R. aux Sioux by D'Anville, 1752 ; but is neither of those now known as the Sioux rivers.

[38] Apparently that river found on some maps by the name of Loupe's branch

[39] Near the mouth of which is Booneville or Boonville, county town of Cooper Co.; across the Missouri is Franklin, Howard Co.    The first large branch of this river is called Salt Fork.    An early name of Mine river was R. au Vermil-

(*p. 12*) which falls into the Missouri from the south, is said to
be navigable for boats 80 or 90 miles, and is about 70 yards
wide at its mouth. It forks about five or six leagues from
the Missouri, and at the point of junction are some very
rich salt springs; the west branch, in particular, is so much
impregnated, that for 20 miles the water is not palatable.
Several branches of the Manitou and Good Woman are
equally tinctured. The French report, also, that lead ore
has been found on different parts of the river. We made
several excursions near the river through the low rich
country on its banks, and after dinner went on to the
island of Mills, where we camped. We met with a party
of three hunters from the Sioux river; they had been out
for twelve months, and collected about $900 worth of pel-
tries and furs. We ascended this river twelve miles.

*June 9th.* We set out early, and reached a cliff called
the Arrow Rock,[40] near to which is a prairie called the
Prairie of Arrows, and Arrow creek, a small stream about
eight yards wide, whose source is in the adjoining prairies
on the south. At this cliff the Missouri is confined within
a bed of 200 yards; and about four miles to the southeast
is a large lick and salt spring of great strength. About three
miles further is Blackbird [now Richland] creek on the north
side, opposite which is an island and a prairie inclosing a

lon of D'Anville, 1752; but it had been called R. à la Mine by Renaudière,
1723. This name has varied to Lamine occasionally. In 1819, when Long
passed, Booneville had eight houses. The earliest settlement in this vicinity
was Boone's Lick, about four miles from Franklin, giving name to the surrounding country. Clark's map of 1814 marks the site of "Boon's Salt Works." An
establishment of this kind was in full blast at the time of Long's visit; Brackenridge, writing of 1811, names one Braxton Cooper in charge of salt works
then, and says that the settlement, though only a year old, consisted of 75 families. Dr. Baldwin, botanist of Long's expedition, died at Franklin, August
31st, 1819.

[40] Present name of the prominent landmark on the south side of the river,
translating Pierre à flèche of the French (D'Anville, 1752). Arrow Rock is
also the present name of a town on the same side of the river, in Saline Co.
Across the river, and a little higher up, is the town of Lisbon, Howard Co.
The rock was so called from being resorted to by Indians for stone arrow-heads.

small lake. Five miles beyond this we camped on the south side, after making, in the course of the day, 13 miles. The land on the north is a high rich plain. On the south it is also even, of a good quality, and rising from 50 to 200 feet.

*June* 10*th*. We passed Deer[41] creek ; and, at the distance of five miles, the two rivers called by the French the two Charatons,[42] a corruption of Thieraton [*read* Charretin], the first of which is 30, the second 70 yards wide. They enter the Missouri together ; both are navigable for boats. The country through which they pass is broken, rich, and thickly covered with timber. The Ayauway[43] nation, (*p.13*)

---

[41] Deer-lick creek of Gass, p. 16 ; present name, Hurricane creek. Just above this, on the same side of the Missouri (right hand, going up), a certain Bear creek comes in, on Owen's map, 1848 ; and the same is indicated on various other maps. This seems to have escaped the attention of Lewis and Clark.

[42] This word has never been satisfactorily explained ; certainly the explanation attempted in the text is itself a misprint or other blunder. It might be either Charleton or Charlatan ; the former is given on p. 387 of the orig. ed.; the latter would match Gasconade, as applied to another river. The various forms in which we find it add to our perplexity. Thus, it is the Chératon of Collot in 1796 ; Charleton is Perrin du Lac's style, 1805 ; Lewis' map of 1806 has Charliton ; Clark's, 1814, prints the two Charatons ; Brackenridge, 1814, gives Chareton and Chariton, p. 211 and p. 265 ; Long, 1823, Charaton ; Nicollet's map, 1843, Chariton ; some of the spurious Lewis and Clark books make it Chareturn ; Gass strikes out for himself with the two Charlottes, p. 16 ; Pike, 1810, is satisfied with two Charlatans ; Lapie, 1821, has but one river, which he calls R. des deux Charlatans. I only discovered what it ought to be on consulting L. and C.'s MSS. (See note under date of June 24th.) The name has now settled into the form Chariton for both rivers, for the county, and for a town. The two rivers were formerly distinguished in French as Grand and Petit Charletons (so Perrin du Lac); they have also been called Great and Little, and West and East. They are probably the pair of rivers called les rivières aux Racines by D'Anville, 1752, though his map runs them separately into the Missouri. These rivers reach the Missouri through Chariton Co., with Howard Co. adjoining at the confluence. The Chicago and Alton R. R. crosses the Missouri a little below this point, and both Charitons are crossed above by the Wabash, St. Louis and Pacific R. R. The streams are straightish, north-south, parallel with many branches of the Grand river, which comes into the Missouri a little higher up. This is the main drainage into the Missouri of the rise to 1,000 feet to the west and north. East of the Charitons the drainage is into the Mississippi.

[43] This word, lacking any true consonants, is fluidic, and varies much in

consisting of 300 men, have a village near its head waters, on the river De Moines.[44] Further on we passed a large island called Chicot[45] or Stump island, and camped on the south, after making ten miles.

A head wind forced us to remain there all the next day, [June 11th], during which we dried the meat we had killed, and examined the surrounding country, which consists of good land, well watered, and supplied with timber. The prairies also differ from those eastward of the Mississippi, inasmuch as the latter are generally without any covering except grass, whilst the former abound with hazel-nuts

orthography. Lewis and Clark spell it several ways, as Ayaway, Ayoway, Ayahwa, Ayawai, etc. Other forms are Ayovai, Ayauvai, Aiaoaez (plural). Another series is Iawai, Iaway, etc. In Lewis' Statistical View it is marked for accent ah -e-o-war'. From the liquid state the word has solidified into our familiar *Iowa*. These Indians on their separation were called Pa-ho-ja (gray snow) ; they are also among the many different Indians who have been styled Pierced-noses. The Iowas were a tribe of the great Siouan family, descendants of the old Missouris. In Lewis and Clark's time they had one village, 40 leagues up the Des Moines river, with a population of 800, of which 200 were warriors. Lewis represents them as turbulent savages, who were at war with many of their neighbors, even of their own kindred, and frequently abused their traders and committed depredations on persons navigating the Missouri, though they were at peace with the Ottoes and Missouris, some of the Sioux and Yankton tribes, and all nations east of the Mississippi. They traded in furs and peltries. (London ed., 1807, p. 22.) The remnants of the Iowas are 165 on the Great Nemaha Reservation in Kansas, 102 on the Sac and Fox Reservation in Oklahoma, five at school at Lawrence, Kas., and one at Carlisle, Pa.—273.

[44] The name of the river Des Moines is obviously French, but it does not mean "of the monks." It is an old word of Algonkin origin, used by Illinois Indians met by Marquette and Joliet. These Indians called their place Moingona, Moingonan, or Mouingouinas—a word found in some form on very old maps (and down to 1843 at least). Later the French clipped the word to Moin, calling the people les Moins, and their river la rivière des Moins. Finally, the name became associated with the Trappist monks (les moines de la Trappe) ; and the river of the Moins became la rivière des Moines, by a spurious etymology. Traces of this history of the name survive in its various spellings, as Des Moins, De Moin, De Moyen, Demoin, Demoir, even "Demon," etc. The Sioux name of the river is Inyanshasha-watpa, literally "stone-red-red-river," or as we should say Redstone river. Compare Nicollet's Report, 1843, p. 22 and map, where Moingonan is used.

[45] Plainly shown on the Mo. R. Commission map, at the 230th mile up the river. Chicot is French, meaning stump. Present name, Harrison island.

[*Corylus americana*], grapes [probably *Vitis cordifolia*], and other fruits, among which is the Osage plum [*Maclura aurantiaca ?*] of a superior size and quality.

*June* 12*th.* In the morning we passed through difficult places in the river, and reached Plum[46] creek on the south side. At one o'clock we met two rafts loaded, the one with furs, the other with the tallow of buffalo; they were from the Sioux nation, and on their way to St. Louis; but we were fortunate enough to engage one of the men, a Mr. Durion,[47] who had lived with that nation more than 20 years and was high in their confidence, to accompany us thither. We made nine miles.

*June* 13*th.* We passed, at between four and five miles, a

[46] No trace of this on either Lewis' or Clark's map. But there are two or three small creeks on the south side, in Saline Co., between Stump island and Bowling Green Bend (L. and C.'s Round Bend below). One of these is marked Edmundson's creek on Owen's map of 1848; one is now called Bear creek; another, Salt creek. Plum creek is probably the first of these.

[47] "Got from them an old Frenchman, who could speak the languages of the Indians up the Missouri, and who agreed to go with us as an interpreter." Gass, p. 17. Irving spells the name Dorion, and thus sketches the old fellow: "Old Dorion was one of those French creoles, descendants of the ancient Canadian stock, who abound on the western frontier, and amalgamate or cohabit with the savages. He had sojourned among various tribes, and perhaps left progeny among them all: but his regular, or habitual wife, was a Sioux squaw. By her he had a hopeful brood of half-breed sons, of whom Pierre was one. The domestic affairs of old Dorion were conducted on the true Indian plan. Father and son would occasionally get drunk together, and then the cabin was the scene of ruffian brawl and fighting, in the course of which the old Frenchman was apt to get soundly belabored by his mongrel offspring. In a furious scuffle of this kind one of the sons got the old man upon the ground, and was on the point of scalping him. 'Hold! my son,' cried the old fellow, in imploring accents, 'you are too brave, too *honorable* to scalp your father.' This appeal touched the French side of the half-breed's heart, so he suffered the old man to wear his scalp unharmed." Astoria, ed. 1861, p. 141.

Pierre appears to have been a sulky brute, who beat his wife and made himself as much of a nuisance as possible in every way. His wife was encumbered with two children already, and had another *en route.* This squaw proved herself a heroine; the parallel between her and Sacajawea, of whom Lewis and Clark tell us much later on, is quite close. Her mongrel spouse was murdered by Indians shortly after the overland expedition of Hunt and his party to Astoria. *Ibid.*, p. 493.

bend of the river, and two creeks on the north, called the Round Bend [48] creeks. Between these two creeks is the prairie, in which once stood the ancient village of the Missouris. [49] Of this village there remains no vestige, nor is there anything to recall this great and numerous nation, except a feeble remnant of about 30 families. They were driven from their original seats by the invasions of the Sauks [Sacs] and other Indians from the Mississippi, who destroyed at this village 200 of them in one contest, and

[48] Marked by a mere scratch on Lewis' map, not lettered ; no trace on Clark's. Larger and later maps usually show these creeks, or one forked creek, at the head of the bend, in Chariton Co. One modern name is Palmer's creek. The Round Bend of the Missouri itself is now known as Bowling Green Bend.

[49] The Missouri or Missouria Indians (*Ni-u'-t'a-tci*) were one of the principal tribes of the great Siouan linguistic stock or family. In Powell's classification they are enumerated as the tenth of eighteen Sioux tribes. Lewis' Statistical View (1806) spells their native name *New'-dar-cha*. Some of the many forms of this name are *Neotacha* and *Neogehe*. The word is said to mean "those who settle at the mouth of a river," *i. e.*, the Missouri. They later moved up to where they were found by the French in about 1700. They lived in one village with the Otoes, mustering a total of 300 persons, with 80 warriors. They traded with the merchants of St. Louis, and their commerce was substantially the same as that of the Otoes. They were at peace with the Pawnees proper, Sacs, and Foxes, but warred with the Omahas, Poncas, Sioux, Osages, Kansas, and Pawnee Loups. At that date they were already the mere remnant of a numerous nation inhabiting the Missouri when first known to the French. Their ancient and principal village was on an extensive and fertile prairie on the north bank of the river, just below the mouth of Grand River. The smallpox, and war with the Sacs and Foxes, reduced them to mere dependence on the Otoes, with whom they resided and hunted in Lewis' time ; though they were viewed by the Otoes as inferiors and sometimes maltreated ; but they were the real owners of the country for a considerable distance above their village, thence to the mouth of the Osage, and on to the Mississippi. In 1752 D'Anville called the Missouri the Pekitanoui, or Rivière des Missouris.

The Sacs and Foxes were in Lewis and Clark's time already so firmly consolidated as to be regarded as one nation, and they have been usually since spoken of together. They are members of the great Algonquian family. The name of the former tribe is rendered by Lewis O'saukee, whence Saukee, Sauk, then Sac or Sacque. They had two villages on the west side of the Mississippi, "140 leagues" above St. Louis, and counted 2,000 population, with 500 warriors. They warred with the Osages, Chippeways, and Sioux, but were at peace with other tribes. The name of the Foxes is rendered by Lewis Ot-tar-går-me ; its French style was Reynard, clipped to Renard and other

sought refuge near the Little Osage, on the other side of the river. The encroachment of the same enemies forced, about 30 years since, both these nations from the banks of the Missouri. A few retired with the Osage, and the remainder found an asylum on the Platte river, among the Ottoes,[50] who are themselves declining. Oppo- (*p. 14*) site the plain there was an island and a French fort, but there is now no appearance of either, the successive inundations having probably washed them away, as the willow-island,

forms. They numbered 1,200, with 300 warriors, and had one village near the Sacs. Of the two tribes together Lewis remarks in 1805 : " They speak the same language. They formerly resided on the east side of the Mississippi, and still claim the land on that side of the river from the mouth of the Oisconsin [Wisconsin] to the Illinois river, and eastward toward Lake Michigan, but to what particular boundary I am not informed ; they also claim, by conquest, the whole of the country belonging to the ancient Missouris, which forms one of the most valuable portions of Louisiana [*i. e.*, of trans-Mississippian regions in the U. S. of 1805], but what proportion of this territory they are willing to assign to the Ayouways [Iowas], who also claim a part of it, I do not know, as they are at war with the Sioux who live N. and N. W. of them, except the Yankton-ahnah. Their boundaries in that quarter are also undefined. Their trade would become much more valuable if peace were established between them and the nations west of the Missouri with whom they are at war. Their population has remained nearly the same for many years. They raise an abundance of corn, beans, and melons. They sometimes hunt in the country west of them, toward the Missouri, but their principal hunting is on both sides of the Mississippi from the mouth of the Oisconsin to the mouth of the Illinois river. These people are extremely friendly to the whites, and seldom injure their traders ; but they are the most implacable enemies of the Indian nations with whom they are at war. To them is justly attributed the almost entire destruction of the Missouris, the Illinois, Cahokias, Kaskaskias, and Piorias." (London ed., 1807, p. 23.) The Sacs and Foxes now number 981 ; there are 515 at their Agency in Indian Terr., 381 at their Agency in Iowa, 77 at the Pottawottomi and Grand Nemaha Agency in Kansas, and eight at the Lawrence, Carlisle, and Hampton schools.

[50] The Otos, Otoes, Ottos or Ottoes, were Indians whose native name Lewis renders *Wâd-doke-tâh-tâh* in his Statistical View of 1806, and Powell spells *Wa-to'-qta-ta* in 1891. Other forms are Wahtohtana, Wahtotata, Wadotan, etc., said to have arisen in a circumstance which occurred on their separation from the Missouris, when their chief abducted a squaw of the latter nation. The French used to call them Othouez, etc. Their single village was shared by the Missouris. They numbered 500, with 120 warriors, and resided on the south side of the Platte,

which is in the situation described by Du Pratz,[51] is small and of recent formation. Five miles from this place is the mouth of Grand river,[52] where we camped. This river follows a course nearly south, or southeast, and is between 80 and 100 yards wide where it enters the Missouri, near a delightful and rich plain. A raccoon [*Procyon lotor*], a bear [*Ursus americanus*], and some deer [*Cariacus virginianus*] were obtained to-day.

*June 14th.* We proceeded at six o'clock in the morning. The current was so rapid, and the banks on the north were falling in so constantly, that we were obliged to approach

15 leagues from its mouth. They traded with the merchants of St. Louis, and made war and were at peace with the same tribes as the Missouris. Lewis remarks : '' They have no idea of the exclusive possession of any country, nor do they assign themselves any limits. I do not believe that they would object to the introduction of any well-disposed Indians ; they treat the traders with respect and hospitality, generally. In their occupations of hunting and cultivation, they are same with the Kansas and Osages. They hunt on the Saline and Nimmehaw [Nemaha] rivers, and west of them in the plains. The country in which they hunt lies well ; it is extremely fertile and well watered ; that part of it which borders on the Nimmehaw and Missouri possesses a good portion of timber. Population rather increasing. They have always resided near the place where their village is situated, and are the descendants of the Missouris.''

There were lately 358 Otoes and Missouris together in the Indian Territory.

[51] Le Page Du Pratz, Hist. de la Louisiane, etc., orig. ed. 3 vols., 12 mo., Paris, 1758 ; English trans., 1763, 1774, etc. Lewis and Clark are clearly mistaken in quoting Du Pratz for the situation of a large island and French fort anywhere along here. Du Pratz says : '' There was a French Fort for some time on an island a few leagues in length over against the Missouris ; the French settled in this fort at the east point, and called it Fort Orleans.'' We have also '' Fort D'Orleans abandonné '' marked on D'Anville's map, pub. 1752, across the Missouri from his Petits Osages et Missouris. This locality is certainly at the large island which the Expedition will pass June 16th, above Malta Bend, 290 miles up river by the Commission map.

[52] Present name : to be distinguished from Grand River in Dakota, greatly higher up the Missouri. It is the first river of any size above the Charitons, and by far the largest of any thence to the Kansas. At its confluence with the Missouri, where it separates Chariton from Carroll Co., is Brunswick, in the latter county. Its mouth is crossed by the W. St. L. and C. R. R., and a railroad follows it up past Chillicothe, continuing nearly in a straight line to Council Bluffs and Omaha. Its name holds over from la rivière Grande of the old French writers, as Renaudière, 1723.

the sand-bars on the south. These were moving continually, and formed the worst passage we had seen, which we surmounted with much difficulty. We met a trading raft from the Pawnee nation on the Platte, and attempted unsuccessfully to engage one of their party to return with us. At the distance of eight miles, we came to some high cliffs, called Snake [53] bluffs, from the number of that animal in the neighborhood; and immediately above these bluffs is Snake creek, about 18 yards wide, on which we camped. One of our hunters, a half-Indian, brought us an account of his having to-day passed a small lake, near which a number of deer were feeding, and in the pond he heard a snake making a guttural noise like a turkey. He fired his gun, but the noise became louder. He adds that he has heard the Indians mention this species of snake, and this story is confirmed by a Frenchman of our party. [54]

*June* 15*th*. The river being very high, the sand-bars were so rolling and numerous, and the current was so strong, that we were unable to stem it even with oars added to our sails. This obliged us to go nearer the banks, which were

[53] This name may be traced to Perrin du Lac, 1805, who speaks of a bluff above la rivière Grande, and marks on his map "Wachanto ou endroit de serpens." Snake creek is lettered on Lewis' map, 1806, on the north side ; it is traced but not named on Clark's, 1814. The present name of a creek on the south near here is Miami ; and a prominent point above, on the north, is White Rock. The stretch of river to-day is between Saline and Carroll Cos., and from 258 to 268 miles up the Missouri. See next note below.

[54] A snake story, told by an Indian and confirmed by a Frenchman, may be taken for what it is worth. Gass omits the story. However this may be, certainly some superstition or tradition concerning serpents has given name to Snake creek—the considerable stream in Carroll Co. now known as Wakenda creek (the Wyaconda river of Nicollet, 1843, whose name is the same word as Perrin du Lac's Wachanto). The first element of this word is the Indian *Wakon* (spelled in a dozen ways or more), meaning "medicine"—that is, anything an Indian does not understand. Various maps consulted differ much in locating the mouth of the stream, which has apparently changed its position by several miles, through a change in the bed of the river. Late maps bring it much nearer the mouth of Grand river than the older ones do. It may have once been above White Rock. The county town of Carrollton is on a branch of this river.

falling in, so that we could not make, though the boat was
occasionally towed, more than 14 miles.   We passed several
islands, and one creek on the south side, and camped on the
north op- (*p. 15*) posite a beautiful plain, which extends as
far back as the Osage river, and some miles up the Missouri.
In front of our camp are the remains of an old village of the
Little Osages, situated at some distance from the river, at
the foot of a small hill.   About three miles above them, in
view of our camp, is the situation of the old village of the
Missouris after they fled from the Sauks [Sacs].[55]   The
inroads of the same tribe compelled the Little Osages to
retire from the Missouri a few years ago, and establish
themselves near the Great Osages.   The river, which is
here about one mile wide, had risen in the morning, but
fell toward evening.

*June* 16*th*.   Early this morning we joined the camp of our
hunters, who had provided two deer and two bear, and then
passing an island and a prairie on the north, covered with
a species of timothy, made our way through bad sand-bars
and a swift current, to a camp for the evening on the north
side, at ten miles' distance.   The timber which we examined
to-day was not sufficiently strong for oars.   The mosquitoes[56] and ticks are exceedingly troublesome.

*June* 17*th*.   We set out early, and having come to a convenient place at one mile's distance, for procuring timber
and making oars, we occupied ourselves in that way on this
and the following day [June 18th].   The country on the
north of the river is rich and covered with timber; among
which we procured the ash for oars.   At two miles it
changes into extensive prairies, and at seven or eight miles'
distance becomes higher and waving.   The prairie and high

[55] The sites of both these Indian tribes (Little Osages and Missouris) are
plainly marked on D'Anville's map of 1752, and also on Perrin du Lac's, 1805.
The location is very near the present Malta Bend, in Saline Co., and a little
above this place is the large island of Du Pratz, where was old Fort Orleans,
to be reached to-morrow.

[56] Spelled throughout the work either musquitoes or musquetoes.   I alter to
the usual orthography.

lands on the south commence more immediately on the river; the whole is well watered and provided with game, such as deer, elk,[57] and bear.   The hunters brought in [58] a fat horse which was probably lost by some war-party—this being the crossing-place[59] for the Sauks [Sacs], Ayauways [Iowas], and Sioux, in their excursions against the Osages.

*June* 19*th.*   The oars being finished, we proceeded under a gentle breeze by two large and some smaller islands. The sand-bars are numerous and so bad that at one place we (*p. 16*) were forced to clear away the driftwood in order to pass; the water too was so rapid that we were under the necessity of towing the boat for half a mile round a point of rocks on the south side.   We passed two creeks; one called Tiger [60] creek, on the north, 25 yards wide, at the extremity of a large island called Panther Island ; the other, Tabo creek, on the south, 15 yards wide.   Along the shores

[57] This animal, which will be repeatedly noticed throughout this work, is the wapiti, *Cervus canadensis.*   "Elk" is most properly the name of a European animal, *Alces machlis,* resembling the American moose ; but "elk" has been, since Lewis and Clark, the almost universal name of the wapiti.

[58] A bear they had killed and

[59] Such a point on the river is marked on Nicollet's map of 1843 as the Grand Pass—but it seems to be a little lower down the river, and to have been passed by Lewis and Clark on the 16th.   South of the northward loop of the river, and west of Malta Bend, is a body of water still called Grand Pass lake on some maps.

[60] I am satisfied of an error here.   The account cannot be squared with geography, and the fact that Gass gives a different itinerary for the 19th and 20th, shows a bad snag here.   Gass says for the 19th :   "Passed Tabo creek on the south side, and a small creek on the north"; and for the 20th :   "Passed Tiger creek, a large creek that flows in from the north."   Now, according to General Land Office and Missouri River Commission maps, which agree well, the stretch of "17½" miles made on the 19th, which separates Carroll from Lafayette Co., shows : (1) A large island, where is now Waverly, Lafayette Co., 300 miles up river ; (2) Another large island, five miles further ; (3) Little Tabo creek on the south, and close to it Big Tabo creek on the same side, with Dover between their mouths, and some small islands in the river, all these points about 310 miles up ; (4) There is no creek on the north large enough to be shown on either of the maps cited ; (5) The "Tiger" creek of both Lewis' and Clark's maps is a sizable stream, but beyond any of the points noted for the 19th.   There-

are gooseberries and raspberries in great abundance. At the distance of 17½ miles we camped on the south, near a lake about two miles from the river and several in circumference, much frequented by deer and all kinds of fowls. On the north the land is higher and better calculated for farms than that on the south, which ascends more gradually, but is still rich and pleasant. The mosquitoes and other animals are so troublesome that mosquito biers [sic—bars] or nets were distributed to the party.

The next morning [June 20th], we passed a large [i. e., Panther] island, opposite which on the north is [Tiger creek and] [61] a large and beautiful prairie, called Sauk prairie, the land being fine and well timbered on both sides the river. Pelicans [*Pelecanus erythrorhynchus*] were seen to-day. We made 6¾ miles, and camped at the lower point of a small island, along the north side of which we proceeded the next

fore we must agree with Gass that Tiger creek was not passed till the 20th, and carry Panther island to this date ; we must suppose Gass' "small creek on the north" to be little Tabo creek, on the *south*, not noted by Lewis and Clark. Then the 19th is all plain sailing, viz., first large island (Dover, 300 miles up); second large island, 305 miles up, between which two islands they had to tow the boat around a bluff, on the south (now known as Sheeps'-nose rock); mouths of both Tabo creeks, some small islands, and present town of Dover, 310 miles up ; then 7½ miles further to camp, on the south, "near a lake." This fetches out exactly ; for a lake, or lake bed, is shown, on the maps cited, at just the right spot. Next morning, the 20th, they speedily reach their "Tiger" creek, now called Crooked creek, which has a large island still at or near its mouth.

Tabo or Tabbo (properly Tabeau, personal name of a certain Canadian who was hereabouts) is still the name of two creeks, distinguished as Big and Little, lying wholly within Lafayette Co. Neither is shown on Lewis' map ; an unlettered trace seems to indicate one of them on Clark's. For Tiger creek, see next note.

[61] See last note. This is Tygers creek of Lewis' map, and Tyger creek of Clark's, now called Crooked creek or river, in Ray Co. L. and C.'s name survived for many years : thus, we find it on Nicollet's map of 1843, with Crooked creek as the name of a branch of this stream. Richmond, the county town of Ray, is on one of its small tributaries. But it had long before been named by D'Anville rivière Vaseuse (Muddy river), and is so marked on his map of 1752. So is Sauk prairie older than L. and C., having been so named by Perrin Du Lac in French form in 1805.

day, *June 21st*, but not without danger, in consequence of the sands and the rapidity of the water, which rose three inches last night. Behind another island come in from the south two creeks, called Eau-beau[62] or Clear-water creeks. On the north is a very remarkable bend, where the high lands approach the river, and form an acute angle at the head of a large island produced by a narrow channel through the point of the bend. We passed several other islands, and camped at 7½ miles on the south.

*June 22d.* The river rose during the night four inches. The water is very rapid and crowded with concealed timber. We passed two large islands and an extensive prairie on the south, beginning with a rich low land, and rising to the (*p. 17*) distance of 70 or 80 feet of rolling clear country. The thermometer at 3 p. m. was at 87° F. After coming

---

[62] Called "Hubert's" island and creek in the Summary Statement at the end of the work, and in Gass given as "Du Beau or Du Bois." In the text above the original misprint was "Eau, Beau, or Clear Water," where the first comma makes it read like three names of the two creeks. Worse is to come in this comedy of errors. Lewis' map of 1806 inscribes Bau-beaux, which also appears on the reduced copy first published November 4, 1887, in *Science*. Clark's map of 1814 traces the creeks but prints no name. Pike's map of 1810 makes the word Eabeace. Nicollet's, of 1843, marks the creeks, without name. Clark's MS. has Eue-bert, for which Biddle substituted Hubert, as above; Lewis' MS. shows Eubert's and Euebaux's. Brackenridge prints Ibar's. All these names refer to some person, represented as a Canadian *coureur de bois* or hunter, named Au Barre, or Herbert, or Hubert, or in some similar style. This being mistaken for a common noun, some maps print Chenal aux Heberts (plural). Now chenal is French for slough, and Major Long (or his printer) tries to explain the name thus : "The Great and Little Chenai au Barre, are two creeks entering the Missouri about a mile and a half from each other. Before the mouths of these two creeks is a large island, the slough or chenai dividing the island from the shore," etc. (Here "chenai" looks as if it were meant for the French chênaie, "oak grove.") Finally, the creeks received their present name of Great and Little Sniabar, or Snibar—a curious word, which I take to be a contraction of Chenal au Barre. Snibar is engraved on the General Land Office maps, and there is also a town of Snibar, in Lafayette Co. Close by the mouths of these creeks on the south of the Missouri are towns bearing the historic names of Wellington and Waterloo. These places are a few miles up river from Lexington, county seat of Lafayette, the future site of which the Expedition passed on the 20th, just 320 miles up the Missouri.

10½ miles we camped on the south, opposite a large creek, called Fire-prairie[63] river.

*June 23d.* The wind was against us this morning, and became so violent that we made only 3½ miles, and were obliged to lie-to during the day at a small island. This is separated from the northern side by a narrow channel which cannot be passed by boats, being choked by trees and drifted wood. Directly opposite, on the south, is a high commanding position, more than 70 feet above high-water mark, and overlooking the river, which is here of but little width. This spot has many advantages for a fort and trading-house with the Indians.* The river fell eight inches last night.

* The United States built, in September, 1808, a factory and a fort on this spot, which is very convenient for trading with the Osages, Ayauways, and Kansas.[64]  [Original note.]

[63] Present name of a creek on the *south* side, in Jackson Co., emptying into the Missouri at or near the junction of Lafayette Co., or shortened usually to Fire creek.  " So called from the circumstance of three or four Indians having been burned to death by the sudden conflagration of the dry grass in the meadows at its source," says Long (vol. i. p. 93 of the London ed., 1823).  But L. and C.'s creek of this name is on the *north*, as per text and Lewis' map, where the creek is laid down and lettered.  Gass also makes camp " on the south side opposite a large creek, called the Fire-prairie, and which is 60 yards wide."  There is no stream of any such size on the north of the Missouri, though there is one now called Clear creek, or Fishing creek, four or five miles higher up the Missouri on the north, which might be stretched to answer to L. and C.'s Fire-prairie creek, especially as its mouth may have shifted since their time.  But to do so would leave the modern Fire or Prairie creek nameless in Lewis and Clark.

[64] This spot is called Fort Point in the Summary Statement at the end of this work.  It is in what is now Jackson Co., Mo., about halfway between Lexington and Independence.  The fort of course is not named in the L. and C. MSS., but it is marked " Fort Clark " on Clark's map, 1814, and is given as " Fort Clark (or Osage) " in Brackenridge's Journal, 1814, p. 265 (to be distinguished from another Fort Clark, at the Mandans, in N. Dak.).  Fort Point also became known as Sibley, the name of the present town of Sibley, at or near the same place.  In 1819 it was the extreme frontier settlement.

Fort Osage was long a notable establishment.  In the summer of 1808 General Clark held a treaty with the Osage Indians, having been escorted to their nation by a troop of cavalry under Capt. M. Wherry from St. Charles, and the fort was built at once thereafter.  It was commanded in 1809 by Capt. Eli B. Clemson, 1st U. S. Infantry.

*June 24th.* We passed, at eight miles' distance, Hay cabin[65] creek, coming in from the south, about 20 yards wide, and so called from camps of straw built on it. To the north are some rocks projecting into the river, and a little beyond them is a creek on the same side, called Charaton Scarty[66]—that is, Charaton like the Otter. We halted,[67] after making 11½ miles, the country on both sides being fine and interspersed with prairies, in which we now see numerous herds of deer, pasturing in the plains or feeding on the young willows of the river.

[65] " Passed a creek on the south side called Depie," Gass, p. 19. This " Depie," elsewhere " Depre " and " Dispre," is meant for *d'Esprits* (of Spirits). No such word occurs here in the MS. of Clark, who writes " Hay Cabbin Creek," and the same is lettered on Lewis' map, 1806. It is now the Little Blue river, in Jackson Co., Mo.

[66] See note at date of June 10th. Since that was penned, I have come into possession of all the original manuscripts of Lewis and Clark which Nicholas Biddle had when he wrote this book, and several other field note-books which were at that time in the hands of President Jefferson. These throw new light on the puzzling word " Charaton." On June 10th, Clark wrote : " passed the two Rivers of Charletons which mouth together " ; on June 24th, he wrote : " Sharreton Carta," as the name of the creek now in question. Lewis' MSS. yield us " Charetton " in one place and " Shariton " in another. Now when Biddle struck these snags he upset, and wrote a letter to Clark (now before me), dated July 7th, 1810, asking : " What is the real name & spelling of the stream called Sharriton Carta, and also the Two Charletons ? Get some of the Frenchmen at St. Louis to put them down exactly as they should be printed." Clark's reply I never saw ; the upshot as above printed has hitherto defied conjecture. But the meaning is now clear. For " Charaton Scarty " read *Charretins écartés*, *i. e.*, two creeks, each named Charretin, which are separated or divergent in their courses, though emptying together into the Missouri. There are a pair of creeks in Clay Co., Mo., which exactly answer this description, and are in just the right place. Then for the attempted explanation, " like the Otter," read simply, "like the *other*," *i. e.*, like the two other rivers called by the same name, having one mouth, though they are separated (écartés) in their courses. The word Charretin (also Chartin) will be found in any good French dictionary. It is a derivative of Charrette, which we have seen before as a place-name on the Missouri.

[67] Gass notes a halt at noon to-day, in order, as he says, to " jirk " some meat which a party had brought in, and he explains that " jirk " is meat cut in small pieces and dried in the sun. Clark writes " jurk." The word as a verb is now generally spelled *jerk*, and jerked meat is known as *jerky*. It has nothing to do with the English verb of the same form (*jerk*), but is a corruption of a Chilian word, *charqui*, meaning sun-dried meat.

*June 25th.* A thick fog detained us till eight o'clock, when we set sail, and at three miles reached a bank of stone-coal on the north, which appeared to be very abundant. Just below it is a creek called after the bank La Charbon-nière.[68] Four miles further, on the southern side, comes in a small creek, called La Bénite.[69] The prairies here approach the river and contain many fruits, such as plums, raspber-ries, wild apples, and nearer the river vast quantities of mul-ber- (*p. 18*) ries. Our camp was at 13 miles' distance, on an island to the north, opposite some hills higher than usual—almost 160 or 180 feet.

*June 26th.* At one mile we passed, at the end of a small island, Blue-water[70] creek, which is about 30 yards wide at its entrance from the south.* Here the Missouri is con-fined within a narrow bed, and the current still more so by counter-currents or whirls on one side and a high bank on the other. We passed a small island and a sand-bar, where our tow-rope broke twice, and we rowed around with great exertions. We saw a number of parroquets [*Conurus carolinensis*], and killed some deer. After 9¾ miles we camped at the upper point of the mouth of the Kansas river.[71]

---

* A few miles up Blue-water creek are quarries of plaster of Paris [gypsum], since worked and brought down to St. Louis. [Original note.]

[68] Clark's MS. has "Chabonea," which Biddle erases and interlines *Charbon*. (See note at May 16th.)    This is now Rush creek, Clay Co., Mo.

[69] Called "Labenile," in Gass, by misprint ; in the original MSS. Benoit's and Bennet's ; Benito's found also. It is a personal name, whether Bénite (blessed) or Benêt (silly) ; one of this name was a factor of the Missouri Fur Co., 1811.    Now Mill creek, Jackson Co., Mo.    The fruits mentioned in this para-graph are : plums, probably *Prunus americana ;* raspberries, *Rubus strigosus ;* wild apples, *Pyrus coronaria ;* mulberries, *Morus rubra.*

[70] This is Perrin du Lac's R. de l'Eau Bleue, now Big Blue river, mouthing in Jackson Co., Mo., about halfway between Independence and Kansas City. Just below it, on the same side, is Rock creek, not noticed in the text—and yesterday the Expedition missed Shoal creek, on the north, in Clay Co.

[71] The Kansas, with its very numerous tributaries, waters the greater part of the present State of the same name, and by its great northern fork, the Republican river, waters also a southern portion of Nebraska. It heads in prairie, between sources of the South Platte and Arkansaw rivers, in the State of Colorado. At

Here we remained two days [June 27th, 28th], during which we made the necessary observations, recruited the party, and repaired the boat. The Kansas river takes its rise in the plains between the Arkansaw and Platte rivers, and pursues a course generally east till its junction with the Missouri, which is in latitude 38° 31' 13"; here it is 340¼ yards wide, though it is wider a short distance above the mouth. The Missouri itself is about 500 yards in width; the point of union is low and subject to inundations for 250 yards; it then rises a little above high-water mark, and continues so as far back as the hills. On the south of the Kansas the hills or high lands come within 1½ miles of the river; on the north of the Missouri they do not approach nearer than several miles; but on all sides the country is fine. The comparative specific gravities of the two rivers are, for the Missouri 78°, the Kansas 72°; the waters of the latter have a very disagreeable taste; the former has risen during yesterday and to-day about two feet. On the banks of the Kansas reside the Indians of the same name,[12] consisting of

its mouth are Wyandotte, Kas., and Kansas City, Mo. The Kansas is still sometimes called the Kaw. Some early French forms of the name on various maps are R. des Quans, R. Cans, R. des Kancés. R. des Padoucas et Kansez, etc., all derived from the Indians of the same names. The Lewis and Clark MSS. spell the name in a dozen different ways. (See note below.) Up to this point the Missouri river has pursued its tortuous way for 388 miles through Missouri State, on the whole nearly east-west. But at the mouth of the Kansas it turns northwesterly, and thence separates the northeast corner of Kansas from Missouri. The Kansas counties ascending are Leavenworth, Atchison, and Doniphan. The Missouri counties are Platte, Buchanan, Andrew, and Holt. The principal points on this section of the river above Wyandotte and Kansas City, are Leavenworth and Atchison, Kas., and St. Joseph, Mo. Some distance up the Kansas river is Topeka. In this corner of Kansas are the Indian Reservations of the Sacs and Foxes, Iowas, Kickapoos, and Pottawattomies.

[12] As already stated, the name is spelled throughout this work Kanzas, which I uniformly alter to the only form now current, Kansas. In books and maps of the period it varies much—with initial c or qu instead of k; first vowel a or o; without final s, in the singular, and in the curious double plural which the word early acquired ending variously in -ces, -cez, -ses, -sez, -sais, etc.; in adjectival form Canzan or Kanzan. The n in the name was scarcely nasalized. Lewis renders the word Kar'sa, in his Statistical View, 1806; Kaw is

two villages, one at about 20, the other 40 leagues (*p. 19*) from its mouth, and amounting to about 300 men. They once lived 24 leagues higher than the Kansas [river], on the south bank of the Missouri, and were then more numerous ; but they have been reduced and banished by the Sauks and Ayauways, who being better supplied with arms have an advantage over the Kansas, though the latter are not less fierce or warlike than themselves. This nation is now hunting on the plains for buffalo,[73] which our hunters have seen for the first time.

from the French rendering, which Lewis prints " Kâh," as a nickname. The Kanza, or Kansa (Ka$^n$'ze) Indians, were a tribe of the great Siouan family, now enumerated as the fifth of eighteen such tribes. The tribe was estimated in Lewis' day at a total of 1,300 ; there are now reported 198 at Osage Agency, Indian Terr., with 15 at school in Lawrence, Kas., and another at Carlisle, Pa. They traded with merchants of St. Louis, warred with all their neighbors, but were sometimes at peace with the Otoes and Missouris, with whom they inter-married to some extent. Lewis represented their population as rather increasing in 1805. " At present they are dissolute, lawless banditti ; frequently plunder their traders and commit depredations on persons ascending and descending the Missouri. . . These people, as well as the Great and Little Osages, are stationary at their villages from about the 15th of March to the 15th of May, and again from the 15th of August to the 15th of October : the balance of the year is appropriated to hunting. They cultivate corn, &c." Statistical View, English ed., 1807, p. 11. See also Say, in Long's Exp. R. Mts., 1823, I., chaps. vi, vii.

[73] The bison, *Bison americanus*, by far the most conspicuous and important animal which our travelers have to notice in this work, where it will be repeatedly mentioned as the buffaloe (which I alter as above ; the L. and C. MSS. usually have buffalow). The present note is instructive in connection with the geographical distribution of the species in 1804.

The Observations, etc., of Wm. Dunbar and Dr. Hunter—the fourth of the documents accompanying President Jefferson's Message communicating to Congress Lewis and Clark's discoveries—first published in 1806, contains a curious passage, which I quote from p. 299 of the English reprint, 1807, not having the original before me as I write :

" The great western prairies, besides the herds of wild cattle, (bison, commonly called buffaloe) are also stocked with vast numbers of wild goat (not resembling the domestic goat) extremely swift footed. As the description given of this goat is not perfect, it may from its swiftness prove to be the antelope or it possibly may be a goat which has escaped from the Spanish settlements of New Mexico. A Canadian, who had been much with the Indians to the westward, speaks of a wool-bearing animal larger than a sheep, the wool much mixed with hair, which he had seen in large flocks. He pretends

*June 29th.* We set out late in the afternoon, and having passed a sand-bar, near which the boat was almost lost, and a large island on the north, we camped at 7¼ miles on the same side in the low lands, where the rushes are so thick that it is troublesome to walk through them.

Early the next morning, [June] 30th, we reached, at five miles' distance, the mouth of a river coming in from the north, and called by the French Petite Rivière Platte, or Little Shallow [74] river; it is about 60 yards wide at its mouth. A few of the party who ascended informed us, that the lands on both sides are good, and that there are several falls well calculated for mills. The wind was from the southwest, and the weather oppressively warm, the thermometer standing at 96° at 3 o'clock p. m. One mile beyond this is a small creek on the south, at five miles from which we camped on the same side, opposite the lower point of an island called Diamond island. The land on the north between the Little Shallow river and the Missouri is not good, and subject to overflow; on the south it is higher and better timbered.

*July 1st.* We proceeded along the north side of Dia-

also to have seen a unicorn, the single horn of which, he says, rises out of the forehead and curls back, conveying the idea of the fossil cornu ammonis."

Here in a few lines of one paragraph are unequivocally noticed four of the most remarkable ruminants of Western North America. 1. The buffalo, *Bison americanus.* 2. The antelope, *Antilocapra americana.* 3. The Rocky Mountain goat, *Haplocerus montanus,* possibly the actual basis of the "woolly horse" legends of the West. 4. The Rocky Mountain sheep, *Ovis montana,* which, though not a "unicorn," has horns quite like the cornu Ammonis, and in fact is a near relative of the Barbary sheep, *Ovis ammon* (aoudad or bearded argali, *Ammotragus tragelaphus*).

The earliest mention I have seen of the antelope in English print occurs in Lewis' Statistical View of the Indians, first published in 1806. There, in his notice of the trade of the Maha (Omaha) Indians, he says (p. 16 of the English ed. of 1807): "Skins of the Missouri antelope, called cabri, by the inhabitants of the Illinois." This word *cabri,* also spelled *cabrit, cabra, cabrie,* and *cabree,* is the Spanish *cabron,* a goat.

[74] Present name, Little Platte. Platte City is on this river, in county of same name, diagonally opposite Leavenworth; at its mouth is Parkville. The position of the mouth of the river has changed much since 1804.

mond [75] island, where a small creek [we] called Biscuit creek empties.   At 1½ miles above the island is a large sand-bar in the middle of the river, beyond which we stopped to re-fresh the men, who suffered very much from the heat.   Here we observed great quantities of grapes and raspberries. Between one and two miles further are three islands, [*p. 20*] and a creek on the south known by the French name of Remore.[76]   The main current, which is now on the south side of the largest of the three islands, ran three years [ago], as we were told, on the north, and there was then no appearance of the two smaller islands.   At 4½ miles we reached the lower point of a cluster of islands, two large and two small, called Isles des Parcs [77] or Field Islands. Paccaun [pecan, *Carya olivæformis*] trees were this day seen, and large quantities of deer and turkeys [*Meleagris americana*] on the banks.   We had advanced 12 miles.

*July 2d.*   We left camp, opposite to which is a high and beautiful prairie on the southern side, and passed up the south of the islands, which are high meadows, and a creek on the north called Parc [or Park] creek.   Here for half an hour the river became covered with drift-wood, which rendered navigation dangerous, and was probably caused by the giving way of some sand-bar, which had detained the wood.   After making five miles we passed a stream on the south called Turkey creek, near a sand-bar, where we could scarcely stem the current with twenty oars and all the poles we had.   On the north at about two miles further is a large island called by the Indians Wau-car-da-

[75] Present name : so called from its shape.   Clark wrote Dimond.   Biscuit creek, so named by Clark, is uncertain ; I find it on no map examined ; possibly it had some connection with a former course of the Little Platte.

[76] " Remore " is certainly a mangled word.   It so stands very plainly in Clark's MS., which perhaps gives us the required clew ; for he says " Remore (or Tree Frog)," whence I conjecture *Grenouille* to be the word intended.   The stream is now known as Nine Mile creek, in Wyandotte Co., Kas.

[77] Isles des Parques in Clark's MS.; Isles des Parcs or Four Islands of Long, 1823 ; one of them is J. de Parc of Perrin du Lac, and Park Island of Nicollet, 1843 ; now Spar island.   The situation is nearly opposite Leavenworth, Kas.

war-card-da,[78] or the Bear-medicine island. Here we landed and replaced our mast, which had been broken three days ago, by running against a tree overhanging the river. Thence we proceeded, and after night stopped on the north side, above the island, having come 11½ miles. Opposite our camp is a valley, in which was situated an old village of the Kansas, between two high points of land, on the bank of the river. About a mile in the rear of the village was a small fort, built by the French on an elevation. There are now no traces of the village, but the situation of the fort may be recognized by some remains of chimneys, and the general outline of the fortification, as well as by the fine spring which supplied it with water. The party who were stationed here were probably cut off by the Indians, as there are no accounts of them.

(*p. 21*) *July 3d.* A gentle breeze from the south carried us 11¼ miles this day, past two islands, one a small willow-island, the other large, and called by the French Isle des Vaches,[79] or Cow island. At the head of this island, on the

[78] *Sic*—one word with five hyphens. At first sight it looks like a misprint meant for two forms of one word, as if "Wau-car-da *or* war-card-da." I have been informed that probably it is meant for *Wakan'da wakhdhi'*, "(where) Wakanda was slain"—Wakanda being somebody or something named after the Thunder-god. This conjecture is borne out by the translation, "Bear Medicine," showing that there was some mystery or superstition about the place, as anything that an Indian does not understand is "medicine." But Clark's MS. gives occasion for a different reading. His words are: "called by the Indians Wau-car-ba War-cand-da [two words, with two hyphens apiece] or the Bear Medesin Island." Here the *second* word, not the first, is "Wakanda" or "Medicine," and the first word has *b* where the text prints *d*. Lewis' MS. has a similar word, not quite the same. The island is marked Wasabe Wakandige on the map of Nicollet, who puts a Kickapoo village on the south bank of the Missouri at the head of it. The island is now on the south side of the river, just above the present site of Fort Leavenworth, and in the immediate vicinity is Kickapoo City, Kas. Its present name is Kickapoo island.

[79] Isle de Vache, in the singular, in Clark's MS. Cow island is the present or a recent name, for which Buffalo island used to be sometimes said, when female buffaloes were the only cows in the country. Long gives Isle au Vache, and notes that Captain Martin's detachment wintered here in 1818-19. Here Major Long held his council with the Kansas, Aug. 24th, 1819.

northern shore, is a large pond containing beaver,[80] and fowls of different kinds. After passing a bad sand-bar, we stopped on the south side at an old trading-house, which is now deserted, and half a mile beyond it camped on the south. The land is fine along the river, and for some distance back. We observed black walnut [*Juglans nigra*] and oak, among the timber; also honeysuckle [*Lonicera* sp.] and the buck's-eye [buckeye, probably *Æsculus glabra*] with the nuts on it.

The morning of the 4th of July was announced by the discharge of our gun. At one mile we reached the mouth of a bayeau [bayou] or creek,[81] coming from a large lake on the north side, which appears as if it had once been the bed of the river, to which it runs parallel for several miles. The water of it is clear and supplied by a small creek and several springs, and the number of goslings which we saw on it induced us to call it Gosling lake. It is about three-quarters of a mile wide, and seven or eight miles long. One of our men was bitten by a snake, but a poultice of bark and gunpowder was sufficient to cure the wound. At 10¼ miles we reached a creek on the south, about 12 yards wide, coming from an extensive prairie which approached the borders of the river. To this creek, which had no name, we gave that of Fourth of July creek; above it is a high mound, where three Indian paths center, and from which is a very extensive prospect. After 15 miles' sail we came-to on the north a little above a creek on the south side, about 30 yards wide, which we called Independence creek, in honor of the day, which we could celebrate only by an evening gun, and an additional gill of whisky to the men.[82]

---

[80] *Castor canadensis*, which becomes extremely abundant higher up the Missouri, and on most of its headwaters, in and near the Rocky mountains.

[81] Called Pond creek in Gass, p. 20. Nicollet notes an old cut-off here (1843). Owen's map marks a Sugar creek and lake.

[82] Gass says of this celebration: "One of our people got snake-bitten, but not seriously;" he discreetly says nothing about the whisky. This man was Joseph Fields. The Expedition to-day passes the present site of Atchison, Kas., be-

*July 5th.* We crossed over to the south and came along the bank of an extensive and beautiful prairie, inter- (*p. 22*) spersed with copses of timber, and watered by Independence creek. On this bank formerly stood the second village of the Kansas; [judging] from the remains it must have been once a large town. We passed several bad sandbars, and a small creek to the south, which we called Yellow-ochre[63] creek, from a bank of that mineral a little above it. The river continues to fall. On the shores are great quantities of summer and fall grapes [*Vitis æstivalis* and *V. cordifolia*], berries, and wild roses [*Rosa setigera*]. Deer are not so abundant as usual, but there are numerous tracks of elk around us. We camped at ten miles' distance on the south side under a high bank, opposite which was a low land covered with tall rushes, and some timber.

*July 6th.* We set sail, and at one mile passed a sand-bar, three miles further an island, and a prairie to the north, at the distance of four miles, called Reevey's[64] prairie, after a man who was killed there; at which place the river is confined to a very narrow channel, and by a sand-bar from the south. Four miles beyond is another sand-bar terminated by a small willow-island, and forming a very considerable bend in the river toward the north. The sand of the bar is light, intermixed with small pebbles and some pit-coal. The river falls slowly; and, owing either to the muddiness of its water, or the extreme heat of the weather, the men perspire profusely. We camped on the south, having made

tween Fourth of July and Independence creeks. The latter stream is still so called. It empties into the Missouri in Atchison Co.

[63] " Yellow-oaker " creek of Clark's MS. which to-day cites De Bourgmont, concerning the Kansas and Missouris, as they were about 1724. The Expedition to-day passes the Wasabi Wachonda of Perrin du Lac (to be distinguished from the island of the same name passed July 2d, see note there), and camps in Doniphan Co., Kas., apparently close by the creek marked Yellow-ochre on Nicollet's map.

[64] So in Clark's MS.; elsewhere, Revoe's. I have no clew to the correct form of the name.

12 miles. The bird called whip-poor-will [*Antrostomus vociferus*] sat on the boat for some time.[85]

*July 7th.* The rapidity of the water obliged us to draw the boat along with ropes. At 6¾ miles we came to a sand-bar, at a point opposite a fine rich prairie on the north, called St. Michael's. The prairies of this neighborhood have the appearance of distinct farms, divided by narrow strips of woodland, which follow the borders of the small runs leading to the river. Above this, about a mile, is a cliff of yellow clay on the north. At four o'clock we passed a narrow part of the channel, where the water is confined within a bed 200 yards wide, the current running directly against the southern bank, with (*p. 23*) no sand on the north to confine it or break its force. We made 14 miles, and halted on the north, after which we had a violent gust about seven o'clock. One of the hunters saw in a pond to the north which we passed yesterday a number of young swans. We saw a large rat,[86] and killed a wolf [*Canis lupus occidentalis*]. Another of our men had a stroke of the sun; he was bled, and took a preparation of niter, which relieved him considerably.

*July 8th.* We set out early, and soon passed a small creek

[85] Gass here names a "Whipperwill" creek from this circumstance, p. 20, apparently that now called Peter's creek, in Doniphan Co., Kas. The Expedition approaches St. Joseph, Mo., to be passed to-morrow.

[86] This is the wood-rat, *Neotoma floridana*, the same species as that mentioned on p. 11. No means of identifying the species is here given, but Gass furnishes the requisite information. He says at this date (p. 20): "Killed a wolf and a large wood-rat on the bank. The principal difference between it and the commoner rat is, its having hair on the tail." *N. floridana* is now known to extend up the Missouri about as far as the mouth of the Niobrara. It was unknown to science when thus discovered by Lewis and Clark. It was rediscovered by Mr. Thomas Say, of Major Long's party, on the Mississippi, a little below St. Louis, at the mouth of the Merameg river, June 7th, 1819. It had been named *Mus floridanus* by Mr. George Ord in 1818 (Bull. Soc. Philom. Phila., 1818, p. 181). In 1825 Messrs. Say and Ord made this species the type of their new genus *Neotoma*, founded in the Journ. Acad. Nat. Sci., Phila., IV. pt. ii. p. 346; see p. 352, pl. x. figs. 1-4. See Long's Exped. R. Mts., I. 1823, p. 54 (p. 50 of the English 3-vol. ed.). Another species of the same genus, *N. cinerea*, of the Rocky mountains, was also discovered on this Expedition.

on the north, which we called Ordway's [87] creek, from our sergeant of that name, who had been sent on shore with the horses, and went up it. On the same side are three small islands, one of which is the Little Nodawa, and a large island called the Great Nowada [*sic*—read Nodawa], extending more than five miles, and containing 7,000 or 8,000 acres of high good land, rarely overflowed ; this is one of the largest islands of the Missouri. It is separated from the northern shore by a small channel from 45 to 80 yards wide, up which we passed, and found near the western extremity of the island the mouth of the river Nodawa.[88] This river pursues nearly a southern course, is navigable for boats to some distance, and about 70 yards wide above the mouth, though not so wide immediately there, as the mud from the Missouri contracts its channel. At 12¼ miles we camped on the north side, near the head of Nodawa island, opposite a smaller one in the middle of the river. Five of the men were this day sick with violent headaches. The river continues to fall.

*July 9th.* We passed the island opposite which we last night camped, and saw near the head of it a creek falling in from a pond on the north, to which we gave the name of Pike pond, from the numbers of that animal which some of our party saw from the shore. The wind changed at eight o'clock from N.E. to S.W., and brought rain. At six miles we passed the mouth of Monter's [89] creek on the

[87] Mentioned, but without name, in Clark's MS. of this date. There is a creek in Andrew Co., Mo., which answers to this ; but its present name I do not know.

[88] Nadawa in Clark's MS., accented Nā-dā-wä ; Nodowa on his map, 1814 ; Nodana on Lewis' map, 1806 ; Nodowa on Pike's, 1810 ; Nodoway in Long's text, 1823 ; Nadoway in Nicollet's ; Perrin du Lac has Madavoay ; Lapie, 1821, marks Nodaoua on his map ; Bradbury spells Naduet. The word is Indian, and means some kind of snake ; hence the river has sometimes been called Snake river. The name settled into Nodoway of present geographers. There is also a Nodoway Co., and a town of the same name, in Andrew Co., Mo. The river separates Holt Co. on the west from portions of Andrew and Nodoway Co. on the east ; higher up it runs entirely in the latter, but quite near the border of Atchison Co. Its sources are still further north.

[89] So in Clark's MS., erased and Montain's interlined by Biddle, but Mon-

south; and two miles above, a few cabins, where one of our party had camped (*p. 24*) with some Frenchmen about two years ago. Further on we passed an island on the north, opposite some cliffs on the south side, near which Loup[90] or Wolf river falls into the Missouri. This river is about 60 yards wide, heads near the same sources as the Kansas,[91] and is navigable for boats at some distance up. At 14 miles we camped on the south side.

*July* 10*th*. We proceeded by a prairie on the upper side of Wolf river, and at four miles passed a creek 15 yards wide, on the south, called Pape's[92] creek after a Spaniard of that name, who killed himself there. At six miles we dined on an island called by the French Isle de Salomon,[93] or Solomon's island, opposite which on the south is a beautiful plain covered with grass, intermixed with wild rye and a kind of wild potato.[94] After making ten miles we stopped for the night on the northern side, opposite a cliff of yellow clay. The river has neither risen nor fallen to-day. On the north the low land is very extensive, and covered with vines; on the south, the hills approach nearer the river, and back of them commence the plains. There are a great many goslings along the banks.

*July* 11*th*. After three miles' sailing we came to a willow-island on the north side, behind which enters a creek called by the Indians Tarkio.[95] Above this creek on the north

ter's restored in the text. The stream is now Charleston creek, Doniphan Co., Kas.

[90] It is the Rivière du Loup of early French maps, now called Wolf river, running in northeastern Kansas, and reaching the Missouri through Doniphan Co. Its mouth is 520 miles up the Missouri. This day's camp was just beyond it.

[91] Not nearly—for this is a comparatively short stream.

[92] Clark wrote "a creek called Pappie"; now Cedar creek, Doniphan Co., Kas.

[93] Clark's MS. has "Isld. called de Salamin," which Biddle altered as above.

[94] The wild rye is probably *Elymus striatus*. The wild potato is questionably a species of *Solanum*; were the locality further northwest, we might identify it as a leguminous plant, the pomme de terre of the French, *Psoralea esculenta*.

[95] "Tarico" in Gass: now Little Tarkio; a sloughy stream, whose waters have leaked into the Missouri in places at least 20 miles apart. The lowermost of these had some connection with the Pike pond of July 9th, close to the Noda-way river. The uppermost, of July 11th, is now at the 530th mile point.

the lowlands are subject to overflow, and further back
the undergrowth, of vines particularly, is so abundant
that they can scarcely be passed. Three miles from the
[Little] Tarkio we camped on a large sand-island on
the north, immediately opposite the [Big] Nemahaw
river.

*July* 12*th.* We remained here to-day for the purpose of
refreshing the party, and making lunar observations. The
[Big] Nemahaw [96] empties into the Missouri from the south,
and is 80 yards wide at the confluence, which is in lat. 39°
55' 56". Captain Clarke ascended it in the perioque [*sic*]
about two miles, to the mouth of a small creek on the lower
side. On going ashore he found on the level plain several
artificial mounds or graves, and on the adjoining hills others
of a larger size. This appearance indicates sufficiently the
former population of this country, the mounds being certainly intended as tombs. The Indians of the Missouri
still preserve the custom of interring the dead on high
ground. From the top of the highest mound a delightful
prospect presented itself ; the level and extensive meadows
watered by the Nemahaw, and enlivened by the few trees
and shrubs skirting the borders of the river and its tributary
streams ; the low land of the Missouri covered with undulating grass, nearly five feet high, gradually rising to a
second plain, where rich weeds and flowers are interspersed
with copses of the Osage plum ; further back are seen small

[96] This is also spelled Nimehaw, Nimmeha, and with several vowel variations ;
on Clark's map, by mistake, engraved Gd. Hemawhaw ; on Pike's map,
Nemshaw ; on Long's, Nemawhaw ; some old French spellings are Nidmahaw
and Nimakas ; the present form of the word is Nemaha. There is a county of
this name in Nebraska. At this point the Expedition has passed that section of
the river which separates the northeast corner of Kansas from Missouri, and is
on that short section where the river separates the southeast corner of Nebraska
from Missouri—with Holt and Atchison Cos., Mo., on the right ascending the
river, and Richardson and Nemaha Cos., Neb., on the left hand going up.
The parallel of 40° N. marks off these two sections of the Missouri, and the
Expedition crossed this parallel July 11th. Hence the latitude given above is
several minutes out of the way, the mouth of the Big Nemaha being north
of 40°, and almost 540 miles up the Missouri.

groves of trees ; an abundance of grapes; the wild cherry [97] of the Missouri, resembling our own, but larger, and growing on a small bush ; and the choke-cherry, which we observed for the first time. Some of the grapes gathered to-day are nearly ripe. On the south of the [Big] Nemahaw, about a quarter of a mile from its mouth, is a cliff of freestone, on which are various inscriptions and marks made by the Indians. The sand-island where we are camped is covered with the two species of willow, broad- and narrow-leaved.

*July* 13*th.* We proceeded at sunrise with a fair wind from the south, and at two miles passed the mouth of a small river on the north, called Big Tarkio.[98]   A channel from the bed of the Missouri once ran into this river, and formed an island called St. Joseph's ;[99] but the channel is now filled up, and the island is added to the northern shore. Further on to the south is situated an extensive plain, covered with a grass resembling timothy in its general appearance, except the seed, which is like flaxseed, and also a number of grape-vines. At twelve miles we passed an island on the north, above which is a large sand-bar [100] covered with willows; and at 20½ miles stopped on a large sand-bar in the middle of the river, opposite a high, handsome prairie which extends to the hills four or five miles distant, though near (*p. 26*) the bank the land is low and subject to be overflowed.

[97] This is probably *Prunus pumila.*   The choke-cherry next named is *P. virginiana.*   The willows are two species of *Salix,* but uncertain ; that called the narrow-leaved may be *S. longifolia.*

[98] Present name ; distinctively Big Tarkio river, to discriminate it from the Little Tarkio, which latter has entered the Missouri at points lower down, one of them near the mouth of the Nodaway. (See note [95], date of July 11th, and recall the creek mentioned on July 9th, as falling in from Pike pond.) Both the Tarkios run in Atchison and thence through Holt Co., Mo.

[99] As by Perrin du Lac, in French form. Just below this, at the 540th mile up the Missouri, is now an island.   This is marked Antelope island on Nicollet's map, 1843.

[100] Now an island which shows on the Mo. R. Comm. map, next below the 560th mile point.   An unnoticed stream passed to-day, on the south, is Winnebago creek, Richardson Co., Neb.

This day was exceedingly fine and pleasant, a storm of wind and rain from the N.N.E., last night, having cooled the air.

*July 14th.* We had some hard showers of rain before seven o'clock, when we set out. We had just reached the end of the sand-island, and seen the opposite banks falling in, and so lined with timber that we could not approach it without danger, when a sudden squall from the northeast struck the boat on the starboard qnarter, and would have certainly dashed her to pieces on the sand-island, if the party had not leaped into the river, and with the aid of the anchor and cable kept her off. The waves dashed over her for the space of 40 minutes; after which, the river became almost instantaneously calm and smooth. The two periogues were ahead, in a situation nearly similar, but fortunately no damage was done to the boats or the loading. The wind having shifted to the southeast, we came, at the distance of two miles, to an island on the north, where we dined. One mile above, on the same side of the river, is a small factory, where a merchant [101] of St. Louis traded with the Ottoes and Pawnees two years ago. Near this is an extensive lowland, part of which is overflowed occasionally; the rest is rich and well timbered. The wind again changed to northwest by north. At 7½ miles, we reached the lower point of a large island, on the north side. A small distance above this point is a river called by the Maha [Omaha] Indians Nishnahbatona. [102] This is a considerable creek, nearly as large as Mine river, and runs parallel to the Missouri the greater part of its course, being 50 yards wide at the mouth. In the prairies or

[101] Clark's MS. says " Mr. Bennet of St. Louis." There was a William Bennet, who is mentioned in Billon's Annals, p. 106, but is not identifiable as this person, especially as there were several persons named Benoit.

[10] Elsewhere in the text Neeshnabatona, as first in Clark's MS.; in Gass Wash-ba-to-nan, p. 22 ; Nishmahbatana of Pike's map ; Nishnabotona of Brackenridge ; Nishnebottona of Long's map; Nishnabatona of Nicollet and of Lapie ; Nichinibatone, of Perrin du Lac ; Nichinanbatonais, of Collot's map. The modern name is commonly Nishnabotona or Nishnabotna. This is a notable side-stream of the Missouri, falling in through Atchison Co.,

glades we saw wild timothy, lamb's-quarter, cuckleberries,[103] and, on the edges of the river, summer grapes, plums, and gooseberries. We also saw to-day, for the first time, some elk, at which some of the party shot, but at too great a distance. We camped on the north side of the island, a little above the Nishnahbatona, having made nine miles. The river fell a little.

(*p. 27*) *July* 15*th.* A thick fog prevented our leaving the camp before seven. At about four miles we reached the extremity of the large island,[104] and crossing to the south, at the distance of 7 miles, arrived at the Little Nemaha [in Nemaha Co., Neb.], a small river from the south, 40 yards wide a little above its mouth, but contracting, as do almost all the waters emptying into the Missouri, at its confluence. At 9¾ miles, we camped on a woody point, on the south. Along the southern bank is a rich lowland covered with pea-vine and rich weeds, and watered by small streams rising in the adjoining prairies. They are rich, and though with abundance of grass, have no timber except what grows near the water; interspersed through both are grape-vines, plums of two kinds, two species of wild cherries, hazel-nuts, and gooseberries. On the south there is one unbroken plain; on the north the river is skirted with some timber, behind which the plain extends four or five miles to the hills, which seem to have little wood.

Mo.; on it is the county town of Rockport. Across the Missouri river here is Nemaha Co., Neb., with Auburn as its county town. Atchison Co. is the extreme northwest corner of the State of Missouri; over the State line is Fremont Co., Ia.; and through the southwest corner of Iowa is most of the extent of the Nishnabotona and its tributaries.

[103] This looks like a misprint for huckleberries; but it is a mistake for cockle-burs, for I find "cuckle burs" in Clark's MS. of this passage. The common cockle-bur or clot-bur is *Xanthium strumarium*, a weedy composite plant with close spiny involucres. The lamb's-quarter is the familiar *Chenopodium album*, a succulent weed often used for greens. The timothy, frequently mentioned in our text, is uncertain. The true timothy is a grass, *Phleum pratense*.

[104] An island answering to this appears at the 570th mile point of the Mo. R. Comm. map, and Gass names an Elk island at this date. This is the Isle Achoven of Perrin du Lac, and Morgan's island of Nicollet's map.

*July* 16*th.* We continued our route between a large island opposite last night's camp and an extensive prairie on the south. About six miles, we came to another large island, called Fairsun [105] island, on the same side; above which is a spot where about 20 acres of the hill have fallen into the river. Near this is a cliff of sandstone for two miles, which is much frequented by birds. At this place the river is about a mile wide, but not deep; as the timber, or saw- yers, [106] may be seen scattered across the whole of its bottom. At 20 miles' distance, we saw on the south an island, called by the French L'Isle Chance [*sic* [107]], or Bald island, opposite a large prairie, which we called Bald-pated prairie, from a ridge of naked hills which bound it, running parallel with the river as far as we could see, at from three to six miles' distance. To the south the hills touch the river. We camped a quarter of a mile beyond this, in a point of woods on the north side. The river continues to fall.

(*p. 28*) *July* 17*th.* We remained here this day, in order to make observations and correct the chronometer, which ran down on Sunday. The latitude we found to be 40° 27′ 5 $\frac{4}{10}$″ north. The observation of the time proved our chro- nometer too slow by 6′ 51 $\frac{6}{10}$″. The highlands bear from our camp N. 25° W., up the river. Captain Lewis rode up the country, and saw the Nishnahbatona, ten or twelve miles from its mouth, at a place not more than 300 yards

[105] *Sic*—one word; properly Fair Sun, as written by Clark, being from the French isle à Beau Soleil; now Sun island, lying halfway between the 580th and 590th mile points.

[106] A sawyer is a snag or timber so fixed in the water that it oscillates or bobs up and down under the varying stress of the current, and forms a special danger to navigation. A firmly embedded snag is called a planter.

[107] Misprint for F. *chauve* (bald). Clark wrote a word now blind, having been over-written and turned into Chauven's, above which Biddle interlined Chauve clearly; but after all this " Chance " was printed. The course of the river pur- sued by the Expedition at this point has altered greatly. It now nowhere approaches the Nishnabotona so closely as the text of July 17th states. In the present shorter and straighter course of the Missouri along here, there is a large island beginning at the 590th mile point. The camp of July 16th–17th is in the N. W. corner of Atchison Co., Mo.

from the Missouri, and a little above our camp. It then passes near the foot of the Bald Hills, and is at least six feet below the level of the Missouri. On its banks are oak, walnut, and mulberry. The common current of the Missouri, taken with the log, is 50 fathoms in 40″, at some places, and even 20″.

*July* 18*th.* The morning was fair, and a gentle wind, from S.E. by S., carried us along between the prairie on the north, and Bald island to the south; opposite the middle of which the Nishnahbatona approaches the nearest to the Missouri. The current here ran 50 fathoms in 41″. At 13½ miles, we reached an island on the north, near to which the banks overflow; while on the south, the hills project over the river and form high cliffs. At one point a part of the cliff, nearly three-quarters of a mile in length, and about 200 feet in height, has fallen into the river. It is composed chiefly of sandstone intermixed with an iron ore of bad quality; near the bottom is a soft slatestone with pebbles. We passed several bad sand-bars in the course of the day, made 18 miles, and camped [108] on the south, opposite the lower point of the Oven islands. The country around is generally divided into prairies, with little timber, except on low points, islands, and near creeks, and that consisting of cottonwood, mulberry, elm, and sycamore.[109] The river falls fast. An Indian dog came to the bank; he appeared to have been lost and was nearly starved; we gave him some food, but he would not follow us.

(*p. 29*) *July* 19*th.* The Oven[110] islands are small and two in

---

[108] In Otoe Co., Neb., a little below Nebraska City. This day's journey carries the Expedition past the boundary between Missouri and Iowa, where they enter upon that section of the river which separates Iowa on the east from Nebraska on the west.

[109] These trees, named in that order, are *Populus monilifera, Morus rubra, Ulmus americana*, and *Platanus occidentalis*. The last is the button-wood or American plane-tree.

[110] Between 600 and 610 miles up river were several islands, sometimes called Oven; for example, Nicollet's map shows two, some distance apart, called Upper and Lower. At the 610th mile point the Mo. R. Comm. map shows two abreast.

number; one near the south shore, the other in the middle
of the river.  Opposite to them is the prairie called Terrien's Oven, from a trader of that name.  At 4½ miles, we
reached some high cliffs of a yellow earth, on the south,
near which are two beautiful runs of water, rising in the
adjacent prairies, one of them with a deer-lick about 200
yards from its mouth.  In this neighborhood we observed
some iron ore in the bank.  At 2½ miles above the runs,
a large portion of the hills, for nearly three-quarters of a
mile, has fallen into the river.  We camped on the western
extremity of an island,[111] in the middle of the river, having
made 10¾ miles.[112]  The river falls a little.  The sand-bars
which we passed to-day are more numerous, and the rolling
sands more frequent and dangerous, than any we have seen ;
these obstacles increasing as we approach the Platte river.
The Missouri here is wider also than below, where the
timber on the banks resists the current ; while here the
prairies which approach are more easily washed and undermined.  The hunters have brought for the last few days no
quadruped but deer ; great quantities of young geese are
seen to-day.  One of the hunters brought calamus, which
he had gathered opposite our camp, and a large quantity of
sweet-flag.[113]

*July 20th.*  There was a heavy dew last night, and this
morning was foggy and cool.  We passed at about three
miles' distance a small willow-island to the north, and a creek
on the south, about 25 yards wide, called by the French

one large and the other small, which may be those of our text, but are certainly
not Nicollet's.  As to the name Terrien's Oven, I suspect a snag.  Clark wrote
twice, July 18th and 19th, a phrase " Four le tourtue," or " tourtu," or
" tourtre "—the last word a little blind in ending, but its first syllable plain, and
a large capital F for the first word.  Then he speaks of the "Baker's Oven
Islands," and Biddle interlines " Baker's Oven " at the entry of the 18th.  This
does not agree with the printed text, and the case remains obscure.

[111] Called Island of Willows by Gass, p. 23.

[112] A little above the present site of Nebraska City, Neb., near the boundary
between Cass and Otoe Cos., Neb. ; on the other hand is Fremont Co., Ia.

[113] Probably by collating different journals, Biddle introduces calamus *and*
sweet-flag.  These are the same well-known plant, *Acorus calamus.*

L'Eau qui Pleure, or the Weeping Water,[114] which empties just above a cliff of brown clay. Thence we made 2½ miles to another island; three miles further to a third, six miles beyond which is a fourth island;[115] at the head of which we camped on the southern shore; in all 18 miles. The party who walked on the shore to-day found the plains to the south rich, but much parched (*p. 30*) with frequent fires, and with no timber, except the scattering trees about the sources of the runs, which are numerous and fine. On the north is a similar prairie country. The river continues to fall. A large yellow wolf was this day killed.

For a month past the party have been troubled with boils, and occasionally with the dysentery. These were large tumors, which broke out under the arms, on the legs, and generally in the parts most exposed to action, which sometimes became too painful to permit the men to work. After remaining some days, they disappeared without any assistance, except a poultice of the bark of the elm, or of Indian meal. This disorder, which we ascribe to the muddiness of the river-water, has not affected the general health of the party, which is quite as good as, if not better than, that of the same number of men in any other situation.

*July* 21*st*. We had a breeze from the southeast, by the aid of which we passed, at about ten miles, a willow-island

[114] "Water-which-cries, or the Weeping stream," Gass, p. 20; "l'Eue que pleure, or the water which cry's," Clark, MS., with "Weeping Water" interlined by Biddle, to whom perhaps we owe the present alliterative name of that stream which makes into the Missouri at the junction of Otoe and Cass Cos. The French form occurs in Perrin du Lac.

[115] Some of these islands are called Trudeau's on Nicollet's map, and others, 5 Barrel islands. Here is also a certain Five Barrel creek on the north, not noticed in our text, but so named on Nicollet's and on Owen's map. Some other points not noted by the Expedition in approaching the Platte, July 20th and 21st, are : a creek on the right hand (in Iowa) marked Kegg creek on Owen's map, and Keg creek on Lieut. G. K. Warren's (about 1859); it retains the latter name. On the left are bluffs, as Calumet point and Rock bluff, near the camp of the 20th, and also a point called Iron Eye hill. The latter name is traceable to the Œil de Fer of Perrin du Lac, an Indian's name (see text of Aug. 19th). "Encamped some distance above a hill called *L'œil effroi*, from an Indian chief who was scaffolded here some years ago," Brackenbridge's Journal, 1814, p. 225.

on the south, near highlands covered with timber at the bank, and formed of limestone with cemented shells. On the opposite side is a bad sand-bar, and the land near it is cut through at high water by small channels forming a number of islands. The wind lulled at seven o'clock, and we reached, in the rain, the mouth of the great river Platte,[116] at the distance of 14 miles. The highlands which had accompanied us on the south for the last eight or ten miles stopped at about three-quarters of a mile from the entrance of the Platte. Captains Lewis and Clark ascended the river in a periogue for about one mile ; they found the current very rapid, rolling over sand and divided into a number of channels, none of which are deeper than five or six feet. One of our Frenchmen, who spent two winters on it, says that it spreads much more at some distance from the mouth ; that its depth is generally not more than five or six feet ; that there are many small islands scattered through it ; and

[116] Falling into the Missouri between Cass Co., Neb., on its right (south) bank, and Sarpy Co., Neb., on the other side. Across the Missouri is Mills Co., Ia. At the confluence, on the south bank, is the county town well named Plattsmouth (" Platte's mouth "). The 1,000 foot contour line, which hugs the Missouri pretty evenly on both sides for some distance below, here recedes westward along the Platte to the mouth of Saline river; but soon hugs the Missouri again on both sides, and crosses the latter river at Council Bluffs and Omaha, a few miles higher up. The Platte is the great western tributary of the Lower Missouri, draining most of Nebraska and portions of Wyoming and Colorado. Its two main courses, the North and South Platte, unite in Nebraska near 101° W. long. The former rises in North Park, Col., runs north into Wyoming, then bends east and southeast to its junction. The latter drains the Rocky mountains from the sources of the Arkansaw in Colorado northward into Wyoming. We commonly use the French form of the name, but the river has also often been called the Nebraska, and Flatwater. Its mouth is marked on the Mo. R. Comm. map 640.8 miles up river—rather more than Lewis and Clark thought. This point conventionally divides the " Lower " from the " Upper " Missouri. We read in Perrin du Lac of the " Premier Poste de la Compagnie du *haut* Missouri," established in 1792 near the mouth of the Platte. " The river Platte is regarded by the navigators of the Missouri as a point of as much importance as the equinoctial line amongst mariners. All those who had not passed it before were required to be shaved, unless they could compromise the matter by a treat. Much merriment was indulged on the occasion. From this we enter what is called the Upper Missouri." Brackenridge's Journal, 1814, p. 226.

that, from its rapidity and the quantity of its sand, it cannot be navigated by boats or periogues, though the In-
(*p. 31*) dians pass it in small flat canoes made of hides.
That the Saline or Salt River, which in some seasons is too
brackish to be drunk, falls into it from the south about 30
miles up, and a little above it [*i. e.*, Salt river] Elk-horn
river [falls into the Platte] from the north, running
nearly parallel with the Missouri [for some little distance].
The river is, in fact, much more rapid than the Missouri,
the bed of which it fills with moving sands, and drives the
current on the northern shore, on which it is constantly
encroaching.    At its junction the Platte is about 600 yards
wide, and the same number of miles from the Mississippi.
With much difficulty we worked around the sand-bars near
the mouth, and came-to above the point, having made 15
miles.    A number of wolves were seen and heard around us
in the evening.

*July 22d.*    This morning we set sail, and having found, at
the distance of ten miles from the Platte, a high and shaded
situation on the north,[117] we camped there, intending to make
the requisite observations, and to send for the neighboring
tribes, for the purpose of making known the recent change
in the government, and the wish of the United States to
cultivate their friendship.

[117] As the Missouri in this section of its course runs approximately south between Iowa and Nebraska, camps on the left bank of the river (right hand going
up) are on the *east* side rather than the north—that is, independently of the minor
bends of the river.    Here I may remark, also, that L. and C.'s MSS. very
seldom have expressions referring to points of the compass in noting sides of the
river they are ascending.    They say "Starboard Side" and "Larboard Side"
almost invariably.    These terms Biddle uniformly edits as "north" and
"south," or otherwise as the case may approximately be.    Moreover, the MSS.
usually abbreviate to "Stard. Sd." and "Lard. Sd.," or simply "S. S." and
"L. S."    Here is a possible source of error, as "S. S." might be read "south
side," and capital "L. S." in manuscript looks very much like "S. S." if the lower
loop of the L is not well formed.    Probably here is the simple explanation of
occasional wrong location of L. and C.'s creeks and camps.    The camp of this
day, July 22d, is on the *east* side of the Missouri, by estimate ten miles above the
Platte; it is therefore on or close to the boundary between Mills and Pottawatamie
Cos., Ia., and nearly or about the same distance below the present site of Council Bluffs and Omaha—past Cerro Gordo, Ia., and Bellevue, Neb.

# CHAPTER II.

## THE MISSOURI FROM THE PLATTE TO VERMILION RIVER.

Butterfly and Mosquito creeks—Elk-horn river—Pawnee Indians—Other Indians—Indian Knob creek—Plants and Animals—Council held with Otto and Missouri Indians, and Council-bluff named—Soldier's river—Detachment islands—A desertion—Little Sioux or Stone river—Lac d'Esprit—Prairie du Chien—Cat river—Pelican island—Coupée à Jacques—Blackbird, an Omaha chief—Bad Spirit creek—Old Fort Charles—Old Omaha village—Omaha creek—Many fish taken—The deserter apprehended—Indian council—Death of Sergeant Charles Floyd—Floyd's river and bluffs—Great Sioux river—Mineral bluffs—Promotion of Patrick Gass—Buffalo prairie—First buffalo killed—The Expedition reaches Whitestone or Vermilion river.

JULY 22d–26th. Our camp is by observation in latitude 41° 3′ 11″. Immediately behind it is a plain about five miles wide, one half covered with wood, the other dry and elevated. The low grounds on the south near the junction of the two rivers are rich, but subject to be overflowed. Further up the banks are higher, and opposite our camp the first hills approach the river, and are covered with timber, such as oak, walnut, and elm. The intermediate country is watered by Papillon[1] or Butterfly creek, about 18 yards wide, and three miles from the Platte; on the north are high open plains and prairies; at nine miles from the Platte are Mosquito[2] creek and two or three small willow-islands.

We stayed here several days, during which we dried our provisions, made new oars, and prepared our dispatches and maps of the country we had passed, for the President

[1] In Sarpy Co., Neb., of which the present town of Papillon or Papillion is the county seat. The name is French for butterfly. Sarpy or Sarpie is a personal name, in this case probably John B.

[2] L. and C. spell the name of this insect musquitoe and musquetoe; in the M'Vickar ed. 1842 it is altered to moscheto; I make it throughout mosquito, pl. mosquitoes. Lewis' map of 1806 runs " Musqueto " creek into the Missouri below Butterfly creek; on Clark's, 1814, it is laid down right. The stream runs chiefly in Pottawattamie Co., Ia., but empties in Mills Co. Its present name is the same.

of the United States, to whom we intend to send them by a periogue from this place. The hunters have found game scarce in this neighborhood; they have seen deer, turkeys, and grouse;[3] we have also an abundance of ripe grapes; and one of our men caught a white catfish,[4] the eyes of which were small, and its tail resembling that of a dolphin. The present season is that in which the Indians go out on the prairies to hunt the buffalo; but as we discovered some hunters' tracks, and observed the plains on fire in the direction of their villages, we hoped that they might have returned to gather the green Indian corn. We therefore dispatched two men[5] to (*p. 33*) the Ottoe or Pawnee villages with a present of tobacco, and an invitation to the chiefs to visit us. They returned after two days' absence. Their first course was through an open prairie to the south, on which they crossed Butterfly creek. They then reached a small beautiful river, called Come [*sic*—read Corne] de Cerf, or Elk-horn[6] river, about 100 yards wide, with clear water and a gravelly channel. It empties a little below the Ottoe village into the Platte, which they crossed, and arrived at the town about 45 miles from our camp. They found no Indians there, though they saw some fresh tracks of a small party.

The Ottoes were once a powerful nation and lived about 20 miles above the Platte, on the southern bank of the Missouri. Being reduced, they migrated to the neighborhood of the Pawnees, under whose protection they now

---

[3] These are the pinnated grouse or prairie-hen, whose best-known technical name is *Cupidonia cupido*, lately changed by the rules of the American Ornithologists' Union to *Tympanuchus americanus*.

[4] *Ictalurus punctatus*. From this fish the present station of the Expedition was named Camp White Catfish. Clark enters in his journal of July 23d: "I commence coppying a map of the river below to send to the P[resident]. U. S."; and 24th: "Capt. Lewis also much engaged in preparing papers to send back by a perogue." But nothing was dispatched to Jefferson till April 7th, 1805.

[5] George Drewyer and Peter Cruzatte.

[6] The French form is iñ Perrin du Lac. Clark here wrote "Corne de Charf or Elk Horn river," and elsewhere "Hartshorn" river.

live. Their village is on the south side of the Platte, about 30 miles from its mouth; and their number is 200 men, including about 30 families of Missouri Indians, who are incorporated with them.

Five leagues above them, on the same side of the river, resides the nation of Pawnees.[7] This people were among the most numerous of the Missouri Indians, but have gradually been dispersed and broken, and even since the year 1797 have undergone some sensible changes. They now consist of four bands; the first is [the Grand Pawnee,] the one just mentioned, of about 500 men, to whom of late

[7] To appreciate the position of the Pawnee nations among Indians we must first distinguish them from any tribes of the great Siouan family, and next recognize their relationship with the Caddoes, as members of the same linguistic stock. Though the Pawnees and Caddoes were long supposed, as by Gallatin and many later writers, to be primitively distinct, they have now been determined to be branches of one family, for which the term Caddoan is selected by Powell as designative. In his clear classification the Caddoans consist: 1. Of a *northern* group, consisting of the Arikara or Ree tribe alone (see beyond). 2. Of a *middle* group, comprising the four nations of Pawnees. 3. Of a *southern* group, including the Caddoes and other tribes which were in Texas, Louisiana, Arkansas, and the Indian Territory.

According to Dr. Dunbar (1806; English ed. 1807, 2d English ed. 1809, p. 15) the original hunting-ground of the Pawnees extended from the river now called Niobrara, in Nebraska, south to the Arkansas river, though no definite boundary can be fixed. In later times they have resided on the Platte river, west of what is now Columbus, Neb. The Pawnee tribes were removed to the Indian Territory in 1876. According to the Indian Report for 1889 they were officially enumerated as 824 in number, representing a little over one-third of the entire remaining Caddoan stock (2,259).

Though Lewis and Clark here spell the name Pawnee, this was not the usual form of the word in their day, when we more frequently find Pani, Pania, or Panea. Lewis uses Pania, plural Panias, in his Statistical View of 1806. The Pawnees of Gallatin (Trans. and Coll. Amer. Antiq., ser. ii. 1836, pp. 128, 306) included all the Pawnees of the Middle Group and also the Ricaras or Black Pawnees. The Pawnees or Panias of Latham (Nat. Hist. Man, 1850, p. 344) included the Loups and Republicans. The Pawnees of Hayden (Cont. Ethnol. and Philol. Missouri Indians, 1862, pp. 232, 345) included the Pawnees and Arikaras, being thus the same as Gallatin's. Gallatin (*l. c.*) renders the word Pawnies. Another form is Pahnies (Berghaus, 1845). Gatschet renders Panis in 1884.

The four principal tribes of the Pawnee nation recognized by Powell in 1891 were: 1. The Grand, or Pawnee proper, as here given by Lewis and Clark.

years have been added the second band, who are called
Republican Pawnees, from their having lived on the
Republican branch of the Kansas river, whence they emigrated to join the principal band of Pawnees; the Republican Pawnees amount to nearly 250 men.  The third are
the Pawnee Loups, or Wolf Pawnees, who reside on the
Wolf fork of the Platte, about 90 miles from the principal
Pawnees, and number 280 men.  The fourth band originally resided on the Kansas and Arkansas, but in their wars
with the Osages were so often defeated that they at last
retired to their present position on the Red river, where

2. The Pawnee Republican, as given by Lewis and Clark.  3. The Tapage,
who did not wander far from their habitat on the Platte.  4. The Skidi, who
are the Pawnee Loups of Lewis and Clark, otherwise called the Pani-mahas.

The Panias proper of Lewis' Statistical View, 1806, also there called Pà-nee,
are represented as speaking their own language, and living in one village
up the Platte, 30 leagues from its mouth, on the south side, and as consisting of 1,600, with 400 warriors.  They were at war with the Pania-pique,
both Osages, Kanzas, Ricaras, Sioux, and some other Indians, but at peace
with the Pawnee Loups, Mahas, Poncas, Ottoes, Missouris, and Ayauways.
They traded with St. Louis merchants.  "With respect to their idea of the
possession of the soil, it is similar to that of the Ottoes ; they hunt on the
south side of the river Platte higher up and on the head of the Kansas.  .  .
They have resided in the country which they now [1805] inhabit, since they
were known to the whites.  .  .  The periods of their residence at their village and hunting, are similar to the Kansas and Osages.  Their population is
increasing.  They are friendly and hospitable to all white persons ; pay great
respect and deference to their traders, with whom they are punctual in the payment of their debts.  They are, in all respects, a friendly, well disposed people.
They cultivate corn, beans, melons, &c." (Lewis' Statist. View, London ed.
1807, p. 14.)

The Republicans are also called by Lewis, in his Statistical View, Ar-râh-pâ-
hoo'—that is, Arapahoes.  He says they lived in 1805 in the same village with
the Panias proper, having a population of 1,400, with 300 warriors.  "About
ten years since [i. e., in 1795 or 1796] they withdrew themselves from the mother
nation, and established a village on a large northwardly branch of the Kanzas,
to which they have given name ; they afterward subdivided and lived in different parts of the country on the waters of Kanzas river ; but being harassed by
their turbulent neighbors, the Kanzas [of Siouan stock], they rejoined the
Panias proper last spring [1804]."  (Stat. View, Eng. ed. 1807, p. 15.)

The third band, Loups or Wolves, Lewis calls in his View Skec'-e-ree, i. e.,
the Skidi of modern nomenclature; they are otherwise known as Pani-mahas.  In
1805 they numbered 1,000, with 280 warriors, as given in the text.  In trade,

(*p. 34*) they form a tribe of 400 men. All these tribes live in villages, and raise corn ; but during the intervals of culture rove in the plains in quest of buffalo.

Beyond them on the river, and westward of the Black mountains, are the Kaninaviesch,[8] consisting of about 400 men. They are supposed to have emigrated originally from the Pawnee nation ; but they have degenerated from the improvements of the parent tribe, and no longer live in villages, but rove through the plains.

Still further to the westward are several tribes, who wander and hunt on the sources of the Platte river, and thence to Rock mountain [*i. e.*, the Rocky mountains].

war and peace, they were similar to those of other Pawnee tribes. " These are also a branch of the Panias proper, who separated themselves from that nation many years since [1805], and established themselves on a north branch of the river Platte, to which their name was also given. These people have likewise no idea of an exclusive right to any portion of the country. They hunt on the Wolf river above their village, and on the river Platte above the mouth of that river [Wolf]. This country is very similar to that of the Panias proper ; though there is an extensive body of fertile well timbered land between the Wolf river below their village and the river Corn [e] de Cerf, or Elkhorn river. They cultivate corn, beans, &c. The particulars related of the other Panias is also applicable to them. They are seldom visited by any trader, and therefore usually bring their furs and peltry to the village of the Panias proper, where they traffic with the whites." (Lewis, *l. c.*)

The " fourth band," mentioned but not named in the text, as being then on the Red river (of Texas), is the same as that mentioned by Gallatin (Trans. and Coll. Am. Antiq. Soc. II. 1836, pp. 117, 128), and doubtfully indicated as of the Pawnee family, but kept separate by Gallatin in Schoolcraft's Indian Tribes, III. 1853, p. 402. See also Panis of Pritchard, Phys. Hist. Mankind, V. 1847, p. 407, and of Latham, Nat. Hist. Man, 1850, p. 344.

From all the indications given by Lewis and Clark, it would properly be supposed that the Pawnees were no Sioux ; and their entire separation from Siouan stock would be justified on other than those linguistic grounds which have occasioned their relegation to Caddoan stock in the scientific classification now adopted.

[8] The Kaninaviesch are called in Lewis' Statistical View Kanenavish, accented Kan-e-nä'-vish, and by the French nickname Gens-des-Vaches (Cowpeople, *i. e.*, Buffalo Indians). He credits them with 150 lodges, 400 warriors, 1,500 people all told, and locates them on the heads of the Paduca fork of the Platte and on the south fork of the Cheyenne river. The name is now preferably written Caninahoic, as by Gatschet, who identifies these Indians with the Arapaho tribe of the great Algonquian family or linguistic stock.

These tribes, of which little more is known than the names and the population, are first, the Staitan[9] or Kite Indians, a small tribe of 100 men. They have acquired the name of Kites from their flying—that is, their being always on horseback, and the smallness of their numbers is to be attributed to their extreme ferocity; they are the most warlike of all the western Indians; they never yield in battle; they never spare their enemies; and the retaliation of this barbarity has almost extinguished the nation. Then come the Wetapahato[10] and Kiawa[11] tribes, associated to-

[9] The Staitan or Kite Indians, Lewis names in his Statistical View Staetan, Sta'-e-tan, with Kite as a nickname. He assigns them 40 lodges, 100 warriors, total population 400, and locates them "on the head of the Chyenne, and frequently with the Kanenavish." They are probably Crows (Siouan family).

[10] The Statistical View of Lewis accents this name We-te-pâ-hà'-to. His census for 1805 is 70 lodges, 200 warriors, and 700 total—this estimate including all the Kiowas. Habitat, Paduca (North) fork of the Platte. He says they maintain a defensive war with the Sioux, but are at war with no other tribes to his knowledge. Of them and the Kiowas together he adds : "They are a wandering nation, inhabit an open country, and raise a great number of horses, which they barter to the Ricaras, Mandans, &c. for articles of European manufactory. They are a well disposed people, and might be readily induced to visit the trading establishments on the Missouri. From the animals their country produces, their trade would, no doubt, become valuable. These people again barter a considerable proportion of the articles they obtain from the Menetares, Ahwahhaways, Mandans, and Ricaras, to the Dotames and Castapanas [sic]." These Indians were allied with the Kiowas, and are now supposed to have formed a part of the Comanches.

[11] Kiawa is a name variously spelled Kiaway, Kioway, Kyaway, etc., now preferably Kiowa, plural Kiowas. Gatschet spells Káyowā (Am. Antiq., Oct., 1882, p. 280, where the phonetics are given). The name is from the Kiowa word, Kói, plural Kó-iqu, meaning Káyowā man; and the Comanche word Káyowā means rat.

The Kiowas represent a distinct linguistic stock now known as the Kiowan family. Kiaways are named by Gallatin in Schoolcraft's Indian Tribes, III. 1853, p. 402, as residing on the upper waters of the Arkansas. The Kioway of Turner (Pac. R. R. Rep. III. pt. iii. 1856, pp. 55, 80) is based only on the Kiowa or Caigua tribe. The conjecture of Lewis and Clark that this tribe and some others they name are but remnants of the great Paduca nation is borne out by Latham (Elem. Comp. Philol., 1862, p. 444), who uses the expression "more Paduca than aught else."

Turner is said to have first formally separated the Kiowan family from all others. "Turner, upon the strength of a vocabulary furnished by Lieut. Whipple, dissents from the opinion expressed by Pike and others to the effect that the language is of the same stock as the Comanche, and while admitting

gether, and amounting to 200 men ; the Castahana,[12] of 300 men ; to which are to be added the Cataka,[13] of 75 men, and the Dotami.[14] These wandering tribes are conjectured to be

that its relationship to Comanche is greater than to any other family, thinks that the likeness is merely the result of long intercommunication. His opinion that it is entirely distinct from any other language has been endorsed by Buschmann and other authorities " (Rep. U. S. Bureau of Ethnol. for 1885–86, pub. 1891, p. 84). Gallatin mentions the tribe with the remark that " both the Kiowas and Kaskaias languages were harsh, guttural, and extremely difficult."

A difficulty of disengaging the Kiowas from their neighbors has been that close association with the Comanches (of a different stock, the Shoshonean) which has tended to obscure the actually existing distinctions. Similarly, it is difficult to determine their original site. Lewis' Statistical View (1806) locates the Kiowas on the Paduca fork of the Platte, and adds that they were frequently with the Wetepahatoes, with whom, indeed, he enumerates them in his census, giving for both a total of 700, warriors 200, lodges 70. By the Medicine Creek treaty of 1867, the Kiowas and Comanches relinquished all their rights to other territory when they were removed to their present location in Indian Territory. Powell adds : " The terms of the cession might be taken to indicate a joint-ownership of territory, but it is more likely that the Kiowan territory adjoined the Comanche territory on the northwest. In fact, Pope (Pacific R. R. Rep. II. pt. iii. 1855, p. 16) definitely locates the Kiowa in the valley of the upper Arkansas and of its tributary, the Purgatory (Las Aminas) river. This is in substantial accord with the statements of other writers of about the same period. Schermerhorn (1812) places the Kiowa on the heads of the Arkansas and Platte. Earlier still they appear on the headwaters of the Platte." This is the position assigned them on the map accompanying Powell's Report, 1891. Lewis states in his Statistical View of 1806 that neither the Kiowas, Wetepa-hatoes, nor Cheyennes " have any idea of exclusive right to the soil."

According to the U. S. Census Report for 1890, there were 1,140 Kiowas on the Kiowa, Comanche, and Wichita Reservation in Indian Territory.

[12] The Castahana are enumerated in the Statistical View, 1806, at 5,000 population, with 1,300 warriors, and 500 lodges ; they are located between the sources of the Paduca (North) fork of the Platte and the Yellowstone. Lewis states that what he says of the Dotami is equally applicable to the Castahana, " except that they trade principally with the Crow Indians, and that they would most probably prefer visiting an establishment on the Yellow Stone river, or at its mouth on the Missouri " (London ed. 1807, p. 24). These are the Comanche Indians (of the Shoshonean or Snake family), and are otherwise called Alliatan, Aiatan, Hietan, Ietan, Jetan, etc.

[13] The Cataka, accented Cat'-a-kâ, are represented in the Statistical View as of 25 lodges, 75 warriors, and total 300. They are located between the north and south forks of the Cheyenne. Lewis' general remarks are to the same effect as those he makes on the Kiowas. This tribe is probably that otherwise known as Kwada, a band of the Comanches.

[14] The Dotami, as here, or Dotame, marked Do-ta'-me, in the Statistical View,

the remnants of the great Padouca nation, who occupied
the country between the upper parts of the Platte and the
Kansas. They were visited by Bourgemont in 1724, and
then lived on the Kansas river. The seats [sites] which he
describes as their residence are now occupied by the Kansas nation; and of the Padoucas there does not now exist
even the name.[15]

*July 27th.* Having completed the object of our stay, we
set sail [at noon], with a pleasant breeze from the N. W.
The two horses swam over to the southern shore, along
which we went, passing by an island, at 3½ miles, formed
by a pond fed by springs. Three miles further is a large
(*p. 35*) sand-island, in the middle of the river; the land on
the south being high, and covered with timber; that on

are located on the heads of the Cheyenne river, with a total of only 120 persons,
including 30 warriors and 10 lodges.  Lewis here remarks : "The information
I possess, with respect to this nation, is derived from Indian information : they
are said to be a wandering nation, inhabiting an open country, and who raise
a great number of horses and mules.  They are a friendly, well disposed
people, and might, from the position of their country, be easily induced to visit
an establishment on the Missouri, about the mouth of Chyenne river.  They
have not, as yet, visited the Missouri."  They are supposed to be a band of the
Comanche tribe, like all the other Indians here noted, excepting the Kiowas
themselves, who are now regarded as forming a distinct linguistic stock or
family.  See note above.

[15] Meaning, of course, that the Padoucas exist only in name.  The name certainly exists, for there it is on the page.  It is now, also, the name of a town in
Kentucky.  The orthography varies as much as is usual with Indian names.  In
his Statistical View, Lewis spells it Padacus (in the plural) and gives Paddo as
a French form.  "This once powerful nation has, apparently," he says, "entirely disappeared ; every inquiry I have made after them has proved ineffectual.
In the year 1724 they resided in several villages on the heads of the Kansas
river, and could, at that time, bring upwards of 2,000 men into the field (see
Du Pratz, Hist. Louisiana, p. 71, and map).  The information that I have received is, that being oppressed by the nations residing on the Missouri, they
removed to the upper part of the river Platte, where they afterwards had but
little intercourse with the whites.  They seem to have given name to the
northern branch of that river, which is still called the Paducas fork.  The most
probable conjecture is, that being still further reduced, they have divided into
small wandering bands, which assumed the names of the subdivisions of the
Paduca nation, and are known to us at present under the appellation of Wetepahatoes, Kiawas, Kanenavish, Katteka, Dotame, &c. who still inhabit the
country to which the Paducas are said to have removed.  The majority of my

the north, a high prairie.   At 10½ miles from our camp, we saw and examined a curious collection of graves or mounds, on the south side of the river.   Not far from a low piece of land and a pond, is a tract of about 200 acres in circumference, which is covered with mounds of different heights, shapes, and sizes ; some of sand, and some of both earth and sand ; the largest being nearest the river.   These mounds indicate the position of the ancient village of the Ottoes, before they retired to the protection of the Pawnees.   After making 15 miles, we camped on the south,[16] on the bank of a high handsome prairie, with lofty cottonwood in groves near the river.

*July 28th.*   At one mile this morning we reached a bluff [17] on the north, being the first highlands which approach the river on that side since we left the Nadawa [river].   Above this is an island, and a creek about 15 yards wide, which, as it has no name, we called Indian Knob [18] [Round Knob, Gass] creek, from a number of round knobs bare of timber, on the highlands to the north.   A little below the bluff, on the north, is the spot where the Ayauway Indians formerly lived.   They were a branch of the Ottoes, and emigrated from this place to the river Des Moines.   At 10¾ miles, we camped on the north [*i. e.*, east], opposite an island in the middle of the river.   The land generally, on the north, consists of high prairie and hills, with timber; on the south, it is low and covered with cottonwood.   Our hunter

information led me to believe that those people spoke different languages, but other and subsequent information has induced me to doubt the fact." (London ed. 1807, p. 39.)   For the case of the Kiowas see above note.

[16] See July 22d, note there.   To-day's camp is on the west side of the river, in Douglas Co., Neb.; and if 15 miles were made, as said, the Expedition is already *past* the present sites of Omaha, Neb., and Council Bluffs, Ia.—a point to be remembered in locating the "Council-bluff" of our text.

[17] At or near which was later built a trading-post, called Fort Croghan—a name to be found on Nicollet's map.

[18] A much-named stream ; Gopher creek of Nicollet's and of Owen's map ; Big Pigeon river of Warren's, and of the G. L. O. (1876) map ; later Indian creek ; arising in Shelby Co., running through Harrison Co. into Pottawattamie Co., and emptying into the Missouri near Crescent City, Ia., a little above the 680th mile point.   To-day's camp is but little above this stream, and on the Iowan (east) side.

brought to us in the evening a Missouri Indian whom he had found, with two others, dressing an elk; they were perfectly friendly, gave him some of the meat, and one of them agreed to accompany him to the boat. He is one of the few remaining Missouris, who live with the Ottoes; he belongs to a small party, whose camp is four miles from the river; and he says that the body of the nation is now hunting buffalo in the plains. He appeared quite sprightly, and his language resembled that (*p. 36*) of the Osages, particularly in his calling a chief "inca." We sent him back with one of our own party next morning,

*July* 29*th*, with an invitation to the Indians to meet us above on the river, and then proceeded. We soon came to a northern bend in the river, which runs within 20 yards of Indian Knob creek, the water of which is five feet higher than that of the Missouri. In less than two miles, we passed Boyer's [19] [or Bowyer's] creek on the north, of 25 yards' width. We stopped to dine under a shade, near the high land on the south, and caught several large catfish, one of them nearly white and all very fat. Above this high land we observed the traces of a great hurricane, which passed the river obliquely from N.W. to S.E. and tore up large trees, some of which, perfectly sound and four feet in diameter, were snapped off near the ground. We made ten miles to a wood on the north, where we camped. The Missouri is much more crooked since we passed the

---

[19] Present name; so also Clark's MS., but Bowyer's on both Lewis' and Clark's maps; misprinted Bayer's and Rowyer's on some maps. It is the Rivière à Boyer of Perrin du Lac. It traverses several counties of western Iowa; at its main forks is Cedar Rapids, Crawford Co., Ia. It was explored by Thomas Say, in 1820, during Major Long's Expedition. Three miles above its mouth, across the Missouri, in what is now Washington Co., Neb., Major Long established himself, Sept. 17th, 1819, and named the place Engineer Cantonment, the latitude of which he determined to be 41° 25′ 03.9″. This spot was half a mile below a trading-post called Fort Lisa (which had been located by the noted Manuel Lisa of the Missouri Fur Company, with whom Clark was at one time in partnership), and five miles below the Council-bluff of Lewis and Clark. This is also the original locality of several of Mr. Say's new species of mammals and birds. When Brackenridge passed here, May 13th, 1811, he saw the houses of the trader McClelland, who had wintered at this place.

Platte, though generally speaking not so rapid ; there is more of prairie, with less timber, and cottonwood in the low grounds, with oak, black walnut, hickory, and elm.

*July 30th.* We went early in the morning 3¼ miles, and camped on the south,[20] in order to wait for the Ottoes. The land here consists of a plain above the high-water level, the soil of which is fertile, and covered with a grass from five to eight feet high, interspersed with copses of large plums, and a currant, like those of the United States. It also furnishes two species of honeysuckle ; one growing to a kind of shrub, common about Harrodsburgh (Kentucky), the other is not so high ; the flowers grow in clusters, are short, and of a light pink color; the leaves too, are distinct [not perfoliate], and do not surround the stalk, as do those of the common honeysuckle of the United States. Back of this plain is a woody ridge about 70 feet above it, at the end of which we formed our camp. This ridge separates the lower from a higher prairie, of a good quality, with grass of ten or twelve inches in height, and extending back about a mile, to another elevation of (*p. 37*) 80 or 90 feet, beyond which is one continued plain. Near our camp, we enjoy from the bluffs a most beautiful view of the river and the adjoining country. At a distance, varying from four to ten miles, and of a height between 70 and 300 feet, two parallel ranges of high land afford a passage to the Missouri, which enriches the low grounds between them. In its winding course it nourishes the willow-islands, the scattered cottonwood, elm, sycamore, lynn [linden, *Tilia pubescens*], and ash ; and the groves are interspersed with hickory, walnut, coffee-nut [*Gymnocladus canadensis*], and oak.

*July 31st.* The meridian altitude of this day made the latitude of our camp 41° 18' 1⁴⁄₁₀". The hunters supplied us with deer, turkeys, geese, and beaver ; one of the last was caught alive, and in a very short time was perfectly

[20] That is, on the west (Nebraskan) side of the river, nearly or exactly at the 690th mile point of the present course of the Missouri. On this matter see further note of August 3d.

tamed. Catfish are very abundant in the river, and we have also seen a buffalo-fish. One of our men brought in yesterday an animal called by the Pawnees chocartoosh, and by the French blaireau,[21] or badger [*Taxidea americana*]. The evening is cool, yet the mosquitoes are still very troublesome.[22]

*August 1st and 2d.* We waited with much anxiety the return of our messenger to the Ottoes. The men whom we dispatched to our last camp returned without having seen any appearance of its having been visited. Our horses too had strayed; but we were so fortunate as to recover them at the distance of twelve miles. Our apprehensions were at length relieved by the arrival of a party of about 14 Ottoe and Missouri Indians, who came at sunset, on the 2d of August, accompanied by a Frenchman[23] who resided among them and interpreted for us. Captains Lewis and Clark went out to meet them, and told them that we would hold a council in the morning. In the mean time we sent them some roasted meat, pork, flour, and meal; in return for which they made us a present of watermelons. We learned that our man Liberté had set out from their camp a day before them. We were in hopes that he had fatigued his horse, or lost himself in the woods, and would soon return; but we never saw him again.

(*p. 38*) *August 3d.* This morning the Indians, with their six chiefs, were all assembled under an awning formed with

[21] This word happens to be here spelled correctly ; nearly always, in this work, it is corrupted to braro, or brairo, or brarow, once braroca, once praro, and in Gass prarow. These forms indicate the Canadian voyageurs' pronunciation, caught by ear by our travelers. Pike has brelau and brelaw.

[22] " *Tuesday* 31st. One of our men went to visit some traps he had set, and in one found a young beaver, but little hurt, and brought it in alive. In a short time he went out again and killed a large buck. Two other hunters came in about twelve, who had killed two deer ; but lost the horses. One of them with two other persons were sent to hunt, who returned at dark without finding them ; and supposed they had been stolen by the Indians," Gass, p. 26. The lost horses were not recovered till Aug. 2d ; and a lost man (Liberté) was never found. Whether this was death or desertion, or both, was never known.

[23] Named as " Mr. Fairfong " in Clark's MS.

the mainsail, in presence of all our party, paraded for the
occasion. A speech was then made announcing to them
the change in the government, our promise of protection,
and advice as to their future conduct. All the six chiefs
replied to our speech, each in his turn, according to rank.
They expressed their joy at the change in the government;
their hopes that we would recommend them to their Great
Father (the President), that they might obtain trade and
necessaries; they wanted arms as well for hunting as for
defense, and asked our mediation between them and the
Mahas, with whom they are now at war. We promised to
do so, and wished some of them to accompany us to that
nation, which they declined, for fear of being killed by
them. We then proceeded to distribute our presents.
The grand chief of the nation not being of the party, we
sent him a flag, a medal, and some ornaments for clothing.
To the six chiefs who were present, we gave a medal of the
second grade to one Ottoe chief, and one Missouri chief; a
medal of the third grade to two inferior chiefs of each nation—the customary mode of recognizing a chief being to
place a medal round his neck, which is considered among
his tribe as a proof of his consideration abroad. Each of
these medals was accompanied by a present of paint, gar-
ters, and cloth ornaments of dress; and to this we added a
cannister of powder, a bottle of whisky, and a few presents to
the whole, which appeared to make them perfectly satisfied.
The air-gun too was fired, and astonished them greatly.
The absent grand chief was an Ottoe named Weahrushhah,
which in English degenerates into Little Thief. The two
principal chieftains present were Shongotongo or Big Horse;
and Wethea or Hospitality; also Shosguscan or White
Horse, an Ottoe; the first an Ottoe, the second a Missouri.[24]
The incident just related induced us to give to this place

[24] In Clark's MS. these names stand as follows : Wearrugenor, Little Thief ;
Shongotongo, Big Horse ; Wethea, Hospatality (*sic*) ; Shonguscan, White
Horse ; with four others not in the text, Waupeuh, Ahhoningga, Bazacouja,
and Ahhonega, all Ottoes.

the name of the Council-bluff;[25] the situation of it (*p. 39*) is
exceedingly favorable for a fort and trading-factory, as the
soil is well calculated for bricks, there is an abundance of
wood in the neighborhood, and the air is pure and healthy.
It is also central to the chief resorts of the Indians; one
day's journey to the Ottoes; 1½ to the great Pawnees; two
days' from the Mahas; 2¼ from the Pawnees Loups village;
convenient to the hunting-grounds of the Sioux; and 25
days' journey to Santa Fee [Fe].

The ceremonies of the council being concluded, we set
sail in the afternoon, and camped at the distance of five
miles, on the south [Nebraskan] side, where we found the
mosquitoes very troublesome.

*August 4th.*   A violent wind, accompanied by rain, puri-
fied and cooled the atmosphere last night.   We proceeded

[25] That is, Council Bluffs, the name of the now flourishing city in Pottawattamie Co., Ia., opposite the still greater city of Omaha, Douglas Co., Neb.
Here is the origin of the name, though the city is much below the exact spot
where these historical incidents took place, and on the other side of the river.
In the text, as above, the name usually stands Council-bluff, in one hyphen-
ated word.   The spot is not marked on Lewis' map of 1806; on Clark's of
1814 the words "Council Bluff" are lettered, but on the Iowan side of the
river, with no mark on the Nebraskan side to indicate the exact spot.   Hence
some confusion arose, and another element of vagueness was introduced by the
fact that some maps extended the name "Council Bluffs" to the whole range of
hills along the river on either side.   The spot is marked on Nicollet's map, as
determined by him in 1839.   It was later the site of Fort Calhoun, in the present Washington Co., Neb.   We must also remember, in attempting to fix this
spot, how much the Missouri has altered its course since 1804.   This shiftiness
of the Missouri is remarked upon by Nicollet (Report, 1843, p. 33), in leaving
Council Bluffs : "Thus we could not recognize many of the bends described
by Lewis and Clark ; and, most probably, those determined by us in 1839, and
laid down upon my map, will ere long have disappeared ; such is the unsettled
course of the river.   Already have I been informed, in fact, that the great bend
opposite Council Bluffs has disappeared since our visit ; and that the Missouri,
which then flowed at the foot of the bluff, is now further removed, by several
miles, to the east of it.   It is, in this respect, curious to compare our journal of
travelling distances with that of Lewis and Clark.   They are found always to
differ, and sometimes considerably.   Yet, on arriving at any prominent station,
as the confluence of a large river, the amount of the partial distances computed
agree as nearly as could be expected, from the methods employed to estimate
them."

early, and reached a very narrow part of the river, where the channel is confined within a space of 200 yards by a sand-point on the north and a bend on the south ; the banks in the neighborhood are washing away, the trees falling in, and the channel is filled with buried logs. Above this is a trading-house on the south, where one of our party [Cru-zatte] passed two years, trading with the Mahas. At nearly four miles is a creek on the south, emptying opposite a large island of sand ; between this creek and our last night's camp the river has changed its bed and encroached on the southern shore. About two miles further is another creek on the south, which, like the former, is the outlet of three ponds, communicating with each other and forming a small lake, which is fed by streams from the high lands.[26] At 15 miles we camped on the south. The hills on both sides of the river are nearly 12 or 15 miles from each other ; those of the north containing some timber, while the hills of the south are without any covering, except some scattering wood in the ravines and near where the creeks pass into the hills ; rich plains and prairies occupy the interme-diate space and are partially covered, near the water, with cotton- (*p. 40*) wood. There has been a great deal of pumice-stone on the shore to-day.[27]

*August 5th.* We set out early, and by means of our oars made 20½ miles, though the river was crowded with sand-bars. On both sides the prairies extend along the river ; the banks being covered with great quantities of grapes, of which three different species are now ripe, one large and resembling the purple grape. We had some rain this morn-

[26] Neither of the creeks mentioned is now identifiable with certainty. To answer to one or the other we find a Beaver creek of Nicollet and of Owen ; a No Heart creek of the G. L. O. map of 1876 (emptying on the boundary between Washington and Burt Co., Neb.), and a Fish creek on the Mo. R. Comm. map. To-day's camp is in Nebraska, near the 700th mile point of the map last named.

[27] Gass notes under this date the desertion of one of the men (not the French-man Liberté), beyond mentioned under date of Aug. 7th. His name does not appear in the text, but was M. B. Reed.

ing, attended by high wind ; but, generally speaking, have remarked that thunder-storms are less frequent than in the Atlantic States, at this season. Snakes too are less frequent, though we killed one to-day of the shape and size of the rattlesnake, but of a lighter color. We fixed our camp on the north side [Harrison Co., Ia.].

In the evening Captain Clark, in pursuing some game in an eastern direction, found himself at the distance of 370 yards from the camp, at a point of the river whence we had come twelve miles. When the water is high, this peninsula is overflowed ; and, judging from the customary and notorious changes in the river, a few years will be sufficient to force the main current of the river across and leave the great bend dry. The whole lowland between the parallel ranges of hills seems formed of mud or ooze of the river, at some former period mixed with sand and clay. The sand of the neighboring banks accumulates with the aid of that brought down the stream, and forms sand-bars projecting into the river ; these drive the channel to the opposite bank, the loose texture of which it undermines, and at length deserts its ancient bed for a new and shorter passage. It is thus that the banks of the Missouri are constantly falling, and the river is changing its bed.

*August 6th.* In the morning, after a violent storm of wind and rain from the N.W., we passed a large island to the north. In the channel separating it from the shore, a creek called Soldier's [28] river enters; the island kept it from our view, but one of our men who had seen it, represents it as about (*p. 41*) 40 yards wide at its mouth. At five miles, we came to a bend of the river toward the north. A sand-bar, running in from the south, had turned its course so as to leave the old channel quite dry. We again saw the same appearance at our camp, 20½ miles distant, on the north side. Here the channel of the river had encroached south, and the old bed was

[28] Also variously Soldier, Soldiers, and Soldiers' ; R. des Soldats of Perrin du Lac ; running in Ida, Crawford, Monona, and Harrison Cos., Ia.

without water, except a few ponds. The sand-bars are
still very numerous.

*August 7th.* We had another storm from the N.W. in
the course of the last evening. In the morning we proceeded, having the wind from the north, and camped on
the northern shore, having rowed 17 miles. The river is
here encumbered with sand-bars, but there are no islands,
except two small ones, called Detachment islands, formed
on the south side by a small stream.

We dispatched four men back to the Ottoe village in
quest of our man Liberté, and to apprehend one of the
soldiers, who left us on the 4th under pretense of recovering a knife which he had dropped a short distance behind,
and who we fear has deserted.[29] We also sent small presents to the Ottoes and Missouris, and requested that they
would join us at the Maha village, where a peace might be
concluded between them.

*August 8th.* At two miles' distance, this morning, we
came to a part of the river where there was concealed
timber difficult to pass. The wind was from the N.W.,
and we proceeded in safety. At six miles, a river empties
on the north side, called by the Sioux Indians Eaneah-
wadepon,[30] or Stone river; and by the French, Petite

[29] "Four of our people were dispatched to the Oto nation of Indians after
the man [M. B. Reed] who had not returned on the 4th, with orders to take
him dead or alive, if they could see him," Gass, p. 27. "At 1 o'clock dispatched George Drewyer, R. Fields, Wm. Bratton & Wm. Labieche back
after the Deserter reed, with order if he did not give up peaceably to put him to
Death," Clark, MS.

[30] Dakotan Indian name, from *inyan*, "stone," and *wa-tpa*, "river," *i. e.*,
Stone river, as in the text. This is the largest of several streams draining
western parts of Iowa into the Missouri, arising near the sources of the Des
Moines in S.W. Minnesota, in a system of prairie lakes, the largest of which,
close by the Des Moines river, is about 7 miles long and broad, and commonly
known as Spirit lake, from the Sioux name Mini-wakon, "spirit" or "medicine"
water. One of its largest tributaries had the Indian name Otcheyedan, derived
from a hill where the Indians went to mourn their dead relatives, the word
meaning "crying-place." This is marked Ocheyedan hillock or Mourning
ground on Nicollet's map. Clark's map (1814) draws a straight line, in part
along the Little Sioux river, from the Missouri to the Des Moines, calling it the

Rivière des Sioux, or Little Sioux river. At its confluence it is 80 yards wide. Our interpreter, Mr. Durion, who has been to the sources of it and knows the adjoining country, says that it rises within about nine miles of the river Des Moines; that within 15 leagues of that river it passes through a large lake nearly 60 miles in circumference, divided into two parts by rocks which approach each other very (*p. 42*) closely; its width is various; it contains many islands, and is known by the name of the Lac d'Esprit; it is near the Dog plains [Prairie du Chien], and within four days' march of the Mahas. The country watered by it is open and undulating, and may be visited in boats up the river for some distance. The Des Moines, he adds, is about 80 yards wide where the Little Sioux river approaches it; it is shoaly, and one of its principal branches is called Cat river. Two miles beyond this [Little Sioux] river is a long island which we called Pelican island,[31] from the numbers of that bird which were feeding on it; one of these being killed, we poured into his bag five gallons of water. An elk was shot, and we had again to remark that snakes are rare in this part of the Missouri. A meridian altitude near the Little Sioux river made the latitude 41° 42' 34". We camped on the north [in Monona Co., Ia.], having come 16 miles.

*August 9th.* A thick fog detained us until past seven o'clock, after which we proceeded with a gentle breeze

Old Route ; and indicates two portages from as many lakes over to the Des Moines. The Little Sioux flows in a general S.W. and S. course, and empties into the Missouri in Harrison Co., Ia. It is the Inyan Yankey of Nicollet's map. Clark's MS. has Eaneahwaudepon and Petite river de Cuouex, and again Little Cuouex, said to pass through a lake called Despree, *i.e.*, d'Esprits. Clark never settled on any spelling of the word Sioux, and his MS. shows great originality and fertility of resource in arranging the letters. I find, for instance, besides Cuouex, Scouex, Suouex, Souex, Souix, Soux, Soues, Sieouex, Sceouex, Sicouex, Seaux. Seauex, Sues, etc., with some remarkable endings for imaginary plurals in -xs and -xes. Some of these permutations persist in his MS. of later years. The uniformity of Sioux in the text is due to Biddle.

[31] Such an island appears on the Mo. R. Comm. map, its head at the 730th mile point.

from the southeast. After passing two sand-bars we reached, at 7½ miles, a point of high land on the left, near which the river has forced itself a channel across a peninsula, leaving on the right a circuit of 12 or 18 miles, which is now recognized by the ponds and islands it contains. At 17½ miles, we reached a point on the north, where we camped. The hills are at a great distance from the river for the last several days; the land on both sides is low, and covered with cottonwood and abundance of grape-vines. An elk was seen to-day, a turkey was shot, and near our camp is a beaver-den; the mosquitoes have been more troublesome than ever for the two last days.

*August 10th.* At 2½ miles, we came to a place called Coupée à Jacques, where the river has found a new bed and abridged a circuit of several miles; at 12½ miles, to a cliff of yellow stone on the left. This is the first high land near the river above the Council-bluff. After passing a number of sand-bars we reached a willow-island at the distance of 22½ miles, which we (*p. 43*) were enabled to do with our oars and a wind from the S.W., and camped on the north side.[32]

*August 11th.* After a violent wind from the N.W. attended with rain, we sailed along the right of the island. At nearly five miles, we halted on the south side for the purpose of examining a spot where one of the great chiefs of the Mahas [Omahas], named Blackbird, who died about

[32] Neither the courses nor distances of Aug. 9th and 10th can now be recognized with any certainty, as the bed of the river has changed greatly, with corresponding alteration of the boundary line between what are now Iowa and Nebraska. Several maps consulted show different courses, cut-offs, and lakes, variously named and hardly identifiable. How these may be formed is indicated in the following : "Passed *la coupe à L'Oiselle.* This name originated in the circumstance of a trader having made a narrow escape, being in the river at the very moment that this cut-off was forming. It was a bend of fifteen miles round, and perhaps not more than a few hundred yards across, the neck, which was suddenly cut through by the river and became the main channel." Brackenridge, Journal, 1814, p. 229. On the whole the river seems to have straightened, as the distances now computed are decidedly less than those estimated by Lewis and Clark. Camp of Aug. 10th is in Monona Co., Ia.

four [in 1800] years ago of the smallpox, was buried. A
hill of yellow soft sandstone rises from the river in bluffs
of various heights, till it ends in a knoll about 300 feet
above the water; on the top of this a mound, of twelve
feet diameter at the base and six feet high, is raised over
the body of the deceased king; a pole of about eight feet
high is fixed in the center, on which we placed a white
flag, bordered with red, blue, and white. Blackbird seems
to have been a personage of great consideration; for ever
since his death he has been supplied with provisions, from
time to time, by the superstitious regard of the Mahas.[33]
We descended to the river and passed a small creek on the
south, called by the Mahas Waucandipeeche[34] (Great Spirit

[33] The following notice of Blackbird, who seems to have been a pretty black
sheep of the Omaha flock, is taken from Brackenridge's Journal (orig. ed.,
Pittsburgh, 1814), p. 229:

"*Saturday* 18*th*. A fine breeze S.W. At seven arrived at the Black-bird
hill. . . It takes its name from a celebrated chief of the Mahas, who caused himself to be interred on the top; a mound has been erected on the pinnacle, with
a branch stuck in it; a flag was formerly attached to it. He was buried sitting
erect on horseback; the reason why he chose this spot was to enable him
to see the traders as they ascended. This chief was as famous in his lifetime amongst all the nations in this part of the world, as Tamerlane or Bajazet
were in the plains of Asia; a superstitious awe is still paid to his grave. Yet
the secret of his greatness was nothing more than a quantity of arsenic which he
procured from some trader. He denounced death against anyone who displeased him or opposed his wishes; it is, therefore, not surprising that he, who
held at his disposal the lives of others, should possess unlimited power and
excite universal terror. The proud savage, whenever this terrible being appeared, rendered the homage of a slave." This immense brute's Indian name
was Wash-ing-guh-sah-ba; he was a great scoundrel and a great soldier. His
own band was called Monekagoha, or the Earth-makers, from their habit of rubbing the body with clay when mourning. During his youth the Omahas were
above the mouth of Floyd's river. He sought to poison Little Bow, an inferior
chief who opposed him; but he failed, and Little Bow maintained a separate
village on the Missouri till Blackbird's death. The successor of Blackbird was
Mushinga or the Big Rabbit, who was shortly succeeded by Tasone, the White
Cow, and he by Ongpatonga, the Big Elk. (See Long's Exp. R. Mts. I., Eng.
ed., pp. 204-207). Tradition has magnified Blackbird's exploits, and the hill
where he was buried still bears his name. His best biography is Irving's
(Astoria, ed. 1861, pp. 161-166).

[34] Elsewhere called "Warcarde or Bad Spirit" creek. The name is spelled

is bad). Near this creek and the adjoining hills the Mahas had a village, and lost 400 of their nation by the dreadful malady which destroyed Blackbird. The meridian altitude made the latitude 42° 1′ 3$\frac{8}{10}$″ north. We camped at 17 miles' distance, on the north side, in a bend of the river.[35] During our day's course it has been crooked ; we observed a number of places in it where the old channel is filled up, or gradually becoming covered with willow and cotton-wood. Great numbers of herrons [herons, *Herodias egretta*] are observed to-day, and mosquitoes annoy us very much.

*August 12th.* A gentle breeze from the south carried us along about ten miles, when we stopped to take a meridian altitude, and sent a man across to our place of observation yesterday. He stepped 974 yards, and the distance we had come round was 18¾ miles. The river is wider and shallower than usual. Four miles beyond this bend a bluff begins, and (*p. 44*) continues several miles; on the south it rises from the water at different heights, from 20 to 150 feet, and higher as it recedes on the river ; it consists of yellow and brown clay, with soft sandstone imbedded in it, and is covered with timber, among which may be observed some red cedar; the lands on the opposite side are low and subject to inundation, but contain willows, cottonwoods, and many grapes. A prairie-wolf [*Canis latrans*] came near the bank and barked at us; we attempted unsuccessfully to take him. This part of the river abounds in beaver. We camped on a sand-island in a bend to the north,[36] having made 20¼ miles.

*August 13th.* Set out at daylight with a breeze from the

Wawandysenche on Clark's map, 1814, and Long's, 1823. The first element in this name is Wakon, Dakotan for " Spirit," " Medicine," or something not understood. This stream is in Thurston Co., Neb., where is now the Omaha Indian Reservation.

[35] Near the present Badger Lake, Monona Co., Ia. Of the " herrons " presently noticed, Lewis' MS. of Aug. 2d gives a long and good description.

[36] Apparently just over the border of Woodbury Co., Ia., and near a lake marked on some maps Crooked lake. But there is now no such bend in the river as the text describes, and the point cannot be located exactly. It should be about the 775th mile point of present charts.

southeast, and passed several sand-bars. Between 10 and 11 miles, we came to a spot on the south where a Mr. Mackay[37] had a trading-establishment in the years 1795 and 1796, which he called Fort Charles. At 14 miles we reached a creek on the south, on which the Mahas[38] reside, and at 17¼ miles, formed a camp on a sand-bar, to the south side of the river, opposite the lower point of a large island. From this place Sergeant Ordway and four men were detached to the Maha village with a flag and a pres-

[37] Lewis' map of 1806 traces " Mr. J. Mackay's Route" from this point along the Loup fork of the Platte, and back by way of the Niobrara to the Missouri. This detail is omitted on Clark's map of 1814, where the Maha village is marked very plainly on a forked creek. This creek had the same name, but its position with respect to the Missouri changed much in the course of years. This day's camp is made very nearly opposite the present site of Omadi, in Dakota Co., Neb., and not far from a creek of the same name.

[38] These Indians are so called throughout, except once or twice when the name is printed Mahar. In the Statistical View Lewis gives Maha and O'mâ-ha. The French nickname he prints "La Mar." The name was often written Omaw'haw (so Long, 1823, chaps. x. et seq., where Say gives their history). The proper phonetic rendering is U-man'-han, with scarcely nasalized n's, and the accent on the second syllable—not on the first, as we now always place it in speaking the name of the great city opposite Council Bluffs. The locality is in Dakota Co., Neb., a little south of Dakota City, north of the present Omaha Indian Reservation.

The Omahas are a tribe of the great Siouan family. They are now at the Omaha and Winnebago Agency in Nebraska, to the reported number of 1,158 ; to which are to be added 19 at school in Carlisle, Pa., 10 at the Hampton school in Virginia, and 10 at the Lawrence school in Kansas ; total 1,197.

In 1805, when Lewis' Statistical View was prepared (pub. 1806 and again 1807), the census was 600, including 150 warriors and 60 lodges. The indication of their family affinities is given by Lewis, who says that they speak "Osage, with different accent ; some words peculiar to themselves." He adds : "About ten years since, they boasted 700 warriors. They have lived in a village on the west bank of the Missouri, 236 miles above the mouth of the river Platte, where they cultivated corn, beans, and melons; they were warlike, and the terror of their neighbours. In the summer and autumn of 1802, they were visited by the small-pox, which reduced their numbers to something less than 300 ; they burnt their village, and have become a wandering nation, deserted by the traders, and the consequent deficiency of arms and ammunition has invited frequent aggressions from their neigbours [sic], which have tended to reduce them still further. They rove principally on the waters of the river Quicurre [Qui court, the Niobrara], or Rapid River. . . The Tetons Bois brûlè [sic] killed and took about 60 of them last summer [1804]." (London ed. 1807, p. 16.)

ent, in order to induce the Mahas to come and hold a council with us. They returned at twelve o'clock the next day, *August 14th.* After crossing a prairie covered with high grass they reached the Maha creek, along which they proceeded to its three forks, which join near the village; they crossed the north branch and went along the south; the walk was very fatiguing, as they were forced to break their way through grass, sunflowers, and thistles, all above ten feet high and interspersed with wild pea. Five miles from our camp they reached the position of the ancient Maha village; it had once consisted of 300 cabins, but was burnt about four years ago, soon after the smallpox had destroyed 400 men and a proportion of women and children. On a hill, in the rear of the village are the graves (*p. 45*) of the nation, to the south of which runs the fork of the Maha creek; this they crossed where it was about ten yards wide, and followed its course to the Missouri, passing along a ridge of hill for 1½ miles, and a long pond between that and the Missouri; they then recrossed the Maha creek, and arrived at the camp, having seen no tracks of Indians nor any sign of recent cultivation.

*August 15th.* In the morning some men were sent to examine the cause of a large smoke from the northeast, which seemed to indicate that some Indians were near; but they found that a small party, who had lately passed that way, had left some trees burning, and that the wind from that quarter blew the smoke directly toward us. Our camp lies about three miles northeast from the old Maha village, and is in latitude 42° 13′ 41″. The accounts we have had of the effects of the smallpox on that nation are most distressing; it is not known in what way it was first communicated to them, though probably by some war-party. They had been a military and powerful people; but when these warriors saw their strength wasting before a malady which they could not resist, their frenzy was extreme; they burnt their village, and many of them put to death their wives and children, to save them from so cruel an affliction, and that all might go together to some better country.

*August 16th.* We still waited for the Indians. A party had gone out yesterday to the Maha creek, which was dammed [39] up by the beaver between the camp and the village. A second went to-day. They made a kind of drag with small willows and bark, and swept the creek. The first company brought 318 fish, the second upward of 800,[40] consisting of pike, bass, fish resembling salmon-trout, red-horse, buffalo-fish, rock-fish, one flat-back, perch, catfish, a small species of perch called on the Ohio silver-fish, a shrimp [41] of the same size, shape, and flavor of those about New Orleans and the lower part of the Mississippi. We also found very fat mussels;[42] and in the river as well as (*p. 46*) the creek, are different kinds of ducks and plovers. The wind, which in the morning had been from the northwest, shifted round in the evening to the southeast, and as usual we had a breeze which cooled the air and relieved us from the mosquitoes, which generally give us great trouble.

*August 17th.* The wind continued from the southeast, and the morning was fair. We observe about us a grass resembling wheat, except that the grain is like rye; also, some similar to both rye and barley, and a kind of timothy, the seed of which branches from the main stock, and is more like a flaxseed than a timothy. In the evening one

---

[39] As to the operations of the beaver, Clark wrote that the creek was damed by them, and the Biddle text makes it damned by them ; I alter as above.

[40] It appears by comparing Gass at Aug. 15th that the veracity of our authors almost extends to reporting fish caught. We here have $318 + 800 = 1,118$ ; Gass says $387 + 709 = 1,096$. Clark's MS. names the camp of Aug. 13th–19th Fishing Camp. I desired to identify to-day's catch, as doubtless among these fishes were species which were then new to science. But after dragging the codices patiently I got only a water-haul, and any identifications I could make on the strength of the bare names would be *ex post facto,* so to speak, or merely based on our present knowledge of Missouri ichthyology.

[41] Not shrimp properly so-called, which are marine crustaceans, but a kind of crawfish common in the Missouri, of the genus *Cambarus.*

[42] Some species of fresh-water bivalve mollusks of the family *Unionidæ.* Clark wrote mustles ; Biddle printed muscles, and I alter as above.

of the party sent to the Ottoes returned with the information that the rest were coming on with the deserter; they had also caught Liberté, but by a trick he had made his escape; they were bringing three of the chiefs in order to engage our assistance in making peace with the Mahas. This nation having left their village, that desirable purpose cannot be effected; but in order to bring in any neighboring tribes, we set the surrounding prairies on fire. This is the customary signal made by traders to apprise the Indians of their arrival; it is also used between different nations as an indication of any event which they have previously agreed to announce in that way, and as soon as it is seen collects the neighboring tribes, unless they apprehend that it is made by their enemies.

*August 18th.* In the afternoon the party arrived with the Indians, consisting of Little Thief and Big Horse, whom we had seen on the 3d, together with six other chiefs and a French interpreter.[43] We met them under a shade, and after they had finished a repast with which we supplied them, we inquired into the origin of the war between them and the Mahas, which they related with great frankness. It seems that two of the Missouris went to the Mahas to steal horses, but were detected and killed; the Ottoes and Missouris thought themselves bound to avenge their companions, and the whole nations were at last obli- (*p. 47*) ged to share in the dispute. They are also in fear of a war from the Pawnees, whose village they entered this summer, while the inhabitants were hunting, and stole their corn.

---

[43] Under this date Gass prints, p. 29 : "The party who had been sent in pursuit of the man who had been absent since the 4th, returned with him and eight Indians and a Frenchman, but left our Frenchman [Liberté] behind, who had gone to hunt the horses." Clark's journal of the 28th finishes the story of the deserter : "Proceeded to the trial of Reed, he confessed that he ' Deserted & Stold a public Rifle shot-pouch Powder & Ball ' and requested we would be as favourable with him as we could consistantly with our Oathes—which we were and only sentenced him to run the gantlet four times through the Party & that each man with 9 switchies should punish him and for him not to be considered in future as one of the Party—"

This ingenuous confession did not make us the less desirous of negotiating a peace for them; but no Indians have as yet been attracted by our fire.   The evening was closed by a dance; and the next day,

*August* 19*th*, the chiefs and warriors being assembled at ten o'clock, we explained the speech we had already sent from the Council-bluffs, and renewed our advice.   They all replied in turn, and the presents were then distributed ; we exchanged the small medal we had formerly given to Big Horse for one of the same size with that of Little Thief ; we also gave a small medal to a third chief, and a kind of certificate or letter of acknowledgment to five of the warriors, expressive of our favor and their good intentions. One of them, dissatisfied, returned us the certificate ; but the chief, fearful of our being offended, begged that it might be restored to him ;  this we declined, and rebuked them severely for having in view mere traffic instead of peace with their neighbors.   This displeased them at first ; but they at length all petitioned that it should be given to the warrior, who then came forward and made an apology to us ; we then delivered it to the chief to be given to the most worthy, and he bestowed it on the same warrior, whose name was Great Blue Eyes.   After a more substantial present of small articles and tobacco, the council was ended with a dram to the Indians.   In the evening we exhibited different objects of curiosity, and particularly the air-gun, which gave them great surprise.   These people are almost naked, having no covering except a sort of breech-cloth round the middle, with a loose blanket or buffalo robe painted, thrown over them.   The names of these warriors, besides those already mentioned, were Karkapaha or Crow's Head, and Nenasawa or Black Cat, Missouris ; Sananona or Iron Eyes, Neswaunja or Big Ox, Stageaunja or Big Blue Eyes, and Wa- (*p. 48*) sashaco or Brave Man, all Ottoes.   These two tribes speak very nearly the same language ; they all begged us to give them whisky.

*August 20th.*   The Indians mounted their horses and left us, having received a canister of whisky at parting.   We then set sail, and after passing two islands on the north, came-to on that side under some bluffs, the first near the river since we left the Ayauwa village.

Here we had the misfortune to lose one of our sergeants, Charles Floyd.   He was yesterday seized with a bilious colic, and all our care and attention were ineffectual to relieve him.   A little before his death he said to Captain Clark, " I am going to leave you ; " his strength failed him as he added, " I want you to write me a letter." He died with a composure which justified the high opinion we had formed of his firmness and good conduct.   He was buried on the top of the bluff with the honors due to a brave soldier ; the place of his interment was marked by a cedar post, on which his name and the day of his death were inscribed.   About a mile beyond this place, to which we gave his name, is a small river about 30 yards wide, on the north, which we called Floyd's [44] river, where we

[44] It may be interesting to reproduce the above paragraph from the original manuscript of Clark's journal, at dates of Aug. 19th and 20th.   It is precisely as follows : " Serjeant Floyd is taken verry bad all at once with a Biliose Chorlick we attempt to reliev him without success as yet, he gets worse and we are much allarmed at his situation, all attention to him . . . Sergeant Floyd much weaker and no better . . . as bad as he can be no pulse and nothing will stay a moment on his stomach or bowels. . . Died with a great deel of composure, before his death he said to me ' I am going away I want you to write me a letter '—— We buried him on the top of the bluff ½ mile below a small river to which we gave his name, he was buried with the Honors of War much lamented, a seeder post with the Name Sergt. C. Floyd died here 20th of August 1804 was fixed at the head of his grave——This man at all times gave us proofs of his firmness and Determined resolution to doe service to his countrey and honor to himself aftes paying all the honor to our Decesed brother we camped in the mouth of *floyds* river about 30 yards wide, a butifull evening."

Floyd's river, first so charted on Lewis' map of 1806, still bears his name ; the bluff is still Floyd's, and his grave is marked on Clark's map of 1814.   Like Blackbird's, it was for many years a landmark.   It shows plainly on Nicollet's map of 1843, and this author, writing of 1839, says : " We stopped before night at the foot of the bluff on which is Floyd's grave ; my men replaced the signal, blown down by the winds, which marks the spot and hallows the memory of the

camped. We had a breeze from the southeast, and made 13 miles.

*August 21st.* The same breeze from the southeast carried us by a small willow creek [45] on the north, about 1½ miles above Floyd's river. Here began a range of bluffs which continued till near the mouth of the Great Sioux river, three miles beyond Floyd's. This river comes in from the north, and is about 110 yards wide. Mr. Durion, our Sioux interpreter, who is well acquainted with it, says that it is navigable upward of 200 miles to the falls, and even beyond them; that its sources are near those of the St. Peter's [Minnesota river]. He also says that below the falls a creek falls in from the eastward, after passing through cliffs of red rock; of this the Indians make their pipes, and the necessity of procuring that article has intro- (*p. 49*) duced a sort of law of nations, by which the banks of the creek are sacred; even tribes at war meet without hostility at these quarries, which possess a right of asylum. Thus we find even among savages certain principles deemed sacred, by which the rigors of their merciless system of warfare are mitigated. A sense of common danger, where stronger ties are wanting, gives all the binding force of more solemn obligations. The importance of preserving the known and settled rules of warfare among civilized nations, in all their integrity, becomes strikingly evident; since even savages, with their few precarious wants, cannot exist in a state of peace or war where this faith is once violated.[46]

brave sergeant who died here during Lewis and Clark's expedition" (Report, p. 34). Another point of the same bluff, a little lower down, is now called Sergeant's bluff. The river with its tributaries drains several northwestern counties of Iowa, and falls into the Missouri a little below Sioux City, lat. approximately 42° 30' N., and a little above the 800th mile point. On the much reduced map of the M'Vickar edition (1842), the name is printed "Castus"—a word I have not found elsewhere.

[45] Now Perry creek. The range of bluffs about to be mentioned is now called Prospect hill. Here is the site of Sioux City, Ia.

[46] The Big Sioux river is to-day not less geographically notable than was it formerly of ethnographic consequence. At its mouth is the southeast corner of South Dakota, meeting here both Nebraska and Iowa. Here the Missouri

The wind became southerly, and blew with such violence that we took a reef in our sail ; it also blew the sand from the bars in such quantities that we could not see the channel at any distance ahead. At 4¼ miles we came to two willow-islands, beyond which are several sand-bars ; and at twelve miles, to a spot where the Mahas once had a village, no longer existing. We again passed a number of sand-bars and camped on the south, having come 24¾ miles. The country through which we passed has the same uniform appearance ever since we left the Platte—rich, low grounds near the river, succeeded by undulating prairies, with timber near the waters. Some wolves were seen to-day on the sand-beaches to the south ; we also procured an excellent fruit, resembling a red currant, growing on a shrub like the privy [privet], and about the height of a wild plum.

*August 22d.* About three miles' distance, we joined the men who had been sent from the Maha village with our horses, and who brought us two deer. The bluffs [elsewhere called Mineral bluffs[47]] or hills which reach the river at this place, on the south, contain alum, copperas, cobalt which had the appearance of soft isinglass, pyrites and sandstone, the two first very pure. Above this bluff comes in a small creek on the south, which we call Rologe [*sic*[48]] creek.

ceases to separate Nebraska from Iowa, and begins to separate Nebraska from South Dakota. The Sioux river itself forms the whole of the boundary between Iowa and South Dakota, from lat. 42° 30' to 43° 30'. It was also called Tchankasndata river (so on Nicollet's map, 1843) ; the name is said to mean that the river is continuously wooded. The upper part was also distinguished as the Watpa-ipak-shan or crooked river, and by the French as la rivière Croche, or, as we should say, Crotchet river. Some sources of the Sioux river, at the head of the Coteau des prairies, are not more than a mile from those of the Minnesota or St. Peter's river.

[47] The bluffs along the river here and higher up, called Mineral bluffs by Lewis and Clark, are named by Nicollet Dixon's bluffs, after William Dixon, a trader. The rocks composing this series of bluffs are geologically considered by Nicollet under the name of Dixon's group, in which he establishes three divisions in ascending order : A, argillaceous limestone ; B, calcareous marl ; C, a slightly ferruginous clay. "This group is the basis of the cretaceous formations of the Missouri."

[48] No clew to this name. Clark's MS. has : "This creek I call Roloje [very

Seven miles above is another cliff, on the ( *p.* 50) same side, of alum rock of a dark brown color, containing in its crevices great quantities of cobalt, cemented shells, and red earth.[49]    From this the river bends eastward, and approaches the [Great] Sioux river within three or four miles. We sailed the greater part of the day, and made 19 miles to our camp on the north side [near Elk Point, Union Co., S. D.].

The sand-bars are as usual numerous ; there are also considerable traces of elk, but none are yet seen.   Captain Lewis, in proving the quality of some of the substances in the first cliff, was considerably injured by the fumes and taste of the cobalt, and took some strong medicine to relieve him from its effects.   The appearance of these mineral substances enabled us to account for disorders of the stomach with which the party had been affected since they left the river Sioux.   We had been in the habit of dipping up the water of the river inadvertently and making use of it till, on examination, the sickness was thought to proceed from a scum covering the surface of the water along the southern shore, but which, as we now discovered, proceeded from these

plainly written] a name I learned last night is "—then the copy is blind, with something like an *m*, a blank space, and then a plain *s*.   There was a person of the American Fur Company named Rolette (so Long), or Rollet (so Pike). This stream is Ayoway creek of Nicollet's map, and now Iowa creek (misprinted Norway creek on the G. L. O. map, 1876), in Dixon Co., Neb., just above the 830th mile point of the Missouri.

[49] The appearances indicate the very great and remarkable change in the geological formation of the country upon which the expedition has now entered. Hitherto it has been palæozoic, and for the most part silurian and permo-carboniferous, especially the latter, which occupies northern and western Missouri, southern Iowa, eastern Kansas, and a small southeastern corner of Nebraska above and below the mouth of the Platte river.   Where the permo-carboniferous ends on the Missouri, above Council Bluffs, Iowa is quaternary to the river, and Nebraska is cretaceous.   At the mouth of Great Sioux river, at the extreme southeast corner of South Dakota, the Expedition has entered upon that vast extent of the cretaceous formation which the Missouri traverses in South and North Dakota and Montana, without a break to the head of navigation of the river.   Almost all of both Dakotas, and the greater part of Montana, are in fact cretaceous.

bluffs. The men had been ordered, before we reached the bluffs, to agitate the water, so as to disperse the scum, and take the water, not at the surface, but at some depth. The consequence was, that these disorders ceased; the boils too which had afflicted the men were not observed beyond the Sioux river.

In order to supply the place of Sergeant Floyd, we permitted the men to name three persons [Gass, Bratton, and Gibson]; and Patrick Gass, having the greatest number of votes, was made a sergeant.[50]

*August 23d.* We set out early, and at four miles came to a small run between cliffs of yellow and blue earth. The wind, however, soon changed and blew so hard from the west that we proceeded very slowly; the fine sand from the bar being driven in such clouds that we could scarcely see. At 3¼ miles beyond this run we came to a willow-island and a sand-island opposite, and camped on the south side, at 10¼ miles. On the north side is an extensive and delightful prairie, which we called Buffalo (*p. 51*) prairie, from our having here killed the first buffalo.[51] Two elk swam the river to-day and were fired at, but escaped; a deer was killed from the boat; one beaver was killed, and several prairie-wolves were seen.

*August 24th.* It began to rain last night and continued this morning; we proceeded, however, 2¼ miles, to the commencement of a bluff of blue clay, about 180 or 190 feet, on the south side; it seems to have been lately on fire, and even now the ground is so warm that we cannot keep our hands in it at any depth; there are strong appearances of coal, and also great quantities of cobalt, or a

[50] His promotion is not mentioned in the journal of the modest Irishman. Clark wrote: "Ordered a vote for a serjeant to chuse one of three . . . P. Gass had 19 votes."

[51] Killed by Captain Clark and one of the men; two barrels of the meat salted, Gass, p. 30. But Clark himself credits the first buffalo to Joseph Fields alone. The extensive prairies above noted are the Hutan Kutey prairies of Nicollet. They recall the famous "American bottom" along the Mississippi below St. Louis. To-day's camp is in Dixon Co., Neb.

crystallized substance resembling it.[52]    There is a fruit now ripe which looks like a red currant, except that it is double the size, and grows on a bush about ten feet high, like a privy [privet,[53] *Ligustrum vulgare*], the size of a damson and of a delicious flavor; its Indian name means rabbit-berries. We then passed, at the distance of about seven miles, the mouth of a creek on the north side, called by an Indian name meaning Whitestone river.[54]    The beautiful prairie of yesterday has changed into one of greater height, very smooth and extensive. We camped on the south side [in-Dixon Co., Neb.], at 10¼ miles, and found ourselves much annoyed by the mosquitoes. (*p. 52*)

[52] This locality is called in the Summary Statement Hot or Burning Bluffs. The formation of these bluffs, and the attendant phenomena suggestive of volcanic action, were very early the subjects of observation and speculation. They may be compared with similar places in various parts of the world known by the French as terrains ardens. Those on the Missouri were called by the voyageurs côtes brulées and collines brulées—burnt bluffs,burnt hills. They were formally styled pseudo-volcanoes by Nicollet in 1843, who also called attention in this connection to the peculiar light, spongy stone which Lewis and Clark repeatedly speak of as pumice, but which he names pumiciform stone, as not being true pumice, but resembling it. He found no hills smoking when he ascended in 1839, nor did Lewis and Clark ; but was credibly informed that such an occurrence had been witnessed in the interim. See his Report, p. 39 *et seq*.

[53] The privet is European, nowhere native in North America. The plant meant is the buffalo-berry, or beefsuet-tree (F. graisse de bœuf), *Shepherdia argentea*, an elæagnaceous shrub abounding in and highly characteristic of the region the Expedition now enters.

[54] This Indian name is Wassisha, Wassesha, Wassecha, etc., to be found on various old maps. The usual translation, White-earth, or White-stone, would be better Smoky-earth. The French name of Perrin du Lac is rivière à Loutre (Otter river). The river is laid down, but unlettered, on Lewis' map of 1806, where it may be identified by the mound inscribed Hill of Little Devils (see next chapter). It is lettered White Stone R. on Clark's map, 1814. This is now called Vermilion or Vermillion river. It reaches the Missouri through Clay Co., S. D., and the county town of Vermilion is at its mouth. It is a short river, some 60 miles long, issuing from some prairie lakes which used to be called by the French les lacs au Bois léger, or Lightwood lakes. The Buffalo prairie of Lewis and Clark ends at this river.

# CHAPTER III.

## THE MISSOURI FROM VERMILION TO TETON RIVER.

Spirit mound, and Indian superstition concerning it—Birds and plants—Petit Arc or Little Bow creek—Jacques, James, or Yankton river—Vicinity of Sioux Indians—Calumet bluff—Visit to the Sioux camp—Council with the Sioux—Characteristics of the Yankton Sioux—Ten tribes of the Sioux or Dakotas—White Bear cliff—Bon Homme or Good Man island—Description and plan of an ancient "fortification"—Plum, White-lime, and White-paint Creeks—L'Eau qui Court, or Rapid river—Pawnee island—Goat creek—Ponca river—Ponca village—Prairie-dog village—Pawnee house—Boat island—Cedar island—Return of George Shannon—Slow progress on account of sand-bars—White river—Corvus creek—Baggage shifted—Oak and other trees—Antelope and other animals—Prospect island—The three Sioux rivers—Elm and Night creeks—Lower island—Grand Détour or Great Bend of the Missouri—Solitary island—Tylor's river—Three Sisters—Cedar island—Loisel's fort—Elk island—Reuben's creek—Large Sioux camps—Highwater creek—Good-humored island—The Expedition reaches Teton river.

UGUST 25th. Captains Lewis and Clark, with ten men, went to see an object deemed very extraordinary among all the neighboring Indians. They dropped down to the mouth of Whitestone river, about 30 yards wide, where they left the boat, and at the distance of 200 yards ascended a rising ground, from which a plain extended as far as the eye could discern. After walking four miles, they crossed the creek where it is 23 yards wide and waters an extensive valley. The heat was so oppressive that we were obliged to send back our dog to the creek, as he was unable to bear the fatigue; and it was not till after four hours' march that we reached the object of our visit. This was a large mound in the midst of the plain, about N. 20° W. from the mouth of Whitestone river, from which it is nine miles distant. The base of the mound is a regular parallelogram, the longest side being about 300 yards, the shorter 60 or 70; from the longest side it rises with a steep ascent from the north and south to the height of 65 or 70 feet, leaving on the top a level plain of 12 feet in breadth and 90 in length. The north and south extremities are connected by two oval borders which serve as new

bases, and divide the whole side into three steep but
regular gradations from the plain. The only thing characteristic in this hill is its extreme symmetry, and this,
together with its being totally detached from (*p. 53*) the
other hills which are at the distance of eight or nine miles,
would induce a belief that it was artificial; but as the earth
and the loose pebbles which compose it are arranged exactly like the steep grounds on the borders of the creek, we
concluded from this similarity of texture that it might be
natural. The Indians have made it a great article of their
superstition; it is called the mountain of Little People, or
Little Spirits,[1] and they believe that it is the abode of
little devils in the human form, about 18 inches high and
with remarkably large heads, armed with sharp arrows,
with which they are very skillful, and always on the watch
to kill those who should have the hardihood to approach
their residence. The tradition is that many have suffered
from these little evil spirits; among others, three Maha
Indians fell a sacrifice to them a few years since. This
has inspired all the neighboring nations, Sioux, Mahas, and
Ottoes, with such terror that no consideration could tempt
them to visit the hill. We saw none of these wicked little
spirits; nor any place for them, except some small holes
scattered over the top; we were happy enough to escape
their vengeance, though we remained some time on the

[1] Marked on Lewis' map of 1806 as the Hill of Little Devils; on Clark's
map of 1814 charted, but unnamed. The tradition has outlived the superstition
to which it owes its origin, and survives in the name Spirit mound, still
applied by settlers, and appearing on modern maps. This elevation is situated
in Clay Co., S. D., in section 14, town 93, range 52; it extends nearly north
and south, being about 1000 feet long, 350 feet wide at the base, and 95 to 115
feet high, though of anything but symmetrical figure. The highest point
is marked by an iron tube, indicating a station of the Missouri River Survey.
The body of the hill is chalkstone of the cretaceous group, to within 30 feet or
less of the top, covered with yellow clay, and this with gravelly loam. A few
miles to the N.W. is a bluff, some 30 to 50 feet higher than this hillock, probably at one time continuous with the latter, the intervening space being due to
erosion. (T. H. Lewis' paper on pseudo-antiquities of the Missouri, in the
Amer. Antiq. and Orient. Journ., xiii. No. 5, Sept. 1891, p. 289.)

mound to enjoy the delightful prospect of the plain, which spreads itself out till the eye rests upon the N.W. hills at a great distance, and those of the N.E. still farther off, enlivened by large herds of buffalo feeding at a distance.

The soil of these plains is exceedingly fine ; there is, however, no timber except on the Missouri, all the wood of the Whitestone river not being sufficient to cover thickly 100 acres. The plain country which surrounds this mound has contributed not a little to its bad reputation ; the wind driving from every direction over the level ground obliges the insects to seek shelter on its leeward side, or to be driven against us by the wind. The small birds, whose food they are, resort of course in great numbers in quest of subsistence ; and the Indians always seem to discover an unusual assemblage of birds as produced by some supernatural (*p. 54*) cause. Among them we observed the brown martin employed in looking for insects, and so gentle that they did not fly until we got within a few feet of them. We have also distinguished, among the numerous birds of the plain, the blackbird, the wren or prairie-bird, and a species of lark about the size of a partridge, with a short tail.[2] The excessive heat and thirst forced us from the hill about one o'clock, to the nearest water, which we found in the creek at three miles' distance, and remained an hour and a half. We then went down the creek, through a lowland about one mile in width, and crossed it three times, to the spot where we first reached it in the morning. Here we gathered some delicious plums, grapes, and blue currants, and afterward arrived at the mouth of the river about sunset. To this place the course from the mound is S. 20 miles, E. 9 miles ; we there resumed our periogue, and on reaching our camp of last night set the prairies on fire, to warn the Sioux of our approach. In the mean time, the boat under Sergeant Pryor had proceeded in the afternoon

---

[2] None of these birds is certainly identifiable (though all are of course now well-known), except the lark, which is the Western field-lark, *Sturnella neglecta.*

one mile, to a bluff of blue clay on the south, and after passing a sand-bar and two sand-islands [his men] fixed their camp at the distance of six miles on the south. In the evening some rain fell. We had killed a duck and several birds; in the boat they had caught some large catfish.[3]

*August 26th.* We rejoined the boat at nine o'clock before she set out; and, then passing by an island and under a cliff on the south, nearly two miles in extent and composed of white and blue earth, camped at nine miles' distance, on a sand-bar toward the north. Opposite to this, on the south, is a small creek called Petit Arc[4] or Little Bow; and a short distance above it, an old village of the same name. This village, of which nothing remains but the mound of earth about four feet high surrounding it, was built by a Maha chief named Little Bow, who being displeased with Blackbird, the late king, seceded with 200 followers and settled at this spot; it is now abandoned, as the two (*p. 55*) villages have reunited since the death of Blackbird. We have great quantities of grapes, and plums of three kinds; two of a yellow color, distinguished by one of the species being longer than

[3] Gass says " nine that would together weigh 300 pounds." The species is doubtless *Amiurus ponderosus.*

[4] Gass makes it Pettit Ark. It has also been known by its Indian name, Hopa-wazhupi. This is the present Bow creek, Cedar Co., Neb. See beyond, under date of Sept. 2d, what is said of some supposed fortifications or other artificial works, stated to have been seen on the upper side of Petit Arc creek, not far from its mouth. Mr. T. H. Lewis, in his paper on the pseudo-antiquities of the Missouri already cited says (p. 290) of the Little Bow Enclosure, that there are " no traces of any village or artificial works of any description to be found in this neighborhood above the mouth of the Bow, the land being low and subject to overflow. There are, however, several natural ridges, similar to those on Bonhomme Point, which run parallel to the current, when the water is high and covers the bottom." In a note Mr. Lewis adds : " On adjacent hills and plateaus there are isolated ruins of old dirt lodges similar to those constructed by the Mandans. There is also an ancient fort on the East or lower side of Bow creek, about two miles from its mouth, and another still further south, near Hartington, but these two forts were unknown to the Lewis and Clark expedition." But it does not seem impossible that the explorers may have actually had these works in view, though by some slip they did not indicate the location correctly.

the other, and a third round and red ; all have an excellent
flavor, particularly those of the yellow kind.

*August 27th.* The morning star appeared much larger
than usual. A gentle breeze from the southeast carried us
by some large sand-bars, on both sides and in the middle
of the river, to a bluff on the south side 7½ miles distant.
This bluff is of white clay or chalk, under which is much
stone, like lime, incrusted with a clear substance, supposed
to be cobalt, and some dark ore. Above this bluff we set
the prairie on fire to invite the Sioux. After 12½ miles we
had passed several other sand-bars, and reached the mouth
of a river called by the French Jacques (James), or Yankton,
from the tribe which inhabits its banks [and now also
Dakota river]. It is about 90 yards wide at the confluence ;
the country which it waters is rich prairie, with little
timber ; it becomes deeper and wider above its mouth, and
may be navigated a great distance, as its sources rise near
those of St. Peter's [the Minnesota, a branch] of the Mississippi, and [those of] the Red river of lake Winnipeg.[5]

[5] The arrangement of the watersheds in Minnesota and eastern North
Dakota is peculiar. The Red river of the North separates these States, flowing
due north ; while on either hand, at a little distance from this river, the watershed is south—on the Minnesota side, the headwaters of the Mississippi ; on
the Dakota side, some tributaries of the Missouri. James river is the first of
any size after the Big Sioux. It rises in a prairie just south of Devil's lake,
in Wells and Foster Cos., N. D., and runs with a general south course into
the Missouri. The lay of the land just south of Devil's lake is specially
remarkable, since with the sources of James river are also the heads of the
principal western tributary of the Red river. Some judicious remarks on the
Coteau des Prairies (also called Coteau de Missouri) will be found in Long's
Expedition to the St. Peter's, Keating's ed., London, 1825, I. pp. 376, 377, and
p. 380, where the deflection of the Missouri from this ridge is noticed. The
western headwaters of the Mississippi are so little separated by any watershed
from those of the Red river of the North, that it has been found actually possible to go in a boat from the lake at the head of the St. Peter's or Minnesota to
that at the head of the Red river ; but a prairie coteau distinctly separates the
sources of James river from any waters of the Red river, and a still stronger
coteau separates the Missouri from any affluent of the Mouse river, a tributary
of the Assiniboin. Says the work just cited (p. 380) : " It is within the recollection of some persons, now [1823] in the country, that a boat once floated
from Lake Travers into the St. Peter. Thus, therefore, this spot offers us one

As we came to the mouth of the river, an Indian swam to the boat; on our landing we were met by two others, who informed us that a large body of Sioux [Yanktons] were camped near us.    They accompanied three of our men, with an invitation to meet us at a spot above the river. The third Indian remained with us; he is a Maha boy, and says that his nation have gone to the Pawnees to make peace with them.    At 14 miles we camped on a sand-bar to the north [near Yankton, S. D.].    The air was cool, the evening pleasant, the wind from the southeast and light. The river has fallen gradually and is now low.

*August 28th.*  We passed, with a stiff breeze from the south, several sand-bars.    On the south is a prairie which rises gradually from the water to the height of a bluff, which is at four miles' distance, of a whitish color, and (*p. 56*) about 70 or 80 feet high.    Further on is another bluff, of a brownish color, on the north side; and at the distance of 8½ miles is the beginning of Calumet bluff on the south, under which we formed our camp [6] in a beautiful plain, to await the arrival of the Sioux.    At the first bluff the young Indian left us and joined their camp.    Before reaching Calumet bluff one of the periogues ran upon a log in the river and was rendered unfit for service, so that all our loading was put into the second periogue.    On both sides of the river are fine prairies, with cottonwood; near the bluff there is more timber in the points and valleys than we have been accustomed to see.

of those interesting phenomena, which we have already alluded to, but which are nowhere perhaps so apparent as they are in this place.    Here we behold the waters of two mighty streams, one of which empties itself into Hudson's Bay at the 57th parallel of north latitude, and the other into the Gulf of Mexico in latitude 29°, rising in the same valley within three miles of each other, and even in some cases affording a direct natural navigation from one into the other."

[6] In Knox Co., Neb., about the 900th river-mile point, and opposite the lower one of two islands to be found on later maps by the name of Buffalo.    By the bluff on the south, first above named, flows Beaver creek, not noted in the text. The Calumet bluff of the text begins at a point where a range of hills approaches the river closely ; but various authors extend the name to this range for several miles up river.

*August 29th.* We had a violent storm of wind and rain last evening, and were engaged during the day in repairing the periogue and other necessary occupations. At four o'clock in the afternoon Sergeant Pryor and his party arrived on the opposite side, attended by five chiefs and about 70 men and boys. We sent a boat for them and they joined us, as did also Mr. [Pierre] Durion, son of our interpreter, who happened to be trading with the Sioux at this time. He returned with Sergeant Pryor to the Indians, with a present of tobacco, corn, and a few kettles; and told them that we would speak to their chiefs in the morning. Sergeant Pryor reported that on reaching their village, which is twelve miles distant from our camp, he was met by a party with a buffalo-robe, on which they desired to carry their visitors—an honor which they declined, informing the Indians that they were not the commanders of the boats. As a great mark of respect, they were then presented with a fat dog, already cooked, of which they partook heartily and found it well flavored. The camps [lodges] of the Sioux are of a conical form, covered with buffalo-robes painted with various figures and colors, with an aperture in the top for the smoke to pass through. The lodges contain from 10 to 15 persons; the interior arrangement is compact and handsome, each lodge having a place for cooking detached from it.[7]

(*p. 57*) *August 30th.* The fog was so thick that we could not see the Indian camp on the opposite side, but it cleared off about eight o'clock. We prepared a speech and some presents, and then sent for the chiefs and warriors, whom we received, at twelve o'clock, under a large oak tree, near which the flag of the United States was flying. Cap-

---

[7] These tents or lodges are more frequently called by their Indian name, *tepee.* "The sergeant who had gone to their camp informed me that their lodges, forty in number, are about nine miles from the Missouri, on the Sacque [Jacques] river. They are made of dressed buffalo and elk skins painted red and white, and are very handsome. He said the women are homely and mostly old, but the young men likely and active. They killed a dog as a token of friendship," Gass, p. 32.

tain Lewis delivered a speech, with the usual advice and counsel for their future conduct. We acknowledged their chiefs, by giving to the grand chief a flag, a medal, a certificate, and a string of wampum ; to which we added a chief's coat—that is, a richly laced uniform of the United States artillery corps, with a cocked hat and red feather. One second chief and three inferior ones were made or recognized by medals, a suitable present of tobacco, and articles of clothing. We smoked the pipe of peace, and the chiefs retired to a bower formed of bushes by their young men, where they divided among one another the presents, smoked, eat, and held a council on the answer which they were to make us to-morrow. The young people exercised their bows and arrows in shooting at marks for beads, which we distributed to the best marksmen. In the evening the whole party danced until a late hour, and in the course of their amusement we threw among them some knives, tobacco, bells, tape, and binding, with which they were much pleased. Their musical instruments were the drum, and a sort of little bag made of buffalo-hide dressed white, with small shot or pebbles in it and a bunch of hair tied to it. This produces a sort of rattling music, with which the party was annoyed by four musicians during the council this morning.

*August* 31*st.* In the morning, after breakfast, the chiefs met and sat down in a row, with pipes of peace highly ornamented ; all pointed toward the seats intended for Captains Lewis and Clark. When they arrived and were seated, the grand chief, whose Indian name Weucha is in English Shake Hand, and in French is called Le Li- (*p. 58*) berateur (the Deliverer), rose and spoke at some length, approving what we had said, and promising to follow our advice.

" I see before me," said he, " my Great Father's two sons. You see me and the rest of our chiefs and warriors. We are very poor ; we have neither powder, nor ball, nor knives ; and our women and children at the village have no clothes. I wish that as my brothers have given me a flag and a medal, they would give something to those poor people, or let them stop and trade with the first boat which comes up the river. I will bring chiefs of the Pawnees and Mahas together, and make peace between them; but it is better that I should do it than my Great Father's sons, for they will listen to me more readily. I will also take some chiefs to your country in the spring; but before that time I cannot leave home. I went formerly to the English, and they gave me a medal and some clothes; when I went to the Spanish they gave me a medal, but nothing to keep it from my skin; but now you give me a medal and clothes. But still we are poor; and I wish, brothers, you would give us something for our squaws."

When he sat down, Mahtoree or White Crane arose.

"I have listened," said he, "to what our father's words were yesterday; and I am to-day glad to see how you have dressed our old chief. I am a young man, and do not wish to take much; my fathers have made me a chief; I had much sense before, but now I think I have more than ever. What the old chief has declared I will confirm, and do whatever he and you please; but I wish you would take pity on us, for we are very poor."

Another chief, called Pawnawneahpahbe, then said:

"I am a young man, and know but little; I cannot speak well; but I have listened to what you have told the old chief, and will do whatever you agree."

The same sentiments were repeated by Aweawechache.

We were surprised at finding that the first of these titles means "Struck by the Pawnee," and was occasioned by some (*p. 59*) blow which the chief had received in battle from one of the Pawnee tribe. The second is in English Half Man, which seemed a singular name for a warrior, till it was explained to have its origin, probably, in the modesty of the chief; who, on being told of his exploits, would say, "I am no warrior; I am only half a man."

The other chiefs spoke very little; but after they had finished, one of the warriors delivered a speech in which he declared he would support them. They promised to make peace with the Ottoes and Missouris, the only nations with whom they were at war. All these harangues concluded by describing the distress of the nation; they begged us to have pity on them; to send them traders; they wanted powder and ball, and seemed anxious that we should supply them with some of their Great Father's milk, the name by which they distinguish ardent spirits. We gave some tobacco to each of the chiefs, and a certificate to two of the warriors who attended the chief. We prevailed on Mr. Durion to remain here, and accompany as many of the Sioux chiefs as he could collect, down to the seat of government. We also gave his son a flag, some clothes and provisions, with directions to bring about a peace between the surrounding tribes, and to convey some of their chiefs to see the President. In the evening they left us and camped on the opposite bank, accompanied by the two Durions. During the evening and night we had much rain, and observed that the river rises a little.

The Indians who have just left us are the Yanktons, a tribe of the great nation of Sioux.[8] These Yanktons are

[8] For the position of the Yanktons and Yanktonnais as members of the great Siouan linguistic stock, and as tribes of the Sioux proper or Dakota Indians, see the classification on p. 100, and note there.

1. These Yanktons, with whom the travelers are holding a council, are enumerated on p. 97 as the First tribe. In Lewis' Statistical View they are those there called Yank'-ton-âh-nâh'; they are credited with 80 lodges, 200 warriors, and 700 total population, and located on the Jacques or James river, the Big and Little Sioux rivers, Floyd's river, and the Des Moines. "These," says Lewis, "are the best disposed Sioux who rove on the banks of the Missouri, and these even will not suffer any trader to ascend the river, if they can possibly avoid it; they have heretofore, invariably, arrested the progress of all those they have met with, and generally compelled them to trade at the prices, nearly, which they themselves think proper to fix on their merchandise. They seldom commit any further acts of violence on the whites. They sometimes visit the river Demoin [Des Moines], where a partial trade has been carried on with them, for a few years past, by a Mr. Crawford. Their trade, if well regulated, might be rendered extremely valuable. Their country is a very fertile one; it consists of a mixture of woodlands and prairies. The land bordering on the Missouri is principally plains with but little timber." (London ed., 1807, p. 18.)

about 200 men in number, and inhabit the Jacques, Des Moines, and Sioux rivers. In person they are stout, well-proportioned, and have a certain air of dignity and bold-ness. In their dress they differ nothing from the other bands of the nation whom we saw and will describe after-ward; they are fond of decorations, and use paint, porcu-pine quills, and feathers. Some of them wore a kind of necklace of white bear's claws three inches long, closely strung (*p. 60*) together round their necks. They have only a few fowling-pieces, being generally armed with bows and arrows, in [using] which, however, they do not appear as expert as the more northern Indians. What struck us most was an institution peculiar to them, and to the Kite

"Yankton" is a word which settled in this orthography, though it formerly fluctuated to the usual extent. The full phonetic rendering is I-hank'-ton-wan. These Indians now number nearly 3,000, of which the majority (1,725) are or were recently on the Yankton Reservation, S. D., and 1,121 at the Fort Peck Reservation in Montana ; a few (123) at Devil's Lake Agency, N. D., and a very few more on the Crow Creek and Lower Brulé Reservations, S. D.

2. The Yanktonnais or Yanktoannans (I-hank'-ton-wan-na) were and still remain more numerous than the Yanktons proper. Lewis called them in his Statistical View the Yanktons of the North or Plains, crediting them with 1,600 popula-tion, 500 warriors, and 200 lodges, and locating them from the St. Peter's and Red rivers to the Great Bend of the Missouri. " This band," he says, " although they purchase a much smaller quantity of merchandise than the Sissatones, still appropriate a considerable proportion of what they do obtain in a similar manner with that mentioned of the Sissatones. This trade, as small as it may appear, has been sufficient to render the Tetons independent of the trade of the Missouri, in a great measure, and has furnished them with the means not only of distressing and plundering the traders of the Missouri, but also of plundering and massacreing [*sic*] the defenceless savages of the Missouri, from the mouth of the river Platte to the Minetares, and west to the Rocky mountains. The country these people inhabit is almost one entire plain, uncovered with timber ; it is extremely level ; the soil fertile, and generally well watered."

The Yanktonnais are now classified and divided as follows: (*a*) Upper Yanktonnais, of whom most are on Standing Rock Reservation, N. D., though a few (of the Cuthead band or Pabaksa subtribe) are on Devil's Lake Reservation. (*b*) Lower Yanktonnais, most of whom are on Crow Creek Reservation, S. D., others at Standing Rock, and others at Fort Peck, Mont. Latest returns give Upper Yanktonnais on Standing Rock Reservation, 1,786 ; Lower Yanktonnais, Crow Creek Reservation, 1,058 ; at Standing Rock Agency, 1,739 : total of both, 4,583.

[Staitan: see p. 58] Indians further to the westward, from whom it is said to have been copied. It is an association of the most active and brave young men, who are bound to each other by attachment, secured by a vow, never to retreat before any danger, or give way to their enemies. In war they go forward without sheltering themselves behind trees, or aiding their natural valor by any artifice. Their punctilious determination not to be turned from their course, became heroic, or ridiculous, a short time since, when the Yanktons were crossing the Missouri on the ice. A hole lay immediately in their course, which might easily have been avoided by going around. This the foremost of the band disdained to do, but went straight forward and was lost. The others would have followed his example, but were forcibly prevented by the rest of the tribe. These young men sit, camp, and dance together, distinct from the rest of the nation; they are generally about 30 or 35 years old, and such is the deference paid to courage that their seats in council are superior to those of the chiefs and their persons more respected. But, as may be supposed, such indiscreet bravery will soon diminish the numbers of those who practice it; so that the band is now reduced to four warriors, who were among our visitors. These were the remains of 22 who composed the society not long ago; but, in a battle with the Kite [Crow] Indians of the Black Mountains, 18 of them were killed, and these four were dragged from the field by their companions. [Cf. Long's Exp. St. Peter's, I. 1825, pp. 436-439.]

Whilst these Indians remained with us we made very minute inquiries relative to their situation, numbers, trade, and manners. This we did very satisfactorily, by means of two different interpreters; and from their accounts, joined to our interviews with other bands of the same nation, and much intelligence acquired since, we were enabled to understand with some accuracy the condition of the Sioux, hitherto so little known.

The Sioux or Dacorta [Dakota] Indians, originally

settled on the Mississippi, and called by Carver Madowe-
sians, are now subdivided into tribes, as follows:[9]

First, Yanktons. This tribe inhabits the Sioux, Des
Moines, and Jacques rivers, and numbers about 200 warriors.

[9] I will give a general account of this great family of Indians, who are among
the most important, both ethnically and politically, of any with whom the
United States has had to reckon. Perhaps we are not quite yet done with
them. My remarks on this difficult subject are mainly a summary of Major
Powell's, in his article on Indian linguistic families, pp. 111–118 of the Report
of the U. S. Bureau of Ethnology for 1885–86, pub. 1891.

The name *Sioux* is not proper to these Indians. It is a corruption of the
Algonkin word *Nadowe-ssi-wag*, meaning the snake-like ones, hence the
enemies, being thus a term of reproach (so Trumbull). But it has been adopted
for the Siouan family, after Gallatin (Trans. and Coll. Amer. Antiq. Soc., II.
1835, pp. 121, 306), back of whom Powell does not go for names of any of his
58 main linguistic stocks or families. Gallatin is followed by Pritchard (Phys.
Hist. Mankind, V. 1847, p. 408), and retains the sense he originally attached
to the name in later works (Trans. Amer. Ethn. Soc., 1848, and Schoolcraft's
Indian Tribes, III. 1853, p. 402). Sioux is in form a French plural, but serves in
English both as singular and plural ; for the singular, it is pronounced " Soo " ;
for the plural, " Sooz "; for the latter, " Siouxs " or " Siouxes " is sometimes very
badly written. The singular is occasionally written " Sue " or " Soo," with a
plural " Sues " or " Soos." Clark's MS. alone furnishes more than a dozen
different spellings, for examples of which see note [30], p. 70. The adjective is now
regularly Siouan.

Gallatin divides his Sioux into four principal groups. 1. Winnebegoes. 2.
Sioux proper and Assiniboins. 3. The Minnetare group. 4. The Osages and
kindred southern tribes. He improperly included his Shyennes among the
Sioux.

" Owing to the fact that ' Sioux ' is a word of reproach and means ' snake '
or ' enemy ' the term has been discarded by many later writers as a family
designation, and ' Dakota,' which signifies ' friend ' or ' ally,' has been employed in
its stead. The two words are, however, by no means properly synonymous. The
term ' Sioux ' was used by Gallatin in a comprehensive or family sense, and was
applied to all the tribes collectively known to him to speak kindred dialects of a
widespread language. It is in this sense only, as applied to the linguistic family,
that the term is here employed. The term ' Dahcota ' was correctly applied by
Gallatin to the Dakota tribes proper as distinguished from the other members of
the linguistic family who are not Dakotas in a tribal sense. The use of the
term with this signification should be perpetuated." (Powell, *l. c.*)

We should observe that Lewis and Clark's use of the term " Sioux " is in its
strict tribal sense, not in the above broad linguistic sense. All the tribes they
call Sioux are Sioux proper or Dakotas, of which they proceed to distinguish
ten tribes. They spell Dakota variously in different places, as " Darcota,"

Second, Tetons of the Burnt Woods [Bois Brulés]. This tribe numbers about 300 men, who rove on both sides of the Missouri, White, and Teton rivers.

"Darcotar," "Dacorta," "Dacotah," etc., which forms I leave as I find them. Observe that the name "Madowesian," misprinted from Carver in the text, is the Algonkin Nadowessiwag, above explained. Carver (ed. 1796 consulted) prints Naudowessies, pl.; other forms are Naudouessies, Nadowasis, etc., earlier in Hennepin (1683) Nadiousioux (whence Carver's corruption), the ending of which form is exactly our Sioux, and first Naduesiu, from Nicolet, 1634-35.

The pristine territory of the Sioux, in the broad linguistic sense of the name, was mainly in one body, the only exceptions being the isolated habitats of the Biloxi, Tutelo, Catawba, and Woccon. The general trend of Siouan migration has been westward. Probably most Siouans were east of the Mississippi in comparatively late prehistoric times. The main Siouan territory extended from about 53° N., in the Hudson's Bay Company's country, to about 33° N., including a considerable part of the Missouri watershed and that of the upper Mississippi. It was bounded on the N.W., N., N.E., and some distance E., by Algonquian territory. South of 45° N. the line ran eastward to Lake Michigan. It extended westward from Lake Michigan through Illinois, crossing the Mississippi at Prairie du Chien, where began Algonquian country. The Siouan tribes claimed all the present States of Iowa and Missouri, excepting parts occupied by Algonkins. The Mississippi divided these two families for a short distance below St. Louis. The line then ran west of Dunklin, New Madrid, and Pemiscot counties, Mo., and Mississippi Co., and those parts of Craighead and Poinsett Cos., Ark., which lie east of the St. Francis river. Once more the Mississippi became the eastern boundary, but in this case separating the Siouan from the Muskhogean family. The Quapaw or Akansa were the most southerly tribe in the main Siouan territory. Southwest of the Siouan family was the Southern Caddoan group, the boundary extending from the west side of the Mississippi river in Louisiana, nearly opposite Vicksburg, and running northwestwardly to the bend of the Red river between Arkansas and Louisiana ; thence northwest along the divide between the Arkansas and Red rivers. In the northwest corner of Indian Territory the Osages (Siouan) came in contact with the Comanche (Shoshonean family), and near the western boundary of Kansas the Kiowa, Cheyenne, and Arapaho barred the westward march of the Kansa or Kaw (Siouan). The Pawnees (Caddoan stock) in western Nebraska and northwestern Kansas separated the Ponka and Dakota on the north from the Kansa on the south, and the Omaha and other Siouan tribes on the east from the Kiowa and other tribes on the west. The Omaha and cognate peoples occupied in Nebraska the lower part of the Platte river, most of the Elk-horn valley, and the Ponka claimed the region watered by the Niobrara in northern Nebraska. There seems reason for assigning to the Crows the N.W. corner of Nebraska and the S.W. part of S. Dakota, as well as the northern part of Wyoming and the southern part of Montana.

The above is the solid body of Siouan territory. The outlying habitats

Third, Tetons Okandandas [Ogallalas], a tribe consisting of about 150 men, who inhabit both sides of the Missouri below the Cheyenne river.

were in Mississippi, for the Biloxi; in Virginia and subsequently in Pennsylvania, for the Tutelo; South Carolina, for the Catawba; North Carolina, for the Woccon.

The whole Siouan stock is divided into 18 principal branches. 1. Dakota or Sioux proper (see above). 2. Assinaboin. 3. Omaha. 4. Ponca. 5. Kaw or Kansa. 6. Osages. 7. Quapaw. 8. Iowa. 9. Oto. 10. Missouri. 11. Winnebago. 12. Mandan. 13. Gros Ventre or Minnetaree or Hidatsa. 14. Crow. 15. Tutelo. 16. Biloxi. 17. Catawba. 18. Woccon. The census of the whole is now about 43,000, of whom only 2,000 are in British America, as against 41,000 in the United States.

We turn now to the first of these 18 branches, the Sioux proper or Dakotas, of whom Lewis and Clark give 10 tribes in the above text, which may be compared with the following tribes and subtribes in Powell's classification:

DAKOTA or SIOUX PROPER.

A. SANTEE. These include the Eighth "Mindawarcarton" (Mde'wa-kanton-wan), and the Ninth "Wahpatoota" (Wa-qpe'-ku-te) tribes of Lewis and Clark. According to U. S. Commissioner's Report for 1889, and the U. S. Census Bulletin for 1890, there were 869 of them together on the Santee Reservation in Nebraska; 292 at Flandreau, Dakota, and 54 at Devil's Lake Agency. Lewis' Statistical View gave for the Eighth of these 120 lodges, 300 warriors, and 1,200 total population; for the Ninth, 60 lodges, 150 warriors, 400 in all. Of the Eighth the View remarks: "'Tis the only band of Sioux that cultivates corn, beans, &c., and even these cannot properly be termed a stationary people. They live in tents of dressed leather, which they transport by means of horses and dogs, and ramble from place to place during the greater part of the year. They are friendly to their own traders; but the inveterate enemies of such as supply their enemies, the Cheppeways, with merchandise. They also claim the country in which they hunt, commencing at the entrance of the river St. Peters, and extending upwards, on both sides of the Mississippi, to the mouth of the Crow-wing river." Of the Ninth tribe the View remarks: "They rove in the country south and west of the river St. Peters, from a place called the Hardwood to the mouth of the Yellow Medicine river; never stationary but when their traders are with them, and that does not happen at any regular or fixed point. At present they treat their traders tolerably well. Their trade cannot be expected to increase much. A great proportion of their country is open plains, lies level, and is tolerably fertile. They maintain a partial traffic with the Yanktons and Tetons to the west of them; to these they barter the articles which they obtain from the traders on the river St. Peters, and receive in return horses, some robes and leather lodges."

B. SISSETON. These are the Tenth tribe of Lewis and Clark's enumeration above, there misprinted "Sistasoone," elsewhere variously spelled "Sissa-

Fourth, Tetons Minnakenozzo [Minneconjou], a nation inhabiting both sides of the Missouri above the Cheyenne river, and containing about 250 men.

ton," "Sisaton," "Sisiton," "Sisitoan," "Cissiton," etc.; in the Statistical View, "Sissatone." The full phonetic form of the word is Si-si'-ton-wan. What is left of them now is divided between the Sisseton Reservation in S. Dakota, where with the Wahpeton they number together 1,522, and Devil's Lake Reservation in N. Dakota, where the Sissetons, Wahpetons, and Yanktonnais together number 857. The Statistical View of 1806 says : "They claim the country in which they rove, embracing the upper portion of the Red river, of Lake Winnipie, and St. Peters ; it is a level country, inter-sected with many small lakes ; the land is fertile and free of stone ; the majority of it open plains. This country abounds more in the valuable fur animals, the beaver, otter and martin, than any portion of Louisiana yet known. This circumstance furnishes the Sissatones with the means of purchasing more merchandise, in proportion to their number, than any nation in this quarter. A great proportion of this merchandise is reserved by them for their trade with the Tetons, whom they annually meet at some point previously agreed on, upon the waters of the James river, in the month of May. This Indian fair is frequently attended by the Yank-tons of the North, and Ahnahs." The View gives the Sissetons 80 lodges, 200 warriors, and 800 total population. (London ed. 1807, p. 17.)

C. WAHPETON. These are Lewis and Clark's Seventh tribe, above spelled "Wahpatone." The full phonetic rendering is Wa-qpe'-ton-wan or Wa-hpe-ton-wah. They are now with the Sissetons at the two Agencies above noted. In 1806 Lewis gives them 80 lodges, 200 warriors, and total 700 population. The Statistical View says of them : "Claim the country in which they rove on the N.W. side of the river St. Peters, from their village to the mouth of the Chippeway river, and thence northeastwardly towards the head of the Mississippi, including the Crow-wing river. Their lands are fertile, and generally well timbered. They are only stationary while the traders are with them, which is from the beginning of October to the last of March. Their trade is supposed to be [now, 1805] at its greatest extent. They treat their traders with respect and seldom attempt to rob them. This, as well as the other Sioux bands, act, in all respects, as independently of each other as if they were a distinct nation."

D. YANKTON. These, the First of Lewis and Clark's ten tribes, have been noticed in full in the note on p. 94.

E. YANKTONNAI. These, the Sixth of Lewis and Clark's ten tribes, are noticed with the Yanktons, p. 95, note.

F. TETON. These include the Second, Third, Fourth, and Fifth of Lewis and Clark's ten tribes ; but there are also others which our authors do not discriminate. The accepted classification of Tetons at present is : (a) *Brulés :* Lewis and Clark's Second tribe. (b) *Sans Arcs :* Lewis and

Fifth, Tetons Saone.[10]  These inhabit both sides of the Missouri below the Warreconne river, and consist of about 300 men.

Sixth, Yanktons of the [North or] Plains, or Big Devils, who rove on the heads of the Sioux, Jacques, and Red

Clark's Fifth tribe (?)  (c) *Blackfeet*.  (d) *Minneconjous*.  Lewis and Clark's Fourth tribe.  (e) *Two Kettles*.  (f) *Ogallalas*, with several subdivisions. (g) *Uncpapas*.  These will be more fully treated beyond, where the Tetons come up for special mention by the authors.

[10] The "Tetons Saone," or Lewis and Clark's Fifth tribe, have given rise to much conjecture and discussion.  From information privately furnished from the U. S. Bureau of Ethnology, based on J. Owen Dorsey, I note the following : A. L. Riggs says "Sanoni wicasa is applied by other Dakota tribes as a sort of nickname."  T. L. Riggs (in the Word Carrier, June, July, 1889, p. 14) says: "The Sicangu, Ogallala and Brulé Sioux formerly spoke of the Itazipco, Minikanojou and Hunkpapa divisions as Sanoni wicasa.  This is also sometimes done at present.  I do not find any evidence to show that either of those divisions ever have designated themselves or each other by that name.  But among the Yanktonnai Dakota part of the Hunkpatina are called San-o-na, 'shot at a white object.'  Maga Bomdu (the Drifting Goose) in 1880 gave Mr. Dorsey Lewis and Clark's Saone as the third gens of the Yanktonnai under Omahankte ; but in the same year Nasuna Tanka (Big Head) and Mato Nonpa (Two Grizzly Bears) gave this as the fourth gens of the Hunkpatina or Lower Yanktonnai, under Wa-un-zo-qi (or Yellow Rump of an Elk)."  J. P. Williamson (in the Word Carrier, June, July, 1889, p. 14) says that Sanona is a division of the Hunkpati, a small band under Omahakte.  The balance of evidence is therefore in favor of our referring L. and C.'s Tetons Saone to the Yanktonnai, whatever the actual scope of our authors' intent may have been.  In the London edition of the Statistical View, 1807, the name is printed "Tetons Sahone" on p. 18 ; on the folding leaf facing p. 24 it stands as "Téton,-sàh-o-né."  No ethnographer who wishes to get at the real facts of L. and C.'s Indian names should fail to examine the original manuscripts in the possession of the American Philosophical Society, and at present in my hands. The variance from the Biddle text as printed is very great, and nowhere greater than in ethnological points.  For example : That portion of Clark's MS. which I have arranged as Codex B, gives at pp. 56, 57 : "The Names of the Defferent Tribes or bands of the Sceoux or Darcotar Nation—1st. *Checher Ree*, Yankton (or bois Ruley) ; 2nd. *Hoindeborto* (Poles) ; 3d. *Memacanjo* (make fence on the river) ; 4th. *Souon-Teton* (People of the Prarie) ; 5th. *Waupacootar* (Leaf Beds) ; 6th. *Tetarton* (or village of Prarie) ; 7th. *Newastarton* (big water Town) ; 8th. *Waupatone* (Leaf Nation) ; 9th. *Cas Carba* (White Man) ; 10th. *Micacuopsiba* (Cut bank) ; 11th. *Souon* ( — ) ; 12th. *Sousitoons* ( — ).  The names of the other bands neither of the Souex's interpters could inform me."  Here are twelve bands instead of ten, and not one of their names is spelled as in the printed text.

rivers; the most numerous of all the tribes, numbering about 500 men.

Seventh, Wahpatone [Waqpetonwan or Wahkpatoan], a nation residing on the St. Peter's, just above the mouth of that river, numbering 200 men.

Eighth, Mindawarcarton [Mdewakantonwan], proper Dacorta [Dakota] or Sioux Indians [Gens du Lac of the French]. These possess the original seat of the Sioux, and are properly so denominated. They rove on both sides of the Mississippi about the falls of St. Anthony, and consist of 300 men.

Ninth, The Wähpatoota [Waqpekute or Wahkpakotoan], or Leaf Beds [Leaf Shooters]. This nation inhabits both sides of the river St. Peter's, below Yellow- (*p. 62*) wood river, amounting to about 150 men.

Tenth, Sistasoone [Sisseton]. This nation numbers 200 men, who reside at the head of the St. Peter's. Of these several tribes more particular notice will be taken hereafter.

*Saturday, September 1st,* 1804. We proceeded this morning under a light southern breeze, and passed Calumet bluffs. These are composed of a yellowish-red and brownish clay as hard as chalk, which it much resembles, and are 170 or 180 feet high. At this place the hills on each side come to the verge of the river, those on the south being higher than [those] on the north. Opposite the bluffs is a large island covered with timber, above which the highlands form a cliff over the river on the north side, called White Bear cliff, an animal of that kind having been killed in one of the holes in it, which are numerous and apparently deep. At six miles we came to a large sand-island covered with cottonwood; the wind was high, the weather rainy and cloudy during the day. We made 15 miles to a place on the north side, at the lower point of a large island called Bon Homme or Good Man island.[11] The country on both sides has the

[11] Between Bon Homme Co., S. D., and Knox Co., Neb., beginning about the 915th river-mile. The island retains its French name, which is also that of

same character of prairies with no timber, but with occasional low lands covered with cottonwood, elm, and oak. Our hunters had killed an elk and a beaver; catfish are in great abundance.

*September 2d.* It rained last night, and this morning we had a high wind from the N.W. We went three miles to the lower part of an ancient fortification on the south side, and passed the head of Bon Homme island, which is large and well timbered. After this the wind became so violent, attended by a cold rain, that we were compelled to land at four miles on the north side, under a high bluff of yellow clay, about 110 feet in height. Our hunters supplied us with four elk; we had grapes and plums on the banks; we also saw the bear-grass [rush, *Juncus angustifolia*] and rue [*Thalictrum* sp.?] on the side of the bluffs. At this place there are high lands on both sides (*p. 63*) of the river, which become more level at some distance back, and contain but few streams of water. On the southern bank, during this day, the grounds have not been so elevated. Captain Clark crossed the river to examine the remains of the fortification we had just passed.

This interesting object[12] is on the south side of the Mis-

the county town. The other island mentioned marks the 910th mile point. Both bluffs named are in continuation of those already noticed.

[12] See plate. The original sketch occupies pp. 81, 82 of Clark, Codex N; only half of it was engraved for the Biddle ed., as now reproduced. The original descriptions are in Clark, Codex B 64, 65, and N 83-85. But this "antient fortification" is simply a natural formation—driftings of sand. This was long ago determined, as by Warren and Hayden in 1855. I examined the place in 1873, and found nothing to support a contrary opinion. It was visited by Mr. T. H. Lewis, of St. Paul, in 1890, and made the subject of an interesting paper entitled "Lewis and Clark and the Antiquities of the Upper Missouri River" (Amer. Antiq. and Orient. Jour., Sept., 1891, pp. 288-293). I cite from pp. 291, 292 :

" The earth-works so glowingly described by Captain Clark as existing on this point are only sand ridges formed by the river, the land being low and subject to overflow. Above the point the river deflects from the Nebraska shore and the strong current strikes the high bank on the Dakota side, and is gradually cutting it away, while at the same time the point is being extended to the north by the accretions from the river. In this way the point has been gradually built, and each successive flood also adds to its general elevation. The sand ridges—

souri, opposite the upper extremity of Bon Homme island, in a low level plain, the hills being three miles from the river. It begins by a wall composed of earth, rising immediately from the bank of the river and running in a direct course S. 76° W. 96 yards; the base of this wall or mound is 75 feet, its height about 8. It then diverges in a course S. 84° W. and continues at the same height and depth to the distance of 53 yards, the angle being formed by a sloping descent; at the junction of these two is an appearance of a hornwork of the same height with the first angle; the same wall then pursues a course N. 69° W. for 300 yards; near its western extremity is an opening or gateway at right angles to the wall and projecting inward; this gateway is defended by two nearly semicircular walls placed before it, lower than the large walls; from the gateway there seems to have been a covered way communicating with the interval between these two walls; westward of

of which there are a number extending across the point—mostly conform to the general direction of the current when the river is at a high stage, for at such times it does not follow the main river bed or channel, but takes a straighter course down the valley between the high banks and bluffs.

"Bonhomme Island is east of and just below the point, but is now connected with it by a bed of sand, the old channel having been filled up within recent years. The general formation and character of the island are similar to that of the point.

"The circular redoubt represented on Lewis and Clark's maps as located on the west side of the island is one of those curious natural sand formations which are occasionally met with along the Missouri Valley. The bank or wall is somewhat irregular in outline and lacks considerable of being a circle. Some enterprising settler has utilized one side of it by building a claim shanty upon it.

"This island is covered with sand-blows, dunes and ridges, and it is rather strange that the elaborate description of the point was not extended so as to include all of the island; but perhaps the greater portion of them have been formed since the time of the expedition, or that the island—then as now—was covered with heavy timber and a dense undergrowth, which hid them from view.

"It may be added that along the Missouri, from the mouth of Knife river to Sioux City, there were many low points and bottoms and some islands, on which there are similar ridges and dunes. Probably the most elaborate of these 'earth-works' are located on the west side, opposite Springfield, South Dakota, and on the west side, opposite to and above Washburn, North Dakota."

the gate, the wall becomes much larger, being about 105 feet at its base, and 12 feet high; at the end of this high ground the wall extends for 56 yards on a course N. 32° W.; it then turns N. 23° W., for 73 yards; these two walls seem to have had a double or covered way; they are from 10 to 15 feet 8 inches in height, and from 75 to 105 feet in width at the base; the descent inward being steep, whilst outward it forms a sort of glacis. At the distance of 73 yards the wall ends abruptly at a large hollow place much lower than the general level of the plain, and from which is some indication of a covered way to the water. The space (*p. 64*) between them is occupied by several mounds scattered promiscuously through the gorge, in the center of which is a deep round hole. From the extremity of the last wall, in a course N. 32° W., is a distance of 96 yards over the low ground, where the wall recommences and crosses the plain in a course N. 81° W. for 1,830 yards to the bank of the Missouri. In this course its height is about 8 feet, till it enters, at the distance of 533 yards, a deep circular pond of 73 yards diameter; after which it is gradually lower, toward the river; it touches the river at a muddy bar which bears every mark of being an encroachment of the water for a considerable distance; a little above the junction is a small circular redoubt. Along the bank of the river, at 1,100 yards' distance in a straight line from this wall, is a second, about 6 feet high and of considerable width; it rises abruptly from the bank the Missouri at a point where the river bends, and goes straight forward, forming an acute angle with the last wall, till it enters the river again, not far from the mounds just described, toward which it is obviously tending. At the bend the Missouri is 500 yards wide; the ground on the opposite side is highlands, or low hills on the bank; where the river passes between this fort and Bon Homme island, all the distance from the bend, it is constantly washing the banks into the stream, a large sandbank being already taken from the shore near the wall. During the whole course of this wall, or glacis, it is covered with trees, among which are many large cottonwoods, two or three feet in diameter. Immediately opposite the citadel, or the part most strongly fortified, on Bon Homme island, is a small work in a circular form, with a wall surrounding it about six feet in height. The young willows along the water, joined to the general appearance of the two shores, induce a belief that the bank of the island is encroaching, and [that] the Missouri indemnifies itself by washing away the base of the fortification. The (*p. 65*) citadel contains about 20 acres, but the parts between the long walls must embrace nearly 500 acres.

These are the first remains of the kind which we have had an opportunity of examining; but our French interpreters [13] assure us that there are great numbers of them on the Platte, the Kansas, the Jacques, etc.; some of our party say that they observed two of those fortresses on the upper side of Petit Arc creek, not far from its mouth, and that the wall was about six feet high and the sides of the angles 100 yards in length.

*September 3d.* The morning was cold, and the wind from the northwest. We passed at sunrise three large sand-bars, and at the distance of ten miles reached a small creek about twelve yards wide, coming in from the north, above a

---

[13] See note [4], Aug. 26th. Old Durion and his hopeful Pierre were not the best ethnological experts in the world, but perhaps the highest authorities that the Expedition had on hand. I suspect much of the French nomenclature was simply Durion's ; some of it certainly was. Clark's Codex B 69 (I have now arranged all the MSS. in codices, and paginated them for reference) has these words : "Two of our party saw two of those antient fortresses on the Pettiet Arc Creek on the upper side near the mouth, each angle of which were 100 yards and about 8 feet high." Mr. T. H. Lewis' paper already cited says : "There are no traces of any village or artificial works of any description to be found in this neighborhood above the mouth of the Bow, the land being low and subject to overflow. There are, however, several natural ridges, similar to those on Bonhomme Point. On adjacent hills and plateaus there are isolated ruins of old dirt lodges similar to those constructed by the Mandans. There is also an ancient fort on the east or lower side of Bow Creek, about two miles from its mouth, and another still further south, near Hartington, but these two forts were unknown to the Lewis and Clark expedition."

white bluff. This creek has obtained the name of Plum [14] creek, from the number of that fruit which are in the neighborhood and of a delightful quality. Five miles further we camped on the south near the edge of a plain. The river is wide and covered with sand-bars to-day; the banks are high and of a whitish color; the timber is scarce, but there is an abundance of grapes. Beaver-houses have been observed in great numbers on the river, but none of the animals themselves.

*September 4th.* We set out early, with a very cold wind from the S.S.E., and at 1½ miles reached a small creek, called White-lime creek, on the south side. Just above this is a cliff covered with cedar trees, and at three miles [15] a creek called White-paint creek, about 30 yards wide; on the same side, and at 4½ miles' distance from White-paint creek, is the [Niobrara, or] Rapid river, or, as it is called by the French, la Rivere qui Court. [16] This river empties into the Missouri in a course S.W. by W. and is 152 yards wide and four feet deep at the confluence. It rises in the Black mountains [17] and passes through a hilly

---

[14] In Bon Homme Co., S. D.; Wananri river of Nicollet's and Warren's maps; Emanuel creek of G. L. O. map, 1879. It empties at the 930th mile point. Clark's B 70 has Plumb creek . . . "abounds with blumbs of a Delicious flavour." The fruit is that of *Prunus americana*.

[15] Text is ambiguous here. For "three miles" read "three miles *from camp*." Clark's B 72 has: "A small creek in a bend to the L. S. [larboard side] called White lime, at 1½ miles higher up passed a large Creek on the L. S. called White paint." His exact courses and distances are: "S. 5° W. 1½ mls. to the mo: of a creek on the L. S. below a Ceeder Clift. S. 35° W. 1½ mls. to the mo: of White Paint River on the L. S." Here 1½ + 1½ = 3 miles from camp. It is not easy to turn tabular data like these into reading-matter without risk of error or ambiguity. Both creeks named are in Knox Co., Neb. White-paint is l'Eau qui Monte of P. du Lac; Wasiska of Nicollet; now called by a name variously spelled Bazille, Bazile, Bozzie, etc.

[16] *Sic*—read la Rivière qui Court, or better L'Eau qui Court, as P. du Lac, usually contracted and corrupted into Quicourre, Quicurre, Quicure, Quecure, sometimes "Quicum" by misprint. The L. and C. codices have many forms; Clark once Ka-cure. The river has also been called Spreading-water and Running-water.

[17] Hardly as far as the Black hills. The Niobrara is almost entirely a

country, with a poor soil.  Captain Clark ascended three miles to a beautiful plain on the upper side, where the Pawnees once (*p. 66*) had a village; he found the river widened above its mouth and much divided by sands and islands, which, joined to great rapidity of the current, makes navigation very difficult, even for small boats. Like the Platte its waters are of a light color; like that river too it throws out into the Missouri great quantities of sand, coarser even than that of the Platte, which forms sand-bars and shoals near its mouth.

We camped just above it, on the south,[18] having made only eight miles, as the wind shifted to the south and blew so hard that in the course of the day we broke our mast.  We saw some deer, a number of geese, and shot a turkey and a duck.  The place in which we halted is a fine low ground, with much timber, such as red cedar [*Juniperus virginianus*], honey-locust, oak, arrow-wood, elm, and coffee-nut [*Gymnocladus canadensis*].

*September 5th.*  The wind was again high from the south. At five miles we came to a large island called Pawnee island, in the middle of the river, and stopped to breakfast at a small creek on the north, which has the name of Goat[19] [*i. e.*, Antelope] creek, at 8½ miles.  Near the mouth of this creek the beaver had made a dam across so as to form a large pond, in which they built their houses.  Above this island the Poncara[20] river falls into the Missouri from the

prairie river, rising with heads of White river between the South Fork of the Cheyenne and the North Platte, in Laramie Co., Wyo.  The Black hills proper are further north, in Crook Co., and all the heads of the South Fork of the Cheyenne intervene.

[18] In South Dakota (Ponca Reservation); for at the mouth of the Niobrara the Missouri ceases to separate Nebraska from South Dakota, and lies entirely within the latter.  The boundary is thence along the Niobrara as far as the mouth of the Keya-paha river, the first large branch of the Niobrara from the north, and thence along that branch to the parallel of 43° N.

[19] Now Choteau or Chouteau creek, bounding Bon Homme Co., S. D., on the west, and emptying about the 950th mile point.  The Nawizi river of Nicollet's map.

[20] Elsewhere Poncar, Poncha, Ponca or Ponka, Punka, Puncah, Puncaw, etc.;

south, and is 30 yards wide at the entrance. Two men whom we dispatched to the village of the same name returned with information that they had found it on the lower side of the creek; but as this is the hunting-season, the town was so completely deserted that they had killed a buffalo in the village itself. This tribe of Poncaras [Poncas], who are said to have once numbered 400 men, are now reduced to about 50, and have associated for mutual protection with the Mahas, who are about 200 in number. These two nations are allied by a similarity of misfortune; they were once both numerous; both resided in villages and cultivated Indian corn; their common enemies, Sioux and smallpox, drove them from their (*p. 67*) towns, which they visit only occasionally for the purposes of trade; and they now wander over the plains on the sources of the Wolf and Quicurre [*sic*] rivers. Between Pawnee island and Goat creek on the north is a cliff of blue earth, under which are several mineral springs, impregnated with salts; near this we observed a number of goats,[21] from which the creek derives its name. At 3½

Ponca is the usual spelling. It is a prairie stream of no great size, north of and parallel with the Niobrara. The word as the name of the Indian tribe about to be mentioned is of equally fluctuating orthography. Lewis' Statistical View gives a French nickname "Les Pongs." They are there credited with 20 lodges, 50 warriors, and a total of 200 population, residing with the Omahas. "The remnant of a nation once respectable in point of numbers. They formerly [before 1805] resided on a branch of the Red River of Lake Winnipie; being oppressed by the Sioux, they removed to the west side of the Missouri, on Poncar river, where they built and fortified a village and remained some years. But being pursued by their ancient enemies the Sioux, and reduced by continual wars, they have joined and now reside with the Mahas, whose language they speak" (English ed. 1807, p. 17).

The Poncas are a tribe of the great Siouan family, but not of the Sioux proper or Dakotas. According to latest returns they now number 847, of whom 605 are in Indian Territory under the Ponca Agent, 217 are in Nebraska under the Santee Agent, 24 are at school in Lawrence, Kas., and one is at the Carlisle school in Pennsylvania.

[21] These "goats" were of course antelopes (*Antilocapra americana*). This animal was new to science when discovered by Lewis and Clark in 1804, and was not technically named till 1815. See note [50], p. 121.

miles from the creek we came to a large island [22] on the south, along which we passed to the head of it, and camped about four o'clock. Here we replaced the mast we had lost with a new one of cedar. Some bucks [*Cariacus virginianus*] and an elk were procured to-day, and a black-tailed deer [*Cariacus macrotis*] was seen near the Poncaras' village.

*September 6th.* There was a storm this morning from the N.W., and though it moderated the wind was still high and the weather very cold ; the number of sand-bars, too, added to the rapidity of the current, obliged us to have recourse to the tow-line. With all our exertions we did not make over 8½ miles, and camped on the north, after passing high cliffs [Ponca bluffs] of soft blue and red colored stone on the southern shore. We saw some goats and great numbers of buffalo, in addition to which the hunters furnished us with elk, deer, turkeys, geese, and one beaver ; a large catfish was caught in the evening. The ground near the camp was a low prairie without timber, though just below is a grove of cottonwood.

*September 7th.* The morning was very cold and the wind southeast. At 5½ miles we reached and camped at the foot of a round mountain on the south, having passed two small islands. This mountain,[23] which is about 300 feet at the base, forms a cone at the top, resembling a dome at a distance, and 70 feet or more above the surrounding highlands.

As we descended from this dome we arrived at a spot, on the gradual descent of the hill, nearly four acres in extent and covered with small holes. These are the residence of

---

[22] Biddle misses a name here. Clark B 77 says : " We came too [read came-to, *i. e.*, stopped the boats] on the upper point of a large Island (which I call *No Preserves* Island)." The cliffs above said are now called Choteau or Chouteau bluffs. Some cliffs opposite, on the south, are the Beauchamp bluffs.

[23] " Resembling a cupola," Clark B 79, and elsewhere called the Dome ; a conspicuous landmark, the Paha Owassoke of Nicollet, also of Catlin, now known as the Tower, near the 970th mile point. As to the islands passed, late maps show a large one, perhaps the J. des Basques of P. du Lac, who marks on the north bank " Second Poste de la Compagnie."

a little animal, called by the (*p. 68*) French petit chien (little dog), which sit erect near the mouth and make a whistling noise, but when alarmed take refuge in their holes. In order to bring them out we poured into one of the holes five barrels of water without filling it, but we dislodged and caught the owner. After digging down another of the holes for six feet, we found, on running a pole into it, that we had not yet dug halfway to the bottom. We discovered, however, two frogs in the hole, and near it we killed a dark rattlesnake, which had swallowed a small prairie-dog; we were also informed, though we never witnessed the fact, that a sort of lizard and a snake live habitually with these animals. The petits chiens are justly named, as they resemble a small dog in some particulars, though they have also some points of similarity to the squirrel. The head resembles the squirrel in every respect, except that the ear is shorter; the tail is like that of the ground-squirrel; the toe-nails are long, the fur is fine, and the long hair is gray.[24]

[24] This is an early description of the prairie-dog, *Cynomys ludovicianus,* then unknown to science, and not technically named till 1815, when it was called *Arctomys ludoviciana* by George Ord, in Guthrie's Geogr., 2d Am. ed., vol. II., pp. 292 and 302. Lewis and Clark's description of 1804 is unmistakable, and it would have prevented some fables which later arose, if their statement of finding a young prairie-dog in the stomach of a rattlesnake they killed had not been overlooked. The snake was probably *Crotalus confluentus,* a species common in Dakota. Our authors do not appear to have observed the burrowing-owl at this stage of their journey. The prairie-dog is called "barking-squirrel" a few paragraphs further on. At this date Gass says "prairie-dog," and gives the same story of trying to drown them out; his published date being 1807. The earliest notice I have seen of the prairie-dog occurs in a letter from Captain Clark to Governor Harrison, dated Fort Mandan, April 2d, 1805, and, I think, published in 1806—if so, before the appearance of Lieut. Z. M. Pike's Travels, 1810. Clark mentions several animals, among them "the ground prairie dog (who burrows in the ground)." Pike is usually cited in this connection before Lewis and Clark; but he must yield to Clark and to Gass in priority. His notice appears at p. 156, at date of Aug. 24th, 1806 (of his MSS.). It begins: "The Wishtonwish of the Indians, prairie-dogs of some travelers, or squirrels as I should be inclined to denominate them," etc. Here is the original application to these rodents of the Indian name which J. Fenimore Cooper applies to the whip-poor-will in his novels. Pike's passage (a footnote

*September 8th.* The wind still continued from the south-east, but moderately. At seven miles we reached a house on the north side, called the Pawnee house, where a trader named Trudeau [25] wintered in the years 1796–97 ; behind this, hills much larger than usual appear on the north, about eight miles off. Before reaching this house, we came by three small islands [26] on the north side, and a small creek on the south ; [27] after leaving it, we reached another island at the end of 17 miles, on which we camped, and called it Boat island. [28] We here saw herds of buffalo, and some elk, deer, turkeys, beaver, a squirrel [29] and a prairie-dog. The party on the north represent the country through which they passed as poor, rugged, and hilly, with the appearance of having been lately burnt by the Indians ; the broken hills, indeed, approach the river on both sides, though each is bordered by a strip of woodland near the water.

(*p. 69*) *September 9th.* We coasted along the island on which we had camped, and then passed three sand- and willow-islands and a number of smaller sand-bars. The river is shallow, joined by two small creeks from the north and one [30] from the south. In the plains to the south are

nearly a page long) is the fountain-head of the standard fables regarding con-sociation of prairie-dogs, owls, and snakes ; but that is not his fault, for all that he actually says is true enough.

[25] " The house of Mr. Troodo," Clark B 82.

[26] The Three Sister islands of Nicollet, Warren, etc. But now there is one large island a little above Fort Randall, at the 980th mile point.

[27] The present site of Fort Randall, where I wintered in 1872–73. On the north side, in Mix Co., is the Yankton Reservation ; but the military reservation includes a section on both sides of the river. Across the river from Fort Randall is a place called Swan, consisting in those years chiefly of a stage station. A creek or coulée leads thence to a lake at a little distance, in Mix Co., which I find named Lake Andes on some maps. It is a sort of a slough, and used to be our resort for duck-shooting. About 1859 Fort Randall was the extreme point on the Missouri where troops were permanently established.

[28] Now called Chicot island ; perhaps the J. de Cèdre of Perrin du Lac.

[29] The western fox-squirrel, *Sciurus ludovicianus*, common at Fort Randall.

[30] Wicha-paha creek of Nicollet ; now Scalp creek, with a large island at its mouth, about the 990th mile point.

great numbers of buffalo, in herds of nearly 500; all the copses of timber appear to contain elk or deer.  We camped on a sand-bar on the southern shore, at the distance of 14¼ miles.

*September* 10*th.*  This day we made 20 miles.  The morning was cloudy and dark, but a light breeze from the southeast carried us past two small islands on the south and one on the north; till, at the distance of 10½ miles, we reached an island extending for two miles in the middle of the river, covered with red cedar, from which it derives its name of Cedar[31] island.  Just below this island, on a hill to the south, is the backbone of a fish[32] 45 feet long, tapering toward the tail and in a perfect state of petrifaction, fragments of which were collected and sent to Washington. On both sides of the river are high dark-colored bluffs. About 1½ miles from the island, on the southern shore, the party on that side discovered a large and very strongly impregnated spring of water; and another, not so strongly impregnated, half a mile up the hill.  Three miles beyond Cedar island are a large island to the north and a number of sand-bars.  After which is another, about a mile in length, lying in the middle of the river and separated by a small channel, at its extremity, from another above it, on which we camped.  These two islands are called Mud

[31] Before this island was reached, the Expedition missed a creek on the south, Miyokendi, or Whet Stone river, of Nicollet, now Whetstone creek.  At its mouth is an island, the J. à Pierre (or Rock island) of P. du Lac, and here is the 1,000th mile point of the Missouri.  "Cedar" is the name which has been applied by various authors to several different islands, many miles apart, in this portion of the river.  That of the text seems to be Rantesha-wita of Nicollet, First Cedar island of Warren, now Little Cedar island ; on the north comes in here Cedar, or Bad creek, in Charles Co.  Next, on the north, in the same county, is Fish creek, of Nicollet's or of Warren's map, and one of these two is marked on some maps as Platte creek.  One of L. and C.'s two Mud islands is now called Snag island.  What with the shiftiness of the islands, and the insignificance of the creeks, exact identifications are difficult between Fort Randall and White river.  To-day's camp is nearly up to the 1,020th mile point, and about on the boundary between Gregory and Todd Cos. (on the south side).

[32] Certainly no "fish," but one of the huge reptiles of the cretaceous period.

islands. The river is shallow during this day's course, and is falling a little. The elk and buffalo are in great abundance, but the deer have become scarce.

*September* 11*th.* At 6½ miles we passed the upper extremity of an island on the south; four miles beyond which is another on the same side of the river; and about a quarter of a mile distant we visited a (*p. 70*) large village of the barking-squirrel.[33] It was situated on a gentle declivity, and covered a space of 970 yards long, and 800 yards wide; we killed four of them. We resumed our course, during 5½ miles passed two islands on the north, and then camped [34] at the distance of 16 miles on the south side of the river, just above a small run. The morning had been clouded, but in the afternoon it began raining, with a high northwest wind, which continued during the greater part of the night. The country seen to-day consists of narrow strips of lowland, rising into uneven grounds, which are succeeded, at the distance of three miles, by rich level plains, without any timber. The river itself is wide, and crowded with sand-bars. Elk, deer, squirrels, a pelican, and a very large porcupine, were our game this day; some foxes were seen, but not caught.[35]

In the morning we observed a man riding on horseback down toward the boat, and we were much pleased to find that it was George Shannon, one of our party, for whose safety we had been very uneasy. Our two horses having strayed from us on the 28th of August, he was sent to search for them. After he had found them he attempted to rejoin us; but seeing some other tracks, which must have been those of Indians, and which he mistook for our own, he concluded that we were ahead, and had been for 16 days following the bank of the river above us. During the first four days he exhausted his bullets, and was then

---

[33] The prairie-dog, *Cynomys ludovicianus.* See note [24], p. 111.

[34] In Gregory Co., just above the 1,030th mile point.

[35] This porcupine is the yellow-haired species, *Erethizon epixanthus.* The "foxes" were probably coyotes.

nearly starved, being obliged to subsist for twelve days on
a few grapes, and a rabbit, which he killed by making use of
a hard piece of stick for a ball.   One of his horses gave out
and was left behind; the other he kept as a last resource
for food.   Despairing of overtaking us, he was returning
down the river, in hopes of meeting some other boat ; and
was on the point of killing his horse, when he was so fortunate as to join us.

   (*p. 71*) *September* 12*th.*   The day was dark and cloudy ;
the wind from the northwest.   At a short distance we
reached an island in the middle of the river, which is covered with timber, a rare object now.   We with great difficulty were enabled to struggle through the sand-bars, the
water being very rapid and shallow, so that we were several
hours in making a mile.   Several times the boat wheeled
on a bar, when the men were obliged to jump out and prevent her from upsetting ; at others, after making a way up
one channel, the shoalness of the water forced us back to
seek the deep channel.   We advanced only four miles in
the whole day and camped on the south.[36]   Along both sides
of the river are high grounds ; on the southern side particularly they form dark bluffs, in which may be observed
slate and coal intermixed.   We saw also several villages
of barking-squirrels, great numbers of growse,[37] and three
foxes.

   *September* 13*th.*   We made twelve miles to-day through
a number of sand-bars, which make it difficult to find the
proper channel.   The hills [38] on each side are high and sepa-

[36] The difficulty of navigating is perhaps the reason why the explorers do not
name a creek from the south to-day.   It is enough of a stream to be laid down
on Clark's map of 1814, where it is lettered Shannon's Cr., though I cannot find
this name in Clark B.   It is also Shannon or Dry R. of Maximilian, 1833.
This looks as if it were named for George Shannon (see Sept. 11th) ; and perhaps it was, by an after-thought of Clark's.   But another name of this creek is
Washinanpi (so Warren), and the two words are suspiciously similar.   Here is
now a place called Rosebud Landing, in Gregory Co.

[37] The sharp-tailed grouse, *Pediœcetes phasianellus columbianus.*

[38] The most conspicuous of these, on the north, in Brulé Co., are called Bijou
or Bijou's hills, after a trader of that name who had a post here, and was killed

rated from the river by a narrow plain on its borders. On the north these lowlands are covered in part with timber, and great quantities of grapes, which are now ripe ; on the south we found plenty of plums, but they are not yet ripe ; and near the dark bluffs, a run tainted with alum and copperas, the southern side being more strongly impregnated with minerals than the northern. Last night four beavers were caught in the traps ; a porcupine was shot as it was upon a cottonwood, feeding on its leaves and branches. We camped on the north side, opposite a small willow-island. At night the mosquitoes were very troublesome, though the weather was cold and rainy, and the wind from the northwest.

*September* 14*th*. At two miles we reached a round island [39] on the northern side ; at about five, a run on the south ; 2½ miles further, a small creek ; [40] and at nine miles camped near the mouth of a creek on the same (*p. 72*) side. The sand-bars are very numerous, and render the river wide and shallow ; this obliged the crew to get into the water and drag the boat over the bars several times. During the whole day we searched along the southern shore, and at some distance into the interior, to find an ancient volcano which we heard at St. Charles was somewhere in this neighborhood ; but we could not discern the slightest appearance of anything volcanic. [41] In the course of their search the party shot a buck-goat [42] and a hare.

The hills, particularly on the south, continue high, but the timber is confined to the islands and banks of the river.

by the Sioux. So Catlin, 1832, and others. The hills are marked on most large maps, as Nicollet's, Warren's, etc.

[39] Sailor island of Nicollet and of Warren.

[40] Ball Cr. of some maps, Water-hole Cr. of others, in **Lyman Co.**, a little above the present site of Brulé City, which is on the north, in county of same name.

[41] There is no trace of anything volcanic in the course of the Missouri till past Milk river, where, in the country on the north, between Maria's and Milk rivers, the evidence of volcanic action first appears.

[42] That is, a male antelope. *Antilocapra americana.* The hare is the northern jackass-rabbit, *Lepus campestris*, of which Clark B 98 gives a good description ; and Lewis Q 37-40 gives over three pages of another account.

We had occasion here to observe the rapid undermining of these hills by the Missouri. The first attacks seem to be on the hills which overhang the river; as soon as the violence of the current destroys the grass at the foot of them, the whole texture appears loosened, and the ground dissolves and mixes with the water; the muddy mixture is then forced over the low grounds, which it covers sometimes to the depth of three inches, and gradually destroys the herbage; after which it can offer no resistance to the water, and becomes at last covered with sand.

*September* 15*th.* We passed, at an early hour, the creek near last night's camp; and at two miles' distance reached the mouth of White [43] river, coming in from the south. We ascended a short distance, and sent a sergeant [Gass] and another man to examine it higher up. This river has a bed of about 300 yards, though the water is confined to 150; in the mouth are a sand-island and several sand-bars. The current is regular and swift, with sand-bars projecting from the points. It differs very much from the Platte and Quicurre [*sic*], in throwing out comparatively little sand, but its general character is like that of the Missouri. This resemblance was confirmed by the sergeant, who ascended about twelve miles; at which distance it was about the same width as near the mouth, and the course, which was generally west, had been (*p. 73*) interrupted by islands and sand-bars. The timber consisted chiefly of elms; he saw pine-burrs [*sic*—pine-cones], and sticks of birch were seen floating down the river; he also met with goats, such as we have heretofore seen, great quantities of buffalo, near which were wolves, some deer, and villages of barking-squirrels.

At the confluence of White river with the Missouri is an

[43] Or White-earth river (to be distinguished from one of that name much lower down the Missouri); rivière Blanche of the French; otherwise Mankizitah river, as Nicollet, etc. White river arises in the N.W. corner of Nebraska, south of the Black hills, and of some headwaters of the South Fork of Cheyenne river, soon enters South Dakota, and courses easterly to the Missouri, falling into this river in Lyman Co., opposite Brulé Co.

excellent position for a town, the land rising by three gradual ascents, and the neighborhood furnishing more timber
than is usual in this country."

After passing high dark bluffs on both sides, we reached
the lower point of an island toward the south, at the distance of six miles. This island bears an abundance of
grapes, and is covered with red cedar; it also contains a
number of rabbits [*Lepus artemisia*]. At the end of this
island, which is small, a narrow channel separates it from a
large sand-island, which we passed, and camped, eight miles
on the north, under a high point of land opposite a large
creek to the south,⁴⁵ on which we observed an unusual quantity of timber. The wind was from the northwest this
afternoon, and high; the weather was cold, and its dreari-
ness increased by the howlings of a number of wolves⁴⁶
around us.

*September* 16*th.* Early this morning, having reached a
convenient spot on the south side at 1¼ miles' distance, we
camped just above a small creek, which we called Corvus,
having killed an animal [a magpie⁴⁷] of that genus near it.
Finding that we could not proceed over the sand-bars as
fast as we desired, while the boat was so heavily loaded,
we concluded not to send back, as we originally intended,

⁴⁴ Brulé City is a little lower down and across the Missouri.

⁴⁵ This blind sentence means, as I learn from Clark B 100, that having made
eight miles in all to-day, they camped on the right hand side (going up river),
opposite a creek which fell in on the other side. This stream is about to be
named Corvus creek, which the G. L. O. map (1879) charts on the wrong side,
in Brulé Co., and by name of American creek.

⁴⁶ The common gray wolf of the West, *Canis lupus occidentalis*, which always
hung about the herds of buffalo. This is quite different from the small barking-
wolf or coyote, *C. latrans.*

⁴⁷ "Killed a bird of the *Corvus* genus and order of the *pica*, about the size of a
jack-daw with a remarkable long tale," Lewis Q 40–44, where are over 4 pp. of
a "tale" about it ; a page is also in Clark B 106. This is the solitary instance
of our authors venturing a technical Latin name in zoölogy. The American
magpie is now called *Pica pica hudsonica.* Corvus creek naturally became Crow
creek of later maps ; someone also named it American river, whence a combina-
tion of the two names, as American Crow creek (so Warren's map). The
sometime important Crow Creek Indian Agency has made the name familiar.

our third periogue, but to detain the soldiers until spring, and in the mean time to lighten the boat by loading the periogue; this operation, added to that of drying all our wet articles, detained us during the day. Our camp is in a beautiful plain, with timber thinly scattered for three-quarters of a mile, and consisting chiefly of elm, cotton-wood, some ash of indifferent quality, and a considerable quantity of a small species of white oak [*Quercus undulata* var. *wrighti.*] This tree seldom rises higher (*p. 74*) than 30 feet, and branches very much; the bark is rough, thick, and of a light color; the leaves are small, deeply indented, and of a pale green; the cup which contains the acorn is fringed on the edges, and embraces it about one-half; the acorn itself, which grows in great profusion, is of an excellent flavor, and has none of the roughness which most other acorns possess. These acorns are now falling, and have probably attracted the number of deer which we saw on this place, as all the animals we have seen are fond of that food. The ground, having been recently burnt by the Indians, is covered with young green grass; in the neighborhood are great quantities of fine plums. We killed a few deer for the sake of their skins, which we wanted to cover the periogues, the meat being too poor for food. The cold season coming on, a flannel shirt was given to each man, and fresh powder to those who had exhausted their supply.[48]

*September* 17*th.* Whilst some of the party were engaged in the same way as yesterday, others were employed in examining the surrounding country. About a quarter of a mile behind camp, at an elevation of 20 feet above it, a plain extends nearly three miles parallel to the river and about a

---

[48] Gass has a separate entry for Sept. 16th, when he was with one man exploring White river. "We set out for the boat across the hills, on the tops of which are level plains with a great number of goats and buffaloe on them. Came to the head-waters of a creek and kept down it a S.E. course, and on our way killed three deer. We proceeded on to its mouth, which I computed to be 14 miles from that of the White river. Having found the boat had passed, we proceeded up the river [Missouri], and came to a handsome bottom, where our people had encamped to dry the provisions and stores."

mile back to the hills, toward which it gradually ascends. Here we saw a grove of plum trees loaded with fruit, now ripe, and differing in nothing from those of the Atlantic States, except that the tree is smaller and more thickly set. The ground of the plain is occupied by the burrows of multitudes of barking-squirrels, who entice hither the wolves of a small kind [*Canis latrans*], hawks, and polecats,[49] all of which animals we saw, and presumed that they fed on the squirrels. This plain is intersected nearly in its whole extent by deep ravines and steep irregular grounds rising from 100 to 200 feet. On ascending the range of hills which border the plain, we saw a second high level plain stretching to the south as far as the eye could reach. To the westward, a high range of hills about 20 miles distant runs nearly north and south, but not to any great ex- (*p. 75*) tent, as their rise and termination is embraced by one view, and they seemed covered with a verdure similar to that of plains. The same view extended over the irregular hills which border the northern side of the Missouri. All around the country had been recently burnt, and a young green grass about four inches high covered the ground, which was enlivened by herds of antelope and buffalo ; the last of which were in such multitudes that we cannot exaggerate in saying that at a single glance we saw 3,000 of them before us.

Of all the animals we had seen the antelope seems to possess the most wonderful fleetness ; shy and timorous, they generally repose only on the ridges which command a view of all the approaches of an enemy ; the acuteness of their sight distinguishes the most distant danger, the delicate sensibility of their smell defeats the precautions of concealment, and when alarmed their rapid career seems more like the flight of birds than the movement of an earthly being. After many unsuccessful attempts, Captain Lewis at last, by winding around the ridges, approached a party of seven which were on an eminence toward which

[49] "Polecat " is here meant for skunk, *Mephitis mephitica.*

the wind was unfortunately blowing. The only male of the party frequently encircled the summit of the hill, as if to announce any danger to the females, which formed a group at the top. Although they did not see Captain Lewis, the smell alarmed them, and they fled when he was at the distance of 200 yards; he immediately ran to the spot where they had been; a ravine concealed them from him, but the next moment they appeared on a second ridge at the distance of three miles. He doubted whether it could be the same band, but their number and the extreme rapidity with which they continued their course convinced him that they must have gone with a speed equal to that of the most distinguished race-horse.[50]

Among our acquisitions to-day were a mule-deer,[51] a magpie, the common deer [*Cariacus virginianus macrurus*], and buffalo. Captain Lewis also saw a hare, and killed a rattlesnake near the burrows of the barking-squirrels.

(*p. 76*) *September* 18*th.* Having everything in readiness we proceeded with the boat much lightened, but the wind being from the N.W. we made but little way. At one mile we reached an island in the middle of the river, nearly a mile in length and covered with red cedar; at its extremity a small creek comes in from the north.[52] We then met

[50] This account of the antelope, much abbreviated by Biddle, forms most of Lewis Ba, Sept. 17th, 1804—the same fragmentary codex including also Sept. 16th. It is an excellent sketch, which should have been printed in full, as at that time the animal was unknown to science.

Gass also does his share of natural history to-day: "Captain Lewis and some men went out to hunt, and killed thirteen common and two black-tailed deer, three buffalo and a goat. The wild goat in this country differ from the common tame goat, and is supposed to be the real antelope. The black-tailed, or mule deer have much larger ears than the common deer and tails almost without hair, except at the end, where there is a bunch of black hair [*Cariacus macrotis*]. There is another species of deer in this country, with small horns and long tails. The tail of one which we killed was eighteen inches long [*Cariacus virginianus macrurus*]. One of our men caught a beaver, and killed a prarie-wolf [*Canis latrans*]. These are a small species of wolves, something larger than a fox, with long tails and short ears."

[51] *Cariacus macrotis*, so called from its large ears and slim tail.

[52] Much early history attaches to this vicinity, a little short of the 1,070th

some small sand-bars, and the wind being very high and ahead, we camped on the south, having made only seven miles. In addition to the common deer, which were in great abundance, we saw goats, elk, buffalo, and black-tailed deer;[53] the large wolves too are very numerous; they have long hair with coarse fur, and are of a light color. A small species of wolf,[54] about the size of a gray fox, was also killed, and proved to be the animal which we had hitherto mistaken for a fox. There are also many porcupines, rabbits, and barking-squirrels in the neighborhood.

*September* 19*th*. We this day enjoyed a cool clear morning and a wind from the southeast. We reached at three miles a bluff on the south, and four miles further the lower point of Prospect[55] island, about 2½ miles in length; opposite this are high bluffs, about 80 feet above the water, beyond which are beautiful plains gradually rising as they recede from the river. These are watered by three streams, which empty near each other. The first is about 35 yards wide, the ground on its sides high and rich, with some timber; the second, about twelve yards wide, but with less timber; the third is nearly of the same size and contains more water, but it scatters its waters over the large timbered plain and empties itself into the river at three places. These rivers are called by the French Les Trois Rivieres des Sioux, the Three Sioux rivers; and as the Sioux generally

mile point, and well within Sioux country. The island noticed but not named in the text is one of several now called Cedar (Second Cedar island of Nicollet's and Warren's maps); the creek from the "north" (rather east) is Nicollet's Rantesha river and Warren's Cedar Island river. On the island was the old site of Fort Recovery; on the west bank of the river was situated Fort Cedar, or aux Cèdres, a post of the Missouri Fur Company.

[53] *Cariacus macrotis*, also called mule-deer. The tail is mostly white, but tipped with black. This species is to be distinguished from one west of the Rocky mountains, *C. columbianus*, which our authors hereafter also call black-tailed.

[54] The coyote, *Canis latrans*.

[55] Present, or a recent name; also called Laurel island, from the French Isle des Lauriers. A little below, on the west bank, about the 1,080th mile point, was built Fort Lookout.

cross the Missouri at this place, it is called the Sioux Pass of the Three Rivers.[56]  These streams have the same right of asylum as the Pipestone creek already mentioned, though in a less degree.

(*p. 77*) Two miles from the island we pass a creek 15 yards wide; eight miles further, another 20 yards wide; three miles beyond which is a third, of 18 yards' width; all on the south side.  The second, which passes through a high plain, we called Elm creek; to the third we gave the name of Night creek, having reached it late at night.[57] About a mile beyond this is a small island on the north side of the river, called Lower island, as it is situated at the commencement of what is known by the name of Grand Detour,[58] or Great Bend, of the Missouri.  Opposite is a creek on the south about ten yards wide, which waters a plain where there are great numbers of the prickly pear,[59]

---

[56] Making into the Missouri from the east, in Buffalo Co., north of Brulé Co.; opposite is Lyman Co., across the river, extending into the bight of the Big Bend of the Missouri.  Various maps consulted chart from two to five rivers, whose nomenclature is much mixed.  It may be well to cite Clark B 111, here: " N. 50° W. 3 miles [from last camp] to a pt. of wood on the S. S. [starboard side] opposit is a bluff on L. S. [larboard side].  North 4 miles to the Lower pt. of Prospect Island opsd. [opposite] the 3 rivers on the S. S.  N. 30° W. 2½ miles to the upper pt. of the Island psd. [passed] the 3 rivers."  So the three rivers emptied within the length of Prospect island.  I am informed by Mr. Henry Gannett, of the U. S. Geological Survey, that present names are, in ascending order: 1. Crow creek; 2. Wolf creek; 3. Campbell creek.  Nicollet's map charts five rivers: 1, 2, 3, nameless; 4. Pokende; 5. Chanpepenan.  Warren's has three: 1. Crow; 2. Shompapi; 3. Campbell's.  Most maps chart several rivers, but name only the first and largest, as Crow creek—to be carefully distinguished from Corvus or Crow creek, lower down and on the other side of the river.  The present Crow creek gives name to the Indian Agency here, where is also the site of Fort Thompson.

[57] Of these three creeks I find the first on some maps by the name of Laurel creek; the second, Elm, I am informed is now called Camel creek (Campbell? Perhaps some confusion here: see last note); the third, Night, is now a certain Fish creek.  Warren's map names the largest branch of Crow creek, Elm creek.

[58] *Sic*—better Détour.  Clark B 115 has " Grand de Tortu," interlined Detour. This remarkable loop of the river takes various English adjectives, as Grand, Long, Great, Big, etc.  An Indian epithet is Karmichigah.

[59] The common species of *Opuntia*, of the Missouri region.

which name we gave to the creek.[60]    We camped on the south, opposite the upper extremity of the island, having made an excellent day's sail of 26¼ miles.    Our game this day consisted chiefly of deer, of which four were black-tails, one a buck with two main prongs of the horns on each side and forked equally.    Large herds of buffalo, elk, and goats were also seen.

*September 20th.*    Finding we had reached the Big Bend, we dispatched two men with our only horse across the neck, to hunt there and await our arrival at the first creek beyond it.    We then set out with fair weather and the wind from the S.E., to make the circuit of the bend.    Near the lower island the sand-bars are numerous, and the river is shallow. At 19½ miles is a sand-island, on the southern side.    About ten miles beyond it is a small island on the south, opposite a small creek [Wassag] on the north.    This island, which is near the N.W. extremity of the bend, is called Solitary [now Cul-de-sac] island.    At about 11 miles further, we camped on a sand-bar, having made 27½ miles.    Captain Clark, who early this morning had crossed the neck of the bend, joined us in the evening.    At the narrowest part the gorge is composed of high and irregular hills of about 180 or (*p. 78*) 190 feet in elevation; from this descends an unbroken plain over the whole of the bend, and the country is separated from it by this ridge.    Great numbers of buffalo, elk, and goats are wandering over these plains, accompanied by [sharp-tailed] grouse and larks.    Captain Clark saw a hare [*Lepus campestris*] also, on the Great Bend.    Of the goats killed to-day, one is a female differing from the male in being smaller in size; its horns too are smaller and straighter, having one sharp prong, and there is no black about the neck.    None of these goats have any beard, but are delicately formed and very beautiful.

*September 21st.*    Between one and two o'clock the sergeant on guard alarmed us, by crying that the sand-bar on which

---

[60] Gass does not notice this, and gives a creek which our authors do not name, between Elm and Night creeks.    He calls it Wash creek.

we lay was sinking. We jumped up, and found that both above and below our camp the sand was undermined and falling in very fast. We had scarcely got into the boats and pushed off, when the bank under which they had been lying fell in, and would certainly have sunk the two periogues if they had remained there. By the time we reached the opposite shore the ground of our camp sunk also. We formed a second camp for the rest of the night, and at daylight proceeded on to the gorge or throat of the Great Bend, where we breakfasted. A man, whom we had dispatched to step off the distance across the bend, made it 2000 yards; the circuit is 30 miles. During the whole course the land of the bend is low, with occasional bluffs; that on the opposite side, high prairie ground and long ridges of dark bluffs. After breakfast, we passed through a high prairie on the north side, and a rich cedar lowland and cedar bluff on the south, till we reached a willow-island below the mouth of a small creek. This creek, called Tyler's [or Tylor's[61]] river, is about 35 yards wide, comes in on the south, and is at the distance of six miles from the neck of the Great Bend.

Here we found a deer and the skin of a white [gray] wolf, left us by our hunters ahead. Large quantities of different kinds of plover and brant are in this neighborhood, collecting and moving toward (*p. 79*) the south. The catfish are small, and not in such plenty as we had found them below this place. We passed several sand-bars, which make the river very shallow and about a mile in width, and camped on the south, at the distance of 11½ miles. On each side the shore is lined with hard, rough gully-stones, rolled from the hills and small brooks. The most common timber is cedar, though, on the prairies, there are great quantities of prickly pear. From this place we passed several sand-

[61] Running chiefly in Presho Co., but emptying about the boundary between that and Lyman Co. Now Medicine, or Medicine Hill river, Indian Pahahwakan, from a hillock which forms a conspicuous landmark near the river, at some little distance from the Missouri.

bars, which make the river shallow and about a mile in width.  At the distance of 11½ miles, we camped on the north at the lower point of an ancient island, which has since been connected with the mainland by the filling up of the northern channel, and is now covered with cotton-wood.  We here saw some tracks of Indians, but they appeared three or four weeks old.  This day was warm.

*September 22d.*  A thick fog detained us until seven o'clock; our course was through inclined prairies on each side of the river, crowded with buffalo.  We halted at a point on the north side, near a high bluff on the south, and took a meridian altitude, which gave us the latitude of 44° 11′ 33$\frac{3}{10}$″.  On renewing our course, we reached first a small island on the south, at the distance of 4½ miles, immediately above which is another island, opposite a creek 15 yards wide.[62]  This creek, and the two islands, one of which is half a mile long and the second three miles, are called the Three Sisters; a beautiful plain extends on both sides of the river.  This is followed by an island on the north, called Cedar island, about 1½ miles in length and the same distance in breadth, deriving its name from the quality of the timber.

On the south side of this island is a fort and large trading-house, built by a Mr. Loisel[63] who wintered here during the last year in order to trade with the Sioux, the remains of

[62] Sentence equivocal, as to which side the creek comes in on.  Clark B 125 has : "Passed a small island on the L. S. imediately above passed a Island situated nearest the L. S. abt. [about] 3 miles long, behind this Isd. on the L. S. a Creek Comes in about 15 yards wide, this Creek and Islands are Called the 3 sisters."  So the creek is on the larboard side or left hand going up river, in Presho Co.  It is much named : Three Sisters creek, as per text ; Third Cedar Island river, Nicollet, 1843; Cedar creek, Reynolds, 1867; Cedar creek, G. L. O. map, 1879 ; now Reynolds' creek, after Capt. W. F. Reynolds, U. S. T. E.

[63] Name correct.  A codex has first a blind word of which Biddle once made Duquett.  Next he wrote to Clark (July 7th, 1810, letter before me) : "What is the name of the trader who built a factory on Cedar island, a Mr. Lucette we have him now?"  Clark B 126 has Louiselle, very plainly ; Codex P 133 is clearly Louasell.  Elsewhere we find Loisell and Loiselle.  Gass prints Lucelle ;

whose camps are in great numbers about this place.    The establishment is 60 or 70 feet square, built with red cedar and pic- (*p. 80*) keted in with the same materials.    The hunters who had been sent ahead joined us here.    They mention that the hills are washed in gullies, in passing over which some mineral substances had rotted and destroyed their moccasins ; they had killed two deer and a beaver.    At 16 miles' distance we came-to on the north side, at the mouth of a small creek.[64]    The large stones which we saw yesterday on the shores are now some distance in the river, and render navigation dangerous.    The mosquitoes are still numerous in the low grounds.

*September 23d.*    We passed, with a light breeze from the southeast, a small island on the north called Goat island ; above which is a small creek called by the party Smoke[65] creek, as we observed a great smoke to the southwest on approaching it.    At ten miles we came to the lower point of a large island, having passed two small willow-islands with sand-bars projecting from them.    This island, which we called Elk island, is about 2½ miles long, and three-quarters of a mile wide, situated near the south, and covered with cottonwood, red currants, and grapes.    The river is here almost straight for a considerable distance, wide and shallow, with many sand-bars.    A small creek on the north, about 16 yards wide, we called Reuben's[66] creek, as Reuben Fields, one of our men, was the first of the party who reached it.

Brackenridge, L'Oiselle (see note [32], p. 71).    One Registre Loisel, b. Lower Canada, came to St. Louis in 1793, and married May 7th, 1800.    (Billon's Annals St. L., 1886, p. 465.)    Gass describes the post more particularly : " The place picketed in is about 65 or 70 feet square, with centry-boxes in two of the angles.    The pickets are 13½ feet above ground.    In this square he built a house 45½ by 32½ feet, and divided it into four equal parts, one for goods, one to trade in, one to be used as a common hall, and the other for a family house."

[64] A creek marked  Baie de  Naples on Nicollet's map answers exactly to this.

[65] Owawichah creek of Nicollet's map ; and the island here called Goat is there shown.    Neither this nor the last creek is charted on ordinary maps.

[66] Wiyo-paha-wakan river of Nicollet, Warren, and Reynolds, translated East Medicine Knoll river, and charted under this name on ordinary maps, in Hughes Co.    Across the Missouri here, in Presho Co., was the site of old Fort George.

At a short distance above this we camped for the night, having made 20 miles.

The country generally consists of low, rich, timbered ground on the north, and high barren lands on the south ; on both sides great numbers of buffalo are feeding.

In the evening three boys of the Sioux [67] nation swam

[67] These were Tetons : '' The Band of Seauex called the Tetongues,'' Clark B 130, where Biddle respells.

Referring to pp. 99-101 and notes there for an outline of the Tetons, the picture of these famous miscreants may be here filled in. I first give the substance of what is in Lewis' Statistical View of 1806, and then add the modern statistics.

Lewis makes four tribes or bands of Tetons, whom he calls (1) Tetons Bois Brulé ; (2) Tetons Okandandas; (3) Tetons Minnakineazzo ; (4) Tetons Sahone. (1) 120 lodges, 300 warriors, 900 total population ; east side of the Missouri, from mouth of the White to the Teton river. (2) 50 lodges, 120 warriors, 360 total ; each side of the Missouri from Teton to Cheyenne river. (3) 100 lodges, 250 warriors, total 750 ; both sides of the Missouri from the Cheyenne river up to the Ricaras. (4) 120 lodges, 300 warriors, total 900, on each side of the Missouri from the Ricaras to Warreconne river. Then in his Remarks (item '' S '' of his schedule) he lumps the four, and proceeds to characterize them thus (p. 18 of the London ed.) :

'' These are the vilest miscreants of the savage race, and must ever remain the pirates of the Missouri, until such measures are pursued by our government, as will make them feel a dependence on its will for their supply of merchandise. Unless these people are reduced to order, by coercive measures, I am ready to pronounce that the citizens of the United States can never enjoy but partially the advantages which the Missouri presents. Relying on a regular supply of merchandise through the channel of the river St. Peters, they view with contempt the merchants of the Missouri, whom they never fail to plunder, when in their power. Persuasion, or advice, with them, is viewed as supplication, and only tends to inspire them with contempt for those who offer either. The tameness with which the merchants of the Missouri have hitherto submitted to their rapacity, has tended not a little to inspire them with contempt for the white persons who visit them, through that channel. A prevalent idea among them, and one that they make the rule of their conduct, is, that the more illy they treat the traders the greater quantity of merchandise they will bring them, and that they will thus obtain the articles they wish on better terms ; they have endeavored to inspire the Ricaras with similar sentiments, but happily without any considerable effect. The country in which these four bands rove is one continued plain, with scarcely a tree to be seen except on the water-courses, or the steep declivities of hills, which last are but rare ; the land is fertile, and lies extremely well for cultivation ; many parts of it are but badly watered. It is from this country that the Missouri derives most of its colouring matter ; the

across the river and informed us that two parties of Sioux were camped on the next river, one consisting of 80 and the second of 60 lodges, at some distance above. After treating them kindly we sent them back with a present of two carrots of tobacco to their chiefs, whom we invited to a conference in the morning.

(*p. 81*) *September 24th.* The wind was from the east, and the day fair. We soon passed a handsome prairie on the north side, covered with ripe plums, and the mouth of

earth is strongly impregnated with glauber salts, alum, copperas, and sulphur, and when saturated with water, immense bodies of the hills precipitate themselves into the Missouri, and mingle with its waters. The waters of this river have a purgative effect on those unaccustomed to use it. I doubt whether these people can ever be induced to become stationary ; their trade might be made valuable if they were reduced to order. They claim jointly with the other bands of the Sioux, all the country lying within the following limits, viz. beginning at the confluence of the river Demoin [Des Moines] and Mississippi, thence up the west side of the Mississippi to the mouth of the St. Peters river, thence on both sides of the Mississippi to the mouth of Crow-wing river, and upwards with that stream, including the waters of the upper part of the same ; thence to include the waters of the upper portion of Red river, of Lake Winnipie [Winnipeg—Red River of the North], and down the same nearly to Pembenar [Pembina] river, thence in a southerly course to intersect the Missouri at or near the Mandans, and with that stream [the Missouri] downwards to the entrance of the Warrecunne creek, thence passing [beyond] the Missouri it [the boundary] goes to include the lower portion of the river Chyenne [Cheyenne], all the waters of White river and river Teton, includes the lower portion of the river Quicurre [Qui court—Niobrara] and returns to the Missouri, and with that stream [goes] downwards to the mouth of Waddipon river, and thence eastwardly to intersect the Mississippi at the beginning [of the boundary thus traced]."

This picture was not overdrawn, if we may judge from the trouble we have always had with these Sioux. But "point of view" must be regarded in judging Sioux and other things. The late General G. K. Warren, who as Lieutenant Warren knew Sioux thoroughly well, has recorded a decision which deserves to be worked in gold thread on the colors of Custer's regiment : "I have always found the Dakotas exceedingly reasonable beings, with a very proper appreciation of their own rights. What they yield to the whites they expect to be paid for, and I have never heard a prominent man of their nation express an opinion in regard to what was due them in which I do not concur. Many of them view the extinction of their race as the inevitable result of the operation of present [1855] causes, and do so with all the feelings of despair with which we should contemplate the extinction of our nationality." (Rep. Expls. Neb. and Dak.,

a creek on the south, called Highwater [68] creek, a little above our camp. At about five miles we reached an island 2½ miles in length, and situated near the south. Here we were joined by one of our hunters [Colter], who procured four elk, but whilst he was in pursuit of the game the Indians had stolen his horse. We left the island, and soon overtook five Indians on the shore; we anchored, and told them from the boat we were friends and wished to continue so, but were not afraid of any Indians ; that some of their young men had stolen the horse which their great father had sent for their great chief, and that we could not treat with them until he was restored. They said that they knew nothing of the horse, but if he had been taken he should be given up. We went on, and at 11½ miles, passed an island

reprint of 1875, p. 54.) Lewis' View of 1806 may be contrasted with the following statistics and present classification of the Tetons—of whom, it must be premised, there are several other bands than those four which Lewis and Clark met on ascending the Missouri in 1804. The Teton (Ti-ton-wan) Indians are now classed as :

1. *Burnt Woods or Bois Brulés*, subdivided into (a) Upper Brulés or High-land Sit-can-xu, and (b) Lower Brulés or Lowland Sit-can-xu. Nearly all the former, to the number of 3,245, are on the Rosebud Reservation, S. D.; the latter number 1,026 at the Crow Creek and Lower Brulé Agency.

2. *Sans Arcs* (Without Bows, I-ta'-zip-tco ) ; mostly on the Cheyenne Reservation, S. D.; some at Standing Rock, N. D.

3. *Blackfeet* (Si-ha'-sa'-pa) ; as (2) ; those at Standing Rock are 545 in number.

4. *Minneconjous* (Mi-ni-ko'-o-ju) ; mostly on the Cheyenne Reservation : with some of the Two Kettles band, they number 2,823 ; others are at Rosebud, and some at Standing Rock.

5. *Two Kettles* (O-o'-he-non-pa, Two Boilings); some with (4), on the Cheyenne Reservation ; 315 on the Rosebud.

6. *Ogallalas* or *Oglalas* (the Okandandas of Lewis and Clark); mostly on Pine Ridge Reservation, S. D., to the number of 4,452 ; some on Standing Rock. Subdivision of the Ogallala tribe gives : (a) Wazaza, Wajaja, or Wazhazha, on the Rosebud, 1,825 ; and (b) Wagluxe, In breeders or Loafers, on the Rosebud, 1,353.

7. *Uncpapas* or *Uncapapas* (Huñk'-pa-pa); on Standing Rock Reservation, now numbering only 571.

[68] Katota Tokah or Cabri river, Nicollet ; Cabri creek, Reynolds ; Antelope or Cabri river, Warren ; Antelope creek or river of present maps, in Presho Co., S. D. Nearly opposite this, on the north, in Hughes Co., is the mouth

on the north, which we called Good-humored [69] island;
it is about 1½ miles long and abounds in elk.    At
13½ miles, we anchored 100 yards off the mouth of
a river on the south side, where we were joined by
both the periogues, and camped; two-thirds of the
party remained on board, and the rest went as a guard
on shore with the cooks and one periogue.    We have
seen along the sides of the hills on the north a great
deal of stone; besides the elk, we also observed a hare.
The five Indians whom we had seen followed us, and slept
with the guard on shore.    Finding one of them was a
chief, we smoked with him and made him a present of
tobacco.    This river is about 70 yards wide, and has a
considerable current.    As the tribe of the Sioux which
inhabit it are called Tetons, we gave it the name of
Teton [70] river. (*p. 82*)

of a considerable stream which the explorers were perhaps too much troubled
by the Indians to notice.    This is the "Padani Tiyohe or Pawnis Deserted R."
of Nicollet; Pawnees Deserted, of Warren; charted, but nameless, on Reynolds'
map.    It is notable, because here, on the north bank of the Missouri, was
the site of *old* Fort Sully, for some time a formidable menace to the turbulent
Tetons.    Another Fort Sully was later built, above Teton river : see note beyond.

[69] Two islands, some distance apart, are charted by Nicollet, Warren, and
Reynolds; one, just above Antelope creek, Warren letters Farm island.    This
is the one noted, but not named, "at about five miles," in the text.    The other,
Good-humored island, is just below Teton river; and I am informed by Mr.
Henry Gannett that it is now called Framboise (Raspberry) island.

[70] The Sioux name—Chicha or Schicha or Shisha, with Watpa or Wakpa
(river) prefixed—means Bad river.    The Teton or Bad river is only a prairie
stream, between and parallel with the White below and the Cheyenne above.
It heads from the direction of the Black hills, but is cut off from these by
the South Fork of the Cheyenne; courses eastward and falls into the Missouri between Stanley and Pratt Cos., opposite Hughes Co.    Three miles
above its mouth, on the right (west) bank of the Missouri, was the site of
old Fort Pierre.    The full name of this establishment was Fort Pierre Chouteau, after P. Chouteau, jr. (b. Jan. 9, 1789, d. Oct. 6, 1865), second son of
(John) Pierre Chouteau, sr., and a member of the family so long famous in the
annals of St. Louis.    The fort was originally a trading-post of the American
Fur Co., at one time in business under the style of P. Chouteau & Co.    The
full name appears on maps of less than fifty years ago; the surname was gradually
dropped, but the Christian name survives as that of Pierre, now the capital of
South Dakota, at the mouth of the river.

# CHAPTER IV.

## THE MISSOURI FROM TETON RIVER TO THE MANDANS.

Council with the Tetons—Trouble with these Indians—Bad-humored island—The Council renewed—Characteristics of the Indians—Smoking, feasting, and dancing—Indian prisoners—Appearance and dress of the Indian men and women—Their lodges—Their police system—Their attempt to detain the party—No-timber creek—Followed by the Tetons—The Cheyenne river—Sentinel and Lookout creeks—Mr. Valle—Lookout bend—Caution island—Many Indians about—Good Hope island—Old Ricara village—White Brant creek—Other Ricara villages—" Pork " (Owl) river—Grouse island—Wetarhoo river—Mr. Gravelines—Visit of the Ricaras—Councils with these Indians—Their three villages—Their characteristics—Civility of their women—Ricara lodges, agriculture, and trade—Stone-idol creek—Ricara legend—Hay creek—Sentence of court martial—More Ricara lodges—Cheyenne creek—Hunting antelope—Cannon-ball river—Fish river—Old Mandan villages—Indian superstition—Teton war-party—Many old Indian villages—Pacific meeting of Mandan and Ricara chiefs—More Mandan and Ricara villages—The Expedition has reached and will winter with the Mandans.

**S**EPTEMBER 25th. The morning was fine, and the wind continued from the southeast. We raised a flagstaff and an awning, under which we assembled at twelve o'clock, with all the party parading under arms. The chiefs and warriors from the camp two miles up the river met us, about 50 or 60 in number, and after smoking we delivered them a speech; but as our Sioux interpreter, Mr. Durion, had been left with the Yanktons, we were obliged to make use of a Frenchman who could not speak fluently, and therefore we curtailed our harangue. After this we went through the ceremony of acknowledging the chiefs, by giving to the grand chief a medal, a flag of the United States, a laced uniform coat, a cocked hat and feather; to the other two chiefs, a medal and some small presents ; and to two warriors of consideration, certificates. The name of the great chief is Untongasabaw or Black Buffalo ; the second Tortohonga or the Partisan ; the third Tartongawaka or Buffalo Medicine ; the name of one of the warriors was Wawzinggo ; that of the second Matocoquepa or Second Bear.

We invited the chiefs on board and showed them the boat, the air-gun, and such curiosities as we thought might amuse them. In this we succeeded too well; for after giving them a quarter of a glass of whisky, which they seemed to like very much, and sucked the bottle, it was with much difficulty that we could get rid of them. They at last accompanied Captain Clark on shore in a periogue with five men; but it seems they had formed a design (*p. 83*) to stop us; for no sooner had the party landed than three of the Indians seized the cable of the periogue, and one of the soldiers of the chief put his arms round the mast. The second chief, who affected intoxication, then said that we should not go on, that they had not received presents enough from us. Captain Clark told them that we would not be prevented from going on; that we were not squaws, but warriors; that we were sent by our great father, who could in a moment exterminate them. The chief replied that he too had warriors, and was proceeding to offer personal violence to Captain Clark, who immediately drew his sword, and made a signal to the boat to prepare for action. The Indians who surrounded him drew their arrows from their quivers and were bending their bows, when the swivel in the boat was instantly pointed toward them, and twelve of our most determined men jumped into the periogue to join Captain Clark. This movement made an impression on them, for the grand chief ordered the young men away from the periogue; they withdrew and held a short council with the warriors. Being unwilling to irritate them, Captain Clark went forward and offered his hand to the first and second chiefs, who refused to take it. He turned from them and got into the periogue, but had not gone more than ten paces when both the chiefs and two of the warriors waded in after him, and he brought them on board. We then proceeded for a mile and anchored off a willow-island, which from the circumstances which had just occurred we called Bad-humored island. [1]

[1] Gass relates the incident thus: "Five of them came on board and remained

*September 26th.* Our conduct yesterday seemed to have inspired the Indians with fear of us, and as we were desirous of cultivating their acquaintance, we complied with their wish that we should give them an opportunity of treating us well, and also suffer their squaws and children to see us and our boat, which would be perfectly new to them. Accord-

about three hours. Captain Clark and some of our men in a periogue went ashore with them ; but the Indians did not seem disposed to permit their return. They said they were poor and wished to keep the periogue with them. Captain Clark insisted on coming to the boat ; but they refused to let him, and said they had soldiers as well as he had. He told them his soldiers were good, and that he had more medicine aboard his boat than would kill twenty such nations in one day. After this they did not threaten any more, and said they only wanted us to stop at their lodge, that the women and children might see the boat. Four of them came aboard, when we proceeded on a mile, and cast anchor at the point of an island in the middle of the river. The Indians remained with us all night " (p. 44). The situation was critical indeed—much more so than one unfamiliar with Sioux might gather from either of the printed texts. Sioux string bows as cowboys draw their six-shooters—that is, for instant use. Lewis was mettlesome ; Clark had red hair, and had been insulted ; both officers were dauntless, and their men were well disciplined. Several lives, possibly the further progress of the Expedition, hung as it were upon the first twang of a bowstring. Clark B 137–139 is therefore worth publishing : " Envited the Chiefs on board to show them our boat and such curiossities as was strange to to them, we gave them ¼ a glass of whiskey which they appeared to be verry fond of, sucked the bottle after it was out & soon began to be troublesom, one the 2d chief assumeing Drunkness, as a Cloaki for his rascally intentions. I went with those chiefs (which left the boat with great reluctiance) to shore with a view of reconseleing those men to us, as soon as I landed the Perogue three of their young men seased the cable of the Perogue, the chiefs soldr. Huged [chief's soldier hugged] the mast, and the 2d chief was verry insolent both in words & justures declareing I should not go on, stateing he had not received presents sufficient from us, his justures were of such a personal nature I felt myself Compeled to Draw my sword, at this motion Capt. Lewis ordered all under arms in the boat, those with me also showed a disposition to Defend themselves and me, the grand chief then took hold of the roap & ordered the young warrers away, I felt myself warn [warm] & spoke in very positive terms. We proceeded about 1 mile & anchored out off a willow Island placed a guard on shore to protect the Cooks & a guard in the boat, fastened the Perogues to the Boat, I call this Island Bad humered Island as we were in a bad humer." Then in a foot-note : " Most of the warrers appeared to have their Bows strung and took out their arrows from the quiver. as I was not permited to return, I sent all the men except 2 Inft. to the boat, the perogue soon returned with about 12 of our determined men, ready for any event."

ingly, after passing at 1½ miles a small willow-island and several sand-bars, (*p. 84*) we came-to on the south side, where a crowd of men, women, and children were waiting to receive us. Captain Lewis went on shore and remained several hours; and observing that their disposition was friendly, we resolved to remain during the night for a dance which they were preparing for us.

Captains Lewis and Clark, who went on shore one after the other, were met on landing by ten well-dressed young men, who took them up in a robe highly decorated and carried them to a large council-house, where they were placed on a dressed buffalo-skin by the side of the grand chief. The hall or council-room was in the shape of three-quarters of a circle, covered at the top and sides with skins well dressed and sewed together. Under this shelter sat about 70 men, forming a circle round the chief, before whom were placed a Spanish flag and the one we had given them yesterday. This left a vacant circle of about six feet diameter, in which the pipe of peace was raised on two forked sticks, about six or eight inches from the ground, and under it the down of the swan was scattered. A large fire, in which they were cooking provisions, stood near, and in the center about 400 pounds of buffalo meat as a present for us. As soon as we were seated, an old man got up, and after approving what we had done, begged us take pity on their unfortunate situation. To this we replied with assurances of protection. After he had ceased, the great chief rose and delivered a harangue to the same effect ; then with great solemnity he took some of the most delicate parts of the dog which was cooked for the festival, and held it to the flag by way of sacrifice ; this done, he held up the pipe of peace, and first pointed it toward the heavens, then to the four quarters of the globe, then to the earth, made a short speech, lighted the pipe, and presented it to us. We smoked, and he again harangued his people, after which the repast was served up to us. It consisted of the dog which they had just been cooking, this being a great dish among the (*p. 85*) Sioux, used on all festivals; to which were added pemitigon [*sic*—read pemmican], a dish made of buffalo-meat, dried or jerked and then pounded and mixed raw with grease; and a kind of ground potato, dressed like the preparation of Indian corn called hominy, to which it is little inferior. Of all these luxuries, which were placed before us in platters, with horn spoons, we took the pemitigon and the potato, which we found good, but we could as yet partake but sparingly of the dog. We eat and smoked for an hour, when it became dark. Everything was then cleared away for the dance, a large fire being made in the center of the house, giving at once light and warmth to the ballroom.

The orchestra was composed of about ten men, who played on a sort of tambourine formed of skin stretched across a hoop, and made a jingling noise with a long stick to which the hoofs of deer and goats were hung; the third instrument was a small skin bag with pebbles in it. These, with five or six young men for the vocal part, made up the band. The women then came forward highly decorated; some with poles in their hands, on which were hung the scalps of their enemies; others with guns, spears, or different trophies, taken in war by their husbands, brothers, or connections. Having arranged themselves in two columns, one on each side of the fire, as soon as the music began they danced toward each other till they met in the center, when the rattles were shaken and they all shouted and returned back to their places. They have no step, but shuffle along the ground; nor does the music appear to be anything more than a confusion of noises, distinguished only by hard or gentle blows upon the buffalo-skin; the song is perfectly extemporaneous. In the pauses of the dance, any man of the company comes forward and recites, in a sort of a low guttural tone, some little story or incident, which is either martial or ludicrous; or, as was the case this evening, voluptuous and indecent; this is taken up by the orchestra and the dancers, who repeat it in a higher strain and dance to it. (*p. 86*) Sometimes they alternate; the orchestra first performing, and when it ceases, the women raising their voices and making a music more agreeable—that is, less intolerable than that of the musicians. The dances of the men, which are always separate from those of the women, are conducted very nearly in the same way, except that the men jump up and down instead of shuffling ; and in the war-dances the recitations are all of a military cast. The harmony of the entertainment had nearly been disturbed by one of the musicians who, thinking he had not received a due share of the tobacco we had distributed during the evening, put himself into a passion, broke one of the drums, threw two of them into the fire, and left the band. They were taken out of the fire ; a buffalo-robe held in one hand and beaten with the other, by several of the company, supplied the place of the lost drum or tambourine, and no notice was taken of the offensive conduct of the man. We stayed till twelve o'clock at night, when we informed the chiefs that they must be fatigued with all these attempts to amuse us, and retired, accompanied by four chiefs, two of whom spent the night with us on board.

While on shore we saw 25 squaws and about the same nnmber of children, who had been taken prisoners two weeks ago in a battle with their countrymen, the Mahas. In this engagement the Sioux destroyed 40 lodges, killed 75 men, of whom we saw many of the scalps, and took these prisoners. Their appearance is wretched and dejected ; the women too seem low in stature, coarse, and ugly—though their present condition may diminish their beauty. We gave them a variety of small articles, such as awls and needles, and interceded for them with the chiefs, to whom we recommended to follow the advice of their great father, to restore the prisoners and live in peace with the Mahas, which they promised to do.

The tribe which we this day saw are a part of the great Sioux nation, and are known by the name of the Teton Okan- (*p. 87*) dandas. They are about 200 men in number, and their chief residence is on both sides of the Missouri between the Chayenne and Teton rivers. In their persons they are rather ugly and ill-made, their legs and arms being too small, their cheek-bones high, and their eyes projecting. The females, with the same character of form, are more handsome, and both sexes appear cheerful and sprightly; but in our intercourse with them we discovered that they were cunning and vicious.

The men shave the hair off their heads, except a small tuft on the top, which they suffer to grow and wear in plaits over the shoulders; to this they seem much attached, as the loss of it is the usual sacrifice at the death of near relations. In full dress, the men of consideration wear a hawk's feather or calumet [2] feather, worked with porcupine-quills, and fastened to the top of the head, from which it falls back. The face and body are generally painted with a mixture of grease and coal. Over the shoulders is a loose robe or mantle of buffalo-skin dressed white, adorned with porcupine-quills loosely fixed so as to make a jingling noise when in motion, and painted with various uncouth figures unintelligible to us, but to them emblematic of military exploits or some other incident. The hair of the robe is worn next the skin in fair weather, but when it rains the hair is put outside, and the robe is either thrown over the arm or wrapped round the body, all of which it may cover. Under this in the winter season they wear a kind of a shirt resembling ours, made either of skin or cloth, and covering the arms and body. Round the middle is fixed a girdle of cloth or dressed elk-skin, about an inch in width, closely tied to the body; to this is attached a piece of cloth or blanket or skin, about a foot wide, which passes between the legs and is tucked under the girdle both before and behind; from the hip to the ankle he is covered by leggings of dressed antelope-skins, with seams at the sides two inches in width, ornamented by little tufts of hair, the produce of the scalps (*p. 88*) taken in war, which are scattered

[2] The feathers most prized as calumets are the tail-feathers of the golden eagle, *Aquila chrysaëtos*, which are about a foot long and white, tipped with black.

down the leg. The winter moccasins are of dressed buffalo-skin, the hair being worn inward, and soled with thick elk-skin parchment; those for summer are of deer or elk-skin, dressed without the hair, and with soles of elk-skin. On great occasions, or whenever they are in full dress, the young men drag after them the entire skin of a polecat fixed to the heel of the moccasin. Another skin of the same animal, either tucked into the girdle or carried in the hand, serves as a pouch for their tobacco, or what the French traders call bois roule.[3] This is the inner bark of a species of red willow, which, being dried in the sun or over the fire, is rubbed between the hands and broken into small pieces, and used alone or mixed with tobacco. The pipe is generally of red earth, the stem made of ash, about three or four feet long, and highly decorated with feathers, hair, and porcupine-quills.

The hair of the women is suffered to grow long and is parted from the forehead across the head, at the back of which it is either collected into a kind of a bag, or hangs down over the shoulders. Their moccasins are like those of the men, as are also the leggings, which do not, however,

---

[3] Read bois roulé, rolled wood; "bau roly" of Clark B 141; best known to us by the name of kinikinik, as it may be most phonetically spelled. This renders an Algonquian word meaning "a mixture," or "that which is mixed." It varies in orthography to a dozen or more forms, with doubling of one or both *n*'s, substitution of single or double *l* for each *n*, and use of *c* for or before a *k*, etc. A form before me is *kinnecanick;* but the vowels are in this word more stable than the consonants, contrary to the rule. Kinikinik is what the Indians smoke as we do tobacco, whatever that may be. It is usually poor tobacco mixed with scrapings or shavings of various other plants. These are, somewhat in the order of their comparative frequency of use: 1. The smooth sumac, *Rhus glabra*, whose crumbled leaves are used. 2. The silky cornel or dogwood, or so-called red-willow, *Cornus sericea*, and related species of *Cornus*, as *C. stolonifera*, or red-osier dogwood, of which the scraped inner bark is used. 3. The bear-berry, *Arctostaphylos uva-ursi*, a trailing ericaceous shrub, hereinafter called sacacommis; the scraped bark used. 4. Species of arrow-wood or *Viburnum*. The various ingredients, properly taken from the respective plants and dried, are rubbed up in the hands as we would treat natural leaf tobacco, and then put in the pipe. The Omaha name of the mixture is ninnegahe, sometimes found as an English word.

reach beyond the knee, where they are met by a long loose
shift of skin which reaches nearly to the ankles ; this is
fastened over the shoulders by a string and has no sleeves,
but a few pieces of the skin hang a short distance down
the arms. Sometimes a girdle fastens this skin around
the waist, and over all is thrown a robe like that worn
by the men. They seem fond of dress.

Their lodges are very neatly constructed, in the same
form as those of the Yanktons ; they consist of about
100 cabins, made of white buffalo-hide dressed, with a
larger one in the center for holding councils and dances.
They are built round, with poles about 15 or 20 feet high,
covered with white skins. These lodges may be taken to
pieces, packed up, and carried with the nation wherever
they go, by dogs, which bear great burdens.[4] The women
are chiefly employed in dressing buffalo-skins ; they seem
perfectly well disposed, but are addicted to stealing anything which they can take without being observed. This
nation, although it makes so many ravages among its neighbors, is badly supplied with guns. The water which they
carry with them is contained chiefly in the paunches of
deer and other animals, and they make use of wooden
bowls. Some had their heads shaved, which we found was
a species of mourning for relations. Another usage, on
these occasions, is to run arrows through the flesh both
above and below the elbow.

While on shore to-day we witnessed a quarrel between
two squaws, which appeared to be growing every moment
more boisterous, when a man came forward, at whose
approach everyone seemed terrified and ran. He took the
squaws and without any ceremony whipped them severely.
On inquiring into the nature of such summary justice, we

---

[4] Gass adds, under date of Sept. 28th : " While I was at the Indian camp yesterday they yoked a dog to a kind of car, which they have to haul their baggage
from one camp to another ; the nation having no settled place or village, but are
always moving about. The dogs are not large, much resemble a wolf, and will
haul about 70 pounds each. "

learned that this man was an officer well known to this and many other tribes. His duty is to keep the peace, and the whole interior police of the village is confided to two or three of these officers, who are named by the chief and remain in power some days, at least till the chief appoints a successor. They seem to be a sort of constable or sentinel, since they are always on the watch to keep tranquillity during the day and guard the camp in the night. The short duration of the office is compensated by its authority. His power is supreme, and in the suppression of any riot or disturbance no resistance to him is suffered ; his person is sacred, and if in the execution of his duty he strikes even a chief of the second class, he cannot be punished for this salutary insolence. In general he accompanies the person of the chief, and when ordered to any duty, however dangerous, it is a point of honor rather to die than to refuse obedience. Thus, when they attempted to stop us yesterday, the chief ordered one of these men to take possession of the boat ; he immediately put his arms around the (*p. 90*) mast, and, as we understood, no force except the command of the chief would have induced him to release his hold. Like the other men his body is blackened, but his distinguishing mark is a collection of two or three ravenskins fixed to the girdle behind the back in such a way that the tails stick out horizontally from the body. On his head too is a raven-skin split into two parts, and tied so as to let the beak project from the forehead.

*September 27th.* We rose early, and the two chiefs took off, as a matter of course and according to their custom, the blanket on which they had slept. To this we added a peck of corn as a present to each. Captain Lewis and the chiefs went on shore to see a part of the nation that was expected, but did not come. He returned at two o'clock, with four of the chiefs, and a warrior of distinction called Wadrapa, or On His Guard ; they examined the boat and admired whatever was strange, during half an hour, when they left it with great reluctance. Captain Clark accompanied them

to the lodge of the grand chief, who invited them to a dance,
where, being joined by Captain Lewis, they remained till a
late hour.   The dance was very similar to that of yesterday.
About twelve we left them, taking the second chief and one
principal warrior on board.   As we came near the boat the
man who steered the periogue, by mistake, brought her
broadside against the boat's cable and broke it.   We called
up all hands to their oars;   our noise alarmed the two
Indians;   they called out to their companions, and immediately the whole camp crowded to the shore;   but after half
an hour they returned, leaving about sixty men near us.
The alarm given by the chiefs was said to be that the Mahas
had attacked us, and that they were desirous of assisting
us to repel the assault;   but we suspected that they were
afraid we meant to set sail and intended to prevent us from
doing so;   for in the night the Maha prisoners had told one
of our men, who understood their language, that we were
to be stopped.   We therefore, (*p. 91*) without giving any
indications of our suspicion, prepared everything for an
attack, as the loss of our anchor obliged us to come-to near
a falling bank, very unfavorable for defense.   We were not
mistaken in these opinions;   for when in the morning,

*Friday, September* 28*th*, after dragging unsuccessfully for
the anchor, we wished to set sail, it was with great difficulty
that we could make the chiefs leave the boat.   At length
we got rid of all except the great chief;   when, just as we
were setting out, several of the chief's soldiers sat on the
rope which held the boat to the shore.   Irritated at this,
we got everything ready to fire on them if they persisted;
but the great chief said that these were his soldiers and only
wanted some tobacco.   We had already refused a flag and
some tobacco to the second chief, who had demanded them
with great importunity;   but, willing to leave them without
going to extremities, we threw him a carrot of tobacco, saying
to him, "You told us that you are a great man and have
influence;   now show your influence, by taking the rope from
those men, and we will then go without any further trou-

ble." This appeal to his pride had the desired effect ; he went out of the boat, gave his soldiers the tobacco, and pulling the rope out of their hands delivered it on board.

We then set sail under a breeze from the S.E. After sailing about two miles we observed the third chief beckoning to us ; we took him on board, and he informed us that the rope had been held by the order of the second chief, who was a double-faced man. A little further on we were joined by the son of this chief, who came on board to see his father. On his return we sent a speech to the nation, explaining what we had done and advising them to peace ; but [assuring them that] if they persisted in their attempts to stop us, we were willing and able to defend ourselves. After making six miles, during which we passed a willow-island on the south and one sand-bar, we camped on another in the mid- (*p. 92*) dle of the river. The country on the south side was a low prairie, that on the north, high land.

*September 29th.* We set out early, but were again impeded by sand-bars, which made the river shallow ; the weather was, however, fair ; the land on the north side, low, and covered with timber, contrasted with the bluffs to the south. At nine o'clock we saw the second chief and two women and three men on shore, who wished us to take the two women offered by the second chief to make friends, which was refused. He then requested us to take them to the other band of their nation, who were on the river not far from us ; this we declined, but in spite of our wishes they followed us along the shore. The chief asked us to give them some tobacco ; this we did, and gave more as a present for that part of the nation which we did not see. At 7½ miles we came to a small creek on the southern side, where we saw great numbers of elk, and which we called No-timber creek [in Stanley Co.] from its bare appearance. Above the mouth of this stream, a Ricara [5] band of Pawnees

---

[5] " Aricaris, commonly called Rickarees, Rickrees, or Rees," Gass, p. 48 ; the codices variant, as usual. The accepted spelling is now Arikara. "No-timber" is now Chankie or Chanker creek ; this name clipped from Sioux Tschehkana-

had a village five years ago; but there are no remains of it except the mound which encircled the town. Here the second chief went on shore. We then proceeded, and at the distance of 11 miles camped on the lower part of a willow-island [Okobojou], in the middle of the river, being obliged to substitute large stones in the place of the anchor which we lost.

*September* 30*th*. The wind was this morning very high from the southeast, so that we were obliged to proceed under a double-reefed mainsail, through the rain. The country presented a large low prairie covered with timber on the north side; on the south, we first had high barren

kasahtapah (so Maximilian), meaning breech-clout. The Arikaras are now confined to a small village on the Fort Berthold Reservation, N. D., which they share with the Mandans and Hidatsans. They are the remnants of ten different tribes of Pawnees (of the *Northern* group of Caddoan stock), driven by the Sioux from their country lower down the Missouri, near the habitat of the Poncas, in what is now northern Nebraska. They numbered 448 in 1889.

Lewis Statistical View of 1806 makes the name Ricârâo, giving Stâr-râh-hé as a primitive form, and La Ree (Les Rees) as the French nickname. He says they speak Pania (Pawnee) with a different accent, and have words peculiar to themselves. They had in 1804 three villages, with 500 warriors and a total population of 2,600, on the S.W. bank of the Missouri, 1,440 miles by his estimate from its mouth. Lewis remarks (item "S" of his tables) that they "are the remains of ten large tribes of Panias who have been reduced, by the smallpox and the Sioux, to their present number. They live in fortified villages, and hunt immediately in their neighbourhood. . . . The remains of the villages of these people are to be seen on many parts of the Missouri from the mouth of the Tetone river to the Mandans. They claim no land except that on which their villages stand, and the fields which they cultivate. Though they are the oldest inhabitants, they may properly be considered the farmers or tenants at will of that lawless, savage and rapacious race the Sioux Teton, who rob them of their horses, plunder their gardens and fields and sometimes murder them, without opposition. If these people were freed from the oppression of the Tetons, their trade would increase rapidly, and might be extended to a considerable amount. They maintain a partial trade with their oppressors the Tetons, to whom they barter horses, mules, corn, beans and a species of tobacco which they cultivate ; and receive in return guns, ammunition, kettles, axes, and other articles which the Tetons obtain from the Yanktons of the N. and Sissatones, who trade with Mr. Cammeron, on the river St. Peters. These horses and mules the Ricaras obtain from their Western neighbours, who visit them frequently for the purpose of trafficking."

hills, but after some miles it [the country] became of the
same character as that of the opposite side. We had not
gone far when an Indian ran after us and begged to be carried on board as far as the Ricaras, which we refused ;
soon after, we discovered on the hills at a distance a
great number of Indians, who came toward the river and
camped ahead of us. We stopped (*p. 93*) at a sand-bar, at
about 11 miles, and after breakfasting proceeded on a short
distance to their camp, which consisted of about 400 souls.

We anchored 100 yards from the shore ; and discovering
that they were Tetons belonging to the band which we
had just left, we told them that we took them by the hand,
and would make each chief a present of tobacco ; that we
had been badly treated by some of their band, and that
having waited for two days below we could not stop here,
but referred them to Mr. Durion for our talk and an explanation of our views. They then apologized for what had
passed, and assured us that they were friendly and very
desirous that we should land and eat with them. This we
refused, but sent the periogue on shore with the tobacco,
which was delivered to one of the soldiers of the chief
whom we had on board. Several of them now ran along the
shore after us, but the chief threw them a twist of tobacco,
and told them to go back and open their ears to our counsels ; on which they immediately returned to their lodges.

We then proceeded past a continuation of the low
prairie on the north, where we had large quantities of
grapes, and on the south [read north] saw a small creek and
an island. Six miles above this, two Indians came to the
bank, looked at us about a half an hour, and then went,
without speaking, over the hills to the southwest. After
some time, the wind rose still higher, and the boat struck a
log, turned, and was very near taking in water. The chief
became so much terrified at the danger that he hid himself
in the boat, and as soon as we landed got his gun and told
us that he wanted to return ; that we would now see no
more Tetons, and that we might proceed unmolested. We

repeated the advice we had already given, presented him with a blanket, a knife, and some tobacco, and after smoking with us he set out. We then continued to a sand-bar on the north side, where we camped, having come 20½ miles.[6] In the course of the day we saw a number of sand-(*p.* 94) bars which impeded navigation. The only animal we observed was the white gull, then in great abundance.

*Monday, October 1st,* 1804. The weather was very cold and the wind high from the southeast during the night, continuing so this morning. At three miles' distance we had passed a large island[7] in the middle of the river, opposite the lower end of which the Ricaras once had a village on the south side of the river ; there are, however, no remnants of it now except a circular wall, three or four feet in height, which encompassed the town. Two miles beyond this island is a river coming in from the southwest, about 400 yards wide ; the current is gentle, discharging not much water and very little sand. It takes its rise in the second range of the Cote [Côte] Noire or Black mountains, and its general course is nearly east. This river has been occasionally called Dog river, under a mistaken opinion that its

[6] And having passed, first, Cow creek (Spring creek of Heap's map), small, in Sully Co., its mouth at point of Hughes Co. ; next, Okobojou creek, large, on which is Clifton, county town of Sully ; thirdly, the "small creek and an island." This creek, on the *right*, in Sully Co., is the site of the important post Fort Sully, in the Military Reservation—to be distinguished from old Fort Sully, below the Teton river. The island is that now called Stanley island. Clark B 165-170, Sept. 30th, has no mention of any creek in connection with this island. There are in fact several creeks from the "south" (west), but these are in Stanley Co., above Stanley island and Fort Sully, and below the Cheyenne. The largest of these is marked on the G. L. O. map Dry creek, with the Cheyenne Agency at its mouth. To-day's camp is in Lookout Bend.

[7] Clark B 165, last course and distance of Sept. 30th : "N. 50° W. 2½ mls. to the Lower pt. of Pania Island situated in the midl. of the river ;" and 171, first course and distance of Oct. 1st : "N. 80° W. 3 mls. to the upper pt. of a large island in the River." So this is "Pania" island of the codex, which makes it three miles long. It shows plainly on Lewis' map, 1806, and Clark's, 1814, where the Arikara village is marked; Nicollet's map charts it, nameless ; Warren's map letters Shyenne, now spelled Cheyenne. By the codex its upper point is two miles below the mouth of "Chien or Dog river," with which the Biddle text agrees.

French name was Chien ; but its true appellation is Chayenne,[8] and it derives this title from the Chayenne Indians.
Their history is the short and melancholy relation of the
calamities of almost all the Indians.    They were a numerous people and lived on the Chayenne, a branch of the
Red river of Lake Winnipeg.    The invasion of the Sioux
drove them westward ; in their progress they halted on
the southern side of the Missouri below the Warreconne,
where their ancient fortifications still exist ; but the same
impulse again drove them to the heads of the Chayenne,
where they now rove and occasionally visit the Ricaras.
They are now reduced, but still number 300 men.[9]

[8] So Biddle text throughout ; in Gass, De Chien ; in Brackenridge, Chienne.
Clark B 172 has "the River Chien (or Dog River)," but the codices yield various
forms of the word ; Schain is one old form ; Chaguyenne and Chaguiene are
others.    Cheyenne is now the accepted spelling.    The Dakotan Indian name
means Good river, by antithesis with the Bad (Teton) river, already treated in
this work.    Lewis' map, 1806, letters Sharha or Chyenne ; Clark's, 1814, gives
Chayenne ; on neither of these is the course well charted.    The upper reaches
are far out of the way on the earlier of these maps, where they were laid down,
of course, from hearsay, and the main course is south instead of north of east.
Nicollet has Shayen, Wasteg or Good river ; Warren and Reynolds both have
Big Shyenne, Wakpa Washte or Good river (where the antithesis of Big is the
Little Cheyenne, for which see beyond).    This is a great river, whose two main
and about equal forks, the North and the South, embrace the Black hills proper,
and drain these outliers of the Rockies by unnumbered tributaries.    The united
waters flow about E.N.E. to join those of the Missouri in Stanley Co., where
there is the notable flexure of the latter river, known as the Little (or Lookout)
Bend, whose bight faces in the opposite direction from that of the Great Bend.

[9] The Cheyennes are Indians of a different linguistic stock from any we
have thus far met in this work, excepting only the Arapahoes.    These two,
Cheyennes and Arapahoes, are of the Algonquian stock.    They became separated from their kindred by forcing their way through hostile tribes, and
formed outliers of the Algonquian family across the Missouri into what is
now the Black Hills country of South Dakota, and parts of Wyoming and
Colorado, thus interpolating themselves between Siouan tribes behind them and
Shoshonean tribes in front, and having on the one hand the Kiowan tribes, and
on the other the Middle Caddoans (Pawnees).

In this place may be offered some general remarks, based on Powell's
monograph, concerning the Algonquian family.    The name is contracted from
Algonequin, an Algonkin word, meaning those across the river—that is, the St.
Lawrence.    The present total of all the Algonquian tribes is about 95,600, of

Although the river does not seem to throw out much sand, yet near and above its mouth we find a great many sand-bars difficult to pass. On both sides of the Missouri, near the Chayenne, are rich, thinly-timbered lowlands, behind which are bare hills. As we proceeded, we found that the sand-bars made the river so shallow, and the wind was so high, that we could scarcely find the channel; at one place were forced to drag the boat over a (*p. 95*) sand-bar, the Missouri being very wide and falling a little. At 7½ miles we came-to at a point and remained three hours, during which time the wind abated; we then passed within

whom 60,000 are in Canada and the rest in the United States. The tribes and subtribes are extremely numerous. The principal of these are, in alphabetical order: Abnaki, Algonkin proper, Arapaho, Cheyenne, Conoy, Cree, Delaware, Fox, Illinois, Kickapoo, Mahican, Massachuset, Menominee, Miami, Micmac, Mohegan, Montagnais, Montauk, Munsee, Nantikoke, Narraganset, Nauset, Nipmuc, Ojibwa, Ottawa, Pamlico, Pennacook, Pequot, Piankishaw, Pottawottomi, Powhatan, Sac, Shawnee, Siksika, Wampanoag, Wappinger. Among these names are some of our most familiar Indian words, and many place-names not less familiar are derived from the same linguistic stock. The area occupied by the Algonquian family was more extensive than that of any other linguistic stock in North America, extending from Labrador to the Rocky mountains, and from Churchill river of Hudson's bay to North Carolina. In the eastern part of this vast area was a region occupied by Iroquoian tribes, almost surrounded by their Algonquian neighbors. On the south the Algonquians were bounded by tribes of Iroquoian stock, and one of Siouan stock (Catawba); on the southwest and west by Muskhogean and Siouan tribes; northwest by the Kitunahan and great Athapascan families; elsewhere they came in contact with the Eskimo. In Newfoundland the Algonquian stock met the single tribe of Beothukan stock. A portion of the Shawnees had early separated from the main body in central Tennessee, and pushed on down the Savannah river in South Carolina, where they became known as Savannahs, and warred with surrounding tribes till about 1700, when they were driven off and joined the Delaware Indians. The rest of the Shawnee tribe was expelled by the Cherokee and Chickasaw soon afterward.

Turning now to Lewis' Statistical View, we find he gives Chyennes, with a form Shâr'-ha as primitive, and the French nickname "la chien" (*i. e.*, le chien, fem. la chienne, pl. les chiens or les chiennes, dogs, bitches). He notes their language by an asterisk, signifying "primitive" in his schedule. He enumerates 110 lodges, 300 warriors, total 1,200, and locates the tribe about the sources of the Cheyenne, now in the Black hills. He puts them at peace with all their neighbors except the Sioux, with whom they were waging defensive warfare, and adds: "They are the remnant of a nation once respect-

four miles two creeks on the south, one of which we called Centinel [10] creek, and the other Lookout [11] creek. This part of the river has but little timber; the hills are not so high as we have hitherto seen, and the number of sand-bars extends the river to more than a mile in breadth. We continued about 4½ miles further, to a sand-bar in the middle of the river, where we spent the night, our progress being 16 miles. On the opposite shore we saw a house among the willows, and a boy whom we called and brought on board. He proved to be a young Frenchman in the employ of a Mr. Valle,[12] a trader who is now here pursuing his commerce with the Sioux.

able in point of number : formerly resided on a branch of the Red River of Lake Winnipie, which still bears their name. Being oppressed by the Sioux, they removed to the west side of the Missouri, about 15 miles below the mouth of Warricunne creek, where they built and fortified a village, but being pursued by their ancient enemies the Sioux, they fled to the Black hills about the head of the Chyenne river, where they wander in quest of the buffalo, having no fixed residence. They do not cultivate. They are well disposed towards the whites, and might easily be induced to settle on the Missouri, if they could be assured of being protected from the Sioux. Their number annually diminishes." (London ed. 1807, p. 20.)

According to the latest returns the Cheyennes now number 3,626. Of Northern Cheyennes there are 517 at Pine Ridge Agency, S. D., and 865 at Tongue River Agency, Mont. There are 2,091 Cheyennes at the Cheyenne and Arapaho Agency in Ind. Terr., and 153 are at school at Lawrence, Kas., and Carlisle, Pa.

[10] " Passed a Creek on the L. S. which we Call the Sentinal," Clark B 173; so also Lewis' map, 1806 ; as per text on Clark's, 1814; charted but unnamed by Warren and by Reynolds ; no trace on G. L. O. map, 1879 ; Pascal creek of Stevens' map ; and now Fox creek. The Missouri is here running nearly from east to west, and the stream comes in from the N.W., in Stanley Co.

[11] " Passed 2 Creeks on the L. S. the upper small," Clark B 171. This upper small creek is Lookout of the text ; shown by a separate scratch on Lewis' map, but apparently charted as a north fork of Sentinel creek on Clark's, though Clark B 174 says, " a small creek above the latter which we call lookout C." There is yet another small creek, just beyond Lookout. I am not informed of a modern name for either of these streams, if either has one.

[12] " A boy came in a canoe & informed that 2 french men were at the house with good to trade with the Seauex whom he expected down from the Rickerees [Arikaras] iverry day. . . This Mr. *Jon Vallie* informs us," etc., Clark B 175.

*October 2d.* There had been a violent wind from the
S.E. during the night, which having moderated we set sail
with Mr. Valle, who visited us this morning and accompanied us for two miles. He is one of the three French
traders who have halted here, expecting the Sioux who are
coming down from the Ricaras, where they now are, for
the purposes of traffic. Mr. Valle tells us that he has
passed the last winter 300 leagues up the Chayenne under
the Black mountains. That river he represents as very
rapid, liable to sudden swells, the bed and shores formed of
coarse gravel, and difficult of ascent even for canoes; 100
leagues from its mouth it divides into two branches, one
coming from the south; the other at 40 leagues from the
junction enters the Black mountains. The land which it
waters, from the Missouri to the Black mountains, resembles the country on the Missouri, except that the former
has even less timber, and of that the greater proportion
is cedar. The Chayennes reside chiefly on the heads of
the river, and steal horses from the Spanish settlement, a
plundering excursion which they perform in a month's
(*p. 96*) time. The Black mountains, he observes, are very
high, covered with great quantities of pine, and in some
parts the snow remains during the summer. There are
also great quantities of goats, white bear, prairie-cocks,
and a species of animal which, from his description, must
resemble a small elk with large circular horns.[13]

[13] Obviously the Rocky Mountain sheep or bighorn, *Ovis montana*, here first
alluded to by our authors. " Saw a spoon made of a horn of an anemele of the
sheep kind," Clark B 149, Sept. 26th, where is an interlineation " mountain ram
or argalia." A codex describes a head and horns which weighed 27 lbs. This
woolless sheep exercised the party a good deal, especially after they discovered
the woolly goat, *Haplocerus montanus*. The codices mostly call it " the big-
horned animal "; sometimes by its Indian name, arsarta or ahsahta—a word
I did not discover in English print till too late to put it in the Century
Dictionary ; sometimes argali or argalia, and again ibex. They give both these
last names to certain creeks higher up the Missouri. Gass says, " Captain
Clarke calls them the Ibex," p. 89, and Gass' editor, David M'Keehan, discusses
this identification with long quotes from Goldsmith's Animated Nature. The
white bear above mentioned is the grizzly, *Ursus horribilis*. The prairie-cock

At 2½ miles we had passed a willow-island on the south ; on the north side of the river were dark bluffs, and on the south low rich prairies.   We took a meridian altitude on our arrival at the upper end of the isthmus of the bend, which we called the Lookout Bend, and found the latitude to be 44° 19′ 36″.[14]   This bend is nearly 20 miles around, and not more than two miles across.

In the afternoon we heard a shot fired, and not long after observed some Indians on a hill.   One of them came to the shore and wished us to land, as there were 20 lodges of Yanktons or Boisbrule [*sic*] there.[15]   We declined doing so, telling him that we had already seen his chiefs, and that they might learn from Mr. Durion the nature of the talk we had delivered to them.   At nine miles we came to the lower point of a long island on the north, the banks of the south side of the river being high, those of the north forming a low rich prairie.   We coasted along this island, which we called Caution[16] island, and after passing a small creek on the south[17] camped on a sand-bar in the middle of the river, having made twelve miles.   The wind changed to the northwest and became very high and cold.   The current of the river is less rapid, and the water, though of the same color, contains less sediment than below the Chayenne, but its width continues the same.   We were not able to hunt to-day, for

is the sage-grouse, *Centrocercus urophasianus*, and the basis of a certain mythical " white booted turkey," Clark B 177 and Lewis Q 44, stated by Mr. Valle to be found in the Black hills.

[14] So Clark B 178, but too far south ; 44° 49′ would be nearer the true latitude of this point on Lookout Bend, which is that already noted, p. 147, as the Little Bend.   At the upper end of the bend is Devil's island.

[15] Gass has "the Jonkta or Babarole band," p. 49.

[16] This is Plum island of Warren's and present maps ; charted, nameless, on Reynolds' ; not shown on Lewis' or on Clark's ; wrongly named Pascal's island by Stevens.   " Observe great caution this day, expecting the Seaux intentions somewhat hostile," Clark C 2, overlapping Codex B in date.

[17] Not identified.   If we could here read *north* for " south," we might suppose this to be the creek marked Inyan Tonka on Heap's map, next above Plum island, on the east or right-hand side going up.   But Clark B 180 has plainly " L. S.," larboard or left-hand side, with which the text agrees.

there were so many Indians in the neighborhood we were in constant expectation of being attacked, and were therefore forced to keep the party together and be on our guard.

*October 3d.*[18]  The wind continued so high from the northwest that we could not set out till after seven.  We then proceeded till twelve o'clock, and landed on (*p. 97*) a bar toward the south, where we examined the periogues and the forecastle of the boat, and found that the mice had cut several bags of corn and spoiled some of our clothes. About one o'clock an Indian came running to the shore with a turkey on his back ; several others soon joined him, but we had no intercourse with them.  We then went on for three miles, but the ascent soon became so obstructed by sand-bars and shoal water that, after attempting in vain several channels, we determined to rest for the night under some high bluffs on the south [now Artichoke butte], and send out to examine the best channel.  We had made eight miles along high bluffs on each side.[19]  The birds we saw were white gulls and brant [*Bernicla brenta*], which were flying to the southward in large flocks.

*October 4th.*  On examination we found that there was no outlet practicable for us in this channel, and that we must retrace our steps.  We therefore returned three miles and attempted another channel, in which we were more fortunate.  The Indians were in small numbers on the shore, and seemed willing, had they been more numerous, to molest us.  They called to desire that we would land,

[18] Clark B ends with this date ; it begins Aug. 15th, to which date Clark A extends.  Up to this point in the History of the Expedition, the Biddle narrative is based almost solely on these two codices—the chief exceptions I have noticed being the account of the antelope, Sept. 17th, which is from the fragmentary Lewis Ba, and of the supposed ancient fortification, the sketch and main description of which are in Clark N 81–85.  Biddle now passes to Codex C, which is mainly a Clark, but with some entries in Lewis' hand.  This we may call " the Mandan Codex," as it extends to April 7th, 1805, and is chiefly the Lewis and Clark journal of their wintering at Fort Mandan, though it includes a good deal of other and miscellaneous matter.  In this respect, as in style of binding and some other particulars, it stands quite alone in the series of codices.

[19] And had overlooked Inyan Tonka of Warren, on the right, now Artichoke creek.

and one of them gave three yells and fired a ball ahead of the boat; we, however, took no notice of it, but landed on the south to breakfast.   One of these Indians swam across and begged for some powder; we gave him a piece of tobacco only.   At 8½ miles we had passed an island in the middle of the river, which we called Goodhope[20] island. At 1½ miles we reached a creek on the south side about twelve yards wide, to which we gave the name of Teal creek.   A little above this is an island on the north side of the current [*i. e.*, channel], about 1½ miles in length and three-quarters of a mile in breadth.   In the center of this island is an old village of the Ricaras, called Lahoocat; it was surrounded by a circular wall, containing 17 lodges. The Ricaras are known to have lived there in 1797, and the village seems to have been deserted about five years since; it does not contain much timber.   We camped on a sand- (*p. 98*) bar making out from the upper end of this island, our journey to-day being twelve miles.

*October 5th.*   The weather was very cold; yesterday evening and this morning there was a white frost.   We sailed along the highlands on the north side, passing a small creek on the south, between three and four miles. At seven o'clock we heard some yells and saw three Indians of the Teton band, who asked us to come on shore and begged for some tobacco; to all which we gave the same

[20] Pascal's island of Warren's but not of ordinary maps, which locate Pascal's island on the parallel of 45° N.   This fixed point is fortunate, for the text of Oct. 4th and 5th is peculiarly difficult to follow.   Clark C 5 has : " Passed a Island in the middle of the river about 3 miles in length, we call Good-hope Island, (2) at 4 miles [further] passed a creek [Teal] on the L. S. about 12 yards wide . . . crossed over to an (3) Island [Lahoocat] situated on the S. S." Thus at the 8½ miles of the text Good Hope (Pascal's of Warren) had been left four miles below Teal creek, instead of only 1½ miles, as the text reads, and Teal creek is close to the island of Lahoocat.   This fetches out exactly for identification of Lahoocat with the island Warren and Heap both called Bullberry, at 45°, between Potter and Dewey Cos., with Teal creek running in the latter county.   The name " Teal " creek is not to be found in the Clark codex ; but it is " Teel " in Gass, p. 50, whence I imagine Biddle took it ; he also had the Gass manuscript in his hands at one time, besides Gass' printed volume

answer as hitherto. At eight miles we reached a small[21] creek on the north. At 14 we passed an island on the south, covered with wild rye ; at the head of it a large creek comes in from the south, which we named Whitebrant creek, from seeing several white brants among flocks of dark-colored ones.[22] At the distance of 20 miles we came to on a sand-bar toward the north side of the river, with a willow-island opposite ; the hills, or bluffs, come to the banks of the river on both sides, but are not so high as they are below ; the river itself, however, continues of the same width, and the sand-bars are quite as numerous. The soil of the banks is dark-colored, and many of the bluffs have the appearance of being on fire. Our game this day was a deer, a prairie-wolf, and some goats [antelope] out of a flock that was swimming across the river.

*October 6th.* The morning was still cold, the wind being from the north. At eight miles we came to a willow-island on the north, opposite a point of timber, where there are many large stones near the middle of the river, which seem

[21] The word "small" does not occur here in Clark C 6-8, Oct. 5th, and the distance from the island of Lahoocat makes this creek, nameless both in the text and in the codex, no other than the Little Cheyenne river, a considerable stream from the "north," *i. e.,* east, in Potter (formerly Ashmore) Co. This is Cut Head R. of Heap, and Hidden creek of Gass, p. 50, who says: "We passed a creek on the north side, called Hidden creek, and high black bluffs on the south side." The Little Cheyenne is well "hidden" in the text. But it is conspicuously traced in Clark's map, 1814, unlettered : see there the stream on the right, next above the parallel of 45°, and next below Otter creek on the same side. There is now a place called Medicine Rock at its mouth. White Brant creek, from the "south," *i. e.,* west, is called White Goat creek in Gass, p. 50, by a slip for White Goose. It is one of two or more streams in Dewey Co., south of Moreau or Owl river, and just below Patched Skin buttes. For future identifications it may be well to give Clark's courses and distances for the 5th, avoiding the peculiarities of his phraseology : N. 63° E. 1½ ms. under high land S. S. E. 3 ms. passing a creek L. S. N. 80° E. 1½ ms. in a bend S. S. N. 30° W. 2 ms. to a point of high land L. S., *passing a creek, S. S.* (Biddle's "small creek on the north "). N. 50° W. 3 ms. to a point S. S. N. 17° W. 3 ms. to a tree on the S. S., passing a small island, " covered with wild rye," above which a creek (White Brant) comes in L. S. N. 16° E. 6 ms., etc. ; total, 20 miles.

[22] The white brant, here first mentioned, is the snow-goose, *Chen hyperbo-reus.* The dark-colored brant is the ordinary species, *Bernicla brenta.*

to have been washed from the hills and high plains on both
sides, or driven from a distance down the stream.   At twelve
miles we halted for dinner at a village which we suppose to
have belonged to the Ricaras.   It is situated in a low plain
on the river, and consists of about 80 lodges of an octagon
form, neatly covered with earth, placed as close to each
other as possible, and picketed around.   The skin canoes,
mats, buckets, and articles of furniture found in the
(*p. 99*) lodges, induce us to suppose that it had been left
in the spring.   We found three different sorts of squashes
growing in the village ; we also killed an elk near it, and
saw two wolves.   On leaving the village the river became
shallow, and after searching a long time for the main channel, which was concealed among sand-bars, we at last
dragged the boat over one of them, rather than go back
three miles for the deepest channel.   At 14½ miles we
stopped for the night on a sand-bar, opposite a creek on
the north [in Walworth Co.], called Otter[23] creek, 22 yards
in width, and containing more water than is common for
creeks of that size.   The sides of the river during the day
were variegated with high bluffs and low timbered grounds
on the banks; the river is very much obstructed by sand-
bars.   We saw geese, swan,[24] brant, and ducks of different
kinds on the sand-bars, and on the shore numbers of the
prairie-hen ; the magpie, too, is very common, but the
gulls and plover, which we saw in such numbers below,
are now quite rare.

*October 7th.*   There was frost again last evening, and

[23] " Beaver or Otter creek," Clark C 10, where Biddle selects the latter name ;
Swamp creek of Stevens ; Swan Lake creek of Heap ; now Swan creek, in Walworth Co., emptying a little below the mouth of Owl or Moreau river.   It is
plainly charted and lettered both on Lewis' and on Clark's maps, but there is no
sign of any such river on either Warren's or Reynolds'; it is charted, but unnamed,
on the G. L. O. map of 1879, and on the latest contour-map of the Geological
Survey.   Gass misses it, unless his " small creek on the *south*," is meant for it.

[24] Probably the common whistling swan, *Cygnus columbianus;* but the trump-
eter, *C. buccinator*, is also found in the Missouri region.   The prairie-hen is the
sharp-tailed grouse, *Pediœcetes phasianellus columbianus.*

this morning was cloudy and attended with rain.  At two
miles we came to the mouth of a river, called by the Ricaras
Sawawkawna,[25] or Pork [*sic*] river; the party who examined
it for about three miles up, say that its current is gentle, and
that it does not seem to throw out much sand.  Its sources
are in the first range of the Black mountains; though it
has now only water of 20 yards' width, yet when full it
occupies 90.  Just below the mouth is another village or
wintering-camp of the Ricaras, composed of about 60
lodges, built in the same form as those passed yesterday,
with willow and straw mats, baskets, and buffalo-skin
canoes remaining entire in the camp.  We proceeded under
a gentle breeze from the southwest.  At ten o'clock we
saw two Indians on the north side, who told us they were
a part of the lodge of Tartongawaka, or Buffalo Medicine,
the Teton chief whom we had seen on [September] the 25th;
that they were on the way to the Ricaras, and begged us
for some- (*p. 100*) thing to eat, which of course we gave them.
At 7½ miles is a willow-island on the north, and another
on the same side five miles beyond it, in the middle of the
river between highlands on both sides.  At 18½ miles is an
island called Grouse island,[26] on which are the walls of an

[25] Elsewhere Sarwarkarna and Sarwarcarna; in Gass Cer-wer-cer-na; in Brackenridge, 1814, Ser-war-cerna, p. 244 and p. 267; on Lewis' map Sar-war-car-na-ho;
" the Ricares call this river Sur-war-kar-na, or Park," Clark C 11, which accounts
for the " Pork " in the text, salted since 1814.  The codices yield some other
forms, which need not be transcribed.  Warren and Reynolds both inscribe on
their maps Hecha or Heecha Wakpa, besides Moreau.  The name on most maps
is Owl river; on the G. L. O. map, 1879, and U. S. Geol. Surv. contour-map,
Moreau or Owl river.  This comes from the 3,000 to 3,500 foot elevation in
Harding and Butte counties, courses east parallel with the Cheyenne below and
the Grand above, through Choteau, Rinehart, Schnasse, and Dewey counties,
falling into the Missouri in the latter opposite Walworth Co.  It drains from
outlying spurs or buttes of the Black hills, and through some Bad Lands.  It
was named for one Moreau, stabbed by a Cheyenne squaw.

[26] " Shaved island," Clark C 12, 13, twice, erased and Grous or Grouse substituted.  This island is described as " nearly 1¼ ms. squar," and on it was
killed a " shee Brarow," being the female blaireau of the text.  Late maps
show two large islands in this day's voyage, but both apparently short of Grouse
island, and seeming to correspond to the other two islands, unnamed in the text.

old village. The island has no timber, but is covered with grass and wild rye, and owes its name to the number of [sharp-tailed] grouse that frequent it. We then went on till our journey for the day was 22 miles. The country presented the same appearance as usual. In the low timbered ground near the mouth of the Sawawkawna we saw the tracks of large white [grizzly] bear, and on Grouse island killed a female blaireau [badger], and a deer of the black-tailed species, the largest [doe] we have ever seen.

*October 8th.* We proceeded early with a cool northwest wind, and at 2½ miles above Grouse island reached the mouth of a creek on the south; then a small willow-island which divides the current equally; and at 4½ miles came to a river on the southern side, where we halted. This river, which our meridian altitude fixes at 45° 39′ 5″ north latitude, is called by the Ricaras Wetawhoo[27] [or Wetarhoo]; it rises in the Black mountains, and its bed, which flows at the mouth over a low soft slate-stone, is 120 yards wide; but the water is now confined within 20 yards and is not very rapid, discharging mud with a small proportion of sand. Here, as in every bend of the river, we again observe the red berries[28] resembling currants, which we men-

On Warren's map these islands are marked Fox (lower) and Blue Blanket (upper). Hills all along the west bank of the Missouri are there inscribed Hawthorne's bluffs. Present Bois Cache creek comes in at Fox island (Walworth Co.).

[27] So first, Clark C 14; also Weterhoo and other forms in the codices; Waterehoo, Brackenridge, p. 267; We-ter-hoo, on Lewis' map; Wetar-hoo, on Clark's; not noted in Gass, p. 51, who instead gives the creek from the south of above text as Slate run, and then proceeds to the Maropa river. The Wetarhoo is the Palanata Wakpa or Ree river of Warren and Reynolds; it is now designated Grand river, duplicating the name of another river so called early in this work (note [52], p. 24). The Grand has its headwaters in Bowman, Ewing, and Harding counties, about the 3,000 to 4,000 feet elevation contours, near the sources of the Little Missouri, which drains north, while the Grand watershed is east. The waters run parallel with those of the Owl below and Cannon-ball above, through Martin, Wagner, Schnasse, and Boreman counties, falling into the Missouri in the latter county on the edge of Dewey; across the Missouri is the line between Campbell and Walworth counties; at the mouth of the Grand is the Indian Agency of the same name.

[28] *Shepherdia argentea :* see note [53], p. 84. "The mandans call a red berry

tioned before. Two miles above the Wetawhoo, and on the same side, is a small river called Maropa [29] [or Marapa or Maripa] by the Indians; it is 20 yards in width, but so dammed up by mud that the stream creeps through a channel of not more than an inch in diameter and discharges no sand. One mile further we reached an island close to the southern shore, from which it is separated by a deep channel of 60 yards. About halfway a number of Ricara Indians came out to see us. We stopped and took a Frenchman on board (*p. 101*), who accompanied us past the island to our camp on the north side of the river, which is at the distance of twelve miles from that of yesterday.

Captain Lewis then returned with four of the party to see the village; it is situated in the center of the island, near the southern shore, under the foot of some high, bald, uneven hills, and contains about 60 lodges. The island itself is three miles long, and covered with fields in which the Indians raise corn, beans, and potatoes. Several Frenchmen living among these Indians as interpreters or traders came back with Captain Lewis, particularly a Mr. Gravelines, a man who has acquired the language. On setting out we had a low prairie covered with timber on the north, and on the south highlands; but at the mouth of the Wetawhoo the southern country changes, and a low timbered plain extends along the south, while the north has a ridge of barren hills during the rest of the day's course.

*October 9th.* The wind was so cold and high last night and during all the day that we could not assemble the

common to the upper part of the Missouri *ăss-dy*. The engages call the same berry Grease de Buff [graisse de bœuf]," Clark C 1.  "The red berry is called by the Rees *Nar-nis*," Clark C, inside front cover of the book.

[29] First, Clark C 14, Rearpar or Beaver Dam R., erased and Maropa interlined; so Lewis' map; Maripa, Clark's map; Marapa in Gass, p. 51; now Rampart creek, as Warren and others. This stream is perfectly well known, but will not be found on ordinary maps; there is no trace of it even on the G. L. O. map of 1879. It is also called Oak creek.

Indians in council; but some of the party went to the village. We received the visits of the three principal chiefs with many others, to whom we gave some tobacco, and told them that we would speak to them to-morrow. The names [30] of these chiefs were : first, Kakawissassa or Lighting Crow ; second chief, Pocasse or Hay ; third chief Piaheto or Eagle's Feather. Notwithstanding the high waves, two or three squaws rowed to us in little canoes made of a single buffalo-skin, stretched over a frame of boughs interwoven like a basket, and with the most perfect composure. The object which appeared to astonish the Indians most was Captain Clark's servant York, a remarkably stout, strong negro. They had never seen a being of that color, and therefore flocked round him to examine the extraordinary monster. By way of amusement he told them that he had once been a wild animal, and caught and tamed by his master ; and to convince them showed them feats of strength (*p. 102*) which, added to his looks, made him more terrible than we wished him to be.[31] Opposite

[30] All these are as Clark C 18. The Mr. Gravelines is Gravellin and Gravolin, Clark C 17, 18 ; Greaveline, Clark C 39, etc. The Mr. Tabeau below named is here Mr. Tabo, elsewhere Taboe, Tabat, Tebaux, etc. See note [66], p. 28.

[31] York was evidently a wag. When he had returned to St. Louis, and been freed, he used to get drunk and tell funny stories, quite in keeping with the above, which revived and rehabilitated the famous old hoax of a nation of bearded, blue-eyed, and red-haired Indians on the Upper Missouri. Accounts of such " White " or " Welsh " Indians, as they were called, are traceable back at least to 1764, when a French trader prepared a list of aborigines in which figure certain " Blancs Barbus, or White Indians with Beard," said to muster 1,500 warriors. Whatever the origin of this relation, it took a new lease of life from the residence of Lewis and Clark's party at the Mandans, in 1804-5, lost nothing at York's glib tongue afterward, and was seriously discussed as an ethnological fact by various eminent authors. Mr. A. J. Hill of St. Paul, my valued correspondent in Lewis and Clark matters, calls my attention to an article in the New York Medical Repository, III. p. 113, 1806, entitled " Bearded and fair People inhabiting the Country high up the Missouri," as an example of the rumors then rife. York's stories grew up with every glass that went down, till Mr. Biddle might have wondered what his History of the Expedition had to do with that multitudinous host who conquered the land, under the leadership of a black drum-major about ten feet tall.

our camp is a small creek on the south, which we distinguished by the name of the chief Kakawissassa.

*October* 10*th*.[32]   The weather was this day fine, and as we
were desirous of assembling the whole nation at once, we
dispatched Mr. Gravelines—who, with Mr. Tabeau, another
French trader, had breakfasted with us—to invite the
chiefs of the two upper villages to a conference.   They
all assembled at one o'clock, and after the usual ceremonies we addressed them in the same way in which we had
already spoken to the Ottoes and Sioux.   We then made
or acknowledged three chiefs, one for each of the three
villages ; giving to each a flag, a medal, a red coat, a cocked
hat and feather, also some goods, paint and tobacco, which
they divided among themselves.   After this the air-gun was
exhibited, very much to their astonishment, nor were they
less surprised at the color and manner of York.   On our
side we were equally gratified at discovering that these
Ricaras made use of no spirituous liquors of any kind, the
example of the traders who bring it to them, so far from
tempting, having in fact disgusted them.   Supposing that it
was as agreeable to them as to the other Indians, we had at
first offered them whisky ; but they refused it with this
sensible remark, that they were surprised that their father
should present to them a liquor which would make them
fools.   On another occasion they observed to Mr. Tabeau
that no man could be their friend who tried to lead them
into such follies.   The council being over they retired to
consult on their answer, and the next morning,

*October* 11*th*, at eleven o'clock, we again met in council at
our camp.   The grand chief made a short speech of thanks
for the advice we had given, and promised to follow it ; add-
ing that the door was now open and no one dare shut it,
and that we might depart whenever we pleased—alluding
to the treatment we had received from the Sioux.   They

[32] Gass says he went this day to the lodges, about sixty in number, which he
thus describes, p. 52 :

" In a circle of a size suited to the dimensions of the intended lodge, they set

also (*p. 103*) brought us some corn, beans, and dried squashes, and in return we gave them a steel mill, with which they were much pleased. At one o'clock we left our camp with the grand chief and his nephew on board, and at about two miles anchored below a creek on the south, separating the second and third village of the Ricaras, which are about half a mile distant from each other. We visited both the villages, and sat conversing with the chiefs for some time, during which they presented us with a bread made of corn and beans, also corn and beans boiled, and a large rich bean which they take from the mice of the prairie, which discover and collect it. These two villages are placed near each other in a high, smooth prairie—a fine situation, except that having no wood the inhabitants are obliged to go for it across the river to a timbered lowland opposite them. We told them that we would speak to them in the morning at their villages separately.

*October* 12*th.* Accordingly, after breakfast, we [Lewis, Clark, and Gass] went on shore to the house of the chief of the second village, named Lassel, where we found his chiefs and warriors. They made us a present of about seven bushels of corn, a pair of leggings, a twist of their tobacco, and seeds of two different species of tobacco. The chief then delivered a speech expressive of his gratitude for the presents and good counsels which we had given him ; his intention of visiting his great father, but

up 16 forked posts five or six feet high, and lay poles from one fork to another. Against these poles they lean other poles, slanting from the ground, and extending about 4 inches above the cross poles ; these are to receive the ends of the upper poles, that support the roof. They next set up 4 large forks, 15 feet high, and about 10 feet apart, in the middle of the area ; and poles or beams between these. The roof poles are then laid on extending from the lower poles across the beams which rest on the middle forks, of such a length as to leave a hole at the top for a chimney. The whole is then covered with willow branches, except the chimney and a hole below to pass through. On the willow-branches they lay grass and lastly clay. At the hole below they build a pen about 4 feet wide and projecting 10 feet from the hut, and hang a buffaloe skin at the entrance of the hut for a door. This labor like every other kind is chiefly performed by the squaws."

for fear of the Sioux; and requested us to take one of the
Ricara chiefs up to the Mandans and negotiate a peace
between the two nations. To this we replied in a suitable
way, and then repaired to the third village. Here we were
addressed by the chief in nearly the same terms as before,
and entertained with a present of ten bushels of corn,
some beans, dried pumpkins, and squashes. After we had
answered and explained the magnitude and power of the
United States, the three chiefs came with us to the boat.
We gave them some sugar, a little salt, and a sun-glass.
Two of them then left us, and the chief of the third [vil-
age], by name (*p. 104*) Ahketahnasha or Chief of the
Town, accompanied us to the Mandans. At two o'clock
we left the Indians, who crowded to the shore to take
leave of us, and after making 7½ miles landed on the
north side, and had a clear, cool, pleasant evening.[33]

The three villages which we have just left are the residence of a nation called the Ricaras [see note [5], p. 143].
They were originally colonies of Pawnees, who established themselves on the Missouri below the Chayenne,
where the traders still remember that twenty years ago
they occupied a number of villages. From that situation
a part of the Ricaras emigrated to the neighborhood of
the Mandans, with whom they were then in alliance. The
rest of the nation continued near the Chayenne till the
year 1797, in the course of which, distressed by their wars
with the Sioux, they joined their countrymen near the
Mandans. Soon after, a new war arose between the
Ricaras and the Mandans, in consequence of which the
former came down the river to their present position. In
this migration, those who had first gone to the Mandans

---

[33] " A curious curstom with the Souex as well as the Reckeres is to give
handsom squars to those whome they wish to show some acknowledgements
to—The Seauex we got clear of without taking their squars, they followed
us with squars two days—The Reckores we put off dureing the time we were
at the Towns but 2 handsom young squars were sent by a man to follow us,
they came up this evening and pursecuted in their civilities," Clark C 27.

kept together, and now live in the two lower villages ; they may hence be considered as the Ricaras proper.   The third village was composed of such remnants of the villages as had survived the wars ; and as these were nine in number, a difference of pronunciation and some difference of language may be observed between them and the Ricaras proper, who do not understand all the words of these wanderers. The villages are within the distance of four miles of each other, the two lower ones consisting of between 150 and 200 men each, the third of 300.

The Ricaras are tall and well proportioned, the women handsome and lively, and as among other savages to them falls all the drudgery of the field and the labors of procuring subsistence, except that of hunting.    Both sexes are poor, but kind and generous, and although they receive with thankfulness what is given to them, do not beg as the Sioux did ; though this praise should be qualified (*p. 105*) by mentioning that an ax was stolen last night from our cooks.   The dress of the men is a simple pair of moccasins, leggings, and a cloth round the middle, over which a buffalo-robe is occasionally thrown ; their hair, arms, and ears are decorated with different ornaments.    The women wear moccasins, leggings, and a long shirt made of goat's skins, generally white and fringed, which is tied round the waist ; to these they add, like the men, a buffalo-robe without the hair, in summer.

These women are handsomer than the Sioux ; both of them are, however, disposed to be amorous, and our men found no difficulty in procuring companions for the night by means of the interpreters.    These interviews were chiefly clandestine, and were of course to be kept a secret from the husband or relations.   The point of honor indeed is completely reversed among the Ricaras ; that the wife or the sister should submit to a stranger's embraces without the consent of her husband or brother is a cause of great disgrace and offense, especially as for many purposes of civility or gratitude the husband and brother will themselves present to a stranger these females, and be gratified by attentions to them. The Sioux had offered us squaws, but we having declined while we remained there, they followed us with offers of females for two days. The Ricaras had been equally accommodating; we had equally withstood their temptation; but such was their desire to oblige us that two very handsome young squaws were sent on board this evening, and persecuted us with civilities. The black man York participated largely in these favors; for, instead of inspiring any prejudice, his color seemed to procure him additional advantages from the Indians, who desired to preserve among them some memorial of this wonderful stranger. Among other instances of attention, a Ricara invited him into his house and, presenting his wife to him, retired to the outside of the door; while there one of York's comrades who was looking for him came to the door, but the gallant hus- (*p. 106*) band would permit no interruption until a reasonable time had elapsed.

The Ricara lodges are in a circular or octagonal form, and generally about 30 or 40 feet in diameter. They are made by placing forked posts about six feet high round the circumference of the circle; these are joined by poles from one fork to another, which are supported also by other forked poles slanting from the ground; in the center of the lodge are placed four higher forks, about 15 feet in length, connected together by beams; from these to the lower poles the rafters of the roof are extended so as to leave a vacancy in the middle for the smoke; the frame of the building is then covered with willow branches, with which is interwoven grass, and over this [is placed] mud or clay; the aperture for the door is about four feet wide, and before it is a sort of entry about ten feet from the lodge. They are very warm and compact.

They cultivate maize or Indian corn, beans, pumpkins, watermelons, squashes, and a species of tobacco peculiar to themselves. Their commerce is chiefly with the traders, who supply them with goods in return for peltries, which they procure not only by their own hunting, but in exchange for corn from their less civilized neighbors. The object chiefly in demand seemed to be red paint, but they would give anything they had to spare for the most trifling article. One of the men to-day gave an Indian a hook made out of a pin, and received in return a pair of moccasins.

They express a disposition to keep at peace with all nations; but they are well armed with fusils, and being much under the influence of the Sioux, who exchange the goods which they get from the British for Ricara corn, their minds are sometimes poisoned and they cannot be always depended on. At the present moment they are at war with the Mandans.

We are informed by Mr. Gravelines, who had passed through that country, that the Yankton or Jacques (*p. 107*) river rises about 40 miles to the east or northeast of this place, the Chayenne branch of the Red river about 20 miles further, passing the Sioux and the St. Peter's about 80.

*October* 13*th.* In the morning our visitors left us, except the brother of the chief who accompanied us, and one of the squaws. We passed at an early hour a camp of Sioux on the north bank, who merely looked at us without saying a word, and from the character of the tribe we did not solicit a conversation. At 10½ miles we reached the mouth of a creek on the north, which takes its rise from some ponds a short distance to the northeast. To this stream we gave the name of Stoneidol creek;[34] for, after passing a willow- and sand-island just above its mouth, we discovered that a few miles back from the Missouri there are two stones resembling human figures, and a third like a dog, all which are objects of great veneration among the Ricaras.

[34] Better Stone Idol Creek, as Clark C 29, where it is said to be 13 yards wide : see his map ; it is Stone creek of Lewis' map. Gass, p. 54, calls it Pond river, 50 yards wide. It is called Bourbeuse river on Warren's map ; Bordache creek, of Heap ; now Spring river, in Campbell Co.

Their history would adorn the Metamorphoses of Ovid. A young man was deeply enamored with a girl whose parents refused their consent to the marriage. The youth went out into the fields to mourn his misfortunes; a sympathy of feeling led the lady to the same spot, and the faithful dog would not cease to follow his master. After wandering together and having nothing but grapes to subsist on, they were at last converted into stone, which, beginning at the feet, gradually invaded the nobler parts, leaving nothing unchanged but a bunch of grapes which the female holds in her hand to this day. Whenever the Ricaras pass these sacred stones, they stop to make some offering of dress to propitiate these deities. Such is the account given by the Ricara chief, which we had no mode of examining, except that we found one part of the story very agreeably confirmed; for on the river near where the event is said to have occurred we found a greater abundance of fine grapes than we had yet seen.

Above this is a small creek, 4½ miles from Stoneidol creek, which is 15 yards wide, comes in from the south, and (*p. 108*) received from us the name of Pocasse or Hay [now Hunkpapa] creek, in honor of the chief of the second village. Above the Ricara island the Missouri becomes narrow and deeper, the sand-bars being generally confined to the points; the current, too, is much more gentle; the timber on the low lands is also in much greater quantities, though the high grounds are still naked. We proceeded on under a fine breeze from the southeast, and after making 18 miles camped [35] on the north near a timbered low plain, after which we had some rain, and the evening was cold. The hunters killed one deer only.

*October 14th.* We set out in the rain, which continued during the day. At five miles we came to a creek on the south, about 15 yards wide, and named by us Piaheto or Eagle's Feather, in honor of the third chief of the Ricaras.

[35] Last camp in South Dakota. To-morrow, before crossing the parallel of 46° N. lat., the Expedition will have passed from South into North Dakota.

After dinner we stopped on a sand-bar, and executed the sentence of a court martial, which inflicted corporeal punishment on one of the soldiers.[36]    This operation affected the Indian chief very sensibly, for he cried aloud during the punishment.    We explained the offense and the reasons of

[36] Private John Newman, U. S. Infantry.    Newman was a good man, and his case a hard one.    Clark C 28–31, Oct. 13th, 14th, has: "One man J. Newmon confined for mutinous expressions. . . We Tried the Prisoner Newmon last night by 9 of his Peers they did 'centence him 75 Lashes & [be] Disbanded the party.' . . halted on a Sand bar & after Dinner executed the Sentence of the Court Martial so far a [as] giving the Corporal punishment, and proceeded on a few miles."    Lewis' autograph muster-roll, now in the War Department archives, is accompanied by a letter in his hand, making certain commentaries on the roll (on which, of course, Newman's name does not appear, as he had been disbanded from the party); and I find the following magnanimous statement: "John Newman was a private in the Infantry of the U' States army who joined me as a volunteer and entered into an inlistment in common with others by which he was held and Mustered as one of the permanent party.    in the course of the expedition, or shortly before we arrived at the Mandan Villages he committed himself by using certain mutinous expressions which caused me to arrest him and to have him tryed by a Court Martial formed of his peers ; they finding him guilty sentenced him to receive seventy five lashes and to be discharged from the permanent party.    this sentence was enforced by me, and the punishment took place.    the conduct of this man previous to this period had been generally correct, and the zeal he afterwards displayed for the benefit of the service was highly meritorious.    in the course of the winter while at Fort Mandan, from an ardent wish to attone for the crime which he had committed at an unguarded moment, he exerted himself on every occasion to become usefull.    This disposition induced him to expose himself too much to the intense cold of that climate, and on a hunting excurtion he had his hands and feet severely frozen with which he suffered extreme pain for some weeks—having recovered from this accident by the 1st. of April 1805.    he asked forgivness for what had passed, and beged that I would permit him to continue with me through the voyage, but deeming it impolitic to relax from the sentence, altho' he stood acquitted in my mind, I determined to send him back, which was accordingly done. since my return I have been informed that he was extremely serviceable as a hunter on the voyage to St. Louis and that the boat on several occasions owed her safety in a great measure to his personal exertions, being a man of uncommon activity and bodily strength.    if under these circumstances it should be thought proper to give Newman the remaining third which will be deducted from the gratuity awarded Paptiest [sic] La Page who occupied his station in the after part of the voyage I should feel myself much gratifyed."    This letter is dated City of Washington, January 15th, 1807, and addressed to General Henry Dearborn, Secretary at War.

it. He acknowledged that examples were necessary, and that he himself had given them by punishing with death; but his nation never whipped even children from their birth. After this we continued with the wind from the northeast, and at the distance of twelve miles we camped [37] in a cove of the southern bank. Immediately opposite our camp, on the north side, are the ruins of an ancient fortification, the greater part of which is washed into the river; nor could we distinguish more than that the walls were eight or ten feet high. The evening is wet and disagreeable, and the river, which is somewhat wider than yesterday, continues to have an unusual quantity of timber. The country was level on both sides in the morning, but afterward we passed some black bluffs on the south.

*October* 15*th.* We stopped at three miles on the north; a little above a camp of Ricaras who are hunting, where- (*p. 109*) we were visited by about 30 Indians. They came over in their skin canoes, bringing us meat, for which we returned them beads and fishhooks. About a mile higher we found another camp of Ricaras on the south, consisting of eight lodges; here we again ate and exchanged a few presents. As we went we discerned numbers of other Indians on both sides of the river. At about nine miles we came to a creek on the south, where we saw many high hills resembling a house with a slanting roof; and a little below the creek, an old village of the Sharha or Chayenne Indians. The morning had been cloudy, but the evening became pleasant, the wind from the northeast. At sunset we halted, after coming ten miles over several sand-bars and points, above a camp of ten Ricara lodges, on the north side. We visited their camp, and smoked and ate with several of them; they all appeared kind and pleased with our attentions, and the fair sex received our men with more than hospitality. York was here again an object of

[37] North Dakota, close to 46°, at a creek now called Thunder-hawk. Piaheto (now Blackfoot) creek meanders the boundary of South Dakota, but empties in North Dakota.

astonishment; the children would follow him constantly, and if he chanced to turn toward them, run with great terror. The country of to-day is generally low and covered with timber on both sides, though in the morning we passed some barren hills on the south.

*October 16th.*[38] At this camp the squaw who accompanied the chief left us; two others were very anxious to go on with us. Just above our camp we passed a circular work or fort where the Sharha or Chayennes formerly lived; and a short distance beyond, a creek [39] which we called Chayenne creek. At two miles is a willow-island with a large sand-bar on both sides above it, and a creek, both on the south, which we called Sohawch, the Ricara name for girl; and two miles above is a second creek, to which we gave the name of Chapawt, which means woman in the same language. Three miles further is an island situated in a bend to the north, about 1½ miles long, and covered with cottonwood. At the lower end of this island (*p. 110*) comes in a small creek from the north, called Keetoosh-

[38] The Indian names in this paragraph are nearly all at variance with Clark C 36, 37, this date. The name of the chief who was aboard the boat is here given as Arketarnashar. The use of "Sharha or Chayennes," one singular and the other plural, is from the expression "Sharha or Chien or Dog Indians" of the codex. The first creek is "Chien," interlined Chayenne or Sharha. The second creek is "Soharch." The third is "Charpart." The fourth is "Keetooch Sarkarnar." The fifth is as printed. The island is said to be named Carp "by Ivens," elsewhere called "Evins," and discredited.

[39] Dissociate this in mind from any other stream called Cheyenne, Chayenne, or Chyenne. It is one of the very few located for right or left hand neither in the codex nor in the printed text. Lewis' map shows three unlettered traces, from the west. Clark's has nothing whatever on this side, from his Maripa (Rampart) to the Cannon-ball. Warren names two creeks on the left, the lower Kichisapi W[akpa], or Battle creek, the upper Pointer creek. The facts are, with modern names: Oct. 15th, Expedition passed, 1, Thunder-hawk creek; 2, Battle creek; 3, Fort Yates; 4, Standing Rock Agency—all these left; 5, Cat-tail creek (Sarbaone of Stevens), right; 6, Porcupine or Pointer creek (Kichisapi or Battle creek of Warren); and camped by an old Cheyenne fort, on the right hand. Now, Oct. 16th, come 1, Cheyenne creek, right? 2, Sohawch, left; 3, Chapawt, left—one of these being Pointer of Warren, but not otherwise identified. For the rest of Oct. 16th, see next two notes.

sahawna [40] or Place of Beaver. At the upper extremity of the island a river empties from the north; it is called Warreconne,[41] or Elk Shed their Horns, and is about 35 yards wide. The island itself was named Carp island by Evans, a former traveler.

As we proceeded there were great numbers of goats [antelopes] on the banks of the river, and we soon after saw large flocks of them in the water. They had been gradually driven into the river by the Indians, who now lined the shore so as to prevent their escape, and were firing on them, while sometimes boys went into the river and killed them with sticks; they seemed to be very successful, for we counted 58 which they had killed. We ourselves killed some, and then passing the lodges to which these Indians belonged, camped at the distance of half a mile on the south, having made 14½ miles. We were soon visited by numbers of these Ricaras, who crossed the river hallooing and singing. Two of them then returned for some goat's flesh and buffalo meat, dried and fresh, with which they made a feast that lasted till late at night, and caused much music and merriment.

*October* 17*th*. The weather was pleasant. We passed a low ground covered with small timber on the south, and barren hills on the north which came close to the river; the wind from the northwest then became so strong that we could not move after ten o'clock until late in the afternoon, when we were forced to use the towline; we therefore made

[40] Sar-har-nar, Lewis' map; Sar-har-ne, Clark's, on the right hand, next below the Warreconne; not to be discovered on ordinary maps; Little Beaver creek of some. The word is Dakotan, and here Lewis and Clark locate their questionable "Teton Saone" Indians, of "300 men" and "1,500 souls" (see note [10], p. 101).

[41] So Clark C 37, and map, plainly; Warreconhe of Lewis' map; elsewhere Warrecunne and Warrecanne; in Le Raye, Warriuna; in Maximilian, Warannano; in Brackenridge, Warecore, p. 268. *This* is the Beaver river of Warren's map, and Beaver creek of Reynolds' and the G. L. O. map; now Big Beaver or Sand creek. It is the largest stream in Emmons Co. It rises by two main affluents in Logan and McIntosh counties respectively, heading in some little lakes, and traverses Emmons Co. westerly to its confluence with the Missouri. The town of Emmonsburg is at its mouth.

only six miles. We all went out hunting and examining the country. The goats, of which we see large flocks coming to the north bank of the river, spend the summer, says Mr. Gravelines, in the plains east of the Missouri, and at the present season are returning to the Black mountains, where they subsist on leaves and shrubbery during the winter, and resume their migrations in the spring.[42] We also saw buffalo, elk, and deer, and a number of snakes; a beaver-house too was seen, and we caught a whippoorwill of a small and uncommon (*p. 111*) kind.[43] The leaves are fast falling; the river is wider than usual and full of sand-bars; on the sides of the hills are large stones, and some rock of a brownish color is in the southern bend below us. Our latitude by observation is 46° 23' 57".

*October* 18*th*. After three miles we reached the mouth of Le Boulet or Cannonball river. This stream rises in the Black mountains[44] and falls into the Missouri on the south [from the west]; its channel is about 140 yards wide, though the water is now confined within 40; its name is derived from the numbers of perfectly round large stones on the shore and in the bluffs just above. We here met

[42] " This chief," who was aboard, "tells me of a number of their tredetions about Turtles, Snakes, &c., and the power of a perticuler rock or cove on the next river which informs of everything none of those I think worth while mentioning," Clark C 40. The hunting party to-day killed six deer, which were " scaffeled up," *i. e.*, scaffolded, out of reach of the wolves.

[43] This is the bird long afterward first described and named by Audubon (Orn. Biog., V, 1839, p. 335) as *Caprimulgus nuttalli* or Nuttall's whippoorwill, now known to science as *Phalænoptilus nuttalli*.

[44] Our authors use the term " Black mountains " in a looser sense than we now say " Black hills," for any of the elevated country to the west of the Missouri in Northern Nebraska and both Dakotas. The codices commonly name them as the Cout or Court noi or nue or nou, *i. e.*, Côte Noir. The Cannon-ball rises by two main branches, north and south, and many tributary streams, somewhat north of the Black hills proper, and east of the Little Missouri river ; flows in a general east course, traversing Hettinger and Morton counties, and falls into the Missouri in Morton Co., on the boundary of Boreman, and opposite Emmons, eight miles below the site of Fort Rice. Its Dakotan name was Inyan Wakarap (so Warren) or Wakahap (so Reynolds). It is also called simply Ball river.

with two Frenchmen in the employ of Mr. Gravelines, who had been robbed by the Mandans of their traps, furs, and other articles, and were descending the river in a periogue ; but they turned back with us in expectation of obtaining redress through our means. At eight miles is a creek on the north [in Emmons Co.], about 28 yards wide, rising in the northeast, and called Chewah[45] or Fish river; one mile above this is another creek on the south [near Fort Rice]. We camped on a sand-bar to the south, at the distance of 13 miles, all of which we have made with oars and poles. Great numbers of goats are crossing the river and directing their course to the westward ; we also saw a herd of buffalo and of elk ; a pelican too was killed, and six fallow-deer, we having found, as the Ricaras informed us, that there are none of the black-tailed species as high up as this place.[46] The country is in general level and fine, with broken short high grounds, low timbered mounds on the river, and a rugged range of hills at a distance.

*October* 19*th*. We set sail with a fine morning and a southeast wind, and at 2½ miles passed a creek on the north side ; at 11½ miles we came to a lake or large pond on the same side, in which were some swans. On both banks of the Missouri are low grounds which have much more timber than lower down the river. The hills are at one or two miles' distance from the banks, the streams which rise in them are brackish, and the mineral salts appear on (*p. 112*) the sides of the hills and edges of the runs. In walking along the shore we counted 52 herds of buffalo, and three of elk, at a single view. Besides these, we also

---

[45] So Clark C 43 ; '' She-wish or Fish Cr.,'' Clark C 250 ; Shewash of Maximilian ; Fish creek on both Lewis' and Clark's maps ; Apple creek of Stevens ; Long Lake creek of later and of present maps, emptying from the east five miles below Fort Rice. A little north of the Chewah was an old trading-house, on the east bank of the Missouri.

[46] The fallow-deer (*Dama platyceros*) is a European species, not found in North America, the animal meant being the Western variety of the Virginia deer. The black-tailed deer has no such restricted range as the paragraph implies, but very likely had been killed off in this particular locality.

observed elk, deer, pelicans, and wolves.  After 17½ miles
we camped on the north, opposite the uppermost of a
number of round hills, forming a cone at the top, one being
about 90, another 60 feet in height, and some of less
elevation.  Our chief tells us that the calumet-bird [47] lives
in the holes formed by the filtration of the water from the
top of these hills through the sides.  Near one of these
moles, on a point of a hill 90 feet above the plain, are the
remains of an old village which is high, strong, and has
been fortified; this our chief tells us is the remains of one
of the Mandan villages, and these are the first ruins which
we have seen of that nation in ascending the Missouri.
Opposite our camp is a deep bend to the south, at the
extremity of which is a pond.  [Camp is in Bismarck Co.]

*October 20th.*  We proceeded early with a southeast wind
which continued high all day, and came to a creek [48] on the
north [in Bismarck Co.] at two miles' distance, 20 yards wide.
At eight miles we reached the lower point of an island [49] in
the middle of the river, though there is no current on the
south.  This island is covered with willows and extends
about two miles, a small creek [50] coming in from the south at
its lower extremity.  After making twelve miles we camped
on the south, at the upper part of a bluff containing stone-

[47] The crevasses and ledges of water-worn or weather-beaten bluffs are favorite
nesting-places for eagles and other large birds of prey in the upper Missouri
country.  I have there examined some nests of enormous size, resorted to year
after year, probably by the same pairs of birds.  They are often inaccessible,
or only to be reached by means of a rope, with much difficulty and danger ; but
sometimes they are built simply on the edge of a bluff, to which one may walk
on smooth ground.  The "callemet bird," Clark C 45, has already been mentioned as the golden eagle, *Aquila chrysaëtos.*

[48] Nameless in the codices, and so in the text, but plainly "Shepherds Cr." of
Lewis' map, and "Shepherd R." of Clark's, with the first (old) Mandan village
marked at its mouth.  Apple creek or Burleigh creek of various late maps,
from the east, in Bismarck Co.

[49] Nameless in the codices, and shown on neither map ; Burnt Boat island of
Warren's ; Sibley's island of the G. L. O. map, 1879 ; very large, in the river
between Bismarck and Morton Cos.

[50] Nameless, and uncharted.  Little Heart or Sturgis river of various maps,
in Morton Co.  Little Heart and Sugar-loaf buttes just south of it.

coal of an inferior quality ; immediately below this bluff and on the declivity of a hill are the remains of a village covering six or eight acres, formerly occupied by the Mandans, who, says our Ricara chief, once lived in a number of villages on each side of the river, till the Sioux forced them 40 miles higher ; whence, after a few years residence, they moved to their present position. The country through which we passed has wider bottoms and more timber than those we have been accustomed to see, the hills rising at a distance and by gradual ascents. We have seen great numbers of elk, deer (*p. 113*), goats, and buffalo, and the usual attendants of these last, the wolves, which follow their movements and feed upon those which die by accident or which are too poor to keep pace with the herd. We also wounded a white bear, and saw some fresh tracks of those animals, which are twice as large as the track of a man.

*October* 21*st*.  Last night the weather was cold, the wind high from the northeast, and the rain which fell froze on the ground. At daylight it began to snow and continued till the afternoon, when it remained cloudy and the ground was covered with snow. However, we set out early, and just above our camp came to a creek on the south, called Chisshetaw,[51] about 30 yards wide and with a considerable quantity of water.

Our Ricara chief tells us that at some distance up this river is situated a large rock, which is held in great venera-

[51] Elsewhere printed Chesshetah and Chesschetar ; in Gass Chischeet ; in Le Raye Chuss-chu ; in the codices variant ; " Ches-che-tar or Heart R." of both maps ; Ta Chanta Wakpa of Warren's and of Reynolds' ; Big Heart river of maps which call Sturgis river Little Heart (see note [50], above). Lewis and Clark's name is uneasy and lapsed ; but it might have survived in the English form of "Chester." This is Heart river, heading mainly in Stark Co., and coursing with a considerable southward loop through Morton Co., to fall into the Missouri opposite Bismarck, now the capital of North Dakota.

At this date the Expedition comes past the point where the Northern Pacific R.R. crosses the Missouri, with Bismarck on the left bank (right as you ascend) and Fort Abraham Lincoln on the right. Here began the series of Mandan villages which extended many miles up river, and here is the present Mandan, county town of Morton, on Heart river, near its mouth.

tion, and visited by parties who go to consult it as to their own or their nation's destinies, all of which they discern in some sort of figures or paintings with which it is covered. About two miles off from the mouth of the river the party on shore saw another of the objects of Ricara superstition ; it is a large oak tree, standing alone in the open prairie, and as it alone has withstood the fire which has consumed everything around, the Indians naturally ascribe to it extraordinary powers. One of their ceremonies is to make a hole in the skin of their necks, through which a string is passed and the other end tied to the body of the tree ; after remaining in this way for some time they think they become braver.

At two miles from our camp we came to the ruins of a second Mandan village, which was in existence at the same time with that just mentioned. It is situated on the north, at the foot of a hill in a beautiful and extensive plain, which is now covered with herds of buffalo ; nearly opposite are remains of a third village, on the south of the Missouri ; and there is another also about two miles further on the north, a little off the river. At the distance of seven miles we camped on the south,[52] and spent (*p. 114*) a cold night. We procured to-day a buffalo and an otter [*Lutra canadensis*] only. The river is wide, the sand-bars are numerous, and a low island is near our camp.

*October* 22d. In the morning we passed an old Mandan village on the south, near our camp ; at four miles another on the same side. About seven o'clock we came-to at a camp of 11 Sioux of the Teton tribe, who are almost perfectly naked, having only a piece of skin or cloth round the middle, though we are suffering from the cold. From their appearance, which is warlike, and from their giving two different accounts of themselves, we believe that they are either going to or returning from the Mandans, to which nation the Sioux frequently make excursions to steal

---

[52] That is, on the west bank of the Missouri, still in Morton Co., but approaching Oliver Co., having passed Burnt Boat or Burnt creek, in Bismarck Co.

horses.   As their conduct displeased us, we gave them
nothing.   At six o'clock we reached an island about one
mile in length, at the head of which is a Mandan village on
the north in ruins ; and two miles beyond is a bad sand-
bar.   At eight miles are remains of another Mandan village
on the south ; at twelve miles we camped on the south.[53]
The hunters brought in a buffalo bull, and mentioned
that of about 300 which they had seen there was not a
single female.   The beaver is here in plenty, and the
two Frenchmen who are returning with us catch several
every night.

These villages, which are nine in number, are scattered
along each side of the river within a space of 20 miles ;
almost all that remains of them is the wall which surrounded them, the fallen heaps of earth which covered
the houses, and occasionally human skulls and the teeth
and bones of men and different animals, which are scattered on the surface of the ground.

*October* 23*d.*   The weather was cloudy and we had some
snow.   We soon arrived at the five lodges where the two
Frenchmen had been robbed, but the Indians had left
them lately, as we found the fires still burning.   The
country consists as usual of timbered low grounds, with
grapes, rushes, and great quantities of a small red acid
fruit [*Shepherdia argentea*], known among the (*p. 115*)
Indians by a name signifying rabbit-berries, and called by
the French graisse de buffle or buffalo-fat.   The river is
obstructed by many sand-bars.   At twelve miles we passed
an old village on the north, which was the former residence
of the Ahwahaways [54] who now live between the Mandans
and the Minnetarees.   After making 13 miles [without
noticing various creeks] we camped on the south.[55]

---

[53] In Oliver Co.   Square Butte creek passed early this morning.

[54] *Sic*—and in the Statistical View spelled Ahwahhaway.   Clark C 54 has
Ahnahawas, otherwise called there Maharha Indians, as a band of Minnetarrees.
See note beyond.

[55] Vicinity of Sanger, Oliver Co., a little south of Deer creek.

*October 24th.* The day was again dark, and it snowed a little in the morning. At three miles we came to a point on the south where the river, by forcing a channel across a former bend, has formed a large island [56] on the north. On this island we found one of the grand chiefs of the Mandans, who, with five lodges, was on a hunting excursion. He met his enemy the Ricara chief with great ceremony and apparent cordiality, and smoked with him. After visiting his lodges, the grand chief and his brother came on board our boat for a short time. We then proceeded and camped on the north, at seven miles from our last night's station, and below the old village of the Mandans and Ricaras. Here four Mandans came down from a camp above, and our Ricara chief returned with them to their camp, from which we augur favorably of their pacific views toward each other. The land is low and beautiful, and covered with oak and cottonwood, but has been too recently hunted to afford much game.

*October 25th.* The morning was cold, and the wind gentle from the southeast. At three miles we passed a handsome high prairie on the south ; and on an eminence, about 40 feet above the water and extending back for several miles in a beautiful plain, was situated an old village of the Mandan nation, which has been deserted for many years. A short distance above it, on the continuation of the same rising ground, are two old villages of Ricaras, one on the top of the hill, the other in the level plain, which were deserted only five years ago. Above these villages is an extensive low ground for several miles, in which are situated, at three or four miles from the Ricara villages, three old vil- (*p. 116*) lages of Mandans near together. Here the Mandans lived when the Ricaras came to them for protection, and from

[56] Very plain on Clark's map, 1814, immediately underneath the word " and " of the sentence there inscribed. There is now nothing of the sort ; instead of which is a considerable lake, indicating the change in the course of the Missouri. This is in McLean Co., above Sanger (Oliver Co.), and below Washburn (McLean Co.), in the vicinity of which latter town to-day's camp is pitched, after passing Deer creek, left, and Painted Wood and Turtle creeks, right.

this they moved to their present situation above. In the low ground the squaws raised their corn, and the timber, of which there was little near the villages, was supplied from the opposite side of the river, where it was and still is abundant.

As we proceeded several parties of Mandans, both on foot and horseback, came along the river to view us, and were very desirous that we should land and talk to them. This we could not do on account of the sand-breaks on the shore, but we sent our Ricara chief to them in a periogue. The wind having shifted to the southwest and being very high, it required all our precautions on board, for the river was full of sand-bars, which made it very difficult to find the channel. We got aground several times, and passed a very bad point of rocks, after which we camped on a sand-point to the north,[57] above a handsome plain covered with timber, opposite a high hill on the south side, at the distance of 11 miles. Here we were joined by our Ricara chief, who brought an Indian to the camp, where he remained all night.[58]

*October 26th.* We set out early with a southwest wind, and after putting the Ricara chief on shore to join the Mandans, who were in great numbers along it, we proceeded to the camp of the grand chiefs, four miles distant. Here we met a Mr. M'Cracken, one of the Northwest or Hudson's Bay Company, who arrived with another person about nine days ago to trade for horses and buffalo-robes. Two of the chiefs came on board with some of their household furniture, such as earthen pots, and a little corn, and went on with us, the rest of the Indians following on shore. At one mile beyond the camp we passed a small creek, and

[57] In McLean Co.; approaching Stanton (on the other side of the river, in Mercer Co.).

[58] Clark C 59, this date, has a relation not in the text. "We are told that the Seaux has latterly fallen in with & stole the horses of the Big bellies [Grosventres], on their way home they fell in with the Ossiniboine who killed them and took their horses—a french man has latterly been killed by the Indians on the Track to the tradeing establishment on the Ossinebine R."

at three [59] more a bluff of coal of an inferior quality, on the south.    After making 11 miles we reached an old field where the Mandans had cultivated grain last summer, and camped for the night on the (*p. 117*) south side, about half a mile below the first village of the Mandans.[60]    In the morning we had a low willow ground on the south and high land on the north, which occasionally varied in the course of the day.    There is but little wood on this part of the river, which is here subdivided into many channels and obstructed by sand-bars.

As soon as we arrived a crowd of men, women, and children came down to see us.    Captain Lewis returned with the principal chiefs to the village, while the others remained with us during the evening.    The object which seemed to surprise them most was a corn-mill fixed to the boat, which we had occasion to use, and delighted them by the ease with which it reduced the grain to powder.    Among others who visited us was the son of the grand chief of the Mandans, who had his two little fingers cut off at the second joints.    On inquiring into this accident, we found that it was customary to express grief for the death of relations by some corporeal suffering, and that the usual mode was to lose two joints of the little fingers, or sometimes of the other fingers.    The wind blew very cold in the evening from the southwest.    Two of the party are affected with rheumatic complaints.

[59] At this, the eighth mile made to-day, Clark C 63 inserts : "**Fort Mandan** stard." in a bold hand, over an erasure made for this later entry—*i. e.*, noting the exact spot where the Fort was presently built, just above the bluff of coal.

[60] The party are to winter in this vicinity, with the Mandans, at a point on the north bank of the river, three miles below here, and seven or eight below the mouth of Knife river.    They will call their winter quarters FORT MANDAN. The locality became better known as Fort Clark, from a trading-post afterward established on the south bank, and therefore in what is now Mercer Co. The spot is marked on some maps of to-day by this name.    The Missouri along here separates McLean from Mercer Co.    Fort Mandan, being on the north bank, was in what is now McLean Co.    The latitude, by observation probably not exact, was 47° 21′ 47″ ; estimated distance up the Missouri, 1,600 miles.

# CHAPTER V.

## WINTERING WITH THE MANDANS.

SATURDAY, October 27th, 1804. At an early hour we proceeded and anchored off the village. Captain Clark went on shore, and after smoking a pipe with the chiefs, was desired to remain and eat with them. He declined on account of being unwell; but his refusal gave great offense to the Indians, who considered it disrespectful not to eat when invited, till the cause was explained to their satisfaction. We sent them some tobacco, and then proceeded to the second village on the north, passing by a bank containing coal, and the second village,[1] and camped at four miles on the north, opposite a village of Ahnahaways. We here met with a Frenchman named Jesseaume, who lives among the Indians with his wife and children, and whom we take as an interpreter. The Indians had flocked to the bank to see us as we passed, and they visited in great numbers the camp, where some of them remained all night. We sent in the evening three young Indians with a present of tobacco

---

[1] " Passed the 2d Village and camped opsd. the Village of the Wetersoon or Ahwahharways," Clark C 65. The Frenchman's name is variable in the codices. Here it is spelled Jessamme or Jessomme. His Christian name was René.

for the chiefs of the three upper villages, inviting them to come down in the morning to a council with us. Accordingly the next day,

*Sunday, October 28th,* we were joined by many of the Minnetarees and Ahnahaways from above; but the wind was so violent from the southwest that the chiefs of the lower (*p. 119*) villages could not come up, and the council was deferred till to-morrow. Meanwhile, we entertained our visitors by showing them what was new to them in the boat; all which, as well as our black servant, they called "great medicine," the meaning of which we afterward learned. We also consulted the grand chief of the Mandans, Black Cat, and Mr. Jesseaume, as to the names, characters, etc., of the chiefs with whom we are to hold the council. In the course of the day we received several presents from the women, consisting of corn, boiled hominy, and garden stuffs; in our turn we gratified the wife of the great chief with a gift of a glazed earthen jar.[2] Our hunter [Drewyer] brought us two beaver. In the afternoon we sent the Minnetaree chiefs to smoke for us with the great chief of the Mandans, and told them we would speak in the morning.

Finding that we shall be obliged to pass the winter at this place, we went up the river about 1½ miles to-day, with the view of finding a convenient spot for a fort; but the timber was too scarce and small for our purposes.

*October 29th.* The morning was fine, and we prepared our presents and speech for the council. After breakfast we were visited by an old chief of the Ahnahaways, who, finding himself growing old and weak, had transferred his power to his son,[3] who is now at war against the Shoshonees. At ten o'clock the chiefs were all assembled under

[2] "I prosent a jah to the chiefs wife who vewed it with much pleasure," Clark C 68, with "earthern jar glazed" interlined in red ink.

[3] "After Brackfust we were visited by the old Cheaf of the *Big bellies* . . . this man was old and had transfired his power to his Sun," Clark C 69—which is the most credible solar myth ever penned by mortal hand.

an awning of our sails, stretched so as to exclude the wind, which had become high. That the impression might be the more forcible, the men were all paraded, and the council was opened by a discharge from the swivel of the boat. We then delivered a speech which, like those we had already made, intermingled advice with assurances of friendship and trade. While we were speaking the old Ahnahaway chief grew very restless, and observed that he could not wait long, as his camp was exposed to the hostilities of the Shoshonees. He was instantly rebuked with great dignity by one of the chiefs for this violation of decorum at such a moment, and remain- (*p. 120*) ed quiet during the rest of the council. Toward the end of our speech we introduced the subject of our Ricara chief, with whom we recommended a firm peace. To this they seemed well disposed, and all smoked with him very amicably. We all mentioned the goods which had been taken from the Frenchmen, and expressed a wish that they should be restored. This being over, we proceeded to distribute the presents with great ceremony. One chief of each town was acknowledged by a gift of a flag, a medal with the likeness of the President of the United States, a uniform coat, hat and feather. To the second chiefs we gave a medal representing some domestic animals and a loom for weaving; to the third chiefs, medals with the impressions of a farmer sowing grain. A variety of other presents were distributed, but none seemed to give them more satisfaction than an iron corn-mill which we gave to the Mandans.

The chiefs who were made to-day are: Shahaka [4] or Big White, a first chief; and Kagohami or Little Raven, a second chief, of the lower village of the Mandans called Matootonha. [5] The other chiefs, of an inferior quality, who were recommended were: 1. Ohheenaw or Big Man, a Chayenne taken prisoner by the Mandans, who adopted him; he now

---

[4] "She-he-ke is a fat man, not much distinguished as a warrior, and extremely talkative," Brackenridge's Journal, 1814, p. 261.

[5] Ma-too-ton'-ka in the Statistical View, 1807.

enjoys great consideration among the tribe. 2. Shotahawrora or Coal, of the second Mandan village, which is called
Rooptahee.[6] We made Poscopsahe or Black Cat, the first
chief of the village and the grand chief of the whole Mandan nation. His second chief is Kagonomokshe or Raven-
Man Chief; inferior chiefs of this village are Tawnuheo
and Bellahsara, of which names we did not learn the translation.

In the third village, which is called Mahawha [or Ma-
haha or Maharhar], and where the Arwacahwas [7] reside, we
made one first chief, Tetuckopinreha or White Buffalo-
Robe Unfolded, and recognized two of an inferior order:
Minnissurraree or Neighing Horse, and Locongotiha or
Old Woman at a Distance.

(*p. 121*) Of the fourth village, where the Minnetarees [8]

[6] Roop-tar'-har in the Statistical View, 1807.

[7] *Sic*—misprint for Ahnahaways or Ahwahhaways, as before. These are the
Indians known to the French as Gens des Souliers ; they are of Siouan stock,
closely related to the Hidatsas, Minnetarees or Grosventres, and are offshoots
of the Crows. The Statistical View gives them a population of 200, with 50
warriors, and notes their defensive warfare with the Sioux and offensive wars with
the Snakes and the Flatheads. "They differ but very little, in any particular,
from the Mandans, their neighbours, except in the unjust war which they, as
well as the Minetares, prosecute against the defenceless Snake [Shoshonean]
Indians, from which, I believe, it will be difficult to induce them to desist. They
claim to have once been a part of the Crow Indians, whom they still acknowledge as relations. They have resided on the Missouri as long as their traditions
will enable them to inform." (London ed. Statistical View, 1807, p. 20.)
They kept up a separate tribal organization for about thirty years after Lewis
and Clark found them, and then merged into the Hidatsas. Their proper name
is Amahami.

[8] The name fluctuates in spelling, much as usual, with one *n* or two, and
variable vowels. The above is good form, and is current : compare Minne-
haha, Minne-apolis, etc. It is the Mandan name of these Indians, not their
own, and means to cross water. The best form is Minitari, or Midi-tadi
(water to cross ; consonants *d*, *n*, *l*, *r* interchangeable). Other forms are
Minatari, Manitari, Minetare, etc. There is less trouble with the word than
with the applications of the name in a narrower or broader sense. It is
co-extensive with F. Grosventres, itself equally misleading. The proper name
of the Minnetarees or Grosventres here in mention by Lewis and Clark, is
Hidatsa, given as E-hât'-sâr by Lewis in the Statistical View, 1807. The village,

live, and which is called Metaharta, we made a first chief, Ompsehara or Black Moccasin; a second chief, Ohhaw or Little Fox. Other distinguished chiefs of this village were Mahnotah or Big Thief, a man whom we did not see, as he was out fighting and was killed soon after; and Mahserassa or Tail of the Calumet-Bird. In the fifth village we made a first chief, Eapanopa or Red Shield; a second chief, Wankerassa or Two-Tailed Calumet-Bird— both young chiefs. Other persons of distinction are: Shahakohopinnee or Little Wolf's Medicine; Ahrattana-mockshe or Wolf Man Chief, who is now at war, and is the son of the old chief we have mentioned, whose name is Caltahcota or Cherry on a Bush.

The presents intended for the grand chief of the Minnetarees, who was not at the council, were sent to him by the

Metaharta is there rendered Me-te-har-tar. Those who wish to learn Hidatsan should consult the valuable vocabulary of Dr. Washington Matthews, U. S. A. I had the manuscript of my esteemed friend officially in hand for some time before I could bring it out, as the Government Printing Office had no sorts for the many orthoëpic marks which the ingenious author used. I caused a special font of type to be cast, and undertook to read the proofs. I have understood that the result was satisfactory. Besides being a dictionary and grammar, this book is replete with ethnographic matter of entire reliability, which furnishes the key to all that Lewis and Clark tell us of the tribes so long and so singularly consociated in these villages. (U. S. Geol. and Geogr. Surv., Misc. Pub. No. 7, Washington, Government Printing Office, 1877. 8vo, pp. vi, 239.)

The census in the View is 2,500, with 600 warriors. "They claim no particular country, nor do they assign themselves any limits : their tradition relates that they have always resided at their present villages. In their customs, manners, and dispositions, they are similar to the Mandans and Ahwahhaways. The scarcity of fuel induces them to reside, during the cold season, in large bands, in camps, on different parts of the Missouri, as high up that river as the mouth of the river Yellow Stone, and west of their villages, about the Turtle mountain. . . These people have also suffered considerably by the small-pox ; but have successfully resisted the attacks of the Sioux. The N.W. company intend to form an establishment in the course of next summer, and autumn, on the Missouri, near these people, which, if effected, will most probably prevent their removal to any point which our government may hereafter wish them to reside at." (London ed. 1807, p. 21.)

According to latest returns, there are 522 Hidatsa Indians on the Fort Berthold Reservation, N. D., where Dr. Matthews studied them in 1871–72, and I visited them in 1874. The Mandans number only 251.

old chief Caltahcota; and we delivered to a young chief
those intended for the chief of the lower village. The
council was concluded by a shot from our swivel; and after
our firing the air-gun for their amusement, they retired to
deliberate on the answer which they are to give to-morrow.

In the evening the prairie took fire, either by accident
or design, and burned with great fury, the whole plain
being enveloped in flames. So rapid was its progress that
a man and a woman were burnt to death before they could
reach a place of safety; another man with his wife and
child were much burnt, and several other persons narrowly
escaped destruction. Among the rest a boy of the half-
white breed escaped unhurt in the midst of the flames;
his safety was ascribed to the great medicine spirit, who
had preserved him on account of his being white. But a
much more natural cause was the presence of mind of his
mother, who,[9] seeing no hopes of carrying off her son, threw
him on the ground and, covering him with the fresh hide
of a buffalo, escaped herself from the flames. As soon as
the fire had passed, she returned and found him untouched,
the skin having prevented the flame from reaching the
grass on which he lay.

(*p. 122*) *October 30th.* We were this morning visited by
two persons from the lower village, one Big White, the
chief of the village, the other the Chayenne called Big
Man; they had been hunting, and did not return yesterday
early enough to attend the council. At their request, we
repeated part of our speech of yesterday, and put a medal
around the neck of the chief. Captain Clark[10] took a periogue and went up the river in search of a good wintering

---

[9] " Who perhaps had more fore Sight for the pertection of her Son and iss
[less] for herself than those who escaped the flame," Clark C 72.  This relation has been prolific of Western legends of the Leather-stocking type.  In one
version it is an old trapper who emerges from under the green hide, and
answers a remark to the effect that he must have perished in the flames, with
" Not by a durned sight ! "

[10] Gass, p. 60, wrongly says Lewis.  " I took 8 men in a small perogue and
went up the river as fur as the 1st. Island about 7 miles," Clark C 76.

place ; he returned after going seven miles to the lower point of an island on the north side, about one mile in length ; he found the banks on the north side high, with coal occasionally, and the country fine on all sides ; but the want of wood and the scarcity of game up the river induced us to decide on fixing ourselves lower down during the winter. In the evening our men danced among themselves, to the great amusement of the Indians.

*October* 31*st.* A second chief arrived this morning with an invitation from the grand chief of the Mandans to come to his village, where he wished to present some corn to us and to speak with us. Captain Clark walked down to his village ; he was first seated with great ceremony on a robe by the side of the other chief, who then threw over his shoulders another robe handsomely ornamented. The pipe was then smoked with several of the old men who were seated around the chief. After some time he began his discourse by observing that he believed what we had told him, and that they should soon enjoy peace, which would gratify him as well as his people, because they could then hunt without fear of being attacked, the women might work in the fields without looking every moment for the enemy, and at night put off their moccasins—a phrase by which is conveyed the idea of security, when the women could undress at night without fear of attack. As to the Ricaras (he continued), in order to show you that we wish peace with all men, that chief (pointing to his second chief) will go with some warriors back to the Ricaras with their chief now here, and smoke with that (*p. 123*) nation. When we heard of your coming, all nations around returned from their hunting to see you, in hopes of receiving large presents ; all are disappointed and some discontented ; for his part he was not much so, though his village was. He added that he would go and see his great father the President. Two of the steel traps stolen from the Frenchmen were then laid before Captain Clark, and the women brought about twelve bushels of corn. After the chief had finished, Captain Clark made an answer to the speech, and then returned to the boat, where he found the chief of the third village and Kagohami (Little Raven), who smoked and talked about an hour. After they left the boat, the grand chief of the Mandans came, dressed in the clothes we had given him, with his two children, and begged to see the men dance, in which they willingly gratified him.

*Thursday, November 1st.* Mr. [Hugh] M'Cracken, the trader whom we found here, set out to-day on his return to the British fort and factory on the Assiniboin river, about 150 miles from this place. He took a letter[11] from

---

[11] Here is this letter, which I happened to find in searching old magazines and newspaper files for the purpose. The original passed into the possession of Roderic McKenzie of Assiniboin, who furnished a copy to Jason Chamberlain, of the University of Vermont, Burlington, who wrote, Feb. 15th, 1812, a letter to the editor of the " Portfolio," a magazine published in Philadelphia in those years, inclosing it for publication. It is printed on pp. 448, 449 of Vol. VII., No. 5, of this periodical, May, 1812—certainly not in the exact words of the original, but no doubt with substantial accuracy. It is very interesting, as being signed by both the great captains, and as a specimen of what they could do as diplomats :

*Upper Mandane Village*, Oct. 31, 1804.

To CHARLES CHABOILLER, Esq. of the N. W. Co.

SIR, On our arrival at this Mandane Village, the 26th instant, we met with Mr. Hugh M'Crachen, who informed us that he was in some measure employed by you in behalf of the North West Company, to traffic with the natives of this quarter ; the return of the man to your parts affords us the means of making, thus early, the present communication ; the contents of which we would thank you to make known, as early as possible, to those engaged, and traders immediately under your direction, as also, if convenient, to the principal representatives of any other company of his Britannic Majesty's subjects, who may reside or trade in this quarter.

We have been commissioned and sent by the government of the United States for the purpose of exploring the river Missouri, and the western parts of the continent of North America, with a view to the promotion of general science. Your government have been advised of the voyage and its objects, as the enclosed copy of a passport, granted by Mr. Edward Thornton, his Britannic Majesty's charge d'affaires to the United States, will evidence.

The cold season having now nearly arrived, we have determined to fortify ourselves, and remain the ensuing winter, in the neighbourhood of this place. During our residence here, or future progress on our voyage, we calculate that

Captain[s] Lewis [and Clark] to [Charles Chaboillez of] the Northwest Company, inclosing a copy of the passport granted by [Edward Thornton] the British minister in the United States.

At ten o'clock the chiefs of the lower village arrived; they requested that we would call at their village for some corn; [they said] that they were willing to make peace with the Ricaras; that they had never provoked the war between them, but as the Ricaras had killed some of their chiefs they had retaliated on them; that they had killed them like birds, till they were tired of killing them; so that they would send a chief and some warriors to smoke with them. In the evening we dropped down to the lower village, where Captain Lewis went on shore, and Captain Clark proceeded to a point of wood on the north side.

*November 2d.* He [Captain Lewis with Sergeant Gass and some of the men] therefore went up to the village, where 11 bushels of corn were presented to him. In the

the injunctions contained in the passport before mentioned will, with respect to ourselves, govern the conduct of such of his Britannic Majesty's subjects as may be within communicative reach of us. As individuals, we feel every disposition to cultivate the friendship of all well disposed persons; and all that we have at this moment to ask of them, is a mutual exchange of good offices. We shall, at all times, extend our protection as well to British subjects as American citizens, who may visit the Indians of our neighbourhood, provided they are well-disposed; this we are disposed to do, as well from the pleasure we feel in becoming serviceable to good men, as from a conviction that it is consonant with the liberal policy of our government, not only to admit within her territory the free egress and regress of all citizens and subjects of foreign powers with which she is in amity, but also to extend to them her protection, while within the limits of her jurisdiction.

If, sir, in the course of the winter, you have it in your power to furnish us with any hints in relation to the geography of the country, its productions, either mineral, animal, or vegetable, or any other information which you might conceive of utility to mankind, or which might be serviceable to us in the prosecution of our voyage, we should feel ourselves extremely obliged by your furnishing us with it.

We are, with much respect,
Your ob't. serv'ts.

[Signed]    MERIWETHER LEWIS, Capt. 1st U. S. R[egt.]. Inf.
WILLIAM CLARK, Capt. [2d. Lt. U. S. Artillerists.]

meantime Captain Clark went down with the boats three miles, and having found a good position where there (*p. 124*) was plenty of timber, camped and began to fell trees to build our huts. Our Ricara chief set out with one Mandan chief and several Minnetaree and Mandan warriors. The wind was from the southeast, and the weather being fine a crowd of Indians came down to visit us.

*November 3d.* We now began the building of our cabins,[12] and the Frenchmen who are to return to St. Louis are building a periogue for the purpose. We sent six men in a periogue to hunt [30 or 40 miles] down the river. We were also fortunate enough to engage in our service a Canadian Frenchman [Lepage], who had been with the Chayenne Indians on the Black mountains, and last summer descended thence by the Little Missouri. Mr. Jessaume, our interpreter, also came down with his squaw and children to live at our camp. In the evening we received a visit from Kagohami or Little Raven, whose wife accompanied him, bringing about 60 [pounds'] weight of dried meat, a robe, and a pot of meal. We gave him in return a piece of tobacco, to his wife an ax and a few small articles, and both of them spent the night at our camp. Two beavers were caught in traps this morning.

*November 4th.*[13] We continued our labors. The timber

---

[12] One of Gass' comical pictures shows this, and he describes the structure as follows : " The huts were in two rows, containing four rooms each, and joined at one end forming an angle. When raised about 7 feet high a floor of puncheons or split plank were [*sic*] laid, and covered with grass and clay ; which made a warm loft. The upper part projected a foot over and the roofs were made shed-fashion, rising from the inner side, and making the outer wall about 18 feet high. The part not enclosed by the huts we intend to picket. In the angle formed by the two rows of huts we built two rooms, for holding our provisions and stores." (Carey's Phila. ed. 1811, p. 60—there are no illustrations in the orig. ed. Pittsburg, 1807.)

[13] Clark C 86, this date, has the first mention I have found of the individual who will figure to the end of the narrative as Chaboneau. " A Mr. Chaubonie, interpreter for the Gross Ventre," interlined " Chaboneau " in red ink. In the codices he has as many aliases as perhaps any other person, place, or tribe in the whole history. He is usually Chabono or Shabono. Lewis' autograph muster-

which we employ is large and heavy, and chiefly consists of cottonwood and elm, with some ash of an inferior size. Great numbers of the Indians passed our camp on their hunting excursions. The day was clear and pleasant, but last night was very cold, and there was a white frost.

*November 5th.* The Indians are all out on their hunting parties. A camp of Mandans caught within two days 100 goats a short distance below us. Their mode of hunting them is to form a large strong pen or fold, from which a fence made of bushes gradually widens on each side. The animals are surrounded by the hunters and gently driven toward this pen, in which they imperceptibly find them- selves inclosed, and are then at the mercy of the hunters. The weather is cloudy and the wind moderate from the northwest. Late at night we were awaked by the sergeant on (*p. 125*) guard to see the beautiful phenomenon called the Northern Light. Along the northern sky was a large space occupied by a light of a pale but brilliant white color which, rising from the horizon, extended itself to nearly 20° above it. After glittering for some time its colors would be overcast and almost obscured, but

roll, Washington, Jan. 15th, 1807, returns him officially as Touisant [Toussaint] Charbono, with the remark : "A man of no peculiar merit. was usefull as an interpreter only, in which capacity he discharged his duties with good faith from the moment of our departure from the mandans on the 7th of April 1805 until our return to that place in August last and received as a compensation 25 dollars pr. month while in service." He seems to have been good-natured, and meant well, no doubt ; but in the light of the narrative he appears to have been a poor specimen, consisting, chiefly, of a tongue to wag in a mouth to fill ; and had he possessed the comprehensive saintliness of his baptismal name, he would have been a minus function still in comparison with his wife Sacajawea, the wonderful "Bird-woman," who contributed a full man's share to the success of the Expedition, besides taking care of her baby.

"We had on board [1811] a Frenchman named Charbonet, with his wife, an Indian woman of the Snake nation, both of whom had accompanied Lewis and Clark to the Pacific, and were of great service. The woman, a good creature, of a mild and gentle disposition, greatly attached to the whites, whose manners and dress she tries to imitate ; but she had become sickly, and longed to revisit her native country ; her husband also, who had spent many years amongst the Indians, was become weary of a civilized life." Brackenridge's Journal, 1814, p. 202.

again it would burst out with renewed beauty; the uniform color was pale light, but its shapes were various and
fantastic. At times the sky was lined with light-colored
streaks rising perpendicularly from the horizon and gradually expanding into a body of light in which we could trace
the floating columns sometimes advancing, sometimes
retreating, and shaping into infinite forms the space in
which they moved. It all faded away before the morning.
At daylight,

*November 6th,* the clouds to the north were darkening;
the wind rose high from the northwest at eight o'clock,
and continued cold during the day. Mr. [Joseph] Gravelines, and four others [Paul Premor? one Laguness? and
two French youths] who came with us, returned to the
Ricaras in a small periogue. We gave him directions to
accompany some of the Ricara chiefs to the seat of government in the spring.

*November 7th.* The day was temperate, but cloudy and
foggy, and we were enabled to go on with our work with
much expedition.

*November 8th.* The morning again cloudy. Our huts
advance very well, and we are visited by numbers of Indians
who come to let their horses graze near us. In the day the
horses are let loose in quest of grass; in the night they are
collected and receive an armful of small boughs of the
cottonwood, which, being very juicy, soft, and brittle, form
nutritious and agreeable food. The frost this morning
was very severe, the weather during the day cloudy, and
the wind from the northwest. We procured from an
Indian a weasel,[14] perfectly white except the extremity of
the tail, which was black. Great numbers of wild geese

[14] This is the *Putorius longicauda,* a species of stoat or ermine, common in
the Missouri region, in winter of the color said, in summer brown and yellowish. I have seen specimens taken near this very locality, and have collected
others in North Dakota and Montana. It was new to science in 1804, and
probably not noticed again till 1829, as by Sir John Richardson, whose remark
in Fn. B.-Am., I. p. 47, caused Prince C. L. Bonaparte to name a *Mustela
longicauda.* The late Prof. S. F. Baird was the first to certainly recognize the

[*Bernicla canadensis*] are passing to the south, but their flight is too high for us to procure any of them.[15]

(*p. 126*) *November 10th.* We had again a raw day with a northwest wind, but rose early in hopes of finishing our works before the extreme cold begins. A chief who is a half Pawnee came to us and brought a present of half a buffalo, in return for which we gave him some small presents and a few articles for his wife and son. He then crossed the river in a buffalo-skin canoe; his wife took the boat on her back and carried it to the village, three miles off. Large flocks of geese and brant, and also a few ducks, are passing toward the south.

*November 11th.* The weather is cold. We received the visit of two squaws [Sacajawea and another], prisoners from the Rock [Rocky] mountains, purchased by Chaboneau. The Mandans at this time are out hunting the buffalo.

*November 12th.* The last night has been cold, and this morning we had a very hard frost; the wind is changeable during the day, and some ice appears on the edges of the rivers; swans are passing to the south. Big White came down to us, having packed on the back of his squaw about 100 pounds of very fine meat, for which we gave him as well as the squaw some presents, particularly an ax to the woman, with which she was very much pleased.

*November 13th.* We this morning unloaded the boat, and stowed away the contents in a storehouse which we have built. At half past ten ice began to float down the river for the first time. In the course of the morning we were visited by Black Cat, Poscapsahe, who brought an Assiniboin chief and seven warriors to see us. This man, whose name is Chechawk,[16] is a chief of one of three bands

species. See his Mamm. N. A., 1857, p. 169, and my Fur-Bearing Animals, 1877, pp. 137-142.

[15] Clark C 90 is a page for Nov. 9th—needless to cite, however, as Biddle has worked the substance of it into his text of other dates.

[16] "Che Chank," plainly, Clark C 95, with Lagree (Legree) noted as a French name of him. He turns up later as Shishank or Shishonk. Clark tagged him neatly by giving him "a gold cord, with a view to know him again," *ibid.*

of Assiniboins who wander over the plains between the
Missouri and Assiniboin [river] during the summer, in the
winter carry the spoils of their hunting to the traders on
the Assiniboin river, and occasionally come to this place.
The whole three bands consist of about 800 men. We
gave him a twist of tobacco to smoke with his people, and
a gold cord for himself. The Sioux also asked for whisky,
which we refused to give them. It snowed all day and the
air was very cold.

(*p. 127*) *November* 14*th.* The river rose last night half
an inch, and is now filled with floating ice. This morning
was cloudy with some snow. About 70 lodges of Assiniboins [17] and some Knistenaux [or Crees] are at the Mandan
village; and this being the day of adoption, and exchange
of property between them all, it is accompanied by a dance,
which prevents our seeing more than two Indians to-day.
These Knistenaux [18] are a band of Chippeways, whose lan-

[17] The Assiniboins are a number of tribes of Indians of Siouan stock, to be
carefully distinguished from the Crees or other members of the Algonquian
family with which they were associated. They have sometimes been called
Stone Sioux, as a translation of the Chippeway name Assinniboan. The
Dakotan name is Hohe. The band spoken of in the text were probably of the
tribe on the Mouse or Souris river, the main southern branch of the Assiniboin,
since they came with the Knisteneaux. The three bands or tribes of Assiniboins mentioned in the preceding paragraph are noted by Lewis in the
Statistical View as : 1. Ma-ne-to'-pâ, or Gens de Canoe, with 100 lodges,
200 warriors, and total of 750 people, living on the Mouse river. (These give
name to the province of Manitoba.) 2. O-see'-gâh or Gens de Tee (misprint for Feuilles. See text, p. 217, near end of this chapter), 100 lodges, 250
warriors, 850 total, from about the mouth of the Little Missouri over to the
Assiniboin. 3. Mâh'-to,-pâ-nà-to or Gens du Grand Diable, 200 lodges, 450
warriors, 1,600 total, on the Missouri about White-earth river and over to the
Assiniboin. Nacota is given as an alternative name with Assiniboin ; the
three bands are said to speak the Sioux language, with some few peculiar
words, and to act entirely independently of one another, though they recognize
their national affinity and never war with one another.

The greater number of Assiniboins are now in British America. Those
officially rated as such in the United States are, according to the latest returns,
952 at Fort Belknap Reservation, Mont., 719 at Fort Peck Reservation, Mont.,
and 2 at Devil's Lake Agency, N. D.

[18] Few names of Indians have been used with more latitude or lack of precision

guage they speak; they live on the Assiniboin and Saskashawan [19] rivers, and are about 240 men.  We sent a man
[Drewyer] down on horseback to see what had become
of our hunters, and as we apprehend a failure of provisions
we have recourse to our pork this evening.  Two Frenchmen who had been below returned with 20 beaver which
they had caught in traps.

*November* 15*th.*  The morning again cloudy, and the ice
running thicker than yesterday; the wind variable.  The
man came back with the information that our hunters were
about 30 miles below, and we immediately sent an order to
them to make their way through the floating ice; to assist
them in which we sent some tin for the bow of the periogue, and a tow-rope.  The ceremony of yesterday seemed
to continue still, for we were not visited by a single Indian.
The swan are still passing to the south.

*November* 16*th.*  We had a very hard white frost this
morning ; the trees are all covered with ice ; the weather is
cloudy.  The men this day moved into the huts, although
they are not finished.  In the evening some horses were
sent down to the woods near us, in order to prevent their
being stolen by the Assiniboins, with whom some difficulty is now apprehended.  An Indian came down with
four buffalo-robes and some corn, which he offered for a
pistol, but was refused.

than Knisteneaux or " Cree," and " Chippeway."   The latter is the same word
as Ojibwa, and is spelled in many other ways.   The Crees proper are British
American Indians, supposed to now number about 17,000.   It is impossible to
say exactly what band of Indians is mentioned in the text, further than that
they were " Crees."   But they were probably not the " Chippeways " or
" Ojibaways " of Lewis' Statistical View, London ed. 1807, p. 28, nor yet the
Algonquins (" Chippeways "), *ibid.* p. 31 ; but the Indians there given, p. 33,
as " Christenoes or Knistenaus," with " Crees," as the French nickname.  These
are said there to speak the language of the " Chippeways, with a different accent,
and many words peculiar to themselves."   They are described as a wandering
nation, though located on the Assiniboin and thence toward the Saskashawan,
which agrees with the text above.   They are credited with 150 lodges, 300
warriors, and a total population of 1,000.

[19] Twenty or more spellings of this could easily be adduced.   Clark C 97 has
Assaskasshawan.   One of our commonest renderings is Saskatchewan.

*November 17th.* Last night was very cold, and the ice in the river to-day is thicker than hitherto. We are totally occupied with our huts, but received visits from several Indians.

(*p. 128*) *November 18th.* To-day we had a cold, windy morning. Black Cat came to see us, and occupied us for a long time with questions on the usages of our country. He mentioned that a council had been held yesterday to deliberate on the state of their affairs. It seems that not long ago a party of Sioux fell in with some horses belonging to the Minnetarees, and carried them off ; but in their flight they were met by some Assiniboins, who killed the Sioux and kept the horses. A Frenchman too, who had lived many years among the Mandans, was lately killed on his route to the British factory on the Assiniboin. Some smaller differences also existed between the two nations ; all of which being discussed, the council decided that they would not resent the recent insults from the Assiniboins and Knistenaux, until they had seen whether we had deceived them or not in our promises of furnishing them with arms and ammunition. They had been disappointed in their hopes of receiving them from Mr. Evans, and were afraid that we too, like him, might tell them what was not true. We advised them to continue at peace ; that supplies of every kind would no doubt arrive for them, but that time was necessary to organize the trade. The fact is that the Assiniboins treat the Mandans as the Sioux do the Ricaras ; by their vicinity to the British they get all the supplies, which they withhold or give at pleasure to the remoter Indians. The consequence is that, however badly treated, the Mandans and Ricaras are very slow to retaliate, lest they should lose their trade altogether.

*November 19th.* The ice continues to float in the river, the wind is high from the northwest, and the weather cold. Our hunters arrived from their excursion below, bringing a very fine supply of 32 deer, 11 elk, and 5 buffalo,[20] all of which was hung in a smokehouse.

[20] Mistake : " 32 Deer, 12 Elk & a Buffalow," Clark C 100.

*November* 20*th.* We this day moved into our huts, which are now completed. This place, which we call Fort Mandan, is situated in a point of low ground, on the north side of the Missouri, covered with tall and heavy cotton-wood. The (*p. 129*) works consist of two rows of huts or sheds, forming an angle where they join each other ; each row containing four rooms, of 14 feet square and 7 feet high, with plank ceiling, and the roof slanting so as to form a loft above the rooms, the highest part of which is 18 feet from the ground ; the backs of the huts form a wall of that height, and opposite the angle the place of the wall is supplied by picketing ; in the area are two rooms for stores and provisions. The latitude by observation is 47° 21′ 47″, and the computed distance from the mouth of the Missouri is 1,600 miles.

In the course of the day several Indians came down to partake of our fresh meat ; among the rest, three chiefs of the second Mandan village. They inform us that the Sioux on the Missouri above the Chayenne river threaten to attack them this winter ; that these Sioux are much irritated at the Ricaras for having made peace through our means with the Mandans, and have lately ill-treated three Ricaras who carried the pipe of peace to them, by beating them and taking away their horses. We gave them assur-ances that we would protect them from all their enemies.

*November* 21*st.* The weather was this day fine, the river clear of ice and rising a little. We are now settled in our new winter habitation, and shall wait with much anxiety the first return of spring, to continue our journey.

The villages near which we are established are five in number, and are the residence of three distinct nations : the Mandans, the Ahnahaways [see note, p. 183], and the Minnetarees [see note, p. 183]. The history of the Man-dans, as we received it from our interpreters and from the chiefs themselves, and as it is attested by existing monu-ments, illustrates more than that of any other nation the unsteady movements and the tottering fortunes of the

American Indians.   Within the recollection of living witnesses, the Mandans were  settled 40 years ago in nine villages, the ruins of which we passed about 80 miles (*p. 130*)
below, seven on the west and two on the east side of the
Missouri.   These two, finding themselves wasting away
before the smallpox and the Sioux, united into one village,
and moved up the river opposite the Ricaras.   The same
causes reduced the remaining seven to five villages, till at
length they emigrated in a body to the Ricara nation,
where they formed themselves into two villages, and joined
those of their countrymen who had gone before them.   In
their new residence they were still insecure, and at length the
three villages ascended the Missouri to their present position.   The two who had emigrated together settled in the
two villages on the northwest side of the Missouri, while
the single village took a position on the southeast side.   In
this situation they were found by those who visited them
in 1796 [*read* David Thompson, Dec. 29th, 1797–Jan. 10th,
1798] ; since which the two villages have united into one.
They are now two villages, one on the southeast of the
Missouri, the other on the opposite side, at the distance of
three miles across.   The first, in an open plain, contains
about 40 or 50 lodges, built in the same way as those of the
Ricaras ;  the second, the  same number ; and both may
raise [*i. e.*, can muster] about 350 men.

On the same side of the river, and at a distance of four
miles from the lower Mandan village, is another called Mahaha [see note on p. 183].   It is situated on a high plain
at the mouth of Knife river, and is the residence of the
Ahnahaways.   This nation, whose name indicates that
they were " people whose village is on a hill," formerly
resided on the Missouri, about 30 miles below where they
now live.   The Assiniboins and Sioux forced them to a
spot five miles higher, where the greatest part of them were
put to death, and the rest emigrated to their present
situation, in order to obtain an asylum near the Minnetarees.   They are called by the French Soulier Noir or

[Black] Shoe Indians;[21] by the Mandans, Wattasoons;[22] and their whole force is about 50 men.

(*p. 131*)   On the south side of the same Knife river, half a mile above the Mahaha [village] and in the same open plain with it, is a village of Minnetarees surnamed Metaharta, who are about 150 men in number.   On the opposite side of Knife river, and one and a half miles above this village, is a second of Minnetarees, who may be considered as the proper Minnetaree nation.   It is situated in a beautiful low plain, and contains 450 warriors.

The accounts which we received of the Minnetarees were contradictory.   The Mandans say that this people came out of the water to the east and settled near them in their former establishment in nine villages; that they were very numerous, and fixed themselves in one village on the southern side of the Missouri.   A quarrel about a buffalo divided the nation, of which two bands went into the plains and were known by the name of Crow[23] and

[21] The French name is given as " Gens de Soulier" in the Statistical View. See note [7], p. 183.

[22] " In the Arickaree language, the Hidatsa are called Witetsaán," Matthews, p. 36.   In the Clark Codex this word wavers in spelling, as usual.   Its translation is disputed.   The Crow name of the Hidatsa is Amasi, which means the dirt lodges in which they lived.   The Sioux name for them is Hewaktokto, of questionable meaning.

[23] The Crows are one of the principal tribes of the Siouan family, related nearest to the Minnetarees or Hidatsans (Grosventres).   Their English name is rendered from the French Gens des Corbeaux.   According to the latest returns there were 2,287 of them on the Crow Reservation in Northern Montana.

In his Statistical View Lewis calls the Crows Kee'-kât-sâ.   Their primitive name is now variously rendered Absaroke, Aubsaroke, Absaruque, etc.   Lewis made their total 3,500, with 900 warriors and 350 lodges, and located them on the Yellowstone, about the mouth of the Bighorn.   He makes their language Minnetaree.   " These people," he continues, " are divided into four bands, called by themselves Ahâh'-âr-ro'-pir-no-pah, Noo'-ta-, Pa-rees-car, and E-hârt'-sâr.   They annually visit the Mandans, Minnetarees, and Ahwahhaways, to whom they barter horses, mules, leather lodges, and many articles of Indian apparel, for which they receive in return guns, ammunition, axes, kettles, awls, and other European manufactures.   When they return to their country they are in turn visited by the Paunch and Snake Indians, to whom they barter most of the articles they have obtained from the nations on the Missouri, for horses

Paunch [24] Indians, and the rest moved to their present establishment. The Minnetarees proper assert, on the contrary, that they grew where they now live and will never emigrate from the spot, the Great Spirit having declared that if they moved they would all die. They also say that the Minnetarees Metaharta—that is, Minnetarees of the Willows, whose language with very little variation is their own, came many years ago from the plains and settled near them. Perhaps the two traditions may be reconciled by the natural presumption that these Minnetarees were the tribes known to the Mandans below, and that they ascended the river for the purpose of rejoining the Minnetarees proper. These Minnetarees are part of the great nation called Fall [25] Indians, who occupy the intermediate

and mules, of which those nations [*i. e.*, Paunch and Snake] have a greater abundance than themselves. They also obtain of the Snake Indians, bridle-bits and blankets, and some other articles which those Indians purchase from the Spaniards. The bridle-bits and blankets I have seen in the possession of the Mandans and Minnetarees." (London ed. 1807, p. 25.)

[24] Lewis in his Statistical View treats these "Paunch" Indians entirely apart from the Grosventres. He gives their native name as Al-la-kâ'-we-âh, with French nickname "Gens de Panse," and locates them along the Yellowstone on both sides, near the Rocky mountains and heads of the Bighorn river, with a population of 2,300, including 800 warriors and 300 lodges. He says they act on the defensive against the Sioux and Ricaras, and have the same alliances as the Wetepahatoes, excepting their wars with the Ricaras. "They are said to be a peaceable, well disposed nation. Their country is a variegated one, consisting of mountains, valleys, plains, and wood-lands, irregularly interspersed. They might be induced to visit the Missouri, at the mouth of the Yellow Stone river; and from the great abundance of valuable furred animals which their country, as well as that of the Crow Indians produces, their trade must become extremely valuable. They are a roving people, and have no idea of exclusive right to the soil." (London ed. 1807, p. 25.)

[25] This is a vague term, due or at least traceable to the trader Edward Umfreville, who was on the Saskatchewan in 1784–87, and who mentions these Indians as living about the falls of the south branch of that river. He says (p. 197) that the French "call them Grosventres or Big-Bellies; and without any reason, as they are as comely and as well made as any tribe whatever, and are very far from being remarkable for their corpulency." On which Matthews, from whom I borrow this quote, remarks (p. 33): "The tribe to which he refers is doubtless that which is now known as the Atsinas or Grosventres of the Prairie. The similarity of the Canadian misnomers led Captain Lewis in

country between the Missouri and the Saskaskawan, and who are known by the name of Minnetarees of the Missouri, and Minnetarees of Fort de Prairie—that is, residing near or rather frequenting the establishment in the prairie on the Saskaskawan [Saskatchewan]. These Minnetarees indeed told us that they had relations on the Saskaskawan, whom they had never known till they met them in war, (*p. 132*) and having engaged in the night were astonished at discovering that they were fighting with men who spoke their own language. The French name of Grosventres, or Bigbellies, is given to these Minnetarees, as well as to all the Fall Indians.

The inhabitants of these five villages, all of which are within the distance of six miles, live in harmony with one another. The Ahnahaways understand in part the language of the Minnetarees. The dialect of the Mandans differs widely from both; but their long residence together has insensibly blended their manners, and occasioned some approximation in language, particularly as to objects of daily occurrence and obvious to the senses.

*November 22d.* The morning was fine, and the day warm. We purchased from the Mandans [26] a quantity of

1804, to speak of the Minnetarees on the Missouri ' as part of the great nation called Fall Indians.' Comparing our Hidatsa words with their synonymes in Umfreville's Fall Vocabulary, or Dr. Hayden's later Atsina Vocabulary, we can discover no affinity between the Fall and Hidatsa tongues." It is necessary for the reader to bear always in mind, that when L. and C. speak of Minnetarees " of the Prairie " and " of the Missouri," they actually designate two entirely different tribes of Indians, the former being Atsinas or the " Fall" Indians, and the latter being the Hidatsas, with whom they are now wintering. Their loose use of " Grosventres" is exactly parallel. For example, see beyond, Jan. 1st, 1805, and note there.

These "Fall" Indians are separately treated by Lewis in the Statistical View. He adopts this name there, and gives the native name A-lân-sâr as synonymous. He estimates their total number at 2,500, with 660 warriors and 260 lodges, and locates them " on the head of the south fork of the Saskshawan [*sic*] river, and some streams supposed to be branches of the Missouri " (perhaps of Milk river : see what is said of the Minnetarees, note [8], p. 183).

[26] " Dispatched a perogue and 5 men under the Derection of Sergeant Pryor

corn of a mixed color, which they dug up in ears from holes made near the front of their lodges, in which it is buried during the winter.

This morning the sentinel informed us that an Indian was about to kill his wife near the fort. We went down to the house of our interpreter, where we found the parties, and after forbidding any violence, inquired into the cause of his intending to commit such an atrocity. It appeared that some days ago a quarrel had taken place between him and his wife, in consequence of which she had taken refuge in the house where the two squaws of our interpreter lived. By running away she forfeited her life, which might have been lawfully taken by the husband. About two days ago she had returned to the village, but the same evening came back to the fort much beaten, and stabbed in three places, and the husband now came for the purpose of completing his revenge.[27] He observed that he had lent her to one of our sergeants for a night, and that if he wanted her he would give her to him altogether. We gave him a few presents and tried to persuade him to take his wife home; the grand chief too happened to arrive at the same moment, and reproached him with his violence; till at length they went off together, but by no means in a state of much apparent love.

(*p. 133*) *November* 23*d*. Again we had a fair and warm day, with the wind from the southeast. The river is now at a stand, having risen four inches in the whole.

*November* 24*th*. The wind continued from the same

to the 2d Village for 100 bushels of Corn in ears which Mr. Jessomme let us have—did not get more than 90 bushels," Clark C 102.

[27] On his wife, not on Sergeant Ordway. " We derected that no man of this party have any intercourse with this woman under the penelty of punishment—he the Husband observed that one of our Serjeants slept with his wife & if he wanted her he would give her to him, I derected the Sergeant Odway to give the man some articles, at which time I told the Indian I believed not one man of the party had touched his wife except the one he had given the use of her for a nite, in his own bed, * * * at this time the grand chief of the nation arrived & lecturd him and they both went off dis[satisfied]," Clark C 103.

quarter, and the weather was warm. We were occupied in finishing our huts and making a large rope of elk-skin to draw our boat on the bank.

*Sunday, November 25th.* The weather is still fine, warm, and pleasant, and the river falls one inch and a half. Captain Lewis went on an excursion to the village, accompanied by eight men. A Minnetaree chief, the first who has visited us, came down to the fort. His name was Waukerassa, but as both the interpreters had gone with Captain Lewis we were obliged to confine our civilities to some presents, with which he was much pleased. We now completed our huts, and fortunately too ; for the next day,

*November 26th,* before daylight the wind shifted to the northwest and blew very hard, with cloudy weather and a keen, cold air, which confined us much and prevented us from working. The night continued very cold.

*November 27th.* The weather was cloudy, the wind continued from the northwest, and the river was crowded with floating ice. Captain Lewis returned with two chiefs : Mahnotah, an Ahnahaway, and Minnessurraree, a Minne-taree ; and a third warrior. They explained to us that the reason of their not having come to see us was that the Mandans had told them that we meant to combine with the Sioux and cut them off in the course of the winter—a suspicion increased by the strength of the fort and the circumstance of our interpreters having both removed there with their families. These reports we did not fail to disprove to their entire satisfaction, and we amused them by every attention, particularly by the dancing of the men, which diverted them highly. All the Indians whom Captain Lewis had visited were very well disposed and received him with great kindness, except a principal chief of one of the upper villages, named Mahpahpaparapassatoo or (*p.134*) Horned Weasel, who[28] made use of the civilized indecorum of refusing to be seen, as when Captain Lewis called he was

[28] " Who did not chuse to be seen by the Capt. and left word that he was not at home &c." Clark C 107.

told the chief was not at home. In the course of the day seven of the Northwest Company's traders arrived from the Assiniboin river; and one of their interpreters having undertaken to circulate among the Indians unfavorable reports, it became necessary to warn them of the consequences if they did not desist from such proceedings.[29] The river fell two inches to-day, and the weather became very cold.

*November 28th.* About eight o'clock last evening it began to snow and continued till daybreak, after which it ceased till seven o'clock, but then resumed and continued during the day, the weather being cold and the river full of floating ice. About eight o'clock Poscopsahe[30] came down to visit us, with some warriors; we gave them presents and entertained them with all that might amuse their curiosity, and at parting we told them that we had heard of the British trader, Mr. Laroche, having attempted to distribute medals and flags among them; but that those emblems could not be received from any other than the American nation without incurring the displeasure of their great father, the President. They left us much pleased with their treatment. The river fell one inch to-day.

*November 29th.* The wind is again from the northwest, the weather cold, and the snow which fell yesterday and last night is 13 inches in depth. The river closed during the night at the village above, and fell two feet; but this afternoon it began to rise a little. Mr. Laroche, the principal of the seven traders, came with one of his men to see us; we told him that we should not permit him to give medals and flags to the Indians; he declared that he had no such intention, and we then suffered him to make use of one of our interpreters, on his stipulating not to touch upon

[29] Clark C 108 names this interpreter Lafrance; and "the principal Mr. Le Rock, & Mr. Mc.Kinsey [Laroche and M'Kenzie of the following text] was informed of the Conduct of their interpeter and the Consiquincies if they did not put a Stop to unfavourable and ill founded assursions."

[30] Variant in text and codices. Clark C 109 has Poss-cop-so-he, as the name of the Mandan Black Cat.

any subject but that of his traffic with them. An unfortunate accident occurred to Sergeant Pryor, who in taking down the boat's (*p. 135*) mast dislocated his shoulder, nor was it till after four trials that we replaced it.

*November 30th.* About eight o'clock an Indian came to the opposite bank of the river, calling out that he had something important to communicate. On sending for him, he told us that five Mandans had been met about eight leagues to the southwest by a party of Sioux, who had killed one of them, wounded two, and taken nine horses; that four of the Wattasoons [31] were missing, and that the Mandans expected an attack. We thought this an excellent opportunity to discountenance the injurious reports against us, and to fix the wavering confidence of the nation. [32]

Captain Clark therefore instantly crossed the river with 23 men strongly armed, and circling the town approached it from behind. His unexpected appearance surprised and alarmed the chiefs, who came out to meet him and conducted him to the village. He then told them that having heard of the outrage just committed, he had come to assist his dutiful children; that if they would assemble their warriors and those of the nation, he would lead them against the Sioux and avenge the blood of their countrymen. After some minutes' conversation, Oheenaw the Chayenne arose: "We now see," said he, "that what you have told us is true, since as soon as our enemies threaten to attack us you come to protect us and are ready to chastise those who have spilt our blood. We did indeed listen to your good talk, for when you told us that the other nations were inclined to peace with us, we went out carelessly in small

[31] "4 of the Wetersoon nation was missing," etc., Clark C 111.

[32] "We thought it well to shew a a Desposition to ade and assist them against their enimies, perticularly those who came in oppersition to our Councils ; and I deturmined to go to the town with Some men, and if the Suoux were comeing to attack the nation to collect the worriers from each village and meet them, those Ideas were also those of Capt. Lewis," Clark C 112. And those warriors would have been " worriers," with a William Clark to lead them.

parties, and some have been killed by the Sioux and Ricaras. But I knew that the Ricaras were liars, and I told the chief who accompanied you that his whole nation were liars and bad men ; that we had several times made a peace with them which they were the first to break; that whenever we pleased we might shoot them like buffalo, but that we had no wish to kill them ; that we would not suffer them to kill us, nor steal our horses ; and that although we agreed to make peace with them, because our two fathers [Lewis and Clark] (*p. 136*) desired it, yet we did not believe that they would be faithful long. Such, father, was my language to them in your presence, and you see that instead of listening to your good counsels they have spilt our blood. A few days ago two Ricaras came here and told us that two of their villages were making moccasins, that the Sioux were stirring them up against us, and that we ought to take care of our horses; yet these very Ricaras we sent home as soon as the news reached us to-day, lest our people should kill them in the first moment of grief for their murdered relatives. Four of the Wattasoons whom we expected back in 16 days have been absent 24, and we fear have fallen. But, father, the snow is now deep, the weather cold, and our horses cannot travel through the plains; the murderers have gone off. If you will conduct us in the spring, when the snow has disappeared, we will assemble all the surrounding warriors and follow you."

Captain Clark replied that we were always willing and able to defend them ; that he was sorry that the snow prevented their marching to meet the Sioux, since he wished to show them that the warriors of their great father would chastise the enemies of his obedient children who opened their ears to his advice; that if some Ricaras had joined the Sioux, they should remember that there were bad men in every nation, and that they should not be offended at the Ricaras till they saw whether these ill-disposed men were countenanced by the whole tribe; that the Sioux possessed great influence over the Ricaras, whom they supplied with military stores and sometimes led astray, because they were afraid to oppose them; but that this should be the less offensive since the Mandans themselves were under the same apprehensions from the Assiniboins and Knistenaux, and that while they were thus dependent, both the Ricaras and Mandans ought to keep on terms with their powerful neighbors, whom they may afterward set at defiance, when we shall supply them with arms and take them under our protection.

(*p. 137*) After two hours' conversation Captain Clark left the village. The chief repeatedly thanked him for the fatherly protection he had given them, observing that the whole village had been weeping all night and day for the brave young man who had been slain, but now they would wipe their eyes and weep no more, as they saw that their father would protect them. He then crossed the river on the ice and returned on the north side to the fort. The day as well as the evening was cold, and the river rose to its former height.

*Saturday, December 1st*, 1804. The wind was from the northwest, and the whole party engaged in picketing the fort. About ten o'clock the half-brother of the man who had been killed came to inform us that six Sharha or Chayenne Indians had arrived, bringing a pipe of peace, and that their nation was three days' march behind them. Three Pawnees had accompanied the Sharhas, and the Mandans being afraid of the Sharhas on account of their being at peace with the Sioux, wished to put both them and the three Pawnees to death; but the chiefs had forbidden it, as it would be contrary to our wishes. We gave him a present of tobacco, and although from his connection with the sufferer he was more embittered against the Pawnees than any other Mandan, yet he seemed perfectly satisfied with our pacific counsels and advice. The Mandans, we observe, call all the Ricaras by the name of Pawnees; the name of Ricaras being that by which the nation distinguishes itself.

In the evening we were visited by a Mr. [G.] Henderson,

who came from the Hudson's Bay Company to trade with the Minnetarees. He had been about eight days on his route in a direction nearly south, and brought with him tobacco, beads, and other merchandise to trade for furs, and a few guns which are to be exchanged for horses.

*December 2d.* The latter part of the evening was warm and a thaw continued till the morning, when the wind shifted to the north. At eleven o'clock the chiefs of (*p. 138*) the lower village brought down four of the Sharhas. We explained to them our intentions and advised them to remain at peace with each other ; we also gave them a flag, some tobacco, and a speech for their nation. These were accompanied by a letter to Messrs. Tabeau and Gravelines [33] at the Ricara village, requesting them to preserve peace if possible, and to declare the part which we should be forced to take if the Ricaras and Sioux made war on those whom we had adopted. After distributing a few presents to the Sharhas and Mandans, and showing them our curiosities, we dismissed them, apparently well pleased at their reception.

*December 3d.* The morning was fine, but in the afternoon the weather became cold, with the wind from the northwest. The father of the Mandan who was killed brought us a present of dried pumpkins and some pemitigon [pemmican], for which we gave him some small articles. Our offer of assistance to avenge the death of his son seemed to have produced a grateful respect from him, as well as from the brother of the deceased, which pleased us much.

*December 4th.* The wind continued from the northwest, the weather cloudy and raw, and the river rose one inch. Oscapsahe [34] and two young chiefs passed the day with us.

The whole religion of the Mandans consists in the belief of one Great Spirit presiding over their destinies. This Being must be in the nature of a good genius, since it is

---

[33] " A letter to Messrs. Tabbo & Gravoline, at the Ricares Village, to interseed in proventing Hostilities," Clark C 121.

[34] *Sic*—usually Poscopsahe in text ; codex here has only "Black Cat " ; see note [30], Nov. 28th, p. 203.

associated with the healing art, and "great spirit" is synonymous with "great medicine," a name applied to everything which they do not comprehend. Each individual selects for himself the particular object of his devotion, which is termed his medicine, and is either some invisible being or more commonly some animal, which thenceforward becomes his protector or his intercessor with the Great Spirit, to propitiate whom every attention is lavished and every personal consideration is sacrificed. "I was lately owner of 17 horses," said a Mandan to us one day, "but I (*p. 139*) have offered them all up to my medicine and am now poor." He had in reality taken all his wealth, his horses, into the plain, and, turning them loose, committed them to the care of his medicine and abandoned them forever. The horses, less religious, took care of themselves, and the pious votary traveled home on foot.

Their belief in a future state is connected with this tradition of their origin: The whole nation resided in one large village underground near a subterraneous lake; a grape-vine extended its roots down to their habitation and gave them a view of the light; some of the most adventurous climbed up the vine and were delighted with the sight of the earth, which they found covered with buffalo and rich with every kind of fruits; returning with the grapes they had gathered, their countrymen were so pleased with the taste of them that the whole nation resolved to leave their dull residence for the charms of the upper region; men women, and children ascended by means of the vine; but when about half the nation had reached the surface of the earth, a corpulent woman who was clambering up the vine broke it with her weight, and closed upon herself and the rest of the nation the light of the sun. Those who were left on earth made a village below, where we saw the nine villages; and when the Mandans die they expect to return to the original seats of their forefathers, the good reaching the ancient village by means of the lake, which the burden of the sins of the wicked will not enable them to cross.

*December 5th.* The morning was cold and disagreeable, the wind from the southeast, accompanied by snow; in the evening there was snow again, and the wind shifted to the northeast. We were visited by several Indians, with a present of pumpkins, and by two of the traders of the Northwest Company.

*December 6th.* The wind was violent from the north-northwest, with some snow, the air keen and cold. At 8 a. m. the themometer stood at 10° above (*p.* 140) zero, and the river rose an inch and a half in the course of the day.

*December 7th.* The wind still continued from the northwest and the day was very cold. Shahaka [Big White], the chief of the lower village, came to apprise us that the buffalo were near, and that his people were waiting for us to join them in the chase. Captain Clark with 15 men went out and found the Indians engaged in killing buffalo. The hunters, mounted on horseback and armed with bows and arrows, encircle the herd and gradually drive them into a plain or an open place fit for the movements of horse; they then ride in among them, and singling out a buffalo, a female being preferred, go as close as possible and wound her with arrows till they think they have given the mortal stroke; when they pursue another, till the quiver is exhausted. If, which rarely happens, the wounded buffalo attacks the hunter, he evades his blow by the agility of his horse, which is trained for the combat with great dexterity. When they have killed the requisite number they collect their game, and the squaws and attendants come up from the rear and skin and dress the animals. Captain Clark killed ten buffalo, of which five only were brought to the fort; the rest, which could not be conveyed home, being seized by the Indians, among whom the custom is that whenever a buffalo is found dead without an arrow or any particular mark, he is the property of the finder; so that often a hunter secures scarcely any of the game he kills, if the arrow happens to fall off. Whatever is left out at night falls to the share of the wolves, who are the constant and numerous attendants of the buffalo. The river closed opposite the fort last night, [with ice] an inch and a half in thickness. In the morning the thermometer stood at 1° below zero. Three men were badly frost-bitten in consequence of their exposure.

*December 8th.* The thermometer stood at 12° below zero —that is, at 42° below the freezing- (*p.* 141) point ; the wind was from the northwest. Captain Lewis, with 15 men, went out to hunt buffalo, great numbers of which darkened the prairies for a considerable distance ; they did not return till after dark, having killed eight buffalo and one deer. The hunt was, however, very fatiguing, as they were obliged to make a circuit at the distance of more than seven miles ; the cold, too, was so excessive that the air was filled with icy particles resembling a fog; the snow was generally 6 or 8 inches deep and sometimes 18, in consequence of which two of the party were hurt by falls, and several had their feet frost-bitten.

*December 9th.* The wind was this day from the east, the thermometer at 7° above zero, and the sun shone clear. Two chiefs visited us, one in a sleigh drawn by a dog and loaded with meat.

*December 10th.* Captain Clark, who had gone out yesterday with 18 men, to bring in the meat we had killed the day before, and to continue the hunt, came in at twelve o'clock. After killing nine buffalo and preparing those already dead, he had spent a cold, disagreeable night on the snow, with no covering but a small blanket, sheltered by the hides of the buffalo they had killed. We observe large herds of buffalo crossing the river on the ice. The men who were frost-bitten are recovering, but the weather is still exceedingly cold, the wind being from the north and the thermometer at 10° and 11° below zero ; the rise of the river is one inch and a half.

*December 11th.* The weather is so intensely cold that we sent for all the hunters who had remained out with Captain

Clark's party, and they returned in the evening, several of them frost-bitten. The wind was from the north and the thermometer at sunrise stood at 21° below zero, the ice in the atmosphere being so thick as to render the weather hazy and give the appearance of two suns reflecting each other. The river continues at a stand. Pocapsahe [*sic*] made us a visit to-day.

(*p. 142*) *December 12th.*[35] The wind is still from the north, the thermometer being at sunrise 38° below zero. One of the Ahnahaways brought us down the half of an antelope killed near the fort. We had been informed that all these animals return to the Black mountains, but there are great numbers of them about us at this season which we might easily kill, were we not unwilling to venture out before our constitutions are hardened gradually to the climate. We measured the river on the ice, and find it 500 yards wide immediately opposite the fort.

*December 13th.* Last night was clear, and a very heavy frost covered the old snow; the thermometer at sunrise being 20° below zero, and followed by a fine day. The river falls.

*December 14th.* The morning was fine, and the weather having moderated so far that the mercury stood at zero, Captain Lewis went down with a party to hunt. They proceeded about 18 miles; but the buffalo having left the banks of the river they saw only two, which were so poor as not to be worth killing, and shot two deer. Notwithstanding the snow, we were visited by a large number of Mandans.

*December 15th.* Captain Lewis finding no game returned to the fort, hunting on both sides of the river, but with

[35] " I line my Gloves and have a Cap made of the Skin of the Louservia (Lynx) (or Wild Cat of the North) the fur near 3 inches long," Clark C 129. An interesting passage, one of the earliest in which *loup-cervier* was ever written in such a form, and also showing that Clark knew the Canada lynx, *Lynx canadensis*, generically and specifically. The Statistical View, 1807, once prints " lynx or louverin." The entry for this date also calls the antelope Cabra or Kokâ, and names as Mocassin Indians those heretofore called Maharhas or Shoes.

no success. The wind was from the north, the mercury at sunrise 8° degrees below zero, and the snow of last night an inch and a half in depth. The Indian chiefs continue to visit us to-day with presents of meat.

*December* 16*th.* The morning is clear and cold, the mercury at sunrise 22° below zero. A Mr. Haney,[36] with two other persons from the British establishment on the Assiniboin, arrived in six days with a letter from Mr. Charles Chabouilles, one of the Company, who with much politeness offered to render us any service in his power.[37]

*December* 17*th.* The weather to-day was colder than any we had yet experienced, the thermometer at sunrise being 45° below zero, and about eight o'clock it fell to 74° below

[36] Name in question. It is certainly not Haney in Clark C 132, where it is twice written Henny or Henry. The other gentleman named in the above paragraph is on the same page **Chaboillez**, in a very firm, heavy hand, which Clark often used when he wished to emphasize a name. The letter referred to was no doubt in answer to the one already quoted, p. 187 ; but I have never seen it.

[37] " The object of the visits we received from the N.W. Company was to ascertain our motives for visiting that country, and to gain information with respect to the change of Government [cession of Louisiana to the United States by the French]," is the shrewd remark of Gass, p. 65, this date.

The Hudson's Bay Company was originally chartered by Charles II. in 1670. In the winter of 1783-84, merchants of Montreal entered in partnership, and amalgamated a rival company in 1787. This was the birth of the famous Northwest Company, consisting of over 20 shareholders and employing 2,000 persons, controlling the fur trade from Montreal through all the regions of the Great Lakes, and thence to Athapasca and Great Slave, and even to the Pacific in British America. The great annual rendezvous of this system was at Fort William, near the Grand Portage of Lake Superior, where the commercial potentates of civilization met their factors, and where swarmed the mongrel legion of their dependants and retainers. Another British association was formed soon after, the Mackinaw, to work the country further south, on the headwaters of the Mississippi. To counteract this, the U. S. government, as early as 1796, sent rival Indian traders ; who, however, were no match for their competitors. About 1794, treaty with Great Britain had opened direct commerce between Canada and the United States. In 1807 Mr. John Jacob Astor embarked in the fur trade on his own account. But the Michilimackinac or Mackinaw corporation was too strong for him. The American Fur Company was incorporated by the State of New York in 1808 or 1809—this concern being practically Mr. Astor himself, who furnished a million of capital. In 1811, an arrangement was made by which Mr. Astor and certain parties of the Northwest Company bought out the Mackinaw,

(*p. 143*) the freezing-point. From Mr. Haney, who is a very sensible, intelligent man, we obtained much geographical information with regard to the country between the Missouri and Mississippi, and the various tribes of Sioux who inhabit it.

*December* 18*th.* The thermometer at sunrise was 32° below zero. The Indians had invited us yesterday to join their chase to-day, but the seven men whom we sent returned in consequence of the cold, which was so severe last night that we were obliged to have the sentinel relieved every half hour. The Northwest traders,[18] however, left us on their return home.

*December* 19*th.* The weather moderated and the river rose a little, so that we were enabled to continue the picketing of the fort. Notwithstanding the extreme cold, we observed the Indians at the village engaged in the open air at a game which resembled billiards more than anything we had seen, and which we inclined to suspect may have been acquired by ancient intercourse with the French of Canada. From the first to the second chief's lodge, a distance of about fifty yards, was covered with timber smoothed and joined so as to be as level as the floor of one of our houses, with a battery at the end to stop the rings. These rings were of clay-stone and flat like the checkers for draughts, and the sticks were about four feet long, with two short pieces at one end in the form of a mace, so fixed that the whole will slide along the board. Two men fix themselves at one end, each provided with a stick, and one

and merged that and the American into one called the Southwest Company ; by which means Mr. Astor acquired one-half of the property and interests which the Mackinaw held in the Indian country of the United States. The *status quo* was suspended by the war of 1812, and after the war the association was dissolved. (Irving's Astoria, *passim.*)

[38] "Messrs. Haney and La Roche," Clark C 133, which continues at this date : "Sent Jessomme to the Main Chief of the Mandans to know the cause of his detaining or takeing a horse of Chabonoe our big belly interpeter, which we found was thro' the rascality of one Lafrance a trader from the N. W. company who told this Chief that Chabonat owd. him a horse."

of them with a ring; they then run along the board, and
about halfway slide the sticks after the ring.

*December 20th.* The wind was from the N.W., the
weather moderate, the thermometer 24° above zero at sunrise. We availed ourselves of this change to picket the
fort near the river.

*December 21st.* The day was fine and warm, the wind
N.W. by W. The Indian who had been prevented a few
days ago from killing his wife came with both his wives to
the fort, and was very desirous of reconciling our interpreter,
a jeal- (*p. 144*) ousy against whom, on account of his wife's
taking refuge in his house, had been the cause of his ani-
mosity. A woman brought her child with an abscess in
the lower part of the back, and offered as much corn as
she could carry for some medicine; we administered it of
course very cheerfully.

*December 22d.* A number of squaws and men dressed
like squaws brought corn to trade for small articles with
the men. Among other things we procured two horns of
the animal called by the French [bélier des Montagnes
Rocheuses, or] the Rock [y] mountain sheep [*Ovis montana*],
and known to the Mandans by the name of ahsahta.[39]  The
animal itself is about the size of a small elk or large deer;
the horns winding like those of a ram, which they resemble
also in texture, though larger and thicker.

*December 23d.* The weather was fine and warm like that
of yesterday. We were again visited by crowds of Indians
of all descriptions, who came either to trade or from mere
curiosity. Among the rest Kagohami or Little Raven,
brought his wife and son loaded with corn, and she then
entertained us with a favorite Mandan dish, a mixture of
pumpkins,[40] beans, corn, and choke-cherries with the stones,

---

[39] " Ar-sar-ta," Clark C 135 ; elsewhere as in the text.  See note [13], p. 150.

[40] " A kittle of boiled Simnins, beens," etc., Clark C 136, using the name
common in the Southern States for summer squashes, and so working a *C* in
with the *S* that it is impossible to say which initial letter was meant to stand.
This is a word the proper spelling of which lexicographers dispute almost as

all boiled together in a kettle, and forming a composition by no means unpalatable.

*December 24th.* The day continued warm and pleasant, and the number of visitors became troublesome. As a present to three of the chiefs, we divided a fillet of sheep-skin, which we brought for sponging, into three pieces, each of two inches in width; they were delighted at the gift, which they deemed of equal value with a fine horse. We this day completed our fort, and the next morning being Christmas,

*Tuesday, December 25th,* we were awaked before day by a discharge of three platoons from the party. We had told the Indians not to visit us, as it was one of our great medicine days; so that the men remained at home and amused themselves in various ways, particularly with danc-ing, in which they take great pleasure. The American flag was hoisted (*p. 145*) for the first time in the fort; the best provisions we had were brought out, and this, with a little brandy, enabled them to pass the day in great festivity.[41]

*December 26th.* The weather is again temperate, but no Indians have come to see us. One of the Northwest traders, who came down to request the aid of our Minne-taree interpreters, informed us that a party of Minnetarees who had gone in pursuit of the Assiniboins who lately stole their horses had just returned. As is their custom, they came back in small detachments, the last of which brought home eight horses which they had captured or stolen from an Assiniboin camp on Mouse river.

*December 27th.* A little fine snow fell this morning, and the air was colder than yesterday, with a high northwest

much as they do *simitar*. Clark's genius led him to choose a form quite near *simnel*, which is probably the best, and certainly better than the usual dialectic variants, *cymlin* and *cymblin*.

[41] "I give them all a little Taffia," Clark C 137, meaning a ration of rum. It is interesting to find written in 1804, on the Upper Missouri, a Malay word which we get from the French by way of the West Indies. We call this liquor Jamaica. Taffia or tafia, spirit distilled from sugar or molasses, seems to be the origin of the familiar name for molasses candy, *taffy*. Compare *ratafia*.

wind. We were fortunate enough to have among our men a good blacksmith, whom we set to work to make a variety of articles. His operations seemed to surprise the Indians who came to see us, but nothing could equal their astonishment at the bellows, which they considered as very great medicine.

Having heretofore promised a more particular account of the Sioux, the following [42] may serve as a general outline of their history :

Almost the whole of that vast tract of country comprised between the Mississippi, the Red river of Lake Winnepeg, the Saskaskawan, and the Missouri, is loosely occupied by a great nation, whose primitive name is Darcota, but who are called Sioux by the French, Sues by the English. Their original seats were on the Mississippi, but they have gradually spread themselves abroad and become subdivided into numerous tribes. Of these, what may be considered as the Darcotas are the Mindawarcarton or Minowakanton, known to the French by the name of the Gens du Lac, or People of the Lake. Their residence is on both sides of the Mississippi near the falls of St. Anthony, and the probable number of their warriors about 300. Above them, on the St. Peter's river, (*p. 146*) is the Wahpatone, a smaller band of nearly 200 men ; and still further up the same river, below Yellow-wood river, are the Wahpatootas or Gens de Feuilles, an inferior band of not more than 100 men ; while the sources of the St. Peter's are occupied by the Sisatoones, a band consisting of about 200 warriors.

These bands rarely, if ever, approach the Missouri, which is occupied by their kinsmen, the Yanktons and the Tetons.

---

[42] What follows is but a slight sketch, which may be passed without comment, and might have been omitted without loss, as it adds scarcely anything to what has been already said : see p. 99 *seq.*, p. 128 *seq.*, and notes there. The fragment indicates, perhaps, a more extended notice which the explorers had intended to give, before they discovered that they had already exhausted their information. But we have a few additional words concerning the Assiniboins.

The Yanktons are of two tribes, those of the Plains, or rather of the North, a wandering race of about 500 men, who roam over the plains at the heads of the Jacques, the Sioux, and the Red river; and those of the South, who possess the country between the Jacques and Sioux rivers and the Desmoine. But the bands of Sioux most known on the Missouri are the Tetons. The first who are met on ascending the Missouri is the tribe called by the French the Tetons of the Boise Brule or Burntwood, who reside on both sides of the Missouri, about White and Teton rivers, and number 200 warriors. Above them on the Missouri are the Teton Okandandas, a band of 150 men living below the Chayenne river, between which and the Wetarhoo river is a third band, called Teton Minnakenozzo, of nearly 250 men; below the Warreconne is the fourth and last tribe of Tetons, of about 300 men, called Teton Saone. Northward of these, between the Assiniboin and the Missouri, are two bands of Assiniboins, one on Mouse river, of about 200 men, called Assiniboin Menatopa, the other, residing on both sides of White river, called by the French Gens des Feuilles, amounting to 250 men. Beyond these, a band of Assiniboins, of 450 men, called [by the French Gens des Grands Diables, or] the Big Devils, wander on the heads of Milk, Porcupine, and Martha's rivers; while still further to the north are seen two bands of the same nation, one of 500 and the other of 200, roving on the Saskaskawan. Those (*p. 147*) Assiniboins are recognized, by a similarity of language and by tradition, as descendants or seceders from the Sioux; though often at war they are still acknowledged as relations. The Sioux themselves, though scattered, meet annually on the Jacques those of the Missouri trading with those of the Mississippi.

# CHAPTER VI.

## WITH THE MANDANS: CONTINUED.

ECEMBER 28th. The wind continued high last night, the frost severe, and the snow drifting in great quantities through the plains.

*December 29th.* There was a frost last night nearly one-quarter of an inch in depth, which continued to fall till the sun had gained some height; the mercury at sunrise stood at 9° below zero ; there were a number of Indians at the fort in the course of the day.

*December 30th.* The weather was cold, and the thermometer 20° below zero. We killed one deer, and yesterday one of the men shot a wolf. The Indians brought corn, beans, and squashes, which they readily gave for getting their axes and kettles mended. In their general conduct during these visits they are honest, but will occasionally pilfer some small article.

*December 31st.* During the night there was a high wind which covered the ice with hillocks of mixed sand and snow. The day was however fine, and the Indians came in great numbers for the purpose of having their utensils repaired.

*Tuesday, January 1st,* 1805. The new year was welcomed by two shots from the swivel and a round of small-arms. The weather was cloudy but moderate ; the mercury, which at sunrise was at 18°, in the course of the day rose to 34° above zero ; toward evening it began to rain, and at night we (*p. 149*) had snow, the temperature for which is about zero. In the morning we permitted 16 men with their music to go up to the first village, where they delighted the whole tribe with their dances, particularly with the movements of one of the Frenchmen, who danced on his head.[1] In return they presented the dancers with several buffalo-robes and quanties of corn. We were desirous of showing this attention to the village, because they had received an impression that we had been wanting in regard for them, and because they had in consequence circulated inviduous comparisons between us and the northern traders. All these, however, they declared to Captain Clark, who visited them in the course of the morning, were made in jest. As Captain Clark was about leaving the village, two of their chiefs returned from a mission to the Grosventres or wandering[2]

---

[1] This statement startled Mr. Biddle, who catechized Captain Clark about it. He was doubtless so much relieved to find that the Frenchman danced on his hands, head downward, that he let it go into type.

[2] A distinction is here drawn between these " wandering " Minnetarees and those whom L. and C. for some reason regarded as Minnetarees proper. Clark C 142 has : " A large party of *Gross Ventres* who were on their way down from their camps 10 miles above to revenge on the *Shoe* tribe an injury," etc. Here it is also well to remark that we must always bear in mind the very broad line to be drawn between any of the " Minnetarees " or " Grosventres " who were sedentary on the Missouri, and those entirely different Indians whom L. and C. will later repeatedly term " Minnetarees of fort de prairie," or call by some equivalent expression. The case will come up again for treatment ; but here I may cite Matthews, p. 33 : " The name [Grosventres] was also applied to a tribe, totally distinct from these [Hidatsans] in language and origin, which lives some hundreds of miles west of Fort Berthold ; and the two nations are now distinguished from one another as Grosventres of the Missouri and Grosventres of the Prairie, names which would lead strangers to suppose that they were merely separate divisions of one tribe."

Minnetarees. These people were camped about ten miles above, and while there one of the Ahnahaways had stolen a Minnetaree girl. The whole nation immediately espoused the quarrel, and 150 of their warriors were marching down to revenge the insult on the Ahnahaways. The chief of that nation took the girl from the ravisher, and giving her to the Mandans requested their intercession. The messengers went out to meet the warriors, delivered the young damsel into the hands of her countrymen, smoked the pipe of peace with them, and were fortunate enough to avert their indignation and induce them to return. In the evening some of the men came to the fort and the rest slept in the village. Pocapsahe also visited us and brought some meat on his wife's back.

*January 2d.* It snowed last night. During this day the same scene of gayety was renewed at the second village, and all the men returned in the evening.[3]

*January 3d.* Last night it became very cold, and this morning we had some snow. Our hunters were sent out for buffalo, but the game had been frightened from the river by the Indians, so that they obtained only one. They however (*b. 150*) killed a hare and a wolf. Among the Indians who visited us was a Minnetaree who came to seek his wife. She had been much abused and came here for protection, but returned with him, as we had no authority to separate those whom even the Mandan rites had united.

*January 4th.* The morning was cloudy and warm, the mercury being 28° above zero; but toward evening the wind changed to northwest, and the weather became cold. We sent some hunters down the river, but they killed only one buffalo and a wolf. We received the visit of Kago-hami, who is very friendly, and to whom we gave a handkerchief and two files.

---

[3] " This day I discovered how the Indians keep their horses during the winter. In the day time they are permitted to run out and gather what they can ; and at night are brought into the lodges, with the natives themselves, and fed on cotton wood branches : and in this way are kept in tolerable case," Gass, p. 68.

*January 5th.*[4] We had high and boisterous winds last night and this morning. The Indians continue to purchase repairs with grain of different kinds. In the first village there has been a buffalo-dance for the last three nights, which has put them all into commotion, and the description which we received from those of the party who visited the village, and from other sources, is not a little ludicrous.

The buffalo-dance is an institution originally intended for the benefit of the old men, and practiced at their suggestion. When buffalo become scarce they send a man to harangue the village, declaring that the game is far off and that a feast is necessary to bring it back; if the village be disposed a day and place is named for the celebration. At the appointed hour the old men arrive and seat themselves cross-legged on skins, round a fire in the middle of the lodge, with a sort of doll or small image, dressed like a female, placed before them. The young men bring with them a platter of provisions, a pipe of tobacco, and their wives, whose dress on this occasion is only a robe or mantle loosely thrown round the body. On their arrival each youth selects the old man whom he means to distinguish by his favor, and spreads before him the provisions, after which he presents the pipe and smokes with him.

Mox senex vir simulacrum parvæ puellæ ostensit. Tunc egrediens cœtu, jecit (*p. 151*) effigium solo et superincumbens, senili ardore veneris complexit. Hoc est signum. Denique uxor e turba recessit, et jactu corporis, fovet amplexus viri solo recubante. Maritus appropinquans senex

---

[4] "I employ myself Drawing a Connection of the Contrey from what information I have received," *i. e.*, making a map on which should be represented, from Indian and other information, parts not charted from his own observations, in ascending the Missouri thus far. This is the very map which was sent to the President, Apr. 7th, 1805, was transmitted by Jefferson to Congress in his message of Feb. 19th, 1806, and was preserved in the archives of the War Department, but never published till Nov. 4th, 1887, when a much reduced copy appeared in *Science*. As draughted by Nicholas King, 1806, this is the map which is repeatedly cited in the present edition as Lewis' map of 1806, it being so legended, as will be seen from the full-sized photographic facsimile, now first published.

vir dejecto vultu, et honorem et dignitatem ejus conservare
amplexu uxoris illum oravit.   Forsitan imprimis ille refellit;
dehinc, maritus multis precibus, multis lacrymis, et multis
donis vehementer intercessit.   Tunc senex amator perculsus
misericordia, tot precibus, tot lacrymis, et tot donis, conju-
gali amplexu submisit.   Multum ille jactatus est, sed debilis
et effœtus senectute, frustra jactatus est.   Maritus interdum,
stans juxta, gaudet multum honore, et ejus dignitate sic
conservata.   Unus nostrum sodalium, multum alacrior et
potentior juventute, hac nocte honorem quatuor maritorum
custodivit.   [Anglicè, Clericus C 144, 145.]

*January 6th.*   A clear, cold morning with high wind.
We caught in a trap a large gray wolf, and last night
obtained in the same way a fox which had for some time
infested the neighborhood of the fort.   Only a few Indians
visited us to-day.

*January 7th.*   The weather was again clear and cold, with
a high northwest wind, and the thermometer at sunrise
22° below zero; the river fell an inch.   Shahaka, the Big
White chief, dined with us, and gave a connected sketch of
the country as far as the mountains.[5]

*January 8th.*   The wind was still from the northwest, the
day cold, and we received few Indians at the fort.   Besides
the buffalo-dance we have just described there is another
called the medicine-dance, an entertainment given by any
person desirous of doing honor to his medicine or genius.
He announces that on such a day he will sacrifice his
horses or other property, and invites the young females of
the village to assist in rendering homage to his medicine;
all the inhabitants may join in the solemnity, which is performed in the open plain and by daylight, but the dance
is reserved for the virgins, or at least the unmarried females,
who disdain the incumbrance or the ornament of dress.

[5] " As far as the high [Rocky] mountains on the south side of the River
Rejone [Roche-jaune, Yellowstone] . . . I continue to Draw a connected plott
from the information of Traders, Indians & my own observations and ideas,"
Clark C 146.

The feast (*p. 152*) is opened by devoting the goods of the master of the feast to his medicine, which is represented by a head of the animal itself, or by a medicine-bag if the deity be an invisible being. The young women then begin the dance, in the intervals of which each will prostrate herself before the assembly to challenge or reward the boldness of the youth, who are often tempted by feeling, or the hope of distinction, to achieve the adventure.

*January 9th.* The weather is cold, the thermometer at sunrise 21° below zero. Kagohami breakfasted with us, and Captain Clark with three or four men accompanied him and a party of Indians to hunt, in which they were so fortunate as to kill a number of buffalo. But they were incommoded by snow, by high and squally winds, and by extreme cold. Several of the Indians came to the fort nearly frozen; others are missing, and we are uneasy for one of our men, who was separated from the rest during the chase, and has not returned.

*January 10th.* This morning, however, he came back, just as we were sending out five men in search of him. The night had been excessively cold; this morning at sunrise the mercury stood at 40° below zero, or 72° below the freezing-point. He had, however, made a fire and kept himself tolerably warm. A young Indian, about 13 years of age, also came in soon after. His father, who came last night to inquire after him very anxiously, had sent him in the afternoon to the fort; he was overtaken by the night, and was obliged to sleep on the snow with no covering except a pair of antelope-skin moccasins and leggings, and a buffalo-robe. His feet being frozen, we put them into cold water, and gave him every attention in our power. About the same time an Indian who had also been missing returned to the fort. Although his dress was very thin, and he had slept on the snow without a fire, he had not suffered the slightest inconvenience. We have indeed observed that these Indians support the rigors of the season in a way which we had hitherto thought (*p. 153*) impossible. A more pleasing reflection occurred at seeing the warm interest which the situation of these two persons had excited in the village. The boy had been a prisoner and adopted from charity, yet the distress of the father proved that he felt for him the tenderest affection. The man was a person of no distinction, yet the whole village was full of anxiety for his safety, and when they came to us, borrowed a sleigh to bring them home with ease, if they survived, or to carry their bodies, if they had perished.

*January* 11*th*. We dispatched three hunters to join the same number whom we had sent below about seven miles to hunt elk. Like that of yesterday, the weather to-day was cold and clear, the thermometer standing at 38° below zero. Poscopsahe and Shotahawrora visited us, and passed the night at the fort.

*January* 12*th*. The weather continues very cold, the mercury at sunrise being 20° below zero. Three of the hunters returned, having killed three elk.

*January* 13*th*. We have a continuation of clear weather and the cold has increased, the mercury having sunk to 34° below zero. Nearly one-half of the Mandan nation passed down the river to hunt for several days. In these excursions, men, women, and children, with their dogs, all leave the village together, and after discovering a spot convenient for the game, fix their tents; all the family bear their part in the labor, and the game is equally divided among the families of the tribe. When a single hunter returns from the chase with more than is necessary for his own immediate consumption, the neighbors are entitled by custom to a share of it; they do not, however, ask for it, but send a squaw, who, without saying anything, sits down by the door of the lodge till the master understands the hint and gives her gratuitously a part for her family. Chaboneau, who with one man had gone to some lodges of Minnetarees near Turtle mountain [on the Little Mo. R.], returned with their faces much frost-bitten. They had (*p. 154*) been about 90 miles distant, and procured from the inhabitants some meat and grease, with which they loaded the horses.   He informs us that the agents of the Hudson's Bay Company at that place had been endeavoring to make unfavorable impressions with regard to us on the mind of the great chief, and that the Northwest Company intended building a fort there.   The great chief had in consequence spoken slightingly of the Americans, but said that if we would give him our great flag he would come and see us.

*January* 14*th.*   The Mandans continued to pass down the river on their hunting-party, and were joined by six of our men [Sergeant Pryor and five privates].   One of those sent on Thursday returned with information that one of his companions [Whitehouse] had his feet so badly frost-bitten that he could not walk home.   In their excursion they had killed a buffalo, a wolf, two porcupines, and a white hare.[6]   The weather was more moderate to-day, the mercury being at 16° below zero, and the wind from the S.E.   We had, however, some snow, after which it remained cloudy.

*January* 15*th.*   The morning is much warmer than yesterday, and the snow begins to melt, though the wind, after being for some time from the S.E., suddenly shifted to the N.W.   Between 12 and 3 o'clock a. m. there was a total eclipse of the moon, from which we obtained a part of the observation[7] necessary for ascertaining the longitude.

We were visited by four of the most distinguished men of the Minnetarees, to whom we showed marked attentions, as we knew that they had been taught to entertain strong prejudices against us ; these we succeeded so well in removing, that when in the morning,

*January* 16*th,* about 30 Mandans, among whom six were chiefs, came to see us, the Minnetarees reproached them with their falsehoods, declaring that they were bad men and ought to hide themselves.   They had told the Minnetarees that we would kill them if they came to the fort ; yet on

[6] *Lepus campestris,* which in this latitude turns white in winter, like *L. americanus,* the American varying hare.

[7] Total obscuration at $12^h\ 57^m\ 54^s$ ; end of do., $1^h\ 44^s$ ; end of eclipse, $2^h\ 39^m\ 10^s$, Clark C 152.

the contrary they had spent a night there and been (*p. 155*) treated with kindness by the whites, who had smoked with them and danced for their amusement. Kagohami visited us and brought us a little corn, and soon afterward one of the first war-chiefs of the Minnetarees came, accompanied by his squaw, a handsome woman, whom he was desirous we should use during the night. He favored us with a more acceptable present, a draft of the Missouri in his manner, and informed us of his intention to go to war in the spring against the Snake Indians. We advised him to reflect seriously before he committed the peace of his nation to the hazard of war; to look back on the numerous nations whom war had destroyed; that if he wished his nation to be happy, he should cultivate peace and intercourse with all his neighbors, by which means they would procure more horses and increase in numbers; and that if he went to war he would displease his great father, the President, and forfeit his protection. We added that we had spoken thus to all the tribes whom we had met; that they had all opened their ears, and that the President would compel those who did not voluntarily listen to his advice. Although a young man of only 26 years of age, this discourse seemed to strike him. He observed that if it would be displeasing to us he would not go to war, since he had horses enough, and that he would advise all the nation to remain at home until we had seen the Snake Indians, and discovered whether their intentions were pacific. The party who went down with the horse for the man who was frost-bitten returned, and we are glad to find his complaint not so serious.

*January* 17*th*. The day was very windy from the north; the morning clear and cold, the thermometer at sunrise being at zero. We had several Indians with us.

*January* 18*th*. The weather is fine and moderate. Messrs. Laroche and M'Kenzie, two of the Northwest Company's traders, visited us with some of the Minnetarees. In the afternoon two of our hunters returned, having killed four [deer, four] wolves and a blaireau [badger].

(*p. 156*) *January 19th.* Another cloudy day. The two traders set out on their return, and we sent two men with the horses 30 miles below to the hunting-camp.

*January 20th.* The day fair and cold. A number of Indians visit us with corn to exchange for articles and to pay for repairs to their household utensils.[8]

*January 21st.* The weather was fine and moderate. The hunters all returned, having killed during their absence three elk, four deer, two porcupines, a fox, and a hare.

*January 22d.* The cold having moderated and the day being pleasant, we attempted to cut the boats out of the ice; but at the distance of eight inches came to water, under which the ice became three feet thick, so that we were obliged to desist.

*January 23d.* The cold weather returned, the mercury having sunk 2° below zero, and the snow fell four inches deep.

*January 24th.* The day was colder than any we have had lately, the thermometer being at 12° below zero. The hunters whom we sent out returned unsuccessful, and the rest were occupied in cutting wood to make charcoal.

*January 25th.* The thermometer was at 25° below zero, the wind from the N.W. and the day fair, so that the men were employed in preparing coal and cutting the boats out of the ice. A band of Assiniboins headed by their chief, called by the French ["Fils de Petit Veau," Clark C 156, or] Son of the Little Calf, have arrived at the villages.

*January 26th.* A fine warm day. A number of Indians

---

[8] " I went up with one of the men to the villages. They treated us friendly and gave us victuals. After we were done eating they presented a bowlful to a buffaloe head, saying 'eat that.' Their superstitious credulity is so great that they believe by using the head well the living buffaloe will come and that they will get a supply of meat," Gass, p. 70.

There was trouble in the little garrison to-day. On the 19th "Jussome's squar " left him, and on the 20th Clark C 155 explains : " A misunderstanding took place between the two inturpeters on account of their squars, one of the squars of Shabowner being sick, I ordered my servent to give her some froot stewed and tee at dift. times which was the cause of the misundrst'd."

dine with us, and one of our men is attacked with a violent
pleurisy.

*January 27th.* Another warm and pleasant day. We
again attempted to get the boat out of the ice. The man
who has the pleurisy was blooded and sweated, and we were
forced to take off the toes of the young Indian who was
frost-bitten some time since. Our interpreter [" Shabonoe "]
returned from the villages, bringing with him three of Mr.
Laroche's horses, which he had sent in order to keep them
out of the way of the Assiniboins. who are very much disposed to steal, and who have just returned to their camp.

(*p. 157*) *January 28th.* The weather to-day is clear and
cold. We were obliged to abandon the plan of cutting the
boat through the ice, and therefore made another attempt
the next day,

*January 29th,* by heating a quantity of stones so as to
warm the water in the boat and thaw the surrounding ice.
But in this too we were disappointed, as all the stones, on
being put into the fire, cracked into pieces. The weather
is warm and pleasant; the man with the pleurisy is recovering.

*January 30th.* The morning was fair, but afterward
became cloudy. Mr. Laroche, the trader from the Northwest Company, paid us a visit, in hopes of being able to
accompany us on our journey westward ; but this proposal
we thought it best to decline.

*January 31st.* It snowed last night and the morning is
cold and disagreeable, with a high wind from the northwest. We sent five hunters down the river. Another man
[Drewyer] is taken with the pleurisy.

*Friday, February 1st.* A cold, windy day. Our hunters
returned, having killed only one deer. One of the Minnetaree war-chiefs, a young man named Maubuksheaho-
keah or Seeing Snake, came to see us and procure a war-
hatchet. He also requested that we would suffer him to
go to war against the Sioux and Ricaras, who had killed a
Mandan some time ago; this we refused, for reasons which

we explained to him.   He acknowledged that we were right, and promised to open his ears to our counsels.

*February 2d.*   The day is fine.   Another deer was killed. Mr. Laroche, who has been very anxious to go with us, left the fort to-day, and one of the squaws of the Minnetaree interpreter is taken ill.

*February 3d.*[9]   The weather is again pleasant.   Disappointed in all our efforts to get the boats free, we occupied ourselves in making iron spikes so as to prize them up by means of long poles.

*February 4th.*   The morning fair and cold, the mercury at sunrise being 18° below zero, and the wind from the northwest.   (*p. 158*) The stock of meat which we had procured in November and December being now nearly exhausted, it became necessary to renew our supply.   Captain Clark therefore took 18 men,[10] and with two sleighs and three horses descended the river for the purpose of hunting, as the buffalo have disappeared from our neighborhood, and the Indians themselves are suffering for want of meat.   Two deer were killed [by Shields] to-day, but they were very lean.

*February 5th.*   A pleasant, fair morning, with the wind from northwest.   A number of the Indians come with corn for the blacksmith, who being now provided with coal has

[9] At this date in the Mandan Codex the hand changes.   Captain Clark is going away to hunt, and Captain Lewis writes the journal to Feb. 12th inclusive.   Feb. 3d has a long account of the attempts to get the boats out of the ice.

[10] Sixteen of the soldiers, and two Frenchmen, Lewis C 162.

Gass was on this trip, which he thus summarizes, p. 71 : " 4th.   A fine day. Captain Clark and 18 men went down the river to hunt.   We proceeded on 20 miles and could see no game.   5th.   We proceeded on to some Indian camps and there we killed three deer.   The next day we went on to more Indian camps and killed some deer.   On the 7th. we camped in a bottom on the south side of the Missouri and next day turned out to hunt.   We killed 10 elk and 18 deer and remained there all night.   On the 9th. we built a pen to secure our game from the wolves, which are very numerous here ; and in the evening went further down and encamped.   The next morning we set out on our return towards the fort ; and killed some elk and deer on our way.   On the 12th. we arrived at the fort ; and found that one of our interpreter's wives [Sacajawea] had in our absence made an addition to our number."

become one of our greatest resources for procuring grain. They seem particularly attached to a battle-ax, of a very inconvenient figure. It is made wholly of iron, the blade extremely thin and from seven to nine inches long; it is sharp at the point and five or six inches on each side, whence the edges converge toward the eye, which is circular and about an inch in diameter, the blade itself being not more than an inch wide; the handle is straight, and 12 or 15 inches long; the whole weighs about a pound. By way of ornament, the blade is perforated with several circular holes. The length of the blade, compared with the shortness of the handle, renders it a weapon of very little strength, particularly as it is always used on horseback. There is still, however, another form which is even worse, the same sort of handle being fixed to a blade resembling an espontoon.[11]

*February* 6*th*. The morning was fair and pleasant, the wind N.W. A number of Indian chiefs visited us, but withdrew after we had smoked with them, contrary to their custom; for, after being once introduced into our apartment, they are fond of lounging about during the remainder of the day. One of the men killed three antelopes. Our blacksmith has his time completely occupied, so great is the demand for utensils of different kinds. The Indians are particularly fond of sheet-iron, out of which they form points for arrows and instruments for scraping hides; and when (*p. 159*) the blacksmith cut up an old cambouse [12] of

---

[11] *Espontoon* or *esponton* is a rare and practically obsolete form of *spontoon*, a word itself now little used. The implement meant is the half-pike, a sort of halberd formerly used by certain officers of the British army. Lewis C 165 gives a neat figure of the Mandan implement, which is fortunate, as the text is not clear. The blade is 12 or 15 inches long, set at right angles in a handle of the same length; the shape of the blade, viewed flat, is a narrow lozenge (like the diamond at cards), sharp at the point, the other end eyed to receive the handle; it is pierced with four holes set in the same diamond figure, and the slant of the two sides of the diamond next to the eyed end results in part from nicking off from each edge a strip of the metal and curling this strip backward.

[12] " Sheet iron callaboos," interlined " camboose, stove," Lewis C 166. *Camboose* and *cambouse* are rare forms of *caboose*, and this from the Dutch name of

metal, we obtained, for every piece of four inches square, seven or eight gallons of corn from the Indians, who were delighted at the exchange.

*February 7th.* The morning was fair and much warmer than for some days, the thermometer being at 18° above zero, and the wind from the S.E. A number of Indians continue to visit us; but learning that the interpreter's squaws had been accustomed to unbar the gate during the night, we ordered a lock put on it, and that no Indian should remain in the fort all night, nor any person be admitted during the hours when the gate is closed—that is, from sunset to sunrise.

*February 8th.* A fair, pleasant morning, with S.E. winds. Pocopsahe came down to the fort with a bow, and apologized for not having finished a shield which he had promised Captain Lewis, and which the weather had prevented him from completing.[13] This chief possesses more firmness, intelligence, and integrity than any Indian of this country, and he might be rendered highly serviceable in our attempts to civilize the nation. He mentioned that the Mandans are very much in want of meat, and that he himself had not tasted any for several days. To this distress they are often reduced by their own improvidence, or by their unhappy situation. Their principal article of food is buffalo-meat, their corn, beans, and other grain being reserved for summer, or as a last resource against what they constantly dread, an attack from the Sioux, who drive off the game and confine them to their villages. The same fear also prevents their going out to hunt in small parties to relieve their occasional wants, so that the buffalo is generally obtained in large quantities and wasted by carelessness.

a ship's galley, or cook's room aboard a vessel; but it is not related to *cala-boose*, which latter word is supposed to be of Arabic derivation, and means a slave-pen. The article which proved so valuable a resource was simply an old sheet iron cooking-stove, which had been burnt out in ascending the Missouri.

[13] " I gave him som small shot 6 fishing-hooks and 2 yards of ribbon his squaw also presented me with 2 pair of mockersons for which in return I gave a small lookingglass and a couple of nedles," Lewis C 167.

*February 9th.*[14]   The morning was fair and pleasant, the wind from the S.E.  Mr. M'Kenzie, from the Northwest Company's establishment, visited us.

*Sunday, February 10th.*  A slight snow fell in the course of the night, the morning was cloudy, and the northwest wind blew so (*p. 160*) high that although the thermometer was 18° above zero, the day was cooler than yesterday, when it was only 10° above the same point.  Mr. M'Kenzie left us, and Chaboneau returned with the information that our horses loaded with meat were below, but could not cross the ice, not being shod.

*February 11th.*  We sent down a party with sleds, to relieve the horses from their loads ; the weather fair and cold, with a N.W. wind.  About five o'clock one of the wives of Chaboneau was delivered of a boy ;[15] this being her first child she was suffering considerably, when Mr. Jessaume told Captain Lewis that he had frequently administered to persons in her situation a small dose of the rattle of the rattlesnake, which had never failed to hasten the delivery.  Having some of the rattle, Captain Lewis gave it to Mr. Jessaume, who crumbled two of the rings of it between his fingers, and mixing it with a small quantity of water gave it to her.  What effect it may really have had it might be difficult to determine, but Captain Lewis was informed that she had not taken it more than ten minutes before the delivery took place.

*February 12th.*  The morning is fair though cold, the mercury being 14° below zero, the wind from the S.E.  About four o'clock the horses were brought in much fatigued ; on giving them meal bran moistened with water they would

[14] " This evening a man by the name of [Thomas P.] Howard whom I had given permission to go [to] the Mandane village returned after the gate was shut and reather than call to the guard to have it opened scaled the works . . . Howard I had comitted to the care of the guard with a determineation to have him tryed by a Courtmartial for this offence.  This man is an old soldier which still hightens this offince," Lewis C 168.

[15] " A fine boy," Lewis C 170 says of Sacajawea's baby.   This little volunteer recruit joined the Expedition, and was brought back safe from the Pacific coast by one of the best of mothers.

not eat it, but preferred the bark of the cottonwood, which, as already observed, forms their principal food during the winter. The horses of the Mandans are so often stolen by the Sioux, Ricaras, and Assiniboins, that the invariable rule now is to put the horses every night in the same lodge with the family. In the summer they ramble on the plains in the vicinity of the camp and feed on the grass, but during cold weather the squaws cut down the cottonwood trees as they are wanted, and the horses feed on the boughs and bark of the tender branches, which are also brought into the lodges at night and placed near them. These animals are very severely treated; for whole days they are pursuing the buffalo, or burdened with the fruits of the chase, during which (*p. 161*) they scarcely ever taste food, and at night return to a scanty allowance of wood; yet the spirit of this valuable animal sustains him through all these difficulties, and he is rarely deficient either in flesh or vigor.

*February* 13*th*.[16]   The morning was cloudy, the thermometer at 2° below zero, the wind from the southeast. Captain Clark returned last evening with all his hunting party. During their excursion they had killed 40 deer, 3 buffalo, and 16 elk; but most of the game was too lean for use, and the wolves, who regard whatever lies out at night as their own, had appropriated a large part of it. When he left the fort on the 4*th* instant, he descended on the ice 22 miles to New Mandan island, near some of the old villages, and camped, having killed nothing, and being therefore without food for the night.

Early on the 5*th*, the hunters went out and killed two buffalo and a deer, but the last only could be used, the others being too lean. After breakfast they proceeded down to an Indian lodge, and hunted during the day. The next morning, the 6*th*, they camped 44 miles from the fort on a sand-point near the mouth of a creek on the south-

[16] Beginning in Lewis' hand, C 173, but continued by Clark, who enters at this date the following account of his hunting-trip, C 174-77, greatly abridged in the text, and then resumes the regular order of the codex.

west side, which they call Hunting creek, and during this
and the following day hunted through all the adjoining
plains with much success, having killed a number of deer
and elk. On the *8th*, the best of the meat was sent by the
horses to the fort; such parts of the remainder as were fit
for use were brought to a point of the river three miles
below, and after the bones were taken out, were secured in
pens built of logs, so as to keep off the wolves, ravens, and
magpies, which are very numerous, and constantly disappoint the hunter of his prey; they then went to the low
grounds near the Chisshetaw [Heart] river, where they
camped, but saw nothing except some wolves on the hills,
and a number of buffalo too poor to be worth hunting. The
next morning, the *9th*, as there was no game and it would
have been inconvenient to send back 60 miles to the fort,
they returned up the river; (*p. 162*) for three days they
hunted along the banks and plains, and reached the fort in
the evening of the *12th*, much fatigued, having walked 30
miles that day on the ice, and through the snow in many
places knee-deep, their moccasins too being nearly worn
out. The only game which they saw, besides what is
mentioned, was some grouse on the sand-bars in the river.

*February* 14*th*. Last night the snow fell three inches deep;
the day was, however, fine. Four men were dispatched
with sleds and three horses to bring up the meat which had
been collected by the hunters. They returned, however,
with the intelligence that about 21 miles below the fort a
party of upward of 100 men, whom they supposed to be
Sioux, rushed on them, cut the traces of the sleds, and
carried off two of the horses, the third being given up by
intercession of an Indian [17] who seemed to possess some
authority over them; they also took away two of the men's

---

[17] " Probably more thro' fear of himself or some of the Indians being killed
by our men who were not disposed to be Robed of all they had tamely," Clark
C 178. This party was led by George Drewyer, the best hunter and shot of all
the men. But four men had no show whatever against " 105 " Indians, and
were lucky to get off alive.

knives and a tomahawk, which last, however, they returned. We sent up to the Mandans to inform them of it, and to know whether any of them would join a party which intended to pursue the robbers in the morning. About twelve o'clock two of their chiefs came down and said that all the young men were out hunting, and that there were few guns in the village. Several Indians, however, armed, some with bows and arrows, some with spears and battle-axes, and two with fusils,[18] accompanied Captain Lewis, who set out,

*February* 15*th*, at sunrise, with 24 men. The morning was fine and cool, the thermometer being at 16° below zero. In the course of the day one of the Mandan chiefs returned from Captain Lewis' party, his eyesight having become so bad that he could not proceed. At this season of the year the reflection from the ice and snow is so intense as to occasion almost total blindness. This complaint is very common ; the general remedy is to sweat the part affected by holding the face over a hot stone, and receiving the fumes from snow thrown on it. A large red fox [*Vulpes macrurus*] was killed to-day.

(*p. 163*) *February* 16*th*. The morning was warm, the mercury at 32° above zero, the weather cloudy. Several of the Indians who went with Captain Lewis returned, as did also one of our men [Howard], whose feet had been frost-bitten.

*February* 17*th*. The weather continued as yesterday, though in the afternoon it became fair. Shotawhorora and his son came to see us, with about 30 pounds of dried buffalo meat and some tallow.

*February* 18*th*. The morning was cloudy with some snow, but in the latter part of the day it cleared up. Mr. M'Kenzie, who had spent yesterday at the fort, now left us. Our stock of meat is exhausted, so that we must confine ourselves to vegetable diet, at least till the return of the party. For this, however, we are at no loss, since both on this and the following day,

---

[18] "Fuzees," Clark C 179 ; old-fashioned flint-lock muskets.

*February* 19*th*, our blacksmith got large quantities of corn from the Indians, who came in great numbers to see us. The weather was fair and warm, the wind from the south.

*February* 20*th*. The day was delightfully fine; the mercury being at sunrise 2°, and in the course of the day 22°, above zero, the wind southerly. Kagohami came down to see us early. His village is afflicted by the death of one of their eldest men, who from his account to us must have seen 120 winters. Just as he was dying, he requested his grandchildren to dress him in his best robe when he was dead, and then carry him on a hill and seat him on a stone, with his face down the river toward their old villages, that he might go straight to his brother, who had passed before him to the ancient village underground. We have seen a number of Mandans who have lived to a great age; chiefly, however, the men, whose robust exercises fortify the body, while the laborious occupations of the women shorten their existence.

*February* 21*st*. We had a continuation of the same pleasant weather. Oheenaw and Shahaka came down to see us, and mentioned that several of their countrymen had (*p. 164*) gone to consult their medicine-stone as to the prospects for the following year. This medicine-stone is the great oracle of the Mandans, and whatever it announces is believed with implicit confidence. Every spring, and on some occasions during the summer, a deputation visits the sacred spot, where there is a thick porous stone 20 feet in circumference, with a smooth surface. Having reached the place, the ceremony of smoking to it is performed by the deputies, who alternately take a whiff themselves and then present the pipe to the stone; after this they retire to an adjoining wood for the night, during which it may be safely presumed that all the embassy do not sleep; and in the morning they read the destinies of the nation in the white marks on the stone, which those who made them are at no loss to decipher. The Minnetarees have a stone of a similar kind, which has the same influence over the nation.[19]

[19] On the subject of the Memahopa, or Minnetaree holy-stone, see Say in

Captain Lewis returned from his excursion in pursuit of the Indians. On reaching the place where the Sioux had stolen our horses, they found only one sled, and several pairs of moccasins which were recognized to be those of the Sioux. The party then followed the Indian tracks till they reached two old lodges where they slept, and the next morning pursued the course of the river till 'they reached some Indian camps, where Captain Clark passed the night some time ago, and which the Sioux had now set on fire, leaving a little corn near the place in order to induce a belief that they were Ricaras. From this point the Sioux tracks left the river abruptly and crossed into the plains; but perceiving that there was no chance of overtaking them, Captain Lewis went down to the pen where Captain Clark had left some meat, which he found untouched by the Indians. He then hunted in the low grounds on the river, till he returned with about 3,000 pounds of meat, some drawn on a sled by 15 of the men, and the rest on horseback; having killed 36 deer, 14 elk, and one wolf.

(*p.* 165) *February 22d.* The morning was cloudy and a little snow fell, but in the afternoon the weather became fair. We were visited by a number of Indians, among whom was Shotawhorora, a chief of much consideration among the Mandans, although by birth a Ricara.

*February 23d.* The day is warm and pleasant. Having worked industriously yesterday and all this morning, we were enabled to disengage one of the periogues and haul it on shore, and also nearly to cut out the second. The father of the boy whose foot had been so badly frozen, and whom we had now cured, came to-day and carried him home in a sleigh.

*February 24th.* The weather is again fine. We succeeded in loosening the second periogue and barge,[2]

---

Long's Exp., I. 1823, London ed., pp. 252, 253, where L. and C. are cited. See also Matthews, p. 50, where he renders Hidatsan Mihopash, and Mandan Mihopinish.

[20] "With the assistance of great prises we lousened her, and turned the second perogue up on the ice, ready to draw out, on lousening the boat from

though we found a leak in the latter. The whole of the next day,

*February 25th,* we were occupied in drawing up the boats on the bank. The smallest one we carried there with no difficulty, but the barge was too heavy for our elk-skin ropes, which constantly broke. We were visited by Orupsehara or Black Moccasin, and several other chiefs, who brought us presents of meat on the backs of their squaws, and one of the Minnetarees requested and obtained permission for himself and his two wives to remain all night in the fort. The day was exceedingly pleasant.

*February 26th.* The weather is again fine. By great labor during the day we got all the boats on the bank by sunset—an operation which attracted a great number of Indians to the fort.

*February 27th.* The weather continues fine. All of us were employed in preparing tools to build boats for our voyage, as we find that small periogues will be much more convenient than the barge in ascending the Missouri.

*February 28th.* The day is clear and pleasant. Sixteen men were sent out to examine the country for trees suitable for boats, and were successful in finding them. Two of the Northwest Company's traders arrived with letters. They had (*p.* 166) likewise a root[21] which is used for the cure of persons bitten by mad dogs, snakes, and other venomous animals. It is found on high grounds and the sides of hills; the mode of using it is to scarify the wound and apply to it an inch or more of the chewed or pounded root, which is to be renewed twice a day; the patient must not, however, chew or swallow any of the root, as an inward application might be rather injurious than beneficial.

the ice some of the corking [calking] drew out which caused her to Leake for a few minits untill we Descovered the Leake & stoped it," Clark C 185.

[21] " Root and top of a plant, presented by Mr. Haney, for the Cure of Mad Dogs, Snakes &c.," Clark C 187. But what was the specific for these afflicted creatures ? The relation is universal tradition in the west ; I have heard it around the camp-fire from the British to the Mexican boundary ; and everybody knows the plant, except the botanists. On primitive Paracelsian principles, it should be the rattle-box, or rattle-wort, a species of *Crotalaria,* whose ripe

Mr. Gravelines, with two Frenchmen and two Indians, arrived from the Ricara nation, with letters from Mr. Anthony Tabeau. This last gentleman informs us that the Ricaras express their determination to follow our advice to remain at peace with the Mandans and Minnetarees, whom they are desirous of visiting; they also wish to know whether these nations would permit the Ricaras to settle near them and form a league against their common enemies, the Sioux. On mentioning this to the Mandans they agreed to it, observing that they always desired to cultivate friendship with the Ricaras, and that the Ahnahaways and Minnetarees have the same friendly views.

Mr. Gravelines states that the band of Tetons whom we had seen was well-disposed toward us, owing to the influence of their chief, Black Buffalo ; but that the three upper bands of Tetons, with the Sisatoons and the Yanktons of the North, mean soon to attack the Indians in this quarter, with a resolution to put to death every white man they encounter. Moreover, that Mr. Cameron of St. Peter's has armed the Sioux against the Chippeways, who have lately put to death three of his men. The men who had stolen our horses we found to be all Sioux, who after com-

---

seeds rattle in hollow pods, and should therefore be good for rattlesnake-bites ; or one of the grape-ferns, *Botrychium virginianum*, whose fruit resembles somewhat the rattles of those reptiles. There are certain orchids, as *Goodyera repens*, called rattlesnake-plantain. The fleabane, baneberry, or black cohosh, *Cimicifuga racemosa*, is a rattlesnake-herb. Some rattlesnake-masters are eupatoriaceous composite plants of the genus *Liatris*, as *L. scariosa*, *L. squarrosa*, and others, called button-snakeroot. Other composites, related to chicory and lettuce, are rattlesnake-roots, as *Prenanthes serpentaria*, in high popular repute for snake-bites, and cancers too. Yet another rattlesnake-weed of the order *Compositæ* is *Hieracium venenosum*, of reputed medicinal virtues. In the West, however, if you should require your old scout or trapper to produce you a genuine "rattlesnake-master," it would probably prove to be a leguminous plant of the genus *Astragalus*, or a related genus, and he would be likely to call it by the Spanish name golondrina. There is no natural reason why the vegetable kingdom should not afford an antidote to certain animal poisons, nor any reason why only one plant should possess such properties ; and I doubt that the belief would have become so universal without some basis of fact.

mitting the outrage went to the Ricara village, where they said that they had hesitated about killing our men who were with the horses, but that in future they would put to death any of us they could, as we were "bad medicines" and deserved to be killed. The Ricaras were displeased at their conduct, and (*p. 167*) refused to give them anything to eat, which is deemed the greatest act of hostility, short of actual violence.

*Friday, March 1st*, 1805. The day is fine and the whole party is engaged, some in making ropes and periogues, others in burning coal and making battle-axes to sell for corn.[22]

*March 2d.* Mr. Laroche,[23] one of the Northwest Company's traders, has just arrived with merchandise from the British establishments on the Assiniboin. The day is fine, and the river begins to break up in some places, the mercury being between 28° and 36° above zero, and the wind from the N.E. We were visited by several Indians.

*March 3d.* The weather pleasant, the wind from the E., with clouds ; in the afternoon the clouds disappeared and the wind came from the N.W. The men are all employed in preparing the boats ; we are visited by Poscapsahe and

---

[22] The main occupation of the month of March seems to have been making canoes to resume the voyage. Gass says, p. 73, that the party of 16 who went on Feb. 28th, about six miles up the river, camped out there till six canoes were made. "On the 20th. and 21st. we carried them to the river about a mile and a half distant :  There I remained with two men to finish them, and to take care of them, until the 26th, when some men came up from the fort, and we put the canoes into the water. As the river had risen there was some water between the ice and the shore. We got three of them safe to the fort ; but the ice breaking before the other three got down, so filled the channel, that we were obliged to carry them the rest of the way by land. On the 27th we put one of the canoes into the water to ascertain what weight they would carry. We found they would not carry as much as was expected, and Captain Lewis agreed to take a large periogue along. The remainder of the month we were employed in preparing our craft for a renewal of our voyage."

[23] "Mr. La Rocque, a Clerk of the NW Company," Clark C 189, who informed them that the Northwest and "X. Y." companies had lately joined, and that Mr. M'Tavish, of Montreal, the head of the former company, was dead. "X. Y." was the cipher name of a certain rival company.

several other Indians with corn.    A flock of ducks passed up the river to-day.

*March 4th.*  A cloudy morning with N.W. wind, the latter part of the day clear.  We had again some Indian visitors with a small present of meat.  The Assiniboins, who a few days since visited the Mandans, returned and attempted to take horses from the Minnetarees, who fired on them ; a circumstance which may occasion some disturbance between the two nations.

*March 5th.*  About four o'clock in the morning there was a slight fall of snow, but the day became clear and pleasant, with the mercury 40° above zero.  We sent down an Indian and a Frenchman to the Ricara villages, with a letter to Mr. Tabeau [Tabbou, Clark C 190].

*March 6th.*  The day was cloudy, and smoky in consequence of the burning of the plains by the Minnetarees ; they have set all the neighboring country on fire in order to obtain an early crop of grass which may answer for the consumption of their horses, and also as an inducement for the buffalo and other game to visit it.  The horses stolen two days ago by the Assiniboins have been returned to the (*p. 168*) Minnetarees.  Ohhaw,[24] second chief of the lower Minnetaree village, came to see us.  The river rose a little and overran the ice, so as to render the crossing difficult.

*March 7th.*  The day was somewhat cloudy and colder than usual ; the wind from the southeast.  Shotawhorora visited us with a sick child, to whom[25] some medicine was

[24] " Oh-harh or the Little fox," Clark C 191 ; where Clark adds that George Shannon cut his foot " with the ads."

[25] " To whome I gave some of rushes pills," Clark C 191.  Dr. Rush's pills were in vogue in those days ; they were a favorite remedy with Captain Clark, who usually tried them first, and then, if the result was not satisfactory, administered Scott's pills.  The codex of this date uses a word which needs explanation.  Among presents enumerated as received by " Shabounar " (Chaboneau) from Mr. Chaboillez, of the Northwest Company, are : " 3 brace of Cloath, . . . a par corduroy overalls, 1 vests, 1 Brace Blu Cloth, 1 Brace red or Scorlet with 3 bars," etc.  What does " brace " mean here ?  It is apparently not " a pair," as

administered.    There were also other Indians who brought
corn and dried buffalo meat, in exchange for blacksmith's
work.

*March 8th.*   The day cold and fair, with a high easterly
wind.   We were visited by two Indians who gave us an
account of the country and people near the Rocky mountains[26] where they had been.

*March 9th.*   The morning cloudy and cool, the wind
from the north.   The grand chief of the Minnetarees, who
is called by the French Le Borgne,[27] from his having but

we have "a par of overalls," and the sense of "pair" does not suit in the
cases of the other articles.    It was probably a trade-word, of whose meaning,
however, I am ignorant.

[26] Here first so called—before "Rock mountain."    "Visited by the Greesey-
head and a Ricara today, those men gave some account of the Indians near the
rockey mountains," Clark C 191.

[27] Brackenridge's Journal is cited for this portrait of Le Borgne : "On
the fourth of July we had something like a celebration of this glorious
anniversary.    The two principal chiefs happened to be with us : the One-ey'd
and the Blackshoe.    The former is a giant in stature, and if his one eye had
been placed in the middle of his forehead, he might have passed for a Cyclops.
His huge limbs and gigantic frame, his bushy hair shading his coarse visage
and savage features, with his one eye flashing fire, constituted him a fearful
demon.    He sways, with unlimited control, all these villages, and is feared by
all the neighbouring nations.    I remarked that on one or two occasions he
treated She-he-ke [Big White] with great contempt.    Lisa having referred to
something said by that chief, ' What,' said the monster, ' what !   Does that
bag of lies pretend to have any authority here ? '    He is sometimes a cruel and
abominable tyrant.    A story was related to me of his cruelty, which has in it
something cf a more refined tragic nature than we usually meet with amongst
these people.    Having fallen in love (for even Polyphemus felt the influence of
the god who spares neither giants nor common men) with the wife of a young
warrior, he went to his lodge during his absence, and carried her off by
force.    The warrior on his return repaired to the One-ey'd demon and demanded
his wife ; but instead of receiving redress, was put to death, while the wretched
object of the dispute was retained in the embraces of her ravisher.    The
mother of the young warrior, whose only child he was, became frantic, lost her
senses from excess of grief, and now does nothing but go about reviling him
[Le Borgne], and loading him with her curses ; yet such is the superstitious
veneration (by the by it deserves a better name on this occasion) for unhappy
objects of this kind [insane persons] that this chief, great as he is, dare not lay
his hand on her, even should she haunt him like one of the Eumenides."    That
sounds like Brackenridge.    I took it long ago from the Analectic Magazine,

one eye, came down for the first time to the fort.   He was received with much attention, two guns being fired in honor of his arrival ; the curiosities were exhibited to him, and as he said that he had not received the presents which we had sent to him on his arrival, we again gave him a flag, a medal, shirt, arm-braces, and the presents usual on such occasions, with all which he was much pleased.   In the course of the conversation, the chief observed that some foolish young men of his nation had told him there was a person among us who was quite black, and he wished to know if it could be true.   We assured him that it was true, and sent for York.   Le Borgne was very much surprised at his appearance, examined him closely, and spit on his finger and rubbed the skin in order to wash off the paint ; nor was it until the negro uncovered his head and showed his short hair, that Le Borgne could be persuaded that he was not a painted white man.

*March* 10*th.*   A cold, windy day.   Tetuckopinreha, chief of the Ahnahaways, and the Minnetaree chief Ompschara, passed the day with us, the former remaining during the night.   We had occasion to see an instance of the summary (*p. 169*) justice of the Indians.   A young Minnetaree had carried off the daughter of Cogonomokshe or Raven Man, second chief of the upper village of the Mandans ; the father went to the village and found his daughter, whom he brought home, and took with him a horse belonging to the offender.   This reprisal satisfied the vengeance of the father and of the nation, as the young man would not dare to reclaim his horse, which from that time became the property of the injured party.

The stealing of young women is one of the most common offenses against the police of the village, and the

VII., Feb., 1816, p. 145.   On turning to Brackenridge, 1814, I find on p. 261 something like it.   But unless the Analectic's reviewer embellished the passage, which he places in quotation marks, he took it from p. 185 of some other edition or work of Brackenridge's, which I have not seen.   However, the passage is too good to cut, and I leave it with this explanation.

punishment of it is always measured by the power or the passions of the kindred of the female. A voluntary elopement is of course more rigorously chastised. One of the wives of Le Borgne deserted him in favor of a man who had been her lover before the marriage and who after some time left her, and she was obliged to return to her father's house. As soon as he heard it Le Borgne walked there and found her sitting near the fire. Without noticing his wife, he began to smoke with the father; when they were joined by the old men of the village, who, knowing his temper, had followed in hopes of appeasing him. He continued to smoke quietly with them till, rising to return, he took his wife by the hair, led her as far as the door, and with a single stroke of his tomahawk put her to death before her father's eyes. Then turning fiercely upon the spectators, he said that if any of her relations wished to avenge her, they could always find him at his lodge; but the fate of the woman had not sufficient interest to excite the vengeance of the family. The caprice or the generosity of the same chief gave a very different result to a similar incident which occurred some time afterward. Another of his wives eloped with a young man, who not being able to support her as she wished, they both returned to the village, and she presented herself before the husband, supplicating his pardon for her conduct. Le Borgne sent for the lover. At the moment when the youth expected that he would be put to death, the chief (*p. 170*) mildly asked them if they still preserved their affection for each other; and on their declaring that want, and not a change of affection, had induced them to return, he gave up his wife to her lover, with the liberal present of three horses, and restored them both to his favor.

*March* 11*th.* The weather was cloudy in the morning, and a little snow fell; the wind then shifted from southeast to northwest, and the day became fair. It snowed again in the evening, but the next day,

*March* 12*th*,[28] was fair, with the wind from the northwest.

[28] Clark C 194, this date, has: "Shabonat deturmins on not proceeding

*March 13th.* We had a fine day and a southwest wind. Mr. M'Kenzie came to see us, as did also many Indians, who are so anxious for battle-axes that our smiths have not a moment's leisure, and procure us an abundance of corn. The river rose a little to-day, and so continued.

*March 14th.* The wind being from the west and the day fine, the whole party were employed in building boats and in shelling corn.

*March 15th.* The day is clear, pleasant, and warm. We take advantage of the fine weather to hang all our Indian presents and other articles out to dry before our departure.

*March 16th.* The weather is cloudy, the wind from the southeast. A Mr. Garrow,[29] a Frenchman who has resided a long time among the Ricaras and Mandans, explained to us the mode in which they make their large beads, an art which they are said to have derived from some prisoners of the Snake Indian nation, and the knowledge of which is a secret even now confined to a few among the Mandans and Ricaras.

The process is as follows:[30] glass of different colors is first pounded fine and washed, till each kind, which is kept separate, ceases to stain the water thrown over it. Some well-seasoned clay, mixed with a sufficient quantity of sand to prevent its becoming very hard when exposed to heat, and reduced by water to the consistency of dough, is then rolled on the palm of the hand, till it becomes of the thickness wanted for the hole in the bead. These sticks of (*p. 171*) clay are placed upright, each on a little pedestal or

with us as an interpeter under the terms mentioned yesterday he will not agree to work let our situation be what it may nor stand a guard, and if miffed with any man he wishes to return when he pleases, also have the disposeal of as much provisions as he chuses." Chaboneau was cooler than the weather at Fort Mandan, and it is a wonder he was not frozen out of the garrison.

[29] I suppose this to be one Pierre Gareau or Garreau, a noted interpreter whose name appears in various books. His Hidatsan name was Mish, or Meesh (also Beesh), from their word for rock, translating *Pierre*, and making a pun—like the translators of Matt. xvi. 18, to whom the R. C. church should be much obliged.

[30] This description is in Clark C 199–202, but in Lewis' hand, of this date, interpolated between March 21st and 22d.

ball of the same material, about an ounce in weight, and distributed over a small earthen platter, which is laid on the fire for a few minutes, when they are taken off to cool. With a little paddle or shovel, three or four inches long and sharpened at the end of the handle, the wet pounded glass is placed in the palm of the hand. The beads are made of an oblong form, wrapped in a cylindrical form around the stick of clay, which is laid crosswise over it and gently rolled backward and forward till it becomes perfectly smooth. If it be desired to introduce any other color, the surface of the bead is perforated with the pointed end of the paddle, and the cavity filled with pounded glass of that color. The sticks with the strings of beads are then replaced on their pedestals, and the platter deposited on burning coals or hot embers. Over the platter an earthen pot containing about three gallons, with a mouth large enough to cover the platter, is reversed, being completely closed except a small aperture at the top, through which are watched the beads. A quantity of old dried wood, formed into a sort of dough or paste, is placed round the pot so as to almost cover it, and afterward set on fire. The manufacturer then looks through the small hole in the pot, till he sees the beads assume a deep red color, to which succeeds a paler or whitish red, or they become pointed at the upper extremity; on which the fire is removed and the pot suffered to cool gradually. At length it is removed, the beads are taken out, the clay in the hollow of them is picked out with an awl or needle, and they are then fit for use. The beads thus formed are in great demand among the Indians, being used as pendants to their ears and hair, and sometimes worn round the neck.

*March* 17*th.* A windy but clear and pleasant day, the river rising a little and open in several places. Our Minnetaree interpreter Chaboneau, whom we intended taking with us to the Pacific, had some days ago been worked (*p. 172*) upon by the British traders, and appeared unwilling to accompany us, except on certain terms—such as his not being subject to our orders, and his doing duty or returning whenever he chose. As we saw clearly the source of his hesitation, and knew that it was intended as an obstacle to our views, we told him that the terms were inadmissible, and that we could dispense with his services. He had accordingly left us with some displeasure. Since then he had made an advance toward joining us, which we showed no anxiety to meet; but this morning he sent an apology for his improper conduct, and agreed to go with us and perform the same duties as the rest of the corps; we therefore took him again into our service.

*March* 18*th.* The weather was cold and cloudy, the wind from the north. We were engaged in packing up the goods into eight divisions, so as to preserve a portion of each in case of accident. We hear that the Sioux have lately attacked a party of Assiniboins and Knistenaux, near the Assiniboin river, and killed 50 of them.

*March* 19*th.* Some snow fell last night; this morning was cold, windy, and cloudy. Shahaka and Kagohami came down to see us, as did another Indian with a sick child, to whom we gave some medicine. There appears to be an approaching war, as two parties have already gone from the Minnetarees, and a third is preparing.

*March* 20*th.* The morning was cold and cloudy, the wind high from the north; the afternoon was pleasant. The canoes being finished, four of them were carried to the river, at a distance of 1½ miles from where they were constructed.

*March* 21*st.* The remaining periogues were hauled to the same place, and all the men except three, who were left to watch them, returned to the fort. On his way down, which was about six miles, Captain Clark passed along the points of the high hills, where he saw large quantities of (*p. 173*) pumice-stone on the foot, sides, and tops of the hills, which had every appearance of having been at some period on fire. He collected specimens of the stone itself, the pumice-stone, and the hard earth; on being put into the furnace the hard earth melted and glazed, the pumice-stone melted, and the hard stone became a pumice-stone glazed.

# CHAPTER VII.

## THE MISSOURI FROM FORT MANDAN TO THE YELLOWSTONE.

First rain ; river rising and ice running—The boats put in order—Indian buffalo-hunt on broken ice—Wildfowl migrating—Thunder and hail-storm—Baggage packed and specimens of natural history to be sent to the President—Indian art—Arrival of a party of Ricaras desiring to visit the President—Departure of the Expedition from Fort Mandan, April 7th, 1805— Roster of the party at this date—Sacajawea and infant—A Mandan goes too—Embarkation in six small and two large boats—The barge sent down river with presents and dispatches —Knife river passed—Miry creek—Minnetaree camps—Bluffs—Pocket-gophers and their food—French trappers overtaken—Little Basin bend of the river—Alkali—The Little Missouri—Description of this river—Onions and dwarf cedar—Onion creek—Goose creek—Old camps of supposed Assiniboins—Indian liquor-trade—Chaboneau's creek—Scarcity of game —Grouse—Goat-pen creek—Minerals and petrifactions—Game—Traces of Assiniboins— Plants and animals—Indian mode of disposing of the dead—The Whiteearth river—Cut bluff—Inconvenience of the sand—Detention by the wind—Approaching the Yellowstone —Captain Lewis goes ahead—The Expedition reaches the Yellowstone, April 26th—Captain Lewis returns and reports—Description of the Yellowstone, so named from the French Rochejaune—Eligible site for a fort.

ARCH 22d. This was a clear, pleasant day, with the wind from the S.S.W. We were visited by the second chief of the Minnetarees, to whom we gave a medal and some presents, accompanied by a speech. Mr. M'Kenzie and Mr. Laroche also came to see us. They all took their leave next day.

*March 23d.* Soon after their departure, a brother of Le Borgne, with other Indians, came to the fort. The weather was fine, but in the evening we had the first rain that has fallen during the winter.

*March 24th.* The morning cloudy, but the afternoon fair, the wind from the N.E. We are employed in preparing for our journey. This evening swans and wild geese flew toward the N.E.

*March 25th.* A fine day, the wind S.W. The river rose nine inches, and the ice began breaking away in several places, so as to endanger our canoes, which we are hauling down to the fort.

*March 26th.* The river rose only half an inch, and being choked up with ice near the fort, did not begin to run till toward evening. This day is clear and pleasant.

*March 27th.* The wind is still high from the S.W. The ice, which is occasionally stopped for a few hours, is then (*p. 175*) thrown over shallow sand-bars when the river runs. We had all our canoes brought down, and were obliged to cauk [calk [1]] and pitch very attentively the cracks so common in cottonwood.

*March 28th.* The day is fair. Some obstacle above has prevented the ice from running. Our canoes are now nearly ready, and we expect to set out as soon as the river is sufficiently clear to permit us to pass.

*March 29th.* The weather clear and the wind from the N.W. The obstructions above gave way this morning, and the ice came down in great quantities, the river having fallen 11 inches in the course of the last 24 hours. We have had few Indians at the fort for the last three or four days, as they are now busy in catching the floating buffalo. Every spring, as the river is breaking up, the surrounding plains are set on fire, and the buffalo are tempted to cross the river in search of the fresh grass which immediately succeeds the burning. On their way they are often insulated on a large cake or mass of ice, which floats down the river. The Indians now select the most favorable point for attack, and, as the buffalo approaches, dart with astonishing agility across the trembling ice, sometimes pressing lightly a cake of not more than two feet square. The animal is of course unsteady, and his footsteps are insecure on this new element, so that he can make but little resistance; and the hunter, who has given him his death-wound, paddles his icy boat to the shore and secures his prey.

*March 30th.* The day was clear and pleasant, the wind N.W., and the ice running in great quantities. All our Indian

---

[1] " Had all the canoes corked pitched & tined [tinned] in and on the cracks and windshakes, which is universially in the cotton wood," Clark C 204. Cracked eggshells, for a voyage of more than a thousand miles !

presents were again exposed to the air, and the barge made ready to descend the Missouri.

*March* 31*st*. Early this morning it rained, and the weather continued cloudy during the day; the river rose nine inches; the ice is not running so much as yesterday. Several flocks of geese and ducks fly up the river.

*Monday, April* 1*st*, 1805. This morning there was a thunder-storm, accompanied by large hail, to which succeeded (*p. 176*) rain for about half an hour. We availed ourselves of this interval to get all the boats into the water. At 4 p. m. it began to rain a second time, and continued till midnight. With the exception of a few drops at two or three different times, this is the first rain we have had since the 15th of October last.

*April* 2*d*. The wind was high last night and this morning from the N.W.; the weather continued cloudy. The Mandans killed yesterday 21 elk, about 15 miles below, but they were so poor as to be scarcely fit for use.[2]

*April* 3*d*. The weather is pleasant, though there was a white frost and some ice on the edge of the water. We were all engaged in packing up our baggage and merchandise.

*April* 4*th*. The day is clear and pleasant, though the wind is high from the N.W. We now packed up in different boxes a variety of articles for the President, which we shall send in the barge.[3] They consisted of a stuffed male and female antelope with their skeletons, a weasel, three squirrels from the Rocky mountains, the skeleton of the prairie-wolf, those of the white and gray hare, a male and female blaireau or burrowing-dog of the prairie [*Taxidea americana*], with a skeleton of the female, two burrowing-squirrels, a white weasel, the skin of the louservia [*sic*], the horns of the

---

[2] " The 2d. Chief of the 2d. Mandan village took a miff at our not attending to him perticularly after being here about ten days and moved back to his village," Clark C 206—but no word of speeding the parting guest !

[3] Clark C 208–211 has the whole invoice, listed by boxes and parcels. The articles reached Mr. Jefferson, and some of them were long on view at Monticello. Others passed to Peale's museum in Philadelphia. I have reason to believe that some of the specimens of natural history are still extant.

mountain ram or bighorn, a pair of large elk horns, the horns and tail of the black-tailed deer, and a variety of skins, such as those of the red fox, white hare, marten [*Mustela americana*], and a yellow bear obtained from the Sioux; also, a number of articles of Indian dress, among which was a buffalo-robe, representing a battle fought about eight years since between the Sioux and Ricaras against the Mandans and Minnetarees, in which the combatants are represented on horseback.

It has of late years excited much discussion to ascertain the period when the art of painting was first discovered. How hopeless all researches of this kind are is evident from the foregoing fact.   It is (*p. 177*) indebted for its origin to one of the strongest passions of the human heart—a wish to preserve the features of a departed friend, or the memory of some glorious exploit.   This inhabits equally the bosoms of all men, either civilized or savage.   Such sketches, rude and imperfect as they are, delineate the predominant character of the savage nations.   If they are peaceable and inoffensive, the drawings usually consist of local scenery and their favorite diversions.   If the band are rude and ferocious, we observe tomahawks, scalping-knives, bows, arrows, and all the engines of destruction.

[Among the articles sent were also] a Mandan bow and quiver of arrows ; also, some Ricara tobacco-seed and an ear of Mandan corn; to which were added a box of plants, another of insects, and three cases containing a burrowing-squirrel, a prairie-hen, and four magpies, all alive.

*April 5th.*   Fair and pleasant, but the wind is high from the northwest.   We were visited by a number of Mandans, and are occupied in loading our boats, in order to proceed on our journey.[4]

---

[4] At this date, p. 74, Gass does a remarkable thing for him—he indulges certain reflections : " If this brief Journal," he says, " should happen to be preserved, and be ever thought worthy of appearing in print ; some readers will expect that, after ou long friendly intercourse with these Indians, among whom we have spent the winter ; our acquaintance with those nations lower down the river ; and the information we received relative to several other nations : we

*April 6th.* Another fine day, with a gentle breeze from the south. The Mandans continued to come to the fort, and in the course of the day informed us of the arrival of a party of Ricaras on the other side of the river. We sent our interpreter to inquire into their reason for coming; and in the morning,

*Sunday, April 7th,* he returned, with a Ricara chief and three of his nation. This chief, whose name[5] is Kagohweto or Brave Raven, brought a letter from Mr. Tabeau, mentioning the wish of the grand chiefs of the Ricaras to visit the President, and requesting permission for himself and four men to join our boat when it descends; to which we consented, as it will then be manned with 15 hands, and be able to defend itself against the Sioux. After presenting the letter, he told us that he was sent, with ten warriors, by his nation, to arrange their settling near the Mandans and Minnetarees, whom they wished to join; that he considered all the neighboring nations friendly except the Sioux (*p. 178*), whose persecution they would no longer withstand, and whom they hoped to repel by uniting with the tribes in this quarter. He added that the Ricaras intended to follow our

ought to be prepared now, when we are about to renew our voyage, to give some account of the fair sex of the Missouri, and entertain them with narratives of feats of love as well as of arms. Though we could furnish a sufficient number of entertaining stories and pleasant anecdotes, we do not think it prudent to swell our Journal with them ; as our views are directed to more useful information. Besides, as we are yet ignorant of the dangers which may await us, and the difficulty of escape, should certain probable incidents occur, it may not be inconsistent with good policy to keep the Journal of as small and portable a size as circumstances will make practicable. It may be observed generally that chastity is not very highly esteemed by these people, and that the severe and loathsome effects of certain French principles are not uncommon among them. The fact is, that the women are generally considered an article of traffic and indulgences are sold at a very moderate price. As a proof of this I will just mention that for an old tobacco-box, one of our men was granted the honor of passing a night with the daughter of the head chief of the Mandan nation. An old bawd with her punks may also be found in some of the villages on the Missouri, as well as in the large cities of polished nations."

[5] " The name of this Chief of War is Kah-kah, We-to—Raven brave," Clark C 213.

advice and live in peace with all nations, and requested that we would speak in their favor to the Assiniboin Indians. This we willingly promised to do, and assured them that their great father would protect them and no longer suffer the Sioux to have good guns, or to injure his dutiful children. We then gave him a small medal, a certificate of his good conduct, a carrot of tobacco, and some wampum, with which he departed for the Mandan village, well satisfied with his reception.[6]

Having made all our arrangements, we left the fort about five o'clock in the afternoon.[7]

The party now consisted of 32 persons.[8] Besides ourselves were Sergeants John Ordway, Nathaniel Pryor, and Patrick Gass. The privates were William Bratton, John Colter, John

[6] The Mandan Codex ends here, at p. 214, in the midst of the Biddle text of April 7th, so far as Clark's journal is concerned. The rest of the codex, pp. 215-274, is a meteorological register, and an elaborate invoice of the stores and presents mentioned in the beginning of Biddle's History, p. 3 of this edition.

[7] The composition of the party at this moment of its division into two—one to go on, the other to go back—is precisely ascertained. Refer now to note [8], p. 3., where it is seen that 45 persons left St. Louis, all told—29 of the permanent party, 16 of the party to return from Mandan. (Several persons, engaged after May 14th, 1804, and discharged before April 7th, 1805, do not affect the present count.) Of the original 29, Floyd was dead, and Liberté lost, leaving 27. To these 27 were added 3—Lepage (vice Newman disbanded), Chaboneau, and Sacajawea, making 30 (without affecting the 16 of the return party). Newman and Reed were transferred to the return party, making the latter 18. Two soldiers of the return party were transferred to the permanent party (vice Reed disbanded, and Liberté lost), leaving the return party 16—strength the same as at the start, but composition different—and making the permanent party 32 in number, all present and accounted for in the text by name. Thus it is seen that of the aggregate of the two parties, 45, 2 had been lost, leaving 43, and 3 had been gained, making 46 to be accounted for. Of these 46, 32 go up river to-day, and 14 are left. For these 14, see note [9].

[8] It is deemed desirable, for historical purposes, to give here a more formal roster of the personnel of this party of 32, with such biographical data as I have been able to discover. Excepting Lewis, Clark, Gass, and Shannon, we know next to nothing more than the names of the men and woman who accomplished an immortal purpose.

### COMMISSIONED OFFICERS (2).

1. MERIWETHER LEWIS, Captain 1st. Regt. U. S. Infantry, Com'd'g. (See Memoirs, anteà.)

Collins, Peter Cruzatte, Reuben Fields, Joseph Fields, Robert Frazier, George Gibson, Silas Goodrich, Hugh Hall,
Thomas P. Howard, Francis Labiche, Baptiste Lapage, Hugh

2. WILLIAM CLARK, Second Lieutenant U. S. Artillerists. (Late Captain
   Clarksville Militia. See Memoir, *anteà*.)

### SERGEANTS (4).

3. JOHN ORDWAY, Odway. No more known of him.
4. NATHANIEL PRYOR, Pryer, Prior. Afterward Ensign, U. S. A. ?
5. †CHARLES FLOYD. " deceased the 20th. of August 1804—a young man
   of much merit—his father, who now resides in Kentucky, is a man
   much rispected, tho' possessed of but moderate wealth. as the son lost
   his life while in this service I considered his father entitled to some gratuity in consideration of his loss, and also, that the deceased being noticed
   in this way will be a tribute but justly due his merit," Lewis' Roll,
   Jan. 15th, 1807. (See p. 79, and note there.)
6. PATRICK GASS. " Promoted to Sergeant 20th of August 1804, in the place
   of Charles Floyd, deceased, in which capacity he continued until discharged at St. Louis Novr. 10th, 1806," Lewis' Roll. (See Memoir,
   *anteà*.)

### PRIVATES (23).

7. WILLIAM BRATTON, Bratten, Brattin. No more known of him.
8. JOHN COLLINS, Collin, Colins. No more known of him.
9. JOHN COLTER, Coulter. Discharged at his own request, at the Mandans,
   Aug. 14th, 1806, and returned to the life of a trapper. See " Colter's
   Route in 1807," as traced on Clark's map of 1814. This is the man who
   had the horrible experience with the Indians on Missouri waters, when his
   comrade Potts was killed. The story has been repeatedly told : see for
   example Bradbury's Travels, p. 17, and Irving's Astoria, p. 146 of the
   1861 edition. It may have been embellished ; but Colter's sufferings
   would be hard to exaggerate. Colter was found near La Charrette, on
   the Lower Missouri, by the overland Astorian party under Hunt, Jan.
   18th, 1811 ; there he had come from the Upper Missouri and Yellowstone
   country in a canoe, and brought accounts of the hatred and fury excited
   among the Indians by Captain Lewis' unfortunate affair on Maria's river,
   July 27th, 1806, when Lewis killed one Indian, and R. Fields another.
   Colter would have joined the Astorians, in spite of his dreadful adventure ; but the charms of a new young wife prevented. No more known
   of this discoverer of sources of the Yellowstone.
10. PETER CRUZATTE of Biddle ; Pier Cruzatte of Lewis' Roll ; Crugatte of
    print, once ; Cruzat, Crouzat, Crusatte, Crusatt, Crusat, Crousatte, Cru-
    zate, etc., of the codices ; real name probably Pierre Croisette or Croix-
    ette ; Canadian French ; one of the " two French watermen " of p. 2 ;
    chief waterman of the Expedition ; accidentally shot Captain Lewis, Aug.
    11th, 1806. No more known of him.

M'Neal, John Potts, John Shields, George Shannon, John B. Thompson, William Werner, Joseph Whitehouse, Alexander Willard, Richard Windsor, Peter Wiser; and Captain

11. JOSEPH FIELDS, and

12. REUBEN FIELDS. Brothers; two of the "nine young men from Kentucky." "Two of the most active and enterprising young men who accompanied us, it was their peculiar fate to have been engaged in all the most dangerous and difficult scenes of the voyage in which they uniformly acquited themselves with much honor," Lewis' Roll, where the names stand Field, and one of them Reubin Field.

13. ROBERT FRAZIER, Fraizer, Frazer, Frasier, Fraser, Frasure. No more known of him.

14. GEORGE GIBSON. From Mercer Co., Pa.; remained in St. Louis; married, and died there 1809; his industrious widow became Mrs. Cartmill, Mrs. Dunleavy, and Mrs. Hayden, successively, and died afterward.

15. SILAS GOODRICH, often in the codices Guthrich. No more known of him.

16. HUGH HALL. No more known of him.

17. THOMAS P. HOWARD. No more known of him.

18. FRANCIS LABICHE, Labishe, Lebiche, Ladishe, on Lewis' Roll Labuiche, in the codices usually Labieshe, which latter is also the common corruption of the name of Lake Labiche ("Elk" Lake, about the sources of the Mississippi); real name François Labiche or La Biche; one of the "two French watermen" of p. 2. "he has received the pay only of a private, tho' besides the duties performed as such, he has rendered me very essential services as a French and English interpreter, and sometimes also as an Indian interpreter; therefore I should think it only just that some small addition to his pay as a private should be added, tho' no such addition has at any time been promised by me," Lewis' Roll.

19. BAPTISTE LEPAGE, or Le Page; in Biddle and the codices usually Lapage or La Page; on the Roll John Bapteist La Page. "entitled to no peculiar merit. was inlisted at Fort Mandan on the 2nd of November [in Biddle Nov. 3d, p. 189] 1804. in order to supply the deficiency in my permanent party occasioned by the discharge of John Newman. he performed this tour to the Pacific Ocean, and returned to St. Louis, where he was discharged in common with others on the 10th of November last. as he did not perform the labours incident to the summer of 1804, it would be proper to give him the grade only of two-thirds as much as is given to others of his rank," Lewis' Roll.

20. HUGH MCNEAL, M'Neal. No more known of him.

21. JOHN POTTS. One Potts was killed when Colter was captured by the Indians; supposably this man; no further evidence.

22. GEORGE SHANNON. Born Pennsylvania 1787, and so a mere lad in his teens when he joined the Expedition. It is said in Billon's Annals of St. Louis, 1888, p. 271, that Mr. Shannon "received a wound in the leg from the Indians, and on his return had his leg amputated at St. Charles, and

Clark's black servant York. The two interpreters were George Drewyer and Toussaint Chaboneau. The wife [Sacajawea] of Chaboneau also accompanied us with her young child, and we hope may be useful as an interpreter among the Snake Indians. She was herself one of that

a wooden one substituted, from which he was ever afterward called ' Peg-leg Shannon.' " But there is no allusion in the Biddle History to any such wound or operation. No man was ever wounded by an Indian on the Expedition. Mr. Shannon suffered the loss of a limb, but under circumstances unknown to me. He was sent by General Clark to Philadelphia (letter before me) to assist Mr. Biddle in preparing the History, and rendered the author important service. He studied law, was admitted to the bar, and began practice in Lexington, Ky. He was a Circuit Judge for some years ; in 1828 he located at Hannibal, Mo., and afterward at St. Charles. He was for a short time State Senator, and United States Attorney for Missouri. He died suddenly, in court, at Palmyra, in 1836, at the age of 49 years. He was a relative of Governor Shannon of Kentucky, and perhaps the one man on the Expedition whom either of the captains would have been most likely to meet at home on terms of social equality.

23. JOHN SHIELDS. " he has received the pay only of a private. nothing was more peculiarly useful to us in various situations than the skill and ingenuity of this man as an artist in repairing our guns and accoutrements, &c. and should it be thought proper to allow him something of an addition to his pay he has deserved it," Lewis' Roll. I think this was the handy and industrious Tubal Cain at Fort Mandan, who earned so much corn and meat from the Indians for the use of the party ; and I fully expected to find him named as this blacksmith in the codices ; but if " Shields " be anywhere there, in this connection, it has escaped careful search for it. A Clatsop codex praises him highly, by name.

24. JOHN B. THOMPSON, Thomson, Tompson, Tomson.

25. WILLIAM WERNER, Warner, Wirner, Wernor.

26. JOSEPH WHITEHOUSE, once White House.

27. ALEXANDER WILLARD, Wilard, Willerd.

28. RICHARD WINDSOR, Windser, Winsor, Winser.

29. PETER WISER, Wisor, Wisert, Wiset. No more known of these six.

### INTERPRETERS (2).

30. GEORGE DREWYER of Biddle and the codices, rarely in the latter Drewer ; Drulyard of Lewis' Roll ; proper name believed to be Drouillard, as appears from an item in the Missouri Gazette of St. Louis, early in 1807 : " In the Spring Manuel Lisa, a trader, and George Drouillard, who had crossed the Rocky mountains to the Pacific with Lewis and Clark, embarked in the Upper Missouri fur trade with the Indians with an out-

tribe, but having been taken in war by the Minnetarees, she was sold as a slave to Chaboneau, who brought her up and afterward married her. One of the Mandans likewise embarked with us, in order to go to the Snake Indians, and obtain a peace with them for his countrymen. All this party

fit of $16,000." (See Billon's Annals, 1888, p. 82.) Drewyer was a half-breed ; the Indian side of him made him the best hunter and woodsman of the party ; he was a crack shot, and simply invaluable. Drewyer and the brothers Fields seem to have been on the whole the most serviceable of the party, exclusive of the sergeants. Lewis' Roll praises Drewyer highly : " A man of much merit ; he has been peculiarly useful from his knowledge of the common language of gesticulation, and his uncommon skill as a hunter and woodsman : those several duties he performed in good faith and with an ardor which deserves the highest commendation. it was his fortune to have encountered on various occasions with either Capt. Clark or myself all the most dangerous and trying scenes of the voyage in which he uniformily acquitted himself with honor. he has served the complete term of the whole tour and received only 25. Dollars pr. month and one ration pr. day, while I am informed that it is not unusual for individuals in similar employment to receive 30 dollars pr. Month.—" Drewyer alone is the " interpreter and hunter " of p. 2.

31. TOUSSAINT CHABONEAU of the text, Touisant Charbono of Lewis' Roll, with twelve or more names in the codices. For this individual, greater in names than in any fact, see note [13], p. 189.

WOMAN (1).

32. SACAJAWEA, otherwise Bird-woman, with her infant, born Feb. 11th, 1805. See note [13], p. 189.

SERVANT (1).

33. YORK, a negro slave, belonging to Captain Clark. See note [31], p. 159.

Deducting from this list of 33 persons one, Sergeant Floyd, who was of the permanent party at the date of his decease, and was returned by Lewis on his Roll, we have accurately the 32 persons (adults) who proceeded from Fort Mandan, and were accompanied for a short distance by an uncounted Mandan Indian, not belonging to the party.

The Muster-roll in the archives of the War Department, above quoted, has no remarks against any of the names, except those which I have transcribed in full. It is entitled : " A Roll of the men who accompanied Captains Lewis & Clark on their late tour to the Pacific Ocean through the interior of the Continent of North America, showing their rank with some remarks on their respective merits and services.—" It is one large double sheet, formed of two sheets of foolscap pasted top to bottom, formally ruled off for the numbered list

with the baggage was stowed in six small canoes and two large periogues.

We left the fort with fair, pleasant weather, though the northwest wind was high, and after making about four miles camped on the north side of the Missouri, nearly (*p. 179*) opposite the first Mandan village.

At the same time that we took our departure, our barge,[9]

of names, rank, remarks, etc.  It is in good preservation and perfectly legible, excepting a few words along the crease of the pasted place.  It ends as follows :

*" General Remarks.*

" With rispect to all those persons whose names are entered on this roll, I feel a peculiar pleasure in declaring, that the ample support which they gave us under every difficulty, the manly firmness which they evinced on every necessary occasion, and the patience and fortitude, with which they submitted to and bore the fatigues and painful sufferings incident to my late tour to the Pacific Ocean entitles them to my warmest approbation and thanks, nor will I suppress the expression of a hope that the recollection of services thus faithfully performed will meet a just reward in an ample remuneration on the part of our government.—

[Signed]    " MERIWETHER LEWIS Capt.
" City of Washington                " 1st. U'S. Regt. Infty.
" January 15th, 1807."

[9] The strength and for the most part the composition of this return party are certain.  The text here indicates ten persons.  The text above (p. 252) indicates that there might be 15 persons (including Mr. Tabeau and his four men).  Gass says, p. 76, this date : " Thirty-one men and a woman went up river and thirteen returned down it in the boat."  Lewis D 3, dated Fort Mandan, April 7th, 1805, is as follows : " Having on this day at 4 p. m. completed every arrangement necessary for our departure, we dismissed the barge and crew with orders to return without delay to St. Louis.  a small canoe with two French hunters accompanyed the barge ; these men had ascended the missouri with us last year as engages [not *engagés* of the Expedition ; simply those two who were picked up at Cannon-ball river, Oct. 18th : see p. 171].  The barge crew consisted of six soldiers [besides Corporal Richard Warfington, in charge, being Privates M. B. Reed and John Newman, disbanded, see note [43] p. 77, note [36] p. 167, note [7] p. 253, and four others], and two Frenchmen ; two Frenchmen and a Ricara Indian also take their passage in her as far as the Ricara Vilages, at which place we expect Mr. Tiebeau [Anthony Tabeau] to embark with his peltry who in that case will make an addition of two, perhaps four men to the crew of the barge. We gave Richard Warfington, a discharged Corpl. the charge of the Barge and crew, and confided to his care likewise our dispatches to the government, letters to our private friends, and a number of articles to the President of the United States.  One of the Frenchmen by the Name of [Joseph, red-inked in by Clark] Gravline an honest discrete man and an excellent boat-man is imployed to con▼

manned with seven soldiers, two Frenchmen, and Mr. [Joseph] Gravelines as pilot, sailed for the United States, loaded with our presents and dispatches.

duct the barge as a pilot ; we have therefore every hope that the barge and with her our dispatches will arrive safe at St. Louis. Mr. Gravlin who speaks the Ricara language extreemly well, has been imployed to conduct a few of the Recara Chiefs to the seat of government who have promised us to decend in the barge to St. Liwis [sic] with that view." So the barge contained the 13 that Gass counts : Corporal Warfington, in charge ; Mr. Gravelines, pilot ; six privates (two of whom were Reed and Newman) ; two Frenchmen—these ten to go to St. Louis, as per text ; with two Frenchmen and an Arikara, to go a short distance. The return of certain members of this party to St. Louis is of course a matter of history, into which, however, a mere foot-note like this can hardly go. But I will give the record of Corporal Warfington, hitherto unpublished. It forms part of the same autograph letter of Lewis' which relates to Private Newman (see note [36], p. 167) accompanying Lewis' official Muster-roll of Jan. 15th, 1807. This letter is in good preservation ; but unluckily some water, or whisky perhaps, got spilled on it, soaked through its three pages, and made the old brown nut-gall ink run in an irregularly circular space of about two inches, so that just there some words are not fairly legible. Yet these can be restored in perfect sense and syntax, by obvious conjecture ; and several experts have agreed in the following rendering :

" Richard Warfington was a Corporal in the Infantry of the U' States army, whom I had occasion to take with me on my voyage as far as the Mandan nation. his term of service expired on the 4th of August [1804] within ? nearly three months previous to my arrival at that place ? nation ? and ? knowing that it would become necessary for me to send back my boat in the spring 1805 with a party of soldiers whose terms of service had not expired ; that it was of some importance that the government should receive in safety the dispatches which I was about to transmit from thence ; that there was not one of the party destined to be returned from thence in whom I could place the least confidence except himself, and that if he was discharged at the moment of the expiration of his term of service that he would necessarily loose his military military [bis—page turns] standing, and thereby lessen the efficiency of his command among the soldiery ; I was induced under these considerations to make an arrangement with him by which it was agreed between us that he should not receive his discharge from the military service untill his return to St. Louis, and that he should in the interim retain his rank and receive only for his services the accustomed compensation. accordingly he remained with me during the winter, and was the next spring in conformity to my plan placed in command of the boat and charged with my dispatches to the government. the duties assigned him on this occasion were performed with a punctuality which uniformly ? characterized ? his conduct while under my command. Taking into view the cheerfulness with which he continued in the service ? after every obligation had ceased to exist, bore ? the exposures ? the fatigues, labour and dangers incident to that service,

*April 8th.*[10]   The day was clear and cool, the wind from the northwest, so that we traveled slowly.   After breakfasting at the second Mandan village, we passed the Mahaha [village] at the mouth of Knife [11] river, a handsome stream about 80 yards wide.   Beyond this we reached the island which Captain Clark had visited on the 30th of October.   This island has timber, as well as the lowlands on the north, but its [*i. e.*, the timber's] distance from the water had prevented

and above all the fidelity with which he discharged this? his? duty, it would seem that when rewards are about to be? distributed among those who were engaged in the enterprise that his claim to something more than his pay of seven dollars Pr. month as corporal cannot be considered unreasonable."

The "distribution of rewards," in which Captain Lewis hopes Corporal Warfington will not be forgotten, though he was not one of the permanent party that returned from the Pacific in 1806, alludes to a certain Act of Congress making grants of land, etc.   The dispatches which the corporal bore were the first direct official word from the Expedition since its departure from St. Louis ; and the last that was heard of or from Lewis and Clark until their return in September, 1806.

[10] The Biddle text, having finished with the Mandan Codex, Clark C, is already *en route* with Codex D, which runs Apr. 7th.–May 23d, 1805.   This is a Lewis, and one of the thirteen " red books."   (See the bibliographical introduction, *anteà.*) The attentive reader will not fail to discern a marked change in the tone or style of the narrative, which has hitherto followed the three Clarks, A, B, C.   It is all Biddle's fabric, of course, but the difference in the raw materials out of which he wove his tissue colors the text accordingly.   Where Clark's syntax is exiguous, Lewis' is redundant, often with singularly intricate constructions, and full stops far apart—where Clark is Doric, Lewis is Corinthian.   For an example at the outset, Lewis D 5 : " Our vessels consisted of six small canoes, and two large perogues.   This little fleet altho' not quite so rispectable as those of Columbus or Capt. Cook, were still viewed by us with as much pleasure as those deservedly famed adventurers ever beheld theirs ; and I dare say with quite as much anxiety for their safety and preservation. we were now about to penetrate a country at least 2000 miles in width, on which the foot of civilized man had never trodden; the good or evil it had in store for us was for experiment yet to determine, and these little vessells contained every article by which we were to expect to subsist or defend ourselves. however as the state of mind in which we are, generally gives the colouring to events, when the immagination is suffered to wander into futurity, the picture which now presented itself to me was a most pleasing one. entertaing as I do the most confident hope of succeeding [page turns] succeeding in a voyage which had formed a darling project of mine for the last ten years, I could but esteem this moment of our departure as among the most happy of my life."

[11] Knife river (Couteau of the French) is the last one of the five considerable streams which seek the Missouri from the west between the Cheyenne below

our camping there during the winter.  From the head of
this island we made 3½ miles to a point of wood on the
north,[12] passing a high bluff on the south, and  having come
about 14 miles [without noticing Spring creek].   In the course
of the day one of our boats filled and was near sinking; we
however saved her with the loss of a little biscuit and powder.

*April 9th.*  We set off as soon as it was light, and proceeded five miles to breakfast, passing a low ground on the
south, covered with groves of cottonwood.   At the distance
of six miles we reached on the north a hunting-camp of
Minnetarees, consisting of 30 lodges, built in the usual form
of earth and timber.   Two miles and a quarter further comes
in on the same side Miry creek,[13] a small  stream about ten
yards wide, which, rising in some lakes near the Mouse [14] [or

and the Little Missouri above, namely : the Owl, Grand, Cannon-ball, Heart,
and Knife.  For this whole distance—in fact from the James river itself—the
Missouri receives from the east no affluent of any size comparable to one of
these.  The five rivers named successively decrease in their respective totals of
length from the Owl to the Knife.  They are included in a somewhat triangular
area embraced by the Cheyenne on the south, the Little Missouri on the west,
and the Missouri on the east ; the points of this triangle being the mouth of the
Little Missouri on the north, the mouth of the Cheyenne on the southeast, and
the Black hills proper on the southwest.  The Knife arises in open broken
country near the Little Missouri and the heads of Heart river, in Dunn, Stark,
and Williams Cos., and courses through Mercer Co. in a general easterly direction to the Missouri.  One of its Indian names is Minah or Meenah Wakpa,
lettered on some maps.  This stream is distinctively Big Knife river (see Little
Knife, beyond).  The county town of Stanton is at its mouth.

[12] Or east (left) bank, about Hancock, McLean Co.  " Capt. Clark myself the
two Interpretters the woman and child sleep in a tent of dressed skins," Lewis D 6.

[13] Now Snake Creek, quite near the boundary between McLean and Stevens
Cos.; R. Bourbeuse (miry, muddy, like Vaseuse) of some French maps.  This
is the only creek from the north or east which the text yields anywhere along
here.  Clark's map, 1814, and Lewis' too, 1806, have *two*, the upper and larger
of these being the Miry or " Mirey."  Lewis D 12 has : " N. 20 W. to the
mouth of Miry creek stard. side, passing a small run and a hill called Snake den."
Here is the first of these creeks ; also, the obvious origin of the modern name
Snake for the second of them.  There are in fact four, of which Snake or Miry
is the second, and the fourth is called Douglass ; between the third and fourth
is Fort Stevenson.  See next two notes.

[14] The Mouse or Souris river is the largest tributary of the Red river of
the North in the United States, joining the Assiniboin in Manitoba, the

Souris] river, passes through beautiful level fertile plains without timber, in a direction nearly southwest, the banks near its entrance being steep and rugged on both sides of the Missouri. Three miles above this creek we came to a hunting-party of Minnetarees, who had prepared a park or inclosure, and were waiting the return of the antelope. These animals, which in the autumn retire for food and shelter to the Black mountains during the winter, recross the river at this season of the year, and spread themselves through the plains on the north of the Missouri. We halted, (*p. 180*) smoked a short time with the Minnetarees, and then proceeded on through handsome plains on each side of the river, and camped at the distance of 23½ miles on the north side.[16] The day was clear and pleasant, the wind high from the south ; but it afterward changed to a western steady breeze.

The bluffs which we passed to-day are upward of 100 feet high, composed of a mixture of yellow clay and sand, with many horizontal strata of carbonated wood resembling pit-coal, from one to five feet in depth, scattered through the

single river thus formed emptying into the Red river at a point where the latter is crossed by the Canadian Pacific R. R. The course of Mouse river is interesting. It heads wholly in the British possessions (north of 49°), west of 105° W. long., runs toward the 49th parallel (northern border of the United States), which it crosses near 103° 30', runs in the United States nearly to 103° long., recrosses 49° lat., then courses north of and nearly parallel with 49° N. lat. to about 102° W. long., when it again crosses 49° lat., re-entering the United States, strikes south and seems about to seek the Missouri. It is " bluffed off " however, by the Coteau du Missouri, representing a general elevation of 2,000 feet, and separating the Missouri watershed from that of the Red river. Thus the Mouse river makes a long loop into North Dakota, and returns upon itself, once more recrossing the parallel of 49° N. lat., at about 101° W. long., west of Turtle mountain, and so on to its junction with the Assiniboin, at a town called Milford, in Manitoba. The southernmost point in the bight of this loop is in McHenry Co., about N.E. of Fort Stevenson on the Missouri, the future site of which the Expedition is now approaching.

[16] Here the Expedition is past the present site of Fort Stevenson, on the north (left) bank of the Missouri, in Stevens Co. (See last two notes.) This fort was flourishing in 1873, in the autumn of which year I came down from the 49th parallel along Mouse river, by an easy wagon road to Stevenson, and thence along the north side of the Missouri to Bismarck.

bluff at different elevations, some as high as 80 feet above the water. The hills along the river are broken, and present every appearance of having been burned at some former period; great quantities of pumice-stone and lava—or rather earth, which seems to have been boiled and then hardened by exposure—being seen in many parts of these hills, where they are broken and washed down into gullies by the rain and melting snow.

A great number of brants pass up the river; some of them are perfectly white,[16] except the large feathers of the first joint of the wing, which are black, though in every other characteristic they resemble common gray brant. We also saw but could not procure an animal that burrows in the ground, and is similar in every respect to the burrowing-squirrel, except that it is only one-third of its size.[17] This may be [is] the animal whose works we have often seen in the plains and prairies; they resemble the labors of the salamander [*Geomys tuza*] in the sand-hills of South Carolina and Georgia, and like him the animals rarely come above ground; they consist of a little hillock of ten or twelve pounds of loose ground, which would seem to have been reversed from a pot, though no aperture is seen through which it could have been thrown. On removing gently the earth, you discover that the soil has been broken in a circle of about an inch and a half diameter, where the ground is looser, though still no opening is perceptible. When we stopped for dinner the squaw went out, and after penetrating with (*p. 181*) a sharp stick the holes of the mice [gophers], near some drift-wood, brought to us a quantity of wild

---

[16] These are the snow-goose, *Chen hyperboreus.*

[17] The animal here indicated by the description of its burrows is a common species of pouched rat or pocket-gopher, either *Geomys bursarius*, closely related to the "salamander" (*G. tuza*) mentioned in the same paragraph, or *Thomomys talpoides*, a species of the next nearest genus; both are common in these parts, and their habits entirely similar. They work extensive underground galleries, throw up loose soil in heaps at intervals, and feed mainly on bulbous roots. See Coues and Allen, Monogr. N. A. *Rodentia*, 4to, Washington, 1877, pp. 612–614, 623–625.

artichokes, which the mice collect and hoard in large numbers. The root is white, of an ovate form, from one to three inches long, and generally of the size of a man's finger, and two, four, and sometimes six roots are attached to a single stalk. Its flavor as well as the stalk which issues from it resemble those of the Jerusalem artichoke,[18] except that the latter is much larger.[19] A larger beaver was caught in a trap last night, and the mosquitoes begin to trouble us.

*April* 10*th*. We again set off early with clear, pleasant weather, and halted about ten o'clock for breakfast, above a sand-bank which was falling in, and near a small willow-island. On both sides of the Missouri, after ascending the hills near the water, one fertile unbroken plain extends as far as the eye can reach, without a solitary tree or shrub, except in moist situations or in the steep declivities of hills, where they are sheltered from the ravages of fire. At the distance of twelve miles we reached the lower point of a bluff on the south, which is in some parts on fire and throws out quantities of smoke, which has as trong sulphurous smell, the coal and other appearances in the bluffs being like those described yesterday.

At one o'clock we overtook three Frenchman, who left the fort a few days before us, in order to make the first attempt on this river of hunting beaver, which they do by means of traps. Their efforts promise to be successful; for they have already caught twelve, which are finer than any we have ever seen. They mean to accompany us as far as the Yellowstone river, in order to obtain our protection against the Assiniboins, who might attack them.

[18] *Helianthus tuberosus*, singularly misnamed "Jerusalem artichoke," as it is not botanically related to the artichoke, and has nothing to do with the city of Zion. The plant belongs to the order *Compositæ*, and to the same genus as the sunflower. The word "Jerusalem" is here a corruption of the Italian *girasole*, of which the French *tourne-sol* and the English *sunflower* (supposed to turn toward the sun) are equivalent in signification. Compare Greek ἡλιοτρόπος, of same sense, but a different word, which we apply to a different flower (heliotrope).

[19] A curiously constructed sentence. It means that the plant named tastes like the Jerusalem artichoke, and has a similar but smaller stalk and root, Lewis D 10.

In the evening we camped on a willow-point to the south,[20] opposite a bluff, above which a small creek falls in, and just above a remarkable bend in the river to the southwest, which we called the Little Basin.      The low grounds which we passed to-day possess more timber than is usual, and are wider; the current is mode- (*p. 182*) rate, at least not greater than that of the Ohio in high tides; the banks fall in but little; so that navigation, comparatively with that lower down the Missouri, is safe and easy.    We were enabled to make 18½ miles.    We saw the track of a large white bear; there were also a herd of antelopes in the plains; the geese and swan were now feeding in considerable quantities on the young grass in the low prairies; we shot a prairie-hen and a bald eagle [*Haliaëtus leucocephalus*], of which latter there were many nests in the tall cottonwood trees; but could procure neither of two elk which were in the plain. Our old companions the mosquitoes have renewed their visits, and give us much uneasiness.

*April 11th.* We set out at daylight, and after passing bare and barren hills on the south, and a plain covered with timber on the north, breakfasted at five miles' distance. Here we were regaled with a deer brought in by the hunters, which was very acceptable, as we had been for several days

[20] Mistake of the text : "S. 52° W. to a point on the Stard. side, opposite a bluf," etc., Lewis D 14, and so on the right hand, left bank or north side of the river.   The bluff and the small creek are both on the south side, in Mercer Co. This is very near the subsequent site of Fort Berthold, which is in lat. 47° 34', long. 101° 48', nearly, at the southeast angle of the Berthold Indian Reservation.

The three Knife River villages were permanent from 1796 at least till after 1837, when the survivors of the epidemic constituted one village on Knife river. The Hidatsas moved up river in 1845 to their present station, about 60 miles by river and 30 by land, where they were joined by the Arikaras in 1862.   This is Fort Berthold, where the American Fur Co. in 1845 built a stockade named for a founder of this company, the Tyrolese, Bartholomew Berthold (b. 1780, d. Apr. 20th, 1831), of St. Louis.   An opposition trading-post was built in the village in 1859, named Fort Atkinson.   This was frozen out by 1862, when the American Fur Company obtained possession, and the name of Berthold was transferred to Atkinson.   The older stockade was burned by the Sioux, Dec. 24th, 1862, and the new one was mostly destroyed by fire, Oct. 12th, 1874.   The "Little Basin" of the text shows on any good map, between Garfield and Mercer Cos.

without fresh meat; the country between this and Fort Mandan being so frequently disturbed by hunters that the game has become scarce. We then proceeded with a gentle breeze from the south, which carried the periogues on very well; the day was, however, so warm that several of the men worked with no clothes except around the waist, which is the less inconvenient, as we are obliged to wade in some places, owing to the shallowness of the river. At seven miles we reached a large sand-bar making out from the north. We again stopped for dinner, after which we went on to a small plain on the north [in Garfield Co.], covered with cottonwood, where we camped, having made 19 miles.[21]

The country around is much the same as that we passed yesterday; on the sides of the hills, and even on the banks of the rivers, as well as on the sand-bars, is a white substance, which appears in considerable quantities on the surface of the earth, and tastes like a mixture of common salt with Glauber's salts. Many of the streams which come from the foot of the hills are so strongly impregnated with this sub- (*p. 183*) stance that the water has an unpleasant taste and a purgative effect.[22]  A beaver was caught last night by one

---

[21] And having passed to-day a stream from the south, in Mercer Co., which has been called Dancing Bear creek—a name which some maps attach to that one from the south near yesterday's camp, in the bight of the Little Basin.

Among the best maps to go by, from Berthold and Stevenson to the Great Falls, are the sectional charts of the Report of the U. S. Northern Boundary Survey, 4to, Washington, 1878, prepared under the direction of the late Major William J. Twining, Corps of Engineers, U. S. A., and Chief Astronomer of the Survey. The topography was done by Lieut. Francis V. Greene, U. S. T. E. The scale is one inch to eight miles. The Missouri was charted for these maps mainly from observations during our trip in Mackinac boats from Benton to Bismarck, in the fall of 1874. We came over 1,100 traditional Missouri river-miles; the actual distance was 805 miles. Miles made for the carrying-trade of the river are naturally stretched to the utmost; Lewis and Clark's are much more reliable. For instance, we made the distance from Knife river to Stevenson 23½ miles; thence to Berthold, 24½; thence to the little Missouri, 23; total, 71 miles. Lewis and Clark's estimates are wonderfully close to this.

[22] This is the famous " alkali" of many parts of the West, often rendering the water undrinkable, and whitening great areas like snow. It consists largely or mainly of the salt named (sulphate of soda).

of the Frenchmen; we killed two geese, and saw some cranes,[23] the largest bird of that kind common to the Missouri and Mississippi, perfectly white except the large feathers on the first joint of the wing, which are black. Under a bluff opposite our camp we discovered some Indians with horses, whom we supposed were Minnetarees, but the width of the river prevented our speaking to them.

*April* 12*th.* We set off early and passed a high range of hills on the south side, our periogues being obliged to go over to the south, in order to avoid a sand-bank which was rapidly falling in. At six miles we came-to at the lower side of the entrance of the Little Missouri, where we remained during the day for the purpose of making celestial obsertions. [Lewis D 17 gives these.]

This river empties on the south side of the Missouri, 1,693 miles from its confluence with the Mississippi. It rises to the west of the Black mountains, across the northern extremity of which it finds a narrow rapid passage along high perpendicular banks, then seeks the Missouri in a northeastern direction, through a broken country with highlands bare of timber, and the low grounds particularly supplied with cottonwood, elm, small ash, box, alder,[24] and an undergrowth of willow, redwood (sometimes called red or swamp willow), red-berry, and choke-cherry. In its course it passes near the northwest side of Turtle mountain, which is said to be only 12 or 15 miles from its mouth in a straight line a little to the south of west; so that both the Little Missouri and Knife river have been laid down too far southwest.[25] It

[23] The great white or whooping crane, *Grus americana*.

[24] The expression " box, alder," does not mean two different plants, but is a mistake for box-elder, the common name of the ash-leaved maple, *Negundo aceroides*, a sapindaceous tree with pinnate leaves, widely distributed and very common on the upper Missouri. The " redwood " presently named is probably *Cornus stolonifera*, one of the ingredients of kinikinik. See note [3], p. 139.

[25] The source of the Little Missouri is stated with sufficient accuracy, but its general course is more nearly north than northeast, to near the Missouri, when it loops about east to the latter river. Note that the Turtle mountain, here said to be 12 or 15 miles from its mouth, is not the same as, but very far from,

enters the Missouri with a bold current, and is 134 yards
wide, but its greatest depth is two feet and a half; which,
joined to its rapidity and its sand-bars, makes the navigation
difficult except for canoes, which may ascend it for a considerable distance.    At the mouth, and as far as we could
(*p. 184*) discern from the hills between the two rivers about
three miles from their junction, the country is much broken,
the soil consisting of a deep rich dark-colored loam, intermixed with a small portion of fine sand, and covered generally
with a short grass resembling blue-grass.    In its color, the
nature of its bed, and its general appearance, it resembles so
much the Missouri as to induce a belief that the countries
they water are similar in point of soil.    From the Mandan
villages to this place the country is hilly and irregular, with
the same appearance of Glauber's salts and carbonated wood;
the low grounds are smooth, sandy, and partially covered with
cottonwood and small ash; at some distance back there are
extensive plains of a good soil, but without timber or water.

We found great quantities of small onions [*Allium* sp.?]
which grow single, the bulb of an oval form, white, about
the size of a bullet, with a leaf resembling that of the shive
[chive].    On the side of a neighboring hill there is a species
of dwarf cedar [*Juniperus sabina* var. *procumbens*]; it spreads
its limbs along the surface of the earth, which it almost con-
ceals by its closeness and thickness, and is sometimes covered
by it; having always a number of roots on the under side,
while on the upper are a quantity of shoots which, with their
leaves, seldom rise higher than six or eight inches; it is an
evergreen, and its leaf is more delicate than that of the common cedar, though the taste and smell are the same.

The country around has been so recently hunted that the

that Turtle mountain which bestrides the 49th parallel east of Mouse river, on
the northern border of N. Dakota.    The general course of the Little Missouri is
approximately parallel with that of Powder river, a branch of the Yellowstone;
and if it went due north, instead of bearing eastward, it would strike about the
mouth of the Yellowstone; but its mouth is in Williams Co.    One Indian name
of it is Wakpa Chan Shoka, meaning heavily wooded river; another is given as
E-wâh-tark , ah-zhah, Clark C 249.

game is extremely shy, so that a white rabbit [*Lepus cam-pestris*], two beaver, a deer, and a bald eagle [*Haliaëtus leu-cocephalus*], were all that we could procure. The weather had been clear, warm, and pleasant in the morning, but about three we had a squall of high wind and rain, with some thunder, which lasted till after sunset, when it cleared off.

*April* 13*th.* We set out at sunrise, and at nine o'clock, having the wind in our favor, went on rapidly past a timbered low ground on the south, and a creek on the north at the distance of nine miles, which we called [Wild] Onion²⁶ creek, from (*p. 185*) the quantity of that plant which grows in the plains near it. This creek is about 16 yards wide at a mile and a half above its mouth; it discharges more water than is usual for creeks of that size in this country, but the whole plain which it waters is totally destitute of timber. The Missouri itself widens very remarkably just above the junction with the Little Missouri. Immediately at the entrance of the latter it is not more than 200 yards wide, and so shallow that it may be passed in canoes with setting-poles, while a few miles above it is upward of a mile in width. Ten miles beyond Onion creek we came to another, discharging itself on the north in the center of a deep bend. On ascending it for about a mile and a half, we found it to be the discharge of a pond or small lake, which seemed to have been once the bed of the Missouri. Near this lake were the remains of 43 temporary lodges which seemed to belong to the Assiniboins, who are now on the river of the same name.

A great number of swan and geese were also in it; from this circumstance we named the creek Goose²⁷ creek, and

²⁶ So Lewis D 23, and Clark's map, 1814 ; Ognion R., Lapie's map, 1821 ; L'eau qui Monte, Heap ; Rising creek, Stevens ; Tide creek, Warren ; Pride creek, G. L. O. map, 1879 ; charted on Twining's and the Milit. map of Dakota, but nameless. It is in Garfield (lately a part of Stevens) Co.

²⁷ " This lake and it's discharge we call goos Egg," Lewis D 24 ; Goose-egg lake of the Summary Statement ; charted on Clark's map, nameless ; Cold Spring lake, Reynolds ; Sparrow creek, Stevens ; now Shell creek, in Garfield Co. There have been great vicissitudes of the Missouri about its mouth. The birds

the lake by the same name. These geese we observe do not build their nests on the ground or in the sand-bars, but in the tops of the lofty cottonwood trees. We saw some elk and buffalo to-day, but at too great a distance to obtain any of them, though a number of the carcasses of the latter animal are strewed along the shore, having fallen through the ice and been swept along when the river broke up. More bald eagles are seen on this part of the Missouri than we have previously met with; the small sparrow-hawk [*Falco sparverius*], common in most parts of the United States, is also found here. Great quantities of geese are feeding on the prairies, and one flock of white brant, or geese with black [-tipped] wings, and some gray brant with them, pass up the river; from their flight they seem to proceed much further to the northwest. We killed two antelopes, which were very lean, and caught last night two beavers. The French hunters, who had procured seven, thinking the neighborhood of the Little Missouri a (*p. 186*) convenient hunting ground for that animal, remained behind there. In the evening we camped on a beautiful plain on the north, 30 feet above the river, having made 22½ miles.²⁸

*April 14th.* We set off early with pleasant and fair weather. A dog joined us, which we supposed had strayed from the Assiniboin camp on the lake. At 2½ miles we passed timbered low grounds and a small creek. In these low

were the common wild or Canada goose, *Bernicla canadensis.* I confirmed the statement of their breeding in trees when I passed this point on the river in 1874. Geese are wise birds, which know enough to get out of the way of wolves, foxes, and badgers. Lewis and Clark's statement of their arboreal nidification used to be much criticised, and discredited. See my Birds N.W., 1874, p. 555.

²⁸ But not without imminent danger. " A sudden squall of wind struck us and turned the perogue so much on the side as to allarm Sharbono who was steering at the time, in this state of alarm he threw the perogue with her side to the wind, when the spritsail gibing was as near oversetting the perogue as it was possible to have missed. . . I ordered Drewyer to the helm," etc., Lewis D 22. This boat had on board the papers, instruments, medicines, and the most valuable part of the merchandise ; to say nothing of both the captains, three men who could not swim, Sacajawea, and the baby—the helmsman being the only part of the lading that might have been lost without inconvenience.

grounds are several uninhabited lodges built with the boughs of the elm, and the remains of two recent camps, which, from the hoops of small kegs found in them, we judged could belong to Assiniboins only, as they are the only Missouri Indians who use spirituous liquors. Of these they are so passionately fond that it forms their chief inducement to visit the British on the Assiniboin, to whom they barter for kegs of rum their dried and pounded meat, their grease, and the skins of large and small wolves and small foxes.[29] The dangerous exchange is transported to their camps with their friends and relations, and soon exhausted in brutal intoxication. So far from considering drunkenness as disgraceful, the women and children are permitted and invited to share in these excesses with their husbands and fathers, who boast how often their skill and industry as hunters have supplied them with the means of intoxication. In this, as in their other habits and customs, they resemble the Sioux, from whom they are descended. The trade with the Assiniboins and Knistenaux is encouraged by the British, because it procures provision for their *engagés* on their return from Rainy lake to the English river and the Athabasky [Athabasca or Athapasca] country, where they winter, these men being obliged during that voyage to pass rapidly through a country scantily supplied with game.

We halted for dinner near a large village of burrowing-squirrels,[30] which we observed generally selected a southeasterly exposure, though they are sometimes found on the plains. At 10¼ miles we came to the lower point of an

[29] The great gray wolf, *Canis lupus occidentalis ;* the coyote or prairie-wolf, *Canis latrans;* and the kit or swift fox, *Vulpes velox.*

[30] This name is applied to any of the spermophiles met with along the river (seldom, however, to the prairie-dog, which the authors call " barking-squirrel "). The most abundant spermophiles on the upper Missouri, and thence through the Milk river region, are *Spermophilus richardsoni,* a tawny, whole-colored species not distantly resembling a prairie-dog, but lighter colored and smaller, with a very short tail ; and *S. tridecemlineatus pallidus,* a pale variety of the thirteen-lined, leopard, or federation spermophile. (See note at date of July 8th, beyond.) All such animals are " gophers " in the local vernacular.

(*p. 187*) island, which, from the day of our arrival there, we called Sunday island. Here the river washes the bases of the hills on both sides and above the island, which, with its sand-bar, extends 1½ miles. Two small creeks fall in from the south ; the uppermost of these, which is the largest, we called Chaboneau's creek,[31] after our interpreter, who once camped on it several weeks with a party of Indians. Beyond this no white man had ever been except two Frenchmen, one of whom (Lapage) is with us, and who, having lost their way, straggled a few miles further, though to what point we could not ascertain. About 1½ miles beyond this island we camped on a point of woodland on the north, having made in all 14 miles.

The Assiniboins have so recently left the river that game is scarce and shy. One of the hunters shot at an otter last evening ; a buffalo was killed, and an elk, both so poor as to be almost unfit for use ; two white bears were also seen, and a muskrat [*Fiber zibethicus*] swimming across the river. The river continues wide and of about the same rapidity as the ordinary current of the Ohio. The low grounds are wide, the moister parts containing timber ; the upland is extremely broken, without wood, and in some places seems as if it had slipped down in masses of several acres in surface. The mineral appearance of salts, coal, and sulphur, with the burnt hill and pumice-stone, continue, and a bituminous water about the color of strong lye, with the taste of Glauber's salts and a slight tincture of alum. Many geese were feeding in the prairies, and a number of magpies, which build their nests much like those of the blackbird, in trees, and composed of small sticks, leaves, and grass, open at the top ; the egg is of a bluish-brown color, freckled with reddish-brown spots. We also killed a large hooting-owl resembling that of the United States [*Bubo virginianus*], except that it was more booted and clad with feathers. On the hills are many aromatic herbs,[32]

---

[31] Called "Sharbons" creek, in Gass, p. 78 ; Sharbono's, Lewis D 31, 32, *bis*. It looks like a large river on Clark's map of 1814, but I can find nothing on present charts with which to identify it.

[32] Lewis D 29 has : "resembling in taste, smel and appearance, the sage,

resembling in taste, smell, and appearance the sage, hyssop, wormwood, southernwood, juniper, and dwarf cedar; a plant also about two or (*p. 188*) three feet high, similar to the camphor in smell and taste; and another plant of the same size, with a long, narrow, smooth, soft leaf, of an agreeable smell and flavor, which is a favorite food of the antelope, whose necks are often perfumed by rubbing against it.

*April* 15*th.* We proceeded under a fine breeze from the south, and with clear, pleasant weather. At seven miles we reached the lower point of an island,[33] in a bend to the south, which is two miles in length. Captain Clark, who went about nine miles northward from the river, reached the high grounds, which, like those we have seen, are level plains without timber. Here he observed a number of drains, which, descending from the hills, pursue a northeast course, and probably empty into Mouse river, a branch of the Assiniboin, which from Indian accounts approaches very near to the Missouri at this place.[34] Like all the rivulets of this neighborhood these drains are so strongly impregnated with mineral salts that they are not fit to drink. He saw also the remains of several camps of Assiniboins. The low grounds on both sides of the river are extensive, rich, and level. In a little pond on the

hysop, wormwood, southernwood, and two other herbs," where the punctuation of the codex, as of the text, makes ambiguity. I do not read here four different plants, but one plant which resembles these. The commonest sage-brush in the West is *Artemisia tridentata,* which we may suppose here meant. *A. abrotanum* is a S. European sage or wormwood, often cultivated in our gardens under the name of southernwood. The juniper is perhaps *Juniperus communis ;* the dwarf cedar is *J. sabina* var. *procumbens,* above described and determined ; the camphor-like plant, and the other aromatic one, remain to be identified.

[33] There is a very large island—large enough to be indicated on the U. S. Geol. Surv. contour-map, and conspicuous on Twining's—six or eight miles below the mouth of the Little Knife river, and thus in about the place of this one.

[34] The Mouse river does in fact approach the Missouri, where it first strikes the parallel of 49° N. lat., though the approach is far from being so near as that which the loop of the Mouse river makes toward the Missouri about Fort Stevenson. The approximation is certainly not such as the text indicates, and nothing like what is legended on Clark's map ("one mile"). We must remember that this consummate geographer never laid eyes on Mouse river, and could only make conjectures as to its true course. See note [14], p. 261.

north we heard for the first time this season the croaking of
frogs, which exactly resembles that of the small frogs in the
United States.   There are also in these plains great quantities of geese, and many of the [sharp-tailed] grouse, or prairie-
hen, as they are called by the Northwest Company's traders ;
the note of the male, as far as words can represent it, is cook,
cook, cook, coo, coo, coo, the first part of which both male
and female use when flying ; the male too drums with his
wings when he flies in the same way, though not so loud, as
the pheasant ; [35] they appear to be mating.   Some deer, elk,
and goats were in the low grounds, and buffalo on the sand-
beaches, but they were uncommonly shy; we also saw a black
bear and two white ones.   At 15 miles we passed on the
north side a small creek 20 yards wide, which we called
Goat-pen creek, [36] from a park or inclosure for the purpose
of catching that animal which those who went up the creek
found (*p. 189*), and which we presume to have been left
by the Assiniboins.   Its water is impregnated with mineral salts, and the country through which it flows consists
of wide and very fertile plains, but without any trees.
We camped at the distance of 23 miles, on a sand-point to
the south.   We passed in the evening a rock in the middle
of the river, the channel of which, a little above our camp,
is confined within 80 yards.

*April* 16*th*.   The morning was clear, the wind light from
the S.E.   The country presents the same appearance of
low plains and meadows on the river, bounded a few miles
back by broken hills, which end in high level fertile lands ;
the quantity of timber is however increasing.   The appearances of minerals continue as usual, and to-day we found
several stones which seem to have been wood, first carbonated, and then petrified by the water of the Missouri,

[35] The ruffed grouse, *Bonasa umbellus*, always called pheasant in Captain
Lewis' Virginian home.

[36] So on Clark's map, 1814 ; but the name does not occur in Lewis D 33–36 of
this date.   The Little Knife or Upper Knife river falls into the Missouri from the
north, in Mountraille Co., 55 miles above the mouth of the Little Missouri,
and thus corresponds to Goat-pen creek.

which has the same effect on many vegetable substances. There is indeed reason to believe that the strata of coal in the hills cause the fire, and appearances which they exhibit of being burned. Whenever these marks present themselves in the bluffs on the river, the coal is seldom seen ; and when found in the neighborhood of the strata of burnt earth, the coal, with the sand and sulphurous matter usually accompanying it, is precisely at the same height and nearly of the same thickness with those strata. We passed three small creeks [37] or rather runs, which rise in the hills to the north. Numbers of geese and a few ducks, chiefly the mallard [*Anas boscas*] and blue-winged teal [*Querquedula discors*], many buffalo, elk, and deer were also observed ; and in the timbered low grounds this morning we were surprised to observe a great quantity of old hornets' nests. We camped in a point of woods [Grand Point, of Gass] on the south, having come 18 miles, though the circuits which we were obliged to make around sandbars very much increased the real distance.

*April 17th.* We set off early, the weather being fine, and the wind so favorable as to enable us to sail the ( *p. 190*) greater part of the course. At 10¾ miles we passed a creek ten yards wide on the south ; at 18 miles a little run on the north, and at night camped in a woody point on the south.[38] We had traveled 26 miles through a country similar to that of yesterday, except that there were greater appearances of burnt hills, furnishing large quantities of lava and pumice-stone, of the last of which we observe

[37] All nameless in the codex of this date. One of them is called " Hall Strand " on Clark's map (next above Goat-pen creek), and also on Lapie's, 1821 ; it is " Hall's strand, lake and creek " of the Summary Statement ; named for Hugh Hall, a member of the Expedition. One of these streams is the Whiteearth river of some maps, 18½ miles by river above the mouth of the Little Knife ; but it is not the Whiteearth river of Lewis and Clark, for which see April 21st, beyond. At the mouth of one of them is the town of Grinnel.

[38] In Wallace Co.; across the river is Flannery Co. No names in Lewis D for to-day ; nothing on Clark's map from the north, between Hall's strand and the White-earth river of our text (now Muddy river) ; only a trace, unlettered, for one creek from the south. (Examine Dry Fork and Reed Bottom of Stevens.)

some pieces floating down the river, as we had previously done as low as the Little Missouri. In all the copses of wood are remains of the Assiniboin camps; around us are great quantities of game, such as herds of buffalo, elk, antelopes, some deer and wolves, and the tracks of bears; a curlue [curlew, *Numenius longirostris*] was also seen, and we obtained three beavers, the flesh of which is more relished by the men than any other food which we have. Just before we camped we saw some tracks of Indians, who had passed 24 hours before and left four rafts, and whom we supposed to be a band of Assiniboins on their return from war against the Indians of the Rocky mountains.

*April* 18*th.* We had again a pleasant day, and proceeded with a westerly wind, which, however, changed to the N.W. and blew so hard that we were obliged to stop at one o'clock and remain four hours, when it abated and we then continued our course.

We camped about dark on a woody bank, having made 13 miles.[39] The country presented the usual variety of highlands interspersed with rich plains. In one of these we observed a species of pea bearing a yellow flower, which is now in blossom, the leaf and stalk resembling the common pea. It seldom rises higher than six inches, and the root is perennial. On the rose-bushes we also saw a quantity of the hair of the buffalo, which had become perfectly white by exposure and resembled the wool of the sheep, except that it was much finer and more soft and silky. A buffalo which we killed yesterday had shed his long hair, and that which remained was about two inches long, thick, (*p. 191*) fine, and would have furnished five pounds of wool, of which we have no doubt an excellent cloth may be made. Our game to-day was a beaver, a deer, an elk, and some geese. The river has been crooked all day and bearing toward the south.

[39] The crookedness of the Missouri along here makes many miles of navigation for comparatively little advance. The Expedition has not yet reached the mouth of Muddy river (Whiteearth river of our text).

On the hills we observed considerable quantities of dwarf juniper, which seldom grows higher than three feet. We killed in the course of the day an elk, three geese, and a beaver. The beaver on this part of the Missouri are in greater quantities, larger and fatter, and their fur is more abundant and of a darker color, than any we have hitherto seen. Their favorite food seems to be the bark of the cottonwood and willow, as we have seen no other species of tree that has been touched by them, and these they gnaw to the ground through a diameter of 20 inches.

The next day, *Friday, April* 19*th*, the wind was so high from the northwest that we could not proceed;[40] but being less violent on

*April* 20*th*, we set off about seven o'clock, and nearly lost one of the canoes as we left the shore, by the falling in of a large part of the bank. The wind became again so strong that we could scarcely make one mile an hour, and the sudden squalls so dangerous to the small boats that we stopped for the night among some willows on the north,[41] not being able to advance more than 6½ miles. In walking through the neighboring plains we found a fine fertile soil covered with cottonwood, some box-elder, ash [*Fraxinus viridis ?*], red elm, and an undergrowth of willow, rose-bushes, honeysuckle, red willow [*Cornus stolonifera*], gooseberry, currant, and service-berries [*Amelanchier alnifolia*], and along the foot of the hills great quantities of hyssop [*Artemisia* sp.]. Our hunters procured elk and deer, which are now lean, and six beaver, which are fatter and more palatable.

Along the plain there were also some Indian camps ; near one of these was a scaffold about seven feet high, on which were two sleds with their harness, and under it the body of a female, carefully wrapped in several (*p. 192*) dressed buf-

[40] "While we lay here, I went out to the hills, which I found very high, much washed by the rain, and without grass. I saw part of a log quite petrified and of which good whetstones or hones could be made," Gass, p. 79, Apr. 19th.

[41] At this point the Expedition has hardly passed Flannery and Wallace Cos., but next camps on the north are in Buford Co., with Allred Co. across the river.

falo-skins; near it lay a bag made of buffalo-skin, containing a pair of moccasins, some red and blue paint, beavers' nails, scrapers for dressing hides, some dried roots, several plaits of sweet grass, and a small quantity of Mandan tobacco. These things, as well as the body itself, had probably fallen down by accident, as the custom is to place them on the scaffold. At a little distance was the body of a dog not yet decayed, who had met this reward for having dragged thus far in the sled the corpse of his mistress, to whom according to the Indian usage he had been sacrificed.

*April 21st.* Last night there was a hard white frost, and this morning the weather was cold, but clear and pleasant; in the course of the day, however, it became cloudy and the wind rose. The country is of the same description as within the few last days. We saw immense quantities of buffalo, elk, deer, antelopes, geese, and some swans and ducks, out of which we procured three deer and four buffalo calves, which last are equal in flavor to the most delicious veal; also two beaver and an otter. We passed one large and two small creeks on the south side, and reached at 16 [½] miles the mouth of Whiteearth[42] [White Clay in Gass] river, coming in from the north.

This river, before it reaches the low grounds near the Missouri, is a fine bold stream, 60 yards wide, and is deep and navigable; but it is so much choked up at the entrance by the mud of the Missouri that its mouth is not more than ten yards wide. Its course, as far as we could discern from the neighboring hills, is nearly due north,[43] passing through

[42] Not that so called on present maps, but the river now named Little Muddy, or simply Muddy; the last considerable stream before the Yellowstone is reached, in Buford Co.; Williston at its mouth, on Gr. Northern Ry.

[43] From the Missouri, *i. e.,* flowing due south to the Missouri. (See back Apr. 16th, 17th, 18th, and notes there.) White-earth or White Earth river is a prairie stream, heading in the Coteau du Missouri near 49°, and thus near the course of the Mouse river, where the latter crosses this parallel of latitude. It is the most considerable stream which has fallen into the Missouri from the N. or E. for many miles. It is not to be confounded with two "Muddy" rivers, the Little and Big, which fall into the Missouri on the same side, but both in Montana (above the mouth of the Yellowstone).

a beautiful and fertile valley, though without a tree or bush of any description.   Half a mile [two miles] beyond this river we camped on the same[44] [opposite] side below a point of highland, which from its appearance we called Cut bluff.

*April 22d.*   The day clear and cold.   We passed a high bluff on the north, and plains on the south, in which were large herds of buffalo, till breakfast, when the wind became so strong ahead that we proceeded with difficulty even with (*p. 193*) the aid of the towline.   Some of the party now walked across to the Whiteearth river, which here, at the distance of four miles from its mouth, approaches very near to the Missouri.   It contains more water than is usual in streams of the same size at this season, with steep banks about ten or twelve feet high ; the water is much clearer than that of the Missouri.   The salts which have been mentioned as common on the Missouri are here so abundant that in many places the ground appears perfectly white, and from this circumstance the river may have derived its name. It waters an open country and is navigable almost to its source, which is not far from the Saskaskawan ;[45] judging from its size and course, it is probable that it extends as far north as the fiftieth [read forty-ninth] degree of latitude. After much delay in consequence of the high wind, we succeeded in making 11 miles, and camped in a low ground on the south, covered with cottonwood and rabbit-berries.

The hills of the Missouri near this place exhibit large irregular broken masses of rocks and stones, some of which, although 200 feet above the water, seem at some remote period to have been subject to its influence, being apparently

[44] " We reached the place of incampment after dark, which was on the Lard. side a little above *White earth* river. . . S. 50° W. to the upper point of the timbered bottom on Lard. side below a high bluff point which we called *Cut bluff*, —at ½ mile pass White Earth river on Stard.," Lewis D 46, 47.   This last course of the day, S. 50° W., was 2½ miles long ; as White Earth river was passed at the first ½ mile of this course, Cut bluff is a point on the *south* side, two miles above this river, in Allred Co., opposite Buford Co.

[45] Read Mouse river, which the head of the river here described approaches. The Saskatchewan is very much further north and west.

worn smooth by the agitation of the water. These rocks
and stones consist of white and gray granite, a brittle black
rock, flint, limestone, freestone, some small specimens of an
excellent pebble, and occasionally broken strata of a black-
colored stone like petrified wood, which makes good whetstones. The usual appearances of coal, or carbonated wood,
and of pumice-stone, still continue, the coal being of a better
quality, and when burnt affording a hot and lasting fire, emit-
ting very little smoke or flame. There are large herds of
deer, elk, buffalo, and antelopes in view of us; the buffalo
are not so shy as the rest, for they suffer us to approach
within 100 yards before they run, and then stop and resume
their pasture at a very short distance. The wolves to-day
pursued a herd of them, and at length caught a calf that
was unable to keep up with the rest; the mothers on these
(*p. 194*) occasions defend their young as long as they
can retreat as fast as the herd, but seldom return any distance to seek for them.

*April* 23*d.* A clear and pleasant morning; but at nine
o'clock the wind became so high that the boats were in danger of upsetting. We therefore were forced to stop at a place
of safety till about five in the afternoon, when the wind being
lower we proceeded, and camped on the north at the distance
of 13½ miles [thus past Painted Wood creek]. The party
on shore brought us a buffalo calf and three black-tailed
deer. The sand on the river has the same appearances as
usual, except that the quantity of wood increases.

*April* 24*th.* The wind blew so high during the whole day
that we were unable to move; such indeed was its violence
that, though we were sheltered by high timber, the waves
wet many articles in the boats. The hunters went out
and returned with four deer, two elk, and some young wolves
of the small kind.

The party are very much afflicted with sore eyes, which we
presume to be occasioned by the vast quantities of sand
which are driven from the sand-bars in such clouds as often
to hide from us the view of the opposite bank. The particles

of this sand are so fine and light that it floats for miles in the air, like a column of thick smoke ; it is so penetrating that nothing can be kept free from it, and we are compelled to eat, drink, and breathe it very copiously.   To the same cause we attribute the disorder of one of our watches,[46] although its cases are double and tight ; since, without any defect in its works that we can discover, it will not run for more than a few minutes without stopping.

*April 25th.*   The wind moderated this morning, but was still high ; we therefore set out early, the weather being so cold that the water froze on the oars as we rowed ; but about ten o'clock the wind increased so much that we were obliged to stop.   This detention from the wind, and the reports from our hunters of the crookedness of the river, in- (*p. 195*) duced us to believe that we were at no great dis- tance from the Yellowstone.   In order, therefore, to prevent delay as much as possible, Captain Lewis determined to go on by land in search of that river, and make the necessary observations, so as to be enabled to proceed immediately after the boats should join him.   He therefore landed about eleven o'clock on the south side, accompanied by four men ; the boats were prevented from going until five in the afternoon, when they went on a few miles further, and we camped for the night at a distance of 14½ miles.

*April 26th.*   We continued our voyage in the morning, and by twelve o'clock camped at eight miles' distance, at the junction of the Missouri and Yellowstone rivers, where we were soon joined by Captain Lewis.

On leaving us yesterday he pursued his route along the foot of the hills, which he descended to the distance of eight miles ; from these the wide plains watered by the Missouri and the Yellowstone spread themselves before the eye, occa- sionally varied with the wood of the banks, enlivened by the

---

[46] " Attribute it to the sand, with which she seems perfectly charged, notwith- standing her cases are double and tight," Lewis D 52.   The codices generally make their watches, chronometers, sextants, octants, guns, and rifles, of the feminine gender, as well as their boats.

irregular windings of the two rivers, and animated by vast herds of buffalo, deer, elk, and antelope.   The confluence of the two rivers was concealed by the wood, but the Yellowstone itself was only two miles distant, to the south.   He therefore descended the hills and camped on the bank of the river, having killed, as he crossed the plain, four buffaloes ; the deer alone are shy and retire to the woods, but the elk, antelope, and buffalo suffered him to approach them without alarm, and often followed him quietly for some distance.

This morning he sent a man up the river to examine it, while he proceeded down to the junction.   The ground on the lower side of the Yellowstone near its mouth is flat, and for about a mile seems to be subject to inundation ; while that at the point of junction, as well as on the opposite side of the Missouri, is at the usual height of 10 to 18 feet above the water, and therefore not overflowed.   There is more timber in the neighborhood of this (*p. 196*) place, and on the Missouri as far below as Whiteearth [Little Muddy] river, than on any other part of the Missouri on this side of the Chayenne.   The timber consists principally of cottonwood, with some small elm, ash, and box-alder [box-elder, *Negundo aceroides*].   On the sand-bars and along the margin of the river grows the small-leaved willow [*Salix longifolia*] ; in the low grounds adjoining are scattered rose-bushes, three or four feet high, the red-berry [*Shepherdia argentea*], service-berry [*Amelanchier alnifolia*], and redwood [*Cornus stoloni fera*].   The higher plains are either immediately on the river —in which case they are generally timbered and have an undergrowth like that of the low grounds, with the addition of the broad-leaved willow, gooseberry, choke-cherry [*Prunus demissa*], purple currant [*Ribes* sp.], and honeysuckle [*Lonicera involucrata*]—or they are between the low grounds and the hills, and for the most part without wood, or anything except large quantities of wild hyssop [sage-brush, *Artemisia* sp.].   This plant rises about two feet high, and, like the willow of the sand-bars, is a favorite food of the buffalo, elk, deer, grouse, porcupine, hare, and rabbit.

This river, which had been known to the French as the Roche jaune, or as we have called it the Yellowstone,[47] rises according to Indian information in the Rocky mountains [in the Yellowstone National Park]; its sources are near those of the Missouri and [not so near those of] the Platte; it may be navigated in canoes almost to its head. It runs first through a mountainous country, in many parts fertile and well-timbered; it then waters a rich, delightful land, broken into valleys and meadows, and well supplied with wood and water, till it reaches near the Missouri open meadows and low grounds, sufficiently timbered on its borders. In the upper country its course is represented as very rapid; but during the two last and largest portions, its current is much more gentle than that of the Missouri, which it resembles also in being turbid, though with less sediment.

[47] In the codices commonly the Yellow Stone river—perhaps a reminiscence of the time when the Missouri was la Rivière Jaune of the French, or the Yellow river; in Gass, "the river jaune or Yellow Stone." The text reads as if the translation of the French was first made by Lewis and Clark, and in this passage. They are doubtless the real authors of the now famous word; but it certainly did not first appear in print in the present connection, though it may have been first penned in a Lewis or Clark MS. I have before me an extremely interesting letter, which in my arrangement makes part of Codex S. This is no other than the *first rough draft* of Lewis' letter to Jefferson, penned at St. Louis, Sept. 23d, 1806—the day the Expedition returned—announcing the happy arrival of the party. It occupies pp. 1-11 of the codex, is signed by Lewis with his official title, and addressed "The President of the United States." The document is full of interlineations and erasures, showing how Lewis studied and no doubt bit his pen in wording so important an announcement, a clean copy of which was to go to the President. This letter is followed by another, now fragmentary, beginning *verso* of the sheet on which the former letter ends, breaking off in the midst of a sentence, and thus making pp. 12-16 of Codex S. It is dated St. Louis, *Sept.* 21*st*, by a slip of the pen, probably for 23d or 24th, as Lewis was not there till about noon of the 23d. Here we read: " at the distance of 1888 miles we reached the entrance of the Yellow Rock river on the 27th [slip for 26th] of Apl.;" and presently: "we examined the country minutely in the vicinity of the entrance of the River Roghejone"—the *g* overwritten for a *c*, but its tail left as long as that of the *j*. In the codices, *passim*, the word ranges from Rejone, through Rejhone, Rochejone, Rochejohn, Rochejhone, etc., to its proper form.

At this point the Expedition is 305 river-miles above Bismarck, and 500 below Benton; lat. 48° N., nearly; long. 104° W., nearly; altitude about 2,000 feet.

The man [48] who was sent up the river reported in the evening that he had gone about eight miles; that during that distance the river winds on both sides of a plain four or five miles wide; that the current was gentle and much obstructed by sand-bars; that at five miles he had met with a large timbered island, three miles beyond which a (*p. 197*) creek [49] falls in on the S.E., above a high bluff, in which are several strata of coal. The country, as far as he could discern, resembled that of the Missouri, and in the plain he met several of the bighorn animals [*Ovis montana*], but they were too shy to be obtained.

The bed of the Yellowstone, as we observed it near the mouth, is composed of sand and mud, without a stone of any kind. Just above the confluence we measured the two rivers, and found the bed of the Missouri 520 yards wide, the water occupying only 330, and the channel deep; while the Yellowstone, including its sand-bar, occupied 858 yards,

---

They are very nearly in the center of a 30-mile square, which extends for 15 miles north and south, and the same east and west, of the intersection of 48° N. with 104° W., and constitutes the Military Reservation of Fort Buford. This became a large and important post, built a couple of miles below the mouth of the Yellowstone, on the north bank of the Missouri. Buford succeeded to the honors of a historic post, Fort Union, long since disestablished. Old Fort Union was built by the American Fur Company in 1830, on the left bank of the Missouri, about 2¾ miles (more by water) above the mouth of the Yellowstone. It was stockaded with hewn timber about 16 feet high, occupied probably 250 feet square, and was furnished with two bastions. This fort was for many years in charge of Mr. Alexander Culbertson, who also exercised supervision over Forts Pierre and Benton.

Captain Clark's party, of the present Expedition, first explored the Yellowstone, on the return journey, in 1806, when Captain Lewis and his men were over on Maria's river. The honor of discovering the (some) sources of the Yellowstone belongs, I think, to Private John Colter, of the Lewis and Clark party. See his route of 1807, as traced on Clark's map.

The next step of the Expedition will take the party beyond 104° W. long., and so from North Dakota into Montana.

[48] Private Joseph Fields—apparently the first white man who ever ascended the Yellowstone. (Qu.: Where was De La Verendrye, about 1744?)

[49] Oak-tan-pas-er-ha of Lewis' map, 1806, later and better named Fields' creek by Clark; still later and much worse, Charbonneau's creek, I know not by what authority. The bluffs which Fields discovered are now called Forsythe's buttes.

with 297 yards of water; the deepest part of the channel is twelve feet; but the river is now falling, and seems to be nearly at its summer height.

*April 27th.* We left the mouth of the Yellowstone. From the point of junction a wood occupies the space between the two rivers, which at the distance of a mile come within 250 yards of each other. There a beautiful low plain commences, widening as the rivers recede, and extends along each of them for several miles, rising about half a mile from the Missouri into a plain twelve feet higher than itself. The low plain is a few inches above high water mark, and where it joins the higher plain there is a channel of 60 or 70 yards in width, through which a part of the Missouri, when at its greatest height, passes into the Yellowstone. At 2½ miles above the junction, and between the high and low plain, is a small lake,[50] 200 yards wide, extending for a mile parallel with the Missouri along the edge of the upper plain.

At the lower extremity of this lake, about 400 yards from the Missouri, and twice that distance from the Yellowstone, is a situation highly eligible for a trading establishment. This is in the high plain which extends back three miles in width, and seven or eight miles in length, along the Yellowstone, where it is bordered by an extensive body of woodland, and (*p. 198*) along the Missouri with less breadth, till three miles above it is circumscribed by the hills within a space four yards in width. A sufficient quantity of limestone for building may easily be procured near the junction of the rivers; it does not lie in regular strata, but is in large irregular masses, of a light color, and apparently of an excellent quality. Game is very abundant, and as yet quite gentle; above all, its elevation recommends it as preferable to the land at the confluence of the rivers, which their variable channels may render very insecure.

[50] Charted on some maps as Elk lake, in connection with a certain Dog creek. The confluence the two mighty rivers has altered much in detail since 1804—verifying the insecurity of the lowland at the point of meeting, which the practiced eye of the Expedition noticed.

The N.W. wind rose so high at eleven o'clock that we were obliged to stop till about four in the afternoon, when we proceeded till dusk. On the south a beautiful plain separates the two rivers, till at about six miles there is a timbered piece of low ground, and a little above it are bluffs, where the country rises gradually from the river; the situations on the north are more high and open. We camped on that side,[51] the wind, the sand which it raised, and the rapidity of the current having prevented our advancing more than eight miles; during the latter part of the day the river becomes wider and crowded with sand-bars. Although the game is in such plenty, we kill only what is necessary for our subsistence. For several days past we have seen great numbers of buffalo lying dead along the shore, some of them partly devoured by the wolves; they have either sunk through the ice during the winter, or been drowned in attempting to cross, or else, after crossing to some high bluff, found themselves too much exhausted either to ascend or swim back again, and perished for want of food; in this situation we found several small parties of them. There are geese in abundance, and more bald eagles than we have hitherto observed; the nest of these last being always accompanied by those of two or three magpies, which are their inseparable attendants.

[51] Site of old Fort Union, nearly if not exactly on the line between North Dakota and Montana; if in the latter territory, in Dawson Co. Lewis D 64 gives elaborate courses and distances for Apr. 27th, from which the exact spot might be determined.

# CHAPTER VIII.

## THE MISSOURI FROM THE YELLOWSTONE TO THE MUSSEL-SHELL.

Mineral appearances—Formidable bears—Death and description of a grizzly—Martha's river—Abundance of elk—Curiosity of the antelope—Advance of vegetation—Beaver as food—Indian rites—Porcupine river—Two-thousand-mile creek—Much game—Large Indian lodges—Geese of several species—Wolves of different species—Measurements of the largest bear killed—Little Dry and Big Dry creeks—Little Dry river—Bald eagles—Milk river reached—Fresh Indian sign—Big Dry river—Anxiety to sight the Rocky mountains—Indian dog in camp—The men suffer from boils—Minerals, pines, and cedars—A bear-hunt—Ferocity and tenacity of life of the grizzly—Pine creek—Gibson's creek—Another bear-hunt—Narrow escape of one of the boats—Cougar wounded—Rattlesnake creek—Rattlesnakes—Indian camp—Alarm of fire—Cordelling up river—Heavy fog—Blowing-fly creek—The Musselshell river reached—Description of this river and surrounding country—Sacajawea's river, a branch of the Musselshell—A spring of pure water—Bend of the Missouri to receive the Musselshell—The Expedition passes Windy island and Grouse creek, and camps some miles above the Musselshell.

$\mathfrak{S}$UNDAY, April 28th, 1805. The day was clear and pleasant ; the wind having shifted to the southeast we could employ our sails, and went 24 miles to a low ground on the north, opposite the steep bluffs. The country on both sides is much broken, the hills approaching nearer to the river and forming bluffs, some of a white and others of a red color, exhibiting the usual appearances of minerals, and some burnt hills, though without any pumice-stone ; the salts are in greater quantities than usual, and the banks and sand-bars are covered with a white incrustation like frost. The low grounds are level, fertile, and partially timbered, but are not so wide as for a few days past. The woods are now green, but the plains and meadows seem to have less verdure than those below. The only streams which we met to-day are two small runs on the north,[1] and one on the south, which rise in the neighboring hills, and have very

---

[1] The second and larger of these, ten or twelve miles by land from Fort Buford, is now called Little Muddy river ; this is the stream marked "Ibex Cr." on Clark's map of 1814 ; at its mouth is town of Hilva, Dawson Co.

little water.  At the distance of 18 miles the Missouri makes a considerable bend to the southeast.  Game is very abundant—the common, and the mule or black-tailed deer, elk, buffalo, antelope, brown bear, beaver, and geese.  The beaver have committed great devastation among the trees, one of which, nearly three feet in diameter, had been gnawed through by them.

(*p. 200*) *April 29th.*  We proceeded early, with a moderate wind.  Captain Lewis, who was on shore with one hunter, met about eight o'clock two white bears.[2]  Of the strength and ferocity of this animal the Indians had given us dreadful accounts.  They never attack him but in parties of six or eight persons, and even then are often defeated with a loss of one or more of their party.  Having no weapons but bows and arrows, and the bad guns with which the traders supply them, they are obliged to approach very near to the bear ; as no wound except through the head or heart is mortal, they frequently fall a sacrifice if they miss their aim.  He rather attacks than avoids a man, and such is the terror which he has inspired, that the Indians who go in quest of him paint themselves and perform all the superstitious rites customary when they make war on a neighboring nation.  Hitherto those bears we had seen did not appear desirous of encountering us ; but although to a skillful rifleman the danger is very much diminished, yet the white bear is still a terrible animal.  On approaching these two, both Captain Lewis and the hunter fired, and each wounded a bear.  One of them made his escape ; the other turned upon Captain

---

[2] Lewis and Clark will have it that these bears are "white"—and the countless repetitions in the books, of adventures with these ferocious beasts, insist on this color—much as if they were speaking of the polar bear (*Thalassarctos maritimus*).  But by "white" we must understand merely some light color (in comparison with the common black bear), translating an Indian name.  Thus Gass, invariably matter-of-fact, remarks :  "The natives call them white, but they are more of a brown-gray;" and Lewis D 66 itself says here, "two brown or white bears."  The species is of course the grizzly, *Ursus horribilis*, new to science in 1805, first described sufficiently in these codices, and not technically named till 1815 (Ord, Guthrie's Geogr., 2d Am. ed., II., pp. 291, 299).

Lewis and pursued him 70 or 80 yards, but being badly wounded the bear could not run so fast as to prevent him from reloading his piece, which he again aimed at him, and a third shot from the hunter brought him to the ground. He was a male, not quite full grown, and weighed about 300 pounds. The legs are somewhat longer than those of the black bear, and the talons and tusks much larger and longer. The testicles are also placed much further forward and suspended in separate pouches from two to four inches asunder, while those of the black bear are situated back between the thighs and in a single pouch like those of the dog. Its color is a yellowish-brown; the eyes are small, black, and piercing; the front of the fore legs near the feet is usually black, and the fur is finer, thicker, and deeper than that of the black bear. Add to which, it is a more furious animal, and very remarkable for the wounds which it will bear without dying.

(*p. 201*) We are surrounded with deer, elk, buffalo, antelopes, and their companions the wolves, which have become more numerous and make great ravages among them. The hills are here much more rough and high, and almost overhang the banks of the river. There are greater appearances of coal than we have hitherto seen, the strata being in some places six feet thick; and there are strata of burnt earth, which are always on the same level with those of coal.

In the evening, after coming 25 miles, we camped at the entrance of a river which empties into a bend on the north side of the Missouri. This stream, which we called Martha's river,[3] is about 50 yards wide, with water for 15

---

[3] " This stream my friend Capt. C. named Martha,s river," Lewis D 69—the name first spelled " Marthy," then the tail of the *y* erased with a knife, and the letter turned into an *a*, with a comma instead of an apostrophe before the *s*; then a line very heavily overwritten with bold backhand strokes. It reads " in honour of Miss M."— followed by an initial of her surname, which I cannot decipher, but which was probably F or T. It is too bad, and we will settle this score with the gallant young captain when we come to Maria's river. Martha's river is now known as the Big Muddy; it is the first considerable stream from the north falling into the Missouri above the mouth of the Yellowstone. It heads by several affluents north of 49°, forms its main stream along

yards; the banks are of earth, and steep, though not high, and the bed is principally of mud. Captain Clark, who ascended it for three miles, found that it continued of the same width, with a gentle current, pursuing its course about N. 30° W. through an extensive, fertile, and beautiful valley, but without a single tree. The water is clear, and has a brownish yellow tint; at this place the highlands [e. g., Stone Point and Hole-in-the-Wall], which yesterday and to-day had approached so near the river, became lower, and, receding from the water, left a valley seven or eight miles wide.

*April 30th.* The wind was high from the north during last evening, and continued so this morning. We however proceeded, and found the river more winding than usual, with a number of sand-islands and bars, on one of which last we camped, at the distance of 24 miles.[4] The low grounds are fertile and extensive, but with very little timber, and that cottonwood, very bad of its kind; being too small for planks, broken and dead at the top, and unsound in the center of the trunk. We passed some ancient lodges of driftwood, which do not appear to have been lately inhabited.

The game continues abundant. We killed the largest male elk we have yet seen; on placing it in its natural erect position, we found that it measured 5 feet 3 inches from

the Wood or Woody mountains about that parallel of latitude, runs S.E. and then S. into the Missouri, 30 miles by land above Fort Buford. The course is approximately parallel with that of Porcupine (Poplar) river, beyond. As to the valley mentioned at the end of the above paragraph, it may be observed that the 2,000-foot contour-line recedes a good deal up Martha's river. This leaves the country flat. On reaching this river in the summer of 1874, we found it unfordable for our wagon-train, and had to wait two days to build a bridge. The officers of the military escort, having nothing else to do, instituted the national game, which was kept up without intermission day and night, by successive relays of players; whence the spot became known as Poker Flats. The E. boundary of Fort Peck Indian Res. meanders Muddy river; Blair is at its mouth.

[4] Thus a little past a place on the north side called Frenchman's Point, about 20 miles above the mouth of the Big Muddy or Martha's river. Here the bluffs come close to the Missouri, and the trail from Fort Buford skirts the north bank of the river. Camp is at town of Brockton. Hence to the next river—Poplar or Porcupine—is only some twelve miles by land, though many more by water.

the point of the hoof to the top (*p. 202*) of the shoulder. The antelopes are yet lean, and the females are with young. This fleet and quick-sighted animal is generally the victim of its curiosity. When they first see the hunters they run with great velocity; if he lies down on the ground and lifts up his arm, his hat, or his foot, the antelope returns on a light trot to look at the object, and sometimes goes and returns two or three times, till it approaches within reach of the rifle. So, too, they sometimes leave their flock to go and look at the wolves, which crouch down, and, if the antelope be frightened at first, repeat the same maneuver, and sometimes relieve each other, till they decoy it from the party, when they seize it. But generally the wolves take them as they are crossing the rivers; for, although swift of foot, they are not good swimmers.

*Wednesday, May 1st.* The wind was in our favor, and we were enabled to use the sails till twelve o'clock, when the wind became so high and squally that we were forced to come-to at the distance of ten miles, on the south, in a low ground stocked with cottonwood, and remain there during the day; one of the canoes being separated from us, and not able to cross over, in consequence of the high waves. The country around is more pleasant than that through which we have passed for several days, the hills being lower and the low grounds wider and better supplied with timber, which consists principally of cottonwood. The undergrowth is willow on the banks and sand-bars, rose-bushes, red-willow, and the broad-leaved willow in the low plains; while the high country on both sides is one extensive plain, without wood, though the soil is a dark, rich, mellow loam. Our hunters killed a buffalo, an elk, a goat, two beaver, and also a bird of the plover kind.[5]

---

[5] Lewis D 72, 73, and Q 49–51; long descriptions. This "plover" is the avocet, *Recurvirostra americana*, which I found very common hereabouts, and in the Milk river region. Lewis' specimen was killed by George Shannon, and the peculiarity of the slender *retroussé* bill struck him: "precisely resembles whalebone," he says.

*May 2d.* The wind continued high during the night; at daylight it began to snow, and did not stop till ten o'clock, when the ground was covered an inch deep, forming a striking contrast with the vegetation, which is now considerably advanced, some flowers having put forth, (*p. 203*) and the cottonwood leaves being as large as a dollar. The wind lulled about five o'clock in the afternoon, and we then proceeded,[6] along wide fertile low grounds and high level plains, and camped at the distance of four miles. Our game to-day was deer, elk, and buffalo; we also procured three beaver, which are quite gentle, as they have not been hunted, though when the hunters are in pursuit they never leave their huts during the day. This animal we esteem a great delicacy, particularly the tail, which when boiled resembles in flavor the fleshy tongues and sounds of the codfish, and is generally so large as to afford a plentiful meal for two men. One of the hunters [J. Fields], in passing near an old Indian camp, found several yards of scarlet cloth, suspended on the bough of a tree as a sacrifice to the deity by the Assiniboins. The custom of making these offerings is common among that people, as indeed among all the Indians on the Missouri.[7] The air was sharp this evening; the water froze on the oars as we rowed, and in the morning,

*May 3d,* the weather became quite cold; the ice was a quarter of an inch thick in the kettle, and the snow still continued on the hills, though it had melted from the plains. The wind continued high from the west, but not so violently as to prevent our going on. At two miles from our camp we passed a curious collection of bushes,

---

[6] " Capt. Clark pursued his walk, while I continued with the party, it being a rule which we had established, never to be absent at the same time from the party," Lewis D 76.

[7] " To offer or sacrefice in this manner to the deity watever they may be possessed of which they think most acceptable to him, and very honestly making their own feelings the test of those of the deity offer him the article which they most prize themselves," etc., Lewis D 75, indicating a species of theology not peculiar to the Assiniboins.

about 30 feet high and 10 or 12 in diameter, tied in the form of a fascine and standing on end in the middle of the low ground. This we supposed to have been left by the Indians as a religious sacrifice. At twelve o'clock, the usual hour, we halted for dinner. The low grounds on the river are much wider than common, sometimes extending from five to nine miles to the highlands, which are much lower than heretofore, not being more than 50 or 60 feet above the lower plain. Through all this valley, traces of the ancient bed of the river are everywhere visible, and since the hills have become lower, the strata of coal, burnt earth, and pumice-stone have in a great measure ceased; (*p. 204*) there being in fact none to-day. At the distance of 14 miles we reached the mouth of a river on the north, which, from the unusual number of porcupines [*Erethizon epixanthus*] near it, we called Porcupine river.[8]

This is a bold and beautiful stream, 112 yards wide, though the water is only 40 yards at its entrance. Captain Clark, who ascended it several miles and passed it above where it enters the highlands, found it continued nearly of the same width and about knee-deep; and as far as he could distinguish, for 20 miles from the hills, its course was from a little to the east of north. There was much timber on the low grounds; he found some limestone also on the surface of the earth in the course of his walk, and saw a range of low mountains at a distance to the west of north, whose direction was northwest; the adjoining country

[8] Now Poplar river, with the flourishing military post of same name at its mouth; Quaking Ash river of Heap, " Porcupine " being now the first branch of Milk river, and forming the western boundary of Fort Peck Indian Reservation. Porcupine river of L. and C. is the second large stream emptying into the Missouri above the mouth of the Yellowstone. It heads north of 49° by several affluents flowing from the 3,000-foot contour-line and upward, and courses S.E. or E. of S., approximately parallel with Martha's river. The statements with which the next paragraph concludes are a good deal out. It appears in various places that our authors never realized the great distance of the nearest Saskatchewan waters, between which and themselves intervened the whole Milk river watershed, of whose extent they were ignorant. Milk river was unknown till discovered by them at its mouth, May 8th.

being everywhere level, fertile, open, and exceedingly beautiful. The water of this river is transparent, and is the only one that is so of all those that fall into the Missouri. Before entering a large sand-bar through which it discharges itself, its low grounds are formed of a stiff blue and black clay, and its banks, which are from eight to ten feet high and seldom if ever overflowed, are composed of the same materials. From the quantity of water which this river contains, its direction, and the nature of the country through which it passes, it is not improbable that its sources may be near the main body of the Saskaskawan, and as in high water it can be no doubt navigated to a considerable distance, it may be rendered the means of intercourse with the Athabasky country, from which the Northwest Company derive so many of their valuable furs.

A quarter of a mile beyond this river a creek falls in on the south, to which, on account of its distance from the mouth of the Missouri, we gave the name of Two-thousand-mile creek.[9] It is a bold stream with a bed 30 yards wide. At 3½ miles above Porcupine river, we reached some high timber on the north, and camped just above an (*p. 205*) old channel of the river, which is now dry. We saw vast quantities of buffalo, elk, deer, principally of the long-tailed kind [*Cariacus virginianus macrurus*], antelope, beaver, geese, ducks, brant, and some swan. The porcupines too are numerous, and so careless and clumsy that we can approach very near without disturbing them, as they are feeding on the young willows. Toward evening we also found for the first time the nest of a goose among some driftwood, all that we had hitherto seen being on the top of a broken tree on the forks, invariably from 15 to 20 or more feet in height.

*May 4th.* We were detained till nine o'clock in order to

---

[9] Now Red-water creek, a considerable stream from the south, which is given on some modern maps as passing into the Missouri a short distance *below* Poplar river. It drains from an elevation of about 3,000 feet, between the Missouri and the Yellowstone. Stevens marks it Little Dry creek, badly.

repair the rudder of one of the boats, and when we set out the wind was ahead; at 6½ [10] miles we passed a small creek in a deep bend on the south, with a sand-island opposite it ; then, passing along an extensive plain, which gradually rises from the north side of the river, we camped at the distance of 18 miles,[11] in a point of woodland on the north. The river is this day wider than usual and crowded with sand-bars on all sides; the country is level, fertile, and beautiful; the low grounds are extensive, and contain a much greater portion of timber than is common. Indeed, all the forepart of the day the river was bordered with timber on both sides, a circumstance very rare on the Missouri, and the first that has occurred since we left the Mandans. There are, as usual, vast quantities of game, extremely gentle; the male buffalo particularly will scarcely give way to us, and as we approach will merely look at us for a moment, as something new, and then quietly resume their feeding.

In the course of the day we passed some old Indian hunting-camps, one of which consisted of two large lodges, fortified with a circular fence 20 or 30 feet in diameter, made of timber laid horizontally, the beams overlying each other to the height of five feet, and covered with the trunks and limbs of trees that have drifted down the river. The lodges themselves are formed by three or more strong sticks about the size of a man's leg or arm and twelve feet long, (*p. 206*) which are attached at the top by a whith [withe] of small willows, and spread out so as to form at the base a circle of 10 to 14 feet in diameter. Against these are placed pieces of driftwood and fallen timber, usually in three ranges, one on the other ; the interstices are covered with leaves, bark,

[10] *Sic*—but 9½ by the codex ; three courses to this creek, of 3, 5, and 1½ miles, respectively, Lewis D 81. This is the creek charted on Clark's map, next above his 2,000-mile creek, with the Indian Fort marked at its mouth. Such a stream also appears on Twining's map, with a large island at its mouth.

[11] This takes the party past Tooly, Tooley, Tulé, or Tulle, also Frog, creek, on the north, only ten miles by the Buford trail from the Poplar river ; but nothing appears in text or code:: about it. Present site of Chelsea, on G. N. Ry.,, also passed.

and straw, so as to form a conical figure about ten feet high, with a small aperture in one side for the door.   It is, however, at best a very imperfect shelter against the inclemencies of the seasons.

*May 5th.*   We had a fine morning, and the wind being from the east we used our sails.   At the distance of five miles we came to a small island, and twelve miles further camped on the north, at the distance of 17 miles.[12]   The country, like that of yesterday, is beautiful in the extreme.

Among the vast quantities of game around us, we distinguish a small species of goose [*Bernicla hutchinsi*] differing considerably from the common Canadian goose [*B. canadensis*]; its neck, head, and beak being much thicker, larger, and shorter in proportion to its size, which is nearly a third smaller; the noise too resembling more that of the brant or of a young goose that has not yet fully acquired its note; in other respects—in color, habits, and the number of feathers in the tail—the two species correspond; this species also associates in flocks with the large geese, but we have not seen it pair with them.   The white brant [*Chen hyperboreus*] is about the size of the common brown brant [*Bernicla brenta*], or two-thirds of the common goose, than which it is also six inches shorter from the extremity of the wings, though the beak, head, and neck are larger and stronger; the body and wings are of a beautiful pure white, except the black feathers of the first joint of the wings; the beak and legs are of a reddish or flesh-colored white; the eye is of moderate size; the pupil is of a deep sea-green, encircled with a ring of yellowish-brown; the tail consists of 16 feathers equally long; the flesh is dark; and [in this respect], as well as in its note, [this brant] differs but little from the common brant, which in form and habits it resembles, and with which it (*p. 207*) sometimes unites in a common flock.   The white brants also

---

[12] "Soon after seting out the rudder irons of the white perogue were broken by her runing fowl on a sawyer, she was however refitted in a few minutes with some tugs of raw hide and nales," Lewis D 82.   Several small streams or runs are passed unnoticed since Tooley, or Frog creek; site of Macon also passed.

associate by themselves in large flocks; but as they do not seem to be mated or paired off, it is doubtful whether they reside here during the summer for the purpose of rearing their young. [They go much further north to breed.]

The wolves are also very abundant, and are of two species. First, the small wolf or burrowing-dog of the prairies [coyote, *Canis latrans*], which is found in almost all the open plains. It is of an intermediate size between the fox and dog, very delicately formed, fleet and active. The ears are large, erect, and pointed; the head is long and pointed, like that of the fox; the tail long and bushy; the hair and fur are of a pale reddish-brown color, though much coarser than that of the fox; the eye is of a deep sea-green color, small and piercing; the talons are rather longer than those of the wolf of the Atlantic States, which animal, as far as we can perceive, is not to be found on this side of the Platte.[13] These wolves usually associate in bands of ten or twelve, and are rarely if ever seen alone. not being able singly to attack a deer or antelope. They live and rear their young in burrows, which they fix near some pass or spot much frequented by game, and sally out in a body against any animal which they think they can overpower; but on the slightest alarm retreat to their burrows, making a noise exactly like that of a small dog.

The second species [*Canis lupus occidentalis*] is lower, shorter in the legs, and thicker than the Atlantic wolf; the color, which is not affected by the seasons, is of every variety of shade, from a gray or blackish-brown to a cream-colored white. They do not burrow, nor do they bark, but howl; they frequent the woods and plains, and skulk along the skirts of the buffalo herds, in order to attack the weary or wounded.

Captain Clark and one of the hunters [Drewyer] met this evening the largest brown bear [grizzly bear, *Ursus horribilis*]

---

[13] A mistake. The common wolf, in some of its varieties, was found in most parts of North America, though it is now exterminated from settled regions. It is this wolf which is described in the next paragraph.

we have seen. As they fired he did not attempt to attack, but fled with a most tremen- (*p. 208*) dous roar; and such was his extraordinary tenacity of life that, although five balls passed through his lungs and he had five other wounds, he swam more than half across the river to a sand-bar, and survived 20 minutes. He weighed between 500 and 600 pounds at least, and measured 8 feet 7½ inches from the nose to the extremity of the hind feet, 5 feet 10½ inches round the breast, 3 feet 11 inches round the neck, 1 foot 11 inches round the middle of the foreleg, and his talons, five on each foot, were 4⅜ inches in length. This differs from the common black bear [*Ursus americanus*] in having its talons much longer and more blunt; its tail shorter; its hair of a reddish or bay brown, longer, finer, and more abundant; his liver, lungs, and heart much larger, even in proportion to his size, the heart being equal to that of a large ox; his maw ten times larger; his testicles pendant from the belly and in separate pouches four inches apart. Besides fish and flesh, he feeds on roots and every kind of wild fruit.

The antelope are now lean and with young, so that they may readily be caught at this season, as they cross the river from S.W. to N.E.

*May 6th.* The morning being fair and the wind favorable, we set sail and proceeded on very well the greater part of the day. The country continues level, rich, and beautiful; the low grounds are wide and, comparatively with the other parts of the Missouri, well supplied with wood. The appearances of coal, pumice-stone, and burnt earth have ceased, though the salts of tartar or vegetable salts continue on the banks and sand-bars, and sometimes in the little ravines at the base of the low hills. We passed three streams on the south : the first, at the distance of 1½ miles from our camp, was about 25 yards wide ; but although it contained some water in standing pools, it discharged none ; this we called Littledry creek, about eight miles beyond which is Bigdry creek, 50 yards wide, without any water ;

the (*p. 209*) third is six miles further, and has the bed of a large river 200 yards wide, yet without a drop of water. Like the other two, this stream, which we called Bigdry[14] river, continues its width undiminished as far as we can dis-cern. The banks are low; the channel is formed of fine brown sand, intermixed with a small proportion of little pebbles of various colors; the country around is flat and without trees. These rivers had recently discharged their waters; from their appearance and the nature of the country through which they pass, we concluded that they rise in the Black mountains, or in the level low plains which are probably between this place and the mountains; that the country being nearly of the same kind and of the same latitude, the rains of spring, melting the snows about the same time, conspire to throw at once vast quantities of water down these channels, which are then left dry during the summer, autumn, and winter, when there is very little rain. We had to-day a slight sprinkling, but it lasted a very short time. The game is in such plenty that it has become a mere amusement to supply the party with provisions.

[14] " Big Dry river " (printed " Bigdry " river) is a mistake for *Little* Dry river, as appears from orig. ed. p. 212, from the Summary Statement at the end of the book, and from the codex : " The first of these we call little dry creek . . . the 2d. 50 yards wide . . . we called it Big dry Creek, the 3d. . . . which we called little dry river," Lewis D 87.   The real Big Dry river is beyond the mouth of Milk river.   The sequence of these " dry " creeks and rivers, or coulées is : 1, Little Dry creek; 2, Big Dry creek ; 3, Little Dry river ; and 4 (beyond Milk river), Big Dry river.   All four of these coulées make into the Missouri from the south.   The statement that the three former of these " rise in the Black mountains," etc., is very far out.   The authors seem to have been misled by the diameters of these coulées, and to have forgotten for the moment that they had passed the mouth of the Yellowstone, the whole watershed of which great river necessarily lay between these coulées and any part of the Black hills—or else, and more likely, they mean by " Black moun-tains " anything mountainous east of the Rockies.   Clark charts all four of these coulées : No. 1, nameless (elsewhere Lackwater creek); Nos. 2, 3, 4, by names, as in this note.   Old Fort Charles was near one of them, on the north bank of the Missouri.   No. 2 is now Elk Prairie creek.   Clark also charts, from the *north*, a stream he calls " Argalia "—a name not in Lewis D, nor in the Sum-mary Statement.   This is Wolf creek of Twining's and other maps ; Wolf Point (town) here now.

We made 25 miles to a clump of trees on the north, where we passed the night.

*May 7th.* The morning was pleasant, and we proceeded at an early hour. There is much driftwood floating; and, what is contrary to our expectation, although the river is rising the water is somewhat clearer than usual. At eleven o'clock the wind became so high that one of the boats was nearly sunk, and we were obliged to stop till one o'clock, when we proceeded, and camped on the south, above a large sand-bar projecting from the north, having made 15 miles.[15]  On the north side of the river are the most beautiful plains we have yet seen; they rise gradually from the low grounds on the water to the height of 50 or 60 feet, and then extend in an unbroken level as far as the eye can reach. The hills on the south are more broken and higher, though at some distance back the country becomes level and fertile. (*p. 210*) There are no more appearances of burnt earth, coal, or pumice-stone, though that of salt still continues, and the vegetation seems to have advanced but little since the 28th of last month. Game is as abundant as usual. The bald eagles, of which we see great numbers, probably feed on the carcasses of dead animals; for on the whole Missouri we have seen neither the blue-crested fisher [kingfisher, *Ceryle alcyon*], nor the fishing-hawk [*Pandion carolinensis*], to supply them with their favorite food; and the water of the river is so turbid that no bird which feeds exclusively on fish can procure a subsistence.

*May 8th.* A light breeze from the east carried us 16 miles, till we halted for dinner at the entrance of a river on the north. Captain Clark, who had walked on the south, on ascending a high point opposite its entrance discovered

---

[15] A place is named in the Summary Statement, "Gulf in the Island Bend," and located 13 miles below Milk river. But no such name appears in the text here or in Lewis D of this date. This is between Bark creek (south, Indian fight there, 1876) and a certain stream or coulée from the north, now called Little Porcupine creek, whose mouth our survey made 15 miles below Milk river; town of Lenox there now.

a level and beautiful country which it watered ; that its course for 12 or 15 miles was N.W., when it divided into two nearly equal branches, one pursuing a direction nearly N., the other to the W. of N.W. Its width at the entrance is 150 yards ; on going three miles up, Captain Lewis found it to be of the same breadth and sometimes more ; it is deep, gentle, and has a large quantity of water ; its bed is principally of mud; the banks are abrupt, about twelve feet in height, and formed of a dark, rich loam and blue clay ; the low grounds near it are wide and fertile, and possess a considerable proportion of cottonwood and willow. It seems to be navigable for boats and canoes ; by this circumstance, joined to its course and quantity of water, which indicates that it passes through a large extent of country, we are led to presume that it may approach the Saskaskawan and afford a communication with that river. The water has a peculiar whiteness, such as might be produced by a tablespoonful of milk in a dish of tea, and this circumstance induced us to call it Milk river.[16]

[16] By far the greatest of all the northern tributaries of the upper Missouri. The surmise of its approach to the Saskatchewan is correct. Some southern sources of the latter head with Milk river in the main divide of the Rocky mountains a little south of 49°, or the northern border of Montana. Milk river skirts this parallel of latitude, a little north of it for some distance, crosses the parallel about 110° 30′ W. long., then runs in Montana approximately eastward, but with general southerly inclination, to the Missouri near 106° 18′ W. long. In its course the Milk river receives many tributaries, from both sides, thus draining the whole country south of the Saskatchewan watershed. These tributaries have mostly a general north and south course, and a number of them cross 49° N. lat., in each of these directions. The largest flow south into Milk river after the latter has entered Montana, as Cottonwood, Frenchman's, Little Rocky, and Big Porcupine rivers. The latter is very large—about like Poplar and Martha's rivers—and is the north "fork" of Milk river which Captain Clark discovered. At the crossing of 49° was a station called Milk River Post ; Fort Assiniboin is now lower down. On Frenchman's river is (or was in 1874, when I was there) Fort M. J. Turnay—a very disagreeable place. The Bear's Paw mountains and the Little Rocky mountains separate the Milk river watershed from that of the Missouri. At the mouth of Milk river the G. N. Ry. leaves the Missouri, along the north bank of which it runs up to here from the Muddy, below the mouth of the Yellowstone, and ascends Milk river, crossing at Glasgow. For the headline of this page, see Lewis' map, 1806.

In the evening we had made 27 miles, and camped on the south [six miles above Milk river, Lewis D 97]. The country on that side consists in general of high bro- (*p. 211*) ken hills, with much gray, black, and brown granite scattered over the surface of the ground. At a little distance from the river there is no timber on either side, the wood being confined to the margin of the river; so that unless the contrary is particularly mentioned, it is always to be understood that the upland is perfectly naked, and that we consider the low grounds well timbered if even a fifth be covered with wood. The wild licorice [*Glycyrrhiza lepidota*] is found in great abundance on these hills, as is also the white-apple [pomme blanche of the French, *Psoralea esculenta*]. As usual, we are surrounded by buffalo, elk, common and black-tailed deer, beaver, antelopes, and wolves. We observed a place where an Indian had recently taken the hair off an antelope's skin, and some of the party thought they distinguished imperfectly some smoke and Indian lodges, up Milk river—marks which we are by no means desirous of realizing, as the Indians are probably Assiniboins, and might be very troublesome.

*May 9th.* We again had a favorable wind, and sailed along very well. Between four and five miles we passed a large island in a deep bend to the north, with a large sandbar at the upper point. At 15¼ miles we reached the bed of a most extraordinary [Big Dry] river, which presents itself on the south.[17] Though as wide as the Missouri itself, —that is, about half a mile,—it does not discharge a drop of water, and contains nothing but a few standing pools. On ascending it three miles we found an eminence from which we saw the direction of the channel, first south for ten or

[17] Had our travelers been as familiar with the Upper Missouri country as they were with the great river itself, they would have thought less of this great dry course. Many of the smaller rivers run dry, and their courses are often road-beds for long distances. This Big Dry river retains its name. (For other such coulées, of similar names, see note [14], May 6th, p. 299.) It is in the bight of a small, sharp bend of the Missouri, on rounding which the Expedition will reach the site of the long celebrated Fort Peck Indian Agency.

twelve miles, then turning to the E.S.E. as far as we could see. It passes through a wide valley without timber; the surrounding country consists of waving low hills, interspersed with some handsome level plains; the banks are abrupt, and consist of a black or yellow clay, or of a rich sandy loam; though they do not rise more than six or eight feet above the bed, they exhibit no appearance of being overflowed; the bed is entirely composed of a light brown sand, the particles of which, like (*p. 212*) those of the Missouri, are extremely fine.    Like the dry rivers we passed before, this seemed to have discharged its waters recently, but the watermark indicated that its greatest depth had not been more than two feet.    This stream, if it deserve the name, we called Bigdry [Big Dry] river.

About a mile below is a large creek on the same side, which is also perfectly dry.    Mineral salts and quartz are in large quantities near this neighborhood.    The sand of the Missouri from its mouth to this place has been mixed with a substance which we had presumed to be a granulated talk [talc], but which is most probably this quartz.    The game is now in great quantities, particularly the elk and buffalo, which last is so gentle that the men are obliged to drive them out of the way with sticks and stones.    The ravages of the beaver are very apparent; in one place the timber was entirely prostrated for a space of three acres in front on the river and one in depth, and great part of it removed, though the trees were in large quantities, and some of them as thick as the body of a man.    At the distance of 24 miles we camped, after making 25½ miles, at the entrance of a small creek in a bend on the north, to which we gave the name of Werner's creek, after one of our men.[18]

[18] William Werner, or Warner; latter in Gass; Werner's run of the Summary Statement, there located nine miles above mouth of Big Dry river; charted as Warner's Run on Clark's map; the first stream from the north above Fort Peck, the site of which has been passed to-day.    The double statements of distances in text, " 24 " and " 25½ " miles, I suppose to be a slip; neither agrees exactly with Lewis D 112, where the distances for May 9th foot up 24½ miles in all.

At this date Lewis D 111 gives a page of description of a remarkable " plover,"

For several days past the river has been as wide as it generally is near its mouth ; but as it is much shallower, crowded with sand-bars, and the color of the water has become much clearer, we do not yet despair of reaching the Rock [Rocky] mountains, for which we are very anxious.

*May 10th.* We had not proceeded more than 4¼ miles when the violence of the wind forced us to halt for the day, under some timber in a bend on the south side. The wind continued high, the clouds thick and black, and we had a

of which he shot four ; the same is in Lewis Q 52, 53. This bird is the semi-palmated tattler or willet, *Symphemia semipalmata*, now a well-known species.

Also at this date Lewis D 109 gives an amusing relation, which I cannot forbear to quote, of Chaboneau's cookery, the result of which must have been a nasty mess, suggesting a cross between a sausage and a suet-pudding. Here is the recipe : " From the cow I killed we saved the necessary materials for making what our wrighthand cook Charbono calls the *boudin blanc* [interlined " poudingue " by Clark in red ink] . . . About 6 feet of the lower extremity of the large gut of the Buffaloe is the first mosel that the cook makes love to ; this he holds fast at one end with the right hand, while with the forefinger and thumb of the left he gently compresses it, and discharges what he says is not good to eat, but of which in the squel [sequel] we get a moderate portion ; the mustle lying underneath the shoulder blade next to the back and fillets are next saught, these are needed [kneaded] up very fine with a good portion of the kidney suit [suet] ; to this composition is then added a just proportion of pepper and salt and a small quantity of flour ; thus far advanced our skillfull opporater C——ɔ seizes his recepticle [*i. e.*, the gut], which has never once touched the water, for that would intirely distroy the regular order of the whole procedure ; you will not forget that the [out] side you now see is that covered with a good coat of fat, provided the anamal be in good order ; the operator seizes the recepticle I say, and tying it fast at one end turns it inwards and begins now with repeated evolutions of the hand and arm, and brisk motions of the finger and thumb to put in what he says is *bon pour manger;* thus by stuffing and compressing he soon distends the recepticle to the utmost limmits of it's power of expansion, and in the course of it's longitudinal progress it drives from the other end of the recepticle a much larger portion of the ——— than was previously discharged by the finger and thumb in a former part of the operation ; thus when the sides of the recepticle are skilfully exchanged the outer for the inner and all is compleatly filled with something good to eat it is tyed at the other end, but not any cut off, for that would make the pattern too scant ; it is then baptised in the missouri with two dips and a flirt, and bobbed into the kettle ; from whence, after it be well boiled it is taken and fryed with bears oil until it becomes brown, when it is ready to esswage the pangs of a keen appetite or such as travelers in the wilderness are seldom at a loss for."

slight sprinkling of rain several times in the course of the day. Shortly after our landing a dog came to us, and as this induced us to believe that we are near the hunting-grounds of the Assiniboins, who are a vicious, (*p. 213*) ill-disposed people, it was necessary to be on our guard. We therefore inspected our arms, which we found in good order, and sent several hunters to scour the country; but they returned in the evening having seen no tents, nor any recent tracks of Indians. Boils[19] and imposthumes are very common among the party, and sore eyes continue in a greater or less degree with all of us; for the imposthumes we use emollient poultices, and apply to the eyes a solution of two grains of white vitriol [sulphate of zinc] and one of sugar-of-lead, with one ounce of water.

*May 11th.* The wind blew very hard in the night; but having abated this morning we went on very well, till in the afternoon the wind arose and retarded our progress; the current, too, was strong, the river very crooked, and the banks, as usual, constantly precipitating themselves in large masses into the water. The highlands are broken, and approach nearer the river than they do below. The soil, however, of both hills and low grounds appears as fertile as that further down the river. It consists of a black-looking loam with a small portion of sand, which covers the hills and bluffs to the depth of 20 or 30 feet, and when thrown in the water dissolves as readily as loaf sugar, and effervesces like marle.[20] There are also great appearances of quartz and mineral salts. The first is most commonly seen in the faces of the bluffs; the second is found on the hills as well as the low grounds, and in the gullies which come down from the hills; it lies in a crust of two

[19] Text and codex have "biles." Imposthumes or impostumes are abscesses, here called by a name now obsolete. Probably the matter with the men was nothing more than bad boils or furuncles, requiring poultices to favor suppuration and discharge of the core.

[20] Old form of the word *marl*. Marl has become a vague term; it is here used in its proper sense of clay containing chalk enough not to be solid, and to disintegrate readily in water or on exposure to the air.

or three inches in depth, and may be swept up with a feather in large quantities. There is no longer any appearance of coal, burnt earth, or pumice-stone.

We saw and visited some high hills on the north side about three miles from the river, whose tops were covered with the pitch-pine. This is the first pine we have seen on the Missouri; it is like that of Virginia [*Pinus rigida*], except that the leaves are somewhat longer. Among this pine is also a dwarf cedar, something between three or four feet high, but generally spreading itself like a vine along the surface (*p. 214*) of the earth, which it covers very closely, putting out roots from the under side. The fruit and smell resemble those of the common red cedar [*Juniperus virginianus*], but the leaf is finer and more delicate. The tops of the hills where these plants grow have a soil quite different from that just described; the basis of it is usually yellow or white clay, and the general appearance light-colored, sandy, and barren, some scattering tufts of sedge being almost its only herbage.

About five in the afternoon one of our men [Bratton], who had been afflicted with boils and suffered to walk on shore, came running to the boats with loud cries, and every symptom of terror and distress. For some time after we had taken him on board he was so much out of breath as to be unable to describe the cause of his anxiety; but he at length told us that about a mile and a half below he had shot a brown bear, which immediately turned and was in close pursuit of him; but the bear being badly wounded could not overtake him. Captain Lewis, with seven men immediately went in search of him; having found his track they followed him by the blood for a mile, found him concealed in some thick brushwood, and shot him with two balls through the skull. Though somewhat smaller than that killed a few days ago, he was a monstrous animal, and a most terrible enemy. Our man had shot him through the center of the lungs; yet he had pursued him furiously for half a mile, then returned more than twice that distance, and with his talons prepared himself a bed in the earth two feet deep and five feet long ; he was perfectly alive when they found him, which was at least two hours after he had received the wound.   The wonderful power of life which these animals possess renders them dreadful ; their very track in the mud or sand, which we have sometimes found 11 inches long and 7¼ wide, exclusive of the talons, is alarming; and we had rather encounter two Indians than meet a single brown bear.   There is no chance of killing them by a single shot unless the ball goes through the brain, and this is very difficult (*p. 215*) on account of two large muscles which cover the side of the forehead and the sharp projection of the center of the frontal bone, which is also thick.

Our camp was on the south, at the distance of 16 miles from that of last night.   The fleece and skin of the bear [21] were a heavy burden for two men, and the oil amounted to eight gallons.

*May 12th.*   The weather being clear and calm, we set out early.   Within a mile we came to a small creek,[22] about 20 yards wide, emptying on the south.   At 11¾ miles we reached a point of woodland on the south, opposite which is a creek of the same width as the last, but with little water, which we called Pine creek.[23]   At 18¾ miles we came to on the south opposite the lower point of a willow-island, situated in a deep bend of the river to the southeast. Here we remained during the day, the wind having risen at twelve so high that we could not proceed ; it continued to

[21] The grizzly bears have by this time won the respect of the party.   Captain Lewis records at this date a very prudent and reasonable resolve : "I most generally went alone, armed with my rifle and espontoon ; thus equiped I feel myself more than a match for a brown bear, provided I get him in open woods or near the water ; but feel myself a little diffident with respect to an attack in the open plains.   I have therefore come to a resolution to act on the defencive only, should I meet these gentlemen in the open country." (D 121.)

[22] Nameless in the codex, as in the text ; charted, unlettered, on Clark's map, where it appears as the first creek on the south above Big Dry river.   Now called Crabb's, Crab's or Crab creek.

[23] So Lewis D 123, and so the Summary Statement ; also charted on Clark's map by this name, on the north, between " Warner's Run " and " Gibson's Cr."

blow violently all night, with occasional sprinklings of rain from sunset till midnight.

On both sides of the river the country is rough and bro-ken, the low grounds becoming narrower ; the tops of the hills on the north exhibit some scattered pine and cedar; on the south the pine has not yet commenced, though there is some cedar on the sides of the hills and in the little ravines. The choke-cherry, the wild hyssop, sage, fleshy-leaved thorn, and particularly the aromatic herb on which the antelope and hare feed, are to be found on the plains and hills. The soil of the hills has now altered its texture considerably. Their bases, like that of the river plains, is as usual a rich, black loam, while from the middle to the summits they are composed of a light brown colored earth, poor and sterile, intermixed with a coarse white sand.

*May* 13*th.* The wind was so high that we could not pro-ceed till about one o'clock, when we had to encounter a cur-rent rather stronger than usual. In the course of 1½ miles we passed two small creeks [24] on the south, (*p. 216*) one of 18 and the other of 30 yards' width, neither of them containing any water, and camped on the south at a point of woodland, having made only seven miles. The country is much the same as yesterday, with little timber in the low grounds, and a small quantity of pine and cedar on the northern hills. The river, however, continues to grow clearer, and this, as well as the increased rapidity [of the current], induces us to hope for some change of country. The game is as usual so abundant that we can get without difficulty all that is necessary.

*May* 14*th.* There was some fog on the river this morn-ing, which is a very rare occurrence. At the distance of 1½ miles we reached an island in a bend on the north, which continued for about half a mile, when at the head of it a large creek comes in on the north, to which we gave

---

[24] No names for these dry runs to be discovered. One of them seems to be indicated on Clark's map by a nameless trace, next before the creek there lettered " Stick lodge Cr."

the name of Gibson's[25] creek. At 7½ miles is a point of rocks on the south, above a creek on the same side, which we called Sticklodge[26] creek; five miles further is a large creek[27] on the south, which, like the two others, has no running water; and at 16½ miles is a timbered point on the north, where we camped for the night. The country is like that of yesterday, except that the low grounds are wider; there are also many high black bluffs along the banks; the game too is in great abundance.

Toward evening the men in the hindmost canoes discovered a large brown bear lying in the open grounds, about 300 paces from the river. Six of them, all good hunters, immediately went to attack him, and concealing themselves by a small eminence came unperceived within 40 paces of him. Four of the hunters now fired, and each lodged a ball in his body, two of them directly through the lungs. The furious animal sprang up and ran open-mouthed upon them;

[25] "Gibson had wounded a very large brown bear, but it was too late to pursue him," Lewis D 124, May 13th, whence the name of this creek, no doubt. It appears in the Summary Statement by the same name, and is so charted on Clark's map.

[26] "A creek on Lard. called Stick Lodge C.," Lewis D 128; "Stick lodge Cr." on Clark's map, where, however, we must observe that it is not brought into the Missouri according to the text, nor agreeably with the courses and distances of the codex of May 14th, for its mouth is charted below instead of above Gibson's creek; and another little creek, nameless on the map, and not noticed in the text, is charted in about the place assigned to Stick Lodge creek in the text. I find no hint in the codex to explain the curious name; May 14th is full of the bear-hunt and the mishap to the perogue. But it refers in some way to the leather tent or lodge of the explorers (compare Burnt Lodge creek of May 17th), or else to an Indian lodge (wickiup) of brushwood.

[27] This creek is named in the Summary Statement "Brown-bear-defeated creek," from the incident about to be narrated. It comes in the Statement between Gibson's and Bratton's creeks, and no Stick Lodge creek is there given. Lewis D 129 has "a large dry creek Lard. the Brown bear Defeat"—which is as doubtful in statement as the bear-hunt itself was for awhile, before the hunters finally defeated the animal by the aid of a re-enforcement from the shore. This creek is charted on Clark's map by the name of "White Beard Cr." This is certainly the same creek; I suppose "Beard" is here a slip of the graver, and we know these bears were variously called "white" or "brown." Clark runs it into the Missouri right for the distances given above Gibson's and below Bratton's creek.

as he came near, the two hunters who had reserved their fire gave him two wounds, one of which, breaking his shoulder, retarded his motion for a moment; but before they could reload he was so near that they were obliged to run to the (*p. 217*) river, and before they reached it he had almost overtaken them. Two jumped into the canoe; the other four separated, and concealing themselves in the willows, fired as fast as each could reload. They struck him several times, but instead of weakening the monster, each shot seemed only to direct him toward the hunter; till at last he pursued two of them so closely that they threw aside their guns and pouches, and jumped down a perpendicular bank of 20 feet into the river. The bear sprang after them and was within a few feet of the hindmost, when one of the hunters on shore shot him in the head and finally killed him. They dragged him to the shore, and found that eight balls had passed through him in different directions. The bear was old and the meat tough, so that they took the skin only, and rejoined us at camp, where we had been as much terrified by an accident of a different kind.[28]

This was the narrow escape of one of our canoes, containing all our papers, instruments, medicine, and almost every article indispensable for the success of our enterprise. The canoe being under sail, a sudden squall of wind struck

---

[28] "Which. . . I cannot recollect but with the utmost trepidation and horror, . . . it happened unfortunately for us this evening that Charbono was at the helm of this Perogue, instead of Drewyer. . . Charbono cannot swim and is perhaps the most timid waterman in the world. . . the perogue then wrighted but had filled within an inch of the gunwals; Charbono still crying to his god for mercy, had not yet recollected the rudder, nor could the repeated orders of the Bowsman, Cruzat, bring him to his recollection untill he threatened to shoot him instantly if he did not take hold of the rudder and do his duty, . . . the fortitude, resolution and good conduct of Cruzat saved her," Lewis D 126, 127. The codex continues with the record of Lewis' wild impulse, for a moment, to jump into the river and swim for the boat, 300 yards away; but adds that he would have paid the forfeit of his life for this madness, which is quite true. When things had quieted down, "we thought it a proper occasion to console ourselves and cheer the sperits of our men and accordingly took a drink." We may hope, for the credit of Sacajawea's feminine instincts, that she viewed the survival of her lord and legal owner with emotions not unmixed.

her obliquely and turned her considerably. The man at the helm, who was unluckily the worst steersman of the party, became alarmed, and instead of putting her before the wind luffed her up into it. The wind was so high that it forced the brace of the square-sail out of the hand of the man who was attending to it, and instantly upset the canoe, which would have been turned bottom upward but for the resistance made by the awning. Such was the confusion on board, and the waves ran so high, that it was half a minute before she righted, and then was nearly full of water; but by bailing out she was kept from sinking until they rowed ashore. Besides the loss of the lives of three men, who not being able to swim would probably have perished, we should have been deprived of nearly everything necessary for our purposes, at a distance of between 2,000 and 3,000 miles from any place where we could supply the deficiency.

(*p. 218*) *May* 15*th.* As soon as a slight shower of rain had passed, we spread out the articles to dry; but the weather was so damp and cloudy that they derived little benefit from exposure. Our hunters procured us deer, buffalo, and beaver.

*May* 16*th.* The morning was fair, and we were enabled to dry and repack our stores. The loss we sustained is chiefly in the medicines, many articles of which are completely spoiled, and others considerably injured.[29] At four o'clock we embarked, and after making seven miles camped on the north near some woods. The country on both sides is broken; the low grounds are narrower and with less timber, though there are some scattered pine and cedar on the steep declivities of the hills, which are now higher than usual. A white bear tore the coat of [Labiche] one of the men, which had been left on shore; and two of the party

[29] Sacajawea's conduct on this occasion is to be admired in itself, as well as by contrast with that of her craven French apology for a male. "The Indian woman, to whom I ascribe equal fortitude and resolution with any person on board at the time of the accident, caught and preserved most of the light articles which were washed overboard," Lewis D 99.

wounded a large panther [cougar, *Felis concolor*], which was feasting on a deer.    We caught some lean antelopes as they were swimming the river, and killed two buffaloes.

*May 17th.*    We set out early and proceeded on very well; the banks being firm and the shore bold, we were enabled to use the towline, which, whenever the banks will permit it, is the safest and most expeditious mode of ascending the river, except under sail with a steady breeze.    At the distance of 10½ miles we came to the mouth of a small creek on the south, below which the hills approach the river, and continue near it during the day.    Three miles further is a large creek [Bratton's[30]] on the north ; and again, 6¾ miles beyond this, is another large creek,[31] to the south ; both containing a small quantity of running water, of a brackish taste.    The last we called Rattlesnake [or Burnt Lodge] creek, from our seeing that animal [*Crotalus confluentus*] near it.    Although no timber can be observed on it from the Missouri, it throws out large quantities of driftwood, among which were some pieces of coal brought down

[30] Named for William Bratton, a private of the party ; so called in the Summary Statement, though no name appears in Lewis D, this date, and consequently Biddle gives none ; charted by Clark under this name.    It is a considerable stream, now known as Timber creek of Heap.    The above mentioned " small creek on the south," before Bratton's is reached, I find no name for anywhere, and cannot identify now.    There is a nameless creek charted by Clark, next before Burnt Lodge creek, but it does not come into the Missouri in the right place to answer for the one here in question, as it is up-river from Bratton's.

[31] Rattlesnake creek does not reappear in the Summary Statement.    There we have, instead, three creeks between Brown Bear Defeated and the mouth of the Musselshell, namely : 1, Bratton's creek, N.; 2, Burnt Lodge creek, S.; 3, Wiser's creek, N.    But Rattlesnake and Burnt Lodge are one creek—the former is Lewis' name of it, the latter is Clark's.    " Capt. Clark narrowly escaped being bitten by a rattlesnake in the course of his walk ; . . . we called this stream rattlesnake creek," Lewis D 102, 103.    Then Clark put it in his Summary Statement as Burntlodge creek, from the other accident which happened this day, when their leather tent was near being destroyed by fire : "notwithstanding the lodge was fifty paces distant from the fire it sustained considerable injury from the burning coals which were thrown on it " by the high wind, Lewis D 103.    Clark's map charts, " Burnt Lodge Cr." plainly—on the S., next to Wiser's, N.    This stream is called Quarrel creek on Heap's map (but it is not Quarrel R. of Stevens', now Killed Woman's creek, on the north).

by the stream.  We continued for 1¼ miles, and camped on the south after making (*p. 219*) 20½ miles.

The country in general is rugged ; the hills are high, with their summits and sides partially covered with pine and cedar, and their bases on both sides washed by the river.  Like those already mentioned, the lower part of these hills is a dark rich loam, while the upper region for 150 feet consists of a whitish-brown sand, so hard in many places as to resemble stone, though in fact very little stone or rock of any kind is to be seen on the hills. The bed of the Missouri is much narrower than usual, being not more than between 200 and 300 yards in width, with an uncommonly large proportion of gravel ; but the sand-bars, and low points covered with willows, have almost entirely disappeared.  The timber on the river consists of scarcely anything more than a few scattered cottonwood trees.  The saline incrustations, along the banks and the foot of the hills, are more abundant than usual.

The game is in great quantities, but the buffalo are not so numerous as they were some days ago ; two rattle-snakes [*Crotalus confluentus*] were seen to-day, and one of them was killed.  It resembles those of the middle Atlantic States [*C. horridus*], being about 30 inches long, of a yellowish brown on the back and sides, variegated with a row of oval dark brown spots lying transversely on the back from the neck to the tail, and two other rows of circular spots of the same color on the sides along the edge of the scuta ; there are 176 scuta on the belly, and 17 on the tail.

Captain Clark saw in his excursions a fortified Indian camp which appeared to have been recently occupied, and was, we presumed, made by a party of Minnetarees who went to war last March.

Late at night we were roused by the sergeant of the guard, in consequence of a fire which had communicated to a tree overhanging our camp.  The wind was so high that we had not removed the camp more than a few minutes when a large part of the tree fell precisely on the spot we had occupied, and would have crushed us if we had not been alarmed in time.

(*p. 220*) *May* 18*th.* The wind continued high from the west, but by means of the towline[32] we were able to make 19 miles, the sand-bars being now few in number, the river narrow, and the current gentle ; the willow has in a great measure disappeared, and even the cottonwood, almost the only timber remaining, is growing scarce. At 12¾ miles we came to a creek [Wiser's[33]] on the north, which was perfectly dry. We camped on the south, opposite the lower point of an island.

*May* 19*th.* Last night was disagreeably cold ; in the morning there was a very heavy fog, which obscured the river so much as to prevent our seeing the way. This is the first fog of any degree of thickness which we have experienced. There was also last evening a fall of dew, the second which we have seen since entering this extensive open country. About eight o'clock the fog dispersed, and we proceeded with the aid of the towline. The island near which we camped was three-quarters of a mile in length. The country resembles that of yesterday, high hills[34] closely

[32] Singular to say, Lewis and Clark never speak of " cordelling," which is the usual expression for the act of pulling a boat up stream by a rope from the shore.

[33] This is Wiser's creek, so called from Peter Wiser, one of the privates of the party. It is nameless in the text, and Lewis D 105, 106, this date, has simply a creek " Stard." But it is Wiser's in the Summary Statement, and charted by this name plainly on Clark's map, where it appears as the last creek on the right hand or starboard, north side, before coming to the Musselshell river. This is now called Fourchette creek—on some maps Pouchette, Ponchette or Ponchet, by mistake. It is a considerable stream—when it is full ; when dry, quite a marked coulée.

[34] Lewis D 107, this date, notes that Capt. Clark, on ascending a height, first sighted the Musselshell, to be presently reached. He also had in prospect from this eminence *a range of mountains*, distant 40 or 50 miles. These were the Little Rocky mountains, of which the narrative will speak in due course by the name of the North mountain. Since the Expedition passed Fort Peck, I have each day expected to find in the codices mention of some other prominent landmarks ; but none appear to have been recorded. One of these is Tiger or Panther butte, 20 miles N.N.W. of Fort Peck. A second is Round butte, south, near the Missouri, about halfway between Big Dry river and the Musselshell ; and a third,

bordering the river. In the afternoon the river became crooked, and contained more sawyers or floating timber than we have seen in the same space since leaving the Platte. Our game consisted of deer, beaver, and elk. We also killed a brown bear, which, though shot through the heart, ran at his usual pace nearly a quarter of a mile before he fell. At 21 miles is a willow-island half a mile in length, on the north side, a quarter of a mile beyond which is a shoal of rapid water under a bluff; the water continued very strong for some distance beyond it ; at half a mile we came to a sand-bar on the north, from which to our camp was another half mile, making in all 22¼ miles. The saline substances which we have mentioned continue to appear ; the men are much afflicted with sore eyes and imposthumes.

*May 20th.* As usual, we set out early, and the banks being convenient for that purpose, we used the towline. (*p. 221*) The river is narrow and crooked, the water rapid, and the country much like that of yesterday. At the distance of 2¼ miles we passed a large creek [from the south], with but little water, to which we gave the name of Blowing-fly [35] creek, from the quantity of those insects [36] found in its neighborhood. They are extremely troublesome, infesting our meat while we are cooking, and at our meals. After making seven miles we reached by eleven o'clock the mouth of a large river on the south, and camped for the day at the upper point of its junction with the Missouri.

This stream, which we suppose to be that called by the Minnetarees [Mahtush-ahzhah [37]] the Muscleshell [Mussel-

near the last, is Church butte. The last two probably were not seen simply because the party were immediately under the high bluffs bordering the river.

[35] Not in the Summary Statement ; not charted on Clark's map ; the last creek from the south in approaching the Musselshell. Lewis D 132 supplies the required data, not in the text: "large creek on Lard. 25 yds. wide, called blowing Fly Cr." This is now Squaw creek.

[36] Blowflies, *Musca vomitoria* or a related species.

[37] So Clark C 249, in a list of Indian names ; the element " ahzhah " is simply river. Lewis D 129, this date, leaves a blank space, not filled in with any Indian name ; hence none appears in the text. For the English name, the

shell] river, empties into the Missouri 2,270 miles above
the mouth of the latter river, in latitude 47° 0′ 24$\frac{6}{10}$″ north.
It is 110 yards wide, and contains more water than streams
of that size usually do in this country; its current is by no
means rapid, and there is every appearance of its being
susceptible of navigation by canoes for a considerable distance. Its bed is chiefly formed of coarse sand and gravel,
with an occasional mixture of black mud; the banks are
abrupt and nearly twelve feet high, so that they are
secure from being overflowed; the water is of a greenish-
yellow cast, and much more transparent than that of the
Missouri, which itself, though clearer than below, still
retains its whitish hue and a portion of its sediment.
Opposite the point of junction the current of the Missouri is gentle, and 222 yards in width; the bed is principally of mud, the little sand remaining being wholly confined to the points, and [the water is] still too deep to
use the setting-pole.

If this be, as we suppose, the Muscleshell, our Indian
information is that it rises in the first chain of the Rocky
mountains not far [see note] from the sources of the Yellowstone, whence in its course to this place it waters a
high broken country, well timbered, particularly on its
borders, and interspersed with handsome fertile plains and

codices usually have Muscleshell, as one or two words; sometimes "Mustle-
shell;" once "Cockkleshell;" occasionally "Shell" river. I prefer to write
Musselshell, but do not alter the text. The river is properly identified, but the
latitude assigned (Lewis D 132) is not far enough north, as the mouth of the
river is nearly up to 47° 30′. It heads in the Little Belt mountains, not far
from a place called White Sulphur Springs, in Meagher Co., east of the Big
Belt mountains, runs easterly between the Big Snowy mountains and Bull mountains, in a course approximately parallel with that of the Yellowstone, to about
107° 30′ W. long., and then turns northward to the Missouri. Its sources are
thus a good deal north of those of the Yellowstone, though approximately on
the same meridian. The Musselshell is geologically interesting as indicating the first changes in the hitherto unbroken cretaceous formation which the
Missouri has so long traversed. Just north of the mouth of the Musselshell
begin the evidences of volcanic action, and some of its tributaries, as well as
the river itself, arise in paleozoic rocks (permo-carboniferous). The course of
the river is, however, mainly through the cretaceous.

meadows. We have reason, however, to believe, from their giving a similar account of the timber (*p. 222*) where we now are, that the timber of which they speak is similar to that which we have seen for a few days past, which consists of nothing more than a few straggling small pines and dwarf cedars on the summits of the hills, nine-tenths of the ground being totally destitute of wood, and covered with short grass, aromatic herbs, and an immense quantity of prickly-pear [*Opuntia fragilis*]; though the party who explored it for eight miles represented the low grounds on the river to be well supplied with cottonwood of a tolerable size, and of an excellent soil. They also report that the country is broken and irregular, like that near our camp; and that about five miles up, a handsome river, about fifty yards wide, which we named after Chaboneau's wife, Sahcajahweah's,[38] or the Birdwoman's river, discharges into the Muscleshell on the north or upper side.

Another party [*i. e.*, John Shields] found at the foot of the southern hills, about four miles from the Missouri, a fine bold spring, which in this country is so rare that since we left the Mandans we have found only one of a similar kind. That was under the bluffs on the south side of the Missouri, at some distance from it, and about five miles below the Yellowstone. With this exception, all the small fountains, of which we have met a number, are impregnated with the salts which are so abundant here, and with which the Missouri is itself most probably tainted, though to us, who have been so much accustomed to it, the taste is not perceptible.

Among the game to-day we observed two large owls [*Bubo virginianus*], with remarkably long feathers resem-

---

[38] Her name is usually spelled Sacajawea. "About five miles abe [above] the mouth of [the Mussel-] Shell river a handsome river of about fifty yards in width discharged itself into the Shell river on the Stard. or upper side ; this stream we called Sâh-câ-gee-me-âh or bird woman's River, after our interpreter the Snake woman," Lewis D 131, with " Sahcagahwea " interlined in red ink by Clark instead of the other form of the name, which he deletes. This river is on recent maps as Crooked creek.

bling ears on the sides of the head, which we presume are the hooting-owls, though they are larger and their colors are brighter than those common in the United States.

*May 21st.* The morning being very fine, we were able to employ the rope,[39] and made 20 miles to our camp on the north. The shores of the river are abrupt, bold, and composed of a black and yellow clay, the bars being formed of black mud and a small proportion of fine sand; the current is strong. In its course the Missouri makes a sudden (*p. 223*) and extensive bend toward the south, to receive the waters of the Muscleshell. The neck of land thus formed, though itself high, is lower than the surrounding country, and makes a waving valley, extending for a great distance to the northward, with a fertile soil which, though without wood, produces a fine turf of low grass, some herbs, and vast quantities of prickly pear. The country on the south is high, broken, and crowned with some pine and dwarf cedar; the leaf of this pine is longer than that of the common pitch or red pine of Virginia [*Pinus rigida*]; the cone is longer and narrower, the imbrications are wider and thicker, and the whole is frequently covered with rosin. During the whole day the bends of the river are short and sudden; the points are covered with some cottonwood, large or broad-leaved willow, and a small quantity of red-wood; the undergrowth consisting of wild roses and the bushes of the small honeysuckle.

The mineral appearances on the river are as usual. We do not find the grouse or prairie-hen so abundant as below, and think it probable that they retire from the river to the plains during this season.

The wind had been moderate during the forepart of the day, but continued to rise toward evening; about dark it veered to the northwest, and blew a storm all night. We had camped on a bar on the north, opposite the lower point of an island, which from this circumstance we called

---

[39] " Imployed the chord principally," Lewis D 133 ; but this useful article of boat-gear is mostly known to the codices as the " toe line."

Windy island ;[40] but we were so annoyed by clouds of dust and sand that we could neither eat nor sleep, and were forced to remove our camp at eight o'clock to the foot of an adjoining hill, which shielded us in some degree from the wind.   We procured elk, deer, and buffalo.

*May 22d.*   The wind blew so violently that it was deemed prudent to wait till it had abated, so that we did not leave camp till ten o'clock, when we proceeded, principally by the towline.   We passed Windy island, which is about three-quarters of a mile in length.   Five and a half miles above it is a large island [41] in a bend to the north ; (*p. 224*) three miles beyond this we came to the entrance of a creek 20 yards wide, though with little water, which we called Grouse creek,[42] from observing near its mouth a quantity of prairie-hens with pointed tails [sharp-tailed grouse, *Pediœcetes columbianus*], the first we have seen in such numbers for several days.   The low grounds are somewhat wider than usual, and apparently fertile, though the short and scanty grass on the hills does not indicate much richness of soil.   The country around is not so broken as that of yesterday, but is still waving, the southern hills possessing more pine than usual, and some appearing on the northern hills, which are accompanied by the usual salt and mineral appearances.

[40] An island answering to this appears on Twining's map, though the distance is considerably less than Lewis and Clark make it from the mouth of the Musselshell.

[41] By Twining's map, and Greene's Missouri distances (less than those of L. and C.), this is Boyd's island, which is 19 or 20 miles up-river from the mouth of the Musselshell.   This was named for one George Boyd, our pilot on the boat-voyage from Benton to Bismarck, who was, and may still be, a noted character in those parts—a good hunter and a good scout, thoroughly acquainted with the country and the Indians.   He had the unusual personal peculiarities of being web-fingered in both hands, and having both feet sadly clubbed ; but he was very quick on the trigger, and could run a footrace with the best of us.

[42] " Passed the entrance of grows [Grouse] creek, . . . on the Stard. side, in a deep bend to the Stard.," Lewis D 135, 136.   This is exactly right for Beauchamp's creek, as it is now called, from the north.   It is not charted on Clark's map.   The Expedition approaches the site of Fort Hawley (or Wilder).

The river continues about 250 yards wide, with fewer sand-bars, and the current more gentle and regular. Game is no longer in such abundance since leaving the Muscle-shell. We have caught very few fish on this side of the Mandans, and these were the white catfish [*Ictalurus punctatus*], of two to five pounds. We killed a deer and a bear. We have not seen in this quarter the black bear [*Ursus americanus*], common in the United States and on the lower parts of the Missouri, nor have we discerned any of their tracks. They may easily be distinguished by the shortness of the talons from the brown, grizzly, or white bear [*Ursus horribilis*], all of which seem to be of the same family [species], which assumes those colors at different seasons of the year. We halted earlier than usual, and camped on the north, in a point of woods, at the distance of 16½ miles [thus past the site of Fort Hawley, on the south].

# CHAPTER IX.

## THE MISSOURI FROM THE MUSSELSHELL TO MARIA'S RIVER.

Frost and ice—Teapot, North Mountain, Little Dog, and South Mountain creeks—High country—Teapot island—Scarcity of buffalo—Windsor's creek—Soft-shelled turtles—First sight of the Rocky mountains, May 26th, 1805—First considerable rapids of the Missouri, named Elk rapids—The river becomes very rapid, with bluffy banks—First thunder since leaving the Mandans—Thompson's and Bull creeks—Abundance of big-horned sheep—A buffalo charges the camp—Judith's river—Large Indian camps—Ash rapids—Herds of buffalo driven over precipices by Indians—Slaughter river—Heavy rain—Difficulty of advancing—Architectural effects of the cliffs—Nearness of some mountains—Encounter with a bear—The Expedition reaches a large river—Uncertainty which of two is the Missouri—Parties sent out to discover—Comparison of the two forks—Captain Lewis explores the north fork—Barn mountain—Lark creek—Tower mountain—A narrow escape.

MAY 23d, 1805. Last night the frost was severe ; this morning the ice appeared along the edges of the river, and the water froze on our oars. At the distance of a mile we passed the entrance of a creek on the north, which we named Teapot[1] creek; it is 15 yards wide, and though it has running water at a small distance from its mouth, yet it discharges none into the Missouri ; thus resembling, we believe, most of the creeks in this hilly country, the waters of which are absorbed by the thirsty soil near the river. They indeed afford but little water in any part, and even that is so strongly tainted with salts that it is unfit for [our] use, though all the wild animals are very fond of it. On experiment it was found to be moderately purgative, but painful to the intestines in its operation. This creek seems to come from a range of low hills,[2] which run from east to

---

[1] "Tea Pot Cr." of Clark's map, the only one charted, either N. or S., between the Musselshell river and North Mountain creek. In fact there are several, exact identification of which is not easy. Teapot is now Yellow creek.

[2] "Low mountains," Lewis D 137, rightly—low hills are not to be seen from a river-bank for 70 miles. Lewis has here in view certain mountains, which to his line of vision seem continuous, but are not. Had he gone out of the site of Carroll, up a sharp ridge S.W., about 900 feet, he would have seen an exten-

west for 70 miles, and have their eastern extremity 30 miles
to the north of Teapot creek.   Just above its entrance is
a large assemblage of the burrowing-squirrels on the north
side of the river.   At nine miles we reached the upper
point of an island in a bend on the south, and opposite the
center of the island, a small dry creek on the north.   Half a
mile further a small creek falls in on the same side.³   At 6½
miles beyond this is another, on the south.⁴   At 4½ miles
(*p. 226*) we passed a small island in a deep bend to the north,
and on the same side, in a deep northeastern bend of the
river, another small island.   None of these creeks, however,
possessed any water, and at the entrances of the islands the
two first are covered with tall cottonwoods, and the last
with willows only.   The river has become more rapid ; the
country is much the same as yesterday, except that there
is rather more rock on the face of the hills, and some small
spruce appears among the pitch-pines.   The wild roses are
very abundant and now in bloom ; they differ from those of
the United States only in having the leaves and the bush
itself of a somewhat smaller size.   We find the mosquitoes
troublesome, notwithstanding the coolness of the morning.

sive prairie N., 30 miles of bad lands S., and these mountains : the Little
Rockies, N. 30 miles ; Bear's Paw, N. W. 70 miles ; Judith's, S. W. 40 miles ;
Big and Little Moccasins, west of and near Judith's ; beyond which latter are
the Snowies, S., and the Little Belts, S. W., the latter separated from each other
by Judith's Gap, through which a head of Judith's river seeks the Missouri.
This gap is due south of the mouth of Judith's river, about 75 miles as the crow
flies.   The "low hills" of the text are at least 5,000 feet high.

³ Immediate vicinity of the present town of Carroll, by Twining's distances
17¼ miles above Beauchamp's creek—practically the identical distance that
Lewis and Clark make it from their Grouse creek.   This point is 640 miles
above Bismarck, and 165 miles below Benton.   It came into existence when the
road was opened from Helena to this point, and in 1875 consisted of 20 or 25
log cabins.

⁴ Nameless in text and codices ; uncharted by Clark.   It shows well on
Twining's map, lettered Hazen river, 6½ miles above Carroll.   This map
charts the identical islands next mentioned in the text ; and a mile or so above
the upper one of these two islands comes in Little Rocky Mountain creek
(Lewis and Clark's North Mountain creek).   It is wonderful how closely these
pioneer explorers' distances agree with the results of the best modern surveys.

The buffalo is scarce to-day, but the elk, deer, and antelope are very numerous. The geese begin to lose the feathers of the wings, and are unable to fly. We saw five bears, one of which we wounded, but in swimming from us across the river he became entangled in some driftwood, and sunk. We formed our camp on the north, opposite a hill and a point of wood in a bend to the south, having made 27 miles.[5]

*May 24th.* The water in the kettles froze one-eighth of an inch during the night; ice appears along the margin of the river, and the cottonwood trees, which have lost nearly all their leaves by the frost, are putting forth other buds. We proceeded, with the towline principally, till about nine o'clock, when a fine breeze sprung up from the S.E., and enabled us to sail very well, notwithstanding the rapidity of the current. At one mile and a half is a large [North Mountain] creek, 30 yards wide, containing some water, which it empties on the north side, over a gravelly bed intermixed with some stone. A man who was sent up to explore the country returned in the evening, after having gone ten miles directly toward the ridge of [the Little Rocky] mountains to the north, which is the source of this, as well as of Teapot creek. The air of these highlands is so pure that objects appear much nearer than (*p. 227*) they really are, so that, although our man went ten miles without thinking himself by any means halfway to the mountains, they do not from the river appear more than 15 miles distant.

This stream we called Northmountain[6] creek.   At 2

[5] Lewis D ends here, so far as the journal is concerned, though the codex includes 5½ leaves more of a meteorological register (now torn out, making a separate codex). The Biddle narrative continues directly with Codex E, which is a Lewis, and will take us to July 16th, at the Gates of the Rocky Mountains.

[6] The North mountain of L. and C. is the Little Rocky mountains of present geographers, rising to height of 5,000 feet or more, running nearly E. and W. on the parallel of 48° N., and across long. 108° 30' W., thus separating the Milk river watershed along here from that of the Missouri itself. From their E. end, westward along the parallel of 48° N. nearly to long. 109° W., and up to Milk

miles higher is a creek on the south, which is 15 yards wide, but without any water, and to which we gave the name of Littledog creek, from a village of burrowing-squirrels opposite its entrance, that being the name given by the French watermen to those animals. Three miles from this a small [now Warm Springs] creek enters on the north; five beyond which is an island,[7] a quarter of a mile in length; and two miles further, a small river. This falls in on the south, is 40 yards wide, and discharges a handsome stream of water; its bed is rocky with gravel and sand, and the banks are high. We called it Southmountain[8] creek, as from its direction it seemed to rise in a range of mountains about 50 or 60 miles to the S.W. of its entrance.

river, is the Fort Belknap Indian Reservation. The St. Paul, Minn. & Man. R. R., or Great Northern Ry., runs along the N. bank of Milk river here. North Mountain creek is the largest northern affluent of the Missouri, above the mouth of the Musselshell and below Judith's river, though not so large as South Mountain river, beyond. It is now called Little Rocky Mountain river or creek—a name often shortened to Little Rocky, or Little Rock.

[7] Named points in the Missouri, above North Mountain creek, are; 1, Bird shoals or rapids, unnoticed in the text, probably on account of the season and consequent state of the river; 2, Emil island, a little above these shoals; and 3, Two Calf islands, a pair close to the mouth of South Mountain creek, doubtless corresponding to the single island of the text.

[8] This is the first stream of any size which falls into the Missouri from the south, above the mouth of the Musselshell. The South mountain of L. and C., in which it heads, is the Judith mountains, with elevations from 5,000 to 6,000 feet. These mountains, and the Snowy mountains south of them, are drained by western and northern tributaries of the Musselshell (especially by the main north fork of this river), by the eastern heads of Judith's river, and by the South Mountain river of our text. The latter is now attempted to be called after some person whose name no geographers seem to know; for he is Arnel, Annel, Amiel, Armel, or Emile, on various maps, and with one *l* or two. In any case, I do not see the sense or justice of thus changing Lewis and Clark's names, when, as in the instances of " North Mountain," and " South Mountain," they are absolutely identifiable, and were properly published. Hundreds of names, which have been superseded by modern inventions, should be restored, not only in equity, but on the plainest principles of the law of priority, which geographers pretend to obey. They must sit at the feet of the zoölogists and botanists, before they can hope for any stability of their own nomenclature. "Annell's creek," forsooth! Why not Tom's, Dick's, or Harry's? If this river is any-body's, it is Lewis and Clark's.

The low grounds are narrow and without timber; the country is high and broken ; a large portion of black rock and brown sandy rock appears in the face of the hills, the tops of which are covered with scattered pine, spruce, and dwarf cedar; the soil is generally poor, sandy near the tops of the hills, and nowhere producing much grass, the low grounds being covered with little else than the hyssop, or southernwood, and the pulpy-leaved thorn [*Sarcobatus vermiculatus* [9]]. Game is more scarce, particularly beaver, of which we have seen but few for several days, and the abundance or scarcity of which seems to depend on the greater or less quantity of timber. At 24½ miles we reached a point of woodland on the south, where we observed that the trees had no leaves, and camped for the night.

The high country through which we have passed for some days, and where we now are, we suppose to be a continuation of what the French traders called the Cote [Côte] Noire or Black hills.

The country thus denominated consists of high, broken, irregular hills, and short chains of mountains, sometimes (*p. 228*) 120 miles in width, sometimes narrower, but always much higher than the country on either side. They commence about the head of the Kansas, where they diverge ; the first ridge going westward, along the northern shore of the Arkansaw. The second approaches the Rock mountains obliquely in a course a little to the W. of N.W., and after passing the Platte above its forks and intersecting the Yellowstone near the Bigbend, crosses the Missouri at this place, and probably swell the country as far as the Saskaskawan, though, as they are represented much smaller here than to the south, they may not reach that river.

*May 25th.* Two canoes which were left behind yesterday, to bring on the game, did not join us till eight o'clock this morning, when we set out with the towline, the use of which the banks permitted. The wind was, however, ahead,

[9] An anomalous apetalous chenopodiaceous plant, well known in the West as greasewood. See Nuttall, Jour. Phila. Acad., I., p. 184.

the current strong, particularly round the points against which it happened to set, and the gullies from the hills having brought down quantities of stone, these projected into the river, forming barriers for 40 or 50 feet around, which it was very difficult to pass.   At the distance of 2¾ miles we passed a small island in a deep bend on the south, and on the same side a creek 20 yards wide, but with no running water.   About a mile further is an island between two and three miles in length, separated from the northern shore by a narrow channel, in which is a sand-island, at the distance of half a mile from its lower extremity.   To this large island we gàve the name of Teapot [10] island; two miles above which is an island a mile long, situated on the south. At 3½ miles is another small island, and one mile beyond it a second, three-quarters of a mile in length, on the north side.   In the middle of the river, two miles above this, is an island with no timber, and of the same extent as this last.

The country on each side is high, broken, and rocky; the rock being either a soft brown sandstone, covered with a thin stratum of limestone, or else a hard black rug- (*p. 229*) ged granite, both usually in horizontal strata, and the sand-rock overlaying the other.   Salts and quartz, as well as some coal and pumice-stone, still appear.   The bars of the river are composed principally of gravel; the river low grounds are narrow, and afford scarcely any timber; nor is there much pine on the hills.   The buffalo have now become scarce ; we saw a polecat [skunk] this evening, which was the first for several days ; in the course of the day we also saw several herds of the big-horned animals [*Ovis montana*] among the steep cliffs on the north, and killed several of them.[11]   At the distance of 18 miles we camped on the south.

[10] This name does not appear in the Summary Statement, instead of which are named two islands, Ibex and Goodrich's, before we reach Windsor's (now Cow) creek.   It is " Tea " island in Lewis E 7.   No such great island as this now exists ; but there are four or more strung along the river for several miles, and at one of them is the shoal now called Picoll's or Picott's rapids (below Cow island and Cow creek).

[11] Lewis E 4–6 gives a long and minute description of the animals, and Gass,

*Sunday, May 26th.* We proceeded at an early hour by means of the towline, using our oars merely in crossing the river, to take advantage of the best banks. There are now scarcely any low grounds on the river, the hills being high, and in many places pressing on both sides to the verge of the water. The black rock has given place to a very soft sandstone, which seems to be washed away fast by the river, and being thrown into the river renders its navigation more difficult than it was yesterday. Above this sandstone, and toward the summits of the hills, a hard freestone of a yellowish-brown color shows itself in several strata of unequal thickness, frequently overlaid or incrusted by a thin stratum of limestone, which seems to be formed of concreted shells. At 8¼ miles we came to the mouth of a creek on the north, 30 yards wide, with some running water and a rocky bed ; we called it Windsor's [12] creek, after one of the party. At 4¾ miles beyond this we came to another [Turtle[13]] creek in a bend to the north, which is 20 yards wide, with a handsome little stream of water ; there is, how-

p. 88, makes much of these bighorns, apparently the first the party actually killed. "Some of the party killed three of what the French and natives call mountain sheep ; but they very little resemble sheep, except in the head, horns and feet. They are of a dun colour except on the belly and round the rump, where they are white. The horns of the male are very large ; those of the female small. Captain Clarke calls them the Ibex, and says they resemble that animal more than any other. They are in size somewhat larger than a deer." May 25th. This account is perfectly diagnostic, and first appeared in 1807. Gass' editor and publisher, David M'Keehan, having a copy of Goldsmith's Animated Nature at hand, quotes that miraculous zoölogist's description of the ibex, and rejects it as inapplicable to the bighorn ; then he proceeds to cite Goldsmith's description of the moufflon or musimon, and comes to the conclusion, fortified by Gass' verbal accounts, that *this* is the animal which our bighorn is like, if not "exactly the same." In which conclusion he is quite right.

[12] Now Cow creek, near the mouth of which is Cow island, above Picoll's rapids and below Burdell's. A branch of Cow creek is Bull creek, and another is called Suction creek, perhaps referring to the calf. But where is Windsor's creek, meanwhile?

[13] Nameless in text and codex, but charted by Clark as Turtle creek, from finding here the turtles which are presently mentioned. This is about the situation of some rapids now known as Budel's, Berdel's, Burdell's or Burdette's, not specified in the text, owing to the state of the Missouri.

ever, no timber on either side of the river, except a few pines on the hills. Here we saw, for the first time since we left the Mandans, several soft-shelled turtles [*Trionyx* (*Aspidonectes*) *spinifer*], though this may be owing rather to the season of the year than to any scarcity of the animal.

It was here (*p. 230*) that, after ascending the highest summit of the hills on the north side of the river, Captain Lewis first caught a distant view of the Rock mountains— the object of all our hopes, and the reward of all our ambition.[14] On both sides of the river, and at no great distance from it, the mountains followed its course. Above these, at the distance of 50 miles from us, an irregular range of mountains spread from west to northwest from his position. To the north of these, a few elevated points, the most remarkable of which bore N. 65° W., appeared above the horizon ; and as the sun shone on the snows of their summits, he obtained a clear and satisfactory view of those mountains which close on the Missouri the passage to the Pacific.

At 4½ miles beyond this [Turtle] creek, we came to the upper point of a small sand-island.[16] At the distance of five

[14] About a year and a half before the day when the Rockies were first sighted in Colorado by Zebulon M. Pike, on the 15th of November, 1806. " This day I first caught sight of the Rocky Mountains the ' Great Divide ' between the Eastern and Western Oceans," is attributed to Pike by a flourishing periodical now published in Denver, which takes this expression as a motto for a standing head. Very likely Pike said something to that effect, somewhere ; what he says in his Journal, orig. ed., Philadelphia, 1810, p. 163, is : " Gave three *cheers* to the *Mexican mountains.* . . Those were a spur of the grand western chain of mountains, which divide the waters of the Pacific from those of the Atlantic oceans," etc., at date of Saturday, Nov. 15th, 1806. Lewis E 7 is delightful here : " While I viewed these mountains I felt a secret pleasure in thus finding myself so near the head of the hitherto conceived boundless Missouri ; but when I reflected on the difficulties which this snowey barrier would most probably throw in my way to the Pacific, and the sufferings and hardships of myself and party in them, it in some measure counterballanced the joy I had felt in the first moments in which I gazed on them ; but as I have always held it a crime to anticipate evils I will believe it a good comfortable road untill I am compelled to believe differently."

[15] About the position of that now called Sturgeon island ; so named, not from

miles, between high bluffs, we passed a very difficult rapid, reaching quite across the river, where the water is deep, the channel narrow, and gravel obstructs it on each side. We had great difficulty in ascending it, though we used both the rope and the pole, and doubled the crews. This is the most considerable rapid [we have thus far found] on the Missouri, and in fact the only place where there is a sudden descent. As we were laboring over the rapids, a female elk with her fawn swam down through the waves, which ran very high, and obtained for the place the name of Elk Rapids.[16] Just above them is a small low ground of cottonwood trees, where, at 22¼ miles, we fixed our camp, and were joined by Captain Lewis, who had been on the hills during the afternoon.

The country has now become desert and barren. The appearances of coal, burnt earth, pumice-stone, salts, and quartz continue as yesterday; but there is no timber except the thinly scattered pine and spruce on the summits of the hills, or along their sides. The only animals we have observed are the elk, the bighorn, and the hare common in this country. In the plain where we lie are two Indian (*p. 231*) cabins [wickiups] made of sticks, and during the last few days we have passed several others in the points of timber on the river.

*May 27th.* The wind was so high that we did not start till ten o'clock, and even then were obliged to use the towline during the greater part of the day. The river has become very rapid, with a very perceptible descent. Its

any ordinary sturgeon, for none such is found in the Missouri, but from the curious shovel-headed or shovel-nosed sturgeon, *Scaphirhynchops platyrhynchus*, a fish I have taken from this very locality.

[16] "A very considerable ripple which we call the Elk rappids," Lewis E 11 ; so charted by Clark, between his Turtle creek and Thompson's (now Birch) creek. Some identify these rapids with Burdell's, near Windsor's (Cow) creek ; others with the Dauphin rapids, which are near Thompson's (Birch) creek. But Elk rapids is neither of these, being certain shoals much below Thompson's or Birch creek, at the distance above Sturgeon island which the text indicates, and now known as the Lone Pine rapids.

general width is about 200 yards ; the shoals are more frequent, and the rocky points at the mouths of the gullies
more troublesome to pass.   Great quantities of stone lie in
the river and on its bank, and seem to have fallen down as
the rain washed away the clay and sand in which they were
imbedded.   The water is bordered by high rugged bluffs,
composed of irregular but horizontal strata of yellow and
brown or black clay, brown and yellowish-white sand, soft
yellowish-white sandstone, and hard dark brown freestone ;
also, large round kidney-formed irregular separate masses
of a hard black ironstone, imbedded in the clay and sand ;
some coal or carbonated wood also makes its appearance in
the cliffs, as do its usual attendants, the pumice-stone and
burnt earth.   The salts and quartz are less abundant, and,
generally speaking, the country is, if possible, more rugged and barren than that we passed yesterday ; the only
growth of the hills being a few pine, spruce, and dwarf cedar,
interspersed with an occasional contrast, once in the course
of some miles, of several acres of level ground, which
supply a scanty subsistence for a few little cottonwoods.

Soon after setting out we passed a small untimbered
island on the south ; at about seven miles we reached a
considerable bend which the river makes toward the southeast, and in the evening, after making 12½ miles, camped
on the south near two dead cottonwoods, the only timber
for fuel which we could discover in the neighborhood.

*May 28th.*   The weather was dark and cloudy ; the air
smoky, and there fell a few drops of rain.   At ten o'clock
(*p. 232*) we had again a slight sprinkling of rain, attended
with distant thunder, which is the first we have heard since
leaving the Mandans.   We employed the towline generally,
with the addition of the pole at the ripples and rocky
points, which we find more numerous and troublesome
than those we passed yesterday.   The water is very rapid
round these points,[17] and we are sometimes obliged to steer

[17] One of these points is that now called Dauphin rapids, about 14 miles
above Lone Pine rapids.

the canoes through the points of sharp rocks rising a few inches above the surface of the water, and so near to each other that if our ropes give way the force of the current would drive the side of the canoe against the rocks, and must inevitably upset the canoe or dash it to pieces. These cords are very slender, being almost all made of elk-skin, now much worn and rotted by exposure to the weather. Several times they gave way, but fortunately always in places where there was room for the canoe to turn without striking the rocks; yet with all our precautions it was with infinite risk and labor that we passed these points. An Indian pole for building floated down the river; it was worn at one end as if dragged along the ground in traveling; several other articles were also brought down by the current, which indicates that the Indians are probably at no great distance above us; judging from a football, which resembles those used by the Minnetarees near the Mandans, we conjecture that they must be a band of the Minnetarees of Fort de Prairie.

The appearance of the river and the surrounding country continued as usual, till toward evening, at about 15 miles, we reached a large creek on the north, 35 yards wide, discharging some water, and named after one of our men Thompson's [18] creek. Here the country assumed a totally different aspect; the hills retired on both sides from the river, which now spreads to more than three times its former size, and is filled with a number of small, handsome islands, covered with cottonwood. The low grounds on the river are again wide, fertile, and enriched with trees; those on the north are particularly wide, the hills being comparatively low, and (*p. 233*) opening into three large valleys, which extend for a considerable distance toward the north. These appearances of vegeta-

[18] Birch creek of various modern maps, as the G. L. O. map of 1879, but not of Twining's, which names a Birch creek above Judith's river, and opposite Arrow river, nor of Ludlow's, which locates Birch creek below Judith's river, about opposite Dog or Bull creek. Clark charts this stream as " Thomson's Cr."; but the soldier's name was John B. Thompson, " with a *p*."

tion are delightful after the dreary hills over which we have passed, and we have now to congratulate ourselves at having escaped from the last ridges of the Black mountains. On leaving Thompson's creek we passed two small islands, and at 23 miles' [total] distance camped among some timber on the north, opposite a small creek, which we named Bull[19] creek. The bighorn is in great quantities, and must bring forth their young at a very early season, as they are now half-grown. One of the party saw a large bear also, but being at a distance from the river, and having no timber to conceal himself, he would not venture to fire.

*May 29th.* Last night we were alarmed by a new sort of enemy. A buffalo swam over from the opposite side to the spot where lay one of our canoes, over which he clambered to the shore; then taking fright he ran full speed up the bank toward our fires, and passed within 18 inches of the heads of some of the men, before the sentinel could make him change his course. Still more alarmed, he ran down between four fires and within a few inches of the heads of the second row of the men, and would have broken into our lodge if the barking of the dog had not stopped him. He suddenly turned to the right, and was out of sight in a moment, leaving us all in confusion, everyone seizing his rifle and inquiring the cause of the alarm. On learning what had happened, we had to rejoice at suffering no more injury than the damage to some guns which were in the canoe which the buffalo crossed.

In the morning early we left our camp, and proceeded as usual by the cord. We passed an island and two sand-bars, and at the distance of 2½ miles came to a handsome river which discharges on the south, and which we ascended to

[19] From the incident narrated May 29th; charted, nameless, by Clark; last creek S. below Judith's river; now called Dog creek, perhaps from some mistaking of L. and C.'s "Littledog" creek of May 24th, now left far behind. This stream is only two or three miles below the mouth of the Judith, and therefore cannot be that Dog river which Twining charts ten or twelve miles lower down. Some cartographer might win fame by inscribing "Bulldog" creek.

the distance of a mile and a half. We called it Judith's[20] river. It rises in the Rock mountains (*p. 234*), in about the same place with the Muscleshell, and near the Yellowstone. Its entrance is 100 yards wide from one bank to the other, the water occupying about 75 yards, and in greater quantity than that of the Muscleshell river; though more rapid, it is equally navigable, there being no stones or rocks in the bed, which is composed entirely of gravel and mud, with some sand. The water is clearer than any which we have yet seen; and the low grounds, as far as we could discern, are wider and more woody than those of the Missouri. Along its banks we observed some box-elder intermixed with cottonwood and willow; the undergrowth consisting of rosebushes, honeysuckles, and a little red-willow. There was a great abundance of the argali or big-horned animal

[20] " Cap. C. who ascended this R. much higher than I did has called it *Judieth's* River," Lewis E 17. The lady thus complimented was Miss Julia Hancock, of Fincastle, Va., familiarly called Judie or Judy by her family and intimate friends. Among the latter was Captain Clark, who perhaps had never heard her called Julia, and naturally supposed her name to be Judith. Miss Julia Hancock was the fourth child and third daughter of George Hancock and Peggy Strother, born Monday, Nov. 21st, 1791 ; married Captain Clark, at Fincastle, Jan. 5th, 1808 ; died at Fotheringay, June 27th, 1820. They had five children, the eldest of whom was Meriwether Lewis Clark, b. St. Louis, Jan. 10th, 1809. All are dead ; for the only surviving son of General and Governor William Clark is issue of a second marriage. This is Jefferson K. Clark, now residing at 3121 Locust st., St. Louis, Mo.

This river was actually first called " Bighorn " by Lewis, from the abundance of these animals (see May 28th). The sentence I have cited above is partly in Lewis' hand, partly in Clark's, interlined and over a careful erasure ; and so near was Miss Julia to losing her fine river that its name still stands " Bighorn," *bis*, in the codex, not deleted, though with " Judith " interlined in Clark's hand. It does not rise so far west as the sources of the Musselshell, and far north of those of the Yellowstone. The Judith heads in the Little Belt and Big Snowy mountains (which are separated by Judith Gap), and runs on an average course due north to the Missouri, passing west of the Judith and both Moccasin mountains. It is by far the largest southern tributary of the Missouri since the Musselshell. Less than a mile above its mouth was old Camp Cook, or Cooke, on the south side of the Missouri, where some of the adobe walls were visible when I passed in 1874. Close by was also built Fort Claggett, a small Indian trading-post, of two loghouses ; and this locality is now the site of the River Crow Agency.

in the high country through which it [Judith's river] passes, and a great number of beaver in its waters.

Just above the entrance of it we saw the fires of 126 lodges, which appeared to have been deserted about 12 or 15 days ; and on the other side of the Missouri, a large camp, apparently made by the same nation. On examining some moccasins which we found here, our Indian woman said that they did not belong to her own nation, the Snake Indians, but she thought that they indicated a tribe on this side of the Rocky mountains, and to the north of the Missouri; indeed it is probable that these are the Minnetarees of Fort de Prairie. At the distance of 6½ miles the hills again approach the brink of the river, and the stones and rocks washed down from them form a very bad rapid, with rocks and ripples more numerous and difficult than those we passed on the 27th and 28th. Here the same scene was renewed, and we had again to struggle and labor to preserve our small craft from being lost. Near this spot are a few trees of the ash, the first we have seen for a great distance, and from which we named the place Ash Rapids.[21] On these hills there is but little timber, but the salts, coal, and other mineral appearances continue.

On the north we (*p. 235*) passed a precipice about 120 feet high, under which lay scattered the fragments of at least 100 carcasses of buffaloes, although the water which had washed away the lower part of the hill must have carried off many of the dead. These buffaloes had been chased down the precipice in a way very common on the Missouri, by which vast herds are destroyed in a moment. The mode of hunting is to select one of the most active and fleet young men, who is disguised by a buffalo-skin round his body; the skin of the head with the ears and horns

[21] This is a bad place at any state of the river. It is now known as Drowned Man's rapids, from an accident which the name expresses. It is marked on Clark's map, just above a nameless creek, from the north, noticed neither in the text nor the codex. This creek has since been called Norris.

being fastened on his own head in such a way as to deceive the buffalo. Thus dressed, he fixes himself at a convenient distance between a herd of buffalo and any of the river precipices, which sometimes extend for some miles. His companions in the meantime get in the rear and side of the herd, and at a given signal show themselves and advance toward the buffaloes. These instantly take the alarm, and finding the hunters beside them, they run toward the disguised Indian or decoy, who leads them on at full speed toward the river; when, suddenly securing himself in some crevice of the cliff which he had previously fixed on, the herd is left on the brink of the precipice. It is then in vain for the foremost buffaloes to retreat or even to stop ; they are pressed on by the hindmost rank, which, seeing no danger but from the hunters, goad on those before them till the whole are precipitated, and the shore is strewn with their dead bodies. Sometimes, in this perilous seduction, the Indian is himself either trodden under foot by the rapid movements of the buffaloes, or missing his footing in the cliff is urged down the precipice by the falling herd. The Indians then select as much meat as they wish ; the rest is abandoned to the wolves, and creates a most dreadful stench. The wolves which had been feasting on these carcasses were very fat, and so gentle that one of them was killed with an espontoon.

Above this place we came-to for dinner at the distance of 17 miles [from camp], opposite a bold running river, 20 yards wide, (*p. 236*) falling in on the south. From the objects we had just passed, we called this river Slaughter river.[22] Its low grounds are narrow, and contain scarcely any

[22] Now Arrow creek or river of ordinary maps, and the first stream from the south of any size above Judith's river. But there may be a snag here, invalidating such identification. L. and C.'s Slaughter river is by codex, text, and Summary Statement, 14½ miles above Judith's river, and is brought in on Clark's map above the Stone Walls. But by Twining's and Ludlow's maps, and by Greene's table of distances, Arrow river is only nine or ten miles above Judith's. Observe, also, that Clark's map charts a certain " Big Horn R." on the south, much below Slaughter river, and thus about in the position of Arrow river of late

timber. Soon after landing it began to blow and rain, and as there was no prospect of getting wood for fuel farther on, we fixed our camp on the north, three-quarters of a mile above Slaughter river. After the labors of the day, we gave each man a dram, and such was the effect of long abstinence from spirituous liquors that, from the small quantity of half a gill of rum, several of the men were considerably affected, and all very much exhilarated. Our game to-day consisted of an elk and two beaver.

*May 30th.* The rain which commenced last evening continued with little intermission till eleven this morning, when the high wind which accompanied it having abated, we set out. More rain has now fallen than we have had since the 1st of September last, and many circumstances indicate our approach to a climate differing considerably from that of the country through which we have been passing. The air of the open country is astonishingly dry and pure. Observing that the case of our sextant, though perfectly seasoned, shrank and the joints opened, we tried several experiments, by which it appeared that a table-spoonful of water, exposed in a saucer to the air, would evaporate in 36 hours, when the mercury did not stand higher than the temperate point [55° F.] at the greatest heat of the day. The river, notwithstanding the rain, is much clearer than it was a few days past; but we advance with great labor and difficulty, the rapid current, the ripples, and rocky points rendering navigation more embarrassing than even that of yesterday; in addition to which, the banks are so slippery after the rain, that the men who draw the canoes can scarcely walk, and the earth and stone, constantly falling down the high bluffs, make it dangerous to pass under them; still, however, we are obliged to make use of the cord, as the wind is strong ahead, the current too rapid for oars, and too deep for the (*p. 237*) pole. In this way

maps. The Big Horn of Clark's map remains unaccounted for; there is no sign of it in our text, and the only river called Big Horn in Lewis E is Judith's river, as we have seen. Here, however, I accept the usual identification.

we passed, at a distance of 5½ miles, a small rivulet in a bend on the north ; two miles further, an island on the same side ; half a mile beyond which we came to a grove of trees, at the entrance of a run in a bend to the south, and camped for the night on the northern shore. The eight miles which we made to-day cost us much trouble. The air was cold and rendered more disagreeable by the rain, which fell in several slight showers in the course of the day; our cords broke several times, but fortunately without injury to the boats.

On ascending the hills near the river, one of the party found that there was snow mixed with the rain on the heights. A little back of these the country becomes perfectly level on both sides of the river. There is now no timber on the hills, and only a few scattering cottonwood, ash, box-elder, and willows along the water. In the course of the day we passed several camps of Indians, the most recent of which seemed to have been evacuated about five weeks since. From the several apparent dates we supposed that they were made by a band of about 100 lodges, who were traveling slowly up the river. Although no parts of the Missouri, from the [village of the] Minnetarees to this place, exhibit signs of permanent settlements, yet none seem exempt from the transient visits of hunting-parties. We know that the Minnetarees of the Missouri extend their excursions on the south side of the river as high as the Yellowstone ; and the Assiniboins visit the northern side, most probably as high as Porcupine [Poplar] river. All the lodges between that place and the Rocky mountains we supposed to belong to the Minnetarees of Fort de Prairie, who live on the south fork of the Saskaskawan.

*May* 31*st.* We proceeded in the two periogues, leaving the canoes to bring on the meat of two buffaloes killed last evening. Soon after we set off it began to rain ; and though it ceased at noon, the weather continued cloudy during the rest of the day. The obstructions of yesterday continue, and fatigue the men excessively. The banks are so slippery (*p. 238*) in some places, and the mud is so adhesive, that they are unable to wear their moccasins; one-fourth of the time they are obliged to be up to their armpits in the cold water, and sometimes they walk for several yards over the sharp fragments of rocks which have fallen from the hills. All this, added to the burden of dragging the heavy canoes, is very painful; yet the men bear it with great patience and good humor. Once the rope of one of the periogues, the only one we had made of hemp, broke short, and the periogue swung and just touched a point of rock, which almost overset her.

At nine miles we came to a high wall[23] of black rock rising from the water's edge on the south, above the cliffs of the river; this continued about a quarter of a mile, and was succeeded by a high open plain, till three miles further a second wall, 200 feet high, rose on the same side. Three miles further a wall of the same kind, about 200 feet high and twelve in thickness, appeared to the north.

These hills and river-cliffs exhibit a most extraordinary and romantic appearance. They rise in most places nearly perpendicular from the water, to the height of between 200 and 300 feet, and are formed of very white sandstone, so soft as to yield readily to the impression of water, in the upper part of which lie imbedded two or three thin horizontal strata of white freestone, insensible to the rain; on the top is a dark rich loam, which forms a gradually ascending plain, from a mile to a mile and a half in extent, when the hills again rise abruptly to the height of about 300 feet

[23] The cañon formation about to be described is called in the Summary Statement the Natural Walls, and is charted by Clark as the Stone Walls. I cannot understand the position assigned to Slaughter river on his map, where it is brought in opposite the upper end of the Stone Walls. I suspect that Slaughter river of the map is *not* the Slaughter river of the text, and that the latter is the Big Horn river of the map. Several special configurations of this cañon have received late names, as Hole in the Wall, Cathedral Rock, and Citadel Rock. Clark's map charts a certain "Crevice Cr." from the south or west, between Slaughter and Stone Wall river; but the text does not notice any such stream. See last and next notes.

more.   In trickling down the cliffs, the water has worn the soft sandstone into a thousand grotesque figures, among which, with a little fancy, may be discerned elegant ranges of freestone buildings, with columns variously sculptured, and supporting long and elegant galleries, while the parapets are adorned with statuary.   On a nearer approach they represent every form of elegant ruins—columns, some with pedestals and capitals entire, others mutilated and prostrate, and some rising pyramidally over each (*p. 239*) other till they terminate in a sharp point.   These are varied by niches, alcoves, and the customary appearances of desolated magnificence.   The illusion is increased by the number of martins [*Petrochelidon lunifrons*, the cliff-swallow], which have built their globular nests in the niches, and hover over these columns, as in our country they are accustomed to frequent large stone structures.   As we advance there seems no end to the visionary enchantment which surrounds us.

In the midst of this fantastic scenery are vast ranges of walls, which seem the productions of art, so regular is the workmanship.   They rise perpendicularly from the river, sometimes to the height of 100 feet, varying in thickness from one to twelve feet, being as broad at the top as below. The stones of which they are formed are black, thick, durable, and composed of a large portion of earth, intermixed and cemented with a small quantity of sand, and a considerable proportion of talk [talc] or quartz.   These stones are almost invariably regular parallelepipeds of unequal sizes in the wall, but equally deep and laid regularly in ranges over each other like bricks, each breaking and covering the interstice of the two on which it rests ; but though the perpendicular interstice be destroyed, the horizontal one extends entirely through the whole work. The stones are proportioned to the thickness of the wall in which they are employed, being largest in the thickest walls.   The thinner walls are composed of a single depth of the parallelepiped, while the thicker ones consist of two or more depths.   These walls pass the river at several places,

rising from the water's edge much above the sandstone
bluffs, which they seem to penetrate ; thence they cross,
in a straight line on either side of the river, the plains
over which they tower to the height of from 10 to 70
feet, until they lose themselves in the second range of
hills. Sometimes they run parallel in several ranges near
each other, sometimes intersect each other at right angles,
and have the appearance of walls of ancient houses or
gardens.

(*p. 240*) The face of some of these river-hills is composed
of very excellent freestone, of a light yellowish-brown
color. Among the cliffs we found a species of pine which
we had not yet seen, differing from the Virginia pitch pine
in having a shorter leaf, and a longer and more pointed
cone. The coal appears only in small quantities, as do the
burnt earth and pumice-stone ; the mineral salts have
abated. Among the animals are a great number of bighorn, a few buffalo and elk, and some mule-deer, but none
of the common deer nor any antelopes. We saw, but could
not procure, a beautiful [cross-] fox, of a color varied with
orange, yellow, white, and black, rather smaller than the
common fox of this country, and about the same size as
the red fox of the United States.

The river to-day has been from about 150 to 250 yards
wide, with but little timber. At the distance of 2½ miles
from the last stone wall is a stream [24] on the north side, 28
yards in width, and with some running water. We camped
just above its mouth, having made 18 miles.

*Saturday, June 1st*, 1805. The weather was cloudy with
a few drops of rain. As we proceeded, by the aid of our
cord, we found the river-cliffs and bluffs not so high as
yesterday, and the country more level. The timber is in
greater abundance on the river, though there is no wood

[24] Not named in the text or codex ; but in the Summary Statement given as
"Stonewall creek, above the Natural Walls," 26 miles from Slaughter creek,
and charted by Clark as "Stone Wall Cr." See next date. This stream will be
found as Key or Key's creek on some maps, and as Eagle creek on better ones.

on the high ground; coal appears in the bluffs. The river is from 200 to 250 feet wide, the current more gentle, the water still clearer, and rocky points and shoals fewer than we met yesterday, though those which we did encounter were equally difficult to pass. Game is by no means in such plenty as below; all that we obtained were one big-horn and a mule-deer, though we saw in the plains a quantity of buffalo, particularly near a small lake about eight miles from the river, to the south. Notwithstanding the wind was ahead all day, we dragged the canoes along the distance of 23 miles. At 14¼ (*p. 241*) miles, we came to a small island, opposite a bend of the river to the north; at 2½ miles, to the upper point of a small island on the north; at five miles, to another island, on the south side and opposite a bluff. In the next two miles we passed an island on the south, a second beyond it on the north, and reached near a high bluff on the north a third, on which we camped.[25]

In the plains near the river are the choke-cherry, yellow and red currant bushes, as well as the wild rose and prickly pear, both of which are now in bloom. From the tops of the river-hills, which are lower than usual, we enjoyed a delightful view of the rich, fertile plains on both sides, in many places extending from the river-cliffs to a great distance back. In these plains we meet, occasionally, large banks of pure sand, which were driven apparently by the south-west winds and there deposited. The plains are more fertile some distance from the river than near its banks, where the surface of the earth is very generally strewed with small pebbles, which appear to be smoothed and worn by the agitation of the waters with which they were, no doubt, once covered. A mountain [Bear's Paw], or part of the North [Little Rocky] mountain, approaches the river within

---

[25] Neither text, codex, nor map has any stream between Stonewall creek and Maria's river. There are several, however, the most notable being the Little Sandy, N., 8½ miles above Citadel Rock, and 23 below Maria's river. This is passed to-day, five miles below camp.

eight or ten miles, bearing north from our camp of last evening; and this morning a range of high mountains [High-
wood] bearing S.W. from us, and apparently running to the
westward, is seen at a great distance, covered with snow.
In the evening we had a little more rain.

*June 2d.* The wind blew violently last night and a slight
shower of rain fell, but this morning was fair. We set out
at an early hour, and although the wind was ahead, by means
of the cord went on much better than for the last two days,
as the banks were well calculated for towing. The current
of the river is strong, but regular; its timber increases in
quantity, the low grounds become more level and extensive,
and the bluffs on the river are lower than usual. In the
course of the day we had a small shower of rain, which lasted
(*p. 242*) a few minutes only.

As game is very abundant, we think it necessary to begin a
collection of hides, for the purpose of making a leathern boat,
which we intend constructing shortly. The hunters, who
were out the greater part of the day, brought in six elk,
two buffalo, two mule-deer, and a bear. This last animal
nearly cost us the lives of two of our hunters, who were
together when he attacked them; one of them narrowly
escaped being caught; the other, after running a considerable distance, concealed himself in some thick bushes, and
while the bear was in quick pursuit of his hiding-place, his
companion came up, and fortunately shot the animal through
the head.

At 6½ miles we reached an island on the northern side;
1¼ miles thence is a timbered low ground on the south; in
the next 2¾ miles we passed three small islands, and came
to a dark bluff on the south; within the following mile are
two small islands on the same side. At 3¼ miles we reached
the lower part of a much larger island near a northern point;
as we coasted along its side, within two miles we passed a
smaller island, and half a mile above reached the head of
another. All these islands are small, and most of them contain some timber. Three-quarters of a mile beyond the last,

and at the distance of 18 miles from our camp, we came-to for the night in a handsome, low cottonwood plain on the south, where we remained for the purpose of making some celestial observations during the night, and of examining in the morning a large [Maria's] river which comes in opposite to us. Accordingly, at an early hour,

*Monday, June 3d,* we crossed and fixed our camp at the point formed by the junction of this river with the Missouri.

It now became an interesting question, which of these two streams is what the Minnetarees call Ahmateahza, or Missouri, which they describe as approaching very near to the Columbia. On our right decision much of the fate of the expedition depends ; since if, after ascending to the Rocky (*p. 243*) mountains or beyond them, we should find that the river we were following did not come near the Columbia, and be obliged to return, we should not only lose the traveling season, two months of which have already elapsed, but probably dishearten the men so much as to induce them either to abandon the enterprise, or yield us a cold obedience, instead of the warm and zealous support which they have hitherto afforded us. We determined, therefore, to examine well before we decided on our future course. For this purpose we dispatched two canoes with three men up each of the streams, with orders to ascertain the width, depth, and rapidity of the current, so as to judge of their comparative bodies of water. At the same time parties were sent out by land to penetrate the country,[26] and discover from the

[26] " The commanding officers could not determine which of these rivers or branches, it was proper to take; and therefore concluded to send a small party up each of them. Myself and two men went up the South branch, and a serjeant and two more up the North. The parties went up the two branches about 15 miles. We found the South branch rapid with a great many islands and the general course South West. The other party reported the North branch as less rapid and not so deep as the other. The North branch is 186 yards wide and the South 372 yards. The water of the South branch is clear, and that of the North muddy. About a mile and a half up the point from the confluence, a handsome little river falls into the North branch, called Rose [or Tansy] river." Gass, p. 94, June 3d. So it seems that Gass and his two men were the first to ascend the Missouri above the mouth of Maria's river.

rising grounds, if possible, the distant bearings of the two rivers; and all were directed to return toward evening.

While they were gone we ascended together the high grounds in the fork of these two rivers, whence we had a very extensive prospect of the surrounding country. On every side it was spread into one vast plain, covered with verdure, in which innumerable herds of buffalo were roaming, attended by their enemies the wolves; some flocks of elk also were seen, and the solitary antelopes were scattered with their young over the face of the plain. To the south was a range of lofty [up to about 6,000 feet; Highwood] mountains, which we supposed to be a continuation of the South [i. e., Judith] mountain, stretching from S.E. to N.W., and terminating abruptly about S.W. from us. These were partially covered with snow; but at a great distance behind them was a more lofty ridge [Little Belt mountains], completely covered with snow, which seemed to follow the same direction as the first, reaching from W. to N. of N.W., where their snowy tops were blended with the horizon. The direction of the rivers could not, however, be long distinguished, as they were soon lost in the extent of the plain. On our return we continued our examination; the width of the north branch [i. e., Maria's river] is (*p. 244*) 200 yards, that of the south is 372. The north, although narrower and with a gentler current, is deeper than the south branch; its waters are of the same whitish-brown color, thickness, and turbidity, and run in the same boiling and rolling manner which has uniformly characterized the Missouri; its bed is composed of some gravel, but principally mud. The south fork [i. e., the Missouri itself] is deeper, but its waters are perfectly transparent; its current is rapid, but the surface smooth and unruffled; and its bed is composed of round and flat smooth stones, like those of rivers issuing from a mountainous country.

The air and character of the north fork so much resemble those of the Missouri that almost all the party believe that to be the true course to be pursued. We, however, though we have given no decided opinion, are inclined to think otherwise; because, although this branch does give the color and character to the Missouri, yet these very circumstances induce an opinion that it rises in and runs through an open plain country, since if it came from the mountains it would be clearer—unless, which from the position of the country is improbable, it passed through a vast extent of low ground after leaving them.  We thought it probable that it did not even penetrate the Rocky mountains, but drew its sources from the open country toward the lower and middle parts of the Saskaskawan, in a direction north of this place.[27]  What embarrasses us most is that the Indians, who appeared to be well acquainted with the geography of the country, have not mentioned this northern river; for "the river which scolds at all others," as it is termed,[28] must be, according to their account, one of the rivers which we have passed; and if this north fork be the Missouri, why have they not designated the south branch, which they must also have passed in order to reach the great falls which they mention on the Missouri?

In the evening our parties returned, after ascending the rivers in canoes for some distance and then continuing on foot, just leaving themselves time to return by (*p. 245*) night. The north fork was less rapid, and therefore afforded the easiest navigation; the shallowest water of the north was five feet deep, that of the south six feet.  At 2½ miles up the north fork is a small river [Teton] coming in on the left or western side, 60 feet wide, with a bold current three feet

[27] But Maria's river does head in the main divide of the Rocky mountains; some of its sources are due west of its mouth; and all the sources of Milk river intervene between any heads of Maria's and the Saskatchewan rivers.  We must remember that the explorers were necessarily ignorant of the very great extent of the Milk river region.  Maria's rises in the Rocky mountains about 48° 30', and runs in a very winding course, though with a general direction little S. of E., its mouth being but little below 48°.  The Great Northern Railway now follows it up to Maria's Pass.

[28] Translation of an Indian name, given as " Ah-mah-tah-ru-spush-sher," Clark C 249, and supposed to be Milk river, not Maria's.  Lewis' map of 1806 (made by Clark) lays down a course, lettered " The Indians call this the River which scolds at all other Rivers," which is not far out for Milk river; and nothing appears there to answer to Maria's.

in depth.  The party by land had gone up the south fork in a straight line somewhat north of west for seven miles, where they discovered that this little river [Teton] came within 100 yards[29] of the south fork; and on returning down it, found it a handsome stream, with as much timber as either of the larger rivers, consisting of the narrow and wide-leaved cottonwood, some birch and box-elder, with an undergrowth of willows, rosebushes, and currants.  They also saw on this river a great number of elk, and some beaver.

All these accounts were, however, very far from deciding the important question of our future route.  We therefore determined, each of us, to ascend one of the rivers during a day and a half's march, or further, if necessary for our satisfaction.  Our hunters killed two buffalo, six elk, and four deer to-day.  Along the plains near the junction are to be found the prickly pear in great quantities; the choke-cherry is also very abundant in the river low grounds, as well as in the ravines along the river-bluffs; the yellow and red currants are not yet ripe; the gooseberry is beginning to ripen, and the wild rose, which now covers all the low grounds near the rivers, is in full bloom.  The fatigues of the last few days have occasioned some falling off in the appearance of the men; who, not having been able to wear moccasins, have had their feet much bruised and mangled in passing over the stones and rough ground.  They are, however, perfectly cheerful, and have an undiminished ardor for the Expedition.

*June 4th.*  At the same hour this morning, Captain Lewis and Captain Clark set out to explore the two rivers.

Captain Lewis, with six men [Sergeant Pryor, Privates Drewyer, Shields, Windsor, Cruzatte, Lepage], crossed the north fork (*p. 246*) near the camp, below a small island, from which he took a course N. 30° W. for 4½ miles, to a commanding eminence.  Here he observed that the North moun-

---

[29] Cracon du Nez is what this narrow isthmus used to be called.  It is given by Governor Stevens as being in 1855 of the same width that is stated in the text (P. R. R. Rep. XII. pt. ii., p. 222, 1860).

tain, changing its direction parallel to the Missouri, turned toward the north, and terminated abruptly at the distance of about 30 miles, the point of termination [north end of Bear's Paw mountains[30]] bearing N. 48° E. The South mountain diverges to the south, and terminates abruptly, its extremity bearing S. 8° W., distant about 20 miles; to the right of and retreating from this extremity is a separate mountain, at the distance of 35 miles, in a direction S. 38° W., which, from its resemblance to the roof of a barn, he called Barn mountain. The north fork, which is now on the [his] left, makes a considerable bend to the N.W., and on its western border a range of hills [Bec d'Outard], about ten miles long, bearing from this spot N. 60° W., runs parallel with it. North of this range of hills is an elevated point of the river-bluff on its south side, bearing N. 72° W., about twelve miles from us. Toward this he directed his course across a high, level, dry, open plain, which in fact embraces the whole country to the foot of the mountains. The soil is dark, rich, and fertile; yet the grass is by no means so luxuriant as might have been expected, for it is short and scarcely more than sufficient to cover the ground. There are vast quantities of prickly-pears, and myriads of grasshoppers [*Caloptenus spretus*], which afford food for a species of curlew [*Numenius longirostris*], which is in great numbers in the plain.

He then proceeded up the river to the point of observation they had fixed on; from which he went two miles N. 15° W., to a bluff point on the north side of the river; thence his course was N. 30° W. for two miles, to the entrance of a large creek[31] on the south. The part of the river along which

---

[30] Bearing in mind Captain Lewis' present point of view, we see that Bear's Paw and the Little Rockies, with the two Medicine Buttes between them (these being collectively his " North " mountain), are in line, so that they seem to end as said. Similarly, his " South " mountain, otherwise Judith's, is, with the two Moccasin Buttes, in line of vision with Highwood mountains; so that the last named are now his " South " mountain, " S. 8° W. about 20 miles," ending on the west (his right hand, as he looks south) in the somewhat isolated elevation he calls Barn mountain, now known as West or Belt Butte of the Highwoods.

[31] Antelope creek has been the first large southern tributary of Maria's river since the Teton broke through the Cracon du Nez into the Missouri.

he passed is from 40 to 60 yards wide, the current strong, the water deep and turbid, the banks falling in; the salts, coal, and mineral appearances are as usual, and in every respect, except as to size, this river resembles the Missouri. The low grounds are narrow, but well supplied with wood; the bluffs are prin- (*p. 247*) cipally of dark brown yellow and some white clay, with freestone in some places. From this point the river bears N. 20° E. to a bluff on the south, at the distance of twelve miles; toward this he directed his course, ascending the hills, which are about 200 feet high, and passing through plains for three miles, till he found the dry ravines [32] so steep and numerous that he resolved to return to the river and follow its banks. He reached it about four miles from the beginning of his course, and camped on the north in a bend among some bushes, which sheltered the party from the wind. The air was very cold, the northwest wind high; the rain wet them to the skin. Besides the game just mentioned, he observed buffalo, elk, wolves, and foxes; he got a blaireau and a weasel,[33] and [Drewyer] wounded a large brown bear, which it was too late to pursue. Along the river are immense quantities of roses, which are now in full bloom, and make the low grounds a perfect garden.

*June 5th.* The rain fell during the greater part of last night, and in the morning the weather was cloudy and cold, with a high northwest wind. At sunrise Captain Lewis proceeded up the river eight miles, to the bluff on the left side, toward which he had been directing his course yesterday. Here he found the bed of a creek 25 yards wide at the entrance, with some timber, but no water, notwithstanding the rain. It is, indeed, astonishing to observe the vast quantities of water absorbed by the soil of the plains, which, being opened in large crevices, presents a fine rich loam. At the

---

[32] One of these is now known as the Black coulée (above Maguire's.)  The road from Benton to the Sweet-grass hills strikes it higher up.  I came down this road with Major Twining in Sept., 1874.  Our trail is marked on his map.

[33] Read beaver.  " I killed a braro and a beaver. . . . also a very fine Mule deer," Lewis E 42.

mouth of this stream, which he called Lark creek, the bluffs
are very steep, and approach the river so that he ascended
them and, crossing the plains, reached the river, which from
the last point bore N. 50° W. four miles from this place; it
extended north two miles.[34] Here he discovered a lofty
mountain, standing alone at the distance of more than 80
miles, in the direction N. 30° W.,[35] and which from its conical
figure he called Tower mountain.

(*p. 248*) He then proceeded on these two hills, and afterward in different courses six miles, when he again changed
for a western course, across a deep bend along the south side.
In making this passage over the plains, he found them like
those of yesterday, level and beautiful, with great quantities
of buffalo, and some wolves, foxes, and antelopes, and inter-
sected near the river by deep ravines. Here at the distance
of from one to nine miles from the river, he met the largest
village of barking-squirrels [36] which he had yet seen; for he

[34] An obscure sentence. Lewis E 43 has : " From the entrance of this Creek
(which I called Lark C.) the river boar [bore] N. 50° W. 4 m. At the entrance
of this creek the bluffs were very steep and approached the river so near on the
Stard. side that we ascended the hills and passed through the plains ; at the
extremity of this course we returned to the river, which there boar North 2 mls."
The creek was called Lark from the abundance of a small bird which Lewis
carefully describes, E 40. This is the black-breasted lark-bunting or longspur,
*Centrophanes* (*Rhynchophanes*) *maccowni*, which abounds in Montana in the
breeding season, together with the chestnut-collared lark-bunting, *C. ornatus*.
See my articles on these birds, in Bull. U. S. Geol. Surv. IV. No. 3, July, 1878,
pp. 579–585. Lewis' Lark creek is the Black coulée.

[35] An unfortunate discrepancy here. Lewis E 43 has : " I discovered a lofty
single mountain which appeared to be at a great distance, perhaps 80 or more
miles, it boar N. 52° W. from it's conic figure I called it tower Mountain."
Here is a difference of 22° from the text. But the text has been corrected
from proper data ; so that Tower mountain is no other than the main peak of the
somewhat famous Three Buttes or Sweet-grass hills, which are cut by the parallel
of 49° N. across their northern foot-hills, and which from Lewis' point of view
would appear as one mountain.

[36] Lewis E 43 has " burrowing or barking squirrels," and no description ;
but I judge from my knowledge of the locality and of the animal, that
the species was not the prairie-dog, but the tawny gopher or spermophile,
*Spermophilus richardsoni*, which abounds in the region of the Milk and Maria's
rivers. See Allen, Monogr. N. A. *Rodentia*, 1877, pp. 848–860, and Coues,

passed a skirt of their territory for seven miles.  He also saw near the hills a flock of the mountain-cock, or a large species of the heath-hen, with a long pointed tail, which the Indians below had informed us were common among the Rocky mountains.  Having finished his course of ten miles west across a bend, he continued two miles N. 80° W., and from that point discovered some lofty mountains [37] to the N.W. of Tower mountain, bearing N. 65° W., at 80 or 100 miles' distance.  Here he camped on the north side in a handsome low ground, on which were several old stick-lodges.  He had seen but little timber on the river in the forepart of the day, but here there is a greater quantity than usual.  The river itself is about 80 yards wide, from six to ten feet deep, and has a strong, steady current.  The party killed five elk and a mule-deer; and by way of experiment roasted some burrowing-squirrels, which they found to be well-flavored and tender.

*June 6th.*  Captain Lewis was now [rightly [38]] convinced that this river pursued a direction too far north for our route to the Pacific, and therefore resolved to return; but waited till noon to take a meridian altitude.  The clouds, however, which had gathered during the latter part of the night, continued and prevented the observation.  Part of the men were sent forward to a commanding eminence, six miles S. 70° W., from which they saw, at the distance of about 15 miles S. 80° W., a point of the south bluff of the river, which

Amer. Nat. IX. 1875, p. 148 *seq.*  It was unknown to science till 1822.  The bird Lewis here mentions is the sage-grouse, *Centrocercus urophasianus*.

[37] These are the other two of the Three Buttes or Sweet-grass hills, now separable by the eye from that one (Tower mountain) which had before intercepted the view of them.  See text of July 19th, 1806.

[38] That is to say, if the Expedition was to explore the Missouri to its source. To have followed up Maria's river and crossed the Continental Divide at Maria's Pass, would have been to discover the present route of the Great Northern Railway, north of Flathead and Pend d'Oreille lakes, over to Clark's fork of the Columbia.  But the glory of the Great Falls—of Smith's, Dearborn's, Gallatin's Madison's, Jefferson's rivers—of nearly the whole Missouri above steamboat navigation—would not then have been Lewis and Clark's.  This was worth striving for, even though it finally brought them to the worst possible point whence to reach the Columbia.

thence bore northwardly. In their absence two rafts had (*p. 249*) been prepared, and when they returned, about noon, the party embarked. But they soon found that the rafts were so small and slender that the baggage was wet; therefore it was necessary to abandon them and go by land. They therefore crossed the plains, and at the distance of twelve miles came to the river, through a cold storm from the northeast, accompanied by showers of rain. The abruptness of the cliffs compelled them, after going a few miles, to leave the river and meet the storm in the plains. Here they directed their course too far northward, in consequence of which they did not strike the river till late at night, after having traveled 23 miles since noon, and halted at a little below the entrance of Lark creek. They had the good fortune to kill two buffalo, which supplied them with supper; but spent a very uncomfortable night without any shelter from the rain, which continued till morning,

*Friday, June 7th,* when at an early hour they continued down the river. The route was extremely unpleasant, as the wind was high from the N.E., accompanied with rain, which made the ground so slippery that they were unable to walk over the bluffs which they had passed on ascending the river. The land is the most thirsty we have ever seen; notwithstanding all the rain which has fallen, the earth is not wet for more than two inches deep, and resembles thawed ground; but if it requires more water to saturate it than the common soils, on the other hand, it yields its moisture with equal difficulty.

In passing along the side of one of these bluffs, at a narrow pass 30 yards in length, Captain Lewis slipped, and but for a fortunate recovery by means of his espontoon, would have been precipitated into the river over a precipice of about 90 feet. He had just reached a spot where by the assistance of his espontoon he could stand with tolerable safety, when he heard a voice behind him cry out, "Good God! Captain, what shall I do?" He turned instantly and found it was Windsor, who had lost his foothold about the middle (*p. 250*) of the narrow pass, and had slipped down to the very verge of the precipice, where he lay on his belly, with his right arm and leg over the precipice, while with the other leg and arm he was with difficulty holding on, to keep himself from being dashed to pieces below.    His dreadful situation was instantly perceived by Captain Lewis, who, stifling his alarm, calmly told him that he was in no danger ; that he should take his knife out of his belt with his right hand, and dig a hole in the side of the bluff to receive his right foot.    With great presence of mind he did this, and then raised himself on his knees. Captain Lewis then told him to take off his moccasins and come forward on his hands and knees, holding the knife in one hand and his rifle in the other.    He immediately crawled in this way till he came to a secure spot.    The men who had not attempted this passage were ordered to return and wade the river at the foot of the bluff, where they found the water breast-high.    This adventure taught them the danger of crossing the slippery heights of the river ; but as the plains were intersected by deep ravines, almost as difficult to pass, they continued down the river, sometimes in the mud of the low grounds, sometimes up to their arms in the water ; and when it became too deep to wade, they cut footholds with their knives in the sides of the banks.    In this way they traveled through the rain, mud, and water, and having made only 18 miles during the whole day, camped in an old Indian lodge of sticks, which afforded them a dry shelter.    Here they cooked part of six deer they had killed in the course of their walk, and having eaten the only morsel they had tasted during the whole day, slept comfortably on some willow-boughs.

END OF VOL. I.

# A CATALOG OF SELECTED
# DOVER BOOKS
## IN ALL FIELDS OF INTEREST

# A CATALOG OF SELECTED DOVER
# BOOKS IN ALL FIELDS OF INTEREST

CONCERNING THE SPIRITUAL IN ART, Wassily Kandinsky. Pioneering work by father of abstract art. Thoughts on color theory, nature of art. Analysis of earlier masters. 12 illustrations. 80pp. of text. 5⅜ × 8½.                23411-8 Pa. $3.95

ANIMALS: 1,419 Copyright-Free Illustrations of Mammals, Birds, Fish, Insects, etc., Jim Harter (ed.). Clear wood engravings present, in extremely lifelike poses, over 1,000 species of animals. One of the most extensive pictorial sourcebooks of its kind. Captions. Index. 284pp. 9 × 12.                23766-4 Pa. $11.95

CELTIC ART: The Methods of Construction, George Bain. Simple geometric techniques for making Celtic interlacements, spirals, Kells-type initials, animals, humans, etc. Over 500 illustrations. 160pp. 9 × 12. (USO)                22923-8 Pa. $8.95

AN ATLAS OF ANATOMY FOR ARTISTS, Fritz Schider. Most thorough reference work on art anatomy in the world. Hundreds of illustrations, including selections from works by Vesalius, Leonardo, Goya, Ingres, Michelangelo, others. 593 illustrations. 192pp. 7⅛ × 10¼.                20241-0 Pa. $8.95

CELTIC HAND STROKE-BY-STROKE (Irish Half-Uncial from "The Book of Kells"): An Arthur Baker Calligraphy Manual, Arthur Baker. Complete guide to creating each letter of the alphabet in distinctive Celtic manner. Covers hand position, strokes, pens, inks, paper, more. Illustrated. 48pp. 8¼ × 11.
24336-2 Pa. $3.95

EASY ORIGAMI, John Montroll. Charming collection of 32 projects (hat, cup, pelican, piano, swan, many more) specially designed for the novice origami hobbyist. Clearly illustrated easy-to-follow instructions insure that even beginning papercrafters will achieve successful results. 48pp. 8¼ × 11.                27298-2 Pa. $2.95

THE COMPLETE BOOK OF BIRDHOUSE CONSTRUCTION FOR WOOD-WORKERS, Scott D. Campbell. Detailed instructions, illustrations, tables. Also data on bird habitat and instinct patterns. Bibliography. 3 tables. 63 illustrations in 15 figures. 48pp. 5¼ × 8½.                24407-5 Pa. $1.95

BLOOMINGDALE'S ILLUSTRATED 1886 CATALOG: Fashions, Dry Goods and Housewares, Bloomingdale Brothers. Famed merchants' extremely rare catalog depicting about 1,700 products: clothing, housewares, firearms, dry goods, jewelry, more. Invaluable for dating, identifying vintage items. Also, copyright-free graphics for artists, designers. Co-published with Henry Ford Museum & Greenfield Village. 160pp. 8¼ × 11.                25780-0 Pa. $9.95

HISTORIC COSTUME IN PICTURES, Braun & Schneider. Over 1,450 costumed figures in clearly detailed engravings—from dawn of civilization to end of 19th century. Captions. Many folk costumes. 256pp. 8⅜ × 11¾.                23150-X Pa. $10.95

PERSPECTIVE FOR ARTISTS, Rex Vicat Cole. Depth, perspective of sky and sea, shadows, much more, not usually covered. 391 diagrams, 81 reproductions of drawings and paintings. 279pp. 5⅜ × 8½. 22487-2 Pa. $6.95

DRAWING THE LIVING FIGURE, Joseph Sheppard. Innovative approach to artistic anatomy focuses on specifics of surface anatomy, rather than muscles and bones. Over 170 drawings of live models in front, back and side views, and in widely varying poses. Accompanying diagrams. 177 illustrations. Introduction. Index. 144pp. 8⅜ × 11¼. 26723-7 Pa. $7.95

GOTHIC AND OLD ENGLISH ALPHABETS: 100 Complete Fonts, Dan X. Solo. Add power, elegance to posters, signs, other graphics with 100 stunning copyright-free alphabets: Blackstone, Dolbey, Germania, 97 more—including many lower-case, numerals, punctuation marks. 104pp. 8⅛ × 11. 24695-7 Pa. $7.95

HOW TO DO BEADWORK, Mary White. Fundamental book on craft from simple projects to five-bead chains and woven works. 106 illustrations. 142pp. 5⅜ × 8. 20697-1 Pa. $4.95

THE BOOK OF WOOD CARVING, Charles Marshall Sayers. Finest book for beginners discusses fundamentals and offers 34 designs. "Absolutely first rate . . . well thought out and well executed."—E. J. Tangerman. 118pp. 7¾ × 10⅝. 23654-4 Pa. $5.95

ILLUSTRATED CATALOG OF CIVIL WAR MILITARY GOODS: Union Army Weapons, Insignia, Uniform Accessories, and Other Equipment, Schuyler, Hartley, and Graham. Rare, profusely illustrated 1846 catalog includes Union Army uniform and dress regulations, arms and ammunition, coats, insignia, flags, swords, rifles, etc. 226 illustrations. 160pp. 9 × 12. 24939-5 Pa. $10.95

WOMEN'S FASHIONS OF THE EARLY 1900s: An Unabridged Republication of "New York Fashions, 1909," National Cloak & Suit Co. Rare catalog of mail-order fashions documents women's and children's clothing styles shortly after the turn of the century. Captions offer full descriptions, prices. Invaluable resource for fashion, costume historians. Approximately 725 illustrations. 128pp. 8⅜ × 11¼. 27276-1 Pa. $10.95

THE 1912 AND 1915 GUSTAV STICKLEY FURNITURE CATALOGS, Gustav Stickley. With over 200 detailed illustrations and descriptions, these two catalogs are essential reading and reference materials and identification guides for Stickley furniture. Captions cite materials, dimensions and prices. 112pp. 6½ × 9¼. 26676-1 Pa. $9.95

EARLY AMERICAN LOCOMOTIVES, John H. White, Jr. Finest locomotive engravings from early 19th century: historical (1804–74), main-line (after 1870), special, foreign, etc. 147 plates. 142pp. 11⅜ × 8¼. 22772-3 Pa. $8.95

THE TALL SHIPS OF TODAY IN PHOTOGRAPHS, Frank O. Braynard. Lavishly illustrated tribute to nearly 100 majestic contemporary sailing vessels: Amerigo Vespucci, Clearwater, Constitution, Eagle, Mayflower, Sea Cloud, Victory, many more. Authoritative captions provide statistics, background on each ship. 190 black-and-white photographs and illustrations. Introduction. 128pp. 8⅞ × 11¾. 27163-3 Pa. $12.95

BRASS INSTRUMENTS: Their History and Development, Anthony Baines. Authoritative, updated survey of the evolution of trumpets, trombones, bugles, cornets, French horns, tubas and other brass wind instruments. Over 140 illustrations and 48 music examples. Corrected and updated by author. New preface. Bibliography. 320pp. 5⅜ × 8½. 27574-4 Pa. $9.95

HOLLYWOOD GLAMOR PORTRAITS, John Kobal (ed.). 145 photos from 1926–49. Harlow, Gable, Bogart, Bacall; 94 stars in all. Full background on photographers, technical aspects. 160pp. 8⅜ × 11¼. 23352-9 Pa. $9.95

MAX AND MORITZ, Wilhelm Busch. Great humor classic in both German and English. Also 10 other works: "Cat and Mouse," "Plisch and Plumm," etc. 216pp. 5⅜ × 8½. 20181-3 Pa. $5.95

THE RAVEN AND OTHER FAVORITE POEMS, Edgar Allan Poe. Over 40 of the author's most memorable poems: "The Bells," "Ulalume," "Israfel," "To Helen," "The Conqueror Worm," "Eldorado," "Annabel Lee," many more. Alphabetic lists of titles and first lines. 64pp. 5³⁄₁₆ × 8¼. 26685-0 Pa. $1.00

SEVEN SCIENCE FICTION NOVELS, H. G. Wells. The standard collection of the great novels. Complete, unabridged. First Men in the Moon, Island of Dr. Moreau, War of the Worlds, Food of the Gods, Invisible Man, Time Machine, In the Days of the Comet. Total of 1,015pp. 5⅜ × 8½. (USO) 20264-X Clothbd. $29.95

AMULETS AND SUPERSTITIONS, E. A. Wallis Budge. Comprehensive discourse on origin, powers of amulets in many ancient cultures: Arab, Persian, Babylonian, Assyrian, Egyptian, Gnostic, Hebrew, Phoenician, Syriac, etc. Covers cross, swastika, crucifix, seals, rings, stones, etc. 584pp. 5⅜ × 8½. 23573-4 Pa. $12.95

RUSSIAN STORIES/PYCCKNE PACCKA3bl: A Dual-Language Book, edited by Gleb Struve. Twelve tales by such masters as Chekhov, Tolstoy, Dostoevsky, Pushkin, others. Excellent word-for-word English translations on facing pages, plus teaching and study aids, Russian/English vocabulary, biographical/critical introductions, more. 416pp. 5⅜ × 8½. 26244-8 Pa. $8.95

PHILADELPHIA THEN AND NOW: 60 Sites Photographed in the Past and Present, Kenneth Finkel and Susan Oyama. Rare photographs of City Hall, Logan Square, Independence Hall, Betsy Ross House, other landmarks juxtaposed with contemporary views. Captures changing face of historic city. Introduction. Captions. 128pp. 8¼ × 11. 25790-8 Pa. $9.95

AIA ARCHITECTURAL GUIDE TO NASSAU AND SUFFOLK COUNTIES, LONG ISLAND, The American Institute of Architects, Long Island Chapter, and the Society for the Preservation of Long Island Antiquities. Comprehensive, well-researched and generously illustrated volume brings to life over three centuries of Long Island's great architectural heritage. More than 240 photographs with authoritative, extensively detailed captions. 176pp. 8¼ × 11. 26946-9 Pa. $14.95

NORTH AMERICAN INDIAN LIFE: Customs and Traditions of 23 Tribes, Elsie Clews Parsons (ed.). 27 fictionalized essays by noted anthropologists examine religion, customs, government, additional facets of life among the Winnebago, Crow, Zuni, Eskimo, other tribes. 480pp. 6⅛ × 9¼. 27377-6 Pa. $10.95

*CATALOG OF DOVER BOOKS*

THE INFLUENCE OF SEA POWER UPON HISTORY, 1660–1783, A. T. Mahan. Influential classic of naval history and tactics still used as text in war colleges. First paperback edition. 4 maps. 24 battle plans. 640pp. 5⅜ × 8½.
25509-3 Pa. $12.95

THE STORY OF THE TITANIC AS TOLD BY ITS SURVIVORS, Jack Winocour (ed.). What it was really like. Panic, despair, shocking inefficiency, and a little heroism. More thrilling than any fictional account. 26 illustrations. 320pp. 5⅜ × 8½. 20610-6 Pa. $7.95

FAIRY AND FOLK TALES OF THE IRISH PEASANTRY, William Butler Yeats (ed.). Treasury of 64 tales from the twilight world of Celtic myth and legend: "The Soul Cages," "The Kildare Pooka," "King O'Toole and his Goose," many more. Introduction and Notes by W. B. Yeats. 352pp. 5⅜ × 8½. 26941-8 Pa. $7.95

BUDDHIST MAHAYANA TEXTS, E. B. Cowell and Others (eds.). Superb, accurate translations of basic documents in Mahayana Buddhism, highly important in history of religions. The Buddha-karita of Asvaghosha, Larger Sukhavativyuha, more. 448pp. 5⅜ × 8½. 25552-2 Pa. $9.95

ONE TWO THREE . . . INFINITY: Facts and Speculations of Science, George Gamow. Great physicist's fascinating, readable overview of contemporary science: number theory, relativity, fourth dimension, entropy, genes, atomic structure, much more. 128 illustrations. Index. 352pp. 5⅜ × 8½. 25664-2 Pa. $8.95

ENGINEERING IN HISTORY, Richard Shelton Kirby, et al. Broad, nontechnical survey of history's major technological advances: birth of Greek science, industrial revolution, electricity and applied science, 20th-century automation, much more. 181 illustrations. ". . . excellent . . ."—Isis. Bibliography. vii + 530pp. 5⅜ × 8¼.
26412-2 Pa. $14.95

*Prices subject to change without notice.*

Available at your book dealer or write for free catalog to Dept. GI, Dover Publications, Inc., 31 East 2nd St., Mineola, N.Y. 11501. Dover publishes more than 500 books each year on science, elementary and advanced mathematics, biology, music, art, literary history, social sciences and other areas.